T0339899

# ROUTLEDGE HANDBOOK OF GENDER AND ENVIRONMENT

The *Routledge Handbook of Gender and Environment* gathers together state-of-the-art theoretical reflections and empirical research from leading researchers and practitioners working in this transdisciplinary and transnational academic field. Over the course of the book, these contributors provide critical analyses of the gender dimensions of a wide range of timely and challenging topics, from sustainable development and climate change politics, to queer ecology and interspecies ethics in the so-called Anthropocene.

Presenting a comprehensive overview of the development of the field from early political critiques of the male domination of women and nature in the 1980s to the sophisticated intersectional and inclusive analyses of the present, the volume is divided into four parts:

- **Part I**: Foundations
- **Part II**: Approaches
- **Part III**: Politics, policy and practice
- **Part IV**: Futures.

Comprising chapters written by forty contributors with different perspectives and working in a wide range of research contexts around the world, this Handbook will serve as a vital resource for scholars, students, and practitioners in environmental studies, gender studies, human geography, and the environmental humanities and social sciences more broadly.

**Sherilyn MacGregor** is Reader in Environmental Politics at the University of Manchester, UK. She has been teaching Environmental Politics and Gender and Environment at undergraduate and postgraduate levels for 15 years and has been an editor and editorial board member of *Environmental Politics* since 2007.

'This impressive collection breaks new theoretical, political and policy ground in the exploration of gender and environment. In challenging us to look beyond conventional narratives, the authors chart new feminist ways forward in this critical time of climate change and right-wing ascendancy. The keys to the future found here unlock our imaginations, allowing us to envision and start building a more just, peaceful and sustainable world.'

— *Betsy Hartmann, Professor Emerita of Development Studies and Senior Policy Analyst, Population and Development Program, Hampshire College, Amherst, Massachusetts, USA*

'More than thirty years of exploring gender and environment interfaces have brought us many different insights and interpretations. This inspirational handbook offers a wide and in-depth overview of feminist analyses and approaches on environment. It will help scholars, students, activists and policy makers to comprehend related politics, policies and practices and build a just and sustainable future.'

— *Irene Dankelman, Radboud University/IRDANA Advice, the Netherlands*

'This remarkable, insightful, and comprehensive handbook analyses the history, problems, and frameworks that characterize the complex relationships between gender and environment. An impressive assemblage of feminist writers from around the world provide powerful insights into the meanings of connections between women, gender, and nature as they have emerged in recent decades. Anyone interested in the history, politics, and real life examples surrounding ecofeminism will want to read this book.'

— *Carolyn Merchant, Professor of Environmental History, Philosophy, and Ethics at the University of California, Berkeley, USA*

'This book goes well beyond categorical framings of gender and environment as "women and nature" to embrace trans-disciplinary, postcolonial and intersectional analyses of heteronormativity, masculinism, racism, transgender and speciesism in the environment–gender nexus. In emphasizing how gender is done and undone, it provides strategies of resistance to environmentally destructive practices and it offers critical hope to enable us to reimagine our relationship with the planet.'

— *Bob Pease, Professor, School of Social Sciences, University of Tasmania, Australia*

'This is the book I've been waiting for. Its focus on gender and environment brings together a hugely impressive range of scholars to explore how gender inequalities and environmental crises are intertwined. The argument that masculinities are associated with exploitative environmental practices is an essential part of developing the policies we need to avoid environmental disaster. Given current political developments it could not be more timely and is certain to become essential reading for scholars and activists alike.'

— *Nickie Charles, Professor and Director of the Centre for the Study of Women and Gender, University of Warwick, UK*

'Sherilyn MacGregor's *Routledge Handbook of Gender and Environment* is more than a reference work, it's a great read. It encompasses the full gamut of gender and environment scholarship over more than three decades. The articles range from meditative and reflective to incendiary and revolutionary, each conveying key insights from engagement with a mix of social movements, activists, and theorists committed to social and ecological justice. MacGregor's introduction is a peerless summary of the issues and debates, and Giovanna Di Chiro's concluding chapter on the white (M)anthropocene is a stunner!'

— *Dianne Rocheleau, Professor of Geography, Clark University, USA*

# ROUTLEDGE HANDBOOK OF GENDER AND ENVIRONMENT

*Edited by Sherilyn MacGregor*

Routledge
Taylor & Francis Group
LONDON AND NEW YORK

earthscan
from Routledge

First published 2017
by Routledge

2 Park Square, Milton Park, Abingdon, Oxfordshire OX14 4RN
52 Vanderbilt Avenue, New York, NY 10017

*Routledge is an imprint of the Taylor & Francis Group, an informa business*

First issued in paperback 2019

*British Library Cataloguing-in-Publication Data*
A catalogue record for this book is available from the British Library

*Library of Congress Cataloging-in-Publication Data*
Names: MacGregor, Sherilyn, 1969– editor.
Title: Routledge handbook of gender and environment / edited by Sherilyn
MacGregor.
Other titles: Handbook of gender and environment
Description: Abingdon, Oxon ; New York, NY : Routledge, 2017. | Series:
Routledge international handbooks | Includes bibliographical references and index.
Identifiers: LCCN 2016057379 | ISBN 9780415707749 (hb) |
ISBN 9781315886572 (ebook)
Subjects: LCSH: Environmentalism—Social aspects. | Women and the
environment. | Ecofeminism. | Green movement—Social aspects.
Classification: LCC GE195 .R678 2017 | DDC 304.2082—dc23
LC record available at https://lccn.loc.gov/2016057379

ISBN: 978-0-415-70774-9 (hbk)
ISBN: 978-0-367-35289-9 (pbk)

Typeset in Bembo
by Apex CoVantage, LLC

# CONTENTS

# ILLUSTRATIONS

## Figures

## Tables

# Boxes

# INTERNATIONAL ADVISORY BOARD

**Bina Agarwal** (School of Environment and Development, University of Manchester, UK and Institute of Economic Growth, Delhi University, India)

**Susan Buckingham** (formerly with the Division of Social Work, Brunel University, UK)

**Irene Dankelman** (Department of Sustainable Resource Management, Radboud University, Netherlands)

**Diana Hummel** (Institute for Social-Ecological Research, Frankfurt am Main, Germany)

**Ana Isla** (Department of Sociology, Brock University, Canada)

**Kuntala Lahiri-Dutt** (Crawford School of Public Policy, The Australian National University, Canberra, Australia)

**Beate Littig** (Institute for Advanced Studies, Vienna, Austria)

**Janet Muthoni Muthuki** (University of KwaZulu-Natal, South Africa)

**Andrea Nightingale** (School of Global Studies, University of Gothenburg, Sweden)

**Bernadette P. Resurrección** (Stockholm Environment Institute, Bangkok, Thailand)

**Catriona Sandilands** (Faculty of Environmental Studies, York University, Toronto, Canada)

**Joni Seager** (Global Studies, Bentley College, United States)

# CONTRIBUTORS

**Seema Arora-Jonsson** is Associate Professor in the Department of Urban and Rural Development at the Swedish University of Agricultural Sciences in Uppsala, Sweden. Her work is situated at the intersection of gender, development, and environmental governance, and spans the Global North and South. Her publications include *Gender, Development and Environmental Governance: Theorizing Connections* (Routledge, 2013); 'Carbon and Cash in Climate Assemblages: The Making of a New Global Citizenship' in *Antipode* 48 (1; 2016); 'Does Resilience Have a Culture? Ecocultures and the Politics of Knowledge Production' in *Ecological Economics* 121 (2016); and 'Across the Development Divide: A North-South Perspective on Environmental Democracy', forthcoming in 2017 in the *Sage Handbook of Nature*.

**Agnes A. Babugura** is Lecturer in the School of Social Science, Geography and Environmental Science at Monash University in South Africa. She has extensive experience working with national governments and international development organizations such as the United Nations Development Programme, United Nations Environmental Programme, Food and Agriculture Organization, the World Bank, and the International Labour Organization on various development issues. Her publications include the chapters in *Geographies of Children and Young People* (Springer, 2016) and in the *Handbook of Hazards and Disasters* (Routledge, 2011) and journal articles in *Children, Youth and Environments* (18/1:2008) and *Natural Hazards Observer* (33/5 2009). She has also written various research reports, including 'Gender Equality as a Means for Promoting Sustainable Agricultural Production and Food Security in the Green Economy' (UNDP Rio+20, 2012).

**Karin Bradley** is Associate Professor at the Department of Urban Planning and Environment, KTH Royal Institute of Technology in Stockholm, Sweden. Her research deals with sociocultural aspects of sustainable urban development, consumption, sharing economies, and alternative futures. Recent publications include 'The sharing economy as the commons of the 21st century' (with Daniel Pargman; 2016), in *Cambridge Journal of Society, Economy & Regions*; 'Open-source urbanism: creating, multiplying and managing urban commons' (2015) in *Footprint Delft Architecture Theory Journal* 16(9); and *Green Utopianism: Perspectives, Politics and Micro-practices* (Routledge, 2014; co-edited with Johan Hedrén).

**Susan Buckingham** is now working independently as a writer and researcher, having spent many years in higher education. Until 2015 she was a Professor in the Centre for Human Geography at Brunel University in London, UK. She has recently published the four volume Routledge major work *Gender and the Environment* (2015) and has a chapter in Friends of the Earth's book *Why Women Will Save the Planet* (2015). She is the editor for Routledge's Gender and Environment series, and is co-editor (with Virginie Le Masson) of *Understanding Climate Change through Gender Relations* (Routledge, 2017).

**Cameron Butler** has a BEng in Bioresource Engineering from McGill University in Montreal, Canada. During his studies he delved into the field of queer ecology and how it can shape environmental activism and engineering practice. Since graduating, he has worked at McGill on developing and delivering student programming related to gender and sexuality, consent and sexual assault, mental health, substance use, race and colonialism, and accessibility. His work has been published in *Convergence; Sprinkle: An Undergraduate Journal of Feminist and Queer Studies; Under-Currents: Journal of Critical Environmental Studies*; and the *Journal of Environmental Management*.

**Chenyang Xiao** is Associate Professor in the Department of Sociology at American University in Washington, D.C, USA. His main research interests include environmental beliefs, attitudes, behaviours, and public opinion over environmental issues. His current project compares the United States and China in terms of environmental concern.

**María Luz Cruz-Torres** is an anthropologist, Associate Professor in the School of Transborder Studies, and a Senior Sustainability Scientist in the Julie Ann Wrigley Institute of Sustainability at Arizona State University in Arizona, USA. She is the author of *Lives of Dust and Water: An Anthropologist of Change and Resistance in Northwestern Mexico* (University of Arizona Press, 2004), and *Voices Throughout Time: Ethnographic Testimonies of Women Shrimp Traders in Southern Sinaloa, Mexico* (University of Sinaloa Press, 2015). She is also the co-author of *Gender and Sustainability: Lessons from Asia and Latin America* (University of Arizona Press, 2012).

**Nicole Detraz** is Associate Professor of Political Science at the University of Memphis in Tennessee, USA. She specializes in international relations and environmental politics. Her research centres on the intersections of security, the environment, and gender. She explores the implications of using one set of narratives over another to understand environmental issues such as climate change. She is the author of *Gender and the Environment* (Polity Press, 2016) and *Environmental Security and Gender* (Routledge, 2014). She has also published articles in journals such as *International Interactions, Security Studies, International Studies Perspectives*, and *International Feminist Journal of Politics*.

**Giovanna Di Chiro** is Professor of Environmental Studies at Swarthmore College in Pennsylvania, USA. She has published widely on the intersections of environmental science and policy, with a focus on racial, gender, and economic disparities and human rights. She is co-editor of the volume *Appropriating Technology: Vernacular Science and Social Power* (2004) and is completing a book titled *Embodied Ecologies: Science, Politics, and Environmental Justice*. Her research, teaching, and activism focus on community-driven approaches to sustainability and the intersections of social justice and environmental change.

**Emma A. Foster** is Lecturer in International Politics and Gender in the Department of Political Science and International Studies at the University of Birmingham, UK. Her research interests include gender and sexuality, environmental politics, and Foucault. She is currently researching issues related to queer ecology and queer(ing) development. She has published in a variety of journals including *Gender, Place and Culture*, the *British Journal of Politics and International Relations* and *Globalizations*.

**Greta Gaard** is Professor of English at the University of Wisconsin-River Falls, USA, and co-founder of Minnesota's Green Party. Her first anthology, *Ecofeminism: Women, Animals, Nature* (1993), positioned interspecies justice as foundational to ecofeminist theory, and was followed by her co-edited *Ecofeminist Literary Criticism* (1998). In *Ecological Politics: Ecofeminists and the Greens* (1998), she documents the evolution of the US Green Movement and evaluates the potentials for radical environmentalism in US electoral politics. Her most recent volumes include *International Perspectives in Feminist Ecocriticism* (2013) and *Critical Ecofeminism* (forthcoming); her eco-memoir, *The Nature of Home* (2007), has been translated into Chinese and Portuguese.

**Margret Grebowicz** is Associate Professor of Philosophy at Goucher College in Baltimore, Maryland, USA. She is author of *The National Park to Come* and *Why Internet Porn Matters* (Stanford University Press, 2015 and 2013), *Beyond the Cyborg: Adventures with Donna Haraway* (Columbia, 2013, with Helen Merrick), and editor of *Gender after Lyotard* (SUNY 2007), among other collections. Her writings and translations have appeared in numerous journals, including *Agni, Guernica, Philosophy of Science, Environmental Humanities, Hypatia, World Literature Today*, and *Humanimalia*. Current projects include a forthcoming book, *Whale Song*, and new work on mobility impairment and adventure culture.

**Ulrika Gunnarsson-Östling** is a researcher in the Department of Sustainable Development, Environmental Science, and Engineering, KTH Royal Institute of Technology, Stockholm, Sweden. Her research is directed toward long-term planning and sustainable development and emanates from environmental justice and gender perspectives. Her publications include 'What about the future? The troubled relationship between futures and feminism' (with H. Bergman, K. Engwall, and L. Johannesson) in *Nordic Journal of Feminist and Gender Research* (2014); 'Politicising planning through images of the future' in *Green Utopianism* (K. Bradley and J. Hedrén, eds., Routledge 2014); and 'Participatory methods for creating feminist futures' in *Futures* (with Å. Svenfelt and M. Höjer, 2012).

**Laura Houlberg** is based in Portland, Oregon, USA. She is a poet, filmmaker, and graduate of the Independent Publishing Resource Center's Poetry Certificate program. Her work has been featured at Fermentation Closet, The Residency in the Garden, Portland Poetry Slam, and Radar Productions. Her book of poetry, *Cautious Delicious*, complicates mainstream conceptions of gender dys/euphoria and naturalness. Laura's chapter for this handbook is adapted from her thesis, 'Exclusive Environments: Transmisogyny in US Environmentalism', which was written for a BA in Environmental Studies at Lewis and Clark College.

**Martin Hultman** is Associate Professor at Linköping University in Sweden, where he is also coordinator of the Environmental PostHumanities and SweMineTech research networks. His publications include 'The Making of an Environmental Hero: A History of Ecomodern Masculinity, Fuel Cells and Arnold Schwarzenegger, Discourses of Global Climate Change' (*Environmental Humanities* 2, 2013, 79–99) and an edited special issue of the Swedish gender studies journal *TGV*. Martin's current research revolves around issues such as posthumanities ethics, ecological masculinities, ecomodern utopias, and ecopreneurship.

**Diana Hummel** is a member of the executive board of ISOE – Institute for Social-Ecological Research in Frankfurt am Main, Germany. Her research focuses on demographic changes, biodiversity and supply systems, societal relations to nature, and gender and environment. She studied educational science, sociology, psychology, and political science at Goethe University Frankfurt. She received her doctorate in 1999 with a thesis on population discourse, demographic knowledge, and political power. In 2009 she received her habilitation in the faculty of social science at Goethe University, where she lecturers in political science.

**Ana Isla** is Professor with a joint appointment in the Sociology Department and the Centre for Women's and Gender Studies (WGST) at Brock University in St. Catharines, Ontario, Canada. Her research focuses on the consequences of the Earth Summits and green capitalism (particularly in Costa Rica and Peru). Her book, *The Greening of Costa Rica: Women, Peasants, Indigenous People, and the Remaking of Nature*, was published by the University of Toronto Press in 2015.

**Stewart Jackson** is Lecturer in the Department of Government and International Relations at the University of Sydney, Australia. He researches Green and environmental parties and politics in the Asia Pacific. He also has research interests in the structure and composition of social movement mobilizations in Australia. His book, *The Australian Greens: From Activism to Australia's Third Party*, was published in 2016.

**Helen Jarvis** is Reader in Urban Social Geography at Newcastle University, UK. Her research considers common dilemmas of work-life reconciliation viewed through a feminist prism of time-space coordination and 'soft' infrastructures of daily life. Her current research shifts attention to the community and alternative paradigms of 'de-growth' through experiments and innovations in collaborative housing and intentional community.

**Beate Littig** is a sociologist, Head of the Division Socio-Ecological Transformation at the Institute for Advanced Studies (IHS) in Vienna, Austria, and a permanent lecturer at the University of Vienna. Her research interests include environmental sociology, sustainable labour societies, participatory technology assessment, gender studies, qualitative research methods, and practice theory and research. In these areas she coordinates several national and international research projects and participates in international research networks.

**Sherilyn MacGregor** is Reader in Environmental Politics at the University of Manchester, where she is joint-appointed to the Sustainable Consumption Institute and the School of Social Sciences. Her research explores synergies and tensions between environmental and feminist politics, with particular interest in questions of justice, sustainability, and strategies for social change. She is author of *Beyond Mothering Earth: Ecological Citizenship and the Politics of Care* (University of British Columbia Press, 2006), *Environment and Politics* (Routledge, 2015), and numerous journal articles on gender and environmental topics. She is also co-editor of the two-volume collection *Environmental Movements Around the World* (Praeger, 2014, with Timothy Doyle) and past editor of the journal *Environmental Politics*.

**Freya Mathews** is Adjunct Professor of Environmental Philosophy at Latrobe University in Australia. Her books include *The Ecological Self* (1991), *Ecology and Democracy* (editor; 1996), *For Love of Matter: A Contemporary Panpsychism* (2003), *Journey to the Source of the Merri* (2003), *Reinhabiting Reality: Towards a Recovery of Culture* (2005), *Ardea: A philosophical novella* (2016), and *Without Animals Life is Not Worth Living* (2016). Her current special interests are in ecological civilization; indigenous (Australian and Chinese) perspectives on 'sustainability' and how these perspectives may be adapted to the context of contemporary global society; panpsychism and the critique of the metaphysics of modernity; and wildlife ethics in the context of the Anthropocene.

**Aaron M. McCright** is Associate Professor of Sociology in Lyman Briggs College, the Department of Sociology, and the Environmental Science and Policy Program at Michigan State University, in Michigan, USA. He was named a 2007 Kavli Frontiers Fellow in the National Academy of Sciences, and has received the 2009 Teacher-Scholar Award and the 2009 Curricular Service-Learning and Civic Engagement Award at MSU, and the 2014 Larry T. Reynolds Award for Outstanding Teaching of Sociology from the Michigan Sociological Association.

**Pamela McElwee** is Associate Professor of Human Ecology at Rutgers, The State University of New Jersey. Her research deals with household impacts of global environmental change, including biodiversity loss and climate change, in Asia. She is the author of the book, *Forests Are Gold: Trees, People, and Environmental Rule in Vietnam* (University of Washington Press, 2016), and is the co-editor, with María Luz Cruz-Torres, of *Gender and Sustainability: Lessons from Asia and Latin America* (University of Arizona Press, 2012).

**Mary Mellor** is Emeritus Professor at Northumbria University, in Newcastle-upon-Tyne, where she was founding chair of the University's Sustainable Cities Research Institute. She has published extensively on alternative economics, integrating socialist, feminist, and green perspectives. Her books include *Breaking the Boundaries: Toward a Feminist Green Socialism* (Virago, 1992); *Feminism and Ecology* (New York University Press, 1997); *The Future of Money: From Financial Crisis to Public Resource* (Pluto, 2010); and *Debt or Democracy: Public Money for Sustainability and Social Justice* (Pluto 2015).

**Helen Merrick** is an independent scholar whose publications include *The Secret Feminist Cabal: A Cultural History of Science Fiction Feminisms* (2009) and the co-authored (with Margret Grebowicz) book *Beyond the Cyborg: Adventures with Donna Haraway* (2013). Her current research focuses on narratives of change and the potential of stories to impact public discourse around social justice issues, particularly climate change and refugee rights.

**Sharlene Mollett** is Assistant Professor in the Department of Human Geography and the Centre for Critical Development Studies at the University of Toronto. As a feminist political ecologist and cultural geographer, her research is positioned at the intersection of postcolonial political ecology and critical feminist/racial studies in the Americas. Her work interrogates the multiple ways racial ideologies and patriarchy shape natural resource conflict and management in Latin America, specifically in Honduras and Panama. Her work is published in such journals as *Antipode, Annals of the Association of American Geographers, Latin American Research Review, Geoforum, Gender, Place and Culture*, and *Cultural Geographies*.

**Karen Morrow** is Professor of Environmental Law at Swansea University in Wales and a founder member of the Global Network for the Study of Human Rights and the Environment. Her research focuses on theoretical and practical aspects of public participation in environmental law and policy and on gender and the environment. Her publications include 'Ecofeminism and the environment: international law and climate change' in M. Davies and V. Munro (eds.), *The Ashgate Companion to Feminist Legal Theory* (Ashgate 2013); and 'Procedural Human Rights in International Law' in A. Grear and L. Kotze (eds.), *Research Handbook on Human Rights and the Environment* (Edward Elgar 2015).

**Bernadette P. Resurrección** is Senior Research Fellow at the Stockholm Environment Institute (SEI) and is Adjunct Associate Professor of the Asian Institute of Technology in Thailand. She has researched and published on varied themes and aspects of gender, environment, and development, ranging from field-based community studies to critical policy analyses. She co-leads the global Gender and Social Equity Programme of SEI, and is exploring how gender and development practices can meaningfully address complex and grounded realities that feminist political ecology research can richly capture.

**Catriona Sandilands** is Professor in the Faculty of Environmental Studies at York University in Toronto, Canada, where she teaches at the intersections of environmental literature and philosophy, queer and feminist studies, and ecological politics. She is also a 2016 Pierre Elliott Trudeau Foundation Fellow. The author of more than 60 published works on topics ranging from national parks to lesbian communities, Walter Benjamin to honeybees, melancholic natures to monstrous plants, she is also known for *The Good-Natured Feminist: Ecofeminism and Democracy* (Minnesota, 1999), *Queer Ecologies: Sex, Nature, Politics, Desire* (Indiana, 2010), and the forthcoming *Green Words/Green Worlds: Environmental Literatures and Politics*.

**Jade Sasser** is Assistant Professor in the Department of Gender and Sexuality Studies at the University of California, Riverside, USA, where she is a core faculty member in the Sustainability Studies major. Her research and teaching lie at the intersections of international development, gender and climate change, and women's health. She is currently completing her first book manuscript, titled *Making Sexual Stewards*.

**Meike Schalk** is Associate Professor at the School of Architecture, KTH Royal Institute of Technology, Stockholm, Sweden. Her research on architecture and urban questions combines critical inquiry into issues of sustainability and resilience; ground research in feminist theory and feminist spatial practices; questions of democracy in planning; critical aesthetic and political practices; and practice-led research. Her recent publications include 'Old News from a Contact Zone. Action Archive in Tensta', in D. Petrescu and K. Trogal (eds.), *The Social (Re)Production of Architecture* (Routledge, forthcoming), and 'Utopian Desires and Institutional Change', in K. Bradley and J. Hedrén (eds.), *Green Utopianism* (Routledge, 2014).

**Joni Seager** is an activist and scholar in feminist environmental analysis and global feminist studies. She is Chair and Professor of Global Studies at Bentley University in Massachusetts, USA. Prior to that, she was Dean of the Faculty of Environmental Studies at York University in Toronto, Canada. The author of dozens of articles, books, and reports, Joni has also worked extensively with the United Nations Environment Programme (UNEP) to bring gendered analysis into their work. Most recently, she was the Lead Coordinating Author of UNEP's first comprehensive global gendered environmental analysis, the 2016 'Global Gender and Environment Outlook'.

**Nicole Seymour** is Assistant Professor of English at California State University, Fullerton, USA. She is the author of *Strange Natures: Futurity, Empathy, and the Queer Ecological Imagination* (University of Illinois Press, 2013), which won the Ecocriticism Book Award from the Association for the Study of Literature and Environment in 2015, and articles published in *Cinema Journal, The Journal of Ecocriticism*, and *Transgender Studies Quarterly*. From 2013–2014 she was a fellow in residence at the Rachel Carson Center for Environment and Society in Munich, Germany. Her current book project focuses on 'inappropriate' affective responses to environmental phenomena, including ambivalence, irreverence, and irony.

**Immanuel Stieß** is Head of the research unit Energy and Climate Protection in Everyday Life of ISOE – Institute for Social-Ecological Research, Frankfurt am Main, Germany. His research focuses on social-ecological life-style analysis and the study of everyday life practices in the fields of housing; energy use and nutrition. He has wide experience in both quantitative and qualitative empirical research.

**Noël Sturgeon** is Dean and Professor of the Faculty of Environmental Studies at York University in Toronto, Canada. She is the author of *Ecofeminist Natures: Race, Gender, Feminist Theory and Political Action* (Routledge, 1997), *Environmentalism in Popular Culture: Gender, Race, Sexuality and the Politics of the Natural* (University of Arizona Press, 2009), and numerous articles on environmentalist, antimilitarist, and feminist movements and theories. She has been a Distinguished Fulbright Lecturer at York; a Rockefeller Fellow at the Center for the Critical Analysis of Contemporary Culture, Rutgers; and a Visiting Scholar at Murdoch University, Australia, the JFK Institute at the Frei Universitat in Berlin, the Center for Cultural Studies, UCSC, and universities in Taiwan, China, Japan, and Ukraine.

**Julie Sze** is Professor and the Chair of American Studies at University of California Davis, in California, USA. She is also the founding director of the Environmental Justice Project for the John Muir Institute of the Environment. Her research investigates environmental justice and environmental inequality; culture and environment; race, gender, and power; and urban/community health and activism. She is the author of *Noxious New York: The Racial Politics of Urban Health and Environmental Justice*, which won the 2008 John Hope Franklin Publication Prize, and *Fantasy Islands: Chinese Dreams and Ecological Fears in an Age of Climate Crisis* (University of California Press, 2015).

**Charis Thompson** is Chancellor's Professor and Chair of Gender and Women's Studies, the University of California, Berkeley and Professor of Sociology, USA, London School of Economics and Political Science, UK. She is the author of *Making Parents: The Ontological Choreography of Reproductive Technologies* (MIT Press, 2005), which won the 2007 Rachel Carson Award from the Society for the Social Study of Science, and *Good Science: The Ethical Choreography of Stem Cell Research* (MIT Press, 2013). Her new book, *Getting Ahead*: *Inequality and Meritocracy in an Age of Technology Elites*, is in preparation.

**Marcela Tovar-Restrepo** is Chair of the Board of Directors of the Women's Environment and Development Organization (WEDO). She has served as an advisor for United Nations agencies (CSD, UNDEF) and international cooperation agencies (GTZ, AECID), as well as for governments, social movements, and NGOs in areas such as gender, ethnic diversity, sustainable development, and human rights. She conducts research and teaches at Columbia University's Graduate School of Architecture, Planning, and Preservation in New York, USA.

**Ines Weller** is Professor at the University of Bremen in Germany, Deputy Chair of the Sustainability Research Center (artec), and coordinator of the research field 'Sociotechnical Systems and Sustainability'. Her research interests focus on sustainability and gender, sustainable consumption and production patterns, and gender and technology. She also has research interests in the links between gender and climate change and climate change adaptation.

# ACKNOWLEDGEMENTS

This handbook has been an enormous undertaking and would not have been possible without the support of a large number of individuals and institutions. My network of editorial advisors offered invaluable suggestions and contacts during the initial stages of developing the contents of the handbook. Conversations with them, by email and Skype, helped me decide on the scope of the topics and identify specialists in the field. Generous support during the commissioning and curating stage was provided by the Rachel Carson Center (RCC), Ludwig Maximilians University in Munich, where I was a Carson Fellow for six months in 2014. I am indebted to Professors Christof Mauch and Helmuth Trischler for seeing the value of this project, and to the many colleagues at the RCC who offered advice and support along the way. Equally generous support, in the form of staff time during the final stages, was provided by the Sustainable Consumption Institute (SCI) at the University of Manchester. Colleagues in the SCI, including Professor Dale Southerton and members of the gender and sustainability reading group, offered invaluable intellectual as well as moral support. Dr. Susan Hogan became my brilliant project manager in the final stages; I could not have completed the handbook without her. Proofreading and copyediting assistance was generously provided by Katrina Farrugia and Anna Wienhues (both of the SCI) and Amy Kings (Keele University). I appreciate the support of editorial assistants at T&F, Helen Bell and Margaret Farrelly, in overseeing the project and bringing it to fruition. It took much longer to complete than expected (in part due to the upheaval created by my move from an established job in the School of Politics, International Relations, and Philosophy at Keele University to a new post at the University of Manchester in November 2015), so the patience of all involved has been much appreciated. Finally, my very special thanks go to the chapter contributors for their work and perseverance, and to Nicole Seymour and Simon Pardoe for their moral support during what was an at-times arduous and lonely process.

# ACRONYMS

This handbook aims to be accessible to a multidisciplinary readership and therefore contributors have tried to keep their use of specialist acronyms to a minimum. Terms in general use, such as EU, UN, US, UK, GNP/GDP, and $CO_2$, are not spelled out.

Some acronyms are highly relevant to discussions of gender and environment, and so have been used frequently. In most cases, they are spelled out when first used in a chapter.

For readers' reference, here is a list:

| | |
|---|---|
| COP | Conference of the Parties to the UNFCCC |
| FPE | feminist political ecology |
| GED | gender, environment, and development |
| IPCC | Intergovernmental Panel on Climate Change |
| LGBTQ | lesbian, gay, bisexual, trans, queer |
| UNCED | United Nations Conference on Environment and Development |
| UNDP | United Nations Development Program |
| UNEP | United Nations Environment Program |
| UNFCCC | United Nations Framework Convention on Climate Change |

# FOREWORD

## Facing the future, honouring the past: whose gender? Whose nature?

### *Noël Sturgeon*

The book you hold in your hands (or have pulled up on one digital platform or another) is the latest effort in a long line of publications that bring together feminist analyses of environmental issues. The history of such edited compilations stretches back before the 1970s, and will continue, I am convinced, into the future. Whether these approaches are called gender and environment, environmental feminism, ecofeminism, feminist environmental justice, or another term, they demonstrate the immense value of feminist thinking about the relationship of social inequalities to environmental problems.

Solving the environmental problems we face means understanding the ways these problems have arisen, developed, and persisted. Critically analyzing environmental problems means identifying the power relations embedded in their production, because otherwise, collective strategies to address them will be ineffective and will increase inequality. If some groups benefit from environmental degradation and exploitation, while others suffer the consequences, then issues of power and inequality must be part of understanding the genesis of environmental problems and identifying adequate solutions.

Feminist theories are powerful tools for critical environmental analysis. Attention to gender is a particularly important aspect of understanding environmental issues because of the long association between concepts of gender and nature, the gendered interaction of human labour with the environment, and the gendered impacts of environmental degradation. Leaving gender out of attempts to conceptualize, examine, and correct environmental problems means that our understanding is deeply inadequate and our solutions at the least partial. At the worst, such insufficient solutions could intensify environmental damage, even if, during the coming shocks of climate change, a few of the world's elite are able to protect themselves and their families. That is the danger we face today. Environmental feminist scholarship teaches us that we must resist apocalyptic calls to 'save the planet' and focus on creating more just societies that reject the continued environmental exploitation that put the marginalized in jeopardy as well as existing ecosystems.

Feminist environmental approaches are also crucially important to feminist theory, and to other critical analyses of social, political, and economic inequalities. As those inequalities have been historically naturalized, a sharp attention to the ways in which concepts of nature are deployed by the dominant culture to justify inequality and colonization is a necessary tool to resist hegemonic structures of exploitation. It's important, as the chapters in this handbook demonstrate, to surface, recognize, and attribute the innovative foundations of such critiques to the scholars who put them forward and influenced later generations of feminist and environmentalist thinkers, with whatever limitations could be found in some earlier ecofeminist efforts.

Bringing together these two streams of analysis – feminist critiques of environmental theory and environmental critiques of feminist theory – as ecofeminism has done for half a century, is even more valuable today, as theories of gender and environment have deepened, become more complex, and become more inclusive of various critical perspectives. Feminist environmentalist analysis has not been static over the last fifty years, but has mutated along with feminist theory itself, changed by activism and academic debate, by challenges to the dominance and complicity of feminists with privilege made by those who were more marginalized. A turn to intersectionality opened up feminist theory to decoloniality, postcoloniality, trans theory, queer theory, women of colour feminism, and critical disability studies; but ecofeminist theory also insisted on attention to animals, land, plants, fungi, water, and in general the exploitation of the nonhuman as part of this growing critical set of tools. Our understanding of environment, of nature, has been deepened considerably as a result. As environmental feminism is now more inclusive, it is closer to achieving answers that take in account all systems of oppression. This more comprehensive and fruitful environmental feminist analysis is apparent throughout the chapters included in this collection.

Similarly, as feminist theory now appears in almost every discipline as a critical analysis, we also find feminist environmental scholarship everywhere: in the humanities, the social sciences, the natural sciences, and all interdisciplinary points in between. This important handbook contains a dizzying array of disciplinary approaches and perspectives, but in each chapter, feminist and environmental tools are deployed simultaneously to give us fresh insights and to surface new debates that must be addressed.

The set of more complex feminist environmentalist analytical tools found in this volume can help us tease out the interaction of social injustice with environmental degradation, an interaction that has created the voracious juggernaut of global capitalism and the disruption of planetary ecosystems, to ends we cannot completely predict but we cannot deny will affect us all. Will these tools be enough? Thankfully, the deepening and complicating of feminist environmentalist analyses is not over, as is clear from the debates internal to this handbook, as well as the challenges these authors offer to other scholars trying to grapple with solutions to environmental and social crises. What will be necessary is to connect these analyses to action, as is being done by movements across the globe. While the differences in theoretical approaches apparent in this collection are important, and debate over strategy, language, and positionality crucial to continued improvement of our understanding of the problems we face and the solutions we need, what shines out clearly from this handbook is the urgent and shared determination to address environmental and social injustice together.

# GENDER AND ENVIRONMENT
## An introduction

*Sherilyn MacGregor*

## Introduction

This handbook presents the 'state of the art' of the academic field of gender and environment. One intention is to showcase the variety of perspectives, themes, and debates that have shaped the intellectual project of understanding the gender-environment nexus within the social sciences and humanities for over four decades. Another is to demonstrate that under the banner of 'gender and environment' sits a diverse, theoretically – sophisticated, and empirically grounded collection of approaches that have a common a set of concerns about gender injustice and the degradation of the natural environment. With some of its roots reaching into the fertile soil of activist movements, this scholarship – particularly within the tradition of ecological feminism – has been motivated by the pursuit of justice in the face of diverse and interlocking forms of oppression. But it has also contributed theoretical insights that in many cases were ahead of their time. Arguably, gender and environment scholarship was *materialist* and *posthumanist* before these concepts gained popularity in the mainstream of Western academia. An *intersectional* analysis of capitalism, rationalist science, colonialism, racism, (hetero) sexism, and speciesism has always been central to feminist environmental scholarship. And, contrary to popular opinion in many corners of environmental studies, this work has very little to do with the claim that 'women are closer to nature than men'. In fact, much of it is aimed at questioning the very ideas of 'women' and 'nature' and at understanding the myriad ways in which gender (as a social category and power relation) shapes and is shaped by inter-human relations as well as human relations with other species and environments. Yet the idea that it is at base a simplistic narrative about women saving the planet persists in spite of the evidence. The *Routledge Handbook of Gender and Environment* aims to dispense with that caricature once and for all.

This chapter provides a comprehensive introduction to the field and to the handbook. It proceeds in two parts. In the first part, after an explanation of the terms 'gender' and 'environment', there is a concise description of the academic field of gender and environment, which includes an account of its evolution and a discussion of its core threads and themes. The second part offers a comprehensive overview of the structure and content of the handbook.

1

## Gender and environment as a field of scholarship

It is inevitably challenging to define an academic field that boasts a long history and a refusal to be contained in a neat disciplinary box. The discussion in this chapter starts from a modest position: it is not the final word but simply a way of introducing the common terms, threads, and themes that run through the chapters in the handbook. The choice of 'gender and environment' is deliberately broad, no doubt too broad, neutral, and bland for those who feel strongly about using the banner of 'ecofeminism' or prefer an agential 'nature' over an anthropocentric 'environment', or who deliberately call it 'ecofeminism' to foreground the politicized nature of this work (cf. Mallory 2009). All of those sentiments can be found in the chapters in this handbook; 'gender and environment' serves as a big tent for housing a wide-ranging and inclusive survey.

The field being mapped here is at the very least committed to sustained and systematic scholarly investigation of how gender shapes human experiences of environments and how environments are interpreted and treated through the lens of gender. The common denominator is the analysis that social oppression and environmental exploitation are inextricably linked to fundamental social constructs that have co-evolved with patriarchal capitalist-colonial power relations. Researchers have both theorized and provided evidence of material, structural, and ideational links between the degradation of the ecosphere and power asymmetries between men and women. They have mapped gender differences in the ways people perceive, experience, and respond to environmental problems in a broad range of social contexts.

Gender and environment scholars are in agreement that gender is missing from most environmental fields and are united in their bafflement at the limited impact that feminist environmental insights and interventions have had on mainstream environmental research (cf. Banerjee and Bell 2007). They share a commitment to the centrality of gender relations to the study of environment, but they by no means agree on the meanings of these terms or on how the gender-environment nexus should be studied.

## *Terms of reference: 'gender' and 'environment'*

'Gender' and 'environment' share a common status as contested terms that are value-laden products of specific historical and cultural contexts. As concepts used in academic research, both can be seen as 'inventions' that do not mean the same thing everywhere in the world. In many places, ideas about gender and conceptions of the environment were imposed as part of the process of colonization. Although humans no doubt have always had ways of understanding and representing differences between the sexes, and between humans and their surroundings, these two concepts have particular meanings and do particular ideological work in the contemporary globalized world. Both gender and environment are taken in this volume, and in the field of gender and environment research more widely, to be *social constructions* rather than empirical objects, there are no such things as 'gender' or 'the environment'. This does not mean that problems such as climate change or transmisogynist violence are not 'real', but rather that they are products of particular social contexts and power relations, and thus how they are understood is malleable, manipulable, and changeable over time. In this handbook, the meanings of gender and environment are consistent with and situated within conversations taking place within the academic field in focus.

They may seem ubiquitous today, but both gender and environment are relatively young concepts. 'The environment' did not enter Western discourse until around the late 1960s (Dryzek 2013). The application of 'gender' to human societies was popularized only as recently as the 1970s.

Their origin in new social movements gives these terms particular political texture and resonance. Environmentalists have objectified the environment in order to advocate its preservation and remediation. Feminists have reified gender in order to politicize inequality, or more precisely the subordinate status of women in all spheres of society. These activist goals have shaped the way the two terms are conceived and studied in their counterpart, interdisciplinary fields of environmental studies and women's and gender studies, each of which have been established in universities for three decades or more.

The academic study of 'the environment' originated in the Anglo-European Global North and has been pursued by a range of scholars, many of whom identify with the field of environmental studies and to some degree with the environmental movement. The concept generally refers to the habitat or living space surrounding all living things, but mostly humans. The dominant use of the term 'the environment' refers to the non-human natural environment or 'nature'. Environment and nature are often used as synonyms, along with 'ecosystem', 'biosphere', and planet earth. In the environmental social sciences and humanities, 'the environment' has been commonly understood as the natural environment, and positioned as being distinct from (albeit interconnected with) human society. Witness the common usage of the binary constructions 'environment and society' and 'human-nature relationship'.

Gender and environment scholars discuss environment in a range of ways, including the biophysical, built (i.e., human-made), and social environments. They share with other heterodox approaches a critical stance toward mainstream conceptions. A point of intersection between gender and environment and environmental justice scholars, for example, is the argument that the mainstream environmental movements and disciplines have adopted a narrow understanding of 'the environment' that excludes the people, places, and practices that are outside the experiences of the privileged and powerful (see Sze Chapter 10). This narrowness has resulted in an anthropocentric approach that places human experiences at the forefront of analyses, with a secondary concern for nature and non-humans subjects. There are others, however, who wish to move to posthumanist (non-speciesist) and 'enlightened' anthropocentric approaches to environment that see humans as embedded in a more-than-human world that has agency and intrinsic value (see, for example, Adams and Gruen 2014; Gaard Chapter 7). The use of 'environment' *without an article* in 'gender and environment' is meant to signal this more inclusive, less objectified interpretation of the term.

In its popular usage, the term 'gender' broadly refers to the collection of characteristics used for categorizing people with reference to dominant understandings of masculinity and femininity. It is typically thought to be the sociocultural layer that sits atop biological sex, such that, for example, those of the male sex tend to be culturally masculine, but even inanimate things without hormones and organs can be gendered. Gender is used as a means to impose expectations and roles upon groups and is claimed and performed as part of an individual's identity. The former definition implies that gender is a tool, not just of simple classification but also of social control: it serves to position people according to the dominant ideology. In this case it is useful to think about gender as a verb, as in 'to gender'. There are sociocultural processes of 'genderization' at work in assigning gendered traits to living beings and inanimate things, as well as to practices, feelings, and roles. It has become common to use the term 'racialized' to refer to a process of ascribing racial and ethnic identities to particular groups with the effect of perpetuating racism. For example, the groups that have been ascribed a race are those who are non-white, because historically white people have had the power to do the naming of others (white people are not considered to have/be a race). A similar kind of process can be theorized for gendering, where particular gender qualities and expectations are ascribed to men and women, but women are 'feminized' in a way that marks them out as distinct from, and inferior to, men. Men, by contrast, are rarely thought of as being gendered. The point is to see these processes through the *lens of power* rather than to see gender and race as essential, biological facts. Both the structural-material and symbolic-cultural dimensions of the genderization process are deconstructed and analyzed with feminist theoretical tools. Gender scholars understand gender as a relational concept, in that one gender is always defined in opposition to the other, and the relationships between genders (including conflict and cooperation) are constitutive of how we think of each gender on its own. The male-female binary is the dominant gender structure in the Anglo-European West, and it has been thus for centuries. Gender and environment scholars have found the analysis of this binary structure particularly important for understanding the links between gender and environment: the analysis of *the naturalization of femininity and the feminization of nature* – and the cultural devaluation of both women and nature are at the core of the analysis. In this line of thinking, gender is deployed as an analytical category and tool for understanding social as well as human-environment relationships.

As several chapters in the handbook point out, it has been, and in some circles remains, common to interpret gender as being synonymous with women. Until relatively recently, most of the research on gender on environment-related topics was conducted by scholars with a particular interest in the experiences of women as women. Reasons for this focus include a political choice to focus on women's lives as interesting in themselves (it was called 'women's studies', after all) and a desire to rectify their historic exclusion from mainstream research. A sole focus on 'women' as a universal and homogenous category, without recognizing/avoiding the pitfalls of doing so, has become rare in recent years; even when researchers study women only, they are attentive to social heterogeneity and frame the analysis with gender as a fluid and relational category. Many chapters in the handbook take the matrix approach of *'intersectionality'*, which now seems de rigueur in feminist environmental analysis. Attempts to analyze gender as a stand-alone category are deemed problematic (see, for example, Mollett Chapter 9). Not only are single-axis analyses prone to embedding assumptions of whiteness in ideas about womanhood and occluding interlocking power dynamics, but they also play into the reification and use of 'women' as a technical category for the neoliberal management of populations (May 2015:7). This latter phenomenon has been identified in gender and development research (see Radcliffe 2015; Arora-Jonsson Chapter 19 for a discussion).

The women-centric and single-axis approach of gender and environment research has been a double-edged sword for the field. On the one hand, those who have focused on women as a category have been criticized for universalizing and essentializing and/or for leaving men, trans, and gender queer people out of the story. As queer scholars have noted, focusing on women only can result in the mistake of treating the experiences of some, usually privileged, Western heterosexual cisgender women as the norm. Used as a catch-all term, 'gender' can mask the fact that women, men, queer, and trans people 'are not situated equally in terms of environmental oppression' (Gaard 2011:42). It can also result in a tendency in some corners of the field to downplay the centrality of racialization to experiences and performances of gender, something that has been problematized in postcolonial and decolonial scholarship. For example, Sharlene Mollett (Chapter 9) argues that 'the mutual constitution of gender and race remains understudied and on the margins' of gender and environment research, and in feminist political ecology in particular.

On the other hand, women as a category are routinely invisibilized in mainstream environmental literature and policy. If feminist scholars and activists do not insert women *qua* women into the discussion, they often remain on the margins or excluded altogether. So 'bringing women in' through the language of gender can sometimes be justified, for example in policy-making through the use of gender mainstreaming (see Buckingham Chapter 26). Gender mainstreaming is a policy approach that has for a long time been a technical euphemism for including women where they would otherwise be forgotten. As Cynthia Enloe (2013) observes, the practice of not taking women seriously, and not including women's experiences and concerns in the (his)stories told about the world, has been the default position in many academic disciplines. At the same time as wanting to treat women as a diverse and contested category, and to attend to the multiple intersections of gender with other axes of social difference, there is still value in taking 'actual women and their activities' seriously (Peterson 2005:500). The work of activists at the front lines of climate change negotiations (e.g., the Women and Gender Constituency of the UNFCCC) and academics who advise and assess sustainable development programmes in the Global South (see Morrow Chapter 27; Babugura Chapter 24; Tovar-Restrepo Chapter 28) demonstrates the strategic dilemmas involved in defending women's gender interests.

Although questions about women still dominate gender studies, understandings of gender have come a long way in the past four decades, resulting in approaches that are more expansive and kaleidoscopic than single-axis, binary constructions of old. Since the 2000s, the cis-trans binary has become common, where 'cis' means having a gender that is on the same side as the biological sex one was born with and where 'trans' means having a gender that is across from one's sex. Within cisgender there are numerous masculinities and femininities, some of which have been theorized as hegemonic and emphasized respectively (cf. Connell 1995, 2009). Femininities have been the default focus of much of the feminist environmental work, with its focus on women. Connections between different masculinities and environmental phenomena have not received much scholarly attention, which is curious given the role that hegemonic forms of masculine power – in institutions of the state such as the military and scientific agencies, as well as in corporations and environmental movement organizations – have played in shaping both environmental problems and how they have (not) been addressed. Bob Pease (2016) argues, for example, that there is a relationship between the exploitation of nature and hegemonic masculinity, with elite men being more likely than any other group to accept environmental risks, to engage in carbon intensive practices (driving cars, eating meat), and to be involved in the quest for profitable, techno-scientific solutions to problems such as global warming (e.g., climate engineering; see Fleming 2007). Similarly, in their groundbreaking article 'Cool Dudes', McCright and Dunlap (2011) provide empirical evidence that it is conservative white men who have played the biggest role in organizing climate denial in the United States (see also Oreskes and Conway 2011). And yet there is very little focus in the academic literature on these aspects of climate change. It is worth noting here that the mainstream of environmental social sciences and humanities is dominated by elite, mostly cisgender, men who it seems have not felt the need to hold up a mirror. Hegemonic masculinity exists as an unmarked category in environmental studies, and to some extent in the gender and environment field (see Anshelm and Hultman 2014; Hultman Chapter 16).

Between the two poles of hegemonic masculinity and emphasized femininity, there is a range of performances of gender, some of which seeking to subvert (or 'to queer') the binary itself. The gender and environment field has gradually expanded to include a much broader interpretation of gender than was adopted in early writings. This move has resulted in genderqueer and LGBT+ becoming an increasingly vibrant part of the gender and environment scholarship – starting in the 1990s as a voice on the margins of radical scholarship. Queer ecology evolved out of ecofeminist theory (Gaard 1997) and took early shape through biologists' studies of the diversity of genders and sexualities that are found in most living species (cf. Bagemihl 1999; Roughgarden 2004). Much of the queer ecology work has been done in the fields of eco-literary criticism and cultural studies, where scholars apply a methodology of queering to deconstruct texts and films (see Mortimer-Sandilands and Erickson 2010). It is increasingly engaging with topics relating to environmental justice in local communities and the discursive framing of environmental policy, such as sustainable development in national and UN-level policy (see, for example, Seymour Chapter 17; Butler Chapter 18). As a consequence of this shift in gender analysis, there is also growing recognition of the workings of non-European gender systems, many of which are non-binary, such as those found in Indigenous American and Asian societies. A survey of the field suggests that more work needs to be done to develop an inclusive framework for understanding the diversity of ways gender is performed in human and other species, and how these ways shape and are shaped by relations to environment.

### Histories, threads, and themes

This handbook contains a collection of chapters that demonstrates the diverse ways in which scholars have analyzed connections between gender and environment. It is a multi-, inter-, and trans-disciplinary body of scholarship that lacks clearly defined boundaries, thus making it a challenge to confect the sense of comprehensiveness that is expected in a handbook. There are no degree programmes or academic journals established in its name, and it is rare to find conference panels, let alone entire conferences, dedicated to themes connecting 'gender and environment'. The aim of this handbook, therefore, is to break new ground by opening up an umbrella over this body of work and calling it a 'field'. This section reviews the histories, threads, and themes that give it a distinctive shape in the 2010s.

The majority of scholarly work on gender and environment is located in the social sciences and the humanities. As it is being mapped in this handbook, it comes out of Western feminist approaches and originated in universities located primarily in Anglo-European countries. It is a much broader and more intellectually diverse field than in often recognized, even by others working in gender studies. For example, as the editors' introduction to the *Routledge Handbook of Gender and Development* explains – by way of distinguishing the gender and development field from gender and environment – 'In the 1980s came the approach of gender and the environment, which was at first based on ecofeminist views, especially Vandana Shiva (1989) and Carolyn Merchant (1992), who identified an essentialist link between women and the environment' (Coles et al. 2015: online). This *Handbook of Gender and Environment* starts from a different understanding of the origins and contemporary contours of gender and environment as a *transdisciplinary academic field* rather than 'an approach'. Although there are important connections and shared analyses between gender and development and gender and environment (they overlap and learn from each other in many ways), a key difference is that gender and environment scholars have looked in their own backyards as much or more than looking at developing country contexts. A significant proportion of the work responds to problems that plague affluent, capitalist, settler-colonial cultures in the Global North, such as the male domination of environmentalism, the pervasiveness of animal exploitation, and the sexist design of cities (to name a few), in addition to what many would call abstract theorizing. A diversity of Western feminist perspectives has shaped the gender and environment field, as have themes and debates over ontology, epistemology, and political strategy that are found with feminist scholarship more broadly.

Excellent histories of ecofeminist traditions of making connections between gender and environment have been written by Sturgeon (1997), Sandilands (1999), Gaard (2011), among others. Greta Gaard's 2011 revisiting of the development of ecofeminism is particularly thorough, and is prefaced by the observation that there is a lack of reflection on the evolution of the field – possibly because the fear of 'contamination-by-association is too strong' (27). In this handbook, Thompson and MacGregor (Chapter 2) provide a potted history, focusing on the failure of ecofeminism to become the 'third wave' of feminism, as it was suggested soon after its inception. They explain that early thinking about women's affinity with nature, starting in the 1970s and 1980s, was connected to the emergence of feminist, peace, and ecology activism in North America and Europe. Frustrations with lack of attention to gender politics in environmentalism, the lack of women in leadership positions in environmental organizations, and the lack of environmental politics in feminism – all while the world was hurtling toward a global eco-crisis – lead to key texts and conferences seeking to make the links. Early actions at Greenham Common in the United Kingdom and the Pentagon in the United States are considered to be the catalysts for the emerging ecological feminist movement. The first texts were written by non-academic writers with an expressly political agenda. French anarchist writer Françoise d'Eubonne, widely credited with coining the term 'écologie-féminisme' in 1974, argued that it was necessary that women bring about an ecological revolution for the survival of the planet ('feminism or death' was the choice she presented; Roth-Johnson 2013). Ten years later, in the United States, Ynestra King (1983:11) wrote that 'our present patriarchy enshrines together the hatred of women and the hatred of nature. In defying this patriarchy we are loyal to future generations and to life and this planet itself'. Conferences were organized and texts were assembled to articulate a feminist plan for 'healing the wounds' (Plant 1989). (See Gaard Chapter 7 for a discussion of how vegan/animal rights feminism fed into the early development of ecofeminist theory.)

From the early 1990s, academics (mostly in the Global North) started to take up the connections between women's subordinate status and the environmental crisis, informed/inspired by examples of women's activism. Scholars responded to activists' claims about women's closeness to nature and moral duty to 'save it', with both excitement and disdain. From the early 1990s onward, several key academic texts were framed by a sense of unease about claims of women's essential connection to nature (see, for example, Merchant 1990; Biehl 1991; Agarwal 1992; Plumwood 1993; Sandilands 1999; MacGregor 2006). Many challenged the rhetoric for its uncritical strategy of reversal, its celebration of a devalued feminine identity created by a patriarchal master logic instead of arguing for its demolition (Plumwood 1993). Some theorists questioned the representation of both ecofeminism and the women about whom it claimed to speak, especially those from the Global South. MacGregor (2006) observes that there was tendency in the nineties to appropriate grassroots subsistence struggles as affirmation of an ideological rather than empirically grounded theory of ecofeminism, a point made by several critics of Vandana Shiva's work on the Indian Chipko Movement (e.g., Agarwal 1992; Sandilands 1999).

For many years a typology of ecofeminism that presented in texts that included cultural, socialist, and social ecofeminism and women in grassroots eco-struggles in the 'third world' (see Merchant 1992). Even though this typology has been reprinted with each new edition of an old text (cf. Dobson 2007:4th edition; Dryzek 2013:2nd edition; Tong 2009:3rd edition), it no longer represents ecofeminist academic work or the broader gender and environment field (if it ever did). One contribution of this handbook is to provide a map of gender and environment scholarship that is fit for the twenty-first century. Rather than draw boxes around camps or categories, as was common in the past, an alternative approach that informs the contents of this handbook is to identify the main threads that are woven together to make the field's rich tapestry.

As discussed later, the first part of the handbook aims at uncovering the intellectual foundations that have shaped the past and are informing the ongoing development of gender and environmental research. Chapters in the three subsequent parts demonstrate the lasting importance of these foundational threads. One thread that can be traced throughout the handbook is *feminist science studies* (FSS), which is concerned with the history and politics of scientific knowledge production. It includes research on the history of modern science, the role of science in naturalizing sex, gender, and sexuality, and the masculine domination of the practice of science. Another thread is *feminist political economy*, which is concerned with the gender division of labour and the feminization and devaluation of life-sustaining and subsistence work under capitalist patriarchy. An important theme in this tradition is the materiality of the natural world and the human body: human embeddedness in the materiality of nature and the inescapable frailties of human embodiment are the analytical starting points. These analyses have also informed research on gender and environment carried out by development scholars in colonized and neoliberalized contexts, which is the *gender, environment, and development* (GED) thread. Insights from feminist geography, political economy, and development studies came together to form the thread of *feminist political ecology* (FPE), which analyzes the co-constitution of gender, nature, and power in different contexts and at multiple scales, from the intimate to the global. It treats gender as a critical variable in determining access to and control over resources, as always interacting with class, caste, culture, race, and ethnicity to shape environmental change. Finally, the *ecofeminist normative theory* thread critically and philosophically interrogates dualism and the conditions necessary for eco-social and interspecies justice. This thread promotes and enacts ethical commitments to inclusivity, intersectionality, and democracy; it demands an end to the exploitation of nature and other species by humans and the dismantling of power structures that sustain white, masculine, heteronormative hegemony within human societies.

These threads and themes, along with others that have not been mentioned here, combine to create a field that is transdisciplinary and *transformative* (Warren 2000). What ties them together is the contention that it is impossible fully to understand the ecologically destructive consequences of human development without understanding their gendered character.

## About this handbook

This handbook contains chapters written by forty academics working in universities and research institutions located primarily but not exclusively in the Global North. It does not claim to offer a fully comprehensive account of the entire gender and environment field; nor is it a random assortment. It is the product of collaboration among scholars from around the world whose contributions offer specialist explanation of particular dimensions of and approaches to academic research on the gender-environment nexus. It has been curated and edited by a scholar with more than twenty years of experience in the field. In the early stages of the project, a group of internationally renowned scholars gave advice on the content and scope of the handbook, as well as suggesting names of authors from whom chapters might be commissioned. Contributors were invited to engage in a cooperative process of developing chapters that give readers an introduction to specific topics, approaches, and bodies of literature, while also offering original and provocative analyses. The outcome of this process is a handbook that fulfils its main purpose: to provide a well-rounded survey of an intellectually rich field.

The intended primary audience of the handbook is academics and university students located in the humanities and social science-based fields of gender studies and environmental studies. The chapters assume a relatively advanced level of understanding of the tools and concepts of academic theorizing. All of the contributing authors are career academics, with the exception of two (Butler and Houlberg) who are recent graduates with connections to activism and the arts. As a result, the majority of chapters are engaged with debates within academic circles as opposed to activism or professional practice. Although it speaks mostly to academic readers, the collection hopefully will be a useful resource for activists, policy makers, practitioners, and lay readers with an interest in the theoretical and empirical linkages between gender and environment. If it can offer help in answering the question, 'What is the connection between gender and environment?', then it will have been worth the time, energy, and paper that has been consumed in the course of its making.

## The grand tour: structure and content of the handbook

The handbook is organized into four parts, each containing chapters written from different approaches and tackling different themes. The rationale for the book's structure is a desire to start (in Part I) from the foundations of the topic, to acknowledge important texts and thinkers and the germinal ideas that were sown in the field from as far back as the 1960s, and then to move (in Part II) to the various ways that scholars interrogate gender-environment connections, theoretically and empirically. The third part provides a selection of policy-focused chapters demonstrating how the concept of gender is used as a tool for uncovering power relations in the ostensibly gender-neutral institutions of environmental governance. Authors use relevant, 'real life' examples to demonstrate how feminist environmental ideas and commitments can inform politics, policy, and practice. The fourth and final section includes chapters that comment on future scenarios that gender and environment scholars have imagined, and in some cases, witnessed. The book concludes on a future-oriented note, drawing on the past and reflecting on the present conjuncture of real crises and crises discourses (all tied into a knot called 'the Anthropocene') to imagine possibilities for change in the coming decades.

## *Part I. Foundations of gender and environment research*

The first part of the handbook offers an overview of some of the most influential ways that scholars have understood connections between gender inequality and the environmental problematique. It begins with a chapter by Joni Seager explaining the important contribution of the American biologist Rachel Carson in putting the human-environment relationship on the political agenda. *Silent Spring* (1962) is a foundational text in environmentalism; it was the first study to make links between the toxification of the oceans and health risks to humans, as well as between science, militarism, and environmental destruction. While not a study of connections between gender and environment, nor written by a self-identified feminist scholar, *Silent Spring* is pivotal because it 'prefigures and points the way to the explicitly feminist analyses that would emerge in the 1980s and 1990s'. Both the book and its author are important for gender and environment scholarship because they shone a bright light on the irrationality of male-dominated scientific progress in the twentieth century. As Seager argues, 'Carson was right' to question the nature of 'progress' and to ask 'big questions' about the role of science in constructing a false narrative of what constitutes human progress. This questioning stance has come to define feminist science and technology studies, as well as feminist environmental scholarship.

Another text that has been foundational in the field is *The Death of Nature: Women, Ecology and the Scientific Revolution* (1980) by environmental historian Carolyn Merchant. It is a watershed book that demonstrates the historical and contemporary links – and the importance of scholarly analysis of these links – between capitalism, colonialism, science, religion, philosophy, the environmental crisis, and patriarchal gender relations (specifically the devaluation and subordination of women). Chapter 2 provides a discussion of the content and context of Merchant's book, along with its role in informing ecofeminist scholarship. The discussion of the interplay between the analysis presented in *The Death of Nature* and the evolution of ecofeminism leads Charis Thompson and Sherilyn MacGregor to criticize the treatment of ecofeminism within feminist scholarly circles. They note that the simplistic ('essentialist') associations of ecofeminism with goddess worship, matriarchy, and feminine eco-virtue was something Merchant criticized in the 1990 second edition of *The Death of Nature*: 'Is not the conflation of woman and nature a form of essentialism? . . . But concepts of nature and women are historical and social constructions. There are no unchanging "essential" characteristics of sex, gender or nature' (1990:xvi). (Note that Merchant is erroneously labelled an 'essentialist' ecofeminist in the quote by Coles et al. 2015 provided previously.)

A similar sense of unease with the activist celebration of women's natural eco-superiority was demonstrated by other key feminist environmental scholars in the 1990s, such as the Australian philosopher Val Plumwood whose work has shaped gender and environment theorizing in profound ways. In *Feminism and the Mastery of Nature* (1993), Plumwood begins by problematizing simplistic associations of women and nature and reminding readers that there is 'enormous variation in ecofeminist literature' (9), which has been ignored by those who would stereotype it 'as theoretically weak and doubtfully liberated' (1). Seeking to respond to the challenge of developing what she called a more theoretically robust ecofeminism, Plumwood goes on to review the history of ideas and structures of thought in Western civilization, from the ancient Greeks to the Enlightenment philosophers. As Freya Mathews explains in Chapter 3, Plumwood's analysis gives ecofeminists and gender and environment scholars tools for critically analyzing the logic of domination that underpins the twin problems of environmental destruction and misogyny. Mathews discusses the importance of dualism, and the philosophical analysis of dualism, as a 'pivot of ecofeminist theorizing'. But she also argues that an approach other than theorizing may be needed if ecofeminists want to escape the dilemma of dualism. Since dualism is inherent in the act of theorizing (a Western invention), she suggests, what are needed are counterdualist practices that are conducive to developing strategic consciousness, such as those found in non-Western traditions (e.g., the Chinese concept of *wu wei*).

Foundations have come from different places. As explained previously, another thick strand of gender and environment research comes from the tradition of gender and development studies, which are largely situated in colonized regions of the Global South. In Chapter 4 Bernadette P. Resurrección provides a comprehensive overview of the evolution of feminist political ecology, which emerged out of feminist geography and is one of the most vibrant scholarly approaches to studying the gender-environment nexus. Important connections continue to exist between academic work in FPE and activists, practitioners, and academics in the development field. While there are many foundations in this strand, as Resurrección explains, the work of Indian academics Vandana Shiva (a physicist) and Bina Agarwal (an economist) have been particularly influential in framing the orientation of FPE, in particular by insisting on an analysis of gender-nature connections that is attendant to colonial power relations and divisions among women along lines of race, ethnicity, class, and caste. Arguably one of the most important articles that has shaped feminist environmental scholarship is Agarwal's 'Gender and environment debate: lessons from India' (1992), which criticized Western ecofeminism for its insufficient attention to diversity and materiality of women's relationships to their environments. Rightly or wrongly, she argued that rather than advance an ideologically driven agenda about women's unique relationship to the earth, ecofeminism (or feminist environmentalism as she called it) should be about challenging and transforming dominant constructions of gender as well as the actual division of labour and resources between men and women (Agarwal 1992:127). Such challenges to Western/Northern ecofeminism were instrumental in bringing about the 'essentialism debate' that has come to define ecofeminist scholarship, and ironically perhaps to distract attention away from its long-standing interest in the materiality of the gender-environment nexus. They have also fuelled the field's movement to a more intersectional approach to gender and to giving much greater attention to studying gendered experiences of grassroots ecological struggles in various local places around the world, through ethnographic and other case study approaches to research. This grassroots challenge was taken up by Dianne Rocheleau, Barbara Thomas-Slayter, and Esther Wangari in their landmark edited collection *Feminist Political Ecology: Global Issues and Local Experiences* (1996), which established the importance of case studies of women's activism. Resurrección's chapter explains the development over time of work in FPE as it has moved away from presenting women as victims of environmental problems toward a more complex analysis of the social construction of vulnerability that results in a wide variety of embodied experiences that are shaped by gender and other axes of power and identity.

Much of the work on women's activism and resistance to environmental exploitation highlights the relations that women in most parts of the world have with their natural environments because of their socially ascribed roles as provisioners and caregivers. Empirical evidence shows that women in practically every society hold a disproportionate amount of responsibility for growing and cooking food, tending to animals, maintaining living spaces, and taking care of the physical and emotional needs of children and dependent adults. The argument that all of this mostly unpaid work that women do provides a base for the functioning of economic systems has been central to feminism since the 1970s, at least since the publication of Esther Boserup's path-breaking book *Women's Role in Economic Development* (1970). In the gender and environment field, analyses have been extended to looking at structural connections between women's unpaid labour and natural resources: that both have been externalized – a free subsidy to capitalism – is their shared trait. Mary Mellor's work over the past three decades has been foundational to ecofeminist critiques of capitalism and orthodox economics as well as offering a vision of what a post-capitalist, ecologically sustainable, and gender-just future society should look like (see, for example, Mellor 1992). In her Chapter 5 on ecofeminist political economy, Mellor connects Marxist, green, and feminist economic arguments to make the case for an alternative approach to political economy capable of redressing the shared exploitation of nature and women's work, which leads her to offer proposals for 'creating socially just societies that live within their ecological means, including sufficiency provisioning and democratizing money'.

The foundations of gender and environment scholarship are built upon a further set of scholarly grounds: what here will be grouped and labelled as feminist materialisms and posthumanisms, both of which seek to depart from humanist traditions of Western (Anglo-European) thought. These fields are related but by no means walk in lock-step; indeed there are tensions and debates within and between, as Greta Gaard's discussion in Chapter 7 makes clear. But the common ground is a radical approach to ontology and epistemology: questioning human exceptionalist understandings of both being and knowing. As noted previously, ecofeminist theory has from the beginning been driven by an understanding of being embodied and embedded in environment/nature and that the practice of knowing, whether through the prism of modern science or through other ways of perceiving the world, is always partial, situated, and political. These signature insights are often associated with the work of Donna Haraway, in such texts as *Primate Visions: Gender, Race and Nature in the World of Modern Science* (1989) and *Simians, Cyborgs and Women: The Reinvention of Nature* (1991). The fact that Haraway's work is cited so frequently in this handbook is a strong indication of her importance in the field of gender and environment. Although she does not comfortably inhabit any particular label or disciplinary pigeonhole, and is rarely categorized as an ecofeminist theorist (although she has called herself one), her 'combination of feminist critique with studies of science [has] produced a distinctive, materialist approach to nature and gender' that has become foundational for ecofeminist theory (Merrick Chapter 6). Haraway is best known for her non-dualist approach to theorizing 'naturecultures', wherein the material and semiotic, the human and the other than human (nature) are relational and co-constructed *all the way down*, and for her presentation of scientific knowledge as a form of story-telling that is inevitably shaped by the situation of the knower. As noted earlier, a critical stance toward how science has defined the nature of gender and the gender of nature is a common quality in the gender and environment field. Merchant has provided an historical explanation of how the birth of modern science led to the death of nature; Haraway has enabled further critical feminist interrogation of how postmodern, capitalist science in the late twentieth and early twenty-first centuries has colonized life and defined relations between 'earthlings'. She has also called for rethinking what it means to be an ethical earthling, and what the political project of resistance should entail (see Grebowicz Chapter 31). As Helen Merrick observes, 'at the heart of [Haraway's] work is the problem of how we craft more ethical, liveable lives for all human and nonhuman organisms, which requires constant critical taking to task of the devastating machines of colonialism, capitalism, and patriarchy'.

While Merrick focusses on the important role played by the writing of Donna Haraway in the development of central lines of ecofeminist thinking, in Chapter 7 Gaard provides a comprehensive review of feminist and ecofeminist engagement with (other) animals, in theory and practice, starting in the 1980s and 1990s with the work of feminist animal theorists such as Carol J. Adams (1990) and Josephine Donovan (1990). She explains how early ecofeminists identified humanism 'as the primary antagonist of both ecological sustainability and feminist environmental justice'. Their analyses of species and ecology were beginning to articulate a *posthumanist* ecofeminism two decades before posthumanism gained academic respectability and popularity. Gaard goes on to bring a postcolonial vegan ecofeminist perspective to her exploration of theories of posthumanism, which include critical animal studies and new materialisms. Her normative analysis embeds criteria for evaluating theoretical turns in academia, of which the posthumanist and new materialist turns are among the latest. In addition to questioning whether (and what) posthumanist theorizing contributes to social justice and ecological sustainability, she asks, 'Is it good for animals?' This leads her to criticize Haraway's work on companion species for defending human objectification and exploitation of other animals as well as to question the privileging of theory (in 'high posthumanism') over praxis (a point made by Mathews in Chapter 3). In her view, posthumanist feminist theory must be tied to politics and activism to end the imprisonment and slaughter of all species.

Standing on solid intellectual foundations, contemporary scholars working in the gender and environment field in general, and in ecofeminist theory in particular, demonstrate political engagement with real world crises of climate change, species extinction and enslavement, and the persistence of colonialism, xenophobia, and white male supremacism (to name a few). As the chapters in this part of the handbook illustrate, the field has grown from critiques of the logics and effects of masculine science and rationality to an increasingly intersectional and expansively political critical-visionary project in the past ten years.

## *Part II. Approaches to gender and environment research*

The second part of the handbook includes a range of approaches to gender and environment research. Authors apply explanatory frameworks and the tools of a range of disciplines, including anthropology, sociology, geography, development, politics and international relations, English literature, and the 'transdiscipline' of environmental studies to understand specific topics. A common theme that emerges in this part is the complicated relationship that has always existed within feminist environmental scholarship between gender (historically the primary interest of feminism) and the other axes of social difference that shape people's lives, such as 'race'/ethnicity, class, caste, sexuality, and geographical location. Sometimes the emphasis has been placed on gender to the neglect of other axes, as Sharlene Mollett observes in Chapter 9. She argues for a critical, postcolonial intersectional version of feminist political ecology. Working within the FPE frame, she uses ethnographic research with Indigenous Miskito women in Honduras to 'show how multiple forms of power and positionings shape natural resource struggles'. The use of case studies, ethnography, and biographical narrative is an important tradition in gender and environment research generally and FPE in particular. Rich descriptions of people's lives are an effective prophylactic against simplistic claims and crude overgeneralizations about 'women's lives'. As María Luz Cruz-Torres and Pamela McElwee explain in Chapter 8, much can be learned from anthropological research on specific instances where gender relations shape resource conflict and management, for example in different Latin American and Asian contexts. Their chapter is based on a thorough review of the sustainable development (SD) literature that focusses on how gender informs people's relationship to land and other necessary resources as they go about the daily pursuit of their livelihoods. Julie Sze's Chapter 10, on the gender dimensions of 'environmental justice' (EJ) as a concept and a political movement, provides similar insights from the context of poor and racialized communities in the United States. These chapters also note the problematic tendency of non-feminist research in SD and EJ to overlook gender dimensions of environmental politics and problems.

While there is no doubt that research connecting gender relations and socio-ecological conditions in the Global South (and the South within the North) has played an important role in shaping the field, analyses of gendered social relations, norms, and values in affluent societies and analyses of global discourses – such as those emanating from the United Nations – have also been common in the literature. How social structures create environmental problems and shape ideas about how they should be addressed is a central concern of mainstream social science disciplines of sociology and political science. And yet gender is often missing from the picture. The sub-field of environmental sociology has been very slow to take up questions of gender, despite empirical evidence of differences in how men and women perceive and respond to environmental problems. Moreover, while environmental sociologists have been collecting data to support the claim that women are more likely than men to express concern for and to take action to protect the environment, there is a 'relatively noncomplex treatment of women in both theory and policy related to the environment' (Huddart Kennedy and Dzialo 2015:921). As Chenyang Xiao and Aaron M. McCright explain in Chapter 11, sociological investigation of gender differences in environmental concern emerged in the 1990s and developed around explanations of difference related to gender socialization and gender roles. It has been hypothesized that women express more concern and are more risk averse than men due to being socialized from childhood to be caring and empathetic and then taking on maternal responsibility for the health and welfare of others (especially children) in adulthood. After testing the dominant hypotheses using Gallup survey data from the United States, Xiao and McCright conclude that gender socialization (rather than gender roles or social structures) offers the most persuasive explanation for why women express more concern and worry than men. Their chapter also demonstrates the use of quantitative methods to test hypotheses about relationships between gender and environmental values, as well as alerting readers to the fact that the data show consistently modest rather than high degrees of gender difference, as is often suggested.

The German tradition of *Soziale Ökologie* (social ecology), mapped out by Diana Hummel and Immanuel Stieß in Chapter 12, is an approach firmly situated within the emerging field of sustainability science. Not well known in the English-speaking community of gender and environment scholars, and yet developing since the mid-1980s, social ecology is a transdisciplinary theoretical approach to analysing how societal relations to nature are shaped and structured by intra-societal relations and vice versa. It transcends the natural science-social science binary and aims to put research to the service of solving problems relevant to policy as well as to everyday life. Because feminist scholars have played an active role in developing social ecology, gender relations figure prominently in all research projects. The key word here is *relations*: gender is theorized as a relational concept that involves inter-social relations as well as social relations with nature in order to transcend the opposition of essentialism and constructivism. And although a distinction is made between physical-material and cultural-symbolic aspects, this approach 'emphasizes the materiality of all the relations between nature and society, while at the same time taking into account their embedding in symbolic orders, interpretive contexts, and social constructions' (Hummel and Stieß Chapter 12). The chapter gives three examples of how the social ecological framework has been applied to specific policy-relevant areas of research, namely food and nutrition, demographic change, and consumption.

Another approach to gender and environment research focuses on political discourse and the politics of discourse within academic, activist, and policy corners of the environmental domain. Discourse analysis is particularly useful in identifying the symbolic ways that gender relations appear (or don't) and the ideological/political work that ideas about gender do within environmental policy. In Chapter 13 Nicole Detraz uses a discourse-analytical approach to understand the narratives of environmental security that have emerged around global climate change. Working within the field of international relations, Detraz examines how the risks, threats, and vulnerabilities stemming from global climate change intersect with gender to produce specific insecurities that reinforce existing patterns and power relations. Her interest lies in developing a feminist approach to climate security, which she defines as 'a gender-sensitive, feminist environmental security discourse [that] highlights issues of human insecurity and environmental instability in ways that are useful for policy-making'. In a similar vein, but looking specifically at the UN discourse of sustainable development (SD) over the past two decades, Emma A. Foster argues that the 'governmental rationalities underpinning environmental decision-making and subjectification are gendered' (Chapter 14). She deploys the Foucault-informed theoretical lens of environmentality to interrogate the interconnections between gendered norms, assumptions, and relations and practices of international environmental governance. Of particular relevance to studies of environmental politics is the way that ecological citizens are not only created but also are enrolled into the state project of SD. These processes include the internalization of values that serve state interests while having specific gender dimensions, such as limiting the number of children and the greening of everyday practices of care and provisioning in the household sphere. Like many other scholars in the gender and environment field, and indeed several others in this handbook (e.g., Butler 18; Sasser 23; Isla 25; Di Chiro 33), Foster uncovers the disciplinary tendencies, entirely consistent with neoliberal capitalism, the lie behind dominant discourses of the green agenda. As she observes, UN documents such as *Agenda 21* (from the 1992 Rio Earth Summit) and *The Future We Want* (Rio 2012) promote a vision of SD that invokes a 'common future' while being built on the erasure of social difference.

In Chapter 15, Catriona Sandilands explains the importance of feminist theorizing of biopolitics, which she defines as 'the intensifying organization of power, in modernity, through bodies and corporeal relations'. Although thinkers within the ecofeminist and feminist science studies traditions have been interrogating the interconnections between biology/bodies and ecology/nature since the 1980s, this work has largely been ignored and misrepresented in wider fields of social and political thought where so-called new materialism has become the rage in recent years. As noted previously, and as several chapters in this handbook demonstrate, theorizing interactions and 'intra-actions' (Barad 2007) of mind and matter, epistemology and ontology, has been central to gender and environment field since its beginning. And how could it not? As Sandilands rightly points out, feminist gender-intersectional analysis deserves to be included in contemporary theorizing of biopolitics and posthumanism and a central text to include in its canon is Haraway's 1985 revolutionary essay 'A Manifesto for Cyborgs'. Sandilands explains the importance of this text and its arguments, along with presenting a powerful critique of contemporary theorists who have failed to give credit where it is due.

A third cluster of approaches in this part of the handbook follows nicely from Sandilands' discussion of biopolitics. A growing body of research on gender and environment deliberately challenges the hitherto traditional focus on women and the narrow conception of gender as referring to the cis-male/cis-female binary, while thus far in the minority of gender and environment research, the approaches of queer ecology, trans ecology, and eco-masculinity studies are blowing open new lines of inquiry and challenging established orthodoxies. As Martin Hultman explains in Chapter 16, there has been very limited interaction between masculinities studies and environmental studies. Hultman offers an overview of the state of research and theorizing on masculinities within the environmental humanities and social sciences, noting that ecofeminists were among the first to pay (limited) attention to the issue, along with a few masculinities studies scholars such as R.W. Connell (1990). Hultman then sets out his own framework for analysing types of masculinities that can be observed in affluent Western societies, namely industrial, eco-modern, and ecological masculinities. A key observation in Hultman's chapter is that gender and environment research has for too long ignored the role of men and masculinities, a curious thing given the prominence of men in the history of environmental destruction and environmentalism as a political movement for change. He argues that not only would more research on men/masculinity and environment fill a large gap in academic knowledge, but 'the future . . . depends on understanding and changing masculinities for the better'.

Whereas Mollett and others have 'troubled' gender from a postcolonial intersectional position, highlighting the problematic tendency to give it a privileged position in FPE; scholars taking a queer and trans ecology approach seek to shake gender out of its binarized rut, or 'to queer' it. One aim is to show 'how cisgender and heterosexual identities have long been implicitly positioned as "natural", to the detriment of transgender and queer identities' and how this naturalization has created and maintained a transphobic climate within environmental research and discourse (Seymour Chapter 17). It is not just gender and environmental scholarship that has been guilty of adopting a heteronormative and cissexist approach to environmental questions; much of the work in environmental studies, including in environmental justice scholarship (which is ostensibly dedicated to inclusivity), has failed to recognize how cissexism has shaped the environmental agenda. As Nicole Seymour argues in Chapter 17, in spite of evidence to show how trans people experience extreme discrimination and marginalization in most parts of the world, there is a significant gap in the environmental justice literature where transgender issues should be. Moreover, she questions recent work in so-called new materialism/material feminisms that appears to call for a return to 'real' rather than socially constructed gender, thereby playing into transphobia. She also takes issue with queer ecology literature that includes trans only as one part of the list LGBTQ+ without sufficient exploration of the specificities of transgenderism. Developing a new theoretical approach that she calls 'trans ecology', Seymour asks a number of questions that turn all environmentalisms on their head, such as why should the gender transitioning process be seen as any less 'natural' than cisgenderism? Similarly, in Chapter 18, Cameron Butler adopts a queer ecological lens to show how heteronormativity (with attendant homophobia and transphobia) shapes the scientific knowledge and policy prescriptions of what he calls the mainstream sustainability movement (MSM). Echoing Seymour, he criticizes the MSM's silence on queer issues and how deep-seated ideological assumptions about the importance of children (as The Future Generation) serve to marginalize all those who don't or won't experience biological reproduction. Butler provides a useful overview of the evolution of queer ecology as a strand within the gender and environment field, along with identifying its core themes and methods: deconstructing binaries, questioning futurity, and the use of irony as a means of queering what is assumed to be normal. He concludes by calling for a politicized approach to queer ecological scholarship and giving some initial thoughts on what a queer sustainability might be.

## *Part III. Gender-environment connections in politics, policy, and practice*

Emerging from a critical position on the margins of mainstream environmental disciplines, gender and environment scholars have developed a set of theoretical and evidence-based claims about the relationship between gender inequality and environmental crisis that seek to change politics, policy, and practice in significant ways. These analytic and empirical insights have been taken up by many practitioners and policy makers, most notably in UN agencies where the concept of 'gender mainstreaming' (i.e., the institutionalization of gender in policy processes) is now central to the environmental agenda. Part III of the handbook contains chapters that explain, illustrate, and critically analyze the ways in which gender, as a concept and a socio-political relation, appears within 'real life' institutions, organizations, and policy fields. Several chapters present specific case examples of how feminist environmental ideas and commitments have been implemented in different sectors and parts of the world.

In Chapter 19 Seema Arora-Jonsson provides a comprehensive overview of the gradual incorporation of gender analysis into environmental policy and management and the effects this incorporation has had in practice over the past forty years. She notes that although academics have tried to work with an inclusive understanding of gender and an analysis of power, gender has always been – and still is – synonymous with women in environmental policy circles. The majority of the work done to incorporate gender/women into environmental policy has been done in contexts of the Global South, as part of sustainable development programmes. Greater gender sensitivity has been driven, for the most part, by a desire to devise policies and programmes that work on the ground, by responding to (and sometimes exploiting) the different interests and roles of men and women. Because women tend to be on the front lines of subsistence – managing resources, tending to crops, and caring for people and animals – their knowledge and labour have been deemed instrumentally valuable to the development process. This acknowledgement has led to greater emphasis on women's participation in governance, to an emphasis on the economic empowerment of women, and to the practice of gender mainstreaming in policy-making and programme design. Arora-Jonsson discusses the logic behind these features and the extent to which they have improved the hitherto gender-blind field of SD policy. However, she also identifies a number of pitfalls. For example, she argues that gender mainstreaming has become a form of 'governance feminism' that pushes forward a specific agenda to help women help the environment while neglecting a wider range of gender issues, such as male violence and male unemployment, and the need for social and economic structural change. In addition, there tends to be a failure to challenge gender stereotypes, such as the male breadwinner and vulnerable, powerless woman. Arora-Jonsson notes that there is comparatively less research and policy work on gender and environment in affluent contexts in the Global North, which stems from the problematic assumption that gender inequality is not a problem in affluent societies – an assumption that falters in the face of examples discussed elsewhere in handbook.

Whereas environmental management often seems to be imposed on the people of the Global South in the name of development, in the North environmentalism is seen as a voluntary stance to be adopted, or not, in democratic arenas. Environmentalism as a political movement is very much a product of Western liberal democracies where citizens have the freedom to question the human abuse of nature and the impacts this abuse has on human well-being (see MacGregor and Doyle 2014). An important part of this history is the emergence and spread of Green political parties in the West since the middle of the twentieth century. In Chapter 20 Stewart Jackson gives a welcome response to the deafening silence on gender in political research on Green parties. He explains that, as products of feminist and ecology movements of the 1960s, Green parties have always embraced and embedded the principle of gender equality, even though in practice they have exhibited a surprising amount of ambivalence toward gender issues. For example, most Green parties have instituted gender parity in leadership roles and have an impressive record of having women elected to parliaments compared to other parties. But there is nothing near gender balance in the rank and file membership of Green parties (men are in the majority) and the masculinist internal dynamics (e.g., male domination of the floor, adversarial debating styles, and meetings without childcare) present barriers to women's full participation in party processes. Jackson laments the lack of research on the gender dimensions of Green party politics, but explains it as wholly consistent with the gender-blindness that afflicts the academic field of environmental politics.

The lack of gender analysis is also evident in research and policy around environmental-economic issues such as green agendas for growth through environmental investment and for reducing $CO_2$ emissions through changes in consumer/citizen choices. In their chapters, Beate Littig and Ines Weller provide introductions to the fields of green economics and sustainable consumption that have been developed in the Global North in recent decades, largely without the benefit of feminist theoretical insights. In Chapter 21 Littig argues that the contemporary discourse of SD is even less engaged with gender analysis than it was in the 1990s, when it was incorporated into key documents emanating from the Rio Earth Summit (e.g., *Agenda 21*). The outcome of Rio+20 was a vision for a green economy, as articulated in *The Future We Want*. The question Littig and many other feminist critics ask is, 'Who is *we*?' Her feminist critique points out that the green economy agenda not only promises to boost growth and employment by investing in technological innovations that create skilled jobs in male dominated sectors (engineering, chemistry), but it also is premised on a very narrow understanding of the contemporary crisis. Feminist economists are critical of ecological modernization and have advanced the notion of a triple crisis – of capitalism, ecology, and care – that leads to holistic policy solutions. These solutions include investment in a caring economy based on meeting human needs through collectivization and redistribution rather than promoting endless growth by greening the capitalist market, which only serves to sustain the ecologically destructive neoliberal status quo.

Ines Weller's Chapter 22 on gender and sustainable consumption is a good partner to Littig's chapter in that it looks at the feminized side of the production-consumption binary. Whereas men have been associated with production and technological know-how, it has long been suggested that women are more likely than men to make pro-environmental purchasing choices, leading to ethical and green products being targeted at women (see Hawkins 2012). Feminists have criticized this targeting as part of the privatization and feminization of environmental responsibility. Green visions for a sustainable future, it would seem, would have men gainfully employed in designing, making, selling, and installing solar panels, while women buy the eco-labelled products and recycle the waste. In addition to looking at how gender differences play out at the individual level, Weller discusses the structural and symbolic dimensions of gender differences in sustainable and unsustainable consumption. These dimensions include analyses of the gender division of labour, specifically the entrenched feminization of housework, as well as how gender norms and identities shape food choices (e.g., masculinity and meat-eating). Both of these chapters demonstrate the transdisciplinary and policy-oriented approach practiced by scholars working in the German tradition of social ecology discussed by Hummel and Stieß in Chapter 12.

As Arora-Jonsson points out, gender has been incorporated into environmental policy since the 1970s. It has been most evident in international policy on SD, as defined and implemented by transnational institutions such as the UN, the World Bank, and the IMF. The Sustainable Development Goals incorporate it in goal no. 5: 'Achieve gender equality and empower all women and girls' (UNDP 2015). And with an emphasis on development in the Global South comes the tendency of policy to be targeted at issues that are seen to affect the livelihoods of poorer and relatively less powerful women. Three chapters in this part of the handbook focus on areas of policy and politics that have received a significant amount of attention by gender and environment scholars: population, food/agriculture, and nature conservation. In Chapter 23 Jade Sasser discusses the politics of population policy that has been a contentious feature of environmentalist discourse since at least the 1970s, and even earlier if one thinks back to Malthus. Focusing on UN summits since the 1990s, Sasser traces the development of the discourse from narratives of control and blame to empowerment: in the twenty-first century the focus of population policy is to empower women to control their fertility. Population has always been a point of contention between feminists and environmentalists, highlighting the conflict of political goals for health and freedom and sustainability and limits respectively (and many feminist environmentalists have written about it; see, for example, Seager 1993; Hartmann 1995; Bandarage 1997). Empowering poor women to limit their reproductivity in the service of global environmental policies that do little to limit the consumption patterns of the rich is not the kind of empowerment most feminists have in mind. Sasser names the intended female target of population policy a 'sexual steward': she is a 'good population-environment-development subject' who 'uses contraceptives consistently and correctly, she values the environment and is motivated to protect its resources, and she views her own childbearing as having direct potential consequences for the environment'. The making of sexual stewards has become all the more important in the light of climate change pressures, and feminists have continued to criticize the focus on marginalized women. However, as with many other topics, the role played by men, male domination, and masculinist worldviews have remained largely absent from policy and activist discussions.

In Chapter 24 Agnes A. Babugura provides an overview of the literature exploring links between gender (in)equality and food (in)security with particular reference to agricultural development in African countries. As with other contributors to this section of the handbook, she discusses the lack of attention to gender concerns within development policy-making and research, leading to a failure to 'reinforce and translate existing gender policy commitments into actions'. Although most countries have signed up for UN commitments to gender equality and the empowerment of women, there is considerable evidence to suggest that women are especially marginalized in the food and agriculture sector, in spite of the fact that they do a disproportionate amount of the work and hold much of the knowledge required to provision food. Babugura argues that recognizing women as farmers and improving the conditions under which women provision food by, for example, giving them access to tools and land and ensuring their participation in decision-making, would go a long way toward ensuring food security. However, current approaches do not seem to 'join up' these essential components of sustainable development. This is a similar finding that is explored in Ana Isla's Chapter 25 on the impacts of the debt-for-nature exchanges that have been part of international conservation policy since the 1980s. Isla uses a case study of Costa Rica to support her argument that such policies, and sustainable development more generally – as conceived and delivered by trans-national intuitions of the UN, World Bank, and IMF – are powerful weapons in neoliberal capitalism's war on subsistence. Gender factors in her analysis in two ways: First, Isla draws on Marxist ecofeminist tools to theorize the historical connections between primitive accumulation and the exploitation of women and feminized nature, as well as to show how capitalism survives by enclosing and appropriating everything involved in subsistence. Second, gender appears as a central thread in her analysis of the on-the-ground impacts of the debt-for-nature swap on all that is feminized (women, children, Indigenous people, and land) in Costa Rica.

Isla explains how the process of greening capitalism by creating conservation/ecotourism areas in exchange for a developing country's debt has resulted in the enclosure of forests, the theft of genetic resources, and the dispossession of Indigenous peoples and rural peasants from their lands and livelihood. Women and children have been especially affected; as the most economically precarious, they have been forced to migrate in search of poorly paid and degrading jobs in cities and in ecotourism resorts, which often end up leaving them even more marginalized and vulnerable to exploitation than they were before.

It should come as no surprise that the politics of climate change – its impacts and policy responses – have attracted the attention of gender and environment scholars in recent years. Whereas in the 2000s very little research on gender and climate change could be found (see MacGregor 2010), by 2017 there is a growing catalogue of texts devoted to understanding climate change through the lens of gender (cf. Buckingham and Le Masson 2017; Nagel 2015). Three chapters in this part of the handbook take up different dimensions of climate change, highlighting a range of ways in which gender relations shape the problem and its proposed solutions. In Chapter 26 Susan Buckingham uses recent national-level climate change policy discussions to critically explore the gender politics within the environmental movement in the UK. As an active member of the Women's Environmental Network, she was in the position to view, first-hand, the difficulties involved in putting gender on the climate policy agenda, which in the UK is dominated by elite men (as it is in most other places). Buckingham goes on to discuss the role of gender in environmental policy-making in Europe, which makes hers a useful complement to Arora-Jonsson's chapter focusing on the Global South. An interesting aspect of this discussion is what she calls the 'culture of masculinity' within the environmental movement, which resonates with Jackson's investigation of the masculinism within Green parties. These findings and the critical analyses provided by gender and environment scholars are significant when viewed alongside the evidence (presented in Chapters 11 and 22) that women express higher levels of concern and are more likely to act on their environmental values than men. Why it is that (white) men take on the leadership of environmental political and policy spheres when it is women who are working on the front lines? This is a question that requires more investigation.

The male domination of environmentalism is even more evident in the global climate change regime, as explained by Karen Morrow in Chapter 27. The United Nations Framework Convention on Climate Change (UNFCCC), established in 1992, is the founding document of this regime. Morrow discusses the marginalization of gender issues and women participants in the UNFCCC process as part of her analysis of the role of the Women and Gender Major Constituency, since it was given constituency status in 2009. She concludes that although it took many years to have their issues recognized by the UNFCCC regime, there have been a number of positive outcomes of feminist lobbying efforts, including an institutional commitment to addressing gender issues and the adoption of 'gender balance' as a goal. There are also more ambiguous aspects that suggest that there is more work to be done: the phrase is 'gender balance' rather than 'gender equality', and the tone is 'determinedly hortatory rather than compulsory'. It is therefore too soon to tell whether the gains made by feminists will amount to more than lip service as the process unfolds. One group that is trying to ensure that it is more than lip service is The Women's Environment and Development Organization (WEDO), which is one of the leading feminist environmental advocacy organizations in the world. In Chapter 28 Marcela Tovar-Restrepo (chair of WEDO's board of directors) provides an overview of the gender dimensions of climate change, which she connects to the findings of action research on REDD+ that was conducted by WEDO in 2011 in Tanzania, Nepal, Ecuador, and Brazil. The research demonstrates how gender, age, location, and ethnicity can be 'mainstreamed' into development plans and policies that are aimed at achieving more sustainable human settlements. Drawing on this research, as well as on the emerging feminist literature on gender and climate change, Tovar-Restrepo argues that 'actions taken to mitigate and/or adapt to climate change should be designed, implemented, and monitored from a gender perspective in order to achieve sustainable resource management, to improve livelihoods, and to promote gender equality'. Her chapter is the most practice-oriented chapter in the collection and resonates with several points raised in theoretical chapters.

## Part IV. Futures

Feminist research on gender and environment is visionary by nature. Rooted in political movements for social change, there is an orientation to the future and a call to imagine, prefigure, and sometimes construct better environments than those currently on offer. Learning from the past plays a central role in this project, as does experimentations in utopian and dystopian thought. These tendencies are displayed in the final part of the handbook, in five chapters that explore the practices of building, making, reconfiguring, reimagining, resisting, and envisioning, and consider why these practices are important for the future of gender and environment research as well as for feminist environmental politics.

A theme that has been important in gender and environment research in the Global North is how gender norms are inscribed on the human-made environment, in city plans and building designs. Assumptions about gender roles and life patterns are literally built into the spaces people inhabit and therefore are difficult to change. Single family dwellings, for example, are designed for the nuclear family, assume a commute to work, and are energy and resource intensive. Changing the design and situation of housing to take diversity, flexibility, and sustainability into account would enable radical changes in the practices that entrench social inequality and resource overconsumption. Ecovillages, smart cities, and the passivhaus concept are often held up as the wave of the (green) future. But is it possible to build differently to live differently? And what is meant by 'differently'? These are the questions animating Helen Jarvis's discussion of intentional communities in Chapter 29. She gives a history of the role of collaborative and cooperative living arrangements in feminist visions of the future, from nineteenth century utopian socialist visionaries to Scandinavian co-housing advocates in the sixties and feminist architects today. Feminists have long been attracted to the idea of co-housing because of its perceived potential to be more democratic, to dissolve the gender division of domestic labour, and to drive cultural change toward egalitarianism (cf. Hayden 1980). Contemporary researchers hold out hope that co-housing can be a concrete strategy for addressing gender inequality and scarce resources simultaneously. However, as Jarvis explains, bringing the goals of gender equality and ecological sustainability together may hold promise, but there is also potential for tensions, conflict, and unintended consequences. Thus far there has been limited empirical research on the effects of co-housing on gender relations and insufficient theorizing of the gender norms that are constructed and reproduced in such arrangements. Research tends to focus on the green credentials of the buildings – such as the energy efficiency and the technical innovation of the design and engineering – rather than on social patterns and practices of the people who live in them (cf. Tummers 2016). While being inspired by the concept, it is important not to overlook the significant obstacles to realizing 'pragmatic utopia' within a capitalist system that privileges waged employment over sharing and caring.

A somewhat more optimistic outlook is offered in Chapter 30 by Meike Schalk, Ulrika Gunnarsson-Östling, and Karin Bradley. They draw on their respective fields of urban planning, architecture, and futures studies to explore pedagogical approaches and practical methods for cultivating more socio-environmentally just relations. This exploration is central to feminist spatial practice, which is about building alternative futures and 'the "productive power of making" to bring new kinds of social and economic realities into existence' (Gibson-Graham 2008:614). After a discussion of the academic work of feminist theorists J. K. Gibson-Graham and Schalk and colleagues give two examples to illustrate what they mean by the term 'critical spatial practice'. The first is British feminist architecture and design collective called Matrix, which worked to design more inclusive spaces and to make the design process more accessible to women from 1980–1994. The second is the Eco Nomadic School, which operates in several European countries to create 'environments for mutual learning and teaching ecocivic practices', including by running seminars for rural women on ecological practices, building ecologically, and alternative economies. Both examples are instructive for feminist theorizing, according to Schalk et al., because they experiment with, create, and live different socio-economic realities. And in so doing they perform what these authors call *lived utopias*. Experimentation and imagination are two key practices that propel the field of gender and environmental research forward in the contemporary period.

Very much in this spirit, Chapter 31 by Margret Grebowicz is a thought-provoking essay that asks the reader to consider the possibility of 'reconfiguring relation'. She explores the challenge of theorizing inter-species relation after the 'end of nature', in contemporary 'conditions of irreducible complexity and claustrophobia'. What this means is that if this is indeed the Anthropocene and humans have colonized the entire planet, then there is no 'nature' to which to escape: a case of 'ontological claustrophobia'. What do/should environmental ethics look like in such claustrophobic conditions? Drawing on Haraway's work in *When Species Meet* (2007) on inter-species relation (e.g., between humans and companion animals) and human animality ('we are not not-animals'), Grebowicz considers the environment side of the gender and environment nexus, thinking specifically about the 'reimagining of what counts as ethics and what makes an environment in the first place'. Drawing also on the work of Lauren Berlant (2011), Grebowicz situates the challenge of reimagining in late capitalism where crisis 'is no longer an event but an environment'. Although she does not offer a prescriptive answer (per se) to her questions, she invites readers to move in a very different direction from that charted in the nineties by ecofeminist theorists of 'partnership ethics', such as Merchant and Plumwood. These are different times.

Another chapter that calls for new directions is Laura Houlberg's Chapter 32 on the problematic approach to gender being displayed in one corner of the contemporary American environmental movement. A radical feminist environmental organization called Deep Green Resistance (DGR) denies membership to transgender people and promotes the future 'end of gender', because gender is seen as an oppressive cultural artefact. Houlberg offers a discussion of the difference between gender essentialism and gender artifactualism, noting that the former is a form of extreme constructivism that cannot abide any suggestion that gender is real, chosen, or meaningful to people. Trans people, especially trans women, are seen by DGR as wilfully upholding an imposed gender system and so are not welcome in a deep green, radical feminist movement for ecological justice. There is in this case an odd mix of old-fashioned cultural feminist belief that only women can be women and an old-fashioned environmentalist *politics of naturalness*, both of which have given queer scholars reason to be sceptical of both feminism and environmentalism. In response to her critique of the transmisogyny displayed by DGR, Houlberg suggests that environmental studies generally, and the gender and environmental field in particular, need new tools with which to discuss the causes of green transmisogyny and ideally to theorize its eradication. She argues that, provided they are incorporated into the canon of environmental studies, the work of trans scholars and activists (such as Eli Clare and Susan Stryker) 'should, and will, guide toward cohesive and groundbreaking terrain, en route to creating more just visions of gender and of environment'.

The concluding chapter in the handbook by Giovanna Di Chiro takes up the politics surrounding the 2016 decision by an international panel of scientists to change the name of the present epoch from Holocene to 'Anthropocene'. This is the name for the period of geological time, in which human activity is considered such a powerful influence on the ecology and climate of the planet that it will leave a long-term signature in the strata record. After identifying a number of problems with this name, including its concealment of social injustice behind a blanket 'Anthro' (man), and the uncritical acceptance of the universal forces of neoliberal capitalism, she argues that Anthropocene discourse is not an appropriate eco-political strategy for the future. In fact, as the title of her Chapter 33 signals, Di Chiro presents a feminist critique of a concept that creates a global 'we' of blame while being exceedingly selective about who will benefit, arguing that it would be better named the 'white m(A)nthropocene'. In characteristic style, she offers a multidimensional, tour de force analysis of the trouble with the Anthropocene meme that has seemingly captured the attention of most of the environmental studies community, including many working in the gender and environment field. Di Chiro's work is cited often in this handbook because it touches on many key themes and synthesizes so much of the gender and environment scholarship. She seamlessly brings together environmental justice, anti-racist queer theory, feminist political ecology, and feminist science studies into a normative framework for revealing the interlocking forms of power that operate below the shiny surface of a popular twenty-first century buzzword.

It is fitting that Di Chiro has the last word in the handbook. Her chapter concludes with a discussion of political resistance movements, such as Idle No More, Black Lives Matter, and Our Power, which are currently working to challenge the 'inhuman humanist' (Luciano 2015) rhetoric of the Anthropocene and to redirect attention to the root causes and differential impacts of injustice. This discussion leads Di Chiro to call for a feminist environmental vision of *sustainability for all*. This vision is 'not a retreat to the façade of Anthropocenic universalism, to the individualism of green consumerism, or to the techno-fixes of the green economy' she writes. Rather, *sustainability for all* aims 'to tell a story and develop practices of collective continuance (Powys-Whyte 2014) in support of just and flourishing communities'. It will be built on the strategies of resistance and resilience that are being practiced by environmental justice and Indigenous activists all over the world, and will be a vision of the future that eschews the gendered, racialized, and ethnocentric environmental politics of the Anthropocene.

Like all contributors to this volume, Di Chiro wrote her chapter before the events of 2016 gave her reason to despair for the future and to doubt the political promise of such visions. As the handbook went to press, an ominous storm cloud was forming on the horizon, threatening to rain on ecofeminist imaginings of a just and sustainable world. Misogynist trolls, climate denialists, and members of the Alt-Right were joining forces to pollute the political sphere with hate. A newly elected US president was promising to rescind the hard-fought rights of women and LGBTQ+ citizens, to destroy the Environmental Protection Agency, and to rip up the 2015 Paris Agreement on global climate change. In the UK, a new but unelected prime minister was displaying a deafening silence on gender equality and declaring her intention to grow the economy by cutting green tape. By pushing for a new airport runway, a new nuclear reactor, and fracking in national parks, she was proving that women most certainly do not have an innate sense of duty toward the environment.

It is reasonable to think that these shifts in the political landscape will present serious challenges, not only for academic research in the gender and environment field, but also for those of us who are called to do it for a living. But environmental destruction and gender injustice, pollution and misogyny, are not new problems; they are escalating every day, everywhere. After nearly four decades of developing tools for understanding the gender-environment nexus, there is still much work to be done.

# References

Adams, C. J. (1990) *The Sexual Politics of Meat: A Feminist-Vegetarian Critical Theory.* New York: Continuum.

Adams, C. J. and Gruen, L. (eds) (2014) *Ecofeminism: Feminist Intersections With Other Animals and the Earth.* London: Bloomsbury.

Agarwal, B. (1992) 'The gender and environment debate: Lessons from India', *Feminist Studies* 18(1): 119–158.

Anshelm, J. and Hultman, M. (2014) 'A green fatwa: Climate change as a threat to the masculinity of industrial modernity', *NORMA: International Journal for Masculinity Studies* 9(2): 84–96.

Bagemihl, B. (1999) *Biological Exuberance: Animal Homosexuality and Natural Diversity.* New York: St. Martin's Press.

Bandarage, A. (1997) *Women, Population and Global Crisis.* London: Zed Books.

Banerjee, D. and Bell, M. (2007) 'Ecogender: Locating gender in environmental social science', *Society and Natural Resources* 20(1): 3–19.

Barad, K. (2007) *Meeting the Universe Halfway: Quantum Physics and the Entanglement of Matter and Meaning.* Durham, NC: Duke University Press.

Berlant, L. (2011) *Cruel Optimism.* Durham, NC: Duke University Press.

Biehl, J. (1991) *Finding Our Way: Rethinking Ecofeminist Politics.* New York: Black Rose Books.

Boserup, E. (1970) *Women's Role in Economic Development.* New York: St. Martin's Press.

Buckingham, S. and Le Masson, V. (eds) (2017) *Understanding Climate Change Through Gender Relations.* London: Routledge.

Carson, R. (1962) *Silent Spring.* New York: Houghton Mifflin.

Coles, A., Gray, L. and Momsen, J. (eds) (2015) *The Routledge Handbook of Gender and Development.* London: Routledge.

Connell, R. W. (1990) 'A whole new world: Remaking masculinity in the context of the environment movement', *Gender and Society* 4(4): 452–478.

Connell, R. W. (1995) *Masculinities.* Cambridge: Polity Press.

Connell, R. W. (2009) *Gender: In World Perspective.* Cambridge: Polity Press.

Dobson, A. (2007) *Green Political Thought* (fourth edition). London: Routledge.

Donovan, J. (1990) 'Animal rights and feminist theory', *Signs: Journal of Women in Culture and Society* 15(2): 350–375.

Dryzek, J. (2013) *The Politics of the Earth: Environmental Discourses* (second edition). Oxford: Oxford University Press.

Enloe, C. (2013) *Seriously! Investigating Crashes and Crises as If Women Mattered.* Berkeley, CA: University of California Press.

Fleming, J. (2007) 'The climate engineers', *The Wilson Quarterly* (Spring): 46–60.

Gaard, G. (1997) 'Toward a queer ecofeminism', *Hypatia* 12(1): 114–137.

Gaard, G. (2011) 'Ecofeminism revisited: Rejecting essentialism and re-placing species in a material feminist environmentalism', *Feminist Formations* 23(2): 26–53.

Gibson-Graham, J. K. (2008) 'Diverse economies: Performative practices for "other worlds"', *Progress in Human Geography* 32(5): 613–632.

Haraway, D. (1989) *Primate Visions: Gender, Race and Nature in the World of Modern Science.* London: Routledge.

Haraway, D. (1991) *Simians, Cyborgs, and Women: The Reinvention of Nature.* New York: Routledge.

Haraway, D. (2007) *When Species Meet.* Minneapolis: University of Minnesota Press.

Hartmann, B. (1995) *Reproductive Rights and Wrongs: The Global Politics of Population Control.* Cambridge, MA: South End Press.

Hawkins, R. (2012) 'Shopping to save lives: Gender and environment theories meet ethical consumption', *Geoforum* 43: 750–759.

Hayden, D. (1980) 'What would a non-sexist city be like? Speculations on housing, urban design, and human work', *Signs* 5(3): 170–187.

Huddart Kennedy, E. and Dzialo, L. (2015) 'Locating gender in environmental sociology', *Sociology Compass* 9(10): 920–929.

King, Y. (1983) 'The ecofeminist imperative', in Caldecott, L. and Leland, S. (eds) *Reclaim the Earth: Women Speak Out for Life on Earth.* London: Women's Press, 9–14.

Luciano, D. (2015) 'The inhuman anthropocene', *LA Review of Books.* Online. Available at: http://avidly.lareviewofbooks.org/2015/03/22/the-inhuman-anthropocene/ (accessed 15 May 2016).

McCright, A. and Dunlap, R. (2011) 'Cool dudes: The denial of climate change among conservative white males in the United States', *Global Environmental Change* 21(4): 1163–1172.

MacGregor, S. (2006) *Beyond Mothering Earth: Ecological Citizenship and the Politics of Care.* Vancouver: University of British Columbia Press.

MacGregor, S. (2010) 'A stranger silence still: The need for feminist social research on climate change', *Sociological Review* 57: 124–140.

MacGregor, S. and Doyle, T. (eds) (2014) *Environmental Movements Around the World: Shades of Green in Politics and Culture.* Santa Barbara, CA: Praeger/ABC-Clio.

Mallory, C. (2009) 'What's in a name? In defense of ecofeminism (not ecological feminisms, feminist ecology, or gender and the environment)', Paper presented at the FEAST: Feminist Ethics and Social Theory Conference, 24–27 September, Clearwater, Florida.

May, V. M. (2015) *Pursuing Intersectionality: Unsettling Dominant Imaginaries.* New York: Routledge.

Mellor, M. (1992) *Breaking the Boundaries: Towards a Feminist Green Socialism.* London: Virago.

Merchant, C. (1980/1990) *The Death of Nature: Women, Ecology and the Scientific Revolution.* New York: Harper and Row.

Merchant, C. (1992) *Radical Ecology: The Search for a Liveable World.* New York: Routledge.

Mortimer-Sandilands, C. and Erickson, B. (eds) (2010) *Queer Ecologies: Sex, Nature, Politics, Desire.* Bloomington: Indiana University Press.

Nagel, J. (2015) *Gender and Climate Change: Impacts, Science, Policy.* London: Routledge.

Oreskes, N. and Conway, E. (2011) *The Merchants of Doubt.* New York: Bloomsbury Press.

Pease, B. (2016) 'Masculinism, climate change and "man-made" disasters: Towards an environmental profeminist response', in Enarson, E. and Pease, B. (eds) *Men, Masculinities and Disaster.* London: Routledge, 21–33.

Peterson, V. S. (2005) 'How (the meaning of) gender matters in political economy', *New Political Economy* 10(4): 499–521.

Plant, J. (1989) *Healing the Wounds: The Promise of Ecofeminism.* Santa Cruz, CA: New Society Publishers.

Plumwood, V. (1993) *Feminism and the Mastery of Nature.* London: Routledge.

Powys-Whyte, K. (2014) 'Indigenous women, climate change impacts and collective action', *Hypatia* 29(3): 599–616.

Radcliffe, S. A. (2015) *Dilemmas of Difference: Indigenous Women and the Limits of Postcolonial Development Policy.* Durham, NC: Duke University Press.

Rocheleau, D. E., Thomas-Slayter, B. P. and Wangari, E. (eds) (1996) *Feminist Political Ecology: Global Issues and Local Experiences*, London: Routledge.

Roth-Johnson, D. (2013) 'Back to the future: Françoise d'Eubonne, ecofeminism and ecological crisis', *The International Journal of Literary Humanities* 10: 52–61.

Roughgarden, J. (2004) *Evolution's Rainbow: Diversity, Gender, and Sexuality in Nature and People.* Berkeley, CA: University of California Press.

Sandilands, C. (1999) *The Good Natured Feminist: Ecofeminism and the Quest for Democracy.* Minneapolis: University of Minnesota Press.

Seager, J. (1993) *Earth Follies: Coming to Feminist Terms With the Global Environmental Crisis.* London: Routledge.

Shiva, V. (1989) *Staying Alive: Women, Ecology and Development.* London: Zed Books.

Sturgeon, N. (1997) *Ecofeminist Natures: Race, Gender, Feminist Theory and Political Action.* London: Routledge.

Tong, R. (2009) *Feminist Thought: A More Comprehensive Introduction* (third edition). Boulder, CO: Westview Press.

Tummers, L. (2016) 'The re-emergence of self-managed cohousing in Europe: A critical review of co-housing research', *Urban Studies* 53(10): 2023–2040.

United Nations Development Program (UNDP) (2015) *Sustainable Development Goals.* Online. Available at: https://sustainabledevelopment.un.org (accessed 12 October 2016).

Warren, K. J. (2000) *Ecofeminist Philosophy: A Western Perspective on What It Is and Why It Matters.* Lanham, MD: Rowman and Littlefield.

# PART I

# Foundations

# 1

# RACHEL CARSON WAS RIGHT – THEN, AND NOW

*Joni Seager*

## Introduction

The 1962 publication of Rachel Carson's *Silent Spring* is universally recognized as a watershed event in the history of modern environmentalism. This book is credited with launching modern environmental movements around the world, catalyzing bans in the United States and many other countries on DDT (dichlorodiphenyltrichloroethane) and cognate pesticides (especially the organochlorines and organophosphates), and framing the first sustained exposé and critique of the depredations wrought by an uncritical embrace of the chemical age. Yet *Silent Spring* offered even more sweeping and radical critiques: of capitalism, productionism, militarism, and corporate control of government agendas. When *Silent Spring* was released, the pesticides narrative was so dominant, and Carson's findings so shocking to most readers, that the larger socio-political critical position within which her pesticides findings were embedded went largely unremarked. A few contemporaneous critics muttered about her being a 'communist', but those seemed mostly to be knee-jerk denouncements, not cogent analyses. Mostly, her anti-capitalist and anti-militarist critiques have only received attention more recently, as the fiftieth anniversary of *Silent Spring* produced a renewed interest in the book.

Quite remarkably and patronizingly, some of the recent assessments of the sweepingly radical nature of *Silent Spring* suggest that Carson herself was not fully aware of her own analysis. For example, in the midst of an overwhelmingly laudatory review of the importance of *Silent Spring*, the former science editor for *The Guardian* suggests that Carson's deeper socio-political critique was not intentionally formed by the author herself:

> [*Silent Spring*] also – although this can hardly have been what she intended – a brilliant critique of free-market capitalism, in which chemical companies concerned only with the balance sheet could persuade government and big business to dust and spray the US mainland with costly, persistent and highly toxic products that bore minimal, and sometimes barely visible, warnings of risk to health; in which research into the consequences of chemical overkill was barely funded, if at all; and in which alternative approaches – among them, biological control – were dismissed because nobody (except perhaps the misinformed farmer and the trusting consumer) would profit from them.
>
> *(Radford 2011:n.p.)*

An attentive reading of *Silent Spring* reveals otherwise; Carson knew exactly what she was doing. Long before it was hip to rage against the machine, Carson was raging (Seager 2014:24).

Rachel Carson's broader political analysis in *Silent Spring* is framed by her proto-feminist environmental analysis. There is no evidence that she defined herself as a feminist; few people did in 1962. Nonetheless, Carson prefigures and points the way to the explicitly feminist analyses that would emerge in the 1980s and 1990s, among them:

- Her critique of the masculinized 'control' of nature, which she saw as the stalking horse for the chemical industry, is a stepping stone for later gender and environment analyses from feminist environmental scholars such as Carolyn Merchant (1980, 2008) and Vandana Shiva (1988; Mies and Shiva 1993).
- She drew attention to the manipulation of gender ideologies deployed to persuade Americans to embrace pesticides for domestic use.
- Carson embraced a subjective engagement with nature and, as a scientist, argued the necessity of incorporating humility and a sense of wonder into modern science. Building on this argument, she laid the groundwork for what would become the 'precautionary principle'.
- Carson was one of the first environmental scientists to draw attention to the then uncertain but, in her view, foreboding indications of potent chemical hormone disruptions and impairment of nonhuman and human reproductive systems (Seager 2003).
- Her positionality as a woman in the natural sciences was never far out of view. This was particularly apparent in the response to *Silent Spring*. Even before the book was published, the major pesticide corporations rolled out a coordinated strategy of attacking Carson's science and *also* attacking her personally through explicit misogyny. The attacks on Carson and *Silent Spring* have become a template for modern corporate denial strategies.

## Raging against the machine

Prior to *Silent Spring*, Carson had made her reputation as a nature writer, with three books on the ocean environment and marine life. The second book, *The Sea Around Us* (1951), captured a wide popular readership and established Carson's place in the pantheon of great nature observers. This book was on the *New York Times* bestseller list for almost 90 weeks, it won the US National Book Award, it was condensed in *Reader's Digest*, and it made Carson a household name. *The Sea Around Us* also gave her the financial independence she needed to resign from her job as chief editor at the US Fish and Wildlife Service to devote herself full time to her writing. In 1955 she followed the success of *The Sea Around Us* with a study of the coastal Atlantic, *The Edge of the Sea*, the third of a trilogy 'biography of the ocean'. By the time *The Edge of the Sea* was released, Carson was famous.

The explosive success of *Silent Spring* is partly explained by this prior reputation. Because Carson was already a household name and a trusted science writer, her 1962 book had an eager, pent-up readership. But her readership might not have been prepared for the *new* Rachel Carson. As an author known for books in the nature-appreciation genre, Carson had been associated with an appropriately womanly and genteel version of science. *Silent Spring* was as sharp a swerve away from genteel nature observation as one might imagine. An unflinching, unrelenting, measured critique of the modernist values emerging in post–World War II America and of the growing corporate control over social priorities and government policy, *Silent Spring* challenged the ascendant view that human progress depended on ever more powerful control over 'nature'.

Her book was one of the first popularized critiques of what we might now call productionist values. Carson devotes considerable space in *Silent Spring* to debunking claims that the use of pesticides increases agricultural production. She was not the first to draw attention to insect resistance and 'flareback', but she was one of the first to bring this into public view. Once started, the process of developing and applying even more powerful chemicals spirals endlessly upward, driven by its own internal logic – and driven by the biological process of resistance. Insects, in what Carson called 'a triumphant vindication of Darwin's principle of the survival of the fittest' (1967:18),[1] rapidly develop resistance to insecticides – thus, different and more powerful insecticides need to be applied, to which *those* insects will develop resistance. Carson documents case after case of the resurgence of insects following pesticide spraying – to which, again, even more spraying seems the only resort. Any initial increases in agricultural production, she argues, were illusory and unsustainable.

But Carson was not primarily concerned with charting a better course to increased production. She questioned whether increased agricultural production in the post-war United States was itself even a desirable goal:

> How could intelligent beings seek to control a few unwanted species by a method that contaminated the entire environment and brought the threat of disease and death even to their own kind? Yet this is precisely what we have done. We have done it, moreover, for reasons that collapse the moment we examine them. We are told that the enormous and expanding use of pesticides is necessary to maintain farm production. Yet is our real problem not one of *overproduction*? Our farms . . . have yielded such a staggering excess of crops that the American taxpayer in 1962 is paying out more than one billion dollars a year as the total carrying cost of the surplus-food storage program.
>
> *(Carson 1967:19)*

Carson's concern about 'productionism' may have been influenced by her friendship with Robert Rudd, a scientist in California who was studying pesticides. Before Carson published *Silent Spring*, Rudd published two articles in *The Nation* in 1959, 'The Irresponsible Poisoners' and 'Pesticides: The *Real* Peril'. Rudd, a sophisticated leftist thinker, argued that the over-use of pesticides such as DDT was based on a misplaced prioritization of 'production' over other values. He wrote, 'Overproduction has settled on us like a plague . . . Chemical use to increase production is continually stressed and few stop to inquire "why?"' (cited in Foster and Clark 2008). It is clear that Carson shared Rudd's view that the problem of pesticides is one of 'values', and that the privileging of productionism and profit-seeking – regardless of collateral damage – is the heart of the problem.

## Little tranquilizing pills of half truth from the gods of profit

Throughout *Silent Spring*, Carson focuses much of her critical analysis on the processes of 'manufacturing consent'.[2] She asks, pointedly and poignantly:

> Who has made the decision that sets in motion these chains of poisonings, this ever-widening wave of death? Who has placed in one pan of the scales the leaves that might have been eaten by the beetles and in the other the pitiful heaps of many-hued feathers, the lifeless remains of the birds that fell before the unselective bludgeon of insecticidal poisons? Who has decided – who has the *right* to decide – for the countless legions of people who were not consulted that the supreme value is a world

without insects, even though it be also a sterile world ungraced by the curving wing of a bird in flight?

*(Carson 1967:118)*

She answers her own rhetorical question with a round condemnation: 'The decision is that of the authoritarian temporarily entrusted with power; he has made it during a moment of inattention by [the] millions to whom beauty and the ordered world of nature still have a meaning that is deep and imperative' (118).

Long before political economy analyses became familiar grist for the environmentalist mill, Carson sounds a presciently radical warning about the dangers of a public policy and science agenda driven by the pursuit of profit by pesticide industries:

It is . . . an era dominated by industry, in which the right to make a dollar at whatever cost is seldom challenged. When the public protests, confronted with some obvious evidence of damaging results of pesticide applications, it is fed little tranquilizing pills of half truth. We urgently need an end to these false assurances, to the sugar coating of unpalatable facts. It is the public that is being asked to assume the risks that the insect controllers calculate.

*(Carson 1967:23)*

Carson saved some of her fiercest criticisms for the cozy collusion she witnessed between industry and supposedly independent university scientists or government officials – the very people who should have provided a firewall against the practices of profit-seeking industries. She decried the influence of money in entomology that drew scientists away from research into non-chemical insect control approaches and that kept them beholden to the chemical companies. Remarking that only about 2 per cent of entomological scientists were then working in the field of biological controls, Carson is palpably pained that most insect scientists are more drawn to the 'exciting' work in chemical control. Carson rhetorically asks 'why', and in answering herself points to the influence of funding. She remarks that chemical companies are pouring money into universities and research labs to support work on insecticides, while biological-control studies have no financial champions. There is no money to be made in biological control, she pointedly remarks.

She goes on to make the point that this cozy financial relationship undercuts the integrity of the pursuit of science. She is mystified that entomologists might ever be leading advocates of chemical control, an improbable position she attributes to the corrupting influence of the financial support of chemical companies. By the time Carson was writing *Silent Spring*, chemical companies had insinuated themselves into research institutes and academia, and were starting to produce privately funded science. The entomologists who promoted chemical controls were, Carson said, most likely supported by the chemical industry itself. Perhaps, she says ruefully, one could not expect them to 'bite the hand that feeds them'. But, she warns, this close relationship between industry funding and the research process means that conclusions that insecticides are 'harmless' had little credibility. As science cozied up to industry, it undercut its own position.

Post–*Silent Spring*, Carson's remarks about industry collusion with science became even sharper still. In a speech to the US Women's National Press Club in 1962, she repeatedly warned against the corrupting influence of chemical companies funding basic science and ended with a rousing denunciation of the 'gods of profit and production':

Support of education is something no one quarrels with – but this need not blind us to the fact that research supported by pesticide manufacturers is not likely to be directed at discovering facts indicating unfavorable effects of pesticides. Such a liaison between science and industry is a growing phenomenon, seen in other areas as well. The AMA [American Medical Association], through its newspaper, has just referred physicians to a pesticide trade association for information to help them answer patients' questions about the effects of pesticides on man . . . We see scientific societies acknowledging as 'sustaining associates' a dozen or more giants of a related industry . . . What does it mean when we see a committee set up to make a supposedly impartial review of a situation, and then discover that the committee is affiliated with the very industry whose profits are at stake? . . .

Is industry becoming a screen through which facts must be filtered, so that the hard, uncomfortable truths are kept back and only the harmless morsels allowed to filter through? I know that many thoughtful scientists are deeply disturbed that their organizations are becoming fronts for industry . . . here the tailoring, the screening of basic truth, is done, not to suit a party line, but to accommodate to the short-term gain, to serve the gods of profit and production.

*(Carson 1998a:208–210)*

Carson's warnings about the 'science-industry' complex came at a distinctive moment in the way Americans were viewing large, powerful institutions. This shift was prompted to a significant extent by President Dwight Eisenhower. It was in 1961, just as Carson would be finishing *Silent Spring*, that Eisenhower (a retired general) surprised Americans in his presidential farewell address with his now-famous warnings about the unwarranted influence and ascendancy of the 'military-industrial complex'.

## The habit of killing: boys with their toys

Carson, too, was worried about the military. She was writing *Silent Spring* in the midst of a post-war technology and power high. The 1950s was an era of unfettered American triumphalism. Boosterism about the triumphs of modern science was ubiquitous. The atomic bomb had won the war (or so it was said). The first patient received a mechanical heart. The polio vaccine was saving lives and lifting a terrifying threat from everyday life. A newfangled device called a computer was making waves. Middle class households could suddenly be stocked with refrigerators, televisions, electric ovens, and a car in every garage; optimistic consumerism was the temper of the times. Commercial airline travel was booming and even ordinary people could imagine flying. The Soviets and the Americans were chasing each other into space. There seemed to be no limits to American ingenuity, American power, American know-how; the prevailing wisdom was that there *shouldn't* be limits.

As the 'American way of life' was being redefined in the Cold War that followed WWII, a significant part of that redefinition involved control over nature. This was not only deemed a necessary element of the American project, but given the tremendous advances in science and technology, it seemed within reach. The US military was the driving force behind much of this post-war, Cold War, enthusiasm for controlling nature. Carson was as worried about the nuclear arms race and radiation in the environment as she was about pesticides. When she was writing *Silent Spring* in the late 1950s and early 1960s, the most disastrous health and environmental consequences of the superpowers' nuclear programs were not yet known and the programs themselves were only in their early years. And yet, alarmed by radiation releases and indeed by the whole nuclear enterprise, Carson was an unwavering critic of the Cold War and its atomic age. She was so attentive to the militarized nuclear threat that the first chemical she mentions in *Silent*

*Spring* is not a pesticide, but strontium-90, a by-product of nuclear explosions. Throughout the book, Carson draws attention to the silent, similar, mechanisms of both pesticides and radiation. Indeed, it is hard for a reader to tell whether the 'white granular powder' that signifies the evil that is visited on her fabled town in her opening chapter is radiation or pesticide residue; it could be either, and that is, perhaps, her point.

To Carson, the parallels between nuclear radiation and pesticides are striking: both posed unseen threats that moved through ecosystems as silent killers; both accumulate in human bodies over several years before their deadly effects are evident; both were alarming new artifices of hubris, developed and unleashed by the military. She was alarmed that while there was growing public concern about radiation, there seemed much less interest in the chemical assault: 'The fact that chemicals may play a [similar] role [as radiation] . . . has scarcely dawned on the public mind, nor on the minds of most medical or scientific workers' (1967:189–190). Further, in Carson's view, it is not just that pesticides and radiation have similar mechanisms or cause similar damage; it is that they are both products of humans' reckless over-reach and the untrammeled use of powers beyond our moral capacity – and, indeed, beyond our control. It is only now, in our modern era, Carson says, that humans have acquired the power to actually alter the nature of the environment that surrounds us – and to do so permanently. And with radiation and pesticides, the character of human interference with nature has shifted from a force of assault to a force of fatal evil, changing both in magnitude and character.

Carson saw considerable similarity between the ideology of the development and use of radiation and the development of synthetic chemicals, and in their similar health and environmental consequences; they were the evil twins of her age. She intensely argued that atomic power and pesticides together represented paramount threats to the very existence of life on the planet:

> Along with the possibility of the extinction of mankind by nuclear war, the central problem of our age has therefore become the contamination of man's total environment with such substances of incredible potential for harm – substances that accumulate in the tissues of plants and animals and even penetrate the germ cells to shatter or alter the very material of heredity upon which the shape of the future depends.
>
> *(Carson 1967:18)*

In Carson's analysis, the 'habit of killing – the resort to "eradicating" any creature that may annoy or inconvenience us' (1967:117) is a product of militarized ideology. She doesn't use that terminology, but she comes very close to it, and an analytical reading of *Silent Spring* leaves no doubt that Carson sees the military as bearing clear responsibility for developing the most egregious killing chemicals. To Carson, it was no coincidence that radioactive materials and pesticides were both products of the military. She is not directly critical of what we would today call militarism, but she plainly places accountability for much environmental and health recklessness with the military. In Chapter 3, 'Elixirs of Death', in which Carson lays out the origins and basic chemical nature of insecticides, she identifies the military origins of the ubiquitous poisoning of humans, animals, and environment by synthetic chemicals. The creation of pesticides was literally a by-product of war: insecticides were discovered as by-products of the laboratory development of chemical weaponry.

DDT was catapulted into large-scale production, and then into civilian life, by the US military. It was not until the US military saw DDT's potential as a chemical weapon against typhus in Europe and malaria in the Pacific that it became a mass-produced chemical – at first, for the exclusive use of the military, and then, as the war was ending, DDT was being pushed into the civilian market as an agricultural and household insecticide. In her narrative of the development of the practice of aerial spraying of pesticides, Carson notes that it was the availability of WWII surplus airplanes that made this possible:

> [Formerly, poisons] were kept in containers marked with skull and crossbones . . . With the development of the new organic insecticides and the abundance of surplus planes after the Second World War, all this was forgotten . . . they have amazingly become something to be showered down indiscriminately from the skies.
>
> *(Carson 1967:141)*

Throughout *Silent Spring*, Carson underscores the point that pesticides derived not only from an ideology of the 'control' of nature but, true to their military origins, represented an ideological proclivity toward outright war *on* nature. She introduces this theme within the first few pages of her book:

> [pesticides] are used in man's war against nature . . . These sprays, dusts, and aerosols are now applied almost universally to farms, gardens, forests, and homes – nonselective chemicals that have the power to kill every insect, the 'good' and the 'bad', to still the song of birds and the leaping of fish in the streams, to coat the leaves with a deadly film, and to linger on in soil – all this though the intended target may be only a few weeds or insects. Can anyone believe it is possible to lay down such a barrage of poisons on the surface of the earth without making it unfit for all life? They should not be called 'insecticides' but 'biocides'.
>
> *(Carson 1967:18)*

Carson railed against the idea that modern 'man' (which she meant in the generic sense) could and should exert mastery over nature at any cost:

> The 'control of nature' is a phrase conceived in arrogance, born of the Neanderthal age of biology and philosophy, when it was supposed that nature exists for the convenience of man. The concepts and practices of applied entomology for the most part date from that Stone Age of science. It is our alarming misfortune that so primitive a science has armed itself with the most modern and terrible weapons, and that in turning them against the insects it has also turned them against the earth.
>
> *(Carson 1967:261–262)*

Throughout *Silent Spring*, Carson returns to the war analogues used by pesticide promoters to validate pesticides in the glow of post-WWII American triumphalism. In one stunning paragraph, she invokes a backslide from peace to war (plowshares being beaten *back* into guns) and the terrible cost of the trivial pursuit of 'the new':

> The chemical weed killers are a bright new toy . . . they give a giddy sense of power over nature to those who wield them, and as for the long-range and less obvious effects – these are easily brushed aside as the baseless imaginings of pessimists. The 'agricultural engineers' speak blithely of 'chemical plowing' in a world that is urged to beat its plowshares into spray guns.
>
> *(Carson 1967:69)*

We might say Carson is previewing here the flip modern gendered colloquialism about 'boys with their toys'.

# Domesticating the poisons: gender marketing

Civilian marketing of synthetic pesticides in the United States began in earnest in 1944, starting with DDT. Marketing pesticides to farmers was easy. The 'need' for pesticides in the agricultural sector seemed self-evident – both then and now. But although farming represented a large sector of the American economy in the 1950s, the pesticide manufacturers had their eyes on another prize, just as big. They wanted to market pesticides to everyone, not just farmers. The newly affluent, expanding, suburbanizing American middle class offered an irresistible opportunity: Americans had to be convinced to bring pesticides home.

Marketing pesticides for household use required their manufacturers to craft a three pronged approach: first, marketing lawn care to men, persuading them that good lawn care (as defined by the pesticide manufacturers) was a mark of good citizenship and manly responsibility; second, marketing to women on the basis that modern pesticides allowed them to protect their children from illnesses borne by insects, and marked them as caring mothers; and, third, marketing to both men and women (though mostly women) for gardening. The campaign to bring pesticides into American households was a carefully contrived and highly gendered effort. This did not escape Carson's analytical attention.

As soon as DDT was released from the military to the civilian market, manufacturers started their campaign to domesticate pesticides. A typical ad in *Women's Day* magazine in 1947, for example, makes, to our modern sensibilities, a horrifying pitch: a photograph shows a typical, white, presumptively middle-class woman bending over a crib that holds a smiling baby, under the large-font banner 'Protect Your Children Against Disease-Carrying Insects'. 'How is she to protect her infant?' the viewer might wonder. DDT-impregnated wallpaper! In Disney 'Jack and Jill' or 'Disney Favorites' patterns, no less. The copy says 'effective against disease-carrying insects for one year' and promises that this DDT-impregnated wallpaper is *'certified* to be absolutely safe for home use'.

This marketing campaign was typical of its time – a direct appeal to the emerging middle class to demonstrate its commitment to family values and a safe modern life through embracing chemicals. Manufacturers of pesticides worked ceaselessly to persuade the American middle class that pesticides would protect their homes and usher their arrival into the American Dream. Carson notes with alarm that use of poisons in the home was made easy and attractive, particularly to appeal to women:

> Kitchen shelf paper, white or tinted to match one's color scheme, may be impregnated with insecticide, not merely on one but on both sides . . . With push-button ease, one may send a fog of dieldrin into the most inaccessible nooks and crannies of cabinets, corners, and baseboards. If we are troubled by mosquitoes, chiggers, or other insect pests . . . we have a choice of innumerable lotions, creams, and sprays for application to clothing or skin. Although we are warned that some of these will dissolve varnish, paint, and synthetic fabrics, we are presumably to infer that the human skin is impervious to chemicals . . . an exclusive New York store advertises a pocket-sized insecticide dispenser, suitable for the purse or for beach, golf, or fishing gear. We can polish our floors with a wax guaranteed to kill any insect that walks over it. We can hang strips impregnated with the chemical lindane in our closets and garment bags or place them in our bureau drawers . . . All these matters attended to, we may round out our day with insecticides by going to sleep under a mothproof blanket impregnated with dieldrin.
>
> *(Carson 1967:158–159)*

Carson goes on to bemoan the fact that government agencies gave their stamp of approval to domesticating the pesticides. *Home and Garden Bulletins* from the US Department of Agriculture, she remarks, regularly encouraged people to spray their clothing with oil solutions of DDT, dieldrin, chlordane, or any of several other moth killers. As appalled as Carson was by the campaigns to make pesticides cozy and convenient, she was even more worried that these advertisements gave no indication that these materials were dangerous.

While manufacturers were appealing primarily to women to keep their homes safe through the liberal use of pesticides, a campaign for the outdoors – designed to appeal primarily to men – was just as intense. Carson decried the 'fad of gardening by poisons' (1967:160), and the slick advertising campaigns mounted to encourage consumers to bring pesticides home. The use of pesticides in and around the home was marketed as a sign of modernity and of middle-class obligation. Gardening, Carson says, is now linked with the super poisons that are available in every hardware store, supermarket, and garden centre. With very little cautionary advice to consumers who are urged to buy deadly materials,

> a constant stream of new gadgets make it easier to use poisons on lawn and garden – and increase the gardener's contact with them. One may get a jar-type attachment for the garden hose, for example, by which such extremely dangerous chemicals as chlordane or dieldrin are applied as one waters the lawn . . . Besides the once innocuous garden hose, power mowers also have been fitted with devices for the dissemination of pesticides, attachments that will dispense a cloud of vapor as the homeowner goes about the task of mowing his lawn.
>
> *(Carson 1967:159)*

Carson was dismayed by the trivial uses for pesticides. She remarked caustically on the role of advertising and the manipulation of class and gender identity by pesticide manufacturers in their effort to mount a campaign against crabgrass on suburban lawns. She and American feminist writer-activist Betty Friedan, who was at the same moment writing her book *The Feminine Mystique* (1963) about the distinctive ways suburban masculinities and femininities were forged, might have had much to say to one another. They were both writing about the toxicities of postwar suburbia, although from different perspectives. Carson literally so:

> The mores of suburbia now dictate that crabgrass must go at whatever cost. Sacks containing chemicals designed to rid the lawn of such despised vegetation have become almost a status symbol. These weed-killing chemicals are sold under brand names that never suggest their identity or nature. To learn that they contain chlordane or dieldrin one must read exceedingly fine print placed on the least conspicuous part of the sack . . . Instead, the typical illustration portrays a happy family scene, father and son smilingly preparing to apply the chemical to the lawn.
>
> *(Carson 1967:161)*

Carson was dismayed that anyone could walk into a store and purchase, without any question or registration or permit required, death-dealing chemicals. In her 1963 testimony before a congressional committee, she implored American lawmakers to restrict the sale and purchase of pesticides

> at least to those capable of understanding the hazards and following directions . . . We place much more stringent restrictions on the sale of drugs – [a man made ill by

spraying] could buy the chemicals that made him ill with no restrictions, but had to have prescriptions to buy the drugs to cure him.

*(Carson 1963:13)*

The manufacturers were astonishingly successful in persuading Americans to bring pesticides home. The American 'home and garden' sector in 2011, fifty years after *Silent Spring*, consumes about seventy million pounds of active pesticide ingredients a year, and accounts for almost one quarter of all pesticide use in the United States; of all insecticides, it accounts for 38 per cent (USEPA 2011:6). The most common pesticide used on home gardens (as a lawn weed killer, used in more than 1,500 pesticide products) is 2, 4-D, a pesticide that Carson warned about in 1962.

## Precaution and humility: prefiguring feminist science

In *Silent Spring*, Rachel Carson keeps drawing attention to how much we *don't* know about pesticides – their persistence, their synergistic and cumulative effects, their transport and spread through ecosystems and across species, their health effects. As she says repeatedly, no one can tell what will be the ultimate ecosystem and health costs and consequences of intensive and extensive exposure to an unpredictable mix of synthetic chemicals. Recently, scholars tallied Carson's use of terminology that framed the rhetorical ways in which she foregrounded uncertainty in *Silent Spring*: they found fourteen uses of 'we do not know'; seven uses of 'potential for harm'; six uses of 'little understood'; four uses of 'more research is needed'; and two uses of 'lack of consensus' (Walker and Walsh 2012:14–15).

At several junctures in the book, she reminds readers that the pesticide promoters had launched us, unwittingly, into a real-time experiment. She means this with reference to specific pesticide programs for which the long-term outcome was entirely uncertain (or even unquestioned), but she also means this as a meta-theme: humanity is running full tilt forward into a yawning unknown, spray-gun in hand. In a 1963, post-*Silent Spring* lecture, Carson quoted ecologist and environmental movement activist Barry Commoner in pointing out that we often defer an inquiry into 'impacts' until it is far too late:

> The lack of foresight [about introducing harmful substances into the environment] is one of the most serious complications . . . we seldom if ever evaluate the risks associated with a new technological program before it is put into effect. We wait until the process has become embedded in a vast economic and political commitment, and then it is virtually impossible to alter.
>
> *(Carson 1998b:232)*

But even were we to be more foresightful – as Carson argues we must – a second kind of uncertainty is not necessarily assuaged: we may 'look before we leap', but when we look, there may be contradictory evidence, or, as in the case of pesticides and human health, often the evidence will only emerge over a long time horizon. What then? Carson answers firmly:

> And if . . . we have concluded that we are being asked to take senseless and frightening risks, then we should no longer accept the counsel of those who tell us that we must fill our world with poisonous chemicals; we should look about and see what other course is open to us.
>
> *(Carson 1967:244)*

In this particular context, Carson's 'other course' was her interest in biological and natural controls. Her warning that too much was at stake to take 'senseless and frightening risks' was one of the overarching themes through *Silent Spring*. Here Carson prefigures the 'precautionary principle' – one of the most progressive and complex contemporary environmental policy vehicles.

Carson was a trained biologist. She understood the norms of science, and then stepped, self-consciously, beyond those normative borders. First and foremost, Carson's approach to science embraced humility, a sense of wonder, and a certainty that 'man' could not and should not control nature. She was not anti-science, far from it, but 'wonder' was a trait she felt had been suppressed by science and by the privileging of science as the primary lens through which to comprehend the world – to humanity's considerable disadvantage. She counterposed the clinical investigation of the laws of nature against an openness to revel in the beauty and marvel of the world. 'Most of us walk unseeing through the world', she writes in *Silent Spring*, 'unaware alike of its beauties, its wonders, and the strange and sometimes terrible intensity of the lives that are being lived about us' (1967:220). She also talks about a notion related to beauty and wonder, humility. 'Humility' often has religious overtones, but Carson's invocation is not a religious one. She is speaking to the rash overconfidence of humans who act as though they can remove themselves from the inescapable truth that humans are part of nature. Humility was embedded in her ecological message that we are all part of nature – and that our efforts to put ourselves outside of natural cycles (or, more likely, above them) will backfire. Humans are not better than, bigger than, stronger than, or outside of nature, Carson would say – and it is when we lose sight of that truth that we get ourselves into trouble.

Carson was not a romantic idealist. She knew that wonder and beauty would not alone catalyze the changes in human behaviour that were needed. But she also knew that the prevailing scientific paradigm was implicated in creating the conditions in which environmental and health assaults were normalized as signs of 'progress'. As a pragmatic matter of science and biology, Carson was certain that there were specific alternatives to the indiscriminate saturation of the environment with pesticides. Chief among those alternatives were natural insect controls, integrated pest management, selective and highly restricted use of chemical controls, and an eagerness to give 'citizen science' a seat at the table of science and policy.

Carson's distinctive approach to science may reflect her positionality as a woman scientist in the 1950s – simply by her presence, she was out of step with the scientific mainstream. Her view that attempts to control nature through the indiscriminate use of chemical poisons would produce environmental calamity was a minority and unpopular one. Feminist scholars of science in the decades after Carson have explicated the gendered implications of this urge to control. The feminist environmental historian Carolyn Merchant (1980, 2008, 2010) argues, for example, that the devaluation of women, long identified with nature, was particularly and specifically integral to the production of the emerging modernist scientific project. As part of the modernist project, Merchant argues, the control of nature was inextricably tied to men's control of women – metaphorically and literally. The 'father of modern science' Francis Bacon's scientific quest was to 'wrest secrets from Nature's grasp' and to reveal the 'secrets locked in nature's bosom'. Bacon talked of dominating and enslaving nature, hounding her, and interrogating her into giving up her secrets (Merchant 2008:754). In the view of many feminist analysts, this is not just rhetorical excess.

Recent feminist environmental analysis makes clear that the association of women with nature – and men's linked domination of both – is not only a seventeenth century artifact. For example, a large corpus of writings on the sexualized representations of associations between animals and women (see Adams 1990; Donovan 1990; Emel 1995), Vandana Shiva's work on contemporary oppressions of women and environment (1993, 1988), Val Plumwood's (1993) critiques of the 'standpoint of mastery', and my own work on masculinized structures of environmental agency (Seager 1993) among many others, extends and deepens Merchant's analysis of the origins of this ideology of dual dominance.

The masculinized domination of nature and, symbiotically, of women is inextricable from the masculinized structure of modern science. To the extent that 'men of reason' structured modern science in their own image as a project to wrest control from a feminized nature, then it follows that women would be placed largely outside the enterprise of science. Feminist historians and philosophers of science such as Donna Haraway, Sandra Harding, and Evelyn Fox Keller have contributed important analyses of the ways in which the standpoints of modern science exclude women or frame women as 'other'. The assumed and structured incompatibility of women and science – and between women and scientific rationality – continues to have enormous salience (see, for example, Noble 1991),[3] as it did in Rachel Carson's own life.

Merchant and scholars of science who have followed in Carson's footsteps not only implicate mechanistic science in creating the most pressing ecological problems of our day; they dare to suggest that women were as much the victims as the beneficiaries of the progress of science. Merchant's analysis, at its core, throws into doubt the 'grand narratives' of science and progress, and questions the previously unexamined ways that modern science is assumed to have manufactured 'progress':

> The notion of a 'Scientific Revolution' in the sixteenth and seventeenth centuries is part of a larger mainstream narrative of Western culture that has propelled science, technology, and capitalism's efforts to 'master' nature – a narrative into which most Westerners have unconsciously been socialized and within which we ourselves have become actors in a storyline of upward progress.
>
> *(Merchant 2006:517)*

This analysis owes a considerable debt to Carson. Two decades earlier, Carson was questioning the nature of 'progress' and asking 'big questions' about the role of science in constructing a false narrative of what constituted progress. She was right then – and now.

## 'Silence, Miss Carson'

Carson's positionality (or her gender) as a woman writing environmental science – and critiquing big business – was never far from view. She kept her personal life well cloaked from the public, especially her intense and years-long romantic involvement with another woman. As she was finishing *Silent Spring* she was dying from breast cancer, another fact she kept hidden from the public and even from many close friends, knowing that her critics would accuse her of having a personal agenda in challenging the proliferation of pesticides. To the public, she presented herself and allowed herself to be presented as a 'spinster'. The 'spinster' role served variously to her advantage and disadvantage throughout her career. On the one hand, an unmarried middle-class white woman such as Carson could be viewed as a stock figure of reliability and respectability in mid-twentieth century America. To many outward appearances, she represented a modest, no-nonsense woman who was briskly and efficiently running her own household, complete with her mother who lived with her throughout much of her adult life. Such a woman was easily typecast as sensible and stable.

The role she forged for herself, prior to *Silent Spring,* as a writer of nature appreciation books fit well with this restrained image, and the two images – spinster and nature appreciator – supported one another in solidifying her public identity as a much admired and 'safe', even sentimental, science writer. In her obituary, the *New York Times* referred to her reputation as 'the essence of gentle scholarship' (Obituary, *NY Times* 1964). Contemporaries apparently not uncommonly referred to her as the 'nun of nature' (Griswold 2012), a peculiar backhanded compliment. A 1951 review of *The Sea Around Us* referred to her, admiringly, as 'the slender, gentle Miss Carson . . .' (cited in Dreier 2012:229), while another review by the science editor of *Time* magazine reassured readers that Carson's book about sea life was 'charming', that the animals she described were her 'friends' whom she loved, and that the very ocean currents themselves were 'dear to her'; he concluded his genteelly paternalistic review wondering what Carson looked like (there was no photo of her on the book's dust jacket), saying 'It would be pleasant to know what a woman looks like who can write about exacting science with such beauty and precision' (Leonard 1951). One can almost feel the pat on the head.

On the other hand, as Carson ventured into more contested terrain with her work leading up to *Silent Spring*, and then with the publication itself, and she started to challenge powerful interests and institutions, her 'spinsterism' was wielded against her. Her critics responded as though being an unmarried, middle-aged woman was a disease or at least a disability. Many of the most ferocious attacks on Carson after *Silent Spring* drew attention to her identity as an unmarried woman – both of which, critics argued, undercut her competence. That a mere woman, let alone a 'spinster', should be taken seriously on scientific matters was unimaginable! The critics were drawing on a long tradition of disdain and distrust of women who did not fulfill the cultural expectations of 'normal' womanhood; the spinster stereotype as a deviant and slightly unhinged woman was a cheap and easily accessible cultural stereotype for Carson's critics to invoke (Faderman 1981; Faludi 1991; Mustard 2000).

Carson was a threat to her detractors not merely because of her message about pesticides, but because she was a woman, an independent scholar whose sex and lack of institutional ties placed her outside the nexus of production and application of conventional scientific knowledge (Smith 2001:734). Invoking a familiar Cold War trope, her loyalty as an American was questioned. Ezra Taft Benson, former agriculture secretary, privately suggested to former President Eisenhower that Carson was 'probably a communist'. A letter to the editor of the *New Yorker* echoed a similar theme:

> Miss Rachel Carson's reference to the selfishness of insecticide manufacturers probably reflects her Communist sympathies, like a lot of our writers these days. We can live without birds and animals, but, as the current market slump shows, we cannot live without business. As for insects, isn't it just like a woman to be scared to death of a few little bugs! As long as we have the H-bomb everything will be O.K.
>
> *(quoted in Stoll 2012, n.p.)*

Sexism knew no bounds. Gender-hazing was used to denigrate Carson and her science, a tactic used by critics to shape the debate over pesticides according to the rules of industrial capitalism which identified itself with a masculine norm. Carson's writing, which combined 'caring' with science, was considered to be well beyond the male pale. Her 'love' of nature was seen as evidence of an unserious author. Many male critics castigated her as a 'bird and bunny lover'. In one remarkable all-in-one critique, the author called her 'part of the vociferous, misinformed group of nature balancing, organic gardening, bird loving, unreasonable citizenry' (quoted in Trost 1984:68).

Carson was portrayed, especially, as a hysterical female who knew little about the ways of the world.[4] A lengthy 1962 review in *Time* magazine (titled, tellingly, 'Pesticides, The Price for Progress') accused her of being emotionally overwrought:

> Many scientists sympathize with Miss Carson's love of wildlife, and even with her mystical attachment to the balance of nature. But they fear that her emotional and inaccurate outburst in *Silent Spring* may do harm by alarming the nontechnical public, while doing no good for the things that she loves.
>
> *(quoted in Lear 1997:430)*

The *Time* review went on to accuse Carson of 'taking up her pen in anger and alarm' (quoted in Trost 1984:68). One now well-cited review in *Chemical and Engineering News* by a medical doctor, William Darby, noted that 'it is doubtful that many readers can bear to wade through its high-pitched sequences of anxieties' (Darby 1962:61). The *National Review* called the book 'simply a long emotional attack' and invoked the need for 'rational' and 'scientific' approaches in place of Carson's screed (quoted in Smith 2001:741). The vilification of Carson invoked notions of the conduct of 'good science' that should be 'rational' and 'unemotional'; Francis Bacon would be pleased.

Much of the story of Carson and her critics echoes with strains of the triumph of Baconian modern (male) science over the unruly forces of (female) nature. Many critics invoked the image of Carson as an anti-science witch. The vice chancellor of the University of California – Riverside, Robert Metcalf, asked whether

> we are going to progress logically and scientifically upward, or whether we are going to drift back to the dark ages where witchcraft and witches reign . . . There are signs people do lean toward 'witchery', and not only on the subject of pesticides. There are food faddists, and quacks in the medical field, and persons who oppose fluoridation of water.
>
> *(Metcalf, quoted in Hazlett 2004:707)*

Other pesticide supporters also invoked the image of Carson as a witch. The cover of the October 1963 issue of the magazine *Farm Chemicals* featured a cartoon in which figures representing three industry spokesmen who testified before Congress forcefully make their case to Uncle Sam, one pounding the table with his fist, another pointing his finger in accusation, and the third gesturing thumbs down. Behind them, a witch on her broomstick flies by (image reproduced in Hazlett 2004:707). Other criticism was equally ugly. Darby's *Chemical and Engineering News* review was titled 'Silence, Miss Carson', tapping the cultural theme that women should know their place – which, the review was clearly suggesting, Carson did not (Darby 1962; see also Domosh and Seager 2001).

Carson died less than two years after *Silent Spring* was published, her voice stilled but not silenced.

## Notes

A prior version of this chapter is published in *Feminist Futures: Reimagining Women, Culture and Development* (second edition), edited by Kum-Kum Bhavnani, John Foran, Priya A. Kurian, and Debashish Munshi, and published by Zed Books, 2016.

1 A note on source: all Silent Spring page references are to the 1967 edition, 5th Fawcett Press printing of Rachel Carson's *Silent Spring* (New York: Fawcett Crest; original work published 1962 by Houghton Mifflin).

2 'Manufacturing consent' is a term credited to Lippmann (1922) and popularized by Herman and Chomsky in the eighties.
3 The precarious position of women in science continues to be well documented. Two of the most prominent recent studies that detail the particulars of this include a 2012 study at Yale University revealing that science professors at American universities widely regard female undergraduates as less competent than male students with the same accomplishments and skills, and would pay them less if they were hiring (Moss-Racusin et al. 2012); and a 1999 study at MIT of the status of women science faculty finding widespread bias and marginalization (Committee on Women Faculty 1999).
4 The tactic of casting women environmentalists as 'hysterical' continues today (see Seager 1996).

# References

Adams, C. J. (1990) *The Sexual Politics of Meat: A Feminist-Vegetarian Critical Theory.* New York: Continuum.
Carson, R. (1951) *The Sea Around Us.* New York: Oxford University Press.
Carson, R. (1955) *The Edge of the Sea.* Boston: Houghton Mifflin Company.
Carson, R. (1962) *Silent Spring.* New York: Houghton Mifflin.
Carson, R. (1963) 'Environmental hazards: Control of pesticides and other chemical poisons', Statement of Rachel Carson before the Subcommittee on Reorganization and International Organizations of the Committee on Government Operations.
Carson, R. (1998a) *The Sense of Wonder.* New York: Harper Collins. (Original publication, 1965).
Carson, R. (1998b) *Lost Woods: The Discovered Writing of Rachel Carson*, Lear, L. (ed). Boston: Beacon Press.
Committee on Women Faculty in the School of Science (1999) *A Study on the Status of Women Faculty in Science at MIT.* Cambridge, MA: MIT Press. Online. Available at: http://web.mit.edu/fnl/women/women.html (accessed 20 December 2012).
Darby, W. J. (1962) 'Silence, Miss Carson', *Chemical and Engineering News* 40(40): 60–63.
Domosh, M. and Seager, J. (2001) *Putting Women in Place: Feminist Geographers Make Sense of the World.* New York: Guilford Press.
Donovan, J. (1990) 'Animal rights and feminist theory', *Signs* 15(2): 350–375.
Dreier, P. (2012) *The 100 Greatest Americans of the 20th Century.* New York: Nation Books.
Emel, J. (1995) 'Are you man enough, big and bad enough? Ecofeminism and wolf eradication in the USA', *Environment and Planning D: Society and Space* 13(6): 707–734.
Faderman, L. (1981) *Surpassing the Love of Men.* New York: Morrow and Company.
Faludi, S. (1991) *Backlash: The Undeclared War Against American Women.* New York: Anchor Books, Doubleday.
Foster, J. B. and Clark, B. (2008) 'Rachel Carson's ecological critique', *Monthly Review* 59(9): 1–17.
Friedan, B. (1963) *The Feminine Mystique.* New York: W.W. Norton.
Griswold, E. (2012) 'The wild life of Silent Spring: How Silent Spring ignited the environmental movement', *New York Times*, 23 September 2012. Online. Available at: www.nytimes.com/2012/09/23/magazine/how-silent-spring-ignited-the-environmental-movement.html?_r=0 (accessed 14 March 2016).
Hazlett, M. (2004) 'Woman vs. man vs. bugs: Gender and popular ecology in early reactions to Silent Spring', *Environmental History* 9(4): 701–729.
Herman, E. S. and Chomsky, N. (1988) *Manufacturing Consent.* New York: Pantheon Books.
Lear, L. (1997) *Rachel Carson: Witness for Nature.* Boston, NY: Houghton Mifflin.
Leonard, J. N. (1951) '. . .And his wonders in the deep', *New York Times.*
Leonard, J. N. (1964) 'Obituary: Rachel Carson dies of cancer', *New York Times.* Online. Available at: www.nytimes.com/books/97/10/05/reviews/carson-obit.html (accessed 14 March 2016).
Lippman, W. (1922) *Public Opinion.* New York: Harcourt Brace & Co.
Merchant, C. (1980) *The Death of Nature: Women, Ecology, and the Scientific Revolution.* San Francisco: Harper Collins.
Merchant, C. (2006) 'The scientific revolution and the *Death of Nature*', *Isis* 97: 513–533.
Merchant, C. (2008) 'The violence of impediments: Francis Bacon and the origins of experimentation', *Isis* 99: 731–760.
Merchant, C. (2010) *Environmentalism: From the Control of Nature to Partnership.* University of California Bernard Moses Lecture, 4 May 2010. Online. Available at: http://nature.berkeley.edu/merchant (accessed 12 December 2012).
Mies, M. and Shiva, S. (1993) *Ecofeminism.* London: Zed Books.

Moss-Racusin, C. A., Dovidio, J. F., Brescoll, V. L., Grahama, M. J. and Handelsman, J. (2012) 'Science faculty's subtle gender biases favor male students', *Proceedings of the National Academy of Sciences* 109(41): 16474–16479.

Mustard, D. (2000) 'Spinster: An evolving stereotype revealed through film', *Journal of Media Psychology*. Online. Available at: www.calstatela.edu/faculty/sfischo/spinster.html (accessed 14 March 2016).

Noble, D. (1991) *A World Without Women: The Evolution of the Masculine Culture of Science*. New York: Knopf.

Plumwood, V. (1993) *Feminism and the Mastery of Nature*. New York: Routledge.

Radford, T. (2011) '*Silent Spring* by Rachel Carson', *The Guardian*. Online. Available at: www.theguardian.com/science/2011/sep/30/silent-spring-rachel-carson-review (accessed 16 March 2016).

Rudd, R. L. (1959) 'The irresponsible poisoners', *The Nation*: 496–497.

Rudd, R. L. (1959) 'Pesticides: The real peril', *The Nation*: 399–401.

Seager, J. (1993) *Earth Follies: Coming to Feminist Terms With the Global Environmental Crisis*. New York: Routledge.

Seager, J. (1996) '"Hysterical housewives" and other mad women: Grassroots environmental organizing in the USA', in Rocheleau, D., Wangari, E. and Thomas-Slater, B. (eds) *Toward a Feminist Political Ecology: Global Perspectives From Local Experience*. New York: Routledge, 271–283.

Seager, J. (2003) 'Rachel Carson died of breast cancer: Feminist environmentalism comes of age', *Signs* 28(3): 945–972.

Seager, J. (2014) *Rachel Carson's Silent Spring*. New York and London: Bloomsbury.

Shiva, V. (1988) *Staying Alive: Women, Ecology and Development*. London: Zed Books.

Smith, M. B. (2001) 'Silence, Miss Carson! Science, gender, and the reception of Silent Spring', *Feminist Studies* 27(3): 733–752.

Stoll, M. (2012) 'Industrial and agricultural interests fight back', *Environment and Society Portal*. Online. Available at: www.environmentandsociety.org/exhibitions/silent-spring/industrial-and-agricultural-interests-fight-back (accessed 14 March 2016).

Trost, C. (1984) *Elements of Risk: The Chemical Industry and Its Threat to America*. New York: Times Books.

USEPA (2011) *Pesticides Industry Sales and Usage: 2006 and 2007 Market Estimates*. Washington, DC: Office of Pesticide Programs.

Walker, K. and Walsh, L. (2012) 'No one yet knows what the ultimate consequences may be: How Rachel Carson transformed scientific uncertainty into a site for public participation', *Journal of Business and Technical Communication* 26(1): 3–34.

# 2

# *THE DEATH OF NATURE*

## Foundations of ecological feminist thought

*Charis Thompson and Sherilyn MacGregor*

### Introduction

Without question, *The Death of Nature: Women, Ecology, and the Scientific Revolution* is one of the most successful and influential books of feminist scholarship ever written. Published in 1980 by American environmental historian Carolyn Merchant, it has remained in print, continuing to sell well and to speak to lay and expert readers alike. The book's continued ability powerfully to connect sexism and other forms of domination prevalent in modern life with a historical and analytic framework for examining ecological devastation remains deeply compelling. One may disagree with the interpretation of a particular piece of evidence in the text, or find the structural explanation to be too sweeping, but the fundamental insight retains its explanatory power. The idea that the rise of modern science, technology, and capitalism produced and relied on the death, domination, and exploitation of a nature gendered female, and that this reinforced and reflected the cultural subordination and exploitation of women, is the kind of provocative thesis of which academia has too few.

In this chapter, we explain the enduring importance of Merchant's ambitious text for the field of gender and environment in general and ecological feminism in particular. We begin with an overview of the books' content and then discuss how it was taken up by ecofeminists in the early phase of that movement. *The Death of Nature* is commonly considered to be one of the founding texts – perhaps *the* founding text – for the articulation of ecofeminism, particularly in Anglo-American circles. It provided a burgeoning movement with historical evidence, academic rigour, and a secular materialist analytic framework that nonetheless appreciated the centrality of relationality and caring in its call for the restoration of an earlier organic and living view of nature. And it established connections between feminism and environmentalism as movements for fundamental social and cultural change. As we are not historians of the sixteenth and seventeenth centuries, we are ill placed to contest Merchant's particular selections of evidence or interpretations of texts. Instead, we argue for the need to resurrect Merchant's analysis in light of the partial sidelining of ecofeminism within academic feminism. As one of the main branches of feminism that attempts to understand the interconnections between gendered injustice and environmental destruction, ecofeminism continues urgently to be needed. Ecofeminism's relative sidelining was in part the result of vital critiques of feminisms that privileged white middle class, Anglophone perspectives and experiences. These critiques – for example, that ecofeminism operated with 'essentialist' understandings of gender and nature, and that ecological politics tended to overlook social differences in the name of protecting 'nature' – should have made the field stronger, but it was to take much of the next thirty years before arguments about race, class, sovereignty, and a multiplicity of views of nature and sexuality and gender were to begin to become more fully incorporated into the ecofeminist analytic that linked feminisms and the environment. The main claims we make in this chapter are, first, that academic feminism has lived to regret the poststructuralist feminist turn away from 'nature' and ecofeminism. And second, that although ecofeminism is becoming better at thinking about *race, class, disability, and coloniality with gender* on issues of science and environment – thanks in particular to decades of work by feminists of colour (e.g., Davis 1983; Mohanty et al. 1991), environmental justice scholars such as Vandana Shiva (1988) writing from the Global South, and to a long history of indigenous feminist thought (Nixon 2015) – there is still some way to go to get an intersectional and trans-national feminist environmental movement off the ground. Going back to Merchant, we argue, can contribute to this effort.

## History turned 'upside down'

*The Death of Nature* is an important example of the claim that 'to write history from a feminist perspective is to turn it upside down – to see social structure from the bottom up and to flip-flop mainstream values' (Merchant 1990:xx). Merchant's book not only offers an interpretation of the male domination of Western science and industrial progress; it also uncovers the ideas and texts of women who had been left out of mainstream history of science texts.[1] It tells the story of how, around the time of the scientific revolution in Western Europe, human societies moved away from living in an 'organic' relationship to the natural world that was defined by subsistence needs and conceptions of nature as a living, nurturing, 'feminized' force. The first part of the book offers detailed examples of how nature and the feminine were closely connected in literature and philosophy from the Ancient Greeks (Aristotle, Plato) to Renaissance poets and polemicists (Donne, Spenser, Agrippa). A recurring theme concerned the earth as 'a beneficent and kindly mother' (so wrote Agricola in 1556) who should be protected from damaging activities such as mining (Merchant 1990:29–41). With the end of feudalism and the rise of commercial and then capitalist economies in the sixteenth century, this view – and its related constraints on human manipulation of the natural world – was undermined to make way for technological progress. Chapter 7 in the book, 'Dominion over Nature', explains the emergence of a mechanistic view and the birth of 'a new ethic sanctioning the exploitation of nature' (164). Here Merchant explores the role of Francis Bacon, founder of both the scientific method and the Royal Society (and Lord Chancellor during King James I's witch trials in England), in shaping a worldview in which nature was cast as at once inert matter and a feminized slave to be dominated (169). The Baconian program, she explains, was a methodology for interrogating nature (described as a 'common harlot') that had much in common with courtroom techniques for extracting the truth out of women accused of witchcraft, including torture, penetration, and restraint (168–171).

Seen from the bottom up, the history of the scientific revolution is a story of violence and exploitation in the name of innovation and progress. Important for our discussion here, Merchant argues persuasively in *The Death of Nature* for a view that subsequently became one of the core tenets of ecofeminism: that the domination of women and the domination of nature are struc-turally linked. She suggests that it is necessary to 're-examine the formation of a world-view and a science that, by reconceptualizing reality as a machine rather than a living organism, sanctioned the domination of both nature and women' (xxi). Not only does the story explain the shift under capitalism from reverence to domination of the environment; she also demonstrates how cultural views and values about women (determined largely by elite White men) shifted over time in ways that appeared to naturalize subordination. Her analysis makes sense of the historical processes whereby women's life-giving and life-protecting capabilities had themselves become the objects of scientific inquiry, thereby objectifying both nature and women. What is more, as outlined in Chapter 6, 'Production, Reproduction and the Female', the triumph of mechanism over organicism resulted in the masculine takeover of reproduction (complete with the persecution of healers and midwives as witches) and the relegation of caring labour to the irrational and devalued domestic sphere. As Merchant explains, the scientific revolution was the beginning of a long process through which '"scientific" authority could be used to keep women in their place as intellectually inferior and economically dependent' (163).

Merchant was motivated by her recognition of an isomorphism in critiques of capitalism in feminism and environmentalism, noting that 'both the women's movement and the ecology movement are sharply critical of the costs of competition, aggression, and domination arising from the market economy's *modus operandi* in nature and society' (xx). In examining the scientific revolution, she made an historical argument that the rise of modern science, and the economies it enabled, were the driving forces behind these twin oppressions. The corollary – that equality for women and care of the environment are two parts of a single remedy to modern exploitation – should unite feminists and ecologists in a call to action. In her detailed elaboration of the 'historical interconnections between women and nature that developed as the modern scientific and economic world took form in the sixteenth and seventeenth centuries' (xx), Merchant provides an empirical and theoretical genealogy of the forms of oppression of women and of the environment that are characteristic of capitalism to argue that the domination of women and of the environment are linked textually, ideologically, and empirically, in the same large historical development – namely, what she termed 'the death of nature'. Much as Robert K. Merton (1938) had done in his work on the Puritan spur to capitalism and to science, Merchant ties science, technology, and the economy to values and beliefs characteristic of modernity. Yet *The Death of Nature* works against the kind of externalism Merton usually employed as much as against the narrow internalism of the majority of the history of science. As Merchant puts it:

> I place less emphasis on the development of the internal content of science than on the social and intellectual factors involved in the transformation. Of course, such external factors do not cause intellectuals to invent a science. . . . Rather, an array of ideas exists, available to a given age; some of these . . . seem plausible . . .; others do not. Some ideas spread; others temporarily die out.
>
> *(Merchant 1990:xxii)*

Her innovative methodology enabled – indeed, was imperative for – this project. Scientific epistemology and 'cultural norms' and 'social ideologies' had to be examined together. Nature could not be reduced to inert and neutral facts about an external observable world – after all, this deadening of nature was exactly what she was examining – and her methodology, along with the social movements and the sciences themselves that motivated her, resurrected nature from its own death. Thus 'through dialectical interaction science and culture develop as an organic whole, fragmenting and reintegrating out of both social and intellectual tensions and tendencies' (xxii–xxiii).

In the epilogue to the book, Merchant comments on the state of mainstream science and environmental politics in the late twentieth century. She notes that the mechanistic view of nature and belief in 'objective, value-free, and context-free knowledge' continue to be dominant in the scientific community (290). The Three Mile Island nuclear reactor accident that took place in the United States in 1979, the year before *The Death of Nature* was published, was for her highly symbolic of the continuation of the same values that have driven mechanistic, for-profit science for centuries. Although she ends with a lament for the 'earth's sickness caused by radioactive wastes, pesticides, plastics, photochemical smog and fluorocarbons' (295), she also implies that readers should find some hope in 'the conjunction of the women's movement with the ecology movement' (294) because they share a commitment to radical change in the political, economic, and scientific systems – in effect, to turning the world upside down.

## Ecological feminism: not 'the third wave'

Not long after the publication of Merchant's text, a new movement seeking to integrate feminist and ecological politics emerged in North America and parts of Europe. Though the concept of ecological feminism was coined in the 1970s by the French feminist writer-activist Françoise D'Eubonne,[2] it was taken up in earnest in the 1980s when it spread inside and outside the academy, especially in the western United States where Merchant was living and working (i.e., Berkeley, California). There was excitement around the rise of ecofeminism as a political movement, prompting predictions (later proved wrong) that it would be part of 'the third wave' of feminism, successor to the first wave, which had achieved some women's enfranchisement from the mid-nineteenth to the early twentieth century, and the second wave, which raised consciousness, condemned work and pay inequities, and exposed the banality that marked the lives of relatively privileged 'first world' women in the mid-twentieth century. Most accounts of ecofeminism's emergence agree that it was the dissatisfaction of feminists with the gender politics inside the radical environmental and anti-nuclear movements that led activists to organize separately around issues of health, non-violence/anti-militarism, anti-colonialism, and animal liberation (for a comprehensive history, see Sturgeon 1997; Mellor 1997; Gaard 2011 and Gaard in this handbook).

Among the first published ecofeminist texts were *Reclaim the Earth: Women Speak Out for Life on Earth* (1983), edited by British feminist activists Leonie Caldecott and Stephanie Leland, and *Reweaving the World: The Emergence of Ecofeminism* (1990), edited by the American feminist academics Irene Diamond and Gloria Feman Orenstein. Connected to these early collections were a number of activist events. One of the first was 'Women and Life on Earth: Ecofeminism in the 1980s', which brought together ecofeminist, anti-nuclear and peace activists for a weekend in Amherst, Massachusetts. It featured the best-known figures of early ecofeminist writing, including Starhawk, Charlene Spretnak, and Susan Griffin (Harris and King 1989). The conference forged a common platform among lesbian feminism, environmentalism, and women's anti-militarist movements, all of which felt a pressing political need to disengage from or otherwise oppose patriarchy and its associated condemnation of the warring inhabitants of the earth to mutually assured destruction. There were two Women's Pentagon Actions in the United States in 1980 and 1981, and the 1981 'Women for Life on Earth' conference in London put the wheels in motion for the first blockade by the women's peace camp at Greenham Common in 1982. The 1987 'Ecofeminist Perspectives: Culture, Nature, Theory' conference organized by Diamond and Orenstein at the University of Southern California was somewhat more spiritual and academic in tone than the Amherst conference, and less directly connected to the anti-nuclear movement, illustrating regional variations as well as temporal changes within ecofeminism. Importantly, though, the presence of Angela Davis and other civil rights activists at the 1987 event tied the oppression of women to other kinds of stratification in society, especially racism, that are linked to sexism in complex ways. This marked an early refusal, at least by some, to allow ecofeminism to rest on easy assumptions about the oneness and benign nature of shared womanhood.

An important theme for some early ecofeminists, the majority of whom were activists rather than academics, was the celebration of women's putative life-giving and holistic reproductive and spiritual capacities. These were seen as gendered qualities that gave women a unique ability to care for and protect the earth from rapacious natural resource extraction, militarism, and ecological disharmony (see Ruether 1975; Griffin 1978; Starhawk 1988; Spretnak 1989). With reference to Merchant's history, it was maintained that women's ways of being and thinking made them 'natural' (in many senses of the word) guardians of nature in an anti-patriarchal and oft-times prelapsarian imaginary. The reclaiming by these ecofeminists of the pairing of women and nature expressed a refusal to base society and community on the power hierarchies of a capitalist patriarchy whose 'invisible hand' operated as if it owned not just the means of production but those of destruction and reproduction as well. For example, in 'The Eco-feminist Imperative', Ynestra King wrote:

> Why women? Because our present patriarchy enshrines together the hatred of women and the hatred of nature. In defying this patriarchy we are loyal to future generations and to life and this planet itself. We have a deep and particular understanding of this both through our natures and through our life experience as women.
>
> *(King 1983:11)*

Writing at the height of the Cold War, soon after a serious nuclear accident and in light of aggressive US foreign policy, King and other early ecofeminists were carrying on the long-standing tradition of using 'women-are-virtuous, men-are-corrupt' arguments to drive their political vision (a tradition used by late-nineteenth century suffragettes). They were arguably engaged in a rhetorical strategy of 'critical otherness' in order to mobilize protest and political solidarity among groups opposed to the dominant order (Sturgeon 1997).

Merchant's preface to the 1990 edition of *The Death of Nature* discusses the rise of early ecofeminism. She writes that

> [d]uring the past decade, women over the entire globe have emerged as ecological activists. . . . Feminist scholars were producing an explosion of books on ancient goddesses that became the basis for a renewed earth-rooted spirituality. . . . Concerts, street theater, solstice and equinoctial rituals, poetry, bookstores, and lecture series celebrated human resonance with the earth.
>
> *(Merchant 1990:xv–xvi)*

Rather than celebrate these developments, however, she goes on to raise questions about the 'inherent contradictions' contained in the identification of women with nature. She asks: 'Is not the conflation of woman and nature a form of essentialism?' and 'If women overtly identify with nature and both are devalued in modern Western culture, don't such efforts work against women's prospects for . . . liberation?' (xvi). These critical questions were harbingers of things to come for the academic standing of ecofeminism as a perspective and political movement.

Despite the 'power and promise' of ecofeminism (Warren 1990) to contribute to debates about the rise and consequences of science, capitalism, and warfare, and despite its ability to unite different strands of radical feminism, by the mid-1990s ecofeminism had largely been relegated to a marginal position in feminist theory in the academy. The reasons were several, and, in the end, this marginalization was perhaps overdetermined. Feminist peace and anti-militarist activism, focused on protesting the nuclear arms race, lost steam at the end of the Cold War. Ecofeminism in the academy was a victim of its own success in crossing the academic/lay boundary and had a race and class problem; cosmopolitan academics distanced themselves from the 'touchy-feely', religious, and reproductive-celebratory strands (jokes about placenta-eating covens of ex-hippies became common). And with the beginning of the third wave of feminism, because of its pre-dominantly white, middle-class ethos and uptake, ecofeminism was seen as irretrievably marred by ethnocentrism and by 'essentialist' beliefs about women.

While the use of waves for understanding the evolution of the feminist movement has been questioned (see, for example, Siegel 1997), it is also common to speak of 'third wave' feminism as a movement for greater inclusivity in the category 'woman' than had been the norm in the previous waves. By the mid-nineties, feminist theory was being challenged from within by explicit and implicit critiques of mind-sets that put women in a single category and called for 'intersectional' analyses that incorporate multiple identities, interests, and axes of oppression, and in which race is non-optional. Far from celebrating the creative and caring unity of all women, this approach showed, for example, how much reproductive and caring labour is outsourced from privileged, predominantly white, men *and* women to women of colour, immigrants, and lower-income women (see Mohanty et al. 1991). Furthermore, feminist understandings of identity, subjectivity, and oppression (among other things) were being revised and reframed in the light of hugely influential poststructuralist thought that was making its way across the Atlantic (for a discussion of third wave feminism, see Snyder 2008).

Poststructuralist feminist theory grew out of the 1960s–1970s poststructuralism of French theorists such as Derrida, Lacan, Foucault, and Althusser. Its strengths have been its repudiation of determinisms and its attention to irreducible complexity, multiplicity, and interpretative flexibility. Feminist science and technology studies (STS; which later spawned so-called feminist new materialisms), even more than poststructuralism, made its argument through 'nature' and scientific knowledge, rejecting a stable nature/culture divide. Both feminist STS and poststructuralist feminism rejected the gender theoretical hallmark of second-wave academic feminisms – namely, the sex/gender divide, arguing instead that biological sex (hence nature) was itself constructed (Alcoff 1988). Feminist STS, postmodern, and poststructuralist feminisms became extremely influential in feminist thinking about nature (see, for example, Soper 1995). A turn to culture and language opened up new types of scholarly projects, including analyses of representations of nature in literature and popular culture. Perhaps because of their deconstruction, 'nature' and 'the environment' – let alone the association of nature with a pre-theoretical womanhood – tended to be sidelined in postmodern and poststructuralist feminisms. The rise of poststructuralist/ postmodernist feminisms became an important factor in the marginalization of ecofeminism in feminist theory (see Alaimo 2000 for a discussion of feminist theory's 'flight from nature' and the 'summary dismissal' of ecofeminism). There was a flurry of new ecofeminist theory texts published the late 1990s and then the field went comparatively quiet.

## Which women? Whose nature?

With the move to decentre and deconstruct nature and women, much of the work that was associated with ecofeminism, including Merchant's, came under criticism and/or was dismissed as problematic. Criticisms ranged from the overtly hostile, in response to a caricature of ecofeminism as being equivalent to intellectually-fluffy goddess worship (Biehl 1991), to the sympathetic-but-troubled and therefore distancing (Agarwal 1992; Jackson 1993; Sargisson 2001).[3] It is instructive to separate the critiques of ecofeminism into those that primarily attack the tenet that involves the structural linking of the domination of women and of nature (the structural argument) and those that primarily attack the romanticization of universal feminine and nurturing values (the anti-essentialist argument). It is our contention that criticisms of the second kind – those against womanly celebration – have little purchase against the arguments presented in Merchant's work. Critiques of the first kind do, however, require an answer. We suggest that, robbed of the second kind of criticism, critiques of the structural argument lose much of their force; indeed, it is important to interrogate feminist poststructuralism and postmodernism from the perspective of the analytic and political clarity that is gained from the structural argument.

Ecofeminism was (and still is) nearly always criticized for its essentialisms in supposedly equating women with nature and conflating one woman with another, without regard for, say, class, race, nation, sexuality, able-bodiedness, or age (see Carlassare 1994). Critics rightly asked, 'Which women?' But while some varieties of ecofeminism may have equated women with nature in an essentialist manner, Merchant's argument does this as an empirical rather than *a priori* fact; indeed she argues expressly against both the error and the dangers of reifying the identification. Similarly, she argues explicitly against the idea that there is a universal female behaviour and against depictions that uniformly cast woman as mother/nurturer. The affiliation between women and nature does interest her, but for the underlying argument, not for its own essential identification: 'Women and nature have an age-old association – an affiliation that has persisted throughout culture, language and history', Merchant tells us. However,

> it is not the purpose of this analysis to reinstate nature as the mother of humankind nor to advocate that women reassume the role of nurturer dictated by that historical identity. Both need to be liberated from the anthropomorphic and stereotypic labels that degrade the serious underlying issues.
>
> *(xix, xxi)*

Of the anti-essentialism arguments, the ones that are most difficult for Merchant's argument are those that question whether an ecological sensibility is (always) a feminist goal. Whose nature is it, anyway? As anti-essentialism insisted, not all women are the same, and many women are part of groups that oppress other women in transnational and intersectional hierarchies of class, race, and nation that cross-cut the question of ecology (Sturgeon 1997). Furthermore, the health risks and other costs of environmental degradation are disproportionately borne by those with control of the fewest resources, as the scholarship on environmental racism and injustice has so compellingly illustrated (see Bullard 1993; Taylor 1997). Thus no one set of values can be assumed to benefit all women equally. The work of feminists of colour and feminists who have tried to connect gender politics to the politics of environmental injustice has made an indelible mark on the field (Mies and Shiva 1993; Di Chiro 1998; see also Sze in this volume).

In addition, calls outside the academy for the preservation of nature are often steeped in deeply sexist, racist, and transnationally unjust imaginaries. Particular visions of nature, especially those of a pristine nature, have been used – implicitly and explicitly – in attitudes toward immigrants and LGBTQ people and in targeting the childbearing patterns and the survival and labour exigencies of the world's poor (see Hartmann 1995, 2006; Bandarage 1997; see also, for example, the chapters by Sasser, Seymour, Butler, and Di Chiro in this volume). 'Pristine nature', and the stereotypical first world environmentalist who works to protect it, are both made possible by profound local and global resource inequity and transnational and domestic divisions of labour. Not all ecological visions are feminist ones, and ecofeminist ones cannot be assumed to apply equally to all women.

Merchant's argument does not support any particular version of nature preservation or conservation, however, and it does not rely on the deep ecological vision of pristine wilderness with which ecofeminism sometimes gets unfairly lumped (see Guha 1989). Indeed, her insistence on 'investigating the roots of our current environmental dilemma and its connections to science, technology, and the economy' (Merchant 1990:xxi) is exactly the kind of political economic purchase for which many third wave feminists have called. The rise of scholarship that connects activism against environmental racism with feminist activism against environmental degradation has articulated what it might mean to take this task as seriously as it warrants (Di Chiro 2008). Equally important are the contributions of postcolonial feminist scholarship and activism and of transnational feminist theory that does make the environment central even while it fundamentally questions patterns of inequity and works from a starting point of the co-constructedness of categories of knowledge and peoplehood (see, for example, Braidotti et al. 1994; Wickramasinghe 1994; also Resurrección, Mollett, and Isla in this volume).

What about the structural component of ecofeminism that Merchant herself has been so influential in formulating, and its critique? Both postmodern and poststructuralist feminism explicitly eschewed ahistorical or a priori appeals to structure; for example, instead of using 'nature' as a given, external, guarantor of truth, they argued that nature, just like writing or avalanches or weapons or envy, cannot be known independently of the lay, juridical, industrial, and any number of other practices that name it, make it, tend it, admire it, destroy it, exploit it, measure it, or render it benign or dangerous. This rejection of structure did not involve taking up structure's modernist twin, agency, because the unified human subject acting with free will had come under the same attack as structure – as the joke ran in feminist circles, no sooner had women begun to get some agency than feminists deconstructed agency. Instead, postmodern and poststructuralist feminists began to develop accounts of subject formation, of gender performativity, and of nature, exercised through continuously and mutually iterating and constructing norms, freedoms, and oppressions (Butler 1990).

Over time, ecofeminist theorists incorporated some poststructuralist, transnational, postcolonial, posthumanist, and other third-wave insights (see Sturgeon 1997; Sandilands 1999; Plumwood 2002; MacGregor 2006; Gaard 2011). Poststructuralist feminist theorists, for their part, began to work in emerging literary and textual fields such as ecocriticism. Having come to understand both 'women' and 'nature' as multiple, contingent, and co-constructed, and nature anything but dead, we tended also to lose the structuralist insight of ecofeminism that yoked together world patterns of environmental degradation and women's oppression. Our mistake, we think, was to see accounts with a structural argument as structuralist in the sense that poststructuralists rejected (i.e., static and hopelessly beguiled by the singularity of truth and reason).

But is Merchant's argument in *The Death of Nature* structuralist in this 'bad' sense? Merchant's argument is one that, far from assuming a fixed structural relation between women, nature, and their joint cause of oppression, tells a historical story in which the structural argument comes as the result of particular patterns of material, ideological, and epistemological exchanges and events that enabled, and were in turn enabled by, the scientific revolution and its continuing legacy. The structural component of her argument is historically constructed; matters have been otherwise in different places and at different times, as Merchant has shown throughout her *oeuvre*. Another thing worthy of notice is how poststructuralist in spirit core parts of Merchant's innovative methodology are – namely, the interaction between science and culture, 'fragmenting and reintegrating out of both social and intellectual tensions and tendencies' (xxiii), that she set out in the book. Arguably, her 'ecological approach to history' gave nature the role of historical agent whose actions 'challenge the very cultural constructions through which it is understood' before it became an accepted approach in humanities and social science scholarship (Merchant 1989; Alaimo 2000:12). Contemporary academic feminist theory, if it is to be as significant as it has the potential to be in countering environmental crises, would do well to resurrect this component of Merchant's path breaking analysis. Academic feminisms would do well to resurrect not just some of the methodological and empirical concerns and insights of ecofeminists such as Carolyn Merchant, but also some of their concomitant strands such as the links to civil rights, economic and technological domination, and to anti-militarisms.[4]

## Conclusion

Returning to Merchant's *The Death of Nature* from the perspective of its contribution to scholarship on gender and environment is a rewarding process. There is no doubt that it has garnered a sustained readership as a foundational text of feminist environmental thinking. Simultaneously, however, ecofeminism itself has been sidelined within feminist theory because of critiques (some fair, others less so) that it is marred by ethnocentrism and by an essentialist identification of women with nature. This sidelining has had multiple causes and has led to what is, in our opinion, a classic case of throwing out the baby with the bathwater.

Rereading Merchant leads to three conclusions: First, Merchant explicitly repudiates ethnocentrism and essentialism, developing instead an archival methodology that grounds the universalizing claims of modern science in time and place, text, and ideology. Second, the central claim of ecofeminism – that the domination of women and of nature has shared roots in the logic of science and capitalism – remains a powerful thesis. Third, ecofeminism brings together anti-militarist feminists and others whose voices are underrepresented in contemporary academic feminism. Combining the critiques of third-wave feminisms with a reevaluation of ecofeminism would greatly strengthen the field.

With more than three decades of hindsight, it is possible to begin the task of rearticulating the central tenet of ecofeminism for which Merchant argues in a way that incorporates the critiques of feminists of colour and of poststructural, postmodern, and transnational feminisms, and to resurrect some of ecofeminism's neglected strengths. We argue that we need to move beyond an implicit choice between taking seriously ecofeminist accounts of nature and the environment, on the one hand, or anti-essentialism about women, feminist poststructuralist explanation, and transnational feminist examination of gendering and racialization, on the other. *The Death of Nature* itself contains the means to begin this work, and Merchant's later writings have gone on to consider many of these intersections in more detail (for example Merchant 1992, 1996). What is perhaps still missing, however, is a widespread recognition among feminist scholars and others of the power of the central analytic of ecofeminism and, indeed, its implicit and powerful critique of postmodern and poststructuralist positions in some of their incarnations. A retrospective look at *The Death of Nature* can begin to draw out these elements. If ever there was a time to bring back serious opposition to militarism, freed from the 'ontology of the enemy' (Galison 1994) of the Cold War, and to combine it with a critique of the profoundly inequitable gendered transnational division of natural resources and labour, then this must surely be that time.

## Notes

This is an extended adaptation by the author and handbook editor of an article that was published in 2006 in the American History of Science journal *Isis* (vol. 97, no. 3). Charis Thompson's essay 'Back to Nature' was originally prepared for the History of Science Society Annual Meeting, Minneapolis, 3–6 November 2005, and presented as part of the twenty-fifth anniversary session in honour of Carolyn Merchant: 'Getting Back to *The Death of Nature*: Rereading Carolyn Merchant'. The editor selected Thompson's essay for inclusion in the handbook not only because it offers a concise overview of the themes and contributions of Merchant's germinal text, but also because it lends insights into debates within ecological feminism and between ecofeminists and other branches of feminist theory that were taking place at the time of writing, and that have been taking place for decades. They are debates that do not appear to have moved on significantly since the mid-2000s. With the author's permission, the editor has added additional material to expand discussion of both the content of Merchant's book and the development of ecofeminism. The original article is at www.jstor.org/stable/10.1086/508080. The editor accepts responsibility for the accuracy of the additional material.

1  In Chapter 11 of *The Death of Nature*, 'Women on Nature', Merchant gives examples of women who contributed to intellectual developments at the time of the scientific revolution, including an account of the ideas of the 'almost forgotten' seventeenth century philosopher Anne Conway, whose writings about vitalism played an important role in the development of Leibniz's thought.
2  A thorough discussion of the life and ideas of Françoise d'Eubonne has been written by Roth-Johnson (2013).
3  Discussions of these criticism and the often nasty fights within ecofeminism and feminist environmental academic circles more broadly can be found in Seager (2003) and Gaard (2011). It is worth noting that Merchant was criticized by Biehl (1991), who questioned her interpretation of the evidence in her history of organicism; Merchant's approach to history has also been questioned by other historians on the grounds that she is selective in her use of evidence or that it is too political to be proper history.
4  Cynthia Enloe (2001) is one of the few feminists who has insisted on continuing to take the connections between gender inequalities, militarism, and environmental destruction seriously (but see also Detraz in this handbook). The emergence of 'new' material feminism in the late 2000s is arguably a sign that feminist theorists have come to regret the poststructuralist/postmodernist turn away from nature and the material world (see Alaimo and Hekman 2008).

# References

Agarwal, B. (1992) 'The gender and environment debate: Lessons from India', *Feminist Studies* 18(1): 119–158.

Alaimo, S. (2000) *Undomesticated Ground: Recasting Nature as Feminist Space.* Ithaca, NY: Cornell University Press.

Alaimo, S. and Hekman, S. (eds) (2008) *Material Feminisms.* Indianapolis: Indiana University Press.

Alcoff, L. (1988) 'Cultural feminism versus post-structuralism: The identity crisis in feminist theory', *Signs: Journal of Women in Culture and Society* 13: 405–536.

Bandarage, A. (1997) *Women, Population, and Global Crisis: A Political-Economic Analysis.* London: Zed Books.

Biehl, J. (1991) *Finding Our Way: Rethinking Ecofeminist Politics.* New York: Black Rose Books.

Braidotti, R., Charkiewicz, E., Hausler, S. and Wieringa, S. (1994) *Women, the Environment and Sustainable Development: Towards a Theoretical Synthesis.* London: Zed Books.

Bullard, R. (ed) (1993) *Confronting Environmental Racism: Voices From the Grassroots.* Boston, MA: South End Press.

Butler, J. (1990) *Gender Trouble: Feminism and the Subversion of Identity.* New York: Routledge.

Caldecott, L. and Leland, S. (eds) (1983) *Reclaim the Earth: Women Speak Out for Life on Earth.* London: The Women's Press.

Carlassare, E. (1994) 'Essentialism in ecofeminist discourse', in Merchant, C. (ed) *Ecology: Key Concepts in Critical Theory.* Atlantic Highlands, NJ: Humanities Press, 220–234.

Davis, A. (1983) *Women, Race and Class.* New York: Vintage Books.

Diamond, I. and Orenstein, G. (eds) (1990) *Reweaving the World: The Emergence of Ecofeminism.* San Francisco: Sierra Club Books.

Di Chiro, G. (1998) 'Environmental justice from the grassroots: Reflections on history, gender, and expertise', in Faber, D. (ed) *The Struggle for Ecological Democracy.* New York: The Guilford Press, 104–136.

Di Chiro, G. (2008) 'Living environmentalisms: Coalition politics, social reproduction, and environmental justice', *Environmental Politics* 17(2): 276–298.

Enloe, C. (2001) *Bananas, Beaches, and Bases: Making Feminist Sense of International Politics.* Berkeley: University of California Press.

Gaard, G. (2011) 'Ecofeminism revisited: Rejecting essentialism and re-placing species in a material feminist environmentalism', *Feminist Formations* 23(2): 26–25.

Galison, P. (1994) 'The ontology of the enemy: Norbert Wiener and the cybernetic vision', *Critical Inquiry* 21: 228–265.

Griffin, S. (1978) *Woman and Nature: The Roaring Inside Her.* New York: Harper and Row.

Guha, R. (1989) *The Unquiet Woods: Ecological Change and Peasant Resistance in the Himalaya.* Delhi: Oxford University Press.

Harris, A. and King, Y. (eds) (1989) *Rocking the Ship of State: Toward a Feminist Peace Politics*. Boulder, CO: Westview Press.

Hartmann, B. (1995) *Reproductive Rights and Wrongs: The Global Politics of Population Control*. Cambridge, MA: South End Press.

Hartmann, B. (2006) 'Liberal ends, illiberal means: National security, "environmental conflict", and the making of the Cairo Consensus', *Indian Journal of Gender Studies* 13(2): 195–218.

Jackson, C. (1993) 'Women/nature or gender history? A critique of ecofeminist development', *Journal of Peasant Studies* 20(3): 389–419.

King, Y. (1983) 'The ecofeminist imperative', in Caldecott, L. and Leland, S. (eds) *Reclaim the Earth: Women Speak Out for Life on Earth*. London: Women's Press, 9–14.

MacGregor, S. (2006) *Beyond Mothering Earth: Ecological Citizenship and the Politics of Care*. Vancouver: University of British Columbia Press.

Mellor, M. (1997) *Feminism and Ecology*. New York: New York University Press.

Merchant, C. (1980/1990) *The Death of Nature: Women, Ecology and the Scientific Revolution*. New York: Harper and Row.

Merchant, C. (1989) *Ecological Revolutions: Nature, Gender and Science in New England*. Chapel Hill: University of North Carolina Press.

Merchant, C. (1992) *Radical Ecology: The Search for a Livable World*. New York: Routledge.

Merchant, C. (1996) *Earthcare: Women and the Environment*. New York: Routledge.

Merton, R. K. (1938/1970) *Science, Technology, and Society in Seventeenth Century England*. New York: Harper and Row.

Mies, M. and Shiva, V. (1993) *Ecofeminism*. London: Zed Books.

Mohanty, C., Russo, A. and Torres, L. (eds) (1991) *Third World Women and the Politics of Feminism*. Bloomington: Indiana University Press.

Nixon, L. (2015) 'Eco-feminist appropriations of indigenous feminisms and environmental violence', *The Feminist Wire*. Online. Available at: www.thefeministwire.com/2015/04/eco-feminist-appropriations-of-indigenous-feminisms-and-environmental-violence/ (accessed 15 October 2016).

Plumwood, V. (2002) *Environmental Culture: The Ecological Crisis of Reason*. London: Routledge.

Roth-Johnson, D. (2013) 'Back to the future: Françoise d'Eubonne, ecofeminism and ecological crisis', *The International Journal of Literary Humanities* 10: 52–61.

Ruether, R. R. (1975) *New Woman/New Earth: Sexist Ideologies and Human Liberation*. New York: Seabury Press.

Sandilands, C. (1999) *The Good-Natured Feminist*. Minneapolis, MN: University of Minnesota Press.

Sargisson, L. (2001) 'What's wrong with ecofeminism?', *Environmental Politics* 10(1): 52–64.

Seager, J. (2003) 'Rachel Carson died of breast cancer: The coming of age of feminist environmentalism', *Signs* 28(3): 945–972.

Shiva, V. (1988) *Staying Alive: Women, Ecology and Survival in India*. London: Zed Books.

Siegel, D. L. (1997) 'Reading between the waves: Feminist historiography in a "post-feminist" moment', in Heywood, L. and Drake, J. (eds) *Third Wave Agenda: Being Feminist, Doing Feminism*. Minneapolis: University of Minnesota Press, 55–84.

Snyder, R. C. (2008) 'What is third wave feminism? A new directions essay', *Signs* 34(1): 175–196.

Soper, K. (1995) *What Is Nature? Culture, Politics, and the Non-Human*. Oxford: Blackwell.

Spretnak, C. (1989) 'Towards an ecofeminist spirituality', in Plant, J. (ed) *Healing the Wounds*. Philadelphia: New Society Publishers, 127–132.

Starhawk (1988) *Spiral Dance: A Rebirth of the Ancient Religion of the Goddess*. San Francisco: HarperCollins.

Sturgeon, N. (1997) *Ecofeminist Natures: Race, Gender, Feminist Theory, and Political Action*. London: Routledge.

Taylor, D. E. (1997) 'Women of color, environmental justice and ecofeminism', in Warren, K. J. (ed) *Ecofeminism: Women, Culture, Nature*. Bloomington: Indiana University Press, 38–81.

Warren, K. J. (1990) 'The power and promise of ecological feminism', *Environmental Ethics* 12(2): 125–146.

Wickramasinghe, A. (1994) *Deforestation, Women and Forestry*. Amsterdam: International Books.

# 3

# THE DILEMMA OF DUALISM

*Freya Mathews*

## Introduction

A defining tenet of feminist environmental scholarship, and ecological feminist theory in particular, is that the domination of women is ideologically linked with the domination of nature. This stems from a recognition that, in Western traditions of thought, the category of the feminine is constructed in opposition to that of masculinity, while the category of nature is constructed in opposition to that of culture; this opposition is an hierarchical one that not only dichotomizes the masculine and feminine but also ranks men above women and culture above nature. Such a dualizing schema is held by ecofeminist theorists to be deeply entrenched, structuring to some degree not only conceptions of gender and nature but also the very foundations of Western knowledge per se. It follows that, from an ecofeminist perspective, neither women nor the natural world may be emancipated unless thinking is freed from the distorting lens of dualism. If the influence of dualism as an organizing principle of thought is so profound, however, we might wonder whether it can be attributed merely to ideology, as much ecofeminist analysis implies. To answer this question of the origins of dualism correctly is surely important, since unless those origins are fully identified it will not be possible to explain how or why dualism has acquired such a hold on Western thought, nor will it be possible to escape its grip.

Most would agree that it was the environmental philosopher, Val Plumwood, who gave definitive form to the ecofeminist analysis of dualism. In this chapter I review the background to her analysis before examining that analysis itself. I shall then suggest that the roots of dualism lie not merely in historical forms of the politics of gender but, insidiously, in the very activity of theorizing itself. If this is true, then counter-dualist theories, and even emancipatory forms of politics based on them, will not help us shake off the shackles of dualism. The way to escape from a dualist mind-set will lie in forms of practice that counter the dualizing tendencies inherent in theory. To make this claim is not merely to argue that dualist habits of thought cannot be broken unless we put theory into practice. Such an argument would indeed be obvious. It is rather to argue that theorizing itself is an exercise, a form of 'practice', that fosters a dualist outlook. If we are to escape such an outlook, then theorizing must be offset by other, countering exercises or practices. As long as ecofeminism continues to define itself in theoretical terms, as philosophical discourse, the consciousness of ecofeminists will arguably remain dualist, however opposed to dualism their theoretical stance might be.

## Environmental philosophy and the critique of dualism

Environmental philosophy emerged as a discipline in the 1970s. Environmental philosophers recognized that the environmental problems that were coming into view at the time were the upshot not merely of flawed policies but of an underlying attitude to the natural world that was built into the very foundations of Western thought. This was the attitude of *anthropocentrism*, the groundless presumption that only human beings matter, morally speaking; to the extent that anything else matters, it does so, from an anthropocentric perspective, only because it has some kind of utility for humanity. Environmental philosophers challenged this view, and declared the need for 'a new, an environmental, ethic', an ethic of nature (Routley 1973).

Val Plumwood (or, as she was then known, Val Routley), together with her husband Richard Routley, was one of the pioneers of this discipline. They joined a handful of colleagues around the English-speaking world in exploring why such a blinding moral prejudice in favour of humanity had developed in the West. It was clear that some kind of dichotomizing tendency was at work, setting the human, in the shape of culture, apart from and above nature. The human stood as the measure of all meaning and value against the brute facticity of nature. But how could this bias in favour of humanity have become justified? What was so special about the human? The assumption underlying this conviction appeared to be the Cartesian one that humans alone possess mental attributes, where it is only mental attributes that confer intrinsic value on things. Without mental attributes of some description, an entity cannot matter to itself or in itself, since it cannot have meaning, value, interests or ends of its own. A being that does matter to itself, that seeks its own good or is invested in its own ends, is surely entitled to moral consideration. If humans alone possess mind, then humans alone are entitled to moral consideration.

Many environmental philosophers sought to show that anthropocentrism was misguided. Clean up the Cartesian fallacies on which it rests, they argued, and the devaluation of nature will be rectified: a whole new respect for nature, figured as an environmental ethic, will come into view.[1] As the only woman among those earliest pioneers of environmental philosophy, Plumwood was perhaps a little more sceptical than her colleagues about the efficacy of argument. Surely anthropocentrism rested on more than a mere mistake, an innocent misunderstanding, that philosophers could put right with corrective arguments? In the years following her divorce from Richard Routley in the early 1980s, Val, who now took the name Plumwood, found herself looking to feminism for clues to the riddle of anthropocentrism and the mind-matter dualism that subtended it. For feminists too had been pondering dualism and the system of human/nature, culture/nature binaries that emanated from it (Ortner 1974; Merchant 1980; see also Thompson and MacGregor in this volume). In feminist theory, however, dualism was intrinsically gendered and it required analysis not merely in logical but in *political* terms. The hold of dualism on the Western imagination had proved resistant to argument and hence correction because it served a political purpose and was held in place by powerful political interests. The political purpose it served was to naturalize and legitimate male domination or, in the lexicon of 1980s feminism, patriarchy.

Feminist theorists were of course no more alone in their focus on dualism than were environmental philosophers, for the analysis of binary oppositions was core to the project of deconstruction that was unfolding in France under the leadership of Jacques Derrida (1970). Many feminists eventually situated their own approach to dualism within a deconstructive framework. The legacy of the Frankfurt School of critical theory, with its emphasis on the role of instrumental reason in constructing a notion of nature as the ultimate object of domination, was also strong at the time. For critical theorists, the domination of nature served as the ideological template for political domination generally (Leiss 1972). In many ways, the quest to dismantle dualism was a defining preoccupation of the twentieth century, as the influence of dualism spread across many of the disciplinary streams of the Western academy. However, it was to the history of feminist thought in particular that Plumwood turned in seeking to clarify the political roots of dualism as they pertained to the fate of the environment.

## The feminist critique of dualism

Recognition of dualism, and in particular the association of women with nature, was not new in feminist thought. Indeed, feminists had remarked on it right from the start. In a sense the whole history of feminist thought in the West has been a struggle with dualism. As far back as 1789, Mary Wollstonecraft noticed the association of women with nature in her *Vindication of the Rights of Women*. Women, she observed, were regarded as creaturely beings, closer than men to the estate of animals, deficient in those higher – rational – faculties of mind definitive of the human. They were accordingly considered uneducable. But, Wollstonecraft insisted, women were kept in such a condition of creatureliness because this was in accordance with the sexual tastes of men. Given a chance at education, women would soon prove themselves to be the equals of men (Wollstonecraft 1985).

For almost two hundred years thereafter, feminists tirelessly protested at the metaphoric assim-ilation of women to nature. Writing within the liberal framework that had set the terms for progressive politics in the seventeenth century 'Age of Reason', they by and large followed Woll-stonecraft in upholding the liberal view of human nature as consisting in the capacity for reason (Jaggar 1984). Any innate deficiency in reason was seen as representing a failure to rise above the estate of nature and become fully human. In other words, liberal feminists tacitly accepted the reason/nature, human/nature dualisms that underpinned liberalism; they merely tried to de-gender these categories, striving to pry apart the notions of woman and nature and attribute the capacity for reason to women as well as men (Friedan 1963; Beauvoir 1965).

While there is no denying that a significant proportion of Western women today owe a huge debt to liberal feminists, who did indeed win the right to equality of opportunity in education, thereby eventually opening up the public sphere and all its powers to (some) women, with historical hindsight we can nevertheless question liberal feminists' acceptance of the dualistic underpinnings of liberalism (Jaggar 1984). Their attempts to demonstrate that women were 'just as good' as men, meaning just as endowed with the capacity for reason, and hence just as removed from nature and mere creatureliness, implicitly condoned the anthropocentrism that demoted nature and everything associated with it to inferior status.

When so-called second wave feminism exploded onto the scene in the 1970s, however, the venerable liberal tradition of feminism was hotly challenged. Did women really want to become like men, or at least as men supposed themselves to be – sober, detached, measured, objective, impartial, the proverbial 'men of reason', the 'masters and possessors of nature', as Descartes put it? No! The new radical, and then 'gynocentric' – or, as they came to be known, 'cultural' – feminists wanted no part of patriarchal identity. The association of woman with embodiment (with fertility, procreation, eros, nurturance, and corporeality) and hence with nature (the terrain of life, purpose, creativity, vulnerability, of intelligence and sentience in a thousand guises, the exuberant and fecund matrix of our existence) was to be ardently embraced. Gynocentric (or woman-centred) feminists repudiated reason as the yardstick of humanness and replaced it with ostensibly feminine attributes, such as the capacities to nurture, feel and care (Rich 1977; Daly 1978; Griffin 1978; Irigaray 1985). Women whose commitment was as much to environmental as to feminist political causes rejoiced in the new valorization of nature and the privileged position to which cultural feminism assigned them as women in relation to it. They recognized that the struggle for nature was inextricable from the feminist struggle, and they adopted the banner of *ecofeminism* to signal this inextricability (King 1983; d'Eaubonne 1994).

Exhilarating and necessary as gynocentric feminism was as an historical moment of female empowerment and recovery; however, it was of course only a halfway house to true liberation, whether for women or nature. Gynocentric feminists had no more dismantled the underlying ideology of subordination – dualism – than liberal feminists had. They had reversed the values attaching to the terms of the dualistic schema but had not sufficiently scrutinized the exclusionary and hierarchical structure of the schema itself (Lloyd 1984; Plumwood 1993). In place of androcentrism and patriarchy, gynocentrists had enshrined gynarchy. The traditional masculine and feminine, and all the exclusive oppositions in terms of which these categories were defined, still remained intact, a schema for domination – whether of women by men or men by women ultimately was not the point.

As the 1980s wore on, feminists of all stripes, including ecofeminists, continued to wrestle with the problem of dualism. It was clear that Western thought had always been organized around a core of dichotomous, hierarchically-ordered categories, such as the following:

mind/matter
mind/body
culture/nature
human/nature
human/animal

These binaries provided the basis for further key oppositions, such as

reason/emotion
reason/intuition
abstract/concrete
universal/particular
subject/object

In new theoretical domains this dualistic core continually threw up new binaries, such as public/ private in the context of liberalism and production/reproduction in the context of Marxism (Ruether 1978; Jaggar 1984; Lloyd 1984). It was also clear that, from the start, dualism as a principle of organization had been inherently gendered: the terms on the higher, left-hand side of the binaries were systematically associated with, and served to define, masculinity, while those on the lower, right-hand side were associated with, and served to define, the feminine.

The whole historical apparatus of dualism had evolved, it seemed, to naturalize and legitimate a particular, specifically patriarchal, system of domination by making the dominance of the masculine appear as a natural characteristic of the universe at large. Everything identified as masculine in the system represented a transcendence of everything identified as feminine, where everything identified as feminine was invariably merely given by nature. Thus men inhabited a *public* sphere of *abstract* and *universal*, *spiritual* and *mental* concerns, whereas women remained immersed in the *concrete* and *particular* realm of the *private*, a *domestic* sphere, bound to the *body* by the requirements of *reproduction*. Woman was, in a word, *nature* to man's *culture*. In transcending nature, man transcended – that is to say, raised himself above – woman, and thereby justified his domination of her.

While feminist theorists agreed on the centrality of dualism to patriarchal ideology, they disagreed on what to salvage of the traditional (dualistically defined) feminine and what to discard.

Deep partings of the way occurred. Some feminists – including some ecofeminists, such as Mary Daly and Susan Griffin – clung uncritically to the gynocentric valorization of woman and nature and continued to insist that the link between them was real, deriving from women's reproductive biology, rather than conceding that the link was an artefact of patriarchal ideology (Plumwood 1993). Other feminists, often described as standpoint feminists, steered away from such biological essentialism, but continued to see an affinity between women and nature on historical materialist grounds: the reproductive work that has traditionally been the province of women remains embedded in the material and the biological rather than the abstract and political, and therefore does indeed give rise to a consciousness and identity attuned to these levels of existence (Salleh 1984, 2005; Hartsock 1985; Harding 1986). The majority of feminists in the Anglophone world however eventually adopted a deconstructive perspective: they saw the link between woman and nature as entirely fabricated, a patriarchal conceit, and accordingly sought to abolish all the identities that supervened on it. Many of these feminists were influenced by the deconstructive movement in France, and particularly by the work of French feminists, such as Luce Irigaray and Julia Kristeva, which tended to place large theoretical frameworks and the categories and identities they subtended in doubt, seeing all such discourse as a political instrument for the naturalizing and legitimating of power relations. The deconstructive turn in feminism led to reluctance to define woman at all (Alcoff 1986; Butler 1990), and it vehemently rejected any actual affinity between women and nature.

Tracking this crisscrossed field of debate throughout the 1980s, Plumwood eventually shot a laser beam of analysis into the fray, crystallizing and clarifying the logical structure and ideological function of dualism as a major organizing principle of Western thought. In her 1993 book *Feminism and the Mastery of Nature*, she skilfully wove together feminist arguments, including those of ecofeminists such as Rosemary Ruether (1978) and Karen Warren (1990), with environmental and post-colonial arguments. Her aim was to show that each term in a binary opposition is not merely dichotomized or *hyper-separated* from its opposite and *ranked* relative to it, but that the term on the right hand side of each pair is *instrumentalized* to, or made to appear as if created for the purpose of serving, the term on the left. So, for example, the body is seen merely as a vessel for the mind, rather than having significance in its own right; the purpose of the private is seen as assuring the material conditions for the all-important affairs of the public. The 'inferior' term in each binary is also *backgrounded* with respect to the 'superior'. Thus, for example, the private sphere figures only as background to the sphere of history and culture, while the dependency of the latter on the private is glossed over, unacknowledged. The lesser term may also be *incorporated* into the greater term, attaining definition only in terms of its lacks or deficiencies relative to the greater. Animals, for example, tend to be measured in terms of their deficiencies relative to humans rather than in terms of their own specific excellences. Lesser terms are also *homogenized* relative to their counterparts, in the sense that they are viewed en masse, as a block, rather than in their richly differentiated specificity. So, again, all sentient life on the planet is lumped together under the category 'animal' in contradistinction to the category 'human', despite the fact that the human is in reality only one animal species among a staggeringly vast and various array of others.

Through this systematic analysis it finally became clear how dualism, or the system of binary oppositions, legitimizes not merely male domination, but domination generally. Dualism as a schema of organization is constantly re-applied in new discursive domains to create categories that serve to naturalize and legitimate domination: civilized/primitive, colonizer/colonized, science/superstition, mental/manual, public/private, production/reproduction, self/other. In Plumwood's (1993) analysis, such categories function within and across discourses to construct a 'master identity', which is gendered but not exclusively *male*. Moreover, this master identity hinges on a particular dualistic pair that Plumwood identified as core to the system, viz the reason/nature pair: reason is defined in opposition to everything associated with feeling and the body and ultimately, and most especially, nature. Reason is, in this system, infiltrated with the meanings of all the terms on the left-hand side of the table of opposites and is, most importantly, that which distinguishes humans from, and raises us above, nature. To the extent that a particular social group can lay a greater claim to reason than another group, it will construct the second group dualistically as in every way exhibiting the opposite of reason: difference, in other words, will be re-worked as dichotomy, and the second group will end up playing nature to the first group's master identity.

Of course, historically the pre-eminent group that laid claim to reason was the class of educated white males; they constituted the reference group for the master identity. But the master identity is sensitive to context. In a colonial context, educated white women might assume the master identity relative to indigenous or colonized peoples, who will then be dichotomously constructed in terms of the attributes on the right hand side of the table of opposites, while the white women will assume, in a kind of honorary capacity and only relative to the indigenous or colonized, all the attributes on the left hand side. In other words, the white women in the colonial context might assume a masculine-tinged identity in relation to the native people, who will be glossed as feminine. It is the native people who will be perceived as irrational, primitive, superstitious, animal, and close to nature compared with the 'civilized' and (in that sense more rational) white women, even though those same women will be constructed as emotional, intuitive, and unstable, subject to hormonal influences and so on, in relation to their male counterparts. In this way Plumwood showed that the master identity is much more than a male identity, even though there is a pre-established fit between this and a certain class of men. The master identity is a dominator identity that can and does constellate itself anew in any context, and in Plumwood's analysis, it revolves around a particular conception of reason on the one hand and nature on the other. Wherever reason in this sense is privileged over other ways of thinking, knowing, and experiencing, there we can expect to find nature construed as a nullity. We can also, in consequence, expect to find complex, mutually reinforcing, and ramifying processes of mastery or domination in train.

The thesis of Plumwood's (1993) *Feminism and the Mastery of Nature*, in sum, is that dualism is not merely a vehicle of male domination, but is the complex and adaptable underlay of domination generally in the West, reiterating itself historically in each major new discourse for the purpose of rationalizing regimes not only of gender, but also of race, class, and species. In light of this finding, neither feminists nor environmentalists – nor, for that matter, post-colonialists, socialists, or the theorists of any other emancipatory discourse – could afford to overlook the workings of dualism. *Feminism and the Mastery of Nature* thus helped clean up and give definitive form to the feminist analysis of dualism, in the process vindicating – and greatly expanding – the ecofeminist proposition that the struggle for the environment was inextricable from the struggle for women, indeed from the struggle for subordinated groups generally. It also exposed the political roots of anthropocentrism, thereby rescuing environmental philosophy from the ineffectuality to which it was doomed as a purely rationalist exercise preoccupied with finding environmentally friendly criteria for moral considerability. Plumwood's analysis showed that anthropocentrism was held in place not merely by defective reasoning but by a potent psychosexual agenda of domination.

## Dismantling dualism

If dualism was the problem, then the solution would presumably lie in the dismantling of dualism. But in what would such a dismantling consist? Would it be a matter simply of putting back together what dualism had sundered, restoring mind to matter, resituating the human in nature, and integrating reason with other faculties of cognition and consciousness, such as intuition and emotion – redefining binary categories in ways that integrated them?

Postmodern/poststructuralist – what I call *deconstructive* – feminist theorists were not at all disposed to put back together again what dualism had split apart. For them, definition itself was the problem, at least where large abstract categories were concerned. To seek new definitions of reason, mind, human, nature, and so on would just be to create new essentialisms, enact new exclusions, and reinscribe relations of power in new ways. Deconstructionists, wary of discourse, were in no way interested in putting together a new, post-dualist paradigm. The politics of emancipation consisted, for them, of keeping up resistance to the narratives inevitably and ongoingly created by relations of power. In other words, their political stance was one of refusal, resistance, demolition; it was a stance that sought to expose the way in which power was turned into prescribed systems of thought and into protocols of performance in human societies (Alcoff 1986; Butler 1990).

But in the minority (and increasingly marginalized) streams of ecofeminism, and in environmental philosophy, intimations of how to put back together what dualism had sundered abounded, and these intimations generally pointed to relationality as the theoretical antidote to dualism. If dualism was a paradigm that defined entities and attributes by hyper-separation, then relationality was the key to a new, emerging paradigm that would define entities and attributes in terms of their constitutive relations with one another, retaining difference and distinctness but construing these not in terms of exclusion, hierarchy, instrumentalism, backgrounding, incorporation, or homogenization, but rather in terms of continuity.

The notion of ecology was, as environmental philosophers were in the process of demonstrating, key to the articulation of relationality (Naess 1985, 1988; Fox 1990; Mathews 1991). Ecophilosophers recognized that mind-matter dualism is correlated with an atomistic assumption about the nature of identity: objects or entities are posited, from this perspective, as 'distinct existences', each one logically independent of all others. Logically speaking, any given individual could conceivably exist independently of all others. Its identity is not a function of the identities of other entities. There is no risk here that if certain entities, such as humans, are attributed with a special attribute, such as mind, this attribute would 'leak out', so to speak, into surrounding entities. Only by way of such an atomistic criterion of individuation could the dualization of mind and matter be accomplished (Mathews 1991).

To overcome mind/matter dualism, then, it was necessary to propose an alternative principle of individuation, one that defined entities in terms of their inter-relations with other entities. An ecological perspective provided a ready-made template for such an alternative. From the viewpoint of ecology – or to be precise, ecology under a philosophical interpretation – entities are defined in terms of their various constitutive relations with other elements of an ecosystem. Consider, for example, the case of Blue Whale and krill. How, from an atomistic perspective, would a Blue Whale be individuated and identified? Presumably via its physical configuration in space and time. Logically (as opposed to causally or materially) speaking, a Blue Whale could exist all by itself in the universe. A universe consisting of just a Blue Whale floating in otherwise empty space would be at least conceivable, in the sense that the entity in question would still count as a Blue Whale, provided it possessed the spatiotemporal configuration, the anatomy, of a Blue Whale. From an ecological perspective, however, a Blue Whale would not be logically isolable in this way. To define a Blue Whale, to say what it is, one has to detail its anatomy, yes, but one also has to mention krill: how the anatomy of the Blue Whale – its huge balleen mouth, for instance, that filters seawater – is only an outward reflection of its constitutive relationship with tiny krill. A Blue Whale is, from this ecological point of view, a creature whose entire being is a reference to krill: Blue Whale and krill are *internally* or *logically* related. They are related not just causally or materially but at the level of identity. This is not to say that they are the same thing, or that the identity of the Blue Whale incorporates or subsumes that of krill, but only that they are behaviourally as well as anatomically mutually configuring.

By the same token, while the Blue Whale might impress us with its prodigious intelligence, this intelligence does not belong exclusively to it but emanates from the ecosystem to which it belongs. Intelligence is here an implicate attribute of the ecosystem, explicated in the Blue Whale but distributed through the system and shared at an implicate level by the humble krill. In a relational schema, in which identity and individuation are logically constituted through the interactivity of entities, mind and matter, intelligence and nature, cannot be dualistically divided and divorced one from the other. Mind/matter dualism is impossible (Mathews 1991).

Human identity, according to ecophilosophers, is no different from Blue Whale identity. It is constituted, through and through, by its relations with other species and communities of life. The human being is no longer a 'higher', mentally endowed self, set apart from and looking down on a 'lower', blind nature, but an *ecological self*, its identity a mesh of relations with other species, its intelligence a function of the intelligence of ecosystems, of the biosphere (Naess 1985, 1988; Fox 1990; Mathews 1991). Both within and beyond environmental philosophy, the relational perspective has spawned a whole new generation of metaphysical theories to replace the materialist metaphysic that, despite dating back to the scientific revolution of the seventeenth century, remains the foundation-stone for modern civilization. These metaphysical theories, sometimes intersecting with contemporary philosophies of consciousness, range from panpsychism (Mathews 2003; Skrbina 2009; Blamauer 2011) and philosophical animism (Harvey 2005; Plumwood 2009) to the so-called new materialisms of the post-deconstructive school (Bennett 2010; Dolphijn and van der Tuin 2012).

Meanwhile, however, as ecophilosophers were exploring relational selfhood in an ecological context in the 1980s and early 1990s, feminists were conducting similar explorations in social and epistemological contexts. In psychology or psychoanalysis, the relational self seeks to build its identity on continuity and affiliation with others rather than on separation from them, as had been assumed in traditional psychoanalytic theory (Chodorow 1979; Benjamin 1988). In science, the 'knower' seeks to understand the 'known' through engagement, empathy, and communication, rather than by assuming the detached, distanced, disinterested, affectless – and often lethal and 'dissecting' – stance of the classical scientist (Keller 1985). The social self, defined by its relations with other humans, sees in communalism rather than in individualism the fundamental estate of the human, thereby confuting the social atomism that had been a premise of the liberal tradition (Jaggar 1984; Miller 1986). For the relational self, respect for others is a corollary of recognition of one's own inextricable entanglement with them. An attitude of care arises spontaneously as a result of the relational approach without need for recourse to formal codes of conduct (Gilligan 1982). In all these contexts, relationality dissolves dualism and reinstates an ethical relationship between self and its world.

In *Feminism and the Mastery of Nature* and her 2003 book, *Environmental Culture*, Plumwood followed this relational path, drawing particularly on feminist standpoint theory to theorize relational alternatives to dualism in politics, epistemology, psychology, and ethics. Such relational thinking was, according to Plumwood, the province of ecological rationality, as distinct from the old divisive, instrumental rationality of dualism.

## But why reason?

Re-reading *Feminism and the Mastery of Nature,* one is struck by the fact that Plumwood never really defines reason. What is reason, exactly? Isn't it a certain set of logical and procedural tools for reflexive thinking? But in the dualist schema it functions more as a signifier of identity.

The form of identity it signifies is one constituted through division, separation, distancing, and domination. But what has thinking logically and reflexively to do with this? Yes, one can think logically and reflexively in the service of a master identity, but one can also think logically and reflexively, as Plumwood herself insists, in the service of relational identities. Why then should it have been reason that was singled out in the dualist schema as the definitive attribute of a dominator identity? True, reason is a marker of mind and hence of value. But why should not some other highly developed mode of cognition have been selected as the marker of mind?

Insofar as there is an answer to these questions in *Feminism and the Mastery of Nature*, it seems to be that the association of reason with a dominator identity is strictly ideological. In the fourth chapter of the book, Plumwood traces the origins of dualism as an ideological construct back to Plato. It was in Plato that the core dichotomy, reason versus nature, took shape for the purpose of opposing everything associated with menials – such as women, slaves, and animals – to the distinctive attributes of the leisured male class whose privileges depended on the services of these menials. The distinctive activity of the leisured class, to which Plato himself of course belonged, was reasoning, as exemplified in philosophical and mathematical thinking. The capacity for reasoning was accordingly selected as the attribute that set the members of this class apart from, and justified their control over, the messy, sweaty realm of reproductive and domestic labour and sheer physical affordance that was the province of the menial classes.

Indeed, the political intent that shaped the reason/nature dualism of Plato's thought, according to Plumwood's analysis, was not merely a matter of the self-legitimation of the elite. At a deeper level it pertained to warfare. Since slaves formed the principal productive base for the intellectual class to which Plato belonged, and since slaves could only be procured through warfare, warfare was the condition for the perpetuation of the Athenian system of privilege. Militarism was accordingly promoted as the pillar of the state in Plato's political philosophy, as evidenced in the *Republic*. But how could one ensure a caste of warriors ready routinely to risk their lives in warfare? It was ultimately in response to this problem, according to Plumwood, that Plato posited a realm of transcendence, the realm of the insensible Forms, imperishable, unchanging, eternal, perfect, and ideal, to which human beings, and only human beings, could gain access, via reason. Death would hold no terrors for the philosopher-warrior who had mentally left behind the world of sensible, mutable particulars – the messy entanglements of labourers, women, and animals – and entered instead a rarefied realm of abstract thought, articulated most fittingly and paradigmatically in mathematics. Plato's thought, then, with its positing of a higher, eternal realm accessible to reason and a lower, perishable realm of nature, served the political purpose of justifying the privilege of his own class and securing the conditions for its perpetuation.[2]

If Plumwood's account of the origins of reason/nature dualism is correct, then we may well wonder why such thinking has retained its appeal. Why has reason endured as the core dualist category through so many centuries of changing social relationships and conditions? Western societies have not continued to depend on slavery and hence on warfare for the procurement of slaves throughout their history, so why should they continue to define ruling male classes in terms of reason? Even if reason as an antidote to death had remained politically relevant, Christianity was soon to offer, only a few centuries after Plato, an entirely different avenue to immortality. According to Christian teaching, the marker of the human, and indeed of immortality, was soul, not reason. So why should reason retain its centrality in dualistic schemas?

I would suggest that reason is indeed integral to dualism, as Plumwood claims, but that the actual roots of dualism lie much deeper in the structure of thought than ad hoc, strictly ideological (or even diffusely psychological) explanations such as Plumwood's allow. Dualism is, I shall argue, a phenomenological corollary of a certain way of thinking that was an innate potential of human cognition. As such it would have been discovered sooner or later in human history regardless of political contingencies. This particular way of thinking did indeed involve reasoning, but it cannot be adequately described merely in terms of logic. Its dualistic character is rather something that is *enacted* in consciousness via a particular cognitive operation, specifically the very act itself of theorizing.

## *Theoria* and *strategia*

It was a brilliant and arresting article by the French philosopher and sinologist Francois Jullien that first set me thinking along these lines. As an environmental philosopher, I had been part of the project of developing a theoretical alternative to the dualist, atomist, and mechanistic paradigm, the alternative favoured by me being a relational and panpsychist one, drawing on the ancient philosophical idea that consciousness – mind or soul (psyche) – is a universal feature of all things. As philosophers, we saw ourselves engaged in a contest of truths – a contest in which we sought to replace the ostensible truths of a worldview based on dualism with the genuine truths of a worldview based on relationality. But Jullien's article, 'Did philosophers have to become fixated on truth?' (2002), signalled the possible contingency of truth as the goal of cognition. And it was the meta-level contrast Jullien drew between the figure of the ancient Greek philosopher and that of the Chinese sage that made plain this contingency of truth as a goal. He observes that while the philosopher set out to explain the world, to provide an accurate and exhaustive representation of it, the sage set out to adapt or accommodate himself to it (both figures are always male in these traditions). The sage sought to identify the tendencies or dispositions at work in particular situations in order to harness those tendencies or dispositions to his own best advantage. To this end he remained open to all points of view instead of insisting, as philosophers did, on a single representation ('the truth') exclusive of others. In describing the sage as seeking 'congruence' with reality, Jullien seems to imply that the thinking of the sage remained inextricable from agency rather than becoming, like the thinking of the Greeks, an end in itself. I would suggest that the contrast drawn by Jullien between the Greek philosopher and the Chinese sage can be further developed to the point where it can shed a deeper light on the origins of dualism.

Let us consider the actual process whereby a philosopher – ancient or modern – seeks truth. Take the case of a thinker who, like the pre-Socratics, is inquiring after the basic constitution of reality. His method is to engage in a particular mental or cognitive operation: he holds an inner mirror up to the manifest world of the senses. In that mirror he constructs an abstract duplicate or conceptual map of the world. Reason, in the sense of the articulation and observance of laws of definition, inference and coherence, is integral to this process, but the actual purpose of the process is not to reason but to mirror (Mathews 2016). As soon as the thinker finds in that abstract duplicate a schema he regards as accurately reflecting the nature of things, he has, he considers, discovered truth. The truth about reality, or some aspect or portion of reality, is ideal and permanent. It is in fact eternal: the world changes, but the truth about the world does not change. Things arise and pass away, moment by moment, but the truth about them is timeless. The goal of thought is, from the perspective of the philosopher, to grasp truth, and the grasping of truth is an end in itself.

Such a notion of truth had not crystallized in other ancient societies in quite the same way as it did among the Greeks, and for this reason philosophy is regarded as a Greek invention. In other ancient societies thinking was still inextricable from agency – humans thought in order to act in some way. Apprehending the world via mythic narratives was inseparable from invoking its divinity or tapping into its agency. In thinking and knowing in these old ways one remained, first and foremost, an agent within the world negotiating one's way around it, rather than a spectator, a looker in an inner mirror that reflected reality. For the Greeks, however, approaching the world through this mental operation of doubling, of re-presenting in abstract what was initially presented to the mind through the senses, reality appeared under a peculiar disembodied, ideal, untouchable aspect, reflective of what-is but inert, unable to act upon the observer or be acted upon by them. While this inertness of the ideal duplicate that was the object of knowledge was not historically accomplished all at once, and traces of the older mythic narratives lingered in the philosophizing of the pre-Socratics, it did become dramatically explicit in Plato, in the shape of the Theory of Forms. The Forms were the abstract, eternal, perfect, and unchanging images to which any actual, concrete, perishable world must conform. The goal of thought was to access this abstract realm and apprehend reality under a timeless rather than an ever-changing aspect. But in positing the Forms, Plato was really no more than describing, in reified terms, the phenomenology of the act of theorizing itself. In projecting a mental reflection or re-presentation or idealized schema of the world onto a kind of abstract screen in an inner theatre, the mind is constituting theory. This mental process has left its trace in etymology: the word 'theory' is derived from the Greek, *theoria*, a looking at, thing looked at; *theoros*, spectator; and *thea*, spectacle.

In the process of theorizing, the human mind subtly removed itself from reality and became reality's spectator, an observer of the drama, invisible from within the constructed drama itself and in this sense invested with a status different from the elements of that drama, the elements of the re-presented reality. The drama itself, the spectacle, was constructed via extrapolation from and idealization of experience. The mind constructed a map or model that was intended to reflect, in outline, the immediate world of experience but also to complete it. Though total, this map or model – *theoria* – was nevertheless a totality that, as something created by the knower, could not include the knower among its contents.

The knower who could not be included in his/her own ideal re-presentation of reality was, I would suggest, the original subject, and the world as ideal projection, or re-presentation in the theatre of the subject's mind, the original object. It was, in other words, via the subtle reification involved in *theoria*, the introjective act of reflective knowing, that the world first became an object for the human mind, inert and untouchable and completely devoid of real presence or agency of its own. And it is in this separation of active, world-constructing subject from the merely acted-upon, constructed object, in which I would further suggest we find the origin of dualism: dualism is a function of the subject-object bifurcation that inevitably occurs as a result of the mental operation involved in that form of knowing here described as theory or *theoria*. Qua active knower, the subject is categorically different from the mere after-image of the world that it projects onto its mental screen, and as a result it inevitably feels the sense of apartness from, and aloofness to, the world that we witness in the history of dualism. Indeed there is a built-in autism, or radical self-centrism, in the standpoint of the subject, in the sense that the subject is developmentally disposed to fail to recognize, in any deeply felt way, the subjectivity of re-presented others. To the extent that self-other relations are mediated by theory then, they will be ethically problematic. The experience of theorizing will effectively block any attempt to allow subjectivity to the world at large.

Much further down the historical track, when the initial Greek objectification of reality for purely explanatory purposes had led to a more accurate, detailed, and comprehensive form of theorization – the body of knowledge known to us as science – humanity would be enabled to exercise its agency, which had initially been bracketed in the search for truth, on an unprecedented scale. But this was a new form of agency, the agency of a subject no longer negotiating the world from within but comprehensively objectifying it in the 'mirror' of *theoria*, and then reflexively premeditating and rehearsing action before carrying it out in actuality. This calculated form of agency, in which the very means for action were themselves theoretically mediated and actualized as technology, turned out to entrain undreamed of efficacy. Such efficacy, combined with the autistic tendency within the dualistic orientation, has in time enabled the wholesale transformation – and degradation – of earth in the service of human ends.

If this argument that the origins of dualism lie in the very activity of theorizing is accepted, then it follows, of course, that we cannot escape dualism by further theorizing. This is not to say that it is impossible to theorize the world in non-dualist and relational ways. It is eminently possible to do so, as the theories of numerous feminists and environmental philosophers and, more recently, new materialists attest. But such theories will lack philosophical traction, because the very experience of thinking them re-enacts at a subconscious level the original subject-object bifurcation. How then can the grip of dualism be broken? Let us return to Jullien's Chinese sage. Where the philosopher became mesmerized by representation and the products of his own thought, and retreated to a 'life of the mind', the sage remained immersed in and engaged with concrete reality. The wisdom of the sage consisted not in theory but in a capacity to live effectively. His definitive discovery was that one lives most effectively by adapting or accommodating oneself to reality. He sought to identify the tendencies or dispositions at work in particular situations not in order to capture them in theory but in order to harness them to his own best advantage. This stance of accommodation, of working with the grain of reality rather than cutting against it in an attempt to impose one's will upon it by sheer force, is enshrined in Chinese tradition as *wu wei*, the stance of effortless action, of swimming with the flow rather than swimming against the current (Lafargue 1992; Mathews 2009).

If we describe the approach of the Chinese sage as *strategic* and define strategists as those who are concerned with the immediate field of influences in which they are immersed and the way in which that field impacts upon their agency, then we might look to strategy for our escape from dualism. Strategists are concerned not with an idealized 'world', conceived under its universal aspect, but with their own immediate situation and how the influences at play in it are impinging on their agency, corporeally and tangibly, in the present moment. One does not need a theory about the nature of reality in order to respond strategically to this field: one can feel the environmental pressure increasing and decreasing as one responds now this way and now that. There is no sense of this world as a completed totality; it extends just as far as the range of one's own sensitivity, and as one moves around in it this range is constantly changing. To train the strategic faculty, one does not teach reason, which is to say, the mental procedures that produce abstract schemas (where these implicate but are not reducible to the rules of logic), but rather sets exercises or practices which increase sensitivity and responsiveness. This is why Chinese sages typically received their training in martial and other Daoist arts rather than in discursive inquiry. Where philosophers theorized, sages *cultivated*.

Etymology is helpful here, as it was in the case of the term 'theory': 'strategy' is derived from the Greek *strategia*, 'office or command or art of a general'; from *stratos*, 'multitude, army, expedition'; and *agein*, 'to lead, guide, drive, carry off'; and from Sanskrit *ajirah*, 'moving, active'. In light of this, strategy may be understood as concerned with the coordination of collective or individual agency. Cognition is required for such coordination, but this is not the kind of cognition involved in *theoria*, which abstracts from the empirical agency of the subject in order to attain a more 'objective' rendering of the world. In *strategia*, cognition remains non-dualist, immersed in the world rather than set apart; it is honed in the service of agency.

## Reviewing the ecofeminist critique of dualism

If dualism is indeed inherent in the act of theorizing, then it would account, I think, for the extraordinary longevity and consistency of dualism as a fundamental schema for the organization of thought. Western civilization, with its origins in ancient philosophy, is uniquely rooted in *theoria*. Science made its first appearance in the West because science is an emanation – indeed the apotheosis – of *theoria*. The immense power over nature that science conferred enabled the West to colonize other societies and subjugate other civilizations (Merchant 1980). *Theoria*, in the shape of science, has been the key, par excellence, to the ascendancy of the West in the modern period. Since *theoria* has in this sense remained the core driver of Western civilization, the West has remained a civilization uniquely fashioned by dualistic logic.

To understand the origins of dualism in this way is to see that the dualistic outlook is not merely an ideological contrivance but the outcome of a particular evolutionary trajectory. In a male-dominated society, such as ancient Greece was, it was inevitable that the primal subject/object bifurcation enacted in the consciousness of the early philosophers should eventually give rise to gendered categories and serve as a vehicle for the legitimation of domination. But if this ideological sequel to the act of theorizing is conflated with the actual source or origin of dualism, we shall fail in our efforts to escape dualism. The primary relationship of domination entrained by the act of theorizing is that of subject versus object: the subject is inherently set apart from and above everything that can become an object of theorization. Since the theorizing subject is inevitably human, the conceptual binary at the core of dualism is that of human versus nature. Only contingently, historically, does this schema furthermore become associated with gender, race, class, and so on.

Male domination by no means inherently requires dualism for its legitimation. It can exist in the absence of a dualistic mind-set, as it did and does, for example, in China. Although Chinese civilization has from the start maintained a deep reverence for nature, as one would expect from its predominantly strategic outlook, it has also been insistently patriarchal. Male domination has been legitimated not in dualistic terms, by denying the subjectivity of women or constructing them as sub-human, but in terms of a core relationship of ruler/ruled that is regarded as structuring the entire yin-yang system of heaven and earth. In this ideological scenario, the ruled are seen as naturally subordinate but not inferior to the ruler. The relationship of ruler to ruled is in this sense genuinely complementary: it is for the sake of harmony at the level of the system as a whole that the ruled must submit to the ruler.[3] That such ideological legitimation of male domination can co-exist with a respectful attitude to ward nature, correlative with China's strategic orientation, is evident from the fact that this ideology takes its cue from nature itself: although all beings are deemed equally important inasmuch as they each have their own intelligent part to play in the order of nature, this order is maintained by way of natural hierarchies – of predator to prey, for example. That nature is in this fashion normative in Chinese culture is indicative of the reverence in which it was traditionally held.[4]

The case of China signals that while adopting a strategic orientation will help to induce a basically respectful attitude to ward nature, it will not of itself preclude stronger parties in society from exercising power over weaker or more vulnerable parties. Dominant groups are inventive in devising ideologies of legitimation. Nonetheless, developing a strategic as opposed to a theoretic orientation will resolve the subject/object split that has powerfully buttressed and legitimated domination in the West. Moreover, by re-attuning us to the manifold forms of intelligence and responsiveness at play in the larger community of life and thereby re-instating our felt sense of the moral significance of the natural world, strategic modalities will help to instil new habits of consciousness, on which new patterns of affiliation and mutuality may be built.

The theory-averseness of the strategic approach seems to chime with, and perhaps add further weight to, the deconstructive approach to feminist theory, touched on earlier, which seeks to dismantle grand narratives without constructing new ones, no matter how ecological or relational such prospective new narratives might be. But the difference from deconstruction is that, rather than remaining in a stance of refusal and resistance, strategists seek alternative, agentic modalities that re-immerse us in reality rather than leaving us stranded as spectators at an epistemic remove from it.

## Strategic modalities

In ancient China, as we have already observed, the sage honed his capacity for acuity, accommodation, and adaptiveness through Daoist exercises, such as martial arts and calligraphy. But such exercises really only represent the refinement of a way of being – an engaged form of agency – that was normal and widespread in early societies, particularly in hunter-gatherer societies. In order to hunt and gather one must apprehend one's own immediate environment not theoretically but concretely, in all its particularity: One must know the plants and animals of the locality, their habits, preferences, idiosyncrasies, their relationships with one another, their particular histories. One must know the landscape intimately and intricately, its terrain, its affordances, its patterns of seasonality. This is not a detached form of knowing but a form of attentiveness to the particular that is guided, like one's responses in a martial context, by one's own vital interests. It is need and danger that open one's eyes to the significance of the particular, and train one's gaze to follow it all the way back to its lair. This is no subject/object standoff, but a push-and-pull contest of flesh with flesh. In coming to such an intimate engagement with the particular, however, one is drawn into affinity of purpose with it, into a kind of ecological collegiality which engenders fellow feeling and respect and hence a natural reticence to overstep the proper sphere of one's own agency. Intimacy, in other words – even the intimacy of the chase – begets an inclination to accommodate and adapt – the disposition toward *wu wei*.[5]

However, the reader may be wondering: How is *strategia* to be cultivated in the context of modern, industrialized, mass societies? Are there practices by which we can today burst the bubble of subject/object dualism and re-immerse ourselves in the living, unpredictable depths of reality? In the 1980s and 1990s, standpoint feminism attempted to demonstrate how the traditional domestic practices of women – childcare, care of the infirm, housework – fostered in women an engagement with the concrete and particular that was in striking contrast to the detached outlook of men preoccupied with the abstract generalities of the public sphere. In light of this legacy of traditional domestic experience, some women in modern societies may be well placed to appreciate the immersive modality of *strategia* and the disposition to accommodate and adapt that accompanies it. This is not to say that women's traditional practices were in themselves sufficient to engender a strategic outlook. The sympathies they produced, however, together with sympathy for indigenous lifeways based on intimate engagement with the particularities of one's environment, may provide a basis for creating new, normative practices that cultivate and hone the strategic faculty. Perhaps then it is a contemporary task for ecofeminist scholars to identify or devise practices whereby *strategia* can be actively cultivated, at both personal and social levels, in order to become reinstated in modern societies as our larger orientation. This is by no means to insist that in a strategic scenario the theoretical approach of science with its managerial corollary be altogether abandoned. Rather, science could be re-situated as one tool among others within the open horizon of a push-and-pull engagement with an always unobjectifiable, and in that sense spontaneous and inexhaustible, reality.

In modern societies reconfigured along the *wu wei* lines of a strategic orientation, social systems would be reconfigured *with* the grain of in situ influences rather than in accordance with the preconceived theoretical impositions of exclusively managerial approaches based on science. Food production, for example, could respond to and nourish local ecologies rather than rendering land a *tabula rasa* for industrial monoculture (Benyus 2002). Manufacture could follow the circular, no-waste model that returns all resource materials back into the twin loops of production and ecology (McDonough 2002). Architecture and engineering could follow the contours of local topography and make full use of local affordances with respect to materials, energy, ventilation, water capture, cycling, and dispersal. Even economics and politics could be conducted on *wu wei* lines, where this would involve a decentralized approach, the nurturing, again, of local affordances: local knowledge and culture, local talent and intelligence, local initiative and responsibility, as well as local physical resources (Gibson-Graham et al. 2013).

## Conclusion

The problem of dualism is indeed the pivot of ecofeminist theorizing which continues to be informed by the writings of Val Plumwood. But I have suggested in this chapter that, philosophically speaking, we cannot escape dualism merely by theoretically deconstructing it or by devising theoretical alternatives to it. Ecofeminism might rather be construed as primarily a discipline of practice, in the manner of traditions such as Daoism, which offer exercises aimed at the cultivation of consciousness rather than discourses that, by their very nature as discourses, perpetuate an underlying dualism of subject versus object. To devise such practices is not merely a matter of reviving, for normative purposes, traditional practices, such as those of women in the domestic sphere or of hunter-gatherer peoples in the subsistence sphere, but of developing contemporary modes of self- and social-cultivation conducive to strategic consciousness. Of course, a place may be – indeed, I think, must be – retained for theory, since in a culture already so profoundly shaped by theory, theory may be required to motivate us to undertake practices intended to transform consciousness. But it will be the practices themselves, re-engaging us with reality, which will release us from the grip of dualism with its unavoidable legacy of domination. Relying on critique and analysis alone may re-entrap us.

## Notes

Some of the text in this chapter has been adapted by the author from Chapter 18, 'Environmental Philosophy', in N. N. Trakakis and G. Oppy (eds), *A History of Australasian Philosophy*, Springer, Dordrecht, 2014, pp. 543–591. Reprinted with permission from Springer.

1 For an excellent introduction to the history of environmental philosophy, see Brennan (2008).
2 The idea that the valorization of reason, under its dualist construction, was somehow tied up with transcendence of death was a theme to which Plumwood returned later in her career when, in a series of powerful articles on death and predation, she sought to re-situate death within ecology, finding consolation for mortality not in a 'higher' realm of abstract existence but in the material continuities of the life process itself. These papers were collected posthumously in Plumwood (2012).
3 See, for example, many passages elaborating this principle in the ancient Chinese text *I Ching*.
4 The fact that a keen aesthetic and spiritual appreciation for nature has always been a defining strand of Chinese civilization has not prevented China from degrading its environment over the millennia (Elvin 2004). But such damage has, until the advent of modernization in China, been inflicted for pragmatic rather than ideological reasons. It might have been much more severe had it been ideologically mandated – as it became after the Communist revolution, when, under the influence of the West, Mao Zedong actually declared a 'war on nature'.
5 I am not for a moment suggesting that hunting – a prime exercise in *strategia* in indigenous contexts – remains morally defensible as a practice in the radically altered circumstances of modern societies (Mathews 2012).

# References

Alcoff, L. (1986) 'Cultural feminism versus poststructuralist theory: The identity crisis in feminist theory', *Signs* 13(7): 405–434.

Beauvoir, S. de (1965) *The Second Sex*. London and New York: Foursquare Books.

Benyus, J. (2002) *Biomimicry: Innovation Inspired by Nature*. New York: Harper Perennial (first published by William Morrow, 1997).

Benjamin, J. (1988) *The Bonds of Love: Psychoanalysis, Feminism and the Problem of Domination*. London: Virago.

Bennett, J. (2010) *Vibrant Matter: A Political Ecology of Things*. Chapel Hill, NC: Duke University Press.

Blamauer, M. (ed) (2011) *The Mental as Fundamental*. Frankfurt Heusenstamm: Ontos Verlag.

Brennan, A. (with Lo, N.) (2008) 'Environmental ethics', *Stanford Encyclopedia of Philosophy*. Online. Available at: http://plato.stanford.edu/entries/ethics-environmental (accessed 9 February 2016).

Butler, J. (1990) *Gender Trouble*. London: Routledge.

Chodorow, N. (1979) *The Reproduction of Mothering*. Berkeley, CA: University of California Press.

Daly, M. (1978) *Gyn/ecology: The Meta-ethics of Radical Feminism*. London: Women's Press.

Derrida, J. (1970) 'Structure, sign and play in the discourse of the human sciences', in Macksey, R. and Donato, E. (eds) *The Languages of Criticism and the Sciences of Man*. Baltimore, MD: Johns Hopkins Press, 247–265.

d'Eubonne, F. (1994) 'The time for ecofeminism', in Merchant, C. (ed) *Ecology: Key Concepts in Critical Theory*. Atlantic Highlands, NJ: Humanities Press, 174–197.

Dolphijn, R. and van der Tuin, I. (2012) *New Materialism: Interviews and Cartographies*. Ann Arbor, MI: Open Humanities Press.

Elvin, M. (2004) *The Retreat of the Elephants: An Environmental History of China*. New Haven, CT: Yale University Press.

Fox, W. (1990) *Towards a Transpersonal Ecology*. Boston, MA: Shambhala.

Friedan, B. (1963) *The Feminine Mystique*. New York: Norton.

Gibson-Graham, J. K. et al. (2013) *Take Back the Economy*. Minneapolis: MN: University of Minnesota Press.

Gilligan, C. (1982) *In a Different Voice*. Cambridge, MA: Harvard University Press.

Griffin, S. (1978) *Women and Nature: The Roaring Inside Her*. New York: Harper and Row.

Harding, S. (1986) *The Science Question in Feminism*. Ithaca, NY: Cornell University Press.

Hartsock, N. C. M. (1985) *Money, Sex and Power*. Boston, MA: Northeastern University Press.

Harvey, G. (2005) *Animism: Respecting the Living World*. New York: Columbia University Press.

Irigaray, L. (1985) *Speculum of the Other Woman*. Translated by Gillian Gill. Ithaca, NY: Cornell University Press.

Jaggar, A. (1984) *Feminist Politics and Human Nature*. Brighton: Harvester.

Jullien, F. (2002) 'Did philosophers have to become fixated on Truth?', Translated by Janet Lloyd. *Critical Inquiry* 28(4): 803–824.

Keller, E. F. (1985) *Reflections on Gender and Science*. New Haven, CT: Yale University Press.

King, Y. (1983) 'The ecofeminist imperative', in Caldecott, L. and Leland, S. (eds) *Reclaim the Earth*. London: The Women's Press, 9–14.

Lafargue, M. (1992) *The Tao of the Tao Te Ching: A Translation and Commentary*. Albany, NY: State University of New York Press.

Leiss, W. (1972) *The Domination of Nature*. New York: George Braziller.

Lloyd, G. (1984) *The Man of Reason*. London: Methuen.

McDonough, W. (2002) *Cradle to Cradle: Remaking the Way We Make Things*. New York: North Point Press.

Mathews, F. (1991) *The Ecological Self*. London: Routledge.

Mathews, F. (2003) *For Love of Matter: A Contemporary Panpsychism*. Albany, NY: SUNY Press.

Mathews, F. (2009) 'Why has the West failed to embrace panpsychism?', in Skrbina, D. (ed) *Mind That Abides: Panpsychism in the New Millennium*. Amsterdam and Philadelphia, PA: John Benjamins, 341–360.

Mathews, F. (2012) 'The anguish of wildlife ethics', *New Formations* 75(Spring): 114–131.

Mathews, F. (2016) 'Do the deepest roots of a future ecological civilization lie in Chinese soil?', in Makeham, J. (ed) *Learning From the Other: Australian and Chinese Perspectives on Philosophy*. Canberra: Australian Academy of the Humanities, 15–27.

Merchant, C. (1980) *The Death of Nature*. San Francisco, CA: Harper and Row.

Miller, J. B. (1986) *Towards a New Psychology of Women.* Harmondsworth: Penguin.

Naess, A. (1985) 'Identification as a source of deep ecological attitudes', in Tobias, M. (ed) *Deep Ecology.* San Diego, CA: Avant Books, 256–270.

Naess, A. (1988) 'Self-realization: An ecological approach to being in the world', in Seed, J. et al. (eds) *Thinking Like a Mountain.* Philadelphia, PA: New Society Publishers, 19–31.

Ortner, S. B. (1974) 'Is female to male as nature is to culture?', in Rosaldo, M. Z. and Lamphere, L. (eds) *Woman, Culture, and Society.* Stanford, CA: Stanford University Press, 67–87.

Plumwood, V. (1993) *Feminism and the Mastery of Nature.* London: Routledge.

Plumwood, V. (2003) *Environmental Culture: The Ecological Crisis of Reason.* London and New York: Routledge.

Plumwood, V. (2009) 'Nature in the active voice', *Australian Humanities Review* 46. Online. Available at: www.australianhumanitiesreview.org/archive/Issue-May-2009/plumwood.html.

Plumwood, V. (2012) *Eye of the Crocodile.* Canberra: ANU Press.

Ruether, R. R. (1978) *New Woman, New Earth.* New York: Seabury Press.

Rich, A. (1977) *Of Woman Born.* London: Virago.

Routley, R. (1973) 'Is there a need for new, an environmental, ethic?', in *Proceedings of the 15th World Congress of Philosophy* (Vol. 1). Sophia: Sophia Press, 205–210.

Salleh, A. (1984) 'Deeper than deep ecology', *Environmental Ethics* 6: 339–345.

Salleh, A. (2005) 'Moving to an embodied materialism', *Capitalism Nature Socialism* 16(2): 9–14.

Skrbina, D. (ed) (2009) *Mind That Abides: Panpsychism in the New Millennium.* Amsterdam and Philadelphia, PA: John Benjamins.

Warren, K. (1990) 'The power and promise of ecological feminism', *Environmental Ethics* 12(2): 121–146.

Wollstonecraft, M. (1985) *Vindication of the Rights of Woman.* London: Everyman Classics.

# 4

# GENDER AND ENVIRONMENT IN THE GLOBAL SOUTH

## From 'women, environment, and development' to feminist political ecology

*Bernadette P. Resurrección*

## Introduction

Interconnections between economic development, environmental change, and gender politics are an important topic of analysis in feminist scholarship. Research into women's roles in resource-based economic development and their work as environmental stewards began to emerge in the 1980s. Inspired by rural women actively resisting deforestation in the Global South, scholars theorized the relationship between people's gender roles and identities and their attitudes toward nature. Case studies of activist struggles and iconic examples of individual 'eco-warriors' became valuable evidence to support new claims. Some scholars adopted an approach that celebrated women's special connection to the earth, while others sought to analyze the material conditions and power relations that shape women's and men's involvement in resource use, their vulnerability to natural forces, and their eco-political agency. Nearly forty years on, debates over theoretical framing as well as over policy and practice continue to drive a vibrant research agenda that integrates several disciplines and employs diverse methodologies. The common ground is a desire to improve the living conditions of the people who are most affected by development-induced environmental change and to influence international policy-making to that end.

This chapter provides an overview of gender, environment, and development scholarship that explains how early ideas and debates have shaped subsequent work. My aim is to demonstrate how this field has evolved over time and how it has now come to understand two of the most pressing challenges of this century: climate change and disaster risk. While there are a number of different approaches to studying gender-environment connections, in the discussion that follows I focus on feminist political ecology (FPE). FPE has evolved as a loose platform of ideas that seeks to theorize differentiated forms of power and resource access primarily but not exclusively in developing country contexts. FPE grew out of a desire to foreground the political aspects of earlier frameworks, as well as to analyze the growing neoliberalization of nature in capitalist development processes. It draws on feminist poststructuralist theory in order to criticize the domination of techno-scientific solutions to environmental change that sidestep more holistic and grounded approaches. I argue that at a time when there is a dire need to address the exigent features of climate change and disaster policy discourses, FPE offers valuable insight into human-nature relations that can contribute to more grounded analyses and better solutions. Understanding how women and men, as embodied and emotional beings, have complex and shifting relationships to the natural world that are embedded in place and shaped by intersections of gender, race, class, caste, culture, age (and so on) is central to the search for environmental and social justice. An FPE lens provides tools for envisioning transformative changes that are much needed in these troubling times.

## Pioneering ideas and debates about gender-environment connections

The academic study of the connections between women, gender roles and relations, and the natural environment (or nature) has evolved over four decades. During that time, the experience and knowledge of academics, activists, and practitioners have played a significant part in the development of scholarly work. In the beginning, in the late 1980s and early 1990s, several strands of thought shaped debates and global policy agendas. One strand was the women, environment, and development (WED) perspective that was closely tied to a version of ecofeminism rooted in the Global South (Shiva 1989; Mies and Shiva 1993). A second strand was a critique put forth by feminist scholars who took issue with the way the women-gender-environment connections were presented in the WED literature (Agarwal 1992a, b; Jackson 1993a, b). It is important to summarize the debate that ensued between these positions because they arguably laid the foundations for the emergence of feminist political ecology as well as being in some ways still apparent in contemporary feminist discussions about climate change and disaster risk.

### *Women, environment, and development (WED)*

Early WED work involved compelling narratives of poor rural and indigenous women (mostly but not only in the Global South) and claims about them being among the hardest hit by – and the most active in trying to address – environmental degradation. These narratives inspired conceptual connections to be made between women and the environment. A result was the recognition that women should play a greater role in environmental programs and policies and that a strong feminist voice in global environmental politics was needed, especially in the run-up to the landmark 1992 UN Conference on Environment and Development (UNCED) in Rio de Janeiro. It is often noted that several of the outcome agreements of UNCED (e.g., *Agenda 21*) incorporated WED principles thanks to the involvement of key activists and academics in the process.[1]

An important figure in the development of WED, and more specifically an Indian ecofeminist approach, was the environmental scholar-activist Vandana Shiva. In her book *Staying Alive: Women, Ecology and Survival in India* (1989), Shiva drew a stark contrast between the dominant forces of science, development, colonialism, patriarchy, and capitalism, which 'destroy life and threaten survival' and 'the suffering and insights of those [women] who struggle to sustain and conserve life' (1989:xii). To illustrate the latter, she celebrated the Chipko movement (a grassroots movement to save forests in northwest India) as a telling example of rural women's leadership in forest and environmental preservation.[2] In doing so, she invoked principles of Hinduism to argue that all pre-colonial societies 'were based on an ontology of the feminine as the living principle (*Prakitri*)' (Shiva 1989:42). In her view, rural indigenous women are the original givers of life and are therefore the rightful caretakers of nature. In *Staying Alive*, and later in a book co-authored with the German sociologist Maria Mies, titled *Ecofeminism* (1993), Shiva suggested that Western patriarchal development (or 'maledevelopment') strategies and Western science have displaced the 'feminine principle' and thus have victimized women, non-Western peoples, and nature. The logical answer, for her, was to learn from 'Third World' women's special knowledge; 'they have privileged access to survival expertise'. She wrote:

> Third World women are bringing the concern with living and survival back to centre stage in human history. In recovering the chances for the survival of all life, they are laying the foundations for the recovery of the feminine principle in nature and society, and through it the recovery of the earth as sustainer and provider.
>
> *(Shiva 1989:214–215)*

Shiva's work influenced the thinking of researchers in the WED strand, but her analysis of rural women's hands-on experience and knowledge of the natural environment was more important for them than her spiritual-culturalist ecofeminist views. It has been noted that because this body of work was largely made of up of development practitioners, it was less theoretical and more based on stories from the field than the work of academic feminists (cf. Jackson 1993a, b). Important for WED writers was to foreground a materialist analysis of the links between women and nature, specifically by pointing to how women's roles brought them into close everyday contact with their environments. They subscribed to the idea that women are materially adversely affected by environmental degradation due to an a priori, and largely universal, gender division of labour, where women are usually disproportionately assigned caring and provisioning roles and obligations (or reproductive labour). Like Shiva's ecofeminism, WED scholarship had an ontology centred on a feminine subject, usually a woman from the Global South who is vulnerable to environmental degradation but at the same time 'agency-endowed' for the tasks of environmental care and protection (Dankelman and Davidson 1988; Sontheimer 1991; Rodda 1993). It is important to note that their focus was on *women* as a group in the development process and as victims/caretakers of their environments rather than on gender as a broad category of analysis.

WED discourses were prominent throughout 1990s and 2000s in gender, livelihoods, and natural resource planning and development organizations. In policy terms, environment and development planners interpreted the feminine subject in these discourses to mean that women are the most effective targets of environment and conservation projects since their daily roles connect them closely with natural resources. As a result, gender planning specialists embraced the simplification of gendered identities, roles, and interests in order to insert gender agendas into institutions that otherwise had different priorities (Cornwall et al. 2007).[3] An unintended consequence of this planning approach was that in many cases 'environmental caretaker' was added to women's already long list of caring roles. Moreover, the 'women as environmental victims' trope also gained political traction in international deliberations around UN conventions, since representing women as such conformed to a requirement of visible politics that needed to be created around a 'centre' (Dirks et al. 1993; see Arora-Jonsson in this handbook for a discussion). At the time, dissatisfaction with this translation of WED thinking into policy ran in parallel with similar critiques levelled at Women in Development (WID) perspectives, which saw women as a stand-alone homogeneous group with a set of static and pre-defined roles.

## Critiques of WED

Intellectual unease with the prominence of a simplified and centred feminine subject in WED and ecofeminist policy discourses spurred new directions in understanding the connections between gender and environment. Criticisms of both WID and WED came from feminist academics working in the development field. For example, Brinda Rao (1991) argued that instead of accepting a priori perceptions of feminine roles, there is a need to contextualize women as they respond to complex environmental realities and to consider how they enter into and engage in social relationships with men within the institutions of their natural resource-dependent societies. An early proponent of the need for a critical gender perspective in unpacking environmental relations, Cecile Jackson (1993a, b) proposed that analysis should focus on power relations between women and men, and that women be treated as a disaggregated group of subjects as gender roles are socially and historically constructed and continually reformulated. Importantly, Jackson challenged the idea of 'women' as a natural constituency for environmental projects, underscoring the contingent nature and fluidity of gender interests.

The scholar who is perhaps most associated with the early critique of ecofeminism and the WED approach, and who has played a significant part in the evolution of gender and environment scholarship, is the Indian feminist economist Bina Agarwal. In a widely cited 1992 article 'The Gender and Environment Debate: Lessons from India', Agarwal offered both a critique of ecofeminism and an alternative to it, which she called 'feminist environmentalism'. She was particularly critical of so-called cultural ecofeminists (such as Sherry Ortner and Ynestra King) who, in her assessment, were viewing women's relationship to nature through an ideological Western feminist lens and failing to understand the diversity of women's experiences and the complex material realties of their interactions with the natural world. Although she argued that Shiva's work 'takes us further than the Western ecofeminists in exploring the links' (1992a:124) between development processes and their impacts on people, livelihoods, and environments, Agarwal also identified a number of similar shortcomings in Shiva's analysis. First, Shiva did not differentiate between 'Third World' women of 'different classes, castes, races, ecological zones and so on' (Agarwal 1992a:125). This homogenization of women, Agarwal suggested, was a form of essentialism and she regarded as questionable the claim that women *qua* women are 'embedded in nature' and having a 'special' relationship with the natural environment (125). Second, she criticized Shiva's use of the Hindu feminine principle as if it applied to all Indian women when in fact it is a very specific interpretation of a pluralistic religion that not all Indians practice. A third shortcoming, according to Agarwal, was that Shiva presented women and nature's oppression in the Third World as 'almost entirely' caused by colonial and patriarchal forms of development, which was in fact a simplification of a complex history that includes the 'very real local forces of power, privilege and property relations that pre-date colonialism'(126).

In response to these criticisms, Agarwal advocated an alternative position, which she called 'feminist environmentalism', that would be both rigorous and transformational. It would take a materialist analytical approach that sees gender and class as intrinsically linked. It would be based on the view that women's specific forms of interaction with the environment are socially constructed: structured by gender, class, and caste divisions of labour and property. These divisions in turn shape their experiences of environmental change and their knowledge of and responses to environmental degradation. In Agarwal's words, her alternative perspective

> would call for struggles over both resources and meanings. It would imply grappling with the dominant groups who have the property, power, and privilege to control resources, and these or other groups who control ways of thinking about them, via educational, media, religious, and legal institutions. On the feminist front there would be a need to challenge and transform both notions about gender and the actual division of work and resources between the genders. On the environmental front there would be a need to challenge and transform not only notions about the relationship between people and nature but also the actual methods of appropriation of nature's resources by a few. Feminist environmentalism underlines the necessity of addressing these dimensions from both fronts.
>
> *(Agarwal 1992a:127)*

Agarwal's critique of the essentializing and single-axis approach found in early ecofeminist work was rooted in her in depth, empirical research in India. The 'lessons from India' that informed her analysis were that it makes no sense to think of women as a unitary category; that environmental degradation and the appropriation of land and resources by the powerful affect poor women the most and result in the loss of their livelihood and knowledge systems; that there is a complex interplay of ideology, power, and inequality behind the destruction of environments and livelihoods; and that it is important to observe and to hear the messages of women and men involved in grassroots resistance the processes, products, people, property, power, and profit-orientation that underlie social inequality and environmental destruction (Agarwal 1992a:150).

Importantly, Agarwal's critique, her analytical and methodological approach, and her lessons from India have provided a model for subsequent research in the gender and environment field. It is apparent from a thorough review of the academic literature that ideologically driven portraits of women's connections to nature are now extremely rare in academic gender and environment research. In fact, the body of research that has been developed under the label of feminist political ecology offers a rich array of local case studies from all regions of the globe that continue to challenge any notions that women as women should be seen as either environmental victims or saviours. It is to this body of work that I now turn.

## The evolution of feminist political ecology

Feminist political ecology (FPE) emerged on the scene in the mid-1990s, arguably as a way to reclaim the feminist politics in environmental engagements and to redress the negative, essentialist reputation of cultural forms of ecofeminism. Whether or not (and how) FPE is connected to ecofeminism or whether it is a rejection of ecofeminist scholarship is beyond the scope of this chapter (see Rocheleau and Nimal 2015 for a review). The discussion in this section offers an overview of its evolution and central themes and concepts.

To begin, no discussion of FPE is ever complete without meandering momentarily into political ecology itself, like a river artery to its source, as FPE is a subfield of political ecology and both perspectives evolved in intellectually integrated and similar ways. Political ecology (PE) is an analytical approach that interrogates the operations of power that define people's unequal and differentiated access and control of resources at local, regional, and global scales. It came to the forefront of human geography in the 1980s, bringing political analysis to the task of understanding the links between environment and society. PE scholars argue that there is no transcendent adaptive or ecological order that can one-sidedly affect human populations, but an ecological system in which capital commodifies and commercializes every aspect of nature and re-configures human communities (Peet et al. 2011; Watts 2015). From its inception, PE scholarship has made deliberate efforts to express how nature and society are understood to co-produce one another, referred to as 'socio-natures'(Castree and Braun 2001). For example, for people involved in environmental justice movements, Loftus says 'the environment is something *lived* as a simultaneously bodily and global process' (2012:x). He draws attention to shack dwellers' struggles to secure water as a political effort that mediates socio-nature relationships, employing the view of 'assemblages' of nature and society that are co-produced and co-evolutionary. By placing the operations of power on the analytical centre stage, political ecology utilizes the theoretical lenses of political economy, human agency, material nature, and discourse, conflict and competition, governmentality, and the creation of environmental subjects (Peet et al. 2011).

FPE emerged out of political ecology's concern for social equity and social justice issues in environmental change, and draws from the intrinsically political character and analytical foci of feminism: power and difference. It was first proposed as a new conceptual framework by Dianne

Rocheleau, Barbara Thomas-Slayter, and Esther Wangari in their landmark 1996 book *Feminist Political Ecology: Global Issues and Local Experiences*. They presented it as a sub-field of political ecology that recognizes gendered power relations as a 'critical variable in shaping resource access and control interacting with class, caste, race, culture, and ethnicity to shape processes of ecological change' (1996:4). In addition to characterizing it as a framework for bringing 'a feminist perspective to political ecology', they explain that it draws on insights from feminist cultural ecology, feminist geography, and feminist political economy. The framework enables a multi-scalar analysis of knowledge production, gendered rights and responsibilities, and more pointedly, the workings of power and politics in the use, access, and distribution of resources in the context of neoliberal economic growth and structural adjustment trajectories.

Also centrally important is a focus on gendered environmental politics and grassroots activism. In contrast to the WED approach, which tended to concentrate on how to help women hurt by the vagaries of environmental destruction, FPE was built on a decade's worth of insights from women's involvement in local environmental struggles and social movement organizing in all parts of the world, in the Global South as well as in the Global North. Notable examples from that time were the Love Canal New York Homeowners' Association, the Kenyan Greenbelt Movement, the Indian Chipko Movement, the anti-toxics campaigns in Cancer Alley (Warren County, North Carolina), and the global Women's Environment and Development Organization (WEDO). Case studies of women's involvement in collective action formed the main content of *Feminist Political Ecology*, thereby establishing the importance of case study and narrative research to the FPE approach. Informed by Rocheleau's and her colleagues' core themes, scholarly work in FPE has since gathered a plethora of qualitative data on gendered experiences and has taken up a range of issues from the workings of gender in contested rights to farms and forests (Schroeder 1999; Cranney 2001; Paulson and Gezon 2005), to struggles over water (Harris 2006; Udas and Zwarteveen 2010), and the changing politics of fisheries (Bavington et al. 2004).

FPE is not a bounded or non-porous framework of ideas and analytical approaches, but rather a living, evolving platform of ideas that draws from the rich history of feminist theory. From its inception in the 1990s, when it aimed to highlight the materiality of women's political struggles[4] around resources and rights (Moeckli and Braun 2001), FPE has in recent years assumed strong post-structuralist leanings that question received wisdoms on the production of gender and other identities. It also brings the staunchly critical reading of the workings of power – neoliberal, androcentric, colonial, and environmental injustices – to new levels of analysis. More than twenty years after the publication of *Feminist Political Ecology*, Rocheleau tells us that

> FPE is more about a feminist perspective and an ongoing exploration and construction of a network of learners than a fixed approach for a single focus on women and/or gender. This constant circulation of theory, practice, policies and politics, and the mixing of various combinations of gender, class, race, ethnicity, sexuality, religion, ontologies and ecologies, with critique of colonial legacies and neoliberal designs, has characterized many feminist political ecologists. It is a work in process.
>
> *(Rocheleau 2015:57)*

Informed by post-structuralist insights, FPE work in the 2010s offers critical perspectives in a growing context of climate change, disasters, and large-scale investments following neoliberal economic growth orientations (see, for example, Harris 2006; Nightingale 2006; Elmhirst 2011; Hawkins and Ojeda 2011; Carney 2014; Buechler and Hanson 2015; Harcourt, Harris and Nelson 2015; Leach 2015; Rocheleau and Nirmal 2015; Sundberg 2017). Economic reform programs that favour accumulation-driven and neoliberal approaches to natural resource management have widened transnationally and deepened their influence in national states' economic growth trajectories. These have led to new exclusions and vulnerabilities, stimulating the creation of platforms for social and environmental justice struggles, and a fresh advocacy of sustainable development. The processes causing the intensification of environmental degradation and climate change (e.g., non-renewable energy markets and fossil fuel dependence, deforestation, desertification, and urbanization on massive scales) have led to more frequent stresses, shocks, and disasters that affect lives and livelihoods, often re-configuring communities in gendered and socially differentiated ways. In turn, solutions for mitigating these stresses – such as for example the emergence of the green economy (with its carbon trade, conservation enclosures, bio-energy development, payment for ecosystem services, etc.) – pose difficult questions regarding trade-offs between environmental sustainability and social well-being. In these emerging contexts, FPE focuses on complex dimensions of gendered and social experiences of loss, disadvantage, dispossession, and displacement within the multiple ecologies in which human beings are embedded.

This focus on multi-dimensional experiences marks out FPE's concern for, first of all, an intersectional analysis of society-environment relations and multi-dimensional gender subjectivities that do not disentangle gender from race, ethnicity, class, disability, and other social categories. Intesectionality is an explicit rejection of single-axis analyses (May 2014). Second, FPE recognizes the importance of conducting 'science from below' or examining people's embodied experiences of resource degradation, disasters, displacements, or dispossessions as these connect with other scales of power and decision-making (Harding 2008; Hanson 2015). And third, FPE interrogates knowledge production, governance, and policy-making, as they herald new forms of intervention and environmental governance that may be shaped by assumptions that deepen differentiated and unjust life opportunities and exclusions. These themes in FPE are elaborated in the context of climate change and disaster risk in the sections that follow.

## A feminist political ecology of climate change and disaster risk: going beyond the vulnerable feminine subject

Interdisciplinary social science research into the politics of climate change and disaster risk is gaining traction today for obvious reasons. It is not necessary to give an explanation of the most significant environmental issue that frames contemporary politics, policy, and academic research: as is reported almost daily in news media, climatic changes brought on by centuries of capitalist development driven by fossil fuels are causing disasters (e.g., extreme weather events such as floods, droughts, storms) and pose severe risks of such disasters in most parts of the globe. But in the face of exigent action and response to disasters, what often goes unquestioned is the identity of the 'disaster victim'.

An important idea that was crystallized quite early by disaster scholars is that disasters put gender and other forms of social inequality into stark relief (Bankoff et al. 2004; Wisner et al. 2004). Popular gender, climate change, and disaster discourses today revolve around a centred feminine subject – that is, the poor rural woman of the Global South who is negatively affected by climate change. A running logic permeates the discussions: climate change is most adversely felt by vulnerable people in the climate hotspots of the Global South, and chief among them are women, who constitute the largest percentage of the world's poorest. Marshalling quantitative evidence, such as the often cited work of Neumayer and Plümper (2007) on how gender shapes people's experiences of and abilities to survive disaster, serves to make the case for including gender in the climate change and disaster agendas at international and local levels of deliberation. This same thinking argues that women are powerful agents of change and that their full participation is critical to the success of adaptation and mitigation programs, and hence it is important that women and gender experts participate in all decisions related to climate change (GenderCC – Women for Climate Justice 2008). Denton (2002) further remarks that threats resulting from global warming have failed to draw attention to the importance of placing women at the centre: 'poor women are generally on the receiving end of the effects of increasing environmental degradation and depletion of natural resources because of their involvement in, and reliance on, livelihood activities which depend directly on the natural environment' (2002:12). Policy makers, and to some extent women's organizations, invoke the flip side of women as victims (i.e., women as agents) with special capacities to adapt, build resilience, or mitigate the effects of degradation or stresses in their homes and communities. This construct translates into treating women as a labour constituency with assigned disaster risk management and climate adaptation tasks that may serve to add to their already long list of caring roles. The discourse of women as chief victim and caretaker in climate change debates and programs thus resonates with the WED ontology of the centred feminine subject who is pre-disposed to specific caring roles (Resurrección 2013).

As an early counterpoint to these WED-oriented framings of women in disaster and climate change contexts described previously, gender and disasters scholar Elaine Enarson (1998) defined a more complex ontological approach that chimes well with contemporary FPE. She warned that gendered vulnerability to disasters and climate risk does not derive from a single factor such as 'being a woman', but instead vulnerability indicates historically and culturally specific patterns of practices, processes, and power relations that render some groups or persons more disadvantaged than others. Enarson's work also takes the view of other scholars on social vulnerability, arguing that vulnerability is an intrinsically differentiating process, a dynamic condition shaped by existing and emerging inequalities in resource distribution and access, the control individuals exert over choices and opportunities, and historical patterns of social domination and marginalization (Bankoff et al. 2004; Wisner et al. 2004; Eakin and Luers 2006 in Enarson 2012). Through such framing, it is possible to understand how people come to be gendered, disciplined, and regulated as women or men – and as a result, differentially vulnerable – under varying conditions of climate change stresses and disaster risks. Additionally, Andrea Nightingale (2006) argues that vulnerability does not stem solely from a set of intrinsic or fixed vulnerable characteristics, but that attention should instead shift to the kinds of climate-related hardships that will result for specific kinds of people (specific classes and ethnic groups of women and men) due to their different political, economic, and social positions and their uneven power relations. This challenges tendencies to rely on typologies of vulnerable groups that are often used in disaster management. Enarson's and Nightingale's contributions to gender, climate change, and disaster literature echo FPE's view that social subjectivities are shaped through, and reflect, differential access to and control over nature and the experiences of disasters and climate change. This work resonates with FPE's position on the production of gender: subjectivities are dynamic and in-process, contingent, and intersectional. Importantly, they depart from the essentialist feminine subject.

In recent gender, climate change, and disaster studies, scholars such as Hyndman (2008), Cupples (2007), and Arora-Jonsson (2011) challenge the tendency to essentialize women's vulnerability to disasters. They emphasize the need to recognize the historical and embodied contexts of women's and men's lives prior to a disaster, which could in large part explain the differentiated vulnerable positions among types of women and men in the wake of a disaster that do not easily fit into the singular and undifferentiated category of 'disaster victim' in popular discourse (Enarson and Chakrabarti 2009; Huynh and Resurrección 2014; Bradshaw 2015; Resurrección and Sajor 2015). These ideas also chime with political ecology's growing concern with 'socio-natures' (Swyngedouw 1999; Castree and Braun 2001), where disasters and disaster identities are viewed as being socially, politically, and biophysically co-produced, but additionally, as Cupples (2007) argues from the perspective of post-structuralist gender and disaster studies, subjectivities are also performed, materialized, and reworked through both extreme and slow-onset disasters.

These ideas draw from the work of Judith Butler as she describes the production of gender as ontologically producing a particular understanding of gender into a 'fact', a repetitive exercise of materializing what is named (Anon. interview 1994). Within FPE, scholars similarly draw from feminist post-structural theory to frame the gendered political ecology subject (see Sundberg 2004; Harris 2006; Nightingale 2006; Elmhirst 2011). No pre-given identities exist; rather, identities are dynamically forged through everyday power-laden practices and discourses in specific ecological contexts. The framing of disasters by aid, disaster, and humanitarian specialists, for example, may tend to define particular identities, such as victims, dependents, survivors, and aid workers. Those left out of the frame may not receive immediate emergency assistance from humanitarian organizations. Emergency response almost always targets 'women and children' first, as men are left to fend for themselves, which in some contexts has led to more male than female fatalities, such as in Nicaragua and Honduras in the wake of Hurricane Mitch in 2000 (Correia 2001).

In a post-disaster context, Hyndman (2008) demonstrates complexity by describing how different social practices throughout two disasters (the Tamil-Singhalese war and later, the Indian Ocean tsunami in 2004) produced subjectivities through the intersections of gender, ethnicity, and religion. The result was a complex mosaic of the performed identities of widows with differentiated gendered and cultural rights and restrictions. War widows affected by the tsunami had very few remaining relations of support since many of their relatives were wiped out by the tsunami; they 'lost everything in one day' and thus sought to remarry. Widows of war still relied on many surviving kinship networks and thus did not remarry. Sinhala women and widows were more economically and socially advantaged compared with Tamil and Muslim widows whose mobility is culturally controlled, and who have fewer employment opportunities. Their embodied experiences of loss, cultural restrictions, and obligations, and their level of access to economic resources, shaped the widows' capacities to fully or only partially recover from disasters. Recovery and resilience-building efforts often gloss over the specific needs of disaster-afflicted women that arise from these experiences and performed intersectional identities in disaster contexts.

## From impacts to embodied knowledge, emotions, and belonging

As discussed previously, international gender and climate change debates largely focus on the *impacts* of climate change and disasters on women, who are often understood as a specifically vulnerable group. 'The notion that women are most vulnerable victims of climate change and its impacts is what makes many [climate change] negotiators receptive to women and gender aspects' (Röhr 2009:59 in Arora-Jonsson 2011:747). The single-axis identity of the 'climate-vulnerable woman' is marshalled to legitimize gender mainstreaming in climate change-related activities. 'Gender' is therefore rarely mentioned in official climate change discourses, except when impacts count women as climate victims or as mothers who defend families and household livelihoods (for a critique, see MacGregor 2010; Tuana 2013; Rocheleau and Nirmal 2015). This can potentially forge dangerous liaisons with positivist and neoliberal managerial approaches that privilege material and measurable impacts to justify interventions and policy change. Climate change and disasters, as a result, can be 'reduced', 'managed', or 'mitigated'[5] through technical means and as scholars caution, in ways that are de-politicized, masculinized, and scientized (MacGregor 2010; Tschakert 2012). This approach in many ways creates persistent silences around the political economic causes of climate change, disasters, and the disadvantage and disempowerment that they exacerbate.

It may be instructive to view the managerial and techno-scientific approaches to climate change that are adopted by the UN and national governments through the lens of feminist critiques of science, where objectivity and value-free knowledge as the goals of scientific inquiry have been questioned. For example, the works of Sandra Harding (1986) and Donna Haraway (1988) challenge the dominant assumption that scientists and decision-makers are separate from their bodies, social position and locations, where objective truth and science arrive as the 'view from nowhere'. Nancy Tuana (2013) points to the feminist search for a 'successor science' that rightfully considers gender as an analytical category richly and complexly situated and intersectional. Informed by this critical perspective, feminist political ecologists accept that knowledge is partial, situated, and emerges from embodied social locations. Empirical evidence collected in the field suggests that gender, if treated as a measurable indicator and stripped of its multi-dimensionality and social embeddedness, can serve to reinforce problematic assumptions about women. What seems to be missing and often overlooked is a FPE analysis that recognizes the complexities of emotions, embodied ways of knowing, and a sense of belonging to place.

In their book *Practicing Feminist Political Ecologies*, Wendy Harcourt, Leila Harris, and Julie Nelson (2015) plead for a practice of theorizing 'from where we are'. By this they mean the need to theorize from everyday, embodied, and affective lives in order to articulate alternatives to neoliberalism, and to serve as correctives to governance scales and priorities that singularly focus on statist or global/transnational interests. These articulations complement Rocheleau's (2011) study in the Dominican Republic that demonstrates how networked and rooted assemblages of resources, animals, landscape features, technologies, institutions, and human beings help us to see embedded, uneven, and dynamic relations of power in everyday life. This analysis applies equally to disaster and climate change contexts.

People's experiences of disasters and extreme or slow-onset climatic changes are themselves meaning-making events. People make sense of their present and future life trajectories as they embody these events, often in emotional terms. Emotions are therefore part of the conscious and unconscious fabric of human action, reaction, and sense- and meaning-making when confronted with changes wrought by disasters, and other environmental and climate impacts. During the Bangkok flood in 2011, for example, I interviewed twelve female residents in a northern peri-urban province near Bangkok whose homes were damaged, and who involuntarily moved to safer places, anxiously returning home at a later time.[6] Their stories revealed that emotions about home unpack how the women lived through their disaster experience, as these same emotions shaped their eventual return home amid the risks of further damage and loss. For the women the flood triggered emotions that were tied to the destruction of their homes and personal possessions. It unsettled their sense of self and place, building fears and anxieties over possible loss of refuge, stable social networks, and ultimately their identity. Once away from home, the flood-displaced women I spoke to expressed that they struggled to re-acquire some cohesive sense of self as they lived temporarily in an alien and distant place with relatives. They sought stability in gender roles by taking up gendered activities such as maternal care for their hosts, while keeping a watch on floodwater levels from a distance, activities normally expected of men. The displaced residents returned to their flooded homes a few weeks after they left. This example shows that the notion of home by itself becomes fixed in emotions and in the imagination as 'something that must be returned to' and re-claimed as part of intimate embodied space and sense of self (Morrice 2012).

Lingering and slow-onset climate changes that deteriorate landscapes and livelihoods have also elicited emotions of growing loss and hopelessness, gradually eroding people's sense of place and belonging. Feminist political ecologist Petra Tschakert and her colleagues (2013) studied people from northern Ghana, some of whom remain in their homelands and others who have left for Accra, the capital. Their study draws attention to the subtle convergence of environmental and social decay in the face of altered landscapes, growing dissatisfaction with life, weak state intervention, and dwindling social networks. Climate change was only one among several reasons why some people chose to leave, a decision that simmered for a long time in their minds, as they witnessed the slow and gradual loss of livelihood options. Those left behind struggle to survive and hold on to their sense of place. Tschakert et al.'s study adopts a grounded and slightly de-centred approach to researching climate change impacts that emphasizes the embodied experiences and place-based manifestations of global and local conditions through landscapes of everyday life. Such a conceptualization of the embodied experiences of climate change could counterweigh dominant managerial approaches that focus on uni-dimensional impacts requiring mitigation. Similarly, this example also shows that through the prism of emotions and embodied experiences, people agonizingly resist being 'dis-placed', thus profoundly challenging growing national security discourses that build spectres of climate change-induced mass migrations. An FPE lens can therefore potentially expose mismatches between people's everyday embodied realities and institutional programs and practices. This point also resonates with the rich tradition of FPE and the pioneering work of Rocheleau et al. (1996) to chronicle struggles of women for survival, voice, and collective action, as they live under risky and degrading environmental conditions, which are outcomes of political economic and ecological power dynamics at multiple scales.

## Conclusion

Some feminists and gender advocates working in the environment and development field continue to define gender, climate change, and disaster agendas in such a way that women are portrayed as victims but with special capabilities and knowledge to enable them to mitigate shocks and stresses. While important in some respects, this approach inadvertently plays into the growing techno-managerial approaches of risk reduction programs, as I have explained. It also sustains the single-axis and essentialist orientation for which criticism has been levelled at WED and ecofeminist development scholars since the 1990s. I argue that the strength of feminist political ecology lies in its possibilities for feminist engagements in ecopolitics without avoiding the workings of power or relying on 'essences' that assume pre-given gender identities and a natural order outside history. FPE frees us to understand that 'nature-as-we-know-it' has become increasingly produced by human activities, which therefore can be re-examined and put in check. It envisions a better world that is socially and environmentally just and free of fossil fuel dependence controlled by big business players. FPE offers nuanced, grounded, and situated research and understandings of emotions and embodied knowing that avoids the shortcomings of universalism and the grand narratives of neoliberal growth and scientific truth.

I have shown in this chapter that there is a growing body of promising work in the field of FPE that uses interdisciplinary theorizing and the analysis of specific case studies that show the ways gender identities and social difference are socially constituted through struggles and embodied experiences of environment, disasters, and climate change. FPE can potentially build on current efforts to explore and enact diverse and fair economies (Gibson-Graham 2008; Gibson-Graham et al. 2013); inspire alternative feminist ethics of care in environment and disaster contexts (Lawson 2007; Jarosz 2011; Whittle et al. 2012); and mitigate the effects of climate change through just and collaborative action in communities (Buechler and Hanson 2015). Solutions and pathways are multiple, and FPE recognizes that there are no one-size-fits-all solutions. And these initiatives help bolster hopes that there is potential for forming coalitions and alliances both transnationally and within national boundaries.

## Notes

1  Notably in the following agreements: *Agenda 21*, the UN Convention on Biological Diversity (1993), and the UN Convention to Combat Desertification (1994). There were no explicit provisions in the UN Framework Convention on Climate Change (1995).
2  Both factual and conceptual assumptions about the Chipko Movement have been called into question by, among others, the contributors to a special collection of journal articles in the *Journal of Peasant Studies* (vol. 25, no. 4, 1998).
3  From the wider field of development policy studies, we are reminded by Lewis and Mosse (2006) that planning exercises have the propensity to mobilize simplifications of policy and politics. Political simplifications, however, are incapable of addressing the complex problems on the ground. It therefore seems far less cumbersome and 'politically acceptable' for planners to relate to the idea of 'women as victims', and thereby view them as agents of positive environmental action, than to address the complex drivers of gendered relations of power within which they are embedded in the first place.
4  Earlier iterations of FPE shared ecofeminism's tendency to bring women's knowledge into environmental decision-making and highlighted the role of women's collective activism around environmental issues (Moeckli and Braun 2001).
5  Peet et al. (2011) pre-dated the UNFCCC COP21 Agreement in their critical assessment of global climate governance as focused largely on emissions counting that obscures and de-politicizes the emissions-producing practices that drive neoliberal economic growth.
6  Primary research was conducted under the project 'Climate change adaptation in peri-urban Southeast Asia', supported by the International Development Research Centre (IDRC), 2012–2015. The author is grateful to Kanophan Jongjarb for her assistance in this project.

## References

Agarwal, B. (1992a) 'The gender and environment debate: Lessons from India', *Feminist Studies* 18(1): 119–158.

Agarwal, B. (1992b) *Gender Relations and Food Security: Coping With Seasonality, Drought and Famine in South Asia*. Boulder, CO: Westview Press.

Anon (1994) *Gender as Performance: An Interview with Judith Butler*. Online. Available at: www.radicalphilosophy.com.ezp.sub.su.se/interview/judith-butler (accessed 7 June 2016).

Arora-Jonsson, S. (2011) 'Virtue and vulnerability: Discourses on women, gender and climate change', *Global Environmental Change* 21(2): 744–751.

Bankoff, G., Hilhorst, D. and Frerks, G. (2004) *Mapping Vulnerability: Disasters, Development and People*. London: Routledge.

Bavington, D., Grzetic, B. and Neis, B. (2004) 'The feminist political ecology of fishing down: Reflections from Newfoundland and Labrador', *Studies in Political Economy* 73(1): 159–182.

Bradshaw, S. (2015) *Gender, Development and Disasters*. Cheltenham: Edward Elgar Publishing.

Buechler, S. and Hanson, A.-M. S. (eds) (2015) *A Political Ecology of Women, Water and Global Environmental Change*. Abingdon: Routledge.

Carney, M. A. (2014) 'The biopolitics of "food insecurity": Towards a critical political ecology of the body in studies of women's transnational migration', *Journal of Political Ecology* 21: 1–18.

Castree, N. and Braun, B. (eds) (2001) *Social Nature: Theory, Practice and Politics*. Oxford: Blackwell Publishing.

Cornwall, A., Harrison, E. and Whitehead, A. (2007) 'Gender myths and feminist fables: The struggle for interpretive power in gender and development', *Development and Change* 38(1): 1–20.

Correia, M. C. (2001) 'Hurricane Mitch: The gender effects of coping and crises', *The World Bank*. Online. Available at: http://documents.worldbank.org/curated/en/2001/09/2011702/hurricane-mitch-gender-effects-coping-crises (accessed 6 June 2016).

Cranney, B. (2001) *Local Environment and Lived Experience: The Mountain Women of Himachal Pradesh*. New Delhi: Sage Publications.

Cupples, J. (2007) 'Gender and Hurricane Mitch: Reconstructing subjectivities after disaster', *Disasters* 31(2): 155–175.

Dankelman, I. and Davidson, J. (1988) *Women and the Environment in the Third World: Alliance for the Future*. London: Routledge.

Denton, F. (2002) 'Climate change vulnerability, impacts, and adaptation: Why does gender matter?', *Gender and Development* 10(2): 10–20.

Dirks, N. B., Eley, G. and Ortner, S. B. (eds) (1993) *Culture / Power / History: A Reader in Contemporary Social Theory*. Princeton, NJ: Princeton University Press.

Eakin, H. and Luers, A. L. (2006) 'Assessing the vulnerability of social-environmental systems', *Annual Review of Environment and Resources* 31(1): 365–394.

Elmhirst, R. (2011) 'Introducing new feminist political ecologies', *Geoforum* 42(2): 129–132.

Enarson, E. (1998) 'Through women's eyes: A gendered research agenda for disaster social science', *Disasters* 22(2): 157–173.

Enarson, E. (2012) *Women Confronting Natural Disaster: From Vulnerability to Resilience*. Boulder, CO: Lynne Rienner Publishers.

Enarson, E. and Chakrabarti, P. G. D. (eds) (2009) *Women, Gender and Disaster: Global Issues and Initiatives*. Los Angeles: Sage Publications.

GenderCC – Women for Climate Justice (2008) 'Recommendations: Network of women ministers and leaders for environment', *Bali*. Online. Available at: www.gendercc.net/fileadmin/inhalte/Dokumente/UNFCCC_conferences/Women_ministers_Bali-Declaration_COP13.pdf.

Gibson-Graham, J. K. (2008) 'Diverse economies: Performative practices for "other worlds"', *Progress in Human Geography* 32(5): 613–632.

Gibson-Graham, J. K., Cameron, J. and Healy, S. (2013) *Take Back the Economy: An Ethical Guide for Transforming Our Communities*. Minneapolis: University of Minnesota Press.

Hanson (2015) 'Shoes in the seaweed and bottles on the beach: Global garbage and women's oral histories of socio-environmental change in coastal Yucatan', in Buechler, S. and Hanson, A.-M. (eds) *A Political Ecology of Women, Water and Global Environmental Change*. Oxon: Routledge, 165–184.

Haraway, D. (1988) 'Situated knowledges: The science question in feminism and the privilege of partial perspective', *Feminist Studies* 14(3): 579–599.

Harcourt, W., Harris, L. and Nelson, I. L. (2015) *Practicing Feminist Political Ecologies: Moving Beyond the 'Green Economy'*. London: Zed Books.

Harding, S. G. (1986) *The Science Question in Feminism*. Ithaca, NY: Cornell University Press.

Harding, S. G. (2008) *Sciences From Below: Feminisms, Postcolonialities, and Modernities*. Durham, NC: Duke University Press.

Harris, L. M. (2006) 'Irrigation, gender, and social geographies of the changing waterscapes of southeastern Anatolia', *Environment and Planning D: Society and Space* 24(2): 187–213.

Hawkins, R. and Ojeda, D. (2011) 'Gender and environment: Critical tradition and new challenges', *Environment and Planning D: Society and Space* 29(2): 237–253.

Huynh, P. T. A. and Resurrección, B. P. (2014) 'Women's differentiated vulnerability and adaptations to climate-related agricultural water scarcity in rural Central Vietnam', *Climate and Development* 6(3): 226–237.

Hyndman, J. (2008) 'Feminism, conflict and disasters in post-tsunami Sri Lanka', *Gender, Technology and Development* 12(1): 101–121.

Jackson, C. (1993a) 'Doing what comes naturally? Women and environment in development', *World Development* 21(12): 1947–1963.

Jackson, C. (1993b) 'Environmentalisms and gender interests in the Third World', *Development and Change* 24(4): 649–677.

Jarosz, L. (2011) 'Nourishing women: Toward a feminist political ecology of community supported agriculture in the United States', *Gender, Place & Culture* 18(3): 307–326.

Lawson, V. (2007) 'Geographies of care and responsibility', *Annals of the Association of American Geographers* 97(1): 1–11.

Leach, M. (2015) *Gender Equality and Sustainable Development*. Oxon: Routledge.

Lewis, D. and Mosse, D. (2006) 'Encountering order and disjuncture: Contemporary anthropological perspectives on the organization of development', *Oxford Development Studies* 34(1): 1–13.

Loftus, A. (2012) *Everyday Environmentalism: Creating an Urban Political Ecology.* Minneapolis: University of Minnesota Press.

MacGregor, S. (2010) 'Gender and climate change: From impacts to discourses', *Journal of the Indian Ocean Region* 6(2): 223–238.

May, V. M. (2014) '"Speaking into the void"? Intersectionality critiques and epistemic backlash', *Hypatia* 29(1): 94–112.

Mies, M. and Shiva, V. (1993) *Ecofeminism.* Halifax, NS: Fernwood Publications.

Moeckli, J. and Braun, B. (2001) 'Gendered natures: Feminism, politics, and social nature', in Castree, N. and Braun, B. (eds) *Social Nature: Theory, Practice and Politics.* Oxford: Blackwell Publishing, 112–132.

Morrice, S. (2012) 'Heartache and Hurricane Katrina: Recognising the influence of emotion in post-disaster return decisions', *Area* 45(1): 33–39.

Neumayer, E. and Plümper, T. (2007) 'The gendered nature of natural disasters: The impact of catastrophic events on the gender gap in life expectancy, 1981–2002', *Annals of the Association of American Geographers* 97(3): 551–566.

Nightingale, A. (2006) 'The nature of gender: Work, gender, and environment', *Environment and Planning D: Society and Space* 24(2): 165–185.

Paulson, S. and Gezon, L. L. (eds) (2005) *Political Ecology Across Spaces, Scales, and Social Groups.* Princeton, NJ: Rutgers University Press.

Peet, R., Robbins, P. and Watts, M. (eds) (2011) *Global Political Ecology.* London: Routledge.

Rao, B. (1991) 'Dominant constructions of women and nature in the social science literature', *CES/CNS Pamphlet 2.* Santa Cruz, CA: University of California.

Resurrección, B. P. (2013) 'Persistent women and environment linkages in climate change and sustainable development agendas', *Women's Studies International Forum* 40: 33–43.

Resurrección, B. P. and Sajor, E. E. (2015) 'Gender, floods and mobile subjects: A post-disaster view', in Lund, R., Doneys, P. and Resurrección, B. P. (eds) *Gendered Entanglements: Revisiting Gender in Rapidly Changing Asia.* Copenhagen, Denmark: Nordic Institute of Asian Studies, 207–234.

Rocheleau, D. E. (2011) 'Rooted networks, webs of relation, and the power of situated science: Bringing the models back down to earth in Zambrano', in Goldman, M. J., Nadasdy, P. and Turner, M. D. (eds) *Knowing Nature.* Chicago: University of Chicago Press, 209–226.

Rocheleau, D. E. (2015) 'A situated view of feminist political ecology from my networks, roots and territories', in Harcourt, W. and Nelson, I. L. (eds) *Practicing Feminist Political Ecologies: Moving Beyond the 'Green Economy'*, London: Zed Books, 29–66.

Rocheleau, D. E. and Nirmal, P. (2015) 'Feminist political ecologies: Grounded, networked and rooted on earth', in Baksh, R. and Harcourt, W. (eds) *The Oxford Handbook of Transnational Feminist Movements.* Oxford: Oxford University Press, 793–814.

Rocheleau, D. E., Thomas-Slayter, B. P. and Wangari, E. (eds) (1996) *Feminist Political Ecology: Global Issues and Local Experiences.* London: Routledge.

Rodda, A. (1993) *Women and the Environment.* London: Zed Books.

Schroeder, R. A. (1999) *Shady Practices: Agroforestry and Gender Politics in the Gambia.* Berkeley, CA: University of California Press.

Shiva, V. (1989) *Staying Alive: Women, Ecology and Development.* London: Zed Books.

Sontheimer, S. (1991) *Women and the Environment.* New York: Monthly Review Press.

Sundberg, J. (2004) 'Identities in the making: Conservation, gender and race in the Maya Biosphere Reserve, Guatemala', *Gender, Place and Culture: A Journal of Feminist Geography* 11(1): 43–66.

Sundberg, J. (2017) 'Feminist political ecology', in Richardson, D. B. (ed) *International Encyclopedia of Geography: People, the Earth, Environment and Technology.* New York: Wiley-Blackwell & Association of American Geographers.

Swyngedouw, E. (1999) 'Modernity and hybridity: Nature, regeneracionismo, and the production of the Spanish waterscape, 1890–1930', *Annals of the Association of American Geographers* 3: 445–463.

Tschakert, P. (2012) 'From impacts to embodied experiences: Tracing political ecology in climate change research', *Geografisk Tidsskrift-Danish Journal of Geography* 112(2): 144–158.

Tschakert, P., Tutu, R. and Alcaro, A. (2013) 'Embodied experiences of environmental and climatic changes in landscapes of everyday life in Ghana', *Emotion, Space and Society* 7: 13–25.

Tuana, N. (2013) 'Gendering climate knowledge for justice: Catalyzing a new research agenda', in Alston, M. and Whittenbury, K. (eds) *Research, Action and Policy: Addressing the Gendered Impacts of Climate Change.* Dordrecht: Springer Netherlands, 17–31.

Udas, P. B. and Zwarteveen, M. Z. (2010) 'Can water professionals meet gender goals? A case study of the Department of Irrigation in Nepal', *Gender & Development* 18(1): 87–97.

Watts, M. J. (2015) 'Now and then: The origins of political ecology and the rebirth of adaptation as a form of thought', in Perreault, T. A., Bridge, G. and McCarthy, J. (eds) *Routledge Handbook of Political Ecology.* Abingdon, UK: Routledge, 19–50.

Whittle, R., Walker, M., Medd, W. and Mort, M. (2012) 'Flood of emotions: Emotional work and long-term disaster recovery', *Emotion, Space and Society* 5(1): 60–69.

Wisner, B., Blaikie, P., Cannon, T. and Davis, I. (2004) *At Risk: Natural Hazards, People's Vulnerability and Disasters* (second edition). London: Routledge.

# 5

# ECOFEMINIST POLITICAL ECONOMY

## A green and feminist agenda

*Mary Mellor*

## Introduction

Ecological feminist political economy is an alternative way of looking at economies that puts forward proposals for meeting human needs in ways that are ecologically sustainable and socially just. It also provides a critique of current economies and mainstream economics that challenges conventional economics' claim to be a value free science. Instead of seeing economies as natural forms based on universal economic laws, ecofeminist political economy sees modern economies as ecologically unsustainable and socially unjust. Current economic structures are not naturally emerging immutable facts, but gendered human constructs. Central to an ecofeminist approach to political economy is the critique of those current economic structures including the concept 'economy' itself. It also challenges economics to return to its roots as a critical perspective.

Political economy was the earliest approach to the study of human economies. It emerged out of moral philosophy to ask fundamental questions about how human beings organize their economies. It originally looked at the complex interconnections between production and trade in relation to law, social customs and government action. It questioned the relationship between individuals and society, states and markets, and the distribution of income and wealth (Barratt Brown 1995). Eventually it was replaced by an approach to economics based on a scientific model that claimed to be a value free study of rational economic actors engaged in market exchange. Ecofeminist political economy returns to the earlier role of economic analysis and challenges both the theory and practice of mainstream economics. It asks fundamental questions about what an economy is and how it is framed in relation to the lives of embodied and gendered subjects (i.e., men and women) and the natural world. In addressing the material basis of human existence in nature, it has roots in Marxist political economy, green economics and feminism (Mellor 1997a, 2007; Salleh 1997, 2009; Perkins and Kuiper 2005).

This chapter provides an overview of an ecofeminist approach to political economy, which arguably has been one of the most important foundations of gender and environment scholarship for the past three decades. It is a perspective that brings together insights from three traditions of heterodox economic thought: Marxian materialism, ecological (or green) economics, and feminist analysis of the gender division of labour and the feminization of unpaid caring and provisioning work (social reproduction). I begin with a discussion of how political economy and the critique of mainstream economics developed in the early political economy of Marx. I will then explore the main arguments of green and feminist economics before bringing them together to make the case for extending political economy to embrace the intersection of the exploitation of nature and the exploitation and marginalization of women's lives and work. I conclude with some proposals for creating socially just societies that live within their ecological means, including sufficiency provisioning and democratizing money.

## Marxian political economy

Marx's theory started from the assertion that the foundation of human economies lay in the interaction between human labour and the environment or the natural world (Marx 1844; Parsons 1977). The way in which this relationship was constructed had evolved through human history. However, under capitalism (and other structures of domination) the relationship between humanity and nature was not direct. Humans did not interact with nature as individuals but as social classes. Ownership was a critical issue: those who owned the natural resources and the means to exploit them dominated those who were without property. The latter had no economic asset other than their capacity to labour. Dominant groups therefore did not interact with nature through their own labour, but the labour of others. Production or other economic activity does not take place because it is necessary for human well-being, but because it is profitable with wages kept as low as possible.

The core of Marxist theory is a study of the material relationship between socio-economic classes and between class-ridden humanity and the natural world. This materialist analysis is also at the centre of ecofeminist political economy, but the focus is upon gender rather than class as the social structure that is exploited. Gendered labour, the exploitation and marginalization of work that is feminized and performed mostly by women (still often regarded as 'women's work'), is seen as key to the destructive relationship between humanity and the natural world. Ecofeminist political economy is therefore Marxian in that it draws analytical frameworks from Marx without being limited to his theories of capitalist production. In focusing upon gender in this context, ecofeminist political economy would not want to ignore or deny other social structures of inequality such as class, heterosexism, racism, and colonialism. Equally, Marx, and particularly Engels, were not blind to gender inequalities, nor the destruction of nature. As Howard Parsons (1977) points out, scattered throughout their work, and in their letters, they express their concern about the destructive impact of human activities on nature. As Vaillancourt notes, Volume 2 of *Capital* (edited by Engels after Marx's death) 'describes the plundering of the forests under capitalism in very modern terms, such as one might easily encounter today in the writings of political ecologists' (1996:55). Although Marx saw humans as materially embedded in nature, he argued that the structures of the capitalist economy alienated humans from it. Dominant classes only saw nature as private exploitable property, while most people had no relation to the natural world, other than as waged labour under which they had no choice but to do what was requested of them however destructive (Marx 1844). In *Origins of the Family, Private Property and the State,* Engels (1884) made a connection between the ownership of private property and the 'enslavement' of women in marriage. While Engels also recognized the importance of domestic and reproductive labour, that is, the labour necessary to reproduce the workforce, these were not reflected in Marxist economic theory, which was focused on production.

## Green economics: saving nature but gender blind

Green economics is a politically engaged form of ecological economics that argues that societies should be embedded within ecosystems, that markets are social structures that should respond to social and environmental priorities, and that economists concerned about sustainability should focus on questions of time, justice, and the irreplaceability of nature.[1] Unlike Marx, who wanted the working class to capture the productive power of capitalism for the benefit of the people under socialism, green economists see modern productivist economies as ecologically unsustainable. Rather than starting from the exploitation of labour, they start from the destructive impact of human activities on nature; a socially just economy must also be an ecologically sustainable one (Cato 2012). Current economies are seen as committed to constant expansion and destructive growth that do not produce real prosperity in terms of human flourishing on a finite planet (Jackson 2011). An important aspect of modern economies is that while they attach a value to most of their activities, they do not acknowledge practically or economically their impact on natural or biophysical environments. Natural resources, particularly those held in common (that is, not privately owned by any economic agent), are treated as a free good. Resource depletion or environmental degradation are not acknowledged or costed into the value of goods and services – in other words, they are *externalized*. Given that depletion and damage is externalized in this way (that is, they are not paid for by the user/polluter), there is no incentive for the abuse of the environment to cease.

Green economists seek 'to build a society in which we can live better lives by working less and consuming less' (Latouche 2009:9). Green proposals range from accommodation with the market economy – through regulation, market measures (e.g., carbon trading) and ecological taxes – to wholesale abandonment of modern economic structures for local subsistence production. Ecofeminist political economy shares the concern of green economics that current economic activities are unsustainable (Bennholdt-Thomsen and Mies 1999). However, there are dangers if the gender implications of green reforms are not considered; women can be disadvantaged by green policies (see the chapter by Littig in this volume). For example, evidence from Costa Rica indicates that poor rural women are paying the price of the Kyoto protocol as they are driven from rainforest areas that have been designated as carbon sinks (Isla 2009 and in this volume). The result is that many are now working in the sex industry.

One of the earliest thinkers directly to link ecological destructiveness with economic structures was the English Nobel laureate Frederick Soddy (Merricks 1996). He drew a distinction between real wealth – that is, the wealth of the environment, and virtual wealth, meaning money and money value (Soddy 1926). He was particularly concerned about debt. He pointed out that natural systems were limited and prone to entropy, which entails moving from usable to unusable states. Debts, on the other hand, grew exponentially. The incompatibility of limited natural systems with growth-oriented economic systems has led to calls for a move toward a 'steady state economy' that reflects the capacity of nature to absorb human activity without degradation (Daly et al. 2013; Czech 2013). This has led to demands for 'degrowth', shrinking resource use back to sustainable levels by unwinding current economic structures.

The demand for degrowth is directed against consumerist economies. It seeks to replace destructive growth with sustainable flourishing (D'Alisa et al. 2015) or sustainable prosperity (Jackson 2011). As a key figure in the degrowth (or décroissance) movement, French economic theorist Serge Latouche sees the potential of a 'concrete utopia' of sustainability if people can be weaned from their commitment to 'the job'. He wants them instead to rediscover what he sees as 'the repressed dimensions of life' (Latouche 2009:40). These are

> the leisure to do one's duty as a citizen, the pleasure of the freedom to engage in freely chosen arts and crafts activities, the sensation of having found time to play, contemplate, meditate, enjoy conversations or quite simply to enjoy being alive.
>
> *(41)*

But what is missing from Latouche's vision, and from many non-feminist (male) writers in this vein, is domestic work. This is because it appears neither in the world of paid work or the world of self-motivated work and leisure. Variously called social reproduction, caring labour or women's work, the low and unpaid work, which is predominantly performed by women, is the focus of feminist economics, the third leg of ecofeminist political economy.

## The roots of feminist economics

The strongest roots of ecofeminist political economy lie in feminist economics, and particularly in the critique of unpaid domestic and community work – the work of the body that I broadly categorize as 'women's work'. However, while all feminists recognize the problem of gender inequalities in the informal (often called private) sphere and the formal economy (that is, activities recognized and rewarded *with money*), there are different emphases on strategies for finding a way forward. A major perspective in feminist economics is concerned with achieving gender equality in the workplace under current economic conditions. Yet doing so would not meet either the Marxist or green agenda as it does not challenge the status quo.

A major movement in early 1970s feminism was the demand that women's domestic work should be given a wage (Dalla Costa and James 1972). This demand was opposed by other feminists on the grounds that it would trap women in low waged household work. Nevertheless the issue of the unfair externalization of women's work was taken up by all sides of the debate. In the same way that green economists wanted to get the work of nature acknowledged, feminist economists sought recognition of the value of women's unpaid work. They demanded that political economy be expanded to include the work of social reproduction; all the work needed to sustain human societies that is not recognized in the more limited concept of 'production' (Picchio 1992). Marilyn Waring's 1989 book *If Women Counted* was a key study that established the need to value and quantify both women's work and the value of unspoilt environments. Nearly thirty years later, however, there is still a question mark over how far feminists in general connect gender inequality with environmental concerns such as climate change (Dankelman 2010; MacGregor 2010).

Ecofeminist political economy therefore brings together insights from the three legs of Marxian materialism, radical green economics and the feminist economic analysis of women's work and gender inequality in order to explore the materiality of human existence in nature. Starting from *human embeddedness in nature* and the *inescapable frailties of human embodiment*, it challenges the way in which current economies are constructed. It draws on Marxian and green analysis to show that human lives and economies are embedded in the environment. It draws from feminism the awareness that human bodies have to be nurtured and sustained in ways that economic theories do not acknowledge. It is important to stress that in doing so, ecofeminist political economy does not draw an essentialist identity between women and nature (a 'crime' of which it has been unfairly accused). Women are not assumed to have a 'natural' affinity with nature. The relationship is a material and structural one; the common experience of exploitation, damage, and marginalization that women and the natural world share. The key argument is that they are both *externalized by current economies*.

## Ecofeminist political economy and the materiality of 'women's work'

When ecofeminism emerged in the early 1970s, it was often criticized for essentialism, seeming to claim that women were more in tune with nature because they shared its work of nourishing life (see Mellor 1997a; Thompson and MacGregor in this volume). Socialist and mainstream liberal feminists were the most critical while radical feminists were more sympathetic. Later, poststructuralist feminists called into question the very category of 'women'. However, the more materialist ecofeminism, upon which ecofeminist political economy is based, always rejected essentialist notions of woman-ness but focused upon women's life and work as the basis of a structural critique (Mellor 1997a, 1997b). It is and has always been a *materialist* approach, in that it is based upon the gendering of work, not the bodily differences between male and female.

Women's work was not analyzed by early materialist ecofeminist scholars in terms of women's essential nature as a mother or caregiver, but as an exploitable resource. The identification of women with nature was not seen as an affinity, but a reflection of the common experience of being externalized yet exploited by modern economies. Externalization, as explained previously, is the failure of formal economic accounting to 'cost in' the work of nature or women's work. One of the works that launched the structural analysis of the exploitation of women's work and its link with the treatment of nature was German sociologist Maria Mies' 1986 book, *Patriarchy and Accumulation on a World Scale*, although a decade earlier Rosemary Radford Ruether had made the same connection:

> Women must see that there can be no liberation for them and no solution to the eco-
> logical crisis within a society whose fundamental model of relationships continues to
> be one of domination. They must unite the demands of the women's movement with
> those of the ecological movement to envision a radical reshaping of the basic socio-
> economic relations and . . . underlying values of . . . society.
>
> *(Ruether 1975:204)*

Contemporary ecofeminist political economy as a body of scholarship remains focused upon the work required to sustain the human body: care, nurture, hygiene, development, and servicing (Mellor 2009). This work is not necessarily exclusively done by women; it can be done by children, low status men or high status men by choice. However, it is work associated with women; it is gendered as feminine, and therefore given low status. To focus on feminized caring and provisioning work is not to argue that other feminist approaches to gender inequality are not important such as the politics of the body (Phipps 2014) or gender injustice (Jaggar 2014). However, the focus of ecofeminist political economy is the gendering of human embodiment in relation to human existence. What has been generally categorized as 'women's work' and often undertaken by women (whether paid or unpaid) is central to the enabling of humans to meet their bodily requirements as physical beings. What is important is that this work is not associated with, or perceived as undertaken by, the construct 'Economic Man'. It is not of concern to conventional 'malestream' economics. For this reason, in this chapter I retain the concept 'women's work' to describe the marginalized work of social reproduction.

While feminists have long debated the 'domestic labour' question, the debate has tended to focus upon its economic relation to the capitalist economy, how surplus value was extracted from women's domestic work, or whether it should be waged (see Weeks 2011). Ecofeminist political economy builds upon these arguments but extends it to the ecological underpinnings of the formal economy. As Adelheid Biesecker and Sabine Hofmeister argue, it is vital to look at the processes of mediation between society and nature, in particular the work of (re)productivity that would recognize that 'the processes involved in the regeneration and restoration of human and nonhuman life are intrinsic to each and every process involving the production of goods and services' (2010:1707). Ariel Salleh (2009) describes this as 'meta-industrial' work that creates 'metabolic value'. She sees capitalism as owing a 'debt' at three levels: social debt to exploited labour, embodied debt to reproductive labour and ecological debt for damage to the natural metabolism (i.e., nature itself; Salleh 2009:24).

The externalization of women's work is ecologically dangerous because women's lives as reflected in domestic and caring work represents the embodiedness of humanity, which in turn reflects human existence as part of the natural world (Mellor 2013). This does not mean that humans are determined by their bodies or their environment, but rather that they cannot ultimately transcend them. What is important about the exclusion of women's lives from the notion of the economic is that women's work has become the repository of the inconvenience of human existence. Women's work represents human immanence, or its embodied materialism (Salleh 2009). This enables a seemingly transcendent construct to emerge: 'Economic Man' (who may be female, but is more generally male). Economic Man appears to be able to escape the limitations of human embodiment and 'his' embeddedness in nature.

## Women's work and the construction of 'Economic Man'

Economic Man (EM) is both real and unreal. 'He' is the image upon which modern economies have been constructed and 'he' is an aspect of many economic participants. At various moments in the days and lives of individuals they may exhibit features of EM, but 'he' cannot exist as a whole person, living a whole day or a whole life. 'He' cannot be embodied or embedded in nature.

Economic Man is assumed to be fit, mobile, able-bodied, and unencumbered by domestic or other responsibilities (Mellor 1997b). 'He' is disembodied, separated from the daily cycle of the life of the body and from the human life cycle. 'He' transcends the real world of the body, as the material body (male or female) lives in *biological time*, the time it takes to rest, recover, grow up, and grow old. EM only lives in the hours of paid work. The economy only values the active worker and takes no responsibility for the rest of 'his' life-cycle or daily cycle. While many people derive high rewards and status in these activities, many more do not. EM may also be a low status and exploited worker.

EM is also alienated from the real life of products and processes. These appear only as traded commodities or consumable conveniences. 'He' takes no responsibility for the life-cycle of those goods or services; they appear and are discarded, vanishing from 'his' gaze. Their origin and disposal is not marked any more than the source of clean water or the disposal of excreta. In the same way as 'he' transcends 'his' bodily life, EM is disembedded from the ecosystem. Consumption is not limited by local growing seasons. The ability to draw on resources from around the world obscures ecological limits or environmental damage. There is no concern about the loss of resources for future generations, loss of habitat for other species, loss of biodiversity, the loss of peace, quiet, and amenity, unless it can be sold. Toxicity and pollution only becomes an issue if there are economic impacts.

In the same way as 'he' is disconnected from biological time, Economic Man is disconnected from *ecological time* – that is, the time it takes to restore the effects of human activity, the life-cycle of renewal and replenishment within the ecosystem. Space and time is also collapsed as transport enables goods and labour to travel long distances while technology enables the twenty-four hour working day. Those responsible for social reproduction – women's work – are much more embedded, leading much less carbon intensive lives, relying more on local public transportation, and living and working close to home (Spitzner 2009).

Distorted and alienated patterns of human activity and economic value emerge because what has become known as 'the economy' is carved out of the complexity of the whole of human and non-human existence, the ecological and social framework of human *being* in its widest sense. Ecofeminist political economy, with its structural material analysis, offers an explanation of how a destructive economic system is constructed. Destructiveness is central to its fundamentally

| HIGHLY VALUED | UN/UNDERVALUED |
|---|---|
| 'Economic Man' | 'Women's work' |
| Market value | Subsistence, provisioning |
| Personal wealth | Social reciprocity |
| Labour/intellect | Body |
| Skills/trade-able knowledge | Feelings, emotions, wisdom |
| Able-bodied workers | Sick, needy, old, young |
| Exploitable resources | Eco-systems, wild nature |
| Unlimited growth | Sufficiency |

*Figure 5.1* Dualistic values hierarchy of Economic Man

gendered structure. The economy valued by money draws on the resources of nature and human labour but prioritizes what dominant Economic Man values (see Figure 5.1). What is unvalued or undervalued is the resilience of the eco-system, unpaid and unrecognized domestic work and social reciprocity, communality, and conviviality in human societies.

EM is not only a social construct, 'he' is an ideological representation of dominant hegemonic structures of thought. One of the early assumptions of the classical political economy of Adam Smith was that humans were naturally drawn to 'truck and barter' and this was taken to the heart of modern 'scientific' economic analysis, particularly so in twentieth and twenty-first century neoliberalism. The image of a profit-making rational actor, *homo economicus* leads to alienated patterns of thought and action that splits people in two: the transcendent economic participant who lives beyond the conditions of 'his' embodiment and embeddedness in nature, and the immanent human being who represents that materiality.

The impossibility of the real existence of EM became clear when neoclassical economics, faced with the reality of human economic behaviour that proved to be too complex and inconvenient to readily reveal its economic paragon of a rational actor, turned to modelling. Ideal worlds were created where there was perfect information, equal playing fields, rational actors, and so on. EM thus became a totally constructed concept, a social and ecological impossibility. However, real economic structures were built that assumed that 'he' could exist and in this lay 'his' social and ecological destructiveness.

## Ecofeminist political economy: challenging 'Economic Man'

Modern economies represent a boundaried system that embraces activities and functions which are valued predominantly through money forms. What the valued economy is not acknowledging is the precariousness of its seemingly transcendent position; its immanence in the sustaining systems that underpin it. As ecofeminist philosopher Val Plumwood puts it so cogently,

> After much destruction, mastery will fail, because the master denies dependence on the sustaining other: he misunderstands the conditions of his own existence and lacks sensitivity to limits and to the ultimate points of Earthian existence.
>
> *(Plumwood 1993:195)*

The failure of contemporary economies to acknowledge their true resource base means that these are both exploited and damaged. The material link between gender and sustainability in ecofeminist political economy starts, therefore, from the need to overcome the money and profit boundary in economic thinking and the purely economistic notion of wealth (Mellor 2016). The notion of 'the economy' needs to be freed from a narrow focus on markets and paid work generally, to a much wider notion of human activities in meeting human needs and sustaining the natural world (Shiva 2005).

What ecofeminist political economy has identified is that the current economy is parasitical upon other aspects of human and natural existence, particularly social reproduction or care work. An ecologically sustainable economy would start from the embodiment and embeddedness of human lives, from the life of the body and the ecosystem. Prioritizing the life-world of women's work would mean that patterns of work and consumption would be sensitive to the human life cycle. Necessary production and exchange would be fully integrated with the dynamics of the body and the environment. Economic Man is unsustainable and human lives based on that model would no longer exist. At present there is a two-step economic structure where people have to find work where they can in order to be able to provide a livelihood for themselves. The aim of an ecofeminist alternative would be a one-step economy where people work to provide for the immediate needs of themselves and others. Work would embrace the whole of the activities needed to maintain human existence in a way that does not deplete or exploit the natural environment.

## Provisioning, not economy

Although the origin of the word economy '*oikonomics*' is related to the provisioning household rather than the money-seeking market (identified as '*chrematistics*' by Aristotle), economy has become associated with the use of money in exchange and the search for profit. That is, it is concerned with exchange value, not use value. In order to break down this boundary and build an economy that embraces the whole of human life in nature, a more useful concept is 'provisioning' which covers all aspects of human needs, including nurturing and emotional support. The notion of provisioning is more comprehensive than economy, as it embraces all aspects of human nourishing: paid and unpaid. Provisioning by integrating 'women's work' would ground Economic Man in conditions of immanence, acknowledging human existence in nature. Provisioning necessary goods and services would be the main focus, prioritizing needs, not wants. It would start from women's work and the vitality of the natural world. Prioritizing the life-world of women's work would mean that patterns of work and consumption would be sensitive to the human life cycle. If the ecofeminist analysis is correct, livelihoods based on provisioning would be sensitive to social and ecological limits.

## Sufficiency provisioning: enough rather than growth

Ecofeminist provisioning would seek to create a socially just society that lives within its ecological means. Central to provisioning would be the idea of sufficiency and social justice. Sufficiency is most clearly defined by what it is not. It is not 'too much' nor 'too little'. Sufficiency is enough. Sufficiency must also be socially just, as sufficiency for one must be sufficiency for all (Mellor 2010b). The only alternative would be to have people with not enough or too much. Salleh argues that what she describes as eco-sufficiency is already 'modelled by the global majority of labour – indigenous, peasant, and care-giving workers' (Salleh 2009:291). The question then becomes, what kind of structures of provisioning would exist? The critique of money-based economies is central to ecofeminist political economy, as money marks the boundary between paid and unpaid women's work and the externalization of nature (Mellor 2010a).

There is a stream within ecofeminism and the ecological movement generally that seeks to exit from money economies entirely and re-establish or retain subsistence economies (Bennholdt-Thomsen and Mies 1999). This would seem logical; after all, it is money that forms the boundary between the economy of Economic Man and the everyday practice of women's work. It is money that turns the natural environment into a commodity. Similar proposals advocate abandoning money and replacing it with provisioning networks (Nelson and Timmerman 2011).

While the image here is of a self-provisioning community reflecting cooperative principles, the notion of subsistence can also be interpreted as individualized self-sufficiency. There is the danger here that a version of Ecological Man emerges where only the fit, young and economically independent can survive – those who have the resources to buy land or the ability to build and cultivate. What will happen when the small-holder grows old or sick or the children need a midwife or an education? What will happen to all the people in the favelas, vast housing estates and refugee camps? Reflecting the ecofeminist critique of contemporary economies, there needs to be gender-based and social justice awareness in proposals for transition to more ecologically sustainable environments.[2]

It is important to acknowledge that in a steady state or degrowth society there may be a conflict between women's desires to be liberated from the burdens of unpaid or underpaid work and green strategies for growth reduction. A particular problem is the need to reduce energy consumption. Limiting energy consuming activities must also include energy used domestically to support unpaid work: fridges, deep freezers, cookers, space heating, washing machines, dishwashers, pumped water, and sewerage. Without these, running a household would become much harder. Around the world women in subsistence economies spend hours fetching water, finding food, tending fires, milling, cooking, as well as growing and tending crops. Green provisioning would thus need to be aware that everyone needs to be responsible for what is now regarded as women's work, which will become more difficult and time-consuming in a post-carbon world. Evidence from studies of pre-industrial ecologically benign societies indicates that women's experience was not good (Mellor 1992). Women were subordinated with heavy workloads as reflected in the testimony of a seventeenth-century traveller about the lives of native American women in a culture often cited in green writing as ecologically benign and socially wise:

> [Women] have almost the entire care of the house and work . . . [they] till the land, plant the corn . . . beat the hemp, spin it . . . making . . . fishing nets and other useful things . . . harvest . . . the corn, attend their husbands from place to place . . . [like] pack-mules . . . carrying the baggage . . . and do a thousand other things . . . All the men do is hunt for deer other animals and fish . . . make their cabins . . . go to war . . . go to other tribes [for] festivities [then] go to sleep which they like to do best of all things.
>
> *(Samuel de Champlain n.d., cited in McLuhan 1971)*

Could the same unbalanced workloads arise in post-industrial degrowth economies? The answer is clearly 'yes', if the green agenda does not embrace a feminist perspective. Provisioning concepts like the 'care economy' could also be misleading.[3] While it refers to the caring activities that need to be carried out in all societies, the implication also is that the providers do that work because they care. Their work is based on love, concern, or empathy. While this may be true for many care providers, others may feel they have little choice but to do this work, as there is no one else to do it. While this work may be carried out as an expression of love and/or duty, for many there is fear of violence and/or lack of any other economic options. I have referred to this as 'imposed altruism' (Mellor 1992:252).

It also needs to be recognized that in modern economies women not only rely heavily on the provision of public services and socialized care (Fawcett Society 2013) but also do most of the nursing, hygiene, childcare, and elderly care involved. As a 2015 study of OECD data showed, on average, women formed 58 per cent of the public sector workforce with up to 70 per cent in Sweden. The public sector, like the wider commercial economy, is highly gendered: management is masculine and front line service provision (taking care of people) is feminine. As a worldwide survey shows, in all bar one country women held under 40 per cent of management posts with Britain at 36 per cent and Japan under 2 per cent (Ernst and Young 2014). Canada stood out at 45.9 per cent. What type of collective public provision would a degrowth system envisage? Who would do the domestic and caring work?

Localism is also a prevalent theme in green economics, but if this is seen as a scaled down version of the market, even with co-operative patterns of ownership, what will happen to more collective public provision, particularly health care or education? For ecofeminist political economy, a green agenda must be a feminist agenda, otherwise green economics, even with the most radical position on sustainability, may solve the problem of unsustainable growth but reinforce gender inequality in more sustainable economies. As Latouche has argued, 'de-growth is conceivable only in a degrowth society . . . based upon a different logic' (Latouche 2009:8). However, if that logic is still gendered, degrowth may be achieved, but gender equality and social justice will not. Although the majority of work in this field is desperately deaf to feminist analyses, some male green theorists have heard the call. For example, John Barry's (2012) *The Politics of Actually Existing Unsustainability* draws on ecofeminism in making his case for green republicanism. One proposal of how to break free of destructive growth economics is to democratize money and make it the servant of humanity not its master (Robertson 2012); to remove the power of money from 'Economic Man' and make it the basis of a gender aware sufficiency provisioning (Mellor 2016).

## Democratize money

The aim of democratizing money presents a direct challenge to the economistic concept of monetary exchange. Conventional theories of money assume that money value is the same as market value. Their solution is to try to put a market value on nature or unpaid work. How much would you pay to preserve this forest? What is care work worth? An ecofeminist political economy approach to money would want to replace such market valuations with democratically agreed priorities. Exchange value for profit would be replaced by exchange value for use in sustainable provisioning. Central to this system would be a right to livelihood, an entitlement to provisioning. A starting point is to challenge the assumption that the use of money must entail commodification and market exchange. While money and commodification is the framework that creates and sustains Economic Man, money itself is not seen as the cause. Monetization is not necessarily the same as commodification.

When Marx made the link between profit and exchange he was clear that exchange took two forms: $C - M - C$ (exchanging one commodity for money in order to buy another commodity) and exchanging solely to achieve a money profit $M - C - M+$ (money invested in a commodity that can be sold at a profit). In contemporary society this has been taken a stage further where money itself has become a commodity $M - M - M+$ (money invested in money to create more money). Money as a medium of exchange therefore is not necessarily money as a medium of profit. Money can be used to exchange use value, that is, it could be used to exchange goods and services based on sufficiency provisioning rather than the maximization of money value.

An historical perspective on money reveals that money is predominantly a social phenomenon, not an economic artefact. It has taken a variety of forms, mostly, like today, without intrinsic value: stone, wood, paper, electronic dots. Money's social origin was as a generally accepted unit of measurement to establish relative values in social relationships: injury payments, gifts, dowries, tithes, entitlements. Money historically was also mainly located in public arenas rather than private economic processes. Money was created and authorized by power-holders rather than created and circulated among private individuals or linked to a market search for profit (Mellor 2010a; Mellor 2016). This is particularly true of precious metal coinage.

The most important aspect of money is not what it is made of, its money-form, but what it does. Money is a measure and representation of value. While occasionally the money-form itself has an equivalent intrinsic value (e.g., precious metal), this should not be taken as its defining feature. The generic role of money is to establish entitlements and obligations in a range of social, public and commercial contexts. These are not necessarily benign. As Graeber puts it, 'the real origins of money are to be found in crime and recompense, war and slavery, honor, debt and redemption' (2011:19). What matters is who owns and controls money and how it is created and circulated. Many people searching for a way out of destructive economic systems are experimenting with forming their own money systems, which I call 'social money'.

## *Social money*

There are many examples of people seeking to set up local money systems as a way of exchanging use values to enable sustainable consumption (Seyfang 2006). Local currencies, local exchange trading schemes (LETS), and time banks are all ways of organizing local provisioning systems. Around the world there are many initiatives and experiments within local communities and across societies that are exploring alternative ways of provisioning (Lewis and Conaty 2012) or looking at more ecologically sustainable models such as a bioregional economy (Cato 2012). A very simple example of a social money system is a baby-sitting circle. Each new member who joins the circle is issued with ten tokens which can be spent and earned. While baby-sitting arrangements could be made on a personal basis, it is much easier to issue tokens to each family to keep account of reciprocal childcare activities.

These initiatives require a conception of wealth that prioritizes community, social and ecological well-being (Large 2010). Wealth here would not be conceived of in asset or profit terms, but as goods and services rendered and security of future provisioning. It would also require a view of monetary exchange as representing obligations and entitlements for social benefit not exchange for profit. Unfortunately, modern money systems have been hijacked by markets and only seen as valuable exchange for profit. This means that activities such as car production, computer production or financial services are seen as a source of wealth, while care provision and other public services are seen as a drain on 'the wealth creating sector'. This failure to recognize the value of public and social life also represents a gendered approach to economic systems. Neoliberalism, in particular, has frequently used the analogy of the public sector as a dependent household to justify its policy of cuts and austerity. The household analogy is based on the assumption that the private sector is the 'breadwinner', the only creator of economic wealth. The public sector is seen as needing to live within a household allowance as determined by the commercial sector. It is limited by the money in its 'handbag' (Mellor 2016:20).

## *Neoliberal 'handbag' economics*

This neoliberal 'handbag economics' with its state-as-housewife analogy reflects the fact that, in many economies, control of money has passed from its historical base in the ruling authority to the commercial banking system. As I have argued elsewhere (Mellor 2010a), the money supply in most modern economies has been privatized. Until the 2008 financial crisis, nearly all new money in market-based economies was created and circulated as debt by banks (Jackson and Dyson 2012). That is, it was created and circulated on a commercial basis. Following the crisis the creation of new money returned to the public monetary authorities, mainly central banks, as the supply of bank-issued money dried up in the 'credit crunch'.

Cash (coin and notes) are only created by public monetary authorities. However, most money in modern societies does not physically exist; it is mainly numbers in accounts. Banks cannot create notes and coin, but they can create new bank accounts – that is, numbers on a bank statement. If people ask for cash, this has to be bought from the central bank out of the bank's reserves. However, as most money transfers don't use cash, by default most of the money created and circulated only exists as bank accounts.

As money is now mainly created and circulated as bank debt, Economic Man is founded not only on the exploitation of 'women's work' and despoiling of the natural environment, but also on the almost totally unregulated creation of debt. This puts a growth dynamic into the economy. Not only do commercial borrowers seek profit; debts have to be repaid with interest. Both commercial investors and banks are seeking to regain more money than they invest/lend. The direction of the economy is therefore driven not by what is necessary, but what is profitable. Those who borrow the most money determine the direction of the economy. This system is bound to end in crisis when those debts turn toxic. At that point the only solution is to pour trillions of newly created public money into the global banking system and financial sector generally, sanitized as being created by 'independent' central banks. The question then becomes, why bail out the financial sector; why not bail out the people or nature? Instead the people are punished through austerity with public services slashed and public assets privatized.

There are many voices now arguing that banks should no longer be granted the privilege of creating new money as bank debt (Mellor 2010a, 2016; Jackson and Dyson 2012; Robertson 2012). The right to create all new money should be placed with the public under democratic control. Banks should be limited to what people think they do, lend savers' money to borrowers. Banks should not be able to generate the public currency out of fresh air as debt. Public currencies in all their forms, including electronic, should only be created by the public for public purposes. Unlike commercially created money, public currencies can be created free of debt, like baby-sitting tokens. They can be spent or allocated into circulation like the experiments in social money. Central to this would be democratic debate about spending priorities. Unlike the commercial creation of money which has largely been uncontrolled in the run up to the crisis, public money creation and circulation would have to be carefully monitored and managed (Jackson and Dyson 2012).

## Conclusion: democratizing money
## for sufficiency provisioning

From an ecofeminist political economy perspective, the starting point for sufficiency provisioning must be to see money as a 'commons' resource like air or water is a natural resource (Mellor 2010a). It should not be privatized or accumulated for private gain. Money should be recognized as social and public in origin rather than emerging only in a market context. Money can represent use value and wealth expressed as provisioning of necessary goods and services as well as commodity value and exchange for profit. Money itself is not the problem; it is who owns and controls its creation and circulation. Money is only a social construction, a token that people acknowledge. Some forms of money have had market value (gold, silver), but throughout history most money forms have only had social value.

As new money in the economy is effectively produced out of thin air, there is an overwhelming case for putting this 'commons' money into the hands of the people as a whole, rather than into the commercial market. This would turn the priorities in the economy around. Rather than being used to create profits, money would be issued to meet needs directly. Money created and circulated as a public resource would create the possibility of sufficiency provisioning because it could be issued debt-free (Mellor 2010b, 2016). The amount of money created and how it is allocated would become a key aspect of public policy with substantial public participation. Money created and circulated under democratic control could be made available to everyone in society on a sufficiency basis. If it was put directly into people's hands as a citizen's income, it could allow people doing 'women's work' access to commercially traded goods and services. Public money could also be used to fund large public infrastructures such as hospitals. It could be used to organize provisioning in large scale societies on the basis of shared necessary work. Certainty of provisioning would be very important so that people felt secure enough to downsize their economic activities. This would provide the basis of a sufficiency economy that could operate without a growth dynamic other than that required to meet needs on an ecologically sustainable basis.

The enduring contribution of ecofeminist political economy is that it offers a fundamental challenge to the gender and nature blindness of current economies and of mainstream/malestream economists and their economic theories. The failure of profit and consumption driven economies to acknowledge their true resource base in women's work and nature means that these are exploited and damaged. Ecofeminist political economy challenges the false boundaries of gendered economies and explores ways to create a provisioning system that will meet human needs and enhance human potential without destroying the life of the planet.

## Notes

1 Ecological economics is an interdisciplinary field of research and a heterodox approach to economic thinking that has been evolving since the 1960s. Green economics is closely related but generally considered to be more radical and politically engaged than ecological economics, in that many of its proponents (e.g., Molly Scott-Cato, Joan Martinez-Allier, New Economics Foundation) are actively involved in environmental social movements and green parties. It should not be confused with 'the green economy' concept that has arrived on the international scene since the Rio+20 Summit in 2012 (for a discussion and critique of that concept, see Littig in this volume).
2 It is worth noting that the Transition movement has yet to be critically analyzed from an ecofeminist political economy perspective.
3 Some feminist political economists use of the term 'caring economy' in a way that unearths and directly challenges assumptions about women's duty to shoulder a disproportionate and unsustainable load of caring labour (see, for example, Wichterich 2014).

## References

Barratt Brown, M. (1995) *Models of Political Economy*. Harmondsworth: Penguin.
Barry, J. (2012) *The Politics of Actually Existing Unsustainability*. Oxford: Oxford University Press.
Bennholdt-Thomsen, V. and Mies, M. (1999) *The Subsistence Perspective*. London: Zed Books.
Biesecker, A. and Hofmeister, S. (2010) 'Focus: (re)productivity. Sustainable relations both between society and nature and between the genders', *Ecological Economics* 69: 1703–1711.

Cato, M. S. (2012) *The Bioregional Economy: Land, Liberty and the Pursuit of Happiness.* London: Routledge.

Champlain, de S. (n.d.) *Voyages of Samuel de Champlain.* Online. Available at: www.fullbooks.com/Voyages-of-Samuel-de-Champlain-V33.html (accessed 16 December 2015).

Czech, B. (2013) *Supply Shock: Economic Growth at the Crossroads and the Steady State Solution.* Gabriola Island, British Columbia: New Society Publishers.

D'Alisa, G., Demaria, F. and Kallis, G. (eds) (2015) *Degrowth: A Vocabulary for a New Era.* Abingdon: Routledge.

Dalla Costa, M. and James, S. (1972) *The Power of Women and the Subversion of Community.* Bristol: Falling Wall Press.

Daly, H., Dietz, R. and O'Neill, D. (2013) *Enough Is Enough: Building a Sustainable Economy in a World of Limited Resources.* London: Routledge.

Dankelman, I. (2010) *Gender and Climate Change.* London: Routledge.

Engels, F. (1884) 'The origins of the family, private property and the state', in Marx, K. and Engels, F. (eds) *Selected Works.* London: Lawrence and Wishart, 461–584.

Ernst and Young (2014) *World Wide Women Public Sector Leaders Index 2014.* Online. Available at: www.ey.com/Publication/vwLUAssets/EY_-_Worldwide_Women_Public_Sector_Leaders_Index_2014/$FILE/EY_Worldwide_Index_of_Women_22Oct14.pdf (accessed 16 December 2015).

Fawcett Society (2013) *The Triple Jeopardy: The Impact of Service Cuts on Women.* Online. Available at: www.fawcettsociety.org.uk/2013/02/services/ (accessed 16 December 2015).

Graeber, D. (2011) *Debt: The First 5,000 Years.* New York: Neville House Publishing.

Isla, A. (2009) 'Who pays for the Kyoto Protocol?', in Salleh, A. (ed) *Eco-Sufficiency and Global Justice.* London: Pluto Press, 199–213.

Jackson, A. and Dyson, B. (2012) *Modernising Money: Why Our Money System Is Broken and How It Can Be Fixed.* London: Positive Money.

Jackson, T. (2011) *Prosperity Without Growth: Economics for a Finite Planet.* London: Routledge.

Jaggar, A. (ed) (2014) *Gender and Global Justice.* Cambridge: Polity.

Large, M. (2010) *Common Wealth for a Free, Equal, Mutual and Sustainable Society.* Stroud: Hawthorn Press.

Latouche, S. (2009) *Farewell to Growth.* Cambridge: Polity.

Lewis, M. and Conaty, P. (2012) *The Resilience Perspective: Cooperative Transitions to a Steady-State Economy.* New York: New Society Publishers.

MacGregor, S. (2010) 'A stranger silence still: The need for feminist social research on climate change', *Sociological Review* 57: 124–140.

McLuhan, T. C. (1971) *Touch the Earth.* New York: Simon and Schuster.

Marx, K. (1844/2005) 'Economic and philosophical manuscripts', in Colletti, L. (ed) *Marx – Early Writings.* Harmondsworth: Penguin e-book, 279–400.

Mellor, M. (1992) *Breaking the Boundaries.* London: Virago.

Mellor, M. (1997a) *Feminism and Ecology.* Cambridge: Polity.

Mellor, M. (1997b) 'Women, nature and the social construction of "economic man"', *Ecological Economics* 20(2): 129–140.

Mellor, M. (2007) 'Ecofeminism: Linking gender and ecology', in Pretty, J., Benton, T., Guivant, J., Lee, D., Orr, D., Pfeffer, M. and Ward, H. (eds) *Handbook on Environment and Society.* London: Sage Publications, 66–77.

Mellor, M. (2009) 'Ecofeminist political economy and the politics of money', in Salleh, A. (ed) *Eco-Sufficiency and Global Justice.* London: Pluto Press, 251–262.

Mellor, M. (2010a) *The Future of Money: From Financial Crisis to Public Resource.* London: Pluto Press.

Mellor, M. (2010b) 'Could the money system be the basis of a sufficiency economy?', *Real-world Economics Review* 54: 79–88. Online. Available at: www.paecon.net/PAERevuew/issue54/Mellor54.pdf

Mellor, M. (2013) 'The unsustainability of economic man', *Okologisches Wirtschaften* 4: 30–33.

Mellor, M. (2016) *Debt or Democracy: Public Money for Sustainability and Social Justice.* London: Pluto.

Merricks, L. (1996) *The World Made New: Frederick Soddy, Science, Politics and Environment.* Oxford: Oxford University Press.

Mies, M. (1986) *Patriarchy and Accumulation on a World Scale.* London: Zed Books.

Nelson, A. and Timmerman, F. (2011) *Life Without Money: Building Fair and Sustainable Economies.* London: Pluto Press.

OECD (2015) *Women in Public Sector Employment.* Online. Available at: www.oecd-ilibrary.org/docserver/download/4215081ec023.pdf?expires=1450265054&id=id&accname=guest&checksum=5831D6BEC42A7EBF017C7B1981A9A639 (accessed 16 December 2015).

Parsons, H. L. (1977) *Marx and Engels on Ecology.* London: Greenwood.

Perkins, E. and Kuiper, E. (eds.) (2005) 'Explorations: Feminist ecological economics', *Feminist Economics* 11(3): 107–148.

Phipps, A. (2014) *The Politics of the Body.* Cambridge: Polity.

Picchio, A. (1992) *Social Reproduction: The Political Economy of the Labour Market.* Cambridge: Cambridge University Press.

Plumwood, V. (1993) *Feminism and the Mastery of Nature.* London: Routledge.

Robertson, J. (2012) *Future Money: Breakdown or Breakthrough.* Totnes: Green Books.

Ruether, R. R. (1975) *New Woman, New Earth.* New York: The Seabury Press.

Salleh, A. (1997) *Ecofeminism as Politics: Nature, Marx and the Postmodern.* London: Zed Books.

Salleh, A. (2009) 'From eco-sufficiency to global justice', in Salleh, A. (ed) *Eco-Sufficiency and Global Justice.* London: Pluto Press, 291–304.

Seyfang, G. (2006) 'Sustainable consumption, the new economics and community currencies: Developing new institutions for environmental governance', *Regional Studies* 40: 781–791.

Shiva, V. (2005) *Earth Democracy: Justice, Sustainability, Peace.* London: Zed Books.

Soddy, F. (1926) *Wealth, Virtual Wealth and Debt.* London: George Allen and Unwin.

Spitzner, M. (2009) 'How global warming is gendered: A view from the EU', in Salleh, A. (ed) *Eco-Sufficiency and Global Justice.* London: Pluto Press, 218–224.

Vaillancourt, J. G. (1996) 'Marxism and ecology: More benedictine than francisan', in Benton, T. (ed) *The Greening of Marx.* London: Guilford Press, 50–63.

Waring, M. (1989) *If Women Counted.* London: Macmillan.

Weeks, K. (2011) *The Problem With Work: Feminism, Marxism, Antiwork Politics, and Postwork Imaginaries.* Durham, NC: Duke University Press.

Wichterich, C. (2014) 'Occupy development: Towards a caring economy', *Development* 56(3): 346–349.

# 6

# NATURECULTURES AND FEMINIST MATERIALISM

*Helen Merrick*

## Introduction

Some of the most original and provocative feminist scholarship on environment and nature is found in Donna Haraway's extensive body of feminist science studies and cultural theory. While she is not primarily identified as an environmental or ecofeminist theorist, the objects of Haraway's inquiries are integral to any contemporary consideration of gender and environment. Spanning a wide array of subjects and disciplines, central to all her writing is the question of how (and why, and in whose interests) we humans encounter nature: materially, discursively, figuratively, and relationally. As Haraway herself has often noted, her work could be considered an ongoing investigation of 'the invention and reinvention of nature – perhaps the most central arena of hope, oppression, and contestation for inhabitants of the planet earth in our times' (Haraway 1991d:1). Haraway's work, like that of French philosopher of science Bruno Latour, presents 'nondualist' theories of nature that 'take nature to be neither reducible to objective reality nor reducible to human subjectivity' (Davison 2005). A nondualist approach at its core resists the whole series of traditional binarisms such as nature/culture and human/nonhuman that inform the reductionist systems ultimately threatening the natural environment.

Like many other feminist scholars of environment and nature, Haraway is concerned to reveal the gendered power relations that shape the construction and deployment of nature in scientific and cultural discourse. Haraway's unique contribution in many ways stems from her combination of passionate socialist feminism and what she calls her 'own contradictory love of science in general, and biology in particular' (Haraway 1997a:123). Trained in zoology, biology, philosophy, and literature, Haraway brings together the reading practices of critical theory with the meticulous observations of life science methodologies, in a relentlessly multidisciplinary approach that refuses to privilege one particular body of knowledge, method, or 'storytelling practice' over another. In Haraway's hands, nature provides the perfect 'object of knowledge' with which to force communication and attempt translation across the divides of the sciences and humanities; every narrative of or about nature – whether literary metaphor or scientific 'fact' – reveals the powerfully gendered and raced histories of human knowledge. Put simply, Haraway's contribution and legacy lie in her refusal to accept the series of oppositional dualisms characterizing the disciplinary fracture between the sciences and humanities; such as nature/culture, fact/story, realist/constructivist, or modernist/postmodernist. Constantly working to unpack these reductive dualisms, Haraway foregrounds nature as one of the central problematics and possibilities for feminist theory and praxis. In other words, from Harawayan viewpoint, we cannot think gender without nature, or nature without gender.

While certain of her works have been taken up widely in various branches of feminist theory (such as the 'Cyborg Manifesto' and her work on 'situated knowledges', published in the 1991 book *Simians, Cyborgs and Women: The Reinvention of Nature*) much of her more challenging and exciting work on nature is less well known. Yet from her earliest publications in the 1970s, Haraway's combination of feminist critique with studies of science produced a distinctive, materialist approach to nature and gender. It is perhaps only with the rise of the so-called new materialism from the mid-2000s that a similar foregrounding of the material has become commonplace in feminist and cultural theory (see Alaimo and Hekman eds 2008; Bennett 2010).

In this chapter, I sketch some of Haraway's engagements with what has come to count as nature, and the resulting challenges and contributions she offers for feminist and environmental theory. In particular I focus on some of the distinctive conceptual tools that Haraway has developed in pursuing her non-dualist approach to nature – namely, resisting the divide between the sciences and humanities; insisting on the indivisibility of nature and culture, or what she terms 'naturecultures'; understanding the complex relations of stories and narratives to the material (the 'material-semiotic'); and her attention to the human/non-human relation. The impact of her work is further explored through her reception in certain areas of feminist theory and intersections with recent developments in 'new materialist' approaches.

## Bridging the sciences and humanities through naturecultures

From her earliest work, Haraway challenged feminist scholars to take account of and to contest the meanings and positioning of technoscience. This was not always a popular or comprehensible position for feminists working within cultural theory or ecofeminist theory. It is now a familiar refrain that early feminist environmental critiques were often framed by calls to privilege the feminine, woman, and (a feminized) 'mother nature' over the masculinized and phallocentric domination of nature seen as the cause of environmental destruction. The role reversal effected by some forms of feminist critique – intended to redress the gendered power imbalance in society as well as in language, theory, and environmental politics – could too easily be expressed as an 'essentialist' position which merely reversed, rather than challenged, gendered binaries (Plumwood 1993). Such a position could also be seen to shore up the notion of biological essentialism underpinning reactionary scientific discourses about women and gender. By the 1990s, the mainstream of feminist theory had shifted to a more postmodern, constructivist position, which focused on language, discourse, the discursive construction of gender and the gendered subject, wherein inclusion of biological 'sex' became almost taboo (for a discussion of this history, see Sturgeon 1997; Thompson and MacGregor in this volume).

Thus Haraway's approach has been challenging for certain branches of feminist theory, as it rests not on a simple rejection of scientific knowledge as hopelessly phallocentric (and potentially politically dangerous in its insistence on the apparent primacy of biology), but a more nuanced critique of how scientific knowledge emerges. Her work deliberately resists the usual modernist versus postmodernist tensions within which arguments around matter, the body, biology, and gender are often framed. In particular, her approach has been concerned with finding a place from which to understand ontology and epistemology in a way that avoids the pitfalls of both modernist and postmodernist approaches to knowledge. Dogged by critique from 'realists' and 'constructivists', and from scientists and cultural critics alike, Haraway has repeatedly argued for a nondualist position that refuses the zero-sum, either-or argument from which such critique emerges.

At the heart of this nondualist conception of nature is a refusal to divide reality (ontology) and human understanding of it (epistemology) into separate spheres of human/nature, culture/nature, or human/non-human. Such a position demands attention to the ways in which both the sciences and humanities disciplines understand and construct nature, as well as relating such constructions to material reality. This commitment is captured in her phrase 'naturecultures', which, like many other of her neologisms, is not mere word play but a serious reminder to the critic and reader that each of these spheres co-produces the other and are always/already in relation. Haraway uses naturecultures to foreground the impossibility of thinking of nature, realism or 'reality' in isolation. From this perspective, everything is a natural-technical system; nothing can be (or ever was) a separate, pristine 'nature' or 'culture'. Her position on nature is equally upsetting to scientists and some environmentalists alike; as Aidan Davison notes, such 'attempts to mess up fixed boundaries between culture and nature, and between technology and ecology, have been met by many nature advocates with deep suspicion' (Davison 2005: online).

A key consequence of thinking in terms of naturecultures is the need to reveal how scientific facts and theories are also marked by specific histories of race, class, and sex, rather than being objective representations of an external 'reality'. The sciences, like all forms of human knowledge, are for Haraway another kind of 'story-telling practice'. While not surprisingly many scientists have viewed such claims as a constructivist refusal of reality, this crucial aspect of Haraway's practice arises from a very serious and considered aspect of her methodology. Just as history, sociology or literature are the stories humans tell ourselves to make sense of human activity or 'culture', the life sciences are the stories humans tell ourselves to make sense of the physical world or 'nature'. This was the central theme of her groundbreaking work *Primate Visions*: 'Scientific practice is above all a story-telling practice. Biology is the fiction appropriate to objects called organisms; biology fashions the facts "discovered" about organic beings' (Haraway 1989:4–5).[1] By insisting on the equivalencies between various forms of knowledge construction, Haraway tries to foreground the constructed and false nature of the binary division between humanities and science, and their separate 'houses' of knowledge, culture, and nature.

## What counts as nature?

'Nature' as term, concept, and relation is an inherently political category for Haraway. As she comments in an interview:

> From the beginning . . . [m]y interest has been in what gets to count as nature and who gets to inhabit natural categories. And furthermore, what's at stake in the judgment about nature and what's at stake in maintaining the boundaries between what gets called nature and what gets called culture in our society.
>
> *(Haraway and Goodeve 2000:50)*

Nature is a slippery figuration that is called upon to perform a multitude of differing political, activist, theoretical, philosophical, representational, and scientific work. It can function at once as supposedly transparent descriptions of the world-as-it-is (or was); serve as justification for normalized patterns of behaviour, forms, and organizations; and be a signifier for that which is somehow outside culture. The human knower of this nature sits in a complex and contradictory relation to this series of meanings: at once both part of nature (the organic) and what is 'natural' (god- or biology-ordained), but also apparently separate from it as the purveyor and originator of culture and discourse (the not-animal). Our definitions and codifications of nature are complexly intertwined with the ways we define 'human' and how/why/when we separate the 'human' from nonhuman.

These layers of meanings lead philosopher Kate Soper (1995) to delineate three differing uses of nature: a metaphysical concept used to signify humanity's 'difference and specificity', which can either signal human continuity with nonhuman or its irreducible difference; the realist concept of the physical structures and processes studied by the natural sciences; and finally the lay use of the word to refer to the nonurban environment or 'wilderness'. Nature, in Haraway's usage, is not so easily segmented, as each of these 'uses' colours and impacts on the rest. In her journeys through naturecultures, Haraway is trying to get at the ways in which the 'reality of nature' cannot be apprehended separately from the nature that has been produced through, and by, Western scientific discourses that are themselves contextualized and bounded by histories marked by race, class, and sex/gender. This is not to say that there is no 'real' or factual element independent of the observations and writings of scientists; as she argued in 'The Past Is the Contested Zone' (one of her 1978 articles in the academic journal *Signs*): 'We can both know that our bodies, other animals, fossils, and what have you are proper objects for scientific investigation, and remember how historically determined is our part in the construction of the object' (Haraway 1991c [1978]:42).

From some of her earliest work, then, Haraway has argued the need for feminists to struggle 'within the belly of the monster', to engage and take seriously the stories of life, nature, and the material that the sciences patrol and are implicated with/in. As she stated in 'Animal Sociology' (also published in 1978),

> we have allowed our distance from science and technology to lead us to misunderstand the status and function of natural knowledge . . . We have challenged our traditional assignment to the status of natural objects by becoming anti-natural in our ideology in a way which leaves the life sciences untouched by feminist needs.
>
> *(Haraway 1991a [1978]:8)*

The ways in which we think, represent, and call upon nature are inherently political, with 'worldly' consequences for the ways we live as humans, societies, and in relation to human and nonhuman others. As Haraway argued in 'The Biological Enterprise' (1979),

> Part of remaking ourselves as socialist-feminist human beings is remaking the sciences which construct the category of 'nature.' . . . In our time, natural science defines the human being's place in nature and history and provides the instruments of domination of the body and the community . . . So science is part of the struggle over the nature of our lives.
>
> *(Haraway 1991b [1979]:43)*

Here, then, are some of the earliest calls for feminists to resist 'antibiologism', which Haraway tried to answer in her own work, insisting on attending to the sciences as a core part of feminist activity. For Haraway, feminist science studies have always been, a priori, feminist theory.

While her later work would frame this argument rather differently, these early works centred on the need for feminists to remain in the contest for what counts as nature. It is worth remembering the very different responses to sociobiology more characteristic of feminist theory at the time. When confronted with a nature that had been 'theorized and developed through the construction of life science in and for capitalism and patriarchy', a common feminist response was rejection of such reductionist biological narratives, rather than, as for Haraway, a renewed reason to engage the sciences. 'To the extent that these practices inform our theorizing of nature, we are still ignorant and must engage in the practice of science. It is a matter for struggle' (Haraway 1991b:68). This imperative to struggle results in Haraway's desire to engage in productive, sometimes contestual, conversations with the kinds of stories the life sciences tell about nature and the effects of these stories on scientific practices. These encounters change our apprehension of and relation to science as much as they do nature: 'If technoscience is, among other things, a practice of materializing refigurations of what counts as nature, a practice of turning tropes into worlds, then how we figure technoscience makes an immense difference' (Haraway 1994:60). Haraway's challenge to feminism (and cultural theory more broadly), then, is to pay attention both to how the humanities and/or science studies figure technoscience as well as to how the sciences 'do' what it is they do.

## None of the above: exploding dualisms

Haraway's ongoing plea to remain attentive to the discourses and practices of science demands a rethinking and repositioning of the historically reified boundaries between disciplines and methodologies, toward a multiliterate transdisciplinarity that encourages the 'traffic between nature and culture' – and thus between and across the two-culture divide of the sciences and humanities. Contextualizing and justifying this divide is the whole series of 'inherited dualisms that run deep in Western cultures' (Haraway 2004:2). All of these dualisms – nature/culture, human/nonhuman, natural/social, sex/gender – are, for Haraway, 'different faces of the same question' (Haraway and Goodeve 2000:106). From this stance emerges a number of challenges for feminist practice and politics. First, there is the epistemological split between science and culture, which then underwrites the positions of realism and constructivism. A second challenge is the sex/gender split, which has facilitated so much of post-second-wave feminist cultural discourse. Finally, and what has arguably become most central to her work, is the challenge of the human/nonhuman binary.

The way Haraway refigures the sciences has entailed relentless attention to the 'materializing of tropes', the language and metaphors of science, and the historically sexed, raced, and classed nature of its construction, constitution, and reproduction. However, approaching the life sciences as 'a story-telling craft', 'political discourses', or 'inherently historical' narratives (Haraway 1989:10, 4) is not to deny the material-semiotic knot that is nature. While *Primate Visions'* (1989) focus on story and narrative fields inclined some readers to see Haraway as a radical constructionist, she was very clear about the dangers of the sorts of social constructionist position suggested by Latour's early work. Just as Haraway does not reduce the natural sciences to 'relativism', neither does her argument 'claim there is no world for which people struggle to give an account, no referent in the system of signs and productions of meanings, no progress in building better accounts within traditions of practice. That would be to reduce a complex field to one pole of precisely the dualisms under analysis' (1989:12). Since *Laboratory Life*, Latour's position has come to be concomitant with Haraway; along with Isabelle Stengers, Latour has distanced himself from the 'social constructivists' who 'confuse what the world is made of with how it is made' (Ihde and Selinger 2003:26). Together, the work of Haraway and Latour demand that we take seriously 'what the world is made of' (some of which is translated through/in science), while also interrogating how it is made – that is, scrutinizing how and why it is science comes to 'know' what it knows.[2]

Simply put (but complexly rendered), Haraway's aim is 'to find a concept for telling a history of science that does not itself depend on the dualism between active and passive, culture and nature, human and animal, social and natural' (1989:8). Despite her respect for – and indeed love of – sciences such as biology, and the meticulous care with which she teases apart and explodes such dualisms, while 'constantly working for ways of connecting that don't resolve into wholes' (Schneider 2005:143), Haraway has not been immune to criticisms of relativism. Reading some of the reductionist reviews of *Primate Visions* or recalling the vitriol of the science wars,[3] it is no surprise that Haraway has since insistently and repeatedly emphasized her stance on the realist/constructivist front. The science wars in particular made evident the dangers of being seen as 'antinatural' (privileging the linguistic over the material; see Ross 1996). Haraway takes the fallout of the science wars and being labelled an 'anti-science person' very seriously:

> I'm not going to let people forget our organic relations with the sciences again . . . me and my buddies, we are not going to be as vulnerable again . . . we became vulnerable to the cheap attacks, as if we were people denying 'reality' in some ways.
>
> *(Schneider 2005:148)*

One of the consequences for Haraway's work has been a need to clearly state her position:

> I am neither a naturalist, nor a social constructionist. Neither-nor. This is not social constructionism, and it is not technoscientific, or biological determinism. It is not nature. It is not culture. It is truly about a serious historical effort to get elsewhere.
>
> *(2004:330)*

Thus Haraway uses naturecultures to foreground the impossibility of talking or thinking nature or reality in isolation, and the turn to a congeries of figures and figurations as a means to 'insist on the join between materiality and semiosis' (Haraway and Goodeve 2000:86). Indeed Haraway tries out different phrases and terms, such as 'being worldly', precisely as 'a way to sidestep the debate between realism and relativism' (110). These questions are pressing for Haraway because they are involved in contests for the world and how we – and others – get to live. That is, these are intensely ontological as well as epistemological concerns. This drive to get beyond and refute a realist/relativist dilemma is at the heart of Haraway's formulations and refashionings of feminist epistemology (such as 'situated knowledges' [1988] and the 'modest witness' [1997b]).

Thinking in terms of naturecultures has consequences for all the other dualisms flowing from their separation – most significantly for a feminist perspective, that of sex/gender. 'Nature/culture and sex/gender are no loosely related pairs of terms; their specific form of relation is hierarchical appropriation . . . symbolically, nature and culture, as well as sex and gender, mutually (but not equally) construct each other' (Haraway 1989:12). Haraway has long reminded us that while a useful and perhaps necessary tool for certain kinds of second wave feminist political and analytical work, the sex/gender divide, and the theories based upon it, depend upon the 'terribly contaminated roots' of an Aristotelian dichotomy (2004:329). It is too easy to commit the sin of 'misplaced concreteness' and mistake the analytical work 'for the thing itself', seeing sex and gender as things, not linguistic tools (330). As she argues from *Primate Visions* onward, 'neither sex nor nature is the truth underlying gender and culture . . . Nature and sex are as crafted as their dominant "other"' (Haraway 1989:12). That is, 'sex' does not ground the mutable discourses of gender; both are bound in an inter-implicated history of relation. Haraway is not alone in this approach; the biologist and gender studies scholar Anne Fausto-Sterling has called for a reconsideration of 'the 1970s theoretical account of sex and gender', which 'assigned biological (especially reproductive) differences to the word sex and gave to gender all other differences' (Fausto-Sterling 2005:1495, 1493).[4]

The environmental social theorist Myra Hird similarly is concerned to pick apart the sex/gender dichotomy and notes that this binary has in fact 'undergone vigorous challenge for some years' (2004b:24). Drawing on nonlinear biology (such as Margulis and Sagan 1997) to sketch her own brand of materialism, she looks to analyses 'that confound the often taken-for-granted immutability of sex and sexual difference found in some cultural theories' (Hird 2004a:231). Like Haraway, critics such as Hird look to science to find different narratives of sex. Hird focuses on the two-sexed system based on sexual difference and a reproductive emphasis secured through heteronormativity as the key shibboleth to be dismantled at least in part by looking to the discursive shifts around sex found in non-linear biology:

> 'sex' is not dichotomous. It makes as much sense, biologically speaking, to talk about zero sexes (we are much more similar than we are different) or a thousand tiny sexes. . . .
> That culture focuses on two sexes is, biologically speaking, arbitrary.
>
> *(Hird 2004b:151)*

In other words, 'while nature emphasizes diversity, culture emphasizes dichotomy'; thus Hird argues feminists should look to the natural sciences 'as a useful site for critiques of this dichotomy' (Hird 2004b:152). Destabilizing sex-gender means also to disrupt the powerful narratives of production and reproduction which discipline nature and remove the grounds for hierarchical human relations with other natural subjects.

One of the most significant consequences of thinking with naturecultures rather than dualisms is that naturecultures are made and inhabited not only for, or by, humans: 'The actors are not all "us"' (Haraway 2004:66). It is in the sense of getting away from the fixed-nature/mutable-culture dualism and the possibility of allowing for non-human agency that Haraway argues for an 'artifactual' understanding of nature – one that she clearly distinguishes from the hyper-productionism which remakes the whole world into a commodity (a move which is also the target of ecofeminism and postcolonial critique). This nature is 'a co-construction among humans and non-humans' (66). One of the most pressing questions, for Haraway and feminist theory, then becomes how we can think relations with a whole host of others. 'How do we designate radical otherness at the heart of ethical relating? That problem is more than a human one . . . it is intrinsic to the story of life on earth' (143).

How, in other words, do we figure the possible conversations, relations, and co-constructions of human and earth others? In the 1992 article 'The Promises of Monsters', well before her 2003 book *Companion Species Manifesto*, Haraway was working toward ways of thinking these relations in terms of articulations rather than representational strategies, or what she terms the 'political semiotics of representation'. This is a key difference in Haraway's approach to nature and socionatural questions, which, as with some of Latour's work, illuminates serious problems in the processes and thinking of deep ecologists and their ilk. Haraway shows that for 'us' to become agents by proxy for various nonhuman actors via questions such as 'Who speaks for the jaguar?' actually involves acts of silencing, disempowerment, and decontextualization of the subject-object: 'the effectiveness of such representation depends on distancing operations. The represented must be disengaged from surrounding and constituting discursive and non-discursive nexuses and relocated in the authorial domain of the representative', who, of course, is always human (Haraway [1992] 2004:87).

Thus those whom Haraway sees as kin in the dance of companion species become, in such representational accounts (whether natural-scientific or ecowarrior), merely the 'recipient of action, never to be a co-actor in an articulated practice among unlike, but joined, social partners' (Haraway [1992] 2004:87). In such a move, even if the politically motivated human has the 'best interests' of the forest/jungle/animal at heart, they refuse these others' agency such that 'the only actor left is the spokesperson, the one who represents' (88). Even more troublesome is that this spokesperson, this sole and singular actor, is historically likely to be a scientist who, within the 'myth of modernity', is seen as 'the perfect representative of nature' (88). In order to co-construct nature, nonproductivist modes of relating between human and nonhuman that are expressed as articulations, relationality, and respect are necessary.

## Feminism revisits materialism

It is precisely issues such as the sex-gender impasse, and human/non-human relationality, which illustrate the continuing theoretical challenges for contemporary feminist and environmental criticism. Increasingly, responses to these issues follow Haraway's lead in negotiating a critical engagement with matter and the material. A sign of how much matter 'has come to matter' (in Karen Barad's [2003] words) within feminist theory is the emergence of a critical 'movement' termed the new materialism: a postconstructivist focus on the material, such as matter, the biological body, and sex.[5] One example is the 2008 collection edited by Stacy Alaimo and Susan J. Hekman, *Material Feminisms*, which argues the need for feminist scholars to (re)engage the material, and brings together an impressive array of feminist theoretical work from the preceding decades including Haraway, Elizabeth Wilson, Vicki Kirby, Karen Barad, Elizabeth Grosz, and Susan Bordo. Such a collection could be seen both as a rather delayed recognition of a longstanding trend in feminist materialism and a mark of the complex theoretical, representational, and political negotiations such work demands.

As Sara Ahmed has noted, what is worrying in calls to recognize or mark out a 'new' feminist materialism is what she calls a 'routinization of the gesture towards feminist anti-biologism or constructionism' (2008:25). As Ahmed observes, critics such as Wilson, Kirby, and Hird have routinely identified (often correctly) an avoidance or distaste for the biological and/or material in feminist theory. Ahmed acknowledges that she admires and is indebted to the work of such theorists, but is concerned that the 'gesturing towards feminism's antibiologism has become a background, something taken for granted' (Ahmed 2008:25). Ahmed's paper prompted a series of responses defending and debating new materialism, signalling the complex and contentious state of feminist historiography in relation to biology, antibiologism, and critiques of biological discourse.[6] What such debates over new materialism make clear is the ongoing difficulty of incorporating bodies, biologies, and matter into feminist theorizing in ways that do not maintain the manufactured separation between science and culture, nature and the social. As Ahmed comments, in contrast to Haraway's material-semiotic natureculture, certain formulations of the new materialism 'seem to return to old binaries – between nature/materiality/biology and culture in the very argument that "matter" is what is missing from feminist work' (34).[7]

What is at stake here, arguably, is a 'forgetting' of the history of feminist engagements with nature, biology, and biological discourses – in particular the long history of feminist science studies. As Haraway has also pointed out, this particular history traverses texts such as the Boston Women's Health Collective's *Our Bodies, Ourselves* (1973) as well as others that Ahmed suggests constitute a shared genealogy for feminist science and cultural studies: the Brighton Women and Science Group's *Alice Through the Microscope* (1980), Emily Martin's *The Woman in the Body* (1987), and the collection edited by Sarah Franklin, Celia Lury, and Jackie Stacey, *Off-Centre: Feminism and Cultural Studies* (1991). These are, of course, all familiar names in Haraway's lineage of feminist science studies. Ultimately, Ahmed suggests that gestures to a 'new materialist' feminist turn construct a particular feminist theory which is 'constituted as anti-biological by removing from the category of "theory" work that engages with the biological, including work within science and technology studies, which has long genealogy, especially within feminism' (2008:26; see also 37n2).

Ahmed's argument is itself the latest in a long history of concerned observations of the schism between feminist work in the sciences and humanities. Back in 1992, Elizabeth Wilson commented that feminist theories of science and technology were an 'exotic' area in comparison with other areas of feminist criticism (Wilson 1992:86). Even in 2004, editors of a special issue on feminism and science could claim that feminist theory had 'betrayed a certain chilliness to feminist science studies' (Squier and Littlefield 2004:123). Whether perceived or real, this disjuncture colours the claims to feminist antibiologism that Ahmed finds worrying: 'it remains inadequate (both theoretically and politically) for feminism simply to reject the biological' (Roberts 2000:1; see also Wilson 1999; Severin and Wyer 2000; Kirby 2008). And yet, just as Ahmed identifies, numerous feminist critics and activists have of course explicitly engaged with the sciences. Speaking to this issue, Vicki Kirby questions what, exactly, the humanities have to offer the sciences, given what she sees as a predilection to critique the 'sins of the sciences' (Kirby 2008:5). In an article on the 'two cultures problem', Kirby argues that '[a]s the humanities have found ways to subject scientific research to textual and cultural analysis, there has been a tendency towards diagnostic fault-finding, suspicion and accusation that militates against more generous styles of engagement' (5). But who, exactly belongs to these 'humanities'? Where does Haraway fit in this schematic? Such questions suggest a falling back into the 'two houses' mentality critiqued by Latour (2004) and the realist-relativist trap in a formulation that does not get at the much more messy way in which feminist engagements with science and nature emerged on a number of fronts.

Indeed, from the very beginnings of so-called 'second wave' feminist theorizing in the 1970s, feminists working across a range of areas were concerned with the constructions of and power over nature, mostly within the domain of what would come to be called feminist science studies. As Haraway suggests, under this umbrella can be gathered the women's health movement, debates about race and IQ, and elements of environmentalism (Schneider 2005:125), as well as critics such as Sandra Harding and Ruth Bleier, who founded the October 29th group.[8] Groups like the Boston Women's Health Collective were well aware of the inter-implications of our fleshy lived reality with the biomedical body object disciplined by the life sciences and related institutions. Feminist cultural work on science and technology has repeatedly called for the pressing need to integrate nature 'including bodily matter, into the extended framework of feminist cultural analysis' (Lykke and Braidotti 1996:243). As Nina Lykke and Rosi Braidotti argued, such a realization proceeds almost inevitably from doing feminist technoscience studies: '"nature" and "matter" are much more difficult to avoid when you move into the monstrous area of feminist studies of the natural, technical and biomedical sciences' (243). Within the 'more unambiguously human' realm of the humanities, they argue, such a realization was slower to emerge (243).

Nevertheless, even in the cyborg-inflected mode of feminist cybercultural studies, consideration of the body and the material has been central, primarily as a way of resisting the notion of the 'disappearing body' that haunts cyberpunk fictions, panic postmodernism, and information theory. Literary theorist N. Katherine Hayles, for example, is concerned to confront the 'dematerialization of embodiment' in both postmodern literary studies and technoscientific narratives so as to understand 'connections between the immateriality of information and the material conditions of its production' (Hayles 1992:148, 1999:192–193). Others, such as Anne Balsamo, come close to Haraway in pointing out the limiting dualistic logic surrounding discussion and construction of the body when reduced to the either/or of a 'flesh and blood entity' versus a 'symbolic construct' (Balsamo 1996:23). The dualist nature of such arguments, Balsamo reminds us, arose from the historical circumstances of feminist challenges to biologically determinist accounts of sex/gender. For Balsamo, the best way to circumvent 'the effectivity of essentialist versus anti-essentialist perspectives' was to focus 'attention on the ways in which nature and culture are mutually determining systems of understanding' (23). Like Hayles, Balsamo links concern about the body directly with developments in postmodern thought, and asks, 'Is it ironic that the body disappears in postmodern theory just as women and feminists have emerged as an intellectual force within the human disciplines?' (31). Balsamo draws on Haraway to argue that 'the cyborg rebukes the disappearance of the body within postmodernism. . . . Ultimately, the cyborg challenges feminism to search for ways to study the body as it is at once both a cultural construction and a material fact of human life' (33).

Ecofeminism is another site of 'humanities feminism' that has been very much concerned with finding ways to account for a realist understanding of nature. Like feminist science studies, ecofeminist theory has a particular (and different) investment in the discursive positioning and uses of nature. Arguably sharing a genealogy stemming from Carolyn Merchant's classic *The Death of Nature* (1980), ecofeminist scholarship has developed along divergent discursive and political paths. Even more so than feminist science studies, ecofeminism has had a precarious relation with feminist theory, not least because many within the academy continue to view ecofeminism with some suspicion as being overly 'essentialist' (for a discussion, see Soper 1995; Sandilands 1997; Sturgeon 1997; MacGregor 2009).

Although Haraway is rarely categorized as an ecofeminist theorist, at the heart of her work is the problem of how we craft more ethical, liveable lives for all human and nonhuman organisms, which requires constant critical taking to task of the devastating machines of colonialism, capitalism, and patriarchy. She is often at pains to point to connections with and inspirations from various ecofeminist scholars such as Val Plumwood, although her stance does not always align with some ecofeminist approaches. As Latour (2004) also notes, historically, the work of many environmental activists and theorists, particularly deep ecologists, has merely reversed the dualism of nature/culture, in the process substituting yet another form of reification. But, as Haraway reminds us, there is no untouched, 'wild' nature to which we can return: 'there is no garden and never has been' (Haraway 2004:83). Nevertheless, in their concern with nature and nonhuman 'earth others', many ecofeminist philosophers, such as Val Plumwood (1993, 2002) and Freya Mathews (this volume), or queer ecofeminist theorists such as Greta Gaard (1997) and Catriona Sandilands (1997), share Haraway's desire to disrupt the nature/culture dualism. Haraway is thus in accord with much ecofeminist theory when she argues that 'we must find another relationship to nature beside reification and possession . . . Neither mother, nurse, nor slave, nature is not matrix, resource, or tool for the reproduction of man' (2004:64, 65).

This brief survey of some feminist efforts to encounter the material and nature suggests the limitations of the badge of new materialism. Most areas of feminist inquiry collected under this label differ little from what we might just as easily term feminist science studies. This begs the question, what (or whose) interests are served by such a rebadging? While it may signal a welcome trend in feminist analysis, the term also works to obscure important lineages and connections with a forty-year history of feminist work and dislocates theorists like Haraway from significant webs of conversation and hard-won alliances. In short, for Haraway, the new materialism is old news.

## Conclusion

How might inhabitable narratives about science and nature be told . . .?

*(Haraway 2004:134)*

In retrospect, Haraway's insistence on accounting for both the material/materialist and the semiotic/discursive in our understanding of nature and environment has often not sat well with the privileged, white, middle-class mainstream of academic Anglo-American feminism. Her refusal to credit nature, gender, or 'woman' as a source for political identity; her insistence that despite their patriarchal, colonialist histories the discourses and matters of the life sciences must be attended to; and her uneasiness about the sex/gender divide as a tool for feminist critique have been, to put it mildly, unsettling for numerous feminist approaches. In the midst of feminist battles over the construction of a female subject – and a politics and theory based on such a subject – a refusal to rely on either essentialism or an antibiologist antiessentialism could well have seemed an impossible position in the late 1970s and early 1980s when Haraway first articulated these critiques. Yet it is precisely this refusal and her attempts to simultaneously occupy contradictory positions that have yielded the complex and relational feminist theory Haraway practices: an anti-racist, anti-imperialist, anti-capitalist, anti-militarist, queer, and multispecies feminism.

While Haraway's complex take on nature and gender do not always align with other ecofeminist or environmental theorists, there is evidently a shared commitment to the ethical, political, and theoretical imperatives of the human/non-human relationship. One of the distinguishing features of Haraway's naturalcultural explorations is her relentless insistence on this relation and the need to articulate our human physical and metaphorical entanglement with non-human actors. A burgeoning array of socio-theoretical movements such as animal studies, Anthropocene studies,[9] and feminist care ethics, have addressed similar concerns about the environment, ecologies, endangered species, and domesticated and domestic food animals, although often from very different critical and political perspectives. What makes Haraway's work simultaneously so challenging and rewarding is her attempt to acknowledge and account for every thread in the naturalcultural tangle that is organic life on planet Earth.

At the base of all Haraway's work is how to have, make, and talk about ethical relations with other beings – organic, inorganic, human, nonhuman, from mitochondria to other people, animals, and machines. Such a desire is imperative for a feminism whose history has been marked by the impossibility of adequately framing such relations due to racism, heterosexism, capitalism, and colonialism. Crucially, Haraway's feminist politics is grounded in a theoretical and critical endeavour that does not seek to prove its epistemological or ontological superiority, to claim a material or discursive connection between 'women' and 'nature', but makes smaller, harder, more complex demands on political movements, theory, and praxis. Her work is about constructing ways to the view the world that can remain accountable to valid and complex accounts of physical reality, and committed to social justice and action, without falling back on flawed systems to justify this stance. This way of 'doing theory' is ethical, personal, and always political; for Haraway, the point is 'to make a difference in the world, to cast our lot for some ways of life and not others. To do that, one must be in the action, be finite and dirty, not transcendent and clean' (Haraway 1997b:36).

# Notes

This chapter has been adapted by Helen Merrick from *Beyond the Cyborg: Adventures with Donna Haraway*, by M. Grebowicz and H. Merrick, © 2013 Columbia University Press. Reprinted by permission of Columbia University Press.

1 While groundbreaking in its feminist deconstruction of primate science, and as an exemplary form of feminist science studies, Haraway's *Primate Visions* received a highly critical, often vitriolic response from scientists. See further discussion below and also the appendix in Grebowicz and Merrick (2013) for more detail on the often mixed critical reception of this and other works by Haraway.

2 In noting this commonality of approach, it is important also to recognize the different intellectual and cultural trajectories that each traversed. While Latour is seen as foundational to science studies and is much cited, Haraway's work developed independently of Latour, although she has long been at pains to cite his work and point out commonalities. But, as she has frequently noted, feminist theorists like herself are often not incorporated into the 'canonized' histories and narratives of science studies: 'after I was already doing what I now call feminist techno-science studies, I read people like, for example, Bruno Latour. So Latour and other authors, which figure prominently in the canonized version of the history of STS [science and technology studies], were not the origin in my story; they came after other events' (Latour 2004:339). See also the introduction and appendix in Grebowicz and Merrick (2013).

3 The 'science wars' is a term applied to a series of (often heated) intellectual debates between scientists and cultural critics and sociologists of science in the 1990s, played out through a number of publications and conferences, especially the journal *Social Text*, including a response from Haraway in issue 50 (1997a); See also Andrew Ross's edited collection *Science Wars* (1996).

4 See also Kirby (1997), Wilson (1998), Hird (2004b), Grebowicz (2005).

5 Since around 2010 there have been numerous collections, monographs, conferences, and research initiatives under the banner of 'new materialisms'. While not all are directly concerned with feminist theory per se as much as a broader theoretical endeavour, many do reference key feminist thinkers such as Donna Haraway, Rosi Braidotti, and Karen Barad. Two useful reference points are Rick Dolphijn and Iris van der Tuin's *New Materialism: Interviews and Cartographies* (2012), which presents interesting claims for new materialism as a 'trend' or theoretical moment; and Peta Hinton and Iris van der Tuin's (2014) 'Preface' in *Women: A Cultural Review* 25(1): 1–8. Special issue 'Feminist Matters: The Politics of New Materialism'.

6 Initial responses included articles by van der Tuin (2008) and Davis (2009); evidence of ongoing debate is found in articles published in later issues of the *European Journal of Women's Studies*: Sullivan (2012) and Irni (2013).

7 While I agree with the general sentiment of Ahmed's argument, I am not as convinced of her critique of Karen Barad's work, which Ahmed sees as participating in such a return to old binaries. See also Davis (2009).

8 This was a discussion group at the University of Wisconsin-Madison of working scientists who were feminists who explored ideas about the possibility of a feminist science, see Witt et al. (1989).

9 Anthropocene studies is an emergent transdisciplinary area encompassing social, political, philosophical and scientific issues relating to anthropogenic climate change.

# References

Ahmed, S. (2008) 'Some preliminary remarks on the founding gestures of the "new materialism"', *European Journal of Women's Studies* 15(1): 23–29.

Alaimo, S. and Hekman, S. (eds) (2008) *Material Feminisms*. Bloomington: Indiana University Press.

Balsamo, A. (1996) *Technologies of the Gendered Body: Reading Cyborg Women*. Durham and London: Duke University Press.

Barad, K. (2003) 'Posthumanist performativity: Toward an understanding of how matter comes to matter', *Signs: Journal of Women in Culture and Society* 28(3): 801–831.

Bennett, J. (2010) *Vibrant Matter: A Political Ecology of Things*. Chapel Hill, NC: Duke University Press.

Boston Women's Health Collective (1973) *Our Bodies, Ourselves*. New York: Simon and Schuster.

Brighton Women and Science Group (1980) *Alice Through the Microscope: The Power of Science Over Women's Lives*. London: Virago.

Davis, N. (2009) 'New materialism and feminism's anti-biologism: A response to Sara Ahmed', *European Journal of Women's Studies* 16(1): 67–80.

Davison, A. (2005) 'Australian suburban imaginaries of nature: Towards a prospective history', *Australian Humanities Review* 37. Online. Available at: http://eprints.utas.edu.au/1515/1/AHR_Davison.htm.

Dolphijn, R. and Tuin, I. v. d. (eds) (2012) *New Materialism: Interviews and Cartographies*. Ann Arbor: Open Humanities Press.

Fausto-Sterling, A. (2005) 'The bare bones of sex: Part 1 – Sex and gender', *Signs* 30(2): 1491–1527.

Franklin, S., Lury, C. and Stacey, J. (1991) *Off-Centre: Feminism and Cultural Studies*. New York: Harper Collins.

Gaard, G. (1997) 'Toward a queer ecofeminism', *Hypatia* 12(1): 112–138.

Grebowicz, M. (2005) 'Consensus, dissensus, and democracy: What is at stake in feminist science studies?', *Philosophy of Science* 72(5): 989–1000.

Grebowicz, M. and Merrick, H. (2013) *Beyond the Cyborg: Adventures With Donna Haraway*. New York: Columbia University Press.

Haraway, D. (1988) 'Situated knowledges: The science question in feminism and the privilege of partial perspective', *Feminist Studies* 14(3): 575–599.

Haraway, D. (1989) *Primate Visions: Gender, Race and Nature in the World of Modern Science*. New York and London: Routledge.

Haraway, D. (1991a) 'Animal sociology and a natural economy of the body politic: A political physiology of dominance', in *Simians, Cyborgs, and Women: The Reinvention of Nature*. New York: Routledge, 7–20.

Haraway, D. (1991b) 'The biological enterprise: Sex, mind, and profit from human engineering to sociobiology', in *Simians, Cyborgs, and Women: The Reinvention of Nature*. New York: Routledge, 43–68.

Haraway, D. (1991c) 'The past is the contested zone: Human nature and theories of production and reproduction in primate behaviour studies', in *Simians, Cyborgs, and Women: The Reinvention of Nature*. New York: Routledge, 21–42.

Haraway, D. (1991d) *Simians, Cyborgs and Women: The Reinvention of Nature*. New York and London: Routledge.

Haraway, D. (1992) 'The promises of monsters: A regenerative politics for inappropriate/d others', in Grossberg, L., Nelson, C. and Treichler, P. A. (eds) *Cultural Studies*. New York and London: Routledge, 295–337.

Haraway, D. (1994) 'A game of cat's cradle: Science studies, feminist theory, cultural studies', *Configurations* 1: 59–71.

Haraway, D. (1997a) 'enlightenment@science_wars.com: A personal reflection of love and war', *Social Text* 15(1): 123–129.

Haraway, D. (1997b) *Modest_Witness@Second_Millenium.FemaleMan©_Meets_OncoMouse™*. New York and London: Routledge.

Haraway, D. (2003) *The Companion Species Manifesto: Dogs, People, and Significant Otherness*. Chicago: Prickly Paradigm Press.

Haraway, D. (2004) *The Haraway Reader*. New York and London: Routledge.

Haraway, D. and Goodeve, T. N. (2000) *How Like a Leaf. Donna J. Haraway: An Interview With Thyrza Nichols Goodeve*. New York: Routledge.

Hayles, K. N. (1992) 'The materiality of informatics', *Configurations* 1: 147–170.

Hayles, K. N. (1999) *How We Became Posthuman: Virtual Bodies in Cybernetics, Literature, and Informatics*. Chicago: University of Chicago Press.

Hinton, P. and Tuin, I. van der (2014) 'Preface [Special Issue: Feminist matters: The politics of new materialism]', *Women: A Cultural Review* 25(1): 1–8.

Hird, M. (2004a) 'Feminist matters: New materialist considerations of sexual difference', *Feminist Theory* 5(2): 223–232.

Hird, M. (2004b) *Sex, Gender, and Science*. New York: Palgrave Macmillan.

Ihde, D. and Selinger, E. (eds) (2003) *Chasing Technoscience: Matrix of Materiality*. Bloomington: Indiana University Press.

Irni, S. (2013) 'The politics of materiality: Affective encounters in a transdisciplinary debate', *European Journal of Women's Studies* 20(4): 347–360.

Kirby, V. (1997) *Telling Flesh: The Substance of the Corporeal*. New York and London: Routledge.

Kirby, V. (2008) 'Subject to natural law: A meditation on the "two cultures" problem', *Australian Feminist Studies* 23(55): 5–17.

Latour, B. (2004) *The Politics of Nature: How to Bring the Sciences Into Democracy*. Cambridge, MA: Harvard University Press.

Lykke, N. and Braidotti, R. (eds) (1996) *Between Monsters, Goddesses and Cyborgs: Feminist Confrontations With Science, Medicine and Cyberspace*. London: Zed Books.

MacGregor, S. (2009) 'Natural allies, perennial foes? On the trajectories of feminist and green political thought', *Contemporary Political Theory* 8(3): 329–339.

Margulis, L. and Sagan, D. (1997) *What Is Sex?* New York: Simon and Schuster.

Martin, E. (1987) *The Woman in the Body: A Cultural Analysis of Reproduction*. Boston: Beacon Press.

Merchant, C. (1980) *The Death of Nature: Women, Ecology, and the Scientific Revolution*. San Francisco: Harper and Row.

Plumwood, V. (1993) *Feminism and the Mastery of Nature*. London: Routledge.

Plumwood, V. (2002) *Environmental Culture: The Ecological Crisis of Reason*. London: Routledge.

Roberts, C. (2000) 'Biological behaviour? Hormones, psychology, and sex', *NWSA Journal* 12(3): 1–20.

Ross, A. (ed) (1996) *Science Wars*. Durham and London: Duke University Press.

Sandilands, C. (1997) 'Mother earth, the cyborg and the queer: Ecofeminism and (more) questions of identity', *NWSA Journal* 9(3): 18–40.

Schneider, J. (2005) *Donna Haraway: Live Theory*. London: Continuum.

Severin, L. and Wyer, M. (2000) 'The science and politics of the search for sex differences: Editorial', *NWSA Journal* 12(3): vii–xvi.

Soper, K. (1995) 'Feminism and ecology: Realism and rhetoric in the discourses of nature', *Science, Technology and Human Values* 20(3): 311–331.

Squier, S. and Littlefield, M. (2004) 'Feminist theory and /of science: Feminist theory special issue', *Feminist Theory* 5(2): 123–126.

Sturgeon, N. (1997) *Ecofeminist Natures*. London: Routledge.

Sullivan, N. (2012) 'The somatechnics of perception and the matter of the non/human: A critical response to the new materialism', *European Journal of Women's Studies* 19(3): 299–313.

Tuin, I. van der (2008) 'Deflationary logic: Response to Sara Ahmed's "Imaginary prohibitions: Some preliminary remarks on the founding gestures of the 'new materialism'"', *European Journal of Women's Studies* 15(4): 411–416.

Wilson, E. A. (1992) 'Is "science" feminism's dark continent?', *Meanjin* 51(1): 77–88.

Wilson, E. A. (1998) *Neural Geographies: Feminism and the Microstructure of Cognition*. New York and London: Routledge.

Wilson, E. A. (1999) 'Introduction, somatic compliance – Feminism, biology and science', *Australian Feminist Studies* 14(29): 7–18.

Witt, P. L., Bauerle, C., Derouen, D., Kamel, F., Kelleher, P., McCarthy, M., Namenwirth, M., Sabatini, L. and Voytovich, M. (1989) 'The October 29th Group: Defining a feminist science', *Women's Studies International Forum* 12(3): 253–259.

# 7

# POSTHUMANISM, ECOFEMINISM, AND INTER-SPECIES RELATIONS

*Greta Gaard*

## Introduction

Initially prompted by post–World War II technologically inflected anxieties about human fallibility, and later influenced by postmodern and poststructuralist theories, posthumanism emerged to critical acclaim through the appearance of texts such as Jacques Derrida's 'The Animal That Therefore I Am (More to Follow)' (2002), Karen Barad's 'Posthumanist Performativity' (2003), Donna Haraway's *The Companion Species Manifesto* (2003), and Cary Wolfe's *Zoontologies: The Question of the Animal* (2003). In the last decade, the academic acclaim for posthumanism's animal studies branch has become widely visible through the presence of new book series at university presses, new journals, new courses in human-animal studies across the curriculum at prestigious universities, numerous conferences, professional societies, and caucuses of professional societies (Wolfe 2009). Of particular interest to feminists, whose work on 'the question of the animal' has been traced from nineteenth century women's activism (ranging from abolitionism to the anti-plumage movement) through Feminists for Animal Rights in the 1980s and beyond (Adams and Gruen 2014), are the ways scholarly interest in posthumanism and animal studies intersects with, builds upon, or ignores feminist and ecofeminist commitments to both theorizing and enacting gender, racial, and inter-species justice. While more than a decade's worth of publications has proven that posthumanist philosophy and animal studies have been good for academic institutions and academic careers, the question remains: Have these scholarly developments also been good for animals?

The capacity to ask this question – indeed, to make it central to one's intellectual, scholarly, and pedagogical work – is the hallmark of feminism. From the start, feminism has been a movement for justice: at its heart is the centrality of *praxis*, the necessary linkage of intellectual, political, and activist work. Feminist methodology – articulated through such foundational texts as *Breaking Out: Feminist Consciousness and Feminist Research* (Stanley and Wise 1983), *Feminism and Methodology* (Harding 1987), and *Feminist Praxis* (Stanley 1990) – requires that feminist research puts the lives of the oppressed (whether by gender, race, species, or other hierarchical systems enforcing inequality) at the centre of the research question, and undertakes studies, gathers data, and interrogates contexts with the primary aim of improving the lives and the material conditions of the oppressed. As bell hooks explains in *Feminism is for Everybody*, visionary feminist thinkers have long dreamed of replacing a

culture of domination with a world of participatory economics grounded in communalism and social democracy, a world without discrimination based on race or gender, a world where recognition of mutuality and interdependency would be the dominant ethos, a global ecological vision of how the planet can survive and how everyone on it can have access to peace and well-being.

*(hooks 2000:110)*

As vegan ecofeminists have long argued, inter-species justice is an integral part of that feminist dream.

When feminist scholars attend to 'the question of the animal', they do so from a standpoint that centres other animal species, makes connections among diverse forms of oppression, and seeks to put an end to animal suffering – in other words, to benefit the subject of the research. Nineteenth-century women's advocacy for animals challenged vivisection, 'plumage' (the practice of wearing birds feathers or even body parts in women's hats), fur-wearing and meat-eating alike (Donovan 1990). Using standard feminist methodology (i.e., asking questions such as 'Where are the women?' and 'Is there an association between ontologizing a being as feminine and that subject's access to social and material goods?'), twentieth-century vegan feminists and ecofeminists[1] sought to end animal suffering in its many manifestations (in scientific research, and specifically in the feminized beauty and cleaning products industries; in dairy, egg, and animal food production [factory farming]; in pet keeping and breeding, zoos, rodeos, hunting, fur, and clothing) by developing a feminist theoretical perspective on the intersections of species, gender, race, class, sexuality, and nature. Motivated by an intellectual and experiential understanding of the mutually reinforcing interconnections among diverse forms of oppression, as well as by many women's interconnected sense of self-identity, a self-in-relationship to other animals (including humans) and environments (specific trees, rivers, plants, as well as places), twentieth and twenty-first century vegan feminists and ecofeminists see their own liberation and well-being as fundamentally connected to the well-being of other animal species; in short, we insist on moving forward together (Harper 2010; Kemmerer 2011).

This commitment to an intersectional[2] approach permeates the *praxis* (or theory-practice) of animal ecofeminists and vegan feminists because, in the words of Martin Luther King Jr., 'Injustice anywhere is a threat to justice everywhere'. For example, when Feminists for Animal Rights (FAR) activists learned that many battered women refused to leave situations of domestic violence, aware that there was no place that would shelter both their children and their companion animals, and fearful that leaving the animals behind would almost ensure the animals' torture, abuse, and death at the hands of the batterer, FAR activists began building coalitions between animal rescue groups and battered women's shelters (Adams 1996). When animal ecofeminists criticized the harms produced by injecting recombinant bovine growth hormone (rBGH) into cows, they addressed the suffering this growth hormone caused to lactating cows already grieving the separation from their own offspring (who would have drank the mother cow's milk, preventing it from being commodified for humans), and ecofeminists also recognized the issue as an opportunity to build coalitions among animal advocates, feminists, small farmers, consumer advocates, and environmentalists alike (Gaard 1994). Such praxis exemplifies vegan feminism and ecofeminism.

The *feminist* empathy for animal suffering (Donovan 2006; Gruen 2009, 2012), initially articulated as an ethic of care (Adams and Donovan 1995; Donovan and Adams 2007), was soon *feminized* and women's activism for animal rights was mocked as a movement of 'little old ladies in tennis shoes': in humanist cultures, the association of women and animals reinforces their subordinate status. Indeed, the animal rights movement of the nineteenth and twentieth centuries was catapulted to academic respectability only when white male philosophers, most notably Tom Regan and Peter Singer, distanced themselves from kindness, empathy, or care, and theorized about the motives for animal liberation as legitimated either by recourse to animal rights (Regan 1983) or an attention to animal suffering (Singer 1975). Nearly thirty years later, Cary Wolfe echoed the Singer/Regan era in his claim that 'taking animal studies seriously thus has nothing to do, strictly speaking, with whether or not you like animals' (2009:567). Between these two eras of animal rights and posthumanism/animal studies prominence, vegan feminist and ecofeminist praxis flourished.

On the feminist belief that the most inclusive theory will be the most accurate, both in describing and in correcting injustices of all kinds (not only gender injustice but also its inter-sectional injustices of race, class, sexuality, species, environments, and more), this essay brings a vegan ecofeminist perspective to explore theories of posthumanism – specifically, its branches of animal studies, critical animal studies, and new feminist materialisms – in the hope of building a more robust and inclusive feminism, one that lives up to the dream bell hooks describes. I begin by defining these fields, each one striving to offer a critical departure from humanism.

## Vegan eco/feminism

When the word *ecofeminism* began to be used and recognized in Anglo-American feminist activ-ism of the early 1980s – as at the US Women's Pentagon Actions in 1981 and 1982, and the Brit-ish Women's Peace Camp at Greenham Common – the term *patriarchy* referenced a set of linked and mutually reinforcing phenomena (*intersectionality* was not yet a term) that ecofeminists saw as lethal to human, animal, and planetary survival: not only male dominance but all the institu-tionalized inequities of sexism, racism, classism, heterosexism, ageism, and anthropocentrism, but-tressed and reinforced through militarism, capitalism, nuclear weapons, and nuclear power. What ecofeminists wanted was articulated in manifestos such as the Unity Statement of the Women's Pentagon Action, in new edited collections of ecofeminist theory (Caldecott and Leland 1983; Plant 1989; Diamond and Orenstein 1990), and in feminist utopian literature (Piercy 1976; Star-hawk 1994). In the two volumes documenting the early visions of this movement, Alice Cook and Gwyn Kirk's *Greenham Women Everywhere* (1983) chronicles the first two years of the move-ment, providing photographs and interview excerpts, while Léonie Caldecott and Stephanie Leland's anthology, *Reclaim the Earth: Women Speak Out for Life on Earth* (1983) offers international feminist perspectives on the intersection of women and ecology, linking the Women's Pentagon Action and the Women's Peace Camp with the politics of women's health, poverty, food security, forestry, urban ecology, indigenous people and environments, technology, the feminist connection to animal rights, birth and female infanticide, work, play, militarism, philosophy, and spirituality. Caldecott and Leland's (1983) volume did not divide theory from activism, but instead offered poetry side by side with scholarship, and writings by a diversity of feminists, including Wan-gari Maathai (Kenya) on the Green Belt movement, Rosalie Bertell (Canada) on nuclear power and health, Wilmette Brown (United Kingdom/United States) on Black ghetto ecology, Marta Zabaleta (Argentina) on the Mothers of the Plaza de Mayo, the Manushi Collective (India) on female infanticide, and Anita Anand (India) on the Chipko Andolan.

At the same time that the peace and anti-nuclear branch of ecofeminism developed, the roots of vegan feminism were articulated in essays by Connie Salamone (1973), Roberta Kalechofsky (1980), and Carol Adams (1975), prompting the formation of Feminists for Animal Rights by Marti Kheel and Tina Frisco in 1982, and Jews for Animal Rights by Roberta Kalechofsky in 1985. By the 1990s, this branch had developed into vegan ecofeminism (at the time called 'ani-mal' or 'vegetarian' ecofeminism) and gained increasing visibility through such publications as Andreé Collard and Joyce Contrucci's *Rape of the Wild* (1989), Carol Adams' *The Sexual Politics of Meat* (1990), three essays (Adams 1991; Curtin 1991; Slicer 1991) developing an ecofeminist critique of speciesism in *Hypatia's* special issue on 'Ecological Feminism' (Warren 1991), and the first anthology to place species at the centre of ecofeminism, *Ecofeminism: Women, Animals, Nature* (Gaard 1993). Ecofeminist philosophy became grounded in a critique of value dualisms and value hierarchies showing that gendered oppression intersected with and reinforced the devaluation of nature and all those others associated with nature via the devalued others of race, class, ethnicity, sexuality, age, ability, and nation (Warren 1990; Plumwood 1993; Gaard 1997).

By the 1990s, *patriarchy* had gone out of fashion (as a term, though not as a practice): in discussions among ecofeminists, deep ecologists, and other radical environmentalists, the term *anthropocentrism* acknowledged that first-world, privileged women were also part of the problem, the *anthros*, suggesting that it was human-centredness as a whole that was killing the planet. As these conversations fragmented by the mid-1990s, ecofeminists pointed out that it was not only anthropocentrism but *androcentrism* that was killing the planet, and that some humans – namely, indigenous societies, many third-world communities both globally and within the first world, non-elite women, and queers – were being destroyed along with the planet. When environmental justice theory first appeared in these environmental ethics debates, with interventions by Ramachandra Guha (1989) among others, ecofeminists recognized its historic connections with not only Vandana Shiva's (1988, 1993, 1997) anti-globalization work but also the women's health movement and the anti-toxics movement; in contrast, deep ecologists charged environmental justice with anthropocentrism, describing its use of environmentalism as just another mask for civil rights discourses. Val Plumwood's (1993) description of Western culture's Master Model (an identity constructed through value dualisms that rely on radical exclusion or hyperseparation, followed by backgrounding, incorporation, instrumentalism, and homogenization) offered a prescient ecological feminist definition of Humanism as the primary antagonist of both ecological sustainability and feminist environmental justice. As their analyses of species and ecology effectively transformed their feminist framework, ecofeminists of the early 1990s were beginning to articulate a posthumanist feminism – twenty years before its time.

What happened next is well known to scholars in the field of gender and environment: environmental justice, feminist, and ecofeminist (Agarwal 1992; Cuomo 1992; Davion 1994) theorists alike provided corrective challenges to gender essentialism in ecofeminism, and this critique served both to splinter and to strengthen ecofeminism, distinguishing essentialist from social constructionist branches, and encouraging theory that became more attentive to differences of race, nation, religion, ethnicity, and so on. In 1994 ecofeminist theorists met at a conference in Montana and debated the place of species in ecofeminist theory, again dividing rather than uniting scholars. Curiously, the outcome of these two challenges was that ecofeminism became caricatured as essentialist, and one prominent ecofeminist scholar vowed to reframe her perspective as 'critical feminist eco-socialism' (Plumwood 2000, 2004) to distinguish it from vegan ecofeminism (Gaard 2011). Though ecofeminists continued to produce theory and engage in activism, many began using other theoretical frameworks (i.e., feminist environmental justice) to continue their work.

For more than twenty years, the spectre of essentialism haunted ecofeminism, pushing away new theorists and activists out of fear that their work would be immediately discredited. Then, something shifted, and Duke University offered the 'New Eco-feminism Project' in 2010. By 2014, ecofeminist dissertations, articles, and book manuscripts were again being written; scholars and activists were seeking out ecofeminist foremothers, recuperating and advancing ecofeminist theories through intersections with new materialist, postcolonial, critical animal studies, and climate justice perspectives. But many ecofeminists seemed wary of 'high post-humanism' (Braidotti 2006:197). Why?

## Humanism and posthumanism, animal studies, and critical animal studies

Dating back to Greek philosophers, and re-emerging through European Renaissance and Enlightenment philosophy, humanism is both a philosophy and theory of human identity that relies on dualisms of self/other, mind/body, culture/nature, human/animal, man/woman, organic/technological. Employing hierarchical differentiation to distinguish the valued half of these pairs, it conceives of humans as autonomous individuals, unique among all life on earth in that humans can reason; it is positivist in asserting that the world can be objectively known, and constructs the knowing subject as superior to the known object(s). Leonardo DaVinci's drawing 'Vitruvian Man' (circa 1487) articulates Renaissance humanism's graphic translation of the Greek humanist philosopher, Protagoras, in his statement that 'man is the measure of all things'. Of course, not all men (and very few women) counted as fully human in humanism, a viewpoint strongly marked by hierarchies of class, race, gender, and nation. Humanism has shaped Western philosophy into modernity and continues to dominate the planet through first-world industrial capitalist humanity's self-centred overconsumption of all other species and life forms, producing today's climate crises, which have prompted the renaming of our era as the Anthropocene (or, as some witty feminist environmental justice scholars suggested at the April 2014 'Anthropocene Feminism' conference at UW-Milwaukee, the '*Andro*cene' or the '*Capitalo*cene').

In contrast with humanism's emphasis on the human as a rational, autonomous, self-determining individual, with distinct and essential traits and qualities, posthumanism positions humans as but one among many life forms on the planet, challenging the myth of human superiority, and exposing both human knowledge and human intelligence as limited and fallible. But unlike vegan eco/feminism, posthumanism's attention to species does not require attention to gender or other intra-human inequities, nor does its scholarship require activism. Perhaps these omissions contribute, in part, to the animal studies branch of posthumanism becoming the most prominent, high-profiled area of humanities research in 2009 through special themed issues of the leading US journals, *Publications of the Modern Language Association (PMLA)* and *The Chronicle of Higher Education*. Articles in both journals carefully distinguished 'between academic and advocate' (Howard 2009), criticizing or simply backgrounding the foundational contributions of activist-scholars Peter Singer (1975) and Tom Regan (1983). For example, in his overview of animal studies for *PMLA*'s special issue, Cary Wolfe positioned animal studies as 'a branch of cultural studies' that poses challenges to both the humanities and to cultural studies on 'the level of content, thematics, and the object of knowledge' as well as 'the level of theoretical and methodological approach': 'just because we study nonhuman animals does not mean that we are not continuing to be humanist – and therefore, by definition, anthropocentric' (2009:568). In contrast, animal studies 'fundamentally challenges the schema of the knowing subject' (Wolfe 2009:568), while the field of cultural studies ends up reproducing a form of the knowing subject who can enact liberal humanism's extension of rights and produce a kind of pluralism that becomes incorporation rather than transformation. Worried that 'animal studies ought not to be viewed as simply the latest flavor of the month' and join the academic fields of 'gender studies, race studies, and cultural studies', Wolfe insists that his preferred form of 'animal studies intersects with the larger problematic of posthumanism'. Moreover, he writes:

> one can engage in a humanist or a posthumanist practice of a discipline . . . Just because a historian or literary critic devotes attention to the topic or theme of nonhuman animals doesn't mean that a familiar form of humanism isn't being maintained through internal disciplinary practices that rely on a specific schema of the knowing subject and the kind of knowledge he or she can have. So even though your external disciplinarity

is posthumanist in taking seriously the existence and ethical stakes of nonhuman beings (in that sense, it questions anthropocentrism) your internal disciplinarity may remain humanist to the core.

*(Wolfe 2009:571–572)*

Wolfe concluded by urging that animal studies locate the animal not just 'out there' in the environment but also 'in here', in the human, thus practicing a *posthumanist* animal studies. It is a worthy challenge that many posthumanisms – animal studies, material feminisms, and posthumanist gender studies – fail to achieve. As Helena Pederson writes,

> What I am concerned with here is whether posthumanism 'works', not only as an impetus to think through or rethink human-animal relationships, but to actually *remake* those relationships. Does posthumanism orient us towards individual and collective actions, habits and lifestyles that, in the end, have a different effect on animals, for instance in the expanding food production system?
>
> *(2011:74–75)*

In fact, it does not.

Critical animal studies (CAS) emerged in 2006 as a corrective to what vegan scholars perceived as the apolitical stance of animal studies. In their 2007 statement of founding principles, CAS scholars criticize animal studies as academically entrenched,

> an abstract, esoteric, jargon-laden, insular, non-normative, and apolitical discipline, one where scholars can achieve recognition while nevertheless remaining wedded to speciesist values, carnivorist lifestyles, and at least tacit – sometimes overt – support of numerous forms of animal exploitation such as vivisection.
>
> *(Best et al. 2007)*

In contrast, CAS is qualified as *critical* because scholars affirm anarchist principles through their position statement that

> rejects apolitical, conservative, and liberal positions in order to advance an anti-capitalist, and, more generally, a radical anti-hierarchical politics . . . [and] seeks to dismantle all structures of exploitation, domination, oppression, torture, killing, and power in favor of decentralizing and democratizing society at all levels and on a global basis.
>
> *(Best et al. 2007)*

They affirm feminist principles through their commitment to advancing 'a holistic understanding of the commonality of oppressions, such that speciesism, sexism, racism, ableism, stateism, classism, militarism and other hierarchical ideologies and institutions are viewed as parts of a larger, interlocking, global system of domination'(Best et al. 2007).

Critical animal studies scholars take as their genealogical roots the work of not just Peter Singer and Tom Regan, but also anarchist philosophers, critical theorists, anarcha-feminists, and animal ecofeminist scholar-activists. Perhaps as a backlash, posthumanist scholars have portrayed CAS scholars as humanists themselves, for perpetuating an all-knowing subject through their 'abolitionist' position to end animal exploitation in all its forms. This charge, invoking the logical fallacy *tu quoque* ('you do it too'), fails to grapple with the real challenge of integrating academic theory and political practice. On this charge, Carol Adams comments:

I know [Donna] Haraway is not alone in viewing 'animal rights' discourse as proscriptive and ideological [i.e., humanist] . . . But in any evolving natureculture, we should stipulate that flesh eating, unlike debates about it, involves more than human beings. Humans consume animal beings. In human-oriented arguments, the fact that others are dictating to animals by eating them disappears . . . at least three beings are involved in a discourse about flesh eating (the speaker, the hearer, and the animal being eaten) . . . there is an a priori deprivation within these critiques that needs to be acknowledged: the death of the animal.

*(Adams 2006:126)*

Convinced of the inseparability of knowledge/research/practice and the interdependence of hierarchical ideologies and systems of domination, CAS scholars implicitly strive to employ a posthumanist methodology and content. Vegan eco/feminists, environmental justice scholar-activists, and other liberatory groups have found strong allies in CAS scholar-activists.[3]

## Vegan eco/feminism meets posthumanist animal studies

It seemed more than coincidence that in the years of ecofeminism's ill repute, posthumanism took the academy by storm, advancing some of the same arguments about species, humanism, and self-identity that were earlier presented by ecofeminist theorists. Given vegan ecofeminism's more than thirty-year commitment to placing species at the centre of ecofeminist theory, crediting ten-year-old posthumanism as inflecting ecofeminism seems less productive than asking, 'What vegan ecofeminist/posthumanist intersections have emerged?' To date, there may be more differences than congruences. Multiple vegan eco/feminist critiques of the key figures in posthumanist animal studies, Wolfe and Haraway, have pointed to the persistent humanism in these theories (Weisberg 2009; Twine 2010; Pederson 2011; Fraiman 2012; Giraud 2013). Is the popularity of their posthumanism a partial product of its penchant for retaining humanist beliefs (i.e., sexism and classism) and thus offering a 'flavour-of-the-month' posthumanism that is less threatening than a methodologically *posthumanist posthumanism*?

In her 2012 essay, 'Pussy Panic versus Liking Animals: Tracking Gender in Animal Studies', Susan Fraiman puzzles over 'the relative slightness of [the] remarks' in Jacques Derrida's 'The Animal That Therefore I Am (More to Follow)' (2002) that have earned him the role of 'forefather of a dramatically renovated version of animal studies'(2012:90–91). According to Fraiman, Wolfe's triumphal proclamation of Derrida's essay as 'arguably the single most important event in the brief history of animal studies' (Wolfe 2009:570) constructs a new patrilineal genealogy of animal studies by articulating critiques of Peter Singer's (1975) utilitarianism and Regan's (1983) rights-based animal ethics for their complicity with Enlightenment ways of knowing – critiques that had been voiced by ecofeminists twenty years earlier (i.e., Adams 1990; Donovan 1990; Luke 1995). Yet Wolfe simultaneously acknowledges and dismisses the work of feminist and ecofeminist animal studies scholarship along with cultural studies, based on their allegedly humanist methodologies and political commitments, when these same 'scholars working on gender, sexuality, and race have themselves been in the forefront of efforts to unseat the normative "liberal humanist" subject' (Fraiman 2012:106). Fraiman distinguishes feminist and ecofeminist animal scholarship as characterized by their well-theorized explications of care, empathy, and attentive listening to other species as the motivations for their scholarship, and activism for inter-species justice as the desired outcomes. Drawing examples from Singer ('We didn't "love" animals'), Regan (who advises animal rights scholars not to 'indulge our emotions or parade our sentiments . . . [make] a sustained commitment to rational inquiry'), and Wolfe (who insists that 'taking animal studies seriously thus has nothing to do, strictly speaking, with whether or not you like animals'; 2009:567), Fraiman concludes 'Real Men Don't Like Animals' (2012:98), for fear that an emotional rather than rational base for theory will lead to its dismissal. Noting Wolfe's *Animal Rites'* distancing itself from ecofeminism and 'disparag[ing] cultural studies', and his relegation of animal studies and feminist/ecofeminist/cultural studies to a paragraph about 'scattered work' in his *PMLA* overview (2009:565), Fraiman revises Wolfe's qualification that 'if taken seriously, animal studies should not be likened to gender studies' to mean 'if animal studies wishes to be taken seriously [in the academy], it must run as fast as it can away from anything resembling gender studies' (2012:107). In sum, Fraiman concludes that the difference between feminist animal studies and Wolfe's animal studies is 'not epistemological so much as political', since both 'protest the exclusion of animals' and 'deconstruct the tenets of humanist thinking', but 'Wolfe does so to ends that are ostensibly theoretical' while 'ecofeminists and their like do so to ends that are avowedly political' (Fraiman 2012:106). And in a 'carnophallogocentric world',[4] claims to be apolitical are themselves highly political, invoking Donna Haraway's 'god-trick', a 'view from nowhere' objectivity that is a hallmark of Cartesian views of knowledge and the knowing subject. Posthumanism does not seem to extrapolate from the understanding that strategies for maintaining the humanist identity – sexism, racism, classism, and other forms of human oppression – are also operating in revisionist genealogies that value reason over emotion, theory over activism, and background the work of non-dominant gendered, raced, and classed scholars (i.e., cultural studies, vegan feminist, and ecofeminist scholars).

But feminist scholars may also perpetuate forms of human exceptionalism in writing about animals. For example, though Donna Haraway describes her approach as 'nonhumanist' (2008), her work is more commonly perceived as, in the terms of Rosi Braidotti, 'high post-humanism' (2006:197). As Twine observes, Haraway

> acknowledges ecofeminist writing on human/animal relations. She professes deep respect for such work and for veganism as a feminist position, whilst also calling for feminists to honour 'animal husbandry' (Haraway 2008:80) . . . [T]hese seem like impossible positions to reconcile. It is difficult to sustain a feminist commitment to both non-violence and to a questioning of 'nature' as normative social relations (be they between humans, or humans and other animals) with any sort of support for animal husbandry, beyond corrective genetics to previous 'husbandry' that has resulted in animal disease.
>
> *(Twine 2010:400–401)*

Indeed, Haraway's work on companion species (2003, 2008) develops a theory that Zipporah Weisberg calls 'sado-humanist' for its anthropocentric logic of mastery that naturalizes human/animal instrumental relations, instead calling them 'mutually beneficial' (2009:27–36); its instrumentalism of canine others (denying their needs in order to produce obedience and a hunger for human rewards); its acceptance of dog breeding (which involves manipulating other species for human purposes, and for capital); and its acceptance of animal experimentation through 'discursive wizardry' that conceals domination.

It is difficult to trace the trajectory that led to this outcome, Weisberg ponders, given that Haraway's *Primate Visions* (1989) once defined sadism and humanism as connected through a narcissistic preoccupation with self-reflection and self-reproduction: 'Sadism produces the self as a fetish, an endlessly repetitive project. Sadism is a shadow twin to modern humanism' (Haraway 1989:233, cited in Weisberg 2009:23). For those with an understanding of speciesism as a form of humanist identity formation (as well as a form of oppression that permeates or 'animalizes' other value dualisms of humanism and humanist identity such as male/female), Haraway's claims that 'inequality in the lab is, in short, not of a humanist kind', or that lab animals 'have many degrees of freedom' and participate in laboratory experiments as 'lab actors' and in factory farming as 'workers' rather than slaves seem disingenuous, to say the least. Haraway goes on to mischaracterize those who exploit animals in laboratories as 'caretakers' or 'caregivers' rather than experimenters, and offers the experimenter's 'sharing' of suffering as an act of 'remaining at risk and in solidarity in instrumental relationships that one does not disavow' (2008:75). But as Weisberg asks, 'If sharing suffering is not meant to stop suffering, what can its purpose really be? What is empathy with the victims of violence, if it does not lead to action to abolish that violence?' (2009:39). Such 'sharing', Weisberg observes, never occurs in reality, for what scientist involved in the use of the estimated hundred million animals annually who die in laboratories around the world would knowingly poison, blind, irradiate, or electrocute themselves in order to express solidarity with their lab animals?

Weisberg's substantial list of 'discursive wizardry' in Haraway's *Companion Species* includes Haraway's defences of experimenting on, killing, and consuming nonhuman animals. Invoking phenomenologist Emmanuel Levinas's language of the 'face', Haraway ascribes face to nonhuman animals and then suggests that one can recognize the face of the Other while still treating the Other as an object for one's use. Playing on the words 'response-able' and 'responsibility', Haraway claims that other animals are equally 'response-able' and 'responsible' in experimental laboratories; she constructs distinctions between 'killing' and 'making killable', which 'distorts the very basis of Levinas' ethics' (Weisberg 2009:41–42). Acknowledging that 'there is no way to eat and not to kill', Haraway (2008:295) then misrepresents veganism as a practice that 'would consign most domestic animals to the status of curated heritage collections or to just plain extermination as kinds and as individuals' when in fact 'one of the central aims of veganism . . . is, of course, to *end* not encourage the extermination of animals as kinds or individuals' (Weisberg 2009:43).

Not unique to Haraway, the posthumanist celebration of boundary-crossing causes concern for feminists, critical animal studies scholars, postcolonialists, and vegan ecofeminists alike. For example, in her discussion of OncoMouse™ – a genetically engineered mouse implanted with an 'oncogene' or cancer-producing DNA from another animals, and used for breast cancer research in laboratories around the world – Haraway (1997) describes OncoMouse™ as 'my sibling, and more properly, male or female, s/he is my sister', a tragically sado-humanist sisterhood of the kind that all feminisms, by definition, should eschew. Here, Haraway's claims that dissolving humanist boundaries will offer radical possibilities in fact involves a 'one-sided imposition of culture (man) onto nature (mouse)', since the primary locus of meaning for her companion species is 'the human and human *discourse about* the nonhuman, not the *nonhuman itself*' (Weisberg 2009:48, 50). Both Weisberg and Eileen Crist (2004) note the resemblance of posthumanist boundary dissolution with political, cultural, and ecological colonialism; through the operation of incorporation, such boundary dissolution invokes Plumwood's (1993) description of the humanist master identity, analogous to the border-crossing freedom of elite travellers versus the border patrol halting of non-dominant groups (most often poor and of colour). As Helena Pederson notes, 'Theorising boundary-dissolution is relatively unproblematic for those who never need to experience oppression. Those to whom life is a constant struggle with suffering imposed by others are likely to be more keen on protecting their subject boundaries from uninvited intervention'(2011:72).

Perhaps the strangest feature of Haraway's 'companion speciesism' (Rossini 2006; Pederson 2011) is her humour, or what Weisberg calls 'wrong laughter' (2009:55), given that feminist, cultural studies, and critical theorist analyses affirm that power is legitimated through humour; oppression and the oppressed are made fun of, and nothing is done to end the oppression. While several cartoons or passages in *When Species Meet* (2008) and *The Companion Species Manifesto*

(2003) exemplify this phenomenon, here one must suffice: Haraway nostalgically reflects on the early days of dog training, when she would '*drive to Burger King for a planet-sustaining health food dinner of burgers, coke, and fries*, and then head to the Santa Cruz SPCA for our lesson' (2003:40, italics mine). With all the available information about fast-food chain restaurants, factory farming and its exacerbation of animal suffering, ecological degradation, abuses of undocumented workers, and the documented effects of fast food on human health, such humour not only perpetuates humanist dualisms and humanist identity but is also completely out of step with contemporary movements for food justice and sustainability, as well as with scholarship in animal studies and vegan ecofeminism. Gendered issues of reproduction and consumption are explored within animal studies, and these topics are simultaneously feminist political issues: across animal species, female bodies do the majority of labour in reproduction, and in most human cultures female bodies both serve and are served as the food. Feminist concerns about reproductive freedom apply not only to elite white women but also to poor women, indigenous women, women of the Global South, and females in factory farming operations; from a vegan ecofeminist standpoint, the reproductive and sexual enslavement of animal bodies *anywhere* is deeply unethical (Gaard 2010). In sum, Haraway's theory of companion species offers companionship to some species while abandoning most others; is this posthumanism, or simply tokenism?

## Vegan ecofeminism and new feminist materialisms

Posthumanist intersections with gender studies have developed through the founding in 2008 of Linköping University's Posthumanities Hub in Sweden, and subsequently the publication of a special issue of *NORA: Nordic Journal of Feminist and Gender Research* (2011) titled 'Post-humanities'. Posthumanist gender studies has also branched into the so-called 'new materialisms' through works such as Diana Coole and Samantha Frost's *New Materialisms* (2010), and into feminist science studies through the work of Karen Barad, Stacy Alaimo, and Myra Hird. These branches of posthumanism share with animal studies an emphasis on the theoretical and academic study of human-animal relations over the applied and activist commitment to animals, oppressed people/women, and interspecies justice that characterizes vegan ecofeminism and critical animal studies.

As Twine (2010) observes, feminist engagement with theories of posthumanism (e.g., Barad 2003) and the emergence of 'new materialist feminists' (e.g., Hird 2004) do not address the relationship between feminism and ecofeminism: many new materialists do not acknowledge ecofeminist scholarship, despite its foundational contributions to new materialist feminisms and the continuing intersections of these two theoretical perspectives. For example, although Linköping's Cecilia Åsberg references 'three decades of technoscience studies and ecofeminist struggles to come to terms with the body, with biology, and with life-changing materialities from a less universalist and more modest standpoint than that of triumphalist Western techno-humanism' (2013:10) and includes 'ecofeminism as a critical form of post-humanism' in her list of 'attempts to challenge humanist frameworks' (Åsberg et al. 2011:226), she otherwise omits feminist animal studies/vegan ecofeminism from her discussions of posthumanism and posthumanist gender studies. Moreover, her description of 'the animal question' as 'no longer a Cassandra cry of teenage animal rights activists and their imagery of tortured rabbits in the cosmetics industry or the beagles used in laboratories worldwide' (Åsberg et al. 2011:220) echoes Haraway's 'wrong laughter' for its caricature of female animal rights activists. While Åsberg's posthumanist stance allows her to recognize biologist Lynda Birke's longstanding contributions to feminist animal studies (Åsberg and Birke 2010) through their shared grounding in science studies, Åsberg is less responsive to Birke's observation that feminist research methodology insists on 'making the research (and the researcher) accountable to the subjects of study', an insistence that makes Birke 'wary of some academic writing on post-humanism' for the ways posthumanist thinkers seem 'preoccupied with transgressing bodily boundaries' and remaining 'oblivious to the politics of our relationships with non-humans' (Birke 2012:151, 152). While Birke emphatically states that 'a politics which does not attempt to consider the perspectives of all those who might be oppressed by existing social institutions is not a feminist politics', and concludes 'we need to start listening' to animal others (2012:153, 155), Åsberg's (2013) writing opens with questions of feminist ethics or a litany of eco-political crises (Åsberg et al. 2011) and ends with perplexingly inert conclusions: 'In any case, the world keeps materializing' (2013) and 'In any case, the world keeps stirring' (2011). Not surprisingly, then, in a comparative study of subjectivity in feminist postcolonial science studies, new feminist materialisms, and queer ecologies, Landon Schnabel laments shortcomings in new feminist materialisms, which pay 'insufficient attention to patriarchal, colonial, racist, and homophobic histories that continue to hierarchize human subjectivity' and fail to offer a 'strong political agenda for mobilizing on behalf of important issues, such as climate change, that threaten life in all its expressions' (Schnabel 2014:15). But Schnabel remains hopeful, noting the strength of new feminist materialisms' locating subjectivity in all expressions of life, including matter, can be 'fruitfully brought into dialogue within interdisciplinary gender studies' as 'White (2012) did with new feminist materialisms and queer ecologies and Gaard (2013) did with postcolonial science studies and new feminist materialisms' (Schnabel 2014:14). Twine believes that 'the emergence of feminist new materialism ought to usher in a renewed conversation between feminism and ecofeminism due to shared interests' (2010:402) – but this conversation has yet to occur.

## Conclusion: toward a material vegan ecofeminism

The preceding critiques and ongoing debates lead us to ask some final questions of feminist research methodology that foreground what these theories are 'good for': are these theories good for animals? Are they good for social and ecological justice, climate justice and sustainability – do they respond helpfully to the gendered eco-politics of our time? And are they good for building greater clarity and insight into the relations among 'earth others' (Plumwood 2004)? In other words, what might feminists – alongside political ecologists, queer ecologists, vegan ecofeminists, eco-anarcha-feminists and others – stand to gain from posthumanist animal studies? My answers are as follows:

1   Renewed academic visibility. *Posthumanism*'s prominence has led mature and emerging scholars to explore its precedents and to recuperate and reinvigorate ecofeminist thought, even when posthumanists have shown little interest in doing so.
2   Extended reach and scope. *Animal studies* scholarship across the disciplines provides greater visibility for interspecies studies and greater opportunities for collaboration.
3   Allies. *Critical animal studies* have developed a strong anarchist and abolitionist articulation of animal studies, prompted by animal rights and vegan feminist activists working undercover as academics and who are exasperated by the largely theoretical approach of animal studies. Vegan ecofeminist and CAS dialogues have proven mutually beneficial.
4   Methodological clarification. Wolfe's posthumanism offers the conceptual tool for emphasizing the distinction between posthumanist *content* and posthumanist *methodology* that has enabled my critique of both posthumanism and animal studies as humanist. My critique in this chapter augments and updates ecofeminism's rebuttals of deep ecology as androcentric and ethnocentric for its idealization of pure wilderness and accompanying devaluation of both ecofeminism and environmental justice as mere civil rights theory.

The vegan ecofeminist challenge to posthumanism is twofold: first, to eschew humanism's sexism, racism, and speciesism in its methodology and content, thereby fulfilling its own goals for becoming a *posthumanist posthumanism*. Valuing emotion as well as reason, and activist praxis as well as theory, will require posthumanism to recuperate vegan feminist and ecofeminist theorizing that both precedes and companions the posthumanist project. A second, equally significant challenge for both posthumanism and critical animal studies is to contextualize these approaches in terms of ecological, economic, and political sustainability by developing theory that responds to the racialized (Coates 2015:150–152) and gendered climate crises of the Anthropocene – for the conditions and relations among and within all species take place in environments that are co-constituted along with these relations (Alaimo 2009).

What emerges from critical explorations of new feminist materialisms and vegan ecofeminism is greater visibility and precision for key concepts of concern to both. Building on the activist observations of women in the anti-toxics, women's health, peace, environmental, animal rights, and LGBT movements, ecofeminists developed theory within a feminist genealogical framework. New feminist materialisms have been informed by some of these key concepts – notably, the empirical data confirming the permeability and exchanges among animal bodies, ecological bodies, and environmental toxins – and shifted to prestige (male) genealogical frameworks, drawing on new materialisms and science studies to develop the concepts of 'intra-action' (Barad 2007), 'transcorporeality' (Alaimo 2008b), and 'posthumanist performativity' (Barad 2003). Arguing that 'ecofeminism has been branded as "essentialist" because nature itself has been understood as the ground of essentialism', Alaimo argues that material feminism 'reconceptualizes nature in such a way that it can no longer serve as the ground of essentialisms, because it is no longer the repository of unchanging truths or determining substances but is itself an active, transforming, signifying, material force' (2008a:302). A *material vegan ecofeminism*, then, would avoid charges of gender and nature essentialism, and be strengthened by new feminist materialisms' recognition of all lives as 'vibrant matter' (Bennett 2010) – but this theoretical interchange would not eliminate charges of universalism and cultural essentialism for vegan eco/feminism. To address such charges, the contextual moral vegetarianism articulated by Deane Curtin (1991, 2014) remains crucial to vegan ecofeminism's intersectional analysis of race, nation, and colonialism.

Making connections among posthumanisms, critical animal studies, interdisciplinary gender studies, new feminist materialisms, and the larger eco-cultural critique of a postcolonial vegan ecofeminism will require extending theory from the realm of the purely intellectual to that of the political. In many cases, such connections expose our own role in oppressive structures – as consumers of suffering, as contributors to climate change, as sponsors of global food scarcity – and such exposure is not flattering. Moreover, these connections uncover the historical role human-animal relations have played in perpetuating colonization (Huggan and Tiffin 2010) – making it paradoxical for posthumanist, animal studies, gender studies, and material feminist scholars alike to continue patronizing institutions of species imprisonment, enslavement, and slaughter. In sum, making these broader connections requires restoring what Adams (1990) calls 'the absent referent', the fragmented bodies of animals, and in the face of such suffering, it requires action.

## Notes

1 In distinguishing the uses of 'vegetarian' and 'vegan' in the 1990s, I quote Richard Twine's excellent explanation: 'During the 1990s . . . the term "vegetarianism" was mostly used instead of "veganism." I would contend three reasons for this. First, I expect some North American writers used vegetarianism but meant veganism. Secondly, since the 1990s . . . vegetarianism has lost a lot of credibility as a consistent ethical position within the animal advocacy movement but at *that* time it was still deemed credible. Thirdly, and relatedly, during the first decade of the twenty-first century, notably in Western countries, there has

been an ethical shift toward, and cultural normalization of, veganism as the preferred and more consistent practice of animal advocates. So much so, that an ecofeminist arguing today for ovo-lacto vegetarianism would suffer from a credibility problem' (Twine 2014:206n4).

2   Feminist scholars have invoked the concept of intersectionality (Collins 1990; Crenshaw 1991) in order to describe the inextricable co-constitution, or 'intra-actions' (Barad 2007) of race, class, gender, sexuality, ethnicity, age, ability, and other forms of human difference, using this analysis to develop more nuanced understandings of power, privilege, and oppression. But fewer scholars have critiqued the humanism of intersectionality (Lykke 2009), or proposed examining the exclusions of species and ecosystems from intersectional identities, addressing the ways that even the most marginalized of humans may participate in the master model process of instrumentalization when it comes to nonhuman nature and *earth others* (Plumwood 2004).

3   In Minnesota's battles over wolf-hunting and indigenous rights, for example, the founder of Idle No More-Duluth and the Northwoods Wolf Alliance, Reyna Crow, has spoken at critical animal studies conferences and at wolf rallies at the state capitol. Environmental justice scholar David Pellow describes these emerging alliances among critical animal studies scholar-activists, eco-anarchists, eco-feminists, Earth First! activists, and environmental justice in his book *Total Liberation* (2014).

4   In a 1990 interview, Jacques Derrida explains the term in this way: 'Our culture rests on a structure of sacrifice. We are all mixed up in an eating of flesh – real or symbolic. In the past, I have spoken about the West's phallic "logocentrism". Now I would like to broaden this with the prefix carno- (flesh): "carnophallogocentrism". We are all – vegetarians as well – carnivores in the symbolic sense' (Birnbaum and Olsson 2009).

# References

Adams, C. J. (1975) 'The Oedible complex', in Covina, G. and Galana, L. (eds) *The Lesbian Reader*. Berkeley, CA: Amazon Press, 145–152.

Adams, C. J. (1990) *The Sexual Politics of Meat: A Feminist-Vegetarian Critical Theory*. New York: Continuum.

Adams, C. J. (1991) 'Ecofeminism and the eating of animals', *Hypatia* 6(1): 125–145.

Adams, C. J. (1996) 'Woman-battering and harm to animals', in Adams, C. J. and Donovan, J. (eds) *Beyond Animal Rights: A Feminist Caring Ethic for the Treatment of Animals*. New York: Continuum, 55–84.

Adams, C. J. (2006) 'An animal manifesto: Gender, identity, and vegan-feminism in the twenty-first century', *Parallax* 12(1): 120–128.

Adams, C. J. and Donovan, J. (eds) (1995) *Animals and Women: Feminist Theoretical Explorations*. Durham, Duke University Press.

Adams, C. J. and Gruen, L. (2014) 'Groundwork', in Adams, C. J. and Gruen, L. (eds) *Ecofeminism: Feminist Intersections With Other Animals and the Earth*. London: Bloomsbury Publishing, 7–36.

Agarwal, B. (1992) 'The gender and environment debate: Lessons from India', *Feminist Studies* 18(1): 119–159.

Alaimo, S. (2008a) 'Ecofeminism without nature? Questioning the relation between feminism and environmentalism', *International Feminist Journal of Politics* 10(3): 299–304.

Alaimo, S. (2008b) 'Trans-corporeal feminism and the ethical space of nature', in Alaimo, S. and Hekman, S. (eds) *Material Feminism*. Bloomington, IN: Indiana University Press, 237–264.

Alaimo, S. (2009) 'Sustainable this, sustainable that: New materialisms, posthumanism, and unknown futures', *PMLA* 127(3): 558–564.

Åsberg, C. (2013) 'The timely ethics of posthumanist gender studies', *Feministische Studien* 31(1): 7–12.

Åsberg, C. and Birke, L. (2010) 'Biology is a feminist issue: Interview with Lynda Birke', *European Journal of Women's Studies* 17(4): 413–423.

Åsberg, C., Koobak, R. and Johnson, E. (2011) 'Post-humanities is a feminist issue', *NORA – Nordic Journal of Feminist and Gender Research* 19(4): 213–216.

Barad, K. (2003) 'Posthumanist performativity: Toward an understanding of how matter comes to matter', *Signs* 28(3): 801–831.

Barad, K. (2007) *Meeting the Universe Halfway: Quantum Physics and the Entanglement of Matter and Meaning*. Chapel Hill, NC: Duke University Press.

Bennett, J. (2010) *Vibrant Matter: A Political Ecology of Things*. Chapel Hill, NC: Duke University Press.

Best, S., Nocella II, A. J., Kahn, R., Gigliotti, C. and Kemmerer, L. (2007) 'Introducing critical animal studies', *The Institute for Critical Animal Studies*. Online. Available at: www.criticalanimalstudies.org/about/ (accessed 6 September 2014).

Birke, L. (2012) 'Unnamed others: How can thinking about "animals" matter to feminist theorizing?', *NORA – Nordic Journal of Feminist and Gender Research* 20(2): 148–157.

Birnbaum, D. and Olsson, A. (2009) 'An interview with Jacques Derrida on the limits of digestion', *e-flux*. Online. Available at: www.e-flux.com/journal/an-interview-with-jacques-derrida-on-the-limits-of-digestion/.

Braidotti, R. (2006) 'Posthuman, all too human: Towards a new process ontology', *Theory, Culture & Society* 23(7–8): 197–208.

Caldecott, L. and Leland, S. (eds) (1983) *Reclaim the Earth: Women Speak Out for Life on Earth*. London: Women's Press.

Coates, T. (2015) *Between the World and Me*. New York: Spiegel & Grau.

Collard, A. and Contrucci, J. (1989) *Rape of the Wild: Man's Violence Against Animals and the Earth*. London: Women's Press.

Collins, P. H. (1990) *Black Feminist Thought: Knowledge, Consciousness, and the Politics of Empowerment*. Boston: Unwin Hyman.

Cook, A. and Kirk, G. (1983) *Greenham Women Everywhere*. London: Pluto Press.

Coole, D. and Frost, S. (eds) (2010) *New Materialisms: Ontology, Agency, and Politics*. Chapel Hill, NC: Duke University Press.

Crenshaw, K. (1991) 'Mapping the margins: Intersectionality, identity politics, and violence against women of color', *Stanford Law Review* 43: 1241–1299.

Crist, E. (2004) 'Against the social construction of nature and wilderness', *Environmental Ethics* 26: 5–24.

Cuomo, C. J. (1992) 'Unravelling the problems in ecofeminism', *Environmental Ethics* 14(4): 351–363.

Curtin, D. (1991) 'Toward an ecological ethic of care', *Hypatia* 6(1): 60–74.

Curtin, D. (2014) 'Compassion and being human', in Adams, C. J. and Gruen, L. (eds) *Ecofeminism: Feminist Intersections With Other Animals and the Earth*. London: Bloomsbury, 39–57.

Davion, V. (1994) 'Is ecofeminism feminist?', in Warren, K. J. (ed) *Ecological Feminism*. New York: Routledge, 8–28.

Derrida, J. (2002) 'The animal that therefore I am (more to follow)', Translated by David Wills. *Critical Inquiry* 28(2): 369–418.

Diamond, I. and Orenstein, G. F. (eds) (1990) *Reweaving the World*. San Francisco: Sierra Club.

Donovan, J. (1990) 'Animal rights and feminist theory', *Signs: Journal of Women in Culture and Society* 15(2): 350–375.

Donovan, J. (2006) 'Feminism and the treatment of animals: From care to dialogue', *Signs: Journal of Women in Culture and Society* 31(2): 305–329.

Donovan, J. and Adams, C. J. (eds) (2007) *The Feminist Care Tradition in Animal Ethics*. New York: Columbia University Press.

Fraiman, S. (2012) 'Pussy panic versus liking animals: Tracking gender in animal studies', *Critical Inquiry* 39(1): 89–115.

Gaard, G. (ed) (1993) *Ecofeminism: Women, Animals, Nature*. Philadelphia: Temple University Press.

Gaard, G. (1994) 'Milking mother nature: An ecofeminist critique of rBGH', *The Ecologist* 24(6): 1–2.

Gaard, G. (1997) 'Toward a queer ecofeminism', *Hypatia* 12(1): 114–137.

Gaard, G. (2010) 'Reproductive technology, or reproductive justice? An ecofeminist, environmental justice perspective on the rhetoric of choice', *Ethics and the Environment* 15(2): 103–129.

Gaard, G. (2011) '"Ecofeminism" revisited: Rejecting essentialism and re-placing species in a material feminist environmentalism', *Feminist Formations* 23(2): 26–53.

Gaard, G. (2013) 'Toward a postcolonial feminist milk studies', *American Quarterly: Special Issue on Race, Gender, Species* 65(3): 595–618.

Giraud, E. (2013) 'Veganism as affirmative biopolitics: Moving towards a posthumanist ethics?', *PhaenEx* 8(2): 47–79.

Gruen, L. (2009) 'Attending to nature: Empathetic engagement with the more than human world', *Ethics and the Environment* 14(2): 23–38.

Gruen, L. (2012) 'Navigating difference (again): Animal ethics and entangled empathy', in Smulewicz-Zucker, G. (ed) *Strangers to Nature: Animal Lives & Human Ethics*. Lanham, MD: Lexington Books, 213–234.

Guha, R. (1989) 'Radical American environmentalism and wilderness preservation', *Environmental Ethics* 11(1): 71–83.

Haraway, D. (1989) *Primate Visions: Gender, Race, and Nature in the World of Modern Science*. New York: Routledge.

Haraway, D. (1997) *Modest_Witness@Second_Millenium.FemaleMan_Meets_OncoMouse: Feminism and Technoscience*. New York: Routledge.

Haraway, D. (2003) *The Companion Species Manifesto: Dogs, People, and Significant Otherness*. Chicago: Prickly Paradigm Press.

Haraway, D. (2008) *When Species Meet*. Minneapolis: University of Minnesota Press.

Harding, S. (ed) (1987) *Feminism and Methodology*. Bloomington: Indiana University Press.

Harper, A. B. (ed) (2010) *Sistah Vegan: Black Female Vegans Speak on Food, Identity, Health, and Society*. Brooklyn, NY: Lantern Books.

Hird, M. J. (2004) 'Feminist matters: New materialist considerations of sexual difference', *Feminist Theory* 5(2): 223–232.

hooks, b. (2000) *Feminism Is for Everybody: Passionate Politics*. Cambridge, MA: South End Press.

Howard, J. (2009) 'Creature consciousness: Animal studies tests the boundary between human and animal – And between academic and activist', *Chronicle of Higher Education*, 18 October. Online. Available at: http://chronicle.com/article/Creature-Consciousness/48504/ (accessed 31 May 2014).

Huggan, G. and Tiffin, H. (2010) *Postcolonial Ecocriticism: Literature, Animals, Environment*. New York: Routledge.

Kalechofsky, R. (1980) *Rejected Essays and Other Matters*. Boston: Micah Publications.

Kemmerer, L. (ed) (2011) *Sister Species: Women, Animals, and Social Justice*. Chicago: University of Illinois Press.

Luke, B. (1995) 'Taming ourselves or going feral? Toward a nonpatriarchal metaethic of animal liberation', in Adams, C. J. and Donovan, J. (eds) *Animals and Women: Feminist Theoretical Explorations*. Durham: Duke University Press, 290–319.

Lykke, N. (2009) 'Non-innocent intersections of feminism and environmentalism', *Kvinder, Køn & Forskning* [Women, Gender & Research] 3–4: 36–44.

Pederson, H. (2011) 'Release the moths: Critical animal studies and the posthumanist impulse', *Culture, Theory and Critique* 52(1): 65–81.

Pellow, D. N. (2014) *Total Liberation: The Power and Promise of Animal Rights and the Radical Earth Movement*. Minneapolis: University of Minnesota Press.

Piercy, M. (1976) *Woman on the Edge of Time*. New York: Alfred A. Knopf.

Plant, J. (ed) (1989) *Healing the Wounds: The Promise of Ecofeminism*. Philadelphia: New Society Press.

Plumwood, V. (1993) *Feminism and the Mastery of Nature*. London: Routledge.

Plumwood, V. (2000) 'Integrating ethical frameworks for animals, humans, and nature: A critical feminist eco-socialist analysis', *Ethics and the Environment* 5(2): 285–322.

Plumwood, V. (2004) 'Animals and ecology: Toward a better integration', in Sapontzis, S. F. (ed) *Food for Thought: The Debate Over Eating Meat*. New York: Prometheus Books, 344–358.

Regan, T. (1983) *The Case for Animal Rights*. Berkeley: University of California Press.

Rossini, M. (2006) 'To the dogs: Companion speciesism and the new feminist materialism', *Kritikos* 3. Online. Available at: http://intertheory.org/rossini (accessed 31 May 2014).

Salamone, C. (1973) 'Feminist as rapist in the modern male hunter culture', *Majority Report*: n.p.

Schnabel, L. (2014) 'The question of subjectivity in three emerging feminist science studies frameworks: Feminist postcolonial science studies, new feminist materialisms, and queer ecologies', *Women's Studies International Forum* 44: 10–16.

Shiva, V. (1988) *Staying Alive: Women, Ecology and Development*. London: Zed Books.

Shiva, V. (1993) *Monocultures of the Mind: Perspectives on Biodiversity and Biotechnology*. London: Zed Books.

Shiva, V. (1997) *Biopiracy: The Plunder of Nature and Knowledge*. Boston: South End Press.

Singer, P. (1975) *Animal Liberation: A New Ethics for Our Treatment of Animals*. New York: Avon Books.

Slicer, D. (1991) 'Your daughter or your dog?', *Hypatia* 6(1): 108–124.

Stanley, L. (ed) (1990) *Feminist Praxis*. New York: Routledge.

Stanley, L. and Wise, S. (1983) *Breaking Out: Feminist Consciousness and Feminist Research*. Boston: Routledge & Kegan Paul.

Starhawk (1994) *The Fifth Sacred Thing*. New York: Bantam.

Twine, R. (2010) 'Intersectional disgust? Animals and (eco) feminism', *Feminism & Psychology* 20(3): 397–406.

Twine, R. (2014) 'Ecofeminism and veganism: Revisiting the question of universalism', in Adams, C. J. and Gruen, L. (eds) *Ecofeminism: Feminist Intersections With Other Animals and the Earth*. New York: Bloomsbury, 191–207.

Warren, K. (1990) 'The power and the promise of ecological feminism', *Environmental Ethics* 12: 125–146.

Warren, K. (ed) (1991) 'Ecological feminism', Special Issue of *Hypatia* 6(1).

Weisberg, Z. (2009) 'The broken promises of monsters: Haraway, animals, and the humanist legacy', *Journal of Critical Animal Studies* 7(2): 21–61.

White, M. A. (2012) 'What's the matter?', *Women's Studies Quarterly* 40(3–4): 339–345.

Wolfe, C. (ed) (2003) *Zoontologies: The Question of the Animal*. Minneapolis: University of Minnesota Press.

Wolfe, C. (2009) 'Human, all too human: "Animal studies" and the humanities', *PMLA: Publications of the Modern Language Association* 124(2): 564–575.

# PART II

# Approaches

# 8

# GENDER, LIVELIHOODS, AND SUSTAINABILITY

## Anthropological research

*María Luz Cruz-Torres and Pamela McElwee*

### Introduction

Anthropological research on gender and environment aims to understand the complexity of the relationship between gender and sustainability and to bring in the interplay between local and global processes that affect the outcome of the human-environment relationships, particularly in countries of the Global South. A gender analysis is necessary in order to understand the roles of households, communities, and nations in creating long-term resource use strategies that could lead to more sustainable outcomes. Often using detailed case studies, anthropologists and ethnographers reveal the multiscale and interconnected dimensions of gender, sustainability, and livelihoods. For example, researchers have examined the impact of development mega-projects on men and women, the gender division of labour in resource-based industries, culturally inscribed gender roles in the use of resources, and women's agency in trying to find more sustainable ways of living. Case studies provide us with valuable lessons and rich insights that illustrate the importance of considering gender when looking for ways to improve the long-term sustainability of natural resource use.

This chapter examines approaches to the study of gender and sustainability and theoretical interconnections between these two concepts, particularly as seen through the lenses of livelihoods and globalization. We draw on anthropological research in the Global South, in Asia and Latin America in particular, to provide evidence to support the claim that gender relations and struggles are intertwined with people's ability to procure and secure sustainable livelihoods. Along with many other scholars, we argue that a gender perspective is critical for assessing the human-environment equation. Our goal here is to show how and why gender is becoming even more crucial for understanding how communities and populations face the challenge of achieving a more sustainable way of life, particularly in the face of such significant pressures as economic globalization and environmental change.

### Gender, livelihoods, and sustainability: conceptual framework

Why does gender matter? Our answer is that a gender-oriented analysis is crucial for examining the complexity of the interactions of women and men with the environment and for understanding local and global processes affecting people's livelihood strategies. Although gender is usually defined as the socioculturally ascribed roles and responsibilities of men and women and their relationships within a given society, the concept is very fluid and varies much throughout the world. Feminist poststructuralist approaches have explored the many additional dimensions of gender, particularly the multiple facets and interactions with other social markers such as power, class, ethnicity, race, sexuality, age, and caste (Verma 2001). It is these many intersections that contribute to making gender a real and lived experience shaping all aspects of life.

The concept of sustainability helps us understand the effects of environmental change upon people and how they develop short- and long-term responses for coping with these changes. Sustainability is traditionally defined as 'the use of environment and resources to meet the needs of the present without compromising the ability of future generations to meet their own needs' (Berkes et al. 2003:3). During the past few decades the notion of sustainability has been gradually broadened beyond simply environmental considerations to include attention to social and economic dimensions and to emphasize its cross-disciplinary nature (Goodland 2002). It is now widely understood that the different dimensions of sustainability overlap; for example, one cannot have environmental sustainability without social and economic sustainability. Feminist environmental scholars working in anthropology and many other fields are concerned with examining the links between two or more of these dimensions of sustainability. For example, social sustainability can be understood through attention to social justice and human rights, social networks, reciprocity, and local knowledge, whereas issues regarding livelihood strategies, development projects, neoliberal economic restructuring, labour mobility, and capital penetration are concerned with the economic dimensions of sustainability. Other approaches to sustainability refer to the idea of 'sustainability science' and argue that this is a more holistic, synergetic approach, and one that pays attention to complexity and uncertainty (Clark and Dickson 2003). An emphasis on the role of global processes as drivers of both unsustainable consumption and potentially more sustainable solutions also characterizes this growing body of literature (Kates et al. 2001; Kates and Parris 2003).

The concept of livelihood also provides us with a useful framework in which to contextualize people's relationship with their environment. Livelihood, simply defined, refers to the ways in which people make a living, taking into consideration the many factors that shape their choices and alternatives. Ellis provides a comprehensive definition of livelihood as 'the assets (natural, physical, human, financial, and social capital), the activities, and the access to these (mediated by institutions and social relations) that together determine the living gained by the individual or household' (2000:10). This definition takes into account the fact that livelihoods might change over time as a result of changes experienced by individuals or households that in turn would increase or limit access to resources and opportunities (Hapke and Ayyankeril 2004). It also emphasizes the various strategies that individuals and households undertake over time in order to cope with uncertainty and vulnerability.

Ethnographic and anthropological research on human-environment relationships in developing countries tends to focus primarily on livelihoods that are directly linked to the use of natural resources, such as water, fish, forests, and wild animals. In many case studies it is evident that access to and use of these resources are being transformed or constrained by factors such as development, overexploitation, environmental change, global demand for commodities, and changes in policies and institutions. These changes, which are happening at multiple scales and caused by multiple drivers, raise a number of important questions. What happens to traditional livelihoods when natural resources are degraded and physical environments change? How do people respond to the threats that environmental change pose to their livelihoods? What sectors of the population will be the most vulnerable to these changes? What might be more sustainable pathways for future livelihoods given these changes? Finally, how does analysis of gender and the differences in men's and women's roles help us understand the outcomes of these questions? Addressing these four questions, particularly from an anthropological perspective and at the local level, requires us to be aware of the drivers of these environmental and livelihoods changes in large regions of the Global South, such as in Asia and Latin America – globalization being chief among them. We therefore pay close attention to the impact of globalization on our themes of gender, livelihoods, and sustainability.

Globalization is the current catchword for the flow of people, commodities, capital, images, and ideas that characterizes the contemporary world (Inda and Rosaldo 2002; Gunewardena and Kingsolver 2007). It is well established that globalization affects women and men differently and that not all women are affected in the same manner, as factors such as class, race, ethnicity, education, and age also structure impacts and responses. For example, global structural adjustment programs and other neoliberal policies implemented during the 1980s and 1990s drove numerous changes in the relationships between people and environments in Asian and Latin American countries, such as the expansion of commodity production for global trade accompanied by the narrowing range of commodities produced, which has had impacts on areas such as land use, labour, food security, and health. These impacts have been particularly severe for poor women (Cupples 2004; Resurrección and Elmhirst 2008). Anthropologists working on globalization agree that our discipline places us in a special and privileged position to study how people experience and respond to these new challenges (Stone et al. 2000; Inda and Rosaldo 2002; Rothstein 2007).

## Theories of gender, environment, and development

Many of the valuable contributions to the field of gender and sustainability can be traced back to earlier efforts of feminist scholars and activists to mainstream gender into development programs. An important pioneer of this work is economist Ester Boserup, who argued in *Women's Role in Economic Development* (1970) that women's responsibilities in household economies and hence national development were seriously undervalued. Her analysis became an essential component of what came to be known as the women in development (WID) approach, which sought to analyze why development projects often failed to take women into consideration and how these failings had differential social, economic, and cultural impacts (Martine and Villarreal 1997; Momsen 2004). Attention to WID culminated in the first UN Conference on Women and Development, which was held in Mexico City in 1975 (Braidotti et al. 1994), with a fourth international UN conference on women taking place on the twentieth anniversary in Beijing, where the focus had shifted to the idea of *gender*, not just women (Rathgeber 2005).

The WID approach, although considered at the time a groundbreaking path in the field of feminist studies, has been subsequently criticized. First, it failed to consider the intersections between women's productive and reproductive roles. Second, most WID programs demanded women's participation without giving them much in return; for example, social anthropologist Melissa Leach noted that 'project "success" has often been secured at women's expense, by appropriating women's labour, unremunerated, in activities which prove not to meet their needs or whose benefits they do not control' (2007:72). Because WID was premised on putting women into traditional development approaches, rather than challenging these approaches as inappropriate or skewed toward so-called First World countries' interests, WID fell prey to the same critiques of conventional development that began to bubble up in the 1980s (Escobar 1988; Escobar 1995). Finally, WID failed to address the roots of women's subordination and oppression within their particular societies (Howard 1995; Burn 2005). For 'Third World' feminists, the WID approach was too focused on a Western-based development model that failed

135

to make women's empowerment a priority (see Sturgeon 1997 for a discussion). Discouraged by this situation, some decided to form their own organization: Development Alternatives with Women for a New Era (DAWN). DAWN, a nongovernmental organization (NGO) composed of feminist scholars and activists from countries in Africa, Asia, Latin America, the Caribbean, and the Pacific, was formed during the 1980s, at a time when most developing countries were battling economic crises and debt that challenged the promotion of equitable development. DAWN sought to advance women's status through cooperation, empowerment, and political mobilization (Burn 2005).

So-called Third World feminists also played a crucial role in urging First World feminists to transform the WID approach into the gender and development approach. Their belief was that unequal gender relations and not women per se should be the focus of development and that the goal should not be to make development better by including women, but to make women's lives better, which might entail the rejection of traditional development altogether (Braidotti et al. 1994). The gender and development (GAD) approach focused in particular on how power relations at various local, regional, and national levels kept women subordinated and marginalized within economic development and decision-making processes (Burn 2005). This approach's concern with women's empowerment led to the creation and implementation of development projects based on a bottom-up approach to encourage women to become the agents of change in their communities and societies.

As development practice in general slowly became attuned to the important need to understand gender as one component, so too did the world of development begin to more explicitly incorporate environmental concerns (Pearce et al. 1990; Kirkby et al. 1995). The use of the term *sustainable development*, rather than simply development, became virtually de rigueur by the early 1990s (Brundtland 1987). With the increasing importance placed on environmental components of development, the trifecta of environment, development, and gender received more attention. Respective oil and fuelwood crises in the First and Third Worlds in the 1970s highlighted these links between environment and development. Because women were the major collectors of fuelwood in the Third World, they were naturally assumed to be both precipitating this crisis and disproportionately affected by it (Braidotti et al. 1994). This new understanding of the roles and relationship of women with their environment became a central focus of what was to become the women, environment, and development (WED) approach. Rooted in the philosophical ideas of the ecofeminist movement of the 1960s and 1970s, and the pioneering work of such figures as Vandana Shiva, Carolyn Merchant, and Rosi Braidotti among others, the WED approach sought to understand the relationship between women and the natural environment, with an emphasis on the 'links between the oppression of women and the degradation of nature' (Braidotti et al. 1994:7).

Much of the WED/ecofeminist perspective at the time assumed women to be more in tune with nature because of their traditionally ascribed caring and nurturing roles (see, for example, Shiva 1988). Two major ideas of early ecofeminism were that women and nature were both subjected to male domination and that Western science and colonialism were responsible for the environmental degradation and the marginalization of women in Third World countries (Momsen 2004). However, because of (some) ecofeminist scholars' apparent ideological preoccupation with female spirituality and biological characteristics, it was labelled as essentialist and too simplistic to be able to properly address the complexity of the relationship between women and the environment (see Resurrección in this volume for a discussion). An important publication at this time was Bina Agarwal's 'The gender and environment debate: lessons from India', in which she argued that Western (largely US) ecofeminism had a problematic tendency to falsely universalize women's experiences and situations and to avoid confronting political economy issues – 'the distribution of power, property, and knowledge' (1992:153). The argument that women's knowledge and action about environmental problems were social artefacts, not biological ones, was a strong one for moving away from the WED approach, which some characterized as a dead-end trap (Jackson 1993).

After a much-heated debate about the strengths and weaknesses of ecofeminism and following feminist scholars' disappointment with the WED approach, a new approach, known as gender, environment, and development (GED), emerged (Chua et al. 2000). The transformation stressed the role gender relations play in shaping and influencing access to and control over natural resources. The approach of feminist political ecology (FPE) has also played an important role in the gender, environment, and development field since, in the words of Dianne Rocheleau et al.,

> [it] treats gender as a critical variable in shaping resource access and control, interacting with class, caste, race, culture, and ethnicity to shape processes of ecological change, the struggle of men and women to sustain ecologically viable livelihoods, and the prospects of any community for 'sustainable development'.
>
> *(Rocheleau et al. 1996:2)*

FPE takes as a core precept the idea that gender is one, but not the only, characteristic of socially differentiated resource use, which must be understood as a complex series of negotiations over access and control (Leach 1994; Agarwal 1997; Schroeder 1999).

Although we appreciate the contributions made by the various approaches of women/gender and development to the contemporary field of gender and sustainability, we echo Lourdes Benería's concerns with development as 'an organizing concept' (2003:1). As scholars working in developing countries, we are fully aware of the many debates and contradictions surrounding the concept of development and its impacts upon the communities and peoples in regions such as Asia and Latin America. Our emphasis is not so much on development per se, as the key word to match with sustainability, but rather on the historical roots and present-day struggles of local people, women and men, to secure decent livelihoods through their access, use, and exploitation of natural resources. Hence, our attention is primarily turned to livelihoods, rather than development, as has been the approach of most previous works on gender and the environment.

## Studying gender and sustainability in local and global contexts: the importance of case study research

The past two decades have witnessed the proliferation of case studies addressing the interconnections between gender and livelihoods in the context of the Global South (see, for example, Bennett 2005; Deere 2005; Fonchingong 2005; Brown 2006; Abbott et al. 2007; Merten and Haller 2007; Rothstein 2007; Turner 2007; Elmhirst 2008; Guhathakurta 2008). From these studies emerges the need to understand how institutions, social relations, and economic opportunities at multiple scales shape livelihood systems. In particular, these studies have focused attention on the many gender-based livelihood strategies that households and individuals employ in various geographic, political, and economic contexts, especially in an era of globalization.

For example, most feminist scholars agree that one of the most visible outcomes of economic globalization has been an increase of women's participation in the labour force. Women constitute the main labour force in nontraditional agricultural exports such as flowers and fruits and vegetables (Ferm 2008). This feminization of labour is partially attributed to socially constructed stereotypes of women as being more patient and docile than men, and willing to perform repetitive and monotonous tasks or even having small hands, among other reasons.

These stereotypes are used to justify the fact that women's work in agriculture, such as in the global cut flower industry, or in maquiladoras (free trade, intensive manufacturing operations in Mexico), is poorly paid and lacks social benefits. Women workers face discrimination, sexual harassment, and health hazards in these new occupations (Iglesias Prieto 1985; Mellon 2002; Salzinger 2004). They also lack social protection and are discouraged from organizing or unionizing. Given all of these constraints, it is not surprising that a great number of women in Asia and Latin America have opted to pursue livelihoods within the informal economic sector instead (Collins 1995; Fonchingong 2005).

Another important theme that emerges from these studies is the concept of 'diversification', defined by Ellis and Allison (2005) as a continuous process through which households add, maintain, or drop activities in order to change their livelihood portfolios. Livelihood diversification is crucial in explaining how individuals and households negotiate improvements to their quality of life. In particular, the gender roles associated with diversification provide important clues about the manner in which men and women adapt and respond to challenges posed by the economic crisis and environmental degradation. Many studies have looked at such outcomes as the flexibilization and feminization of labour as part of household diversification, whether it is in fisheries, agriculture, offshore data processing centres, transnational factories and maquiladoras, tourism, or the global sex trade (see, for example, Burn 2005; Mendez 2005; Neis et al. 2005; Pongsapich 2007; Rothstein 2007; Muñoz 2008; Cabezas 2009).

But these changes in livelihoods cannot be understood merely as a one-way process of global changes pressing down on local existence and constraining choices. Outcomes such as the expansion of women's agency, empowerment, and resistance can also been seen. People can resist and respond to the risks and opportunities imposed by globalization upon their livelihoods, often in innovative and surprising ways, such as in the formation of new institutions, social relationships, and management practices for resources (Reed 2003; Bury 2004; Pongsapich 2007). In traditional communities in Latin America, for instance, strategies or responses to global pressures have included 'forming labour unions; promoting health and educational activities; working with activist religious, environmental, and feminist groups and NGOs' (Heyck 2002:20). Feminist scholars have noted the many strategies that women in the Global South and Global North use in order to counteract the negative effects of globalization (Naples and Desai 2002; Gunewardena and Kingsolver 2007). For example, one of the most common and effective ways in which women respond to globalization is through collective organization, and women's agency can be enacted in such spaces as local grassroots social movements, NGOs, and transnational feminism (Naples and Desai 2002; Reed 2003).

Case study research allows scholars to take what is known about gender, livelihoods, and globalization and to position this knowledge at the intersection of recent attention to sustainability. Despite both areas being important fields of study for some time, very little literature specifically highlighting the interconnections between gender and sustainability has been published. For example, only a small number of papers specifically on women or gender have been published in the journal *Sustainable Development* since its inception. A 2006 citation index search of the main environmental social science journals revealed that references to gender or sex or feminism only occurred in 3.9 per cent of articles published (Banerjee and Bell 2007); this situation has not changed significantly in the ten years since. Furthermore, many indicators becoming popular in sustainability approaches, such as ecological footprinting, fail to address gender as something that affects people's lifestyles and consumer choices, as people are aggregated into averages of generic indicators, such as gross domestic product per capita. We are concerned that social sustainability issues, among them livelihoods and gender, may fail to be at the forefront of analysis in these approaches.

## Lessons from Asia and Latin America

In this section, we offer an overview of key themes in empirical research on gender and sustainability in three areas – forestry, water, and fisheries – that we cover in our edited book *Gender and Sustainability: Lessons from Asia and Latin America*, published in 2012. The chapters in that collection, along with our review of the literature from Asian and Latin American country contexts, yield a number of lessons, or key themes, that are commonly explored in anthropological and ethnographic research on gender and sustainability. These lessons are drawn out of research that is ethnographically grounded and include:

* the potential sustainability of the livelihood diversification and occupational pluralism that has been a result of globalization and has brought women into new roles and new jobs;
* the duality of the private-public spheres that women must occupy, and the roles they must negotiate in each realm, particularly with regard to access to resources and participation in decision-making processes;
* the manner in which women situate their households to sustain both traditional and newly developed livelihoods in light of uncertainty and risk brought about by globalization, the declining availability of natural resources, and climate change;
* the myriad changes in local environments caused by expanded global commodity markets, and how women and communities manoeuvre around the pressures and unsustainable exploitation often exerted by these global demands;
* the emergence of political activism to resist the challenges posed by global economic, social, and environmental change, and the strategies women have deployed to exert agency, resist local and global threats, and empower themselves.

### Gender and forests

In Asia and Latin America, women tend to use forests to meet the subsistence needs of their households. They collect wood for fuel, plants for cooking and medicinal purposes, and other forest products for sale, such as seeds, nuts, or flowers, to help supplement the incomes of their families. In contrast, men tend to rely on forests for timber, charcoal, and wild animals, due to perceptions of the labour and time efforts and potential dangers involved in these activities. When major environmental changes such as deforestation occur, it is mostly women who are affected (Agarwal 2001). When forest resources are not available nearby, it means that women must travel longer distances searching for wood and wild plants, reducing their available time to take care of children and perform household tasks. Women and men have different relationships with forests; women are less likely to be involved in decision-making processes regarding policies on access and exploitation of forest resources than men. In response to these gender inequalities, researchers have highlighted the many ways in which women engage in resistant practices and collective action to deal with their exclusion from forest resources or to protect them, particularly from new threats (Agarwal 2010).

For example, in 'Democratic Spaces across Scales: Women's Inclusion in Community Forestry in Orissa, India', Neera Singh (2012) focuses on women's exclusion within community forest management in Orissa and examines a case in which increased roles for women within a local federation of villages led to the transformation of this male-dominated realm. She explores how democratic spaces for women's participation and action emerged across spatial scales, allowing previously immobile women to move away from their proscribed gender roles. Singh makes explicit both her own positionality and her role in this case study by bringing into the discussion the dilemmas of representation as one balances the imperatives of engagement with that of scholarship and knowledge production.

Another interesting example of research on gender and forest livelihoods is discussed in 'The Gender Dimensions of the Illegal Trade in Wildlife: Local and Global Connections in Vietnam' by Pamela McElwee (2012). Her study looks at the role of men and women in the illegal bushmeat trade and notes that any attempt to regulate this trade toward more sustainability must take into account gender. Here gender is not used as a synonym for women; McElwee argues that in the case of forest bushmeat, a gender analysis would focus primarily on the roles of men. She shows there are important cultural notions of masculinity in Vietnam among both the consumers of wild species, such as urban men who desire the prestige of eating in wild-game restaurants, and among the suppliers of wild animals, such as the hunters in remote forested regions who previously used to hunt for family subsistence, but who now primarily hunt for the global trade. As a result of overhunting, local extinctions have occurred, limiting local access to fresh meat and driving many nonprofessional hunters out of the trade entirely. This has had differential consequences for both women's and men's roles and workloads within households.

## Gender and water

Access to clean water is a major human right, but in many places, access to water is dictated by gender norms. Women are often responsible for making sure their families have sufficient supplies to drink, cook, clean, bathe, irrigate crops, and raise livestock. When deteriorating water quality and scarcity occur, it is often women who are most affected.

A good illustration of this lesson is provided by Amber Wutich (2012) in 'Gender, Water Scarcity, and the Management of Sustainability Tradeoffs in Cochabamba, Bolivia', where she examines how gendered water management norms become blurred in the face of severe water scarcity in a squatter settlement on the outskirts of an urban area. Although women had long been the primary procurers of household water supplies, gender roles shifted as men became actively engaged in the household's struggle to obtain subsistence-level water provision. Yet, outside the household, men's dominance in decision-making was subverted, as women took more responsibility for the enforcement of institutional rules and protection of scarce groundwater resources in the community's water system. Wutich's research offers some indication that sustainability challenges may create new opportunities for women to provide leadership in community decision-making.

Stephanie Buechler (2012) focuses on gendered agricultural production and home processing of fruits and vegetables in San Ignacio, a farming community in Sonora, Mexico, near the border with the United States. Her chapter sheds light on environmental and livelihood sustainability under conditions of growing water scarcity and climate change. She reveals that women and men have different visions of the future of small-scale, water-dependent, non-capitalist household production and that changes in this economic sector will have ramifications for community and cross-border social and economic relations. Moreover, the effects of climate change are already being seen, and this has led to increased vulnerability of women and small-scale home enterprises, in particular.

In 'Meaningful Waters: Women, Development, and Sustainability along the Bhagirathi Ganges', Georgina Drew (2012) focuses on the Indian Himalayas along the primary tributary of the Ganges River, the Bhagirathi. She argues that notions of sustainability can and should be broadened to include the maintenance of diverse relationships between humans and the non-human world. That is, the women highlighted by Drew who are fighting dams upstream from their villages are protesting not just the economic impacts of water scarcity, but loss of cultural relationships and notions of place that influence human behaviour. While pointing out the potential for greater inclusion and collaboration between women and groups organizing in defense of the Bhagirathi Ganges, Drew notes that such efforts should be sensitive to women's personal needs, time constraints, social and structural limitations, and goals for involvement.

## Gender and fisheries

Although fisheries are one of the most important resources and industries in the world, very little research in terms of women's roles has been published. As Choo et al. note, 'gender and fisheries research is a potentially rich field because of its relative novelty and the great diversity of issues and situations' (2008:178). In the Asian and Latin American regions, fisheries tend to be highly gender segregated. For the most part, women are more visible in the marketing and processing of seafood, whereas men tend to fish. However, this is changing as aquaculture takes over traditional fishing activities, and more women enter into this field. A number of case studies discuss the feminization of labour within the fishing and aquaculture industries, alternative livelihoods for women in fishing families, and women's resistance and unionization to deal with exclusion from fishery resources.

For example, in 'Gender, Sustainability, and Shrimp Farming: Negotiating Risky Business in Vietnam's Mekong Delta', Hong Anh Vu (2012) questions whether shrimp aquaculture can be a sustainable livelihood for rural households in coastal Vietnam. She looks at the issues women and men face when engaging in aquaculture, particularly how households negotiate and make decisions regarding their entering into a risky venture such as shrimp farming. She argues that the marked gender division of labour prevalent in shrimp farming, along with cultural proscriptions and taboos, is partly responsible for keeping women at the margin of this activity. She notes that this marginalization has likely increased the economic risks for households as a whole.

James Eder's (2012) research focuses on alternative coastal zone livelihood programs for resource management in overfished areas of the Philippines. He examines the key role of women in establishing new household enterprises that redirect the labour of male household members away from fishing and into more sustainable economic activities. He concludes that efforts of community-based conservation projects, microfinance programs, and others to develop these new sustainable livelihoods need to build on the important role that women play in household economic affairs, otherwise they risk ignoring an important part of household economic structure.

In 'Contested Livelihoods: Gender, Fisheries, and Resistance in Northwestern Mexico', María Luz Cruz-Torres (2012) discusses how gender shapes access to control over fishing resources in southern Sinaloa, Mexico. She examines past and present struggles of women in claiming access to the use of the shrimp resources, traditionally allocated to males organized into fishing cooperatives. She also traces the emergence of women's collective action undertaken to assure the continuity of their livelihoods as shrimp traders and how local institutions shape the course of their actions. Using a feminist political ecology framework, this case study also analyzes the manner in which gender interacts with state policies and local norms of resource allocation to understand the role of women within the Mexican fishing industry.

## Conclusion

This chapter has highlighted the many challenges involved in addressing the interconnections between very broad and encompassing concepts such as gender, livelihoods, globalization, and sustainability. As might be expected, many creative tensions arise within the process of giving context and meaning to the many dimensions associated with these concepts. However, rather than being seen as an obstacle or excuse, we hope it motivates more anthropologists, and more environmental studies scholars, to actively engage in rethinking how gender and sustainability are inexorably rooted and embedded in the daily lives of millions of people around the world.

The value of case studies is that they give us first-hand insight into myriad ways that the social reproduction of households and communities in the Global South is interconnected not only to culturally constructed notions of gender, but also to local and global processes shaping people's abilities to secure meaningful livelihoods. The fact that in most of the cases it is women who struggle to procure or protect these livelihoods also highlights the need to understand the differential gender impacts of global and local economic, political, environmental, and social processes. However, men and women in the Global South are not just passive victims, and it is important to note how in many instances they engage, resist, contest, negotiate, and create their own means for dealing with these processes.

If we as anthropologists are truly concerned about how to mitigate human impacts upon the natural resources that would guarantee our survival as a species, then our approach as academics and practitioners should include a careful examination of specific case studies such as those referred to here. Anthropological and ethnographic research provides us with the necessary tools to understand the various strategies and actions people in diverse cultural and geographic settings undertake in order to survive and whether these strategies will be able to lead to a greater balance between the need to sustain and expand human life.

## Note

This chapter has been adapted by the editor from *Gender and Sustainability: Lessons from Asia and Latin America,* edited by M. L. Cruz-Torres and P. McElwee. © 2012 The Arizona Board of Regents. Reprinted by permission of the University of Arizona Press.

## References

Abbott, J., Campbell, L. M., Hay, C. J., Naesje, T. F. and Purvis, J. (2007) 'Market-resource links and fish vendor livelihoods in the Upper Zambezi River floodplains', *Human Ecology* 35: 559–574.

Agarwal, B. (1992) 'The gender and environment debate: Lessons from India', *Feminist Studies* 18(1): 119–158.

Agarwal, B. (1997) 'Gender, environment, and poverty interlinks: Regional variations and temporal shifts in rural India, 1971–91', *World Development* 25(1): 23–52.

Agarwal, B. (2001) 'Participatory exclusions, community forestry, and gender: An analysis for South Asia and a conceptual framework', *World Development* 29(10): 1623–1648.

Agarwal, B. (2010) *Gender and Green Governance: The Political Economy of Women's Presence Within and Beyond Community Forestry.* Oxford: Oxford University Press.

Banerjee, D. and Bell, M. (2007) 'Ecogender: Locating gender in environmental social science', *Society and Natural Resources* 20: 3–19.

Benería, L. (2003) *Gender, Development, and Globalization: Economics as If All People Mattered.* New York: Routledge.

Bennett, E. (2005) 'Gender, fisheries and development', *Marine Policy* 29: 451–459.

Berkes, F., Colding, J. and Folke, C. (2003) 'Introduction', in Berkes, F., Colding, J. and Folke, C. (eds) *Navigating Social-ecological Systems: Building Resilience for Complexity and Change.* Cambridge: Cambridge University Press, 1–29.

Boserup, E. (1970) *Woman's Role in Economic Development.* London: George Allen and Unwin.

Braidotti, R., Chatkiewicz, E., Hausler, S. and Wieringa, S. (1994) *Women, the Environment and Sustainable Development: Towards a Theoretical Synthesis.* London: Zed Books.

Brown, A. (ed) (2006) *Contested Space: Street Trading, Public Space, and Livelihoods in Developing Cities.* Warwickshire, UK: ITDG Publishing.

Brundtland, G. H. (1987) *Our Common Future.* Oxford: Oxford University Press.

Buechler, S. J. (2012) 'Gendered fruit and vegetable home processing near the US-Mexico border: Climate change, water scarcity, and noncapitalist visions of the future', in Cruz-Torres, M. L. and McElwee, P. (eds) *Gender and Sustainability: Lessons From Asia and Latin America*. Tucson: The University of Arizona Press, 121–141.

Burn, S. (2005) *Women Across Cultures: A Global Perspective* (second edition). New York: McGraw-Hill.

Bury, J. (2004) 'Livelihoods in transition: Transnational gold mining operations and local change in Cajamarca, Peru', *The Geographical Journal* 170(1): 78–91.

Cabezas, A. (2009) *Economies of Desire: Sex and Tourism in Cuba and the Dominican Republic*. Philadelphia, PA: Temple University Press.

Choo, P. S., Nowak, B. S., Kusakabe, K. and Williams, M. J. (2008) 'Guest editorial: Gender and fisheries', *Development* 51: 176–179.

Chua, P., Bhavnani, K.-K. and Foran, J. (2000) 'Women, culture, development: A new paradigm for development studies?', *Ethnic and Racial Studies* 23(5): 820–841.

Clark, W. C. and Dickson, N. M. (2003) 'Sustainability science: The emerging research program', *Proceedings of the National Academy of Sciences* 100(14): 8059–8061.

Collins, J. (1995) 'Transnational labor processes and gender relations: Women in fruit and vegetable production in Chile, Brazil and Mexico', *Journal of Latin American Anthropology* 1(1): 178–199.

Cruz-Torres, M. L. (2012) 'Contested livelihoods: Gender, fisheries, and resistance in northwestern Mexico', in Cruz-Torres, M. L. and McElwee, P. (eds) *Gender and Sustainability: Lessons From Asia and Latin America*. Tucson: The University of Arizona Press, 207–230.

Cupples, J. (2004) 'Rural development in El Hatillo, Nicaragua: Gender, neoliberalism and environmental risk', *Singapore Journal of Tropical Geography* 25(3): 343–357.

Deere, C. (2005) *The Feminization of Agriculture? Economic Restructuring in Rural Latin America*. Occasional paper 1. Geneva: United Nations Research Institute for Social Development.

Drew, G. (2012) 'Meaningful waters: Women, development, and sustainability along the Bhagirathi Ganges', in Cruz-Torres, M. L. and McElwee, P. (eds) *Gender and Sustainability: Lessons From Asia and Latin America*. Tucson: The University of Arizona Press, 142–164.

Eder, J. (2012) 'The role of gender in the reduction of fishing effort in the coastal Philippines', in Cruz-Torres, M. L. and McElwee, P. (eds) *Gender and Sustainability: Lessons From Asia and Latin America*. Tucson: The University of Arizona Press, 187–206.

Ellis, F. (2000) *Rural Livelihoods and Diversity in Developing Countries*. Oxford: Oxford University Press.

Ellis, F. and Allison, E. (2005) *Linking Livelihood Diversification to Natural Resources in a Poverty Reduction Context*. Online. Available at: www.uea.ac.uk/polopoly_fs/1.53420!2005%20fao%20div%20briefing.pdf.

Elmhirst, R. (2008) 'Multi-local livelihoods, natural resource management and gender in upland Indonesia', in Resurrección, B. and Elmhirst, R. (eds) *Gender and Natural Resource Management: Livelihoods, Mobility and Interventions*. Sterling, VA: Earthscan, 67–86.

Escobar, A. (1988) 'Power and visibility: Development and the invention and management of the Third World', *Cultural Anthropology* 3(4): 428–443.

Escobar, A. (1995) *Encountering Development: The Making and Unmaking of the Third World*. Princeton, NJ: Princeton University Press.

Ferm, N. (2008) 'Non-traditional agricultural export industries: Conditions for women workers in Colombia and Peru', *Gender & Development* 16(1): 13–26.

Fonchingong, C. (2005) *Negotiating Livelihoods Beyond Beijing: The Burden of Women Food Vendors in the Informal Economy of Limbe, Cameroon*. Oxford: Blackwell Publishing.

Goodland, R. (2002) *Sustainability: Human, Social, Economic and Environmental*. Washington, DC: The World Bank.

Guhathakurta, M. (2008) 'Globalization, class and gender relations: The shrimp industry in southwestern Bangladesh', *Development* 51: 212–219.

Gunewardena, N. and Kingsolver, A. (eds) (2007) *The Gender of Globalization: Women Navigating Cultural and Economic Marginalities*. Santa Fe, NM: School of American Research Press.

Hapke, H. and Ayyankeril, D. (2004) 'Gender, the work-life course, and livelihood strategies in a South Indian fish market', *Gender, Place and Culture* 11(2): 229–256.

Heyck, D. L. D. (2002) *Surviving Globalization in Three Latin American Communities*. Peterborough, Ontario: Broadview Press.

Howard, R. (1995) 'Women's rights and the right to development', in Peters, J. and Wolper, A. (eds) *Women's Rights, Human Rights: International Feminist Perspectives*. New York: Routledge, 301–316.

Iglesias Prieto, N. (1985) *La flor más bella de la maquiladora*. Mexico City, Secretaría de Educación Pública and Centro de Estudios Fronterizos del Norte de México.

Inda, J. and Rosaldo, R. (2002) *The Anthropology of Globalization: A Reader*. Malden, MA: Blackwell Publishers.

Jackson, C. (1993) 'Doing what comes naturally? Women and environment in development', *World Development* 21(12): 1947–1963.

Kates, R. W., Clark, W. C., Corell, R., Hall, J. M., Jaeger, C. C., Lowe, I., McCarthy, J. J., Schellnhuber, H. J., Bolin, B., Dickson, N. M., Faucheux, S., Gallopin, G. C., Grübler, A., Huntley, B., Jäger, J., Jodha, N. S., Kasperson, R. E., Mabogunje, A., Matson, P., Mooney, H., Moore III, B., O'Riordan, T. and Svedin, U. (2001) 'Environment and development: Sustainability science', *Science* 292(5517): 641–642.

Kates, R. W. and Parris, T. M. (2003) 'Long-term trends and a sustainability transition', *Proceedings of the National Academy of Sciences* 100(14): 8062–8067.

Kirkby, J., O'Keefe, P. and Timberlake, L. (1995) *The Earthscan Reader in Sustainable Development*. London: Earthscan.

Leach, M. (1994) *Rainforest Relations: Gender and Resource Use Among the Mende of Gola, Sierra Leone*. Washington, DC: Smithsonian Institute Press.

Leach, M. (2007) 'Earth mother myths and other ecofeminist fables: How a strategic notion rose and fell', *Development and Change* 38(1): 67–85.

McElwee, P. (2012) 'The gender dimensions of the illegal trade in wildlife: Local and global connections in Vietnam', in Cruz-Torres, M. L. and McElwee, P. (eds) *Gender and Sustainability: Lessons From Asia and Latin America*. Tucson: The University of Arizona Press, 71–96.

Martine, G. and Villarreal, M. (1997) *Gender and Sustainability: Reassessing Linkages and Issues*. Rome: Sustainable Development Department, Food and Agriculture Organization of the United Nations.

Mellon, C. (2002) *Deceptive Beauty: A Look at the Global Flower Industry*. Victoria, BC: Victoria International Development Education Association.

Mendez, J. (2005) *From the Revolution to the Maquiladoras: Gender, Labor, and Globalization in Nicaragua*. Durham, NC: Duke University Press.

Merten, S. and Haller, T. (2007) 'Culture, changing livelihoods, and HIV/AIDS discourse: Reframing the institutionalization of fish-for-sex exchange in the Zambian Kafue Flats', *Culture, Health and Sexuality* 9(1): 69–83.

Momsen, J. (2004) *Gender and Development*. New York: Routledge.

Muñoz, C. B. (2008) *Transnational Tortillas: Race, Gender, and Shop-floor Politics in Mexico and the United States*. Ithaca, NY: Cornell University Press.

Naples, N. and Desai, M. (eds) (2002) *Women's Activism and Globalization: Linking Local Struggles and Transnational Politics*. New York: Routledge.

Neis, B., Binkley, M. and Gerard, S. (eds) (2005) *Changing Tides: Gender, Fisheries and Globalization*. Halifax, Nova Scotia: Fernwood Publishing.

Pearce, D., Barbier, E. and Markandya, A. (1990) *Sustainable Development: Economics and Environment in the Third World*. Aldershot: E. Elgar Publishers.

Pongsapich, A. (2007) 'Women's movements in the globalizing world: The case of Thailand', in Jaquette, J. and Summerfield, G. (eds) *Women and Gender Equity in Development Theory and Practice: Institutions, Resources, and Mobilization*. Durham, NC: Duke University Press, 219–239.

Rathgeber, E. (2005) 'Gender and development as a fugitive concept', *Revue Canadienne d'Etudes du Developpement* 26: 579–591.

Reed, M. (2003) *Taking Stands: Gender and the Sustainability of Rural Communities*. Vancouver: University of British Columbia Press.

Resurrección, B. and Elmhirst, R. (eds) (2008) *Gender and Natural Resource Management: Livelihoods, Mobility and Interventions*. Sterling, VA: Earthscan.

Rocheleau, D., Thomas-Slayter, B. and Wangari, E. (eds) (1996) *Feminist Political Ecology: Global Issues and Local Experiences*. New York: Routledge.

Rothstein, F. (2007) *Globalization in Rural Mexico: Three Decades of Change*. Austin: University of Texas Press.

Salzinger, L. (2004) 'From gender as object to gender as verb: Rethinking how global restructuring happens', *Critical Sociology* 30: 43–62.

Schroeder, R. (1999) *Shady Practices: Agroforestry and Gender Politics in The Gambia*. Berkeley, CA: University of California Press.

Shiva, V. (1988) *Staying Alive: Women, Ecology and Development*. London: Zed Books.

Singh, N. M. (2012) 'Democratic spaces across scales: Women's inclusion in community forestry in Orissa, India', in Cruz-Torres, M. L. and McElwee, P. (eds) *Gender and Sustainability: Lessons From Asia and Latin America*. Tucson: The University of Arizona Press, 50–70.

Stone, M., Haugerud, A. and Little, P. (2000) 'Commodities and globalization: Anthropological perspectives', in Haugerud, A., Stone, M. and Little, P. (eds) *Commodities and Globalization: Anthropological Perspectives*. New York: Rowman & Littlefield, 1–29.

Sturgeon, N. (1997) *Ecofeminist Natures: Race, Gender, Feminist Theory and Political Action*. New York: Routledge.

Turner, S. (2007) 'Trading old textiles: The selective diversification of highland livelihoods in northern Vietnam', *Human Organization* 66(4): 389–404.

Verma, R. (2001) *Gender, Land, and Livelihoods in East Africa*. Ottawa, Ontario: International Development Research Centre.

Vu, H. A. (2012) 'Gender, sustainability, and shrimp farming: Negotiating risky business in Vietman's Mekong Delta', in Cruz-Torres, M. L. and McElwee, P. (eds) *Gender and Sustainability: Lessons From Asia and Latin America*. Tucson: The University of Arizona Press, 165–186.

Wutich, A. (2012) 'Gender, water scarcity, and the management of sustainability tradeoffs in Cochabamba, Bolivia', in Cruz-Torres, M. L. and McElwee, P. (eds) *Gender and Sustainability: Lessons From Asia and Latin America*. Tucson: The University of Arizona Press, 97–120.

# 9

# GENDER'S CRITICAL EDGE

## Feminist political ecology, postcolonial intersectionality, and the coupling of race and gender

*Sharlene Mollett*

## Introduction

Feminist political ecology (FPE) is an important and influential approach to gender and environment research in the social sciences. In this chapter, I discuss how feminist political ecology and increased attention to social difference provides a useful conceptual terrain for interrogating environmental change and mainstream international development policies. While recognizing the importance of gender in feminist political ecology, and in gender and environment literature more generally, I want to problematize the privileging of gender over other forms of difference in FPE. Drawing on the insights from feminist geography and black feminist theorizing, I argue for a *postcolonial intersectionality* as a way to unleash the multidimensional and radical potential of gender in environmental scholarship. This chapter also serves to illuminate the way colonial practices and stereotypes remain embedded in development practice, even after colonialism. Then, I demonstrate how a postcolonial intersectional analysis can be used to understand environmental conflicts by applying it to ethnographic research conducted in Honduras. I provide a partial view of the life experiences of two similar, but different Miskito women to show how multiple forms of power and positionings shape natural resource struggles. To close, I argue that gender and race together, as a mutually constituted coupling, offer great insight to the illumination of the power dynamics embedded in natural resource contests. As such, postcolonial intersectional analyses help to advance FPE research and to procure a robust critique of modernist development thought and practice.

## Feminist political ecology

Feminist political ecology emerged as a subfield of mainstream political ecology during the early 1990s. Political ecology is a diverse field of scholarship with an aim to blend political economy with multiple notions of ecology (Blaikie and Brookfield 1987; Neumann 1997). It is a popular arena of geographic inquiry and has applications across numerous themes: poverty, environmental degradation, biodiversity conservation, mining, and extraction, to name a few. With a strong focus on social justice, political ecologists work to disclose how societal inequalities are structural – namely that the various ideologies that underpin power relations (gender, race, nation, sexuality,

146

class) are part of the central organizing logics of societies. A core theme is that power structures are woven into the production of space and have material and symbolic outcomes.

Feminist political ecology emerged to counter the tendency within political ecology to illuminate class logics and inequalities and state and global scaled struggles, rather than gender and patriarchal struggles at more micro-locales, such as within communities and households. Feminist critics, largely working within geography and development fields, problematized the focus on male resource users to the neglect of questions about how women and gendered power relations factored into understandings of environmental change. In 1996 Dianne Rocheleau, Barbara Thomas-Slayter, and Esther Wangari published the landmark volume *Feminist Political Ecology: Global Issues and Local Experiences*. In it they insist that as a conceptual framework for critiquing international development, FPE must employ gender as 'a critical variable in shaping resource access and control, interacting with class, caste, race, culture and ethnicity to shape processes of ecological change' (1996:4).

Notwithstanding this stated openness to several different axes of social difference within early FPE scholarship, feminist political ecological analyses tend to regard gender as the most significant factor in resource struggles and environmental change, rights, and knowledges across scales. From global environmental policies to national development projects to household livelihood struggles, FPE highlights how gender and patriarchy are privileged forms of difference that shape struggles over access to, and control of, the environment; mobilization for rights; and the recognition of environmental knowledges. Such struggles unfold in everyday practices and engender body politics (Rocheleau et al. 1996; Mackenzie 1998; Jarosz 1999; Gezon 2006). Attention to gender difference improves our understandings of how international development projects, such as land administration, export-led industrial agriculture, mining and resource extraction, water privatization, sanitation services, urban gentrification, and resettlement affect women and men in distinct ways.

In FPE, gender differences are often viewed at the household level. Analyzing household relations provides a nuanced conceptualization of gender relations in the context of development interventions both nationally and internationally. Judith Carney, for instance, writes that a focus on the household 'brings attention to the crucial role of family authority relations of property in structuring the gendered division of labour and access to rural resources' (1996:165). For example, social and historical land use changes in the Gambian wetlands illustrate how women's reduced control over wetlands takes place simultaneously with the devaluation of women's labour and therefore disclose the various ways environmental and societal change are interwoven in rural Gambia (Carney 1996, 2004). A focus on the household and environmental change challenges the disparate spheres of production and distribution evident in mainstream development economic thinking regarding household decision-making (Kabeer 1994:126). FPE also offers an excellent vantage point for understanding how 'the forms of patriarchy present women with distinct "rules of the game" and call for different strategies to maximize security and optimize life options with varying potential for active or passive resistance in the face of oppression' (Kandiyoti 1988:274; see also Mollett 2010). As a result, women's empowerment and an acknowledgement of women's agency, however paradoxical in a variety of environmental struggles and tensions, remain a key focus in the FPE scholarship (Rocheleau et al. 1996; Sundberg 2004; Harris 2006; Rocheleau 2008; Mollett 2010). In the context of agrarian restructuring in Botswana, for instance, the push toward commercial production and agribusiness has led women to embrace their traditional roles as small scale farmers where women participate in the commercial urban agriculture sector without the dependence on male relatives that is common in agrarian landscapes. While the sector puts the squeeze on many rural families, women working as individuals are able to gain formal rights to land and to find indirect access to household necessities such as water. Moreover, because poultry farming is classified in Botswana as 'women's work', low and middle-income women have been able to participate in the poultry subsector and are 'ultimately making new claims over commercial agriculture production from which they have been largely excluded' (Hovorka 2006:220). Hovorka explains that women have welcomed their subjugated gender identities and see 'poultry work' as a way to resist exclusion from traditional male oppression in commercial agriculture. The women in Hovorka's research reflect what Nightingale (2011) refers to as 'resilient contestations', whereby gender boundaries that would normally exclude women are 'side-stepped'. Such a move complicates and challenges male privilege in the distribution of development benefits.

## Gender and race in feminist political ecology

In more recent years, FPE has moved toward 'troubling' a primary focus on gender in natural resource struggles. 'New Feminist Political Ecologies', as coined by Rebecca Elmhirst (2011), builds upon poststructural and postcolonial theorizing to shape the foci within FPE toward other kinds of differences beyond gender and to understand the ways development practices take shape through the environment in the Global South. In this vein, I look to contribute to 'New Feminist Political Ecologies' by making visible the way race and gender, through the concept of *postcolonial intersectionality* cannot be separated, and that gender does not act alone. Like gendered oppression and patriarchal practice, race and racialization operate through everyday practices where struggles over rights and resources are spatialized in reference to, and through presumed essence within, racialized and gendered bodies. While FPE is seemingly open to interrogating how gender is understood through connections to other kinds of differences (Gururani 2002; Sundberg 2004; Nightingale 2006; Asher 2009; Sultana 2011), very few analyses stray from privileging *gender* in shaping 'the struggles of men and women to sustain ecologically viable livelihoods' (Rocheleau et al. 1996:4). Take, for instance, the important work by Hapke and Ayyankeril (2004) on fisher folk in Kerala. These scholars examine the various shapings of urban-rural localities in the context of economic restructuring in the fishing sector. This work includes a description of how fisher folk, practicing a caste-based identity have 'lagged considerably far behind the rest of Keralan society in terms of social and economic welfare and have ranked among the poorest communities in the state' (Hapke and Ayyankeril 2004:235). However, there is no mention of the process through which caste and religious power inequalities create or limit choices for women and men from Christian and Muslim fishing communities in Kerala. Instead, caste and religious differences are explained in economic terms, while 'gender norms and divisions of labour and their interactions with institutions, events and individualized household circumstances to create particular experiences of work for men and women' (Hapke and Ayyankeril 2004:251) remain central to their argument. This is *not* a critique of Hapke and Ayyankeril's work, but rather an example of the way gender is predominantly approached and positioned in the field of FPE. Their piece reflects for us the prevailing ambivalence toward differences that has been apparent in the subfield since the 1990s, with only a limited number of exceptions (see Sundberg 2004; Mollett 2010; Nightingale 2011).

Ambivalence toward difference unfolds in a number of ways. First, while FPE has tended to homogenize groups of women, ambivalence around difference is also illustrated by the way scholars rarely account for how men and their gendered identities are shaped by racial, ethnic, and caste racializations as positioned vis-à-vis development interventions at the village level and beyond. Feminist theory acknowledges the existence of 'paradoxical space' occupying a place on the margin and the centre simultaneously (hooks 1984; Collins 1990; Rose 1993). Such paradoxical spatialities occur for men too: they may be at the patriarchal centre of the household and village life, but due to their racialized identities in the nation, as tribal, black, nomadic, and/ or indigenous, they may simultaneously exist at the margins of societies (Jarosz 1992; Mollett

2006, 2011; Li 2007). Such complexities have contradictory positions for women, as I will illustrate later in the chapter. After feminist postcolonial theorist Chandra Mohanty, I argue that 'the privileged positioning and exploratory potential of gender difference as the origin of oppression' is questionable (1991:59).

Second, this paucity of difference may be linked to operations of whiteness in our own scholarly knowledge production. In fact, our 'whiteness', as feminist geographers and geographers more broadly, possibly constrains the recognition of race and racialization where we seek to understand struggles to secure natural resource access in the Global South. Certainly, the fact that whiteness (as a cultural project) and white bodies (as phenotypical traits) remain the norm against which difference is fashioned, in the discipline of geography and around the world (Bonnett 2000; Kobayashi and Peake 2000; Pulido 2000; Sundberg 2005), has shaped knowledge production. Such a history converges in a tendency for black and brown bodies to become the most common object of analysis (Collins 1990; Mohanty 1991).

Third, in feminist geography, and in FPE more specifically, gender is often understood as shorthand for other differences. This is troubling, and while my reasons for being troubled echo similar critiques of feminism that have been articulated by women of colour and Third World feminists for almost three decades, they are worth repeating. Indeed, as Crenshaw has argued, 'it is fairly obvious that treating different things the same can generate as much inequality as treating the same things differently' (1997:285). Obscuring race behind gender elicits the notion of a monolithic 'women's experience' that unfolds autonomously with other social axes of power (Harris 1997:31). Furthermore, to use gender as code for other kinds of differences ignores the hierarchical positions of FPE scholars and the communities that we study. Such erasure reinforces 'whiteness as the constitutive racial component of gender', or what Gillman calls 'a white cultural narrative of race', whereby race is placed beyond the arena of gender. In such narratives race intersects with gender oppression but in a way that obfuscates racial power, 'keeping difference from making a difference' (2007:120). This may present a practical challenge; the 'problem occurs when thinkers reify their respective starting points and cease to examine the assumptions that frame them' (Collins 2008:71), a practice I believe marginalizes race repeatedly.

Lastly, this lack of racial inquiry in FPE may be rooted in more practical barriers. I admit, as black feminist scholar Patricia Hill Collins has noted, that given the complexities of a truly intersectional analysis, we have to 'decide which systems of power to bracket as so-called background systems and which two or three entities of the pantheon of systems of power to emphasize in the foreground' (2008:73). However, in light of the entanglements of race and gender, Crenshaw and Collins wrote from their own positions as African American women/activists/scholars and at a particular moment in US racial history and spatial landscape: democratic promises of individual freedom amidst persistent segregation. The fact that the specific, racialized space from which they wrote and lived demands an understanding of oppression beyond gender discrimination is important for feminist political ecologists to consider. It demonstrates that the operations of race are deeply spatial and temporal. As such, an understanding of gender in 'New Feminist Political Ecologies' (Elmhirst 2011) would be richly served by careful theorizations of the 'colonial present' articulated through race, racialization, and whiteness, as well as structural and enduring socio-economic inequalities between the Global North and Global South.

## Postcolonial intersectionality

So, how can feminist political ecologists think gender differently? Since becoming visible in the 1980s, intersectionality remains a useful concept for making sense of how 'any particular individual stands at the crossroads of multiple groups' (Minow 1997:38 in Valentine 2007:12).

The concept of intersectionality is credited to critical race theorist Kimberlé Crenshaw (1989), who worked to understand race, gender, sexuality, class, and ethnicity as interdependent and interlocking, rather than disparate and exclusive, social categories. As Crenshaw writes, 'I used the concept of intersectionality to denote the various ways in which race and gender interact to shape the multiple dimensions of black women's employment experiences' (1991:1241). Joined by other notable scholars and women of colour, namely bell hooks and Patricia Hill Collins, feminist theory could no longer ignore the mutual constitution of race and gender and their underpinning ideologies as a way to understand and write about women's subjugation. In particular, these feminists also sought to reveal the ways black women in the United States had been excluded not only from feminism's intellectual project, but its political project as well, and sought a discursive and material attention to racial difference (Collins 1990). This multi-scalar 'buzzword' (Davis 2008) highlights how gender and race are mutually constituted, whereby their unstable dynamic is experienced simultaneously and therefore autonomous social categories cannot be simply added to the mix (Anthias and Yuval-Davis 1992:62–63 in Valentine 2007; Crenshaw 1989, 1991; Gillman 2007).

With this in mind, I employ a *postcolonial intersectionality* that acknowledges the way patriarchy and racialized processes are consistently bound in a postcolonial genealogy that embeds race and gender ideologies within nation-building and international development processes. This concept reflects the way women and men are always marked by difference whether or not they fit nicely into colonial racial categorizations, as cultural difference is also racialized (McEwan 2001:104; Radcliffe 2005; Sundberg 2007). Like postcolonial development, geography seeks to decentre the material and symbolic legacies of the colonial period and serves as an important challenge to understanding Global North-South relations in simply economistic terms (Radcliffe 2005). Postcolonial intersectionality in FPE would help to better differentiate among women in the same way that feminism was forced to confront its historical engagement with 'imperialist origins' through the work of Mohanty, hooks, Collins, and many others (McEwan 2001:97). Postcolonial intersectionality addresses Mohanty's warnings against the construction of a 'third world woman' and prioritizes a grounded and spatially informed understanding of patriarchy constituted in and through racial power.

## Understanding race, gender, and whiteness in Honduras: postcolonial intersectional analysis at work

In the remainder of this chapter, I demonstrate how the mutual entanglement of race and gender in FPE advances our understandings of the multiple kinds of oppressions and privileges people face in natural resource struggles. I draw from ethnographic fieldwork in Honduras to illustrate how people's multiple identities are entangled as seen through the guise of postcolonial intersectionality.[1]

### *The Miskito peoples of Honduras*

The Miskito people are an indigenous group who live in the Honduran Mosquitia region and share Amerindian, African, and European ancestry. Such ancestry is embodied in visible racial mixes where people phenotypically appear black, white, Indian, and a mixture of these and other racial heritages. In Honduras, the Miskito occupy a subjugated position in the context of Honduran racial hierarchies where the dominant ethnic identity, in number and in power, is the *ladino*. *Ladino* bloodlines (European ancestry) and cultural symbols such as Spanish language, Western dress, sedentary land use practices, and urban residence are often equated with progress and modernity at the national level and are seen as superior to Miskito cultural practices such as swidden agriculture, Miskito language, subsistence production, and forest residence inside the Mosquitia. As a result, the Honduran state has historically tried to integrate the Mosquitia region and its natural resources through a continual devaluation of Miskito (and indigenous peoples) cultural and land use practices. Such practices are consistently subjugated and Miskito people's development contributions are historically placed in relation to *ladino* and white bodies (Mollett 2006).

Since independence, the state has made a persistent attempt to populate the Honduran Mosquitia with Europeans, Americans, and other 'white' bodies through a number of legal, social, and environmental measures. These development discourses operate in the name of civilization, integration, poverty reduction, sustainable development, multicultural reforms, and land regularization (Mollett 2011). State goals to 'whiten' the Mosquitia build upon a broader regional political discourse known as *mestizaje,* which means racial mixing. This nineteenth and twentieth century ideology posited racial mixtures as a form of racial improvement. Within the narrative it was assumed that blacks and Indians would be elevated from elite imaginings of primitiveness, barbarism, and backwardness, and their concomitant cultural land use practices would be transformed. Inherent in this discourse is a racialized process known as *blanquemiento* (or whitening) where citizenship was imbued with Creole (Mesoamerican born Europeans) ideals of 'whiteness and masculinity' evidenced by 'literacy, property ownership and individual autonomy' (Appelbaum et al. 2003:4). Those rendered outside these ideals (Indians, blacks, mestizos, and women), while theoretically capable of social mobility, were presupposed as biologically and culturally inferior. This racialized subjectivity justified their exclusion from the rights as citizens and such ideals of whiteness were imbued in progress and modernity (Bonnett 2000; Sundberg 2008).

Presently this hierarchy unfolds on the north coast of the Honduran Mosquitia and inside the Rio Platano Biosphere Reserve. As a key aspect of sustainable development, the Honduran state is looking to regularize the collective territories of the reserve's indigenous peoples. Over the last ten years, this has been a particularly contentious intervention since the state prefers to title lands individually. This is in contrast to Miskito claims for collective territorial demarcation. And while options for agricultural lands include collective arrangements, village lands are expected to be individuated, where ownership risks being reduced to a single 'male' holder despite matrilineal and matriarchal customs in Nabeel (Mollett 2010). These tensions over individual and collective land demarcation disclose the ways Miskito land practices are racialized vis-à-vis *ladino campesinos,* elite commercial farmers, and the state. They are also gendered, in part, in the ways in which land encroachments are led by *ladino* men. At the same time, state practice assumes Miskito men as the beneficiaries of land registration. In this context, as the lens of postcolonial intersectionality makes clear 'it becomes impossible to separate out "gender" from the political and cultural intersections in which it is inevitably produced and maintained' (Butler 1990:3). I illustrate this point with an excerpt from my field notes.

\* \* \*

Lina and Alia are Miskito women from the Miskito village of Nabeel. Nabeel is located on the Atlantic coast inside the reserve's cultural zone, home to the roughly 20,000 Miskito peoples and other indigenous peoples. Farming and wage labour are the main livelihood activities. The majority of Miskito people self-identifies as poor and uses various signifiers to define a Miskito identity. Widows in their sixties, Lina and Alia are both mothers with young children living in their homes. As both women are well known, local discourse often describes these widows as '*viejitas*' – an affectionate way to describe an old woman. In relation, both women commonly complain of illness, aching feet, hands and having a 'weak body', ailments that render them motionless for days on end. While village narratives represent both *viejitas* as 'needy' and 'weak', the local hierarchies of race and religion situate them differently in both ideological and material ways.

## Lina

Lina is Miskito with dark brown skin and long, black, straight hair. She lives with her two sons in the coastal community of Nabeel. Lina's youngest son is twelve years old and attends the local elementary school. While her middle son Tonio has work through the lobster industry, according to Lina, 'he often drinks his salary'. Throughout research in Nabeel, Lina often described herself as 'very poor'. She, like other Miskito women, often raised her hands and proclaimed 'that God will lift [her] out of this misery'. In the meantime, Lina sells fruit harvested from four enormous fruit trees (mango and plum) inherited from her parents.

In addition to *viejita*, Lina's neighbours describe her as 'poor', 'hardworking', and 'persistent'. Lina has earned her status as a 'hard worker' through her work cleaning the offices of a local missionary development group and the laundry services she provides the staff and their guests. She is also known to clean the homes of foreign volunteers and development workers who rent homes within the village. For Lina, employment with foreigners is 'better than working for a Honduran'. Foreigners 'always give you extra, invite you to eat with them and you can often take something home for the next day'. While Lina is happy to be employed, the unpredictable cycles of international development funding means that 'sometimes I work for months at the [mission] and then nothing'. Lina explicitly links her vulnerability to intense poverty to being a widow, which she insists leaves her 'disadvantaged'. She adds 'if my husband was alive, I wouldn't have to pay for a *mozo* [field labourer] to clear and fence my land and we would always have food on the table'. In Nabeel, the 'poor are women like me, alone without a man to clear the land'. Lina's claim that poverty is embodied in women 'without men to clear the land' is a common refrain in Nabeel.

Lina's poverty narrative situates her in a gendered division of labour where Miskito men customarily clear land and women plant seeds and harvest food alongside male relatives. While fencing is relatively new in Nabeel, fence building is considered a male activity. In addition, her reliance on male labour, for clearing and fencing, also reveals the contextual limits to matriarchal land rights in Nabeel. While Lina's land was inherited from her mother, her ability to maintain this land is in peril in the context of impending land regularization. Land competition in the village is at its highest and new land is impossible to locate. These tensions make Lina's uncleared and unfenced lands vulnerable to encroachment by Miskito and non-Miskito men. Such vulnerability is not simply because she is a *viejita*, but because mandatory land registration increases state intervention and concomitant tenure rules, like clearing and fencing lands to show possession (practices more common to ladino land use practices; see Mollett 2006, 2011). Furthermore for Lina, her inability to access male labour may mean that even if she can formally register her village plot in her own name, formalization does not secure her access to her parcel as her access to land as a *viejita* remains dependent on male labour (either remunerated or bartered). As FPE scholars note, such struggles commonly emerge as a result of changing agrarian reform (Carney 1996, 2004; Jarosz 1999). However, gendered (and aged) vulnerability to displacement is provoked by land registration in Nabeel. State pressures to regularize Miskito lands are imbued with racialized processes of development, where a single model of Euro-American ideals for land individuation is part of a broader spatialized genealogy of whitening imbued in nation-building. This genealogy shapes the everyday practices of Lina's racialized and gendered subjectivity as an indigenous Miskito *viejita* in the Mosquitia.

According to the local health clinic, Lina's poverty narrative is common. The Nabeel Health clinic reports that single mothers make up roughly 30 per cent of Nabeel households (Mollett, field notes 2008). While most villagers call themselves 'poor' and 'humble' (*humilde*), there is consensus that 'single mothers' (*madres solteras*) and widows are 'those who struggle most' in Nabeel. They are often described as '*pobrecitas*' (poor little ones), seen as the village's 'needy population'. At first glance, village consensus appears to support Lina's poverty narrative. However, ad hoc conversational interviews and village gossip present Lina's case in a different light. Instead, village discourse suggests that Lina 'struggles' because she 'is in bed with the devil'. In 1999, the Moravian Church, after almost two hundred years of unified practice, divided into two sects throughout most villages inside the Mosquitia. This split was a violent and galvanizing process that divided families and communities. Those that mobilized a separation from the church, known as *Renovados* (Renewed Moravians) became more evangelical and many believed themselves to be 'prophets'. *Tradicionales* (Traditional Moravians) rejected this evangelical move and warned villagers against believing in 'false prophets'. Instead *Tradicionales* blamed this mobilization on 'greed' and 'ignorance' led by a younger and more 'selfish' Miskito generation. Reinforcing this critique, in 2000, the *Renovada* leadership was able to secure control over US donations that were still funnelling in since Hurricane Mitch pummelled Honduras in 1998. *Renovados* were accused of becoming 'thieves' and being 'sneaky like *los morenos*'. *Los morenos* refers to the Garifuna, an Afro-indigenous community who lives in close proximity to Nabeel. While the *Renovados* were able to mobilize foreign donations, by 2001, initial energy for this mobilization began to wane as people decided that they missed their families and their community and 'didn't want to be mad anymore'. This collective epiphany overwhelmingly saw people return to the Traditional church. A former *Renovado* suggests 'we are all Moravians and stronger together than divided'. As a consequence, those who had participated in the split were now seen with much suspicion.

For Lina, the decision to become a *Renovada* made her the subject of village rumours that posited her as a 'harlot' and 'bad mother'. According to many villagers, Renovado church seminars were often held at a neighbouring village overnight. As one Miskito woman expressed '*las morenas* sleep outside the house, they are easy and foolish, but a Miskito woman sleeps in her home with her family, she is a good girl, a good mother'. Again, Lina's behaviour is understood through Miskito stereotypes about Garifuna women. These racial ideologies are infused with a devaluation of blackness (despite African ancestry among the Miskito). Other rumours posit her decline as inevitable due to the fact she was 'too *india*' (docile) and 'followed bad influences'. These narratives together draw upon colonial racial hierarchies that essentialize Indians as 'docile' and 'obedient' and blacks as 'wild', 'promiscuous', and 'hardheaded' (Mollett 2006).

Lina's active racialization was not simply discursive, but material. Prior to the split, Lina enjoyed credit at many of the small home stores in Nabeel because she was a cousin of a well-respected *Tradicional* Moravian elder and because 'everybody knew she worked for the *gringos*, she had a good job'.[2] But shortly after the split Lina temporarily lost her job, and at the same time her access to credit in village shops was abruptly cut. In reflecting on this horrible moment, Lina laments that she is even disrespected by the village children, who compete with her in gathering fallen fruit from *her own* fruit trees and call her '*tonta vieja*' (dumb old lady) as her ailing body makes it impossible for her to chase them away. Lina's village status and her racialized gender subjectivity are remade through religious and generational logics. While once admired and granted credit for being close to white foreigners, Lina is now racialized through stereotypical narratives regarding blackness and indianness. While a genealogy of these discourses point to a time and space dominated by Euro-American postcolonial ambitions embodied in state practice, the contemporary naturalizations of racial hierarchies are also fulfilled by Miskito society (Mollett 2006), and shape Lina's ability to access and formalize her customary rights to land and natural resources in Nabeel.

## *Alia*

To be sure, racial and gendered subjectivities not only close opportunities for environmental rights, but may create openings as well. Like Lina, Alia is a Miskito widow in her mid-sixties. She is also referred to as *una viejita*, and people often refer to her as 'almost white' in reference to her light skin colour. Alia is raising her two grandsons, but unlike Lina, villagers insist that Alia 'doesn't have to struggle' because people like to help Alia, 'she is good'. Alia is referred to by many as '*una viejita con fuerza*' (a little old lady with fight). While she no longer works her land, her brother, a farmer, brings her a variety of produce from her land for household consumption and to sell in her small home shop.

Alia's favourable status in Nabeel is shaped by both the logic of religious and racial ideologies specific to the Mosquitia, informed by global interactions. For many villagers, Alia does better than most widows and single mothers as 'Alia is fortunate; God granted her "white skin" so that people will always help her even when she doesn't ask for it'. Like Lina, Alia considers herself to be poor. She often refers to the incomplete construction of her home as evidence of her poverty. Despite the house, Alia admits that '[she] was blessed to marry a [religious elder] because his work brought white people from around the world to Nabeel to pray, eat, and learn ways to understand Miskito culture'. This conflation of blessing and whiteness is common. A well-known Miskito doctor, who describes herself as a 'white Miskito' describes Alia's house as '*sana*' (clean and pure) and fit for '*meriki*' (foreigners) and the 'educated'.[3] Such affinity for whiteness is not masked by Alia's enthusiasm and her tales of past and present visitors, namely missionaries, researchers and tourists, all of whom, as described by Alia, are '*hablas ingles, ninos de Dios y blanco*' (English speaking, children of God and white).

The ways in which Alia's privilege is justified by her (almost) white phenotype and affiliation with the Traditional Moravian church vis-à-vis Lina exemplifies how the concept of intersectionality is useful in illustrating how space and processes of subject formation are fluid and inextricably bound. While both stories illustrate Miskito gender relations (i.e., how Miskito women look to men to help support and maintain farming and access to land) faith, age, and particularly race help explain the different lived experiences of these two *viejitas* in Nabeel. While both describe themselves as poor Miskito women, Lina's choice to support a faction of the Moravian church that soon became seen as '*sucia*' (dirty) informed her racialization as paradoxically 'promiscuous' and 'too docile'. Her new status undermined her ability to be self-sufficient and maintain access to her land and credit as it was now thinkable (due to racializing/gendered logics) among villagers in Nabeel to marginalize her.

In contrast, Alia's favourable status in the village as 'clean', 'moral', and 'educated' (even though Alia was pulled from formal education in the second grade) is upheld through continuous relations with white foreigners. This status garnished both her brother's labour and access to land and natural resources. In fact, when the local municipal official came to Nabeel to register her village land in the context of state's land regularization program the local official enthusiastically registered her land in her name, and never collected the fee from her (Mollett, field notes 2008). Such 'Anglo-affinity' (whiteness) in the Miskito geographic imagination secures both symbolic and material outcomes, for Alia, and in particular access and rights to land.

## Postcolonial intersectionality and feminist political ecology

These stories demonstrate the extent to which racialization and whiteness are relevant to feminist political ecological analysis and natural resource struggles. Postcolonial intersectionality, in this regard, permits us to understand the different lived experiences of the *viejitas* not as stable or given forms/structures but as multiple and 'situated accomplishments' (West and Fenstermaker 1995). As Lina and Alia actively negotiate, contest and acquiesce to differential forms of power hierarchies, 'the intersections of identities' blur rather than reinforce the boundaries of social categorization (Valentine 2007:14). In particular, theorizing intersectionality as a process of postcolonial becoming and unbecoming makes visible the ways in which whiteness shapes material and ideological possibilities and how *racialized genders* emerge out of the everyday practices of livelihood and natural resource struggles in Nabeel. A postcolonial intersectionality contests designations of legible forms of the dominant and the subaltern. Lina and Alia are not simply 'needy', Moravian, or 'old' women compelled to make 'strategic bargains'. Instead the power of racial logics that shape religious conflict and struggles over land marginalize one widow and privileges another.

Postcolonial intersectionality fits well with the aims of FPE to 'build an approach towards power relations taking into full account not only male dominance, but mainstream and privileged attitudes and control over the environment' (Rocheleau et al. 1996:306). Gender and race together comprise a historically important coupling that shapes and is shaped by space. Take, for example, the 'myth of virgin land' in former 'colonies' where women and land are posited in the colonial texts to be 'discovered', 'named', and 'owned', and where indigenous peoples are made invisible by male conquerers. Another instance is the entanglement of race and gender in the spaces of the auction block in the history of transatlantic slavery where the 'black women's body as a fertile commodity of exchange' (McKittrick 2006) was central to its reproduction. And today we can look at national ideologies that are premised on either homogenous or heterogeneous citizenry but that both rely on the active policing of women's sexuality and bodies. As McClintock (1995) writes, the co-production of race and gender as degenerative tropes brought about a particular modern form of racialized hegemony by the late nineteenth century. These legacies live on and are simultaneously contested and re-entrenched in the everyday material and discursive practices of survival and international development in Honduras and elsewhere. As Asher notes, in reference to violent displacements in Colombia, *Afro-Colombiana* resistance 'emerges in the context of multifaceted, inter-twined, and mutually constitutive relations of power of gender (as women) of race or culture (as black) of class (as poor people) and of location (as rural Pacific residents)' (2009:152). With this in mind, I argue for a *postcolonial intersectionality* in FPE that is attentive to the changing and unstable contradictions of racial and gender 'identities in the making' (Sundberg 2004) in a way that illustrates the messy, conflicting, and partial makeup of the subjectivities that we encounter.

## Conclusion: racialized gender in feminist political ecology research

Over time, feminist political ecology has become more attentive to the use of intersectionality to understand environmental change (Mollett and Faria 2013; Buechler and Hanson 2015; Harcourt and Nelson 2015). However, the mutual constitution of gender and race remains understudied and on the margins. Thus I argue that this entanglement be moved to the fore of the FPE research agenda. Taking heed of the mutual entanglements of gender and race communicates that people in the Global South do not exist in separate worlds or 'contexts' different from the Global North, but that the racist structures and inequalities that shape their lives, also shape our lives as feminist political ecology scholars. As feminist geographers, we too are historically and spatially constituted subjects woven in racialized and gendered relationships of power in relation to those we write about. For now, I humbly suggest that future work in FPE should reflect how gender does not act alone 'as an optic for analyzing the power effects of the social constitution of difference' (Elmhirst 2011). In fact, FPE needs race. This point is crucial, not simply because race and racialization are understudied and grossly misunderstood, and because development problems require explanations and strategies found outside political economic reforms, but for the sake of gender as well. Indeed, increased attention to race may open more critical analysis of natural resource control, distribution, and access as a way to help 'mainstream' gender in development policy and planning, in a more meaningful and plural fashion. It will compel feminist political ecologists to see race in places we tend to take as race-less, such as 'the environment'. Without such engagement, FPE scholarship will remain ahistorical and out of place.

Finally, I posit postcolonial intersectionality as a way to 'trouble gender' or to 'mess with gender' – to re-theorize it in such a way that refuses to silence, elide or side-step race but instead to accommodate a more complex understanding of the entanglement of racialized and gendered power. This approach demands an acknowledgment of the postcolonial moment of development's interventions in the Global South. And it is a stance that feminist political ecology can and must take on.

# Notes

This paper is a partial reproduction of Mollett, S. and Faria, C. (2013). 'Messing with Gender in Feminist Political Ecology', *Geoforum*, 45: 116–125. Permission granted December 2015.

1 This example emerges from ethnographic fieldwork conducted over two months in summer 2008. However, this work builds on a larger research project culminating in almost 24 months in Nabeel (Mollett 2010; Mollett 2011). Ethnographic collection was supplemented by interviews (60 household interviews, 134 surveys, and more than 50 interviews with state personnel in areas of biodiversity conservation and development) as well as historical data collection and discourse analysis of news media and government documents in Honduras.
2 'Gringo' is the Spanish term for foreigner. In Honduras a gringo is first assumed to be white.
3 It must be noted this Miskito term is also racialized, similar to 'gringo'. Both terms in Honduras refer to specifically white foreigners. In particular 'meriki' in reference to the author was always followed by sixsa, which means 'black' in Miskito.

# References

Anthias, F. and Yuval-Davis, N. (1992) *Racialized Boundaries: Race, Nation, Gender, Colour and Class and Anti-racist Struggle*. London: Routledge.
Appelbaum, N., Macpherson, A. and Rosemblatt, K. (2003) 'Racial nations', in Appelbaum, N., Macpherson, A. and Rosemblatt, K. (eds) *Race and Nation in Modern Latin America*. Chapel Hill: University of North Carolina Press, 1–31.
Asher, K. (2009) *Black and Green: Afro-Colombians, Development and Nature in the Pacific Lowlands*. Durham: Duke University Press.
Blaikie, P. and Brookfield, H. (1987) *Land Degradation and Society*. London: Routledge.
Bonnett, A. (2000) *White Identities: Historical and International Perspectives*. Harlow: Pearson.
Buechler, S. and Hanson, A.-M. (2015) *A Political Ecology of Women, Water and Global Environmental Change*. London: Routledge.
Butler, J. (1990) *Gender Trouble: Feminism and the Subversion of Identity*. New York: Routledge.
Carney, J. A. (1996) 'Converting the wetlands, engendering the environment: The intersection of gender with agrarian change in Gambia', in Peet, R. and Watts, M. (eds) *Liberation Ecologies: Environment, Development, and Social Movements*. London: Routledge, 165–187.
Carney, J. A. (2004) 'Gender conflict in Gambian wetlands', in Peet, R. and Watts, M. (eds) *Liberation Ecologies: Environment, Development, and Social Movements*. London: Routledge, 289–305.
Collins, P. H. (1990) *Black Feminist Thought: Knowledge, Consciousness, and the Politics of Empowerment*. New York: Routledge.
Collins, P. H. (2008) *Black Feminist Thought: Knowledge, Consciousness, and the Politics of Empowerment*. New York: Routledge Classics.
Crenshaw, K. (1989) 'Demarginalizing the intersection of race and sex: A black feminist critique of antidiscrimination doctrine, feminist theory and antiracist politics', *University of Chicago Legal Forum*: 139–167.

Crenshaw, K. (1991) 'Mapping the margins: Intersectionality, identity politics, and violence against women of colour', *Stanford Law Review* 43: 1241–1299.

Crenshaw, K. (1997) 'Colour blindness, history and the law', in Lubiano, W. (ed) *The House That Race Built: Original Essays by Toni Morrison, Angela Y. Davis, Cornel West, and Others on Black Americans and Politics in America Today.* New York: Pantheon, 280–288.

Davis, K. (2008) 'Intersectionality as buzzword: A sociology of science perspective on what makes a feminist theory successful', *Feminist Theory* 9(1): 67–85.

Elmhirst, R. (2011) 'Introducing new feminist political ecologies', *Geoforum* 42(2): 129–132.

Gezon, L. L. (2006) *Global Visions, Local Landscapes: A Political Ecology of Conservation, Conflict, and Control in Northern Madagascar.* Lanham, MD: Altamira Press.

Gillman, L. (2007) 'Beyond the shadow: Re-scripting race in women's studies', *Meridians: Feminism, Race, Transnationalism* 7(2): 117–141.

Gururani, S. (2002) 'Forests of pleasure and pain: Gendered practices of labour and livelihood in the forests of the Kumaon Himalayas, India', *Gender, Place and Culture: A Journal of Feminist Geography* 9(3): 229–243.

Hapke, H. and Ayyankeril, D. (2004) 'Gender, the work-life course, and livelihood strategies in a South Indian fish market', *Gender, Place and Culture: A Journal of Feminist Geography* 11(2): 229–256.

Harcourt, W. and Nelson, I. (2015) *Practising Feminist Political Ecologies: Moving Beyond the Green Economy.* London: Zed Books.

Harris, A. (1997) 'Race and essentialism in feminist legal theory', in Wing, A. K. (ed) *Critical Race Feminism: A Reader.* New York: New York University Press, 34–41.

Harris, L. (2006) 'Irrigation, gender, and social geographies of the changing waterscapes of southeastern Anatolia', *Environmental and Planning D: Society and Space* 24: 187–213.

hooks, b. (1984) *Feminist Theory From Margin to Center.* Boston, MA: South End Press.

Hovorka, A. (2006) 'The no. 1 ladies' poultry farm: A feminist political ecology of urban agriculture in Botswana', *Gender, Place and Culture: A Journal of Feminist Geography* 13(3): 207–225.

Jarosz, L. (1992) 'Constructing the dark continent: Metaphor as geographic representation of Africa', *Geografiska Annaler* 74 B(2): 105–115.

Jarosz, L. (1999) 'A feminist political ecology perspective', *Gender, Place and Culture: A Journal of Feminist Geography* 6(4): 390.

Kabeer, N. (1994) *Reversed Realities: Gender Hierarchies in Development Thought.* New Delhi: Kali for Women.

Kandiyoti, D. (1988) 'Bargaining with patriarchy', *Gender and Society* 2(3): 274–290.

Kobayashi, A. and Peake, L. (2000) 'Racism out of place: Thoughts on whiteness and an anti-racist geography in the new millennium', *Annals of the Association of American Geographers* 90(2): 393–397.

Li, T. (2007) *The Will to Improve: Governmentality, Development, and the Practice of Politics.* Durham: Duke University Press.

McClintock, A. (1995) *Imperial Leather: Race, Gender and Sexuality in the Colonial Contest.* New York: Routledge.

McEwan, C. (2001) 'Postcolonialism, feminism and development: Intersections and dilemmas', *Progress in Development Studies* 1(2): 93–111.

Mackenzie, A. F. D. (1998) *Land, Ecology and Resistance in Kenya, 1880–1952.* Portsmouth: Heinnemann.

McKittrick, K. (2006) *Demonic Grounds: Black Women and the Cartographies of Struggle.* Minneapolis: University of Minnesota Press.

Minow, M. (1997) *Not Only for Myself: Identity, Politics and the Law.* New York: The New Press.

Mohanty, C. (1991) 'Under western eyes: Feminist scholarship and colonial discourses', in Mohanty, C., Russo, A. and Torres, L. (eds) *Third World Women and the Politics of Feminism.* Bloomfield: Indiana University Press, 51–80.

Mollett, S. (2006) 'Race and natural resource conflicts in Honduras: The Miskito and Garifuna struggle for Lasa Pulan', *Latin American Research Review* 41(1): 76–101.

Mollett, S. (2010) 'Esta Listo (Are you ready)? Gender, race and land registration in the Rio Platano Biosphere Reserve', *Gender, Place and Culture: A Journal of Feminist Geography* 17(3): 357–375.

Mollett, S. (2011) 'Racial narratives: Miskito and colono land struggle in the Honduran Mosqutia', *Cultural Geographies* 18(1): 43–62.

Mollett, S. and Faria, C. (2013) 'Messing with gender in feminist political ecology', *Geoforum* 45: 116–125.

Neumann, R. P. (1997) 'Primitive ideas: Protected area buffer zones and the politics of land in Africa', *Development and Change* 28(3): 559–582.

Nightingale, A. (2006) 'The nature of gender: Work, gender and environment', *Environment and Planning D: Society and Space* 24(2): 165–185.

Nightingale, A. (2011) 'Bounding difference: Intersectionality and the material production of gender, caste, class and environment in Nepal', *Geoforum* 42(2): 153–162.

Pulido, L. (2000) 'Rethinking environmental racism: White privilege and urban development in Southern California', *Annals of the Association of American Geographers* 90(1): 12–40.

Radcliffe, S. (2005) 'Development and geography: Towards a postcolonial development geography?', *Progress in Human Geography* 29(3): 291–298.

Rocheleau, D. (2008) 'Political ecology in the key of policy: From chains of explanation to webs of relation', *Geoforum* 39(2): 716–727.

Rocheleau, D., Thomas-Slayter, B. and Wangari, E. (eds) (1996) *Feminist Political Ecology: Global Issues and Local Experience.* London: Routledge.

Rose, G. (1993) *Feminism and Geography: The Limits of Geographical Knowledge.* Minneapolis: University of Minnesota Press.

Sultana, F. (2011) 'Suffering for water, suffering from water: Emotional geographies of resource access, control and conflict', *Geoforum* 42: 163–172.

Sundberg, J. (2004) 'Identities-in-the-making: Conservation, gender, and race in the Maya Biosphere Reserve, Guatemala', *Gender, Place and Culture: A Journal of Feminist Geography* 11(1): 44–66.

Sundberg, J. (2005) 'Looking for the critical geographers, or why bodies and geographies matter to the emergence of critical geographies of Latin America', *Geoforum* 36: 17–28.

Sundberg, J. (2007) 'Reconfiguring North-South solidarity: Critical reflections on experiences of transnational resistance', *Antipode* 39(1): 144–166.

Sundberg, J. (2008) 'Placing race in environmental justice research in Latin America', *Society and Natural Resources* 21(7): 569–582.

Valentine, G. (2007) 'Theorizing and researching intersectionality: A challenge for feminist geography', *The Professional Geographer* 59: 10–21.

West, C. and Fenstermaker, S. (1995) 'Doing difference', *Gender and Society* 9(1): 8–37.

# 10

# GENDER AND ENVIRONMENTAL JUSTICE

*Julie Sze*

## Introduction

How are gender and environmental justice linked? Answering this question depends, in some part, on what is meant by both of these terms. Gender spans the gamut from sexual identity to sociocultural characteristics associated with masculinity and femininity. Initially, the concept of environmental justice was connected to the movement aimed at contesting and resisting the disproportionately high levels of exposure to toxic pollution that racialized minorities face. It began in the grassroots struggle of American minority groups against environmental racism but has since spread to other parts of the world, from Canada, the UK, and Australia to many parts of Latin America and Africa. The environmental justice frame extends to criticisms of the exclusivity of mainstream environmentalism and serves to recalibrate the very notion of 'environment', beyond the idea of pristine nature to the places where people 'live, work, and play' (Novotny 2000). Alongside the work of activists, an academic field of research has developed, including work by scholars in disciplines including geography, sociology, planning, political science, and even literature. Although it comes from a diversity of perspectives and deploys a range of different methods, two common goals of this research are to gather empirical evidence to support the claim that poor people tend to live in poor quality environments and to assert the normative position that this situation is unjust (Walker 2012). The existence of environmental injustice is a reminder that people's experiences of 'nature' are shaped by their experiences of social, economic, and political inequalities. Race and class are powerful determinants of environmental health and well-being. From a feminist perspective, it stands to reason that gender also plays a significant part in causing and sustaining environmental injustice. In general, however, the vast majority of environmental justice scholarship does not tend to take gender seriously as a category, despite evidence that men and women are affected differently by toxics (for example) and that women have played a pivotal role in environmental justice movements. But this blindness to gender may be starting to change.

In this chapter, I examine how debates and discussions about gender and environmental justice (EJ) have changed over time. I do not offer an exhaustive review of the scholarship; rather, my purpose is to explain general trends, key questions, and notable changes that have taken place over time. The themes in this discussion are centred around debates about the relationship between race and gender; how race and gender figure into debates about bodies, biology, and environmental exposures; issues of social power; and the increasing prominence of intersectional analyses and theories of transcorporeality in feminist engagements with environmental justice issues. I use illuminating and illustrative case studies to show how contemporary environmental justice scholarship is beginning to take gender seriously in understanding the historical roots of environmental inequalities and how they affect gendered bodies in space and time. I demonstrate how gender has been an important, albeit underwritten, part of the history of environmental justice activism and scholarship in the United States. In other words, I aim to retell the standard narrative of environmental justice movements and scholarship in the 1970s to the early 2000s in the United States by highlighting that gender was and remains a central component, even if it was not understood to be so.

## The early days of environmental justice: race not gender

A large strand of the early US environmental justice scholarship was dedicated to finding the shared, historical roots of concerns around race and class inequality and environmental quality. A small number of scholars locate the ideological roots of the contemporary environmental justice movement (EJM) in the Progressive Era (1890s to 1920s; Hood-Washington 2004; Taylor 2009). This period saw the rise of movements to clean up urban environments, for example through the establishment of settlement houses by activists such as Jane Adams and Alice Hamilton, and the early worker's, occupational health, sanitation, and clean food movements. The role of women in the Progressive Era and settlement house movements has been well established (Gottlieb 2005). Thus EJ scholars who have focused on these roots implicitly endorse a narrative of environmental justice that has gender at its centre. However, the vast majority of EJ scholars locate the origins of the EJM in the United States in the 1960s as a hybrid of the civil rights, farm workers' rights, Native American rights, and mainstream environmental movements. Cole and Foster (2001) call these the 'tributaries' that feed into the environmental justice movement; they do not name Progressive Era activism as a tributary.

Throughout the 1980s, as a result of a number of high profile protests in communities of colour against toxic and industrial facilities, a number of studies by US government agencies, community organizations, and scholars focused on the question of whether communities of colour (e.g., Black, Latino, and Native American) were disproportionately exposed to pollution. One of the important early conflicts was in Warren County, North Carolina, where in 1982 a primarily low-income African American community protested a controversial toxic waste dump. This protest symbolically initiated the EJM across the United States (McGurty 2009). EJ activism targeted the 'unequal protection' of minority populations from environmental pollution by local, state and national regulatory agencies. For example, early research from the *National Law Journal* suggested that there may be lower penalties for environmental violations in minority communities and slower clean-up times than in affluent and white communities (Lavelle and Coyle 1993).

The movement also developed as an explicit reaction to the lack of adequate attention to race and class issues by mainstream environmental movement organizations. Up until then, the US environmental movement was focused more on saving pristine natural environments and their non-human inhabitants than protecting the lives and environments of diverse human communities. In 1990 a letter was written by Richard Moore of the Southwest Organizing Project and co-signed by one hundred community-based activists to the heads of eight prominent national environmental organizations. This letter highlighted not only the narrow focus, but also the lack of diversity of staff and of programs in the mainstream environmental movement as well as its reliance on corporate funding (Tokar 1997; for a reappraisal of that conflict, see Sandler and Pezzullo 2007).

The 'Principles of Environmental Justice', adopted at the 1991 First People of Color Environmental Leadership summit and widely circulated, can be considered the founding vision document that catalyzed the movement. The principles provided an alternative framework for environmentalism by moving beyond the class and racial biases in mainstream environmental groups, and combating the abuses of corporate polluters and complicity of regulatory agencies. The document embraced a wide spatial and temporal scale, addressing histories of colonialism, imperialism, and genocide of indigenous cultures. The only mention of anything gender-related in that founding document is in the first principle, that 'Environmental Justice affirms the sacredness of Mother Earth, ecological unity and the interdependence of all species, and the right to be free from ecological destruction'.[1]

In response to pressure from social and environmental movements – and informed by empirical research by epidemiologists and others – since the 1990s US government agencies have incorporated EJ as a basis for public policy in the federal, state, regional and even local levels. The policy that initiated such public sector efforts was President Clinton's Executive Order of 1994 (no. 12898), which directed all federal agencies to 'make achieving environmental justice part of its mission by identifying and addressing, as appropriate, disproportionately high and adverse human health or environmental effects of its programs, policies, and activities'. As progressive as this development may seem, it is limited by the fact that gender has not been considered a central part of these policies.

The lack of explicit focus on gender in standard narratives of EJ history is not surprising. As a scholarly field it has consistently struggled over the definitions and parameters of race and racism, largely ignoring gender and sexism and their interconnections with race and racism. 'Environmental racism', the term used in the earliest literature in the field (e.g., Chavis and Lee 1987), describes the disproportionate effects of environmental pollution on racial minorities. Because it describes the disproportionate relationship between high levels of pollution exposure for people of colour and the low level of environmental benefits they enjoy, environmental racism can be defined as the unequal distribution of environmental benefits and pollution burdens based on race. 'Environmental inequality' has emerged more recently to encompass a range of factors besides race that are associated with disproportionate environmental impacts on certain groups, such as class, gender, dis/ability, age, and immigration status, as well as the interconnections between these factors (Pellow 2000, 2007). However, much of the quantitative research on EJ has moved away from using the (politicized) terms environmental racism and injustice as organizing principles and analytic categories. There is a relationship between the choice of terms and the questions that get asked. To generalize, quantitative academic research tends to try to ascertain which is a greater contributing factor to pollution exposure: race or class – or which came first, the non-white community or polluting facilities. Do chemical companies and waste incinerators get sited in poor communities because they are poor and powerless, or are these communities poor and powerless because they are stuck in degraded environments? The aim in much of the research has been to describe 'what is' (a la positivist social science) rather than make a claim for 'what ought to be' (see Walker 2012 for a discussion). And this line of research tends not to focus significantly on gender.

Sociologist and EJ scholar David Pellow's (2000, 2007) work has been influential in refocusing environmental justice scholarship away from narrow quantitative questions (such as 'does race or class affect an exposure?') to broader socio-historical questions of power and power relations. In doing so, Pellow maintains a focus on power and exploitation, while allowing for terms that are more capacious analytically. Thus, while early attempts to redefine environmental justice/injustice, environmental racism/environmental inequality were met by activists and the first generation of scholars as diluting the critique of the movement, Pellow and others have focused on the same political and cultural questions, while allowing for different analyses that foreground race in relation to gender and other intersecting categories as well as global and geopolitical factors (see also Sze 2007).

## Unearthing connections between gender and environmental justice

### Women and local environmental justice movements in the United States

We can trace debates about how to account for intersections of gender/race/class in environmentalism by looking back to one of the most iconic US-based environmental struggles in the post-civil rights era. Among the earliest and most high-profile cases of anti-toxics activism in the 1970s were the struggles at Love Canal in New York State. In 1978 Lois Gibbs, a working-class white woman, discovered that her son's school was built on top of a toxic waste dump. It was subsequently revealed that the surrounding housing development had also been contaminated, with some families finding pools of mysterious liquid in their basements. Gibbs became a major leader in the successful effort to evacuate the Love Canal neighbourhood. The activism of the organization she founded, the Love Canal Homeowners Association, which was mostly made up of local women, helped to spur regulatory change at the US Environmental Protection Agency. It also helped to catalyze broad public concern around exposure to toxics in private homes as opposed to industrial workplaces. The Love Canal protest is often cited as a major event in the history of the US-based environmental justice movement.

Because the media and public discourse about Gibbs focused on her identity as a mother, the perception was that her environmental activism was motivated primarily by her concerns about the contamination of her house and related threats to her children's health. She was criticized in the press as a 'hysterical housewife' (Seager 1996; Blum 2008). Perkins (2012) describes the social construction of Lois Gibb's experience as an iconic example of 'the pathway into environmental activism' narrative, in which apolitical women personally experience an environmental problem that launches them into a life of activism to protect the health of their families. Elements of this narrative are reductionist, in that they conflate gender and motherhood: they define women's roles in their culturally acceptable frame, as reproductive beings, and assume that women prioritize threats to their children as first among their political concerns as citizens (see MacGregor 2006 for a sustained analysis of the 'eco-maternalist' narrative).

This gendered narrative of politicization, which focuses largely on white women, ignores the historical realities and complicated race and class politics in operation at Love Canal, and elsewhere. For example, historian Elizabeth Blum has more fully analyzed the complex relationships between race, class and gender in her book *Love Canal Revisited* (2008). Blum focuses on communities largely ignored in media accounts of Love Canal, specifically the stories of black women in public housing and white middle-class religious activists. She also identifies the many tensions between different groups and their relationship to narratives of feminism and women's rights. Her work is therefore important for interweaving contested accounts of environmental activism with a deeply historical, spatial and political analysis. Unlike the iconic story of Love Canal, with Gibbs as the lone heroine following in the footsteps of Rachel Carson, Blum's is a more complex story about race, class, gender, and activism, where there are many actors and conflicts within and between different communities. Her work is emblematic of EJ scholarship that situates contemporary conflicts within a historical framework, whether those conflicts are over nuclear contamination on Native American lands or occupational health hazards in Silicon Valley.

In addition to complicating simplistic narratives, since the late 1990s and into the 2000s, a growing body of EJ research has begun to take gender more seriously as a category of analysis.

In general, this research has approached gender in less biologically reductionist or essentialist ways than the first generation that fought to legitimize environmental justice as a serious body of scholarship, where women were often treated as a homogenous category. Informed by the feminist theoretical concept of intersectionality (see Crenshaw 1991), recent generations of EJ researchers have continued to focus on gender and race but have treated them as interrelated and intersecting categories of analysis in highlighting the impact of pollution on the health and bodies of differently situated people. A sustained focus on health and bodies by researchers can be explained, in part, by the fact that in utero exposures to pollution are a very visible way in which exposures and their health effects are registered inter-generationally, with differing outcomes depending on class, race, and other axes of social power.

One example is the elevated levels of pollution within indigenous Arctic communities as a result of persistent organic pollutants (POPs). POPSs are a set of extremely toxic, long-lasting, chlorinated, organic chemicals that can travel long distances from their emissions source (often created through industrial pollution thousands of miles away) and that bio-accumulate in animals and ecosystems. In the 1980s scientists observed high levels of toxic chemicals (pesticides, insec-ticides, fungicides, industrial chemicals and waste combustion) far from their sites of production. An Inuit midwife in Nunavik (a province in the Canadian Arctic) collected breast milk samples as a control from a 'clean' environment, but instead, researchers were surprised to find that Inuit women had POP concentrations in their breast milk five to ten times higher than women in southern Canada and among the highest ever recorded. The health effects include high rates of infectious diseases and immune dysfunction, negative effects on neuro-behavioural development, and negative effects on height. This problem of breast milk contamination has local effects but was created in global economic-political and scientific-ecological contexts (Downie and Fenge 2003). Therefore a multi-scalar analysis is necessary in order to fully comprehend the concentrated local effects of POP pollution in its historical, spatial, political, and biological dimensions. This issue is an environmental justice (or injustice) concern due to disproportionality: in other words, those with the least culpability for causing the problem face the worst impacts of this pollution.

Another example is female workers employed in computer processing and garment factories in the United States. In the 1990s, over half of all textile and apparel workers in the United States were immigrant Asian women. Garment workers in sweatshops face increased exposure to fibre particles, dyes, formaldehydes, and arsenic, leading to high rates of respiratory illness. More than 70 per cent of computer production workers in Silicon Valley were immigrant women who held jobs where occupational illness rates were more than three times those of any other industry. Pellow and Park (2002) document the occupational health hazards computer production-line workers in Silicon Valley face, and discuss the fact that most of these labourers are non-unionized, low-income Asian and Latina immigrant women. The health and environmental effects of com-puter production-line labour are numerous, and there are particular harms to reproductive and nervous systems (such as triggering higher rates of miscarriages). Although much of this work has since moved overseas, the problems have only intensified and increased in their scope.

A final example comes from my own research on asthma activism in New York City. Here gender became a significant category of analysis not only in terms of maternal health and breast milk contamination, but also in terms of chronic childhood illnesses. My study documents how the different aspects of gender, household dynamics, and childhood motivate asthma activism in NYC. In certain urban communities of colour, child asthma rates are four times the average rate, contributing to overall levels of poor health, high stress, and premature death (Sze 2007). Gender is a factor in the questions of causation (what causes asthma and prenatal exposures), treatment (blaming mothers for poor housekeeping), and in the activism itself (the family and childhood focus on the activism in public rallies and campaign documents).

## *Making global connections*

In the 1990s EJ scholarship moved from local to global. Researchers moved beyond a local US focus and began to develop critical analyses of the global expansion of neoliberalism and privatization. The sophisticated spatial analysis that has become the norm in EJ literature echoes the links that environmental justice activists have made between local and global forces and phenomena. Although the following examples are based in the United States, they show how activists have analyzed their problems across national borders. What has become apparent is that environmental justice and community organizing are gendered, as argued by scholars such as Giovanna Di Chiro and Bindi Shah.

Di Chiro's oeuvre over two decades has focused squarely on the central interconnections between environmental justice and gender in social movements, both local and global (1992, 1997, 1998, 2005, 2008, and a chapter in this handbook). In 'Living Environmentalisms: Coalition Politics, Social Reproduction and Environmental Justice', Di Chiro (2008) examines the intersectional links forged by activists in US environmental justice and women's rights organizations and how they exercise coalition politics using a strategic-relational vision of social and environmental change. Framed by the feminist concept of social reproduction, which refers to the mostly unpaid work of caring for and sustaining life, Di Chiro examines the complex ways that globalized capitalism has downloaded state and corporate responsibilities for social reproduction on to the backs of local communities and individual women. She writes, 'Social reproduction is the intersecting complex of political-economic, sociocultural, and material-environmental processes required to maintain everyday life and to sustain human cultures and communities on a daily basis and intergenerationally' (2008:281). Using empirical examples, Di Chiro effectively analyzes the intertwining of gender and environmental justice movements that are theoretically informed by feminist, social movement, and science and technology studies scholarship.

Examples of the embodiment of a 'living environmentalism' lie, according to Di Chiro, in the coalition politics of a growing international network committed to 'climate justice': the aim of making visible the disproportionate impact of global warming on poor and marginalized communities throughout the world. For example, poor, rural African American communities in the southern United States were among the first to use the term environmental racism in the fight against toxic siting. Gulf Coast African American EJ activists have been leaders of the national movement, in part because of the extensive problems they face from toxic-chemical pollution from oil refineries and petrochemical facilities. The state of Louisiana is home to more than 125 oil and chemical plants in the corridor known by some as 'Cancer Alley', between New Orleans and Baton Rouge, where a series of low-income, predominantly African American, rural communities live. Most well-known perhaps is Margie Eugene-Richard, who won the Goldman Prize (which some refer to as environmentalism's Nobel Prize) in 2004. The first African American to win the award, Richard had, with fellow residents of Diamond, waged a thirty-year campaign against Shell Chemicals. She travelled internationally to address the transnational corporation and its board of trustees, as well as forging an alliance with the Ogoni peoples in Nigeria who were also fighting Shell – a fight that led to the death of writer and EJ activist Ken Saro-Wiwa in 1995 (Lerner 2006).

Local communities fighting transnational oil companies realized that they needed to network transnationally. These activist networks crossed between Louisiana, to Nigeria, and back to Richmond, a city in Contra Costa County in northern California, which is home to the Chevron/Texaco oil refinery and more than 350 industrial facilities, including chemical plants and chemical and petroleum-based industries. Some of the facilities have suffered major industrial accidents over the past thirty years. The Chevron refinery, the largest oil refinery in the western United

States, has been a major source of pollution, toxic releases, and industrial accidents that have threatened the health and safety of workers and community members. Against this backdrop of urban pollution, the Laotian Organizing Project (LOP) emphasizes direct organizing and youth mobilization within the Laotian community in Richmond. This population, primarily refugees who entered the United States after the 1970s, is predominantly low-income. The LOP was formed in 1995 to work on community empowerment through direct organizing on issues of community concern. One concrete result of the LOP was a victory of a multilingual warning system for toxic releases, whereas previously the warning system was only in English. The LOP was successful in emphasizing the community's unique cultural and linguistic resources and needs as well as because it worked for years developing community-based leadership, especially among Laotian youth as discussed in Bindi Shah's book *Laotian Daughters: Working toward Community, Belonging and Environmental Justice* (2011).

Shah offers a well-researched and broad-ranging theoretical account of Laotian teenage girls involved in a four-year Asian American Youth Leadership Project run by an EJ organization called the Asian Pacific Environmental Network (APEN). The participants are second-generation Laotian teenage girls living at the intersection of multiple identities – as teenage girls, racialized minorities, and refugees in a hyper-polluted urban context with complex interracial encounters. Through this engagement with members of a relatively small youth leadership development project, her participants experience new understandings of belonging, citizenship, and national identity that change longstanding debates about assimilation. Her contribution is to outline what she calls 'the cultural politics of critical incorporation', which she defines as a 'set of practices that challenge, accommodate, or transform power relations within the national, civil society and the (Laotian) family' (Shah 2011:8). These practices represent the exercise of symbolic, cultural, and social capital outside the bounds of legal categories of citizenship and formal politics. Through engagement with Laotian female teenagers' experiences, she highlights how they 'jump' spatial scales through which to 'negotiate the contradiction between the liberal ideology of universal citizenship and the collective boundaries of race, class, nationality, gender and life stage that define substantive citizenship' (Shah 2011:8). Gender is at the *core* of EJ activism in Richmond, connected to multiple frames. For Shah, gender is not a function of essentialist reproductive identity; rather it is deeply connected to class, race, refugee status, the historical context of US military incursions in their 'home' countries, and the social lives of the communities themselves. These identities are interrelated, developed, and transformed in the particular urban landscape in Richmond, just as they are also shaped by the polluting practices of transnational oil and energy corporations. It is precisely this *interrelationship* between gender and race, space, power, and geo-politics that makes much contemporary EJ activism and scholarship so compelling.

## A focus on bodies

More recently, EJ research has moved to another scale of analysis: the body. To some extent this move has been sparked by the attentiveness to the material interchanges between bodies and environments that has been observed in other fields of environmental scholarship. This 'material turn' away from the postmodern focus on discourse has not brought the body 'back in' in essentialist or determinist ways, but rather in ways that involve properly theorizing 'the often unpredictable an unwanted actions of human bodies, nonhuman creatures, ecological systems, chemical agents, and other actors' (Alaimo 2010). These interchanges and actions across bodies add up to what feminist environmental scholar Stacey Alaimo calls 'transcorporeality'. In her book *Bodily Natures: Science, Environment, and the Material Self,* Alaimo writes that 'the human is always the very stuff of the messy, contingent, emergent mix of the material world' (2010:11), and she uses a number of texts and case studies, including from environmental justice issues, to support this claim. The body is enmeshed in social and material systems and systems of domination that are enacted in individual and community bodies, cultural representations, and modes of knowing and thinking. Thus, while earlier accounts of gender and environmental justice draw on essentialist constructions of women and motherhood that ignore complicated politics of class, race and gender (as in Love Canal), contemporary theories of transcorporeality take disputes over environmental injustices and situate them in all their complexity, including in systems of risk and knowledge production. A good example to illustrate this approach is the political struggle over the links between toxic contamination and congenital disorders.

In a forthcoming piece, I examine how racialized images of motherhood and childbirth are a central component of the activist organizing strategy in Kettleman City, California. Kettleman City was an early, iconic example of EJ mobilizing against toxics, where a poor, primarily rural and Latino (95 per cent) community fought the siting (in 1975), and later expansion of the largest PCB facility west of the Mississippi in the 2000s. In 2009, community residents, with help from environmental and social justice allies, sought to connect the high rate of congenital disorders, and in particular, cleft palates, to their exposure to hazardous waste. Activists used maternalist discourse as a counterweight to the highly technical knowledge about toxic exposures used by regulatory agencies and polluters. I argue that the Kettleman City cleft palate controversy is an example of where reproductive and environmental justice meet, through what might be called 'racialized transcorporeality', to de-normalize the embodied toxicity operating at multiple spatial and temporal scales, including bodily and regional. Specifically, the activist politics of race, gender, and toxic exposure are being constructed through the frames of motherhood and children's health, which rely, in complicated ways, on normative ideologies of bodily health, even as their critique challenges the social and economic structures that deny the normative bodily health of these women of colour and their babies. The politics of gender and motherhood are being mobilized by EJ activists, in the context of anti-immigrant and anti-natalist politics, in contrast to polluter and State attempts to reject the claims of the activists who use complex cumulative impact analysis to argue for a relationship between their health and elevated pollution exposure (Sze forthcoming).

The examples I have discussed in this section – Inuit women's breast milk contamination; Asian and Latina immigrant occupational exposures, whether from garment work, farm work, or computer production; and children born with cleft palates in California – all exemplify the racialized and gendered ways in which transcorporeality is lived and experienced. In other words, while transcorporeality is a broad condition of contemporary life, the particular economic and environmental conditions for women of colour and indigenous women ensure that they suffer particular burdens from the global toxic production system. The question here is not whether or how these populations 'choose' the conditions of their life and labour. Rather, the racialized dimensions of transcorporeality necessitate particular burdens on their bodies. These racialized and gendered burdens have reproductive consequences that lay bare the brutalities of the current economic and environmental system, overlaid with histories of domination and violence.

## Conclusion

Gender has always been part of the story of environmental justice activism, whether or not it has been properly recognized or analyzed as such. As I have argued in this chapter, while early scholarship on environmental racism largely neglected gender, gender was always an important part of the story of the larger environmental justice movement. As the field has matured, and thrived, a new generation of scholars is tackling environmental justice issues using diverse interdisciplinary methods and tools. As a result, the prominence of gender in environmental justice scholarship has come to the fore.

Scholarship on gender and environmental justice is diverse in every sense of the word: in terms of the issues it addresses, the theoretical frameworks and methodologies that are used, and the geographical and historical scope of analyses. What ties this vast field together is a shared concern with the question of how identities, in particular, but not exclusively race, gender, and class, shape the experiences of individuals and communities in a world marked by injustice at multiple scales. Many, although by no means all, of the problems discussed in the gender and EJ scholarship remain centred on the bodily scale, on maternal and child health and the negative effects of toxic exposures. This gendered focus on bodies is less a function of woman-as-body/nature, as it is a function of the hyper-polluted realities in which much of the contemporary world lives. Environmental contamination is never simply a local concern; there are links to people and places and corporations to be analyzed and challenged. Contamination is intensifying as a result of development and globalization. In the current context of global climate change, which is posing existential threats to the collective continuance of many communities, including indigenous, small-island states and others, EJ research is moving into debates about climate justice (see, e.g., Whyte 2013, 2014). Recent work is increasingly looking at the gender dimensions of climate change and sustainable development, which also have implications for health and well-being (see, e.g., Nagel 2016). As conditions of environmental degradation and impacts from climate change intensify, scholarship that uses interdisciplinary methods, political frameworks and analyses that understand the complex relationship between gender, environmental justice, race and social movements have become even more necessary.

## Note

1 Of course, this reference to Mother Earth has a long and contested history, between those ecofeminists who celebrate the connection between women/nature and those who object to this relationship on philosophical, epistemological and pragmatic grounds.

## References

Alaimo, S. (2010) *Bodily Natures: Science, Environment, and the Material Self.* Bloomington, IN: Indiana University Press.

Blum, E. (2008) *Love Canal Revisited: Race, Class, and Gender in Environmental Activism.* Lawrence, KA: University of Kansas Press.

Chavis, B. Jr. and Lee, C. (1987) *United Church of Christ Commission on Racial Justice, Toxic Wastes and Race in the United States: A National Report on the Racial and Socio-Economic Characteristics of Communities With Hazardous Waste Sites.* New York: United Church of Christ.

Cole, L. and Foster, S. (2001) *From the Ground Up: Environmental Racism and the Rise of the Environmental Justice Movement.* New York: New York University Press.

Crenshaw, K. (1991) 'Mapping the margins: Intersectionality, identity politics, and violence against women of color', *Stanford Law Review* 43(6): 1241–1299.

Di Chiro, G. (1992) 'Defining environmental justice: Women's voices and grassroots politics', *Socialist Review* 22(4): 93–130.

Di Chiro, G. (1997) 'Local actions, global visions: Remaking environmental expertise', *Frontiers: A Journal of Women Studies* 8(2): 203–231.

Di Chiro, G. (1998) 'Environmental justice from the grassroots: Reflections on history, gender, and expertise', in Faber, D. (ed) *The Struggle for Ecological Democracy: Environmental Justice Movements in the United States.* New York: Guilford, 104–136.

Di Chiro, G. (2005) 'Performing a "global sense of place": Women's actions for environmental justice', in Nelson, L. and Seager, J. (eds) *A Companion to Feminist Geography.* Oxford: Blackwell Publishers, 496–516.

Di Chiro, G. (2008) 'Living environmentalisms: Coalition politics, social reproduction, and environmental justice', *Environmental Politics* 17(2): 276–298.

Downie, D. and Fenge, T. (eds) (2003) *Northern Lights Against Pops: Toxic Threats in the Arctic.* Montreal and Kingston: McGill University Press.

Gottlieb, R. (2005) *Forcing the Spring: The Transformation of the American Environmental Movement.* Washington, DC: Island Press.

Hood-Washington, S. (2004) *Packing Them in: An Archaeology of Environmental Racism in Chicago, 1865–1954.* Lanham, MD: Lexington Books.

Lavelle, M. and Coyle, M. (1993) 'Unequal protection: The racial divide in environmental law', in Hofrichter, R. (ed) *Toxic Struggles: The Theory and Practice of Environmental Justice.* Philadelphia, PA: New Society, 136–143.

Lerner, S. (2006) *Diamond: A Struggle for Environmental Justice in Louisiana's Chemical Corridor.* Cambridge, MA: MIT Press.

MacGregor, S. (2006) *Beyond Mothering Earth: Ecological Citizenship and the Politics of Care.* Vancouver, BC: University of British Columbia Press.

McGurty, E. (2009) *Transforming Environmentalism: Warren County, PCBs, and the Origins of Environmental Justice.* Newark, NJ: Rutgers University Press.

Nagel, J. (2016) *Gender and Climate Change: Impacts, Science, Policy.* New York: Routledge.

Novotny, P. (2000) *Where We Live, Work and Play: The Environmental Justice Movement and the Struggle for a New Environmentalism.* Praeger Series in Transformational Politics and Political Science. Westport, CT: Praeger.

Pellow, D. N. (2000) 'Environmental inequality formation', *American Behavioral Scientist* 43: 581–601.

Pellow, D. N. (2007) *Resisting Global Toxics: Transnational Movements for Environmental Justice.* Cambridge, MA: MIT Press.

Pellow, D. N. and Park, L. (2002) *The Silicon Valley of Dreams: Environmental Injustice, Immigrant Workers and the High-Tech Global Economy.* New York: New York University Press.

Perkins, T. (2012) 'Women's pathways into activism: Rethinking the women's environmental justice narrative in California's San Joaquin Valley', *Organization & Environment* 25(1): 76–94.

Principles of Environmental Justice (1991) Online. Available at: www.ejnet.org/ej/principles.html (accessed 23 August 2016).

Sandler, R. and Pezzullo, P. C. (eds) (2007) *Environmental Justice and Environmentalism: The Social Justice Challenge to the Environmental Movement.* Cambridge, MA: MIT Press.

Seager, J. (1996) '"Hysterical housewives" and other mad women: Grassroots environmental organizing in the United States', in Rocheleau, D., Thomas-Slayter, D. and Wangari, E. (eds) *Feminist Political Ecology.* London: Routledge, 271–283.

Shah, B. (2011) *Laotian Daughters: Working Toward Community, Belonging and Environmental Justice.* Philadelphia, PA: Temple University Press.

Sze, J. (2007) *Noxious New York: The Racial Politics of Urban Health and Environmental Justice.* Cambridge, MA: MIT Press.

Sze, J. (forthcoming) 'De-normalizing embodied toxicity: The case of Kettleman City', in Leilani Nishimi, L. and Williams, K. H. (eds) *Racial Ecologies.* London: Routledge.

Taylor, D. (2009) *The Environment and the People in American Cities, 1600s–1900s: Disorder, Inequality, and Social Change.* Durham, NC: Duke University Press.

Tokar, B. (1997) *Earth for Sale: Reclaiming Ecology in the Age of Corporate Greenwash.* Boston, MA: South End Press.

Walker, G. (2012) *Environmental Justice: Concepts, Evidence and Politics.* London: Routledge.

Whyte, K. P. (2013) 'Justice forward: Tribes, climate adaptation and responsibility', *Climatic Change* 120: 517–530.

Whyte, K. P. (2014) 'Indigenous women, climate change impacts and collective action', *Hypatia* 29(3): 599–616.

# 11

# GENDER DIFFERENCES IN ENVIRONMENTAL CONCERN

## Sociological explanations

*Chenyang Xiao and Aaron M. McCright*

### Introduction

Research on environmental concern in the past few decades consistently finds that women express slightly greater environmental concern than men. This modest gender difference exists whether environmental concern is operationalized via items measuring environment/economic tradeoffs, participation in pro-environmental activities, pro-environmental attitudes or an ecological worldview, or perceived seriousness of different types of environmental problems. The greatest gender differences are generally seen in studies dealing with the last type of indicator – worry about specific environmental problems, especially those local problems with clear health risks to family and community.

The prevailing sociological explanations for gender differences in environmental concern are derived from either gender socialization theory or perspectives emphasizing the social roles that men and women differentially perform in society. When environmental concern is operationalized as perceived seriousness or worry about specific environmental problems, some scholars have argued that the gender divide largely reflects underlying gender differences in perceptions of health and safety risks to individuals or their families (see also Slovic 1999).

In this chapter, we review relevant sociological literature on gender differences in environmental concern. This work provides an analytical model for a study conducted to examine the existing explanations for such gender differences with recent data. Such a study will update our knowledge of gendered patterns in environmental concern.

We integrate insights from Bord and O'Connor (1997) on gendered risk perceptions while testing a number of hypotheses to explain gender differences in environmental concern that have been identified by Davidson and Freudenburg (1996) and Blocker and Eckberg (1997). These hypotheses expect connections between gender differences and (1) safety concerns; (2) religiosity; (3) economic salience; (4) family roles; and (5) parenthood. We use a data set derived from six Gallup surveys of the US general public between 2001 and 2008, which includes multi-item measures of (1) worry about health-related environmental problems, (2) worry about global environmental problems, and (3) generalized risk perception. This data set also offers the advantage of examining the performance of key variables across multiple years. To test the above hypotheses adequately, we apply structural equation modelling for the examination of the direct and indirect effects of gender and other key variables.

After explaining our analytical model in part one of the chapter, we go on describe our data set and variables before presenting the results of our analyses in part two. We end with a discussion of fruitful avenues for future research on gender differences in environmental concern.

## Part one: explanations of gender differences in environmental concern

Sociological research on how men and women perceive and respond to environmental problems began to develop in the 1990s. Among the most cited early articles are by Davidson and Freudenburg (1996) and Blocker and Eckberg (1997), which presented what have since become the prevailing hypotheses for explaining gender differences on environmental concern. Like others have done before us, we place these explanations into two groups: those emphasizing gender socialization processes and those emphasizing the different social roles that men and women tend to perform. Since these explanations were formed based upon the results of empirical studies with data collected two decades ago, we believe it is time to re-examine these explanations using more recent data. As we explain in part two, our data set allows us to test two of the five major socialization hypotheses and each of the three major social roles hypotheses. We limit our discussion here to only those hypotheses we test later in the chapter.

### *Gender socialization hypotheses*

How individuals come to develop an understanding of themselves as a member of a gender group (i.e., how they gain a gender identity) to which are attached particular norms and behaviours (i.e., gender roles) is a central question for sociologists. Gender socialization theorists emphasize the different values and social expectations that are internalized by boys and girls through socialization into their society's dominant culture (see, for example, classic texts by Chodorow 1978; Gilligan 1982). Briefly, in most societies boys learn that masculinity means being competitive, independent, and unemotional, and entails objectively exerting mastery and control over other people and things. Also, boys realize they are expected to economically provide for their family when they grow up and become fathers. On the other hand, girls learn that femininity means being compassionate, cooperative, and empathetic, and entails connecting with other people and expressing concern about their well-being. Also, girls realize they are expected to enact an ethic of care as a nurturing caregiver when they grow up and become mothers. In short, a masculine identity emphasizes detachment, control, and mastery, while a feminine identity stresses attachment, empathy, and care (e.g., Keller 1985; Kimmel 2009).

Many scholars have invoked gender socialization theory to explain why women are more concerned than are men about local environmental problems that pose significant health and safety risks for community members (e.g., Mohai 1992; Greenbaum 1995; Freudenburg and Davidson 2007). This line of reasoning has become known as the 'Concerns about Health and Safety' hypothesis (Blocker and Eckberg 1997) or 'Safety Concerns Hypothesis' (Davidson and Freudenburg 1996), and it enjoys considerable support in the literature.

Given this level support, we designed a study to test this safety concerns hypothesis by examining gender differences in concern for health-related environmental problems (e.g., air pollution) and in concern for global environmental problems (e.g., global warming). At its most basic level, the safety concerns hypothesis expects that *women express greater concern than do men about health-related environmental problems, especially when controlling for key social roles variables* (this is our Hypothesis 1, or H1). While women may indeed express greater concern than do men for both types of environmental problems, the safety concerns hypothesis expects that *the effect of gender is greater in models explaining concern for health-related environmental problems than in models explaining concern for global environmental problems* (our H2).

A few other theoretical arguments extend the gender socialization perspective. Each argues that men and women socialized respectively into masculine and feminine identities differ on key *beliefs and values* that directly influence environmental concern. A strict interpretation of each argument holds that these beliefs and values – as intervening variables – greatly mediate the relationship between gender and environmental concern. Scholars have identified four such arguments; we only discuss one here since data limitations preclude testing the other three.[1]

A few scholars reviewed in a pioneering article by Blocker and Eckberg (1997) argued that differences between men and women in religious beliefs and religiosity explain gender differences in environmental concern. Briefly, women tend to express stronger religious beliefs and greater levels of religiosity than do men (e.g., Batson et al. 1993), and religiosity is associated negatively with environmental concern (e.g., Eckberg and Blocker 1989, 1996; Hayes 2001). This religiosity hypothesis expects that *religiosity has a negative effect on environmental concern* (our H3) and that *inclusion of religiosity as an intervening variable between gender and environmental concern greatly mediates the relationship between gender and environmental concern* (our H4).

## Social roles hypotheses

While gender socialization theories emphasize the development of masculine and feminine values and identities, another set of theoretical arguments gives greater attention to the influences of the social roles and types of work that men and women differentially perform in society. Greenbaum captures the general sentiment of these arguments: 'The different attitudes of men and women . . . reflect the different experiences, competencies, interests, and dispositions that come from performing (and being socialized to perform) these different roles' (1995:134). For the most part, scholars focus on three productive or reproductive roles: employment status, homemaker status, and parenthood.

Several scholars investigate the influence of men's and women's differential paid labour force participation on their environmental concern – the 'Economic Growth Orientation' (Blocker and Eckberg 1997) or 'Economic Salience Hypothesis' (Davidson and Freudenburg 1996). Building upon the socialization perspectives discussed above, some early research argued that conventional gender socialization leads males to internalize a 'marketplace mentality' and females to internalize a 'motherhood mentality'. While the former favours economic growth and exploitation of natural resources for human benefit, the latter favours protection of nature and other species. Early studies assumed that these two orientations were activated by the greater participation of males than females in the paid labour force in past decades. Most of this research has produced mixed and generally inconclusive results (see a review by Blocker and Eckberg 1997).

Yet scholars more recently seek to examine the direct effect that labour force participation has on environmental concern independent of gender, arguing that employment for pay outside the home leads to greater concern for economic issues and lesser concern for environmental issues for both men and women. Overall, the results for this hypothesis have been mixed (Davidson and Freudenburg 1996; Hayes 2001). A few studies have even found that people who are employed full-time are more concerned about the environment than are those who are not (e.g., Blocker and Eckberg 1989; Mohai 1992). Further, Mohai (1992) has reported that women employed full time are still more concerned about the environment than are men employed full time.

As a corollary to this employment hypothesis, some argue that a woman's decision to be a homemaker triggers her values of nurturance, compassion, and empathy in such a way as to increase environmental concern: the 'Family Roles and Environmentalism' hypothesis (Blocker and Eckberg 1997). For example, Mohai (1992) and Blocker and Eckberg (1989, 1997) have examined this hypothesis and found – contrary to expectations – that women with some labour force experience express more pro-environmental beliefs than do women who are homemakers. The economic salience hypothesis expects that *full-time employment has a negative effect on environmental concern* (our H5), and the family roles hypothesis expects that *homemaker status has a positive effect on environmental concern* (our H6).

Finally, some scholars also investigate the effect that parenthood has on men's and women's environmental concern. This is the 'Parenthood Status' hypothesis (Blocker and Eckberg 1997) or 'Parental Roles Hypothesis' (Davidson and Freudenburg 1996). Briefly, theorists expect that parenthood increases 'parents' attentiveness to consequences bearing on their sex-typed roles in families: for mothers, concern for their children's health; for fathers, concern for the material well-being of the family' (Stern et al. 1993:331). Consequently, mothers with more concern about the health and safety of their children as caregiver of the family become more concerned about the environment, while fathers with stronger concern with economic growth as economic provider of the family become less concerned about the environment (Greenbaum 1995). Some studies in this area have found that motherhood increases environmental concern for women (e.g., Blocker and Eckberg 1989; Davidson and Freudenburg 1996), though slightly fewer studies have found that fatherhood decreases environmental concern for men (e.g., Blocker and Eckberg 1989). Several other studies have found either mixed results or overall non-significance for parenthood status (e.g., Freudenburg 1993; Blocker and Eckberg 1997). The parenthood hypothesis expects that *parenthood has a positive effect on women's environmental concern and a negative effect on men's environmental concern* (this is our H7).

## *Gendered risk perceptions*

One of the most consistent patterns in the expansive literature on risk perception is that women tend to judge a wide range of risks as more problematic than do men (e.g., Slovic 1999, 2001). For instance, analyzing nationally representative data from telephone surveys conducted between late 1997 and early 1998, Finucane et al. (2000) found that a greater percentage of females than males rated twelve of thirteen different hazardous activities and technologies as high risk to themselves and their families. These activities and technologies ranged from nuclear power plants to street drugs and from lead in dust and paint to electromagnetic fields. This pattern of gender difference in risk perception continues to the present, as recent studies consistently find greater risk perception among women on issues such as HIV/AIDS (e.g., Robertson et al. 2006; Hillman 2008), smoking and other health risks (e.g., Duckworth et al. 2002; Lundborg and Andersson 2008), crime and victimization (e.g., May et al. 2010), as well as technological risks (e.g., Siegrist et al. 2005; Smith et al. 2008).

Drawing upon this risk perception literature, Bord and O'Connor (1997) re-interpreted the gender divide in environmental concern. Since well-publicized environmental hazards and disasters of the late 1970s and early 1980s (most notably the Love Canal toxic chemical waste disaster), the authors claimed that the US general public has linked concern about the environment to health and well-being risks (see the chapter by Sze in this handbook). Bord and O'Connor (1997) further argued that the gender difference in environmental concern may be due to a gender difference in perceived vulnerability to risk and not necessarily due to differences in ecological sensibilities. This is especially the case when environmental beliefs and attitudes are assessed in ways that trigger women's heightened sensitivity to risk. This includes, for example, survey questions about environmental issues widely perceived as risks (e.g., radioactive waste) and question formats that ask for levels of 'worry', 'concern', or 'seriousness'.

Through this lens of risk, Bord and O'Connor (1997) reorganized the empirical studies reviewed by Davidson and Freudenburg (1996). They discovered that 92 per cent of those studies conducted in the 1980s and 1990s support their argument. Bord and O'Connor (1997) then performed their own empirical analysis of responses to questions about hazardous chemical waste sites and global warming in a 1991 survey. Briefly, they found that the statistically significant gender divide on the perceived seriousness of these problems disappears when they account for perceptions of health risks due to these problems. This risk perception argument advanced and confirmed by Bord and O'Connor (1997) provides us with an additional hypothesis deserving examination. The gendered risk perception hypothesis expects that *inclusion of generalized risk perception as an intervening variable between gender and environmental concern greatly mediates the effect of gender on environmental concern* (our H8).

The eight hypotheses identified in the foregoing discussion provide collective insights on the causes of the modest gender differences in environmental concern persistently observed in empirical data. Of course, it is worth noting that this list is not complete. As mentioned previously, we limit our discussion to only those hypotheses for which we have data to perform statistical tests. In part two, we present the procedures as well as results of these tests.

## Part two: examining gender differences in environmental concern in the United States, 2001–2008

In our study, we utilize structural equation modelling (SEM), a tool that has proven particularly effective for analyzing mediating effects (e.g., Dietz at al. 2007) and for its ability to construct theoretically guided models and estimate both direct and indirect effects simultaneously.[2] Further, SEM incorporates in the overall structural model the measurement modules of latent factors while controlling measurement errors and their correlations (e.g., Bollen 1989). The three figures illustrate the conceptual path diagrams we use to conduct our SEM analyses. In each diagram, all arrows indicate direct paths of influence.

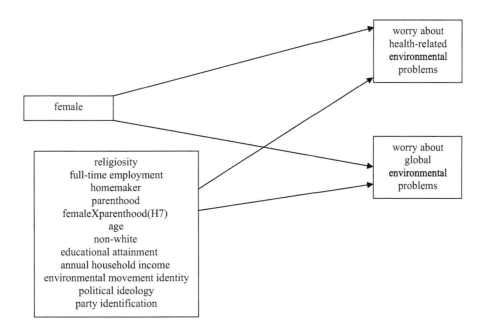

*Figure 11.1* Model A: the parenthood hypothesis

To accommodate data availability and theoretical arguments, we conducted three SEM analyses. Figure 11.1 illustrates Model A for the test of the parenthood hypothesis (H7). Gallup did not ask about parenthood status in its 2008 survey, so we examined this hypothesis in a separate model. Including parenthood status in the other models illustrated in Figure 11.2 and 11.3 would have prohibited us from using the 2008 data. Figure 11.2 illustrates Model B for the examination of the mediating effect of religiosity (H3 and H4). Figure 11.3 illustrates Model C for the examination of the mediating effect of generalized risk perception (H8).

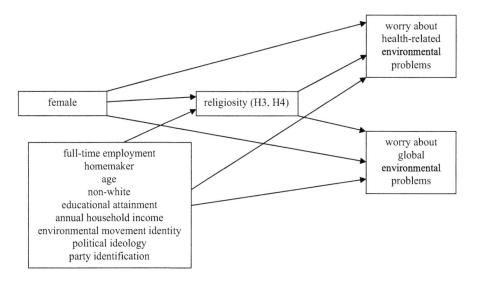

*Figure 11.2*   Model B: the religiosity mediating effect

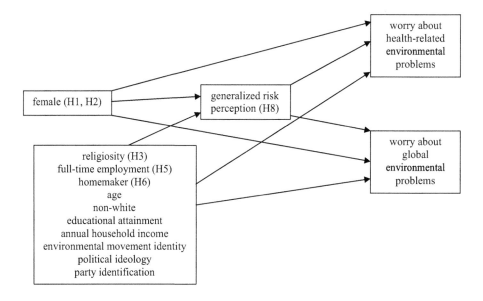

*Figure 11.3*   Model C: the generalized risk perception mediating effect

As we discuss later, Model C offers the best fit to our data, so we test the remaining hypotheses with this model. Female (H1, H2) is the primary independent variable, and full-time employment (H5) and homemaker (H6) are also crucial for our tests of hypotheses. Both employment and homemaker status are arguably mediating factors as suggested by the social roles hypotheses. Yet, the results of Models A and B show that neither factor has a statistically significant effect on any dependent variable. Thus there is no empirical basis to further examine their potential mediating effects. In all models, we also control for respondents' age, race, educational attainment, annual household income, environmental movement identity, political ideology, and party identification.[3] All of these variables are considered observed.

Three latent variables, which have multiple survey items as measurement indicators, are 'generalized risk perception', 'worry about health-related environmental problems', and 'worry about global environmental problems'. We incorporated these latent variables and their corresponding survey items directly into our SEM analyses as measurement modules, which we discuss in greater detail in the next section. As this discussion will show, the two latent factors of environmental concern are highly correlated. Thus we allowed for correlation between the disturbance terms of these two latent factors for more efficient parameter estimations as in 'seemingly unrelated regression estimation' (e.g., Greene 2000). We tested each of the three models (illustrated in Figures 11.1, 11.2, and 11.3) with six yearly samples separately but simultaneously using the 'comparing groups' feature of SEM to examine long-term consistency of various effects, using AMOS 16.0.

To save space, we present tables of results only from the generalized risk perception model (Figure 11.3), with which we test H1, H2, H5, H6, and H8. We briefly discuss in the text the results of the parenthood hypothesis model (Figure 11.1) and the religiosity hypothesis model (Figure 11.2).

## Data and variables

Our data come from the Gallup Organization's annual environment survey, conducted each March in anticipation of Earth Day (April 22). The six Gallup surveys (2001, 2002, 2004, 2006, 2007, 2008) are based on telephone interviews with nationally representative samples of 1,000 to 1,060 adults (age eighteen years or older) in the United States. The 2001 survey was the first to include all of the key variables employed in this study. The surveys in 2003, 2005, 2009, and 2010 were excluded from our study, since they did not measure several key variables.

Gender was coded 0 for 'male' and 1 for 'female'. Religiosity ranged from 1 for 'never attend church' to 5 for 'attend church once a week'. Three dichotomous variables (coded 0 for 'no' and 1 for 'yes') measured whether or not respondents were employed full time, were a homemaker, and were a parent of a child living at home. To test the parenthood hypothesis, we created a 'female × parenthood' interaction term. We control for several demographic, social, and political variables believed to correlate with environmental concern: age (in actual years), race (white = 0, non-white = 1), educational attainment (high school graduate or less = 1 to more than college graduate = 4), annual household income (less than \$20,000 = 1 to more than \$75,000 = 5), environmental movement identity (unsympathetic to environmental movement = 1 to active participant in environmental movement = 4),[4] political ideology (very conservative = 1 to very liberal = 5, with middle-of-the-road = 3), and party identification (Republican = 1 to Democrat = 5, with Independent = 3).

We modelled both dependent variables ('worry about health-related environmental problems' and 'worry about global environmental problems') and an intervening variable ('generalized risk perception') as latent factors measured by relevant survey items (see Table 11.1 for details). These measurement modules were confirmatory factor analyses (CFAs). The items we

Table 11.1 Survey items for the three latent factors in our analytical model

| Latent factors | Survey items | Factor Loadings | Reliability (Alpha) |
|---|---|---|---|
| | Gallup wording: 'Next I'm going to read a list of problems facing the country. For each one, please tell me if you personally worry about this problem a great deal, a fair amount, only a little, or not at all. First, how much do you personally worry about:' | | |
| **Generalized risk perception** | | | .77–.82 |
| | Hunger and homelessness | 0.62–0.69 | |
| | Crime and violence | 0.48–0.59 | |
| | The availability and affordability of health care | 0.58–0.62 | |
| | Drug use | 0.37–0.55 | |
| | Race relations | 0.46–0.52 | |
| | Availability and affordability of energy | 0.40–0.57 | |
| | The economy | 0.54–0.70 | |
| | Unemployment | 0.66–0.71 | |
| | Gallup wording: 'I'm going to read you a list of environmental problems. As I read each one, please tell me if you personally worry about this problem a great deal, a fair amount, only a little, or not at all. First, how much do you personally worry about:' | | |
| **Worry about health-related environmental problems** | | | .85–.87 |
| | Pollution of rivers, lakes, and reservoirs | 0.77–0.82 | |
| | Air pollution | 0.77–0.79 | |
| | Contamination of soil and water by toxic waste | 0.78–0.83 | |
| | Pollution of drinking water | 0.75–0.79 | |
| **Worry about global environmental problems** | | | .84–.87 |
| | Damage to the earth's ozone layer | 0.75–0.79 | |
| | The loss of tropical rain forests | 0.69–0.75 | |
| | The 'greenhouse effect' or global warming | 0.70–0.76 | |
| | Extinction of plant and animal species | 0.70–0.79 | |

*Note:* All items in this table have the same coding scheme: not at all = 1; only a little = 2; a fair amount = 3; and a great deal = 4. Factor loadings reported are the minimum and maximum loadings of each item over six years. Cronbach's alpha values reported are the minimum and maximum values over six years.

used to measure generalized risk perception come from a regular question asked prior to the set of questions for the dependent variables, which are typically in the middle of the environmental issues section.

The Gallup environment surveys asked respondents how much they worried about a list of different economic and social problems. We excluded the 'quality of the environment' item, since it overlapped with our two dependent variables. We examined the remaining nine items via a CFA of six years' data. Results showed that the 'illegal immigration' item's factor loadings are too low (less than 0.20) in all years, so we dropped this item. The remaining eight items have adequate to good factor loadings in all years and form a coherent measure of 'generalized risk perception'. An independent CFA of this single-factor measurement model showed a good model fit: goodness-of-fit index (GFI) = 0.98; adjusted goodness-of-fit index (AGFI) = 0.96; incremental fit index (IFI) = 0.96; comparative fit index (CFI) = 0.96; root mean squared error of approximation (RMSEA) = 0.03.

For our dependent variables we used eight items asking respondents how much they worried about a list of different environmental problems (see Table 11.1). To test the safety concerns hypothesis (H1 and H2), we separated the four health-related environmental problems from those global environmental problems (see, e.g., Stern et al. 1992) and tested a two-factor measurement model via CFA. All items have good to very good factor loadings in all years, and the entire model has a good fit: GFI = 0.97; AGFI = 0.94; IFI = 0.98; CFI = 0.98; RMSEA = 0.03. These two latent factors have very strong correlations, 0.85–0.91, indicating that these eight items are essentially unidimensional. For the purpose of our study, however, we maintained the separation when we incorporated the measurement model into our final structural models.

## Results and discussion

We begin by briefly discussing the results of Model A for the test of the parenthood hypothesis (H7) and Model B for the test of the religiosity mediating effect (H3 and H4). We then discuss the results of Model C, the generalized risk perception mediator model, with which we test the remaining hypotheses.

For the parenthood hypothesis (parenthood has a positive effect on women's environmental concern and a negative effect on men's environmental concern), we examined the effect of the 'female × parenthood' interaction term. Limited data availability only allowed us to test the parenthood hypothesis with data from five of six years (omitting data from 2008). Results show that neither parenthood nor the interaction term has a statistically significant effect on either of the two latent factors of environmental concern in any year, clearly not supporting the parenthood hypothesis. Thus, we conclude that there is no need to examine the parenthood hypothesis (H7) in our other models.

In Model B we examined the direct effect (H3) and mediating effect (H4) of religiosity on environmental concern. Our female dummy variable has a weak but statistically significant, positive effect on religiosity in all six years (standardized regression weights from 0.06 to 0.13), which is consistent with the literature that women tend to be more religious than men (e.g., Batson et al. 1993; Blocker and Eckberg 1997). Yet, religiosity fails to have much influence on either factor of environmental concern. Its effect on worry about health-related environmental problems is statistically significant only in 2002, with a very weak standardized regression weight of –0.07, while its effect on worry about global environmental problems is only statistically significant in 2002 and 2007 – and its respective standardized regression weights of -0.11 and –0.09 were small. This provides only weak support for H3. Gender's standardized indirect effects (through religiosity) on both factors of environmental concern were all close to zero (0.01 or less in all years). We thus conclude that there is no support for H4 in our study; there is no need to model religiosity as an intervening variable.

Model C, the generalized risk perception mediator model, has a good fit (GFI = 0.94, AGFI = 0.91, IFI = 0.94, CFI = 0.94, RMSEA = 0.02). To fully analyze this model, we first examine predictors of generalized risk perception. As shown in Table 11.2, gender is a statistically significant predictor of generalized risk perception in all years but 2006; women have greater risk perception than do men, as expected. In most years (2001, 2007, and 2008), gender's effects are also relatively strong, typically ranked as the second or third among 11 independent variables.

*Table 11.2* Standardized direct effects of demographic, social, and political characteristics on generalized risk perception

| Predictors | 2001 | 2002 | 2004 | 2006 | 2007 | 2008 |
|---|---|---|---|---|---|---|
| Female | 0.14* | 0.09* | 0.06* | 0.05 | 0.20* | 0.13* |
| Religiosity | 0.09* | 0.00 | 0.06 | 0.06 | 0.04 | 0.10* |
| Full-time employment | 0.03 | 0.00 | −0.02 | 0.06 | −0.01 | −0.01 |
| Homemaker | 0.03 | 0.05 | −0.01 | 0.04 | 0.00 | −0.03 |
| Age | 0.09* | 0.02 | 0.01 | −0.05 | 0.02 | 0.10* |
| Non-white | 0.12* | 0.16* | 0.08* | 0.08* | 0.13* | 0.08* |
| Educational attainment | −0.18* | −0.10* | −0.07* | −0.16* | −0.17* | −0.12* |
| Annual household income | −0.07* | −0.09* | −0.09* | −0.09* | −0.03 | −0.10* |
| Environmental movement identity | 0.20* | 0.15* | 0.13* | 0.28* | 0.20* | 0.21* |
| Political ideology | 0.04 | −0.02 | 0.10* | 0.04 | 0.07* | 0.05 |
| Party identification | 0.12* | 0.21* | 0.32* | 0.24* | 0.23* | 0.24* |
| **$R^2$** | **0.18** | **0.17** | **0.26** | **0.26** | **0.25** | **0.25** |
| Sample size | 1060 | 1006 | 1005 | 1000 | 1009 | 1012 |

\* $p < .05$

Further, non-whites and respondents with lower socio-economic status (e.g., educational attainment and annual household income) perceive the group of social and economic problems as posing greater risk than do their white and higher socio-economic status counterparts, respectively. These results are all consistent with robust findings in the risk perception literature (e.g., Slovic 2001), evidence that our measure of generalized risk perception has considerable construct validity. In addition, identification with the environmental movement and Democratic Party increases this perceived risk quite consistently over the years. Effects of other social demographical variables are much less consistent, while employment status and homemaker status have no statistically significant effect on generalized risk perception across all years.

We now shift to the tests of our remaining hypotheses. Tables 11.3 and 11.4 present the standardized direct and total effects of demographic, social, and political variables on worry (i.e., concerns or stress) about health-related environmental problems (Table 11.3) and on worry about global environmental problems (Table 11.4). Each variable's total effect is the sum of its direct effect and its indirect effect through generalized risk perception. For H1, H2, H5, and H6, we examined the total effect of relevant variables on both factors of environmental concern. For H8, we examined the direct effect of gender.

Results show that there is weak but somewhat consistent support for the safety concerns hypothesis. This hypothesis expects that women express greater concern than do men about health-related environmental problems, especially when controlling for key social roles variables (H1) and that the effect of gender is greater in models explaining concern for health-related environmental problems than in models explaining concern for global environmental problems (H2). In three of the six years (2001, 2002, and 2007), women indeed reported greater worry about health-related environmental problems than men, even after controlling for ten other demographic, social, and political variables, although the gender differences we found are rather modest. Further, women reported greater worry about global environmental problems than men

*Table 11.3* Standardized direct and total effects of demographic, social, and political characteristics and generalized risk perception on worry about health-related environmental problems

| Predictors | 2001 | | 2002 | | 2004 | | 2006 | | 2007 | | 2008 | |
|---|---|---|---|---|---|---|---|---|---|---|---|---|
| | *Direct* | *Total* | *Direct* | *Total* | *Direct* | *Total* | *Direct* | *Total* | *Direct* | *Total* | *Direct* | *Total* |
| Female | -0.01 | 0.07* | 0.02 | 0.08* | -0.03 | 0.02 | -0.04 | -0.01 | -0.04 | 0.09* | -0.06 | 0.02 |
| Religiosity | -0.02 | 0.03 | -0.07* | -0.07* | -0.09* | -0.05 | -0.02 | 0.02 | -0.07* | -0.05 | -0.05 | 0.01 |
| Full-time employment | 0.01 | 0.03 | 0.02 | 0.03 | 0.02 | 0.00 | -0.03 | 0.01 | -0.05 | -0.06 | 0.04 | 0.03 |
| Homemaker | -0.06* | -0.05 | 0.03 | 0.06 | 0.02 | 0.01 | -0.02 | 0.01 | -0.03 | -0.03 | 0.00 | -0.02 |
| Age | 0.01 | 0.06 | 0.04 | 0.06 | 0.02 | 0.03 | 0.03 | 0.00 | 0.00 | 0.01 | 0.03 | 0.09* |
| Non-white | 0.03 | 0.10* | 0.04 | 0.15* | -0.01 | 0.04 | 0.02 | 0.08* | 0.00 | 0.07* | 0.04 | 0.08* |
| Educational attainment | -0.10* | -0.20* | -0.08* | -0.14* | -0.08* | -0.13* | -0.02 | -0.12* | -0.03 | -0.14* | -0.03 | -0.10* |
| Annual household income | 0.03 | -0.01 | 0.03 | -0.03 | -0.01 | -0.07* | -0.03 | -0.09* | -0.02 | -0.04 | -0.06 | -0.12* |
| Environmental movement identity | 0.17* | 0.29* | 0.14* | 0.24* | 0.23* | 0.31* | 0.23* | 0.40* | 0.15* | 0.27* | 0.21* | 0.34* |
| Political ideology | 0.02 | 0.05 | 0.03 | 0.02 | 0.01 | 0.08* | 0.07* | 0.10* | -0.03 | 0.01 | 0.05 | 0.08* |
| Party identification | 0.08* | 0.15* | 0.04 | 0.18* | -0.02 | 0.18* | -0.04 | 0.11* | 0.06* | 0.20* | 0.00 | 0.15* |
| Generalized risk perception | 0.57* | – | 0.64* | – | 0.64* | – | 0.64* | – | 0.62* | – | 0.60* | – |
| **R²** | **0.46 (0.19)** | | **0.53 (0.18)** | | **0.55 (0.24)** | | **0.58 (0.28)** | | **0.49 (0.21)** | | **0.52 (0.24)** | |
| Sample size | 1060 | | 1006 | | 1005 | | 1000 | | 1009 | | 1012 | |

*Note:* The R-squared coefficients in parentheses exclude the contribution of generalized risk perception.

\* $p < .05$

Table 11.4 Standardized direct and total effects of demographic, social, and political characteristics and generalized risk perception on worry about global environmental problems

| Predictors | 2001 | | 2002 | | 2004 | | 2006 | | 2007 | | 2008 | |
|---|---|---|---|---|---|---|---|---|---|---|---|---|
| | Direct | Total | Direct | Total | Direct | Total | Direct | Total | Direct | Total | Direct | Total |
| Female | -0.03 | 0.05 | -0.03 | 0.03 | -0.03 | 0.01 | -0.04 | -0.01 | -0.05 | 0.06* | -0.04 | 0.02 |
| Religiosity | -0.08* | -0.03 | -0.11* | -0.11* | -0.09* | -0.06* | -0.08* | -0.05 | -0.12* | -0.10* | -0.10* | -0.04 |
| Full-time employment | -0.01 | 0.00 | 0.02 | 0.02 | 0.01 | 0.00 | 0.02 | 0.06 | -0.04 | -0.05 | -0.01 | -0.02 |
| Homemaker | -0.03 | -0.02 | 0.04 | 0.01 | -0.03 | -0.03 | 0.00 | 0.02 | -0.05 | -0.05 | 0.02 | 0.00 |
| Age | -0.05 | -0.01 | -0.03 | -0.01 | -0.01 | -0.01 | 0.04 | 0.02 | -0.06* | -0.05 | -0.05 | 0.01 |
| Non-white | -0.04 | 0.02 | -0.01 | 0.08* | -0.01 | 0.03 | 0.01 | 0.06 | -0.01 | 0.06 | 0.02 | 0.06* |
| Educational attainment | -0.06 | -0.16* | -0.01 | -0.07* | -0.05 | -0.09* | 0.04 | -0.06 | 0.01 | -0.08* | 0.01 | -0.05 |
| Annual household income | 0.04 | 0.00 | 0.02 | -0.04 | -0.03 | -0.08* | 0.00 | -0.06 | -0.06 | -0.07* | -0.06* | -0.11* |
| Environmental movement identity | 0.24* | 0.35* | 0.26* | 0.35* | 0.29* | 0.36* | 0.23* | 0.39* | 0.24* | 0.35* | 0.29* | 0.41* |
| Political ideology | 0.11* | 0.13* | 0.05 | 0.04 | 0.13* | 0.19* | 0.15* | 0.17* | 0.05 | 0.09* | 0.10* | 0.13* |
| Party identification | 0.15* | 0.22* | 0.10* | 0.22* | -0.01 | 0.16* | 0.02 | 0.16* | 0.12* | 0.25* | 0.10* | 0.22* |
| Generalized risk perception | 0.55* | – | 0.58* | – | 0.54* | – | 0.58* | – | 0.54* | – | 0.52* | – |
| R² | 0.51 (0.27) | | 0.53 (0.25) | | 0.55 (0.33) | | 0.58 (0.33) | | 0.56 (0.34) | | 0.60 (0.39) | |
| Sample size | 1060 | | 1006 | | 1005 | | 1000 | | 1009 | | 1012 | |

Note: The R-squared coefficients in parentheses exclude the contribution of generalized risk perception.

* $p < .05$

only in 2007; thus there is virtually no gender difference in worry about global environmental problems.

The results in Tables 11.3 and 11.4 indicate no support for the economic salience hypothesis (H5) and the family roles hypothesis (H6). The former expects that full-time employment has a negative effect on environmental concern, and the latter expects that homemaker status has a positive effect on environmental concern. As in Models A and B, neither full-time employment status nor homemaker status have a statistically significant total effect on either factor of environmental concern in any year in the study. Combined with the absence of support for the parenthood hypothesis discussed above, this provides further evidence that gender differences in environmental concern are not due to the social roles that men and women perform in society (see also McCright 2010).

The gendered risk perception hypothesis (H8) expects that the intervening variable of generalized risk perception greatly mediates the direct effect of gender on environmental concern. This hypothesis includes three sub-hypotheses: (1) gender influences risk perception; (2) risk perception predicts environmental concern; and (3) gender has little or no statistically significant direct effect on environmental concern with risk perception in the model. The results reported in Tables 11.2, 11.3, and 11.4 indicate that all three sub-hypotheses are supported over the years of this study.

According to Table 11.2, women perceived the group of social and economic problems as posing greater personal risks than men in all years but 2006. Tables 11.3 and 11.4 show that generalized risk perception is the most influential predictor of environmental concern in all years (standardized regression weights of 0.57–0.64). In fact, generalized risk perception alone is responsible for half or more than half of the explained variation in concern for environmental problems in all of our models (see the R-squared coefficients in Tables 11.3 and 11.4 for details). Finally, Tables 11.3 and 11.4 also show that the direct effect of gender is not statistically significant in all years with generalized risk perception in the model. Yet, as discussed previously, gender does have a statistically significant total effect on worry about health-related environmental problems in 2001, 2002, and 2007, and on worry about global environmental problems in 2007. Thus these results provide consistent support for H8; gender's effect on environmental concern is largely mediated by generalized risk perception.

The key upshot of this study is that women's slightly greater environmental concern than that of men is largely due to the former's heightened risk perception. This seems especially the case when we use indicators of environmental risks to measure environmental concern. Scientists, activists, journalists, and policy makers who inform the general public about environmental problems should be aware that employing a risk frame, and especially highlighting health and safety risks to individuals, their families, and their communities, will likely provoke greater attention and response from women than men. Further, women may be more likely than men to support those public policies meant to protect or conserve environmental quality that are couched in terms of minimizing or managing risk.

The results presented in Tables 11.3 and 11.4 also bear upon the performance of other demographic, social, and political variables. In general, the demographic variables are poor and inconsistent predictors of worry about environmental problems. Combining the six years and the two factors of environmental concern, each independent variable has twelve total effects. Respondents' age only has one statistically significant total effect, with age increasing worry about health-related environmental problems in 2008. Yet, seven total effects of race are statistically significant but weak, with non-whites expressing slightly greater worry about health-related environmental problems in five years and slightly greater worry about global environmental problems in two years than their white counterparts.

Socio-economic status has a negative effect on environmental concern. Educational attainment, with ten statistically significant total effects, is a bit more robust than is income, which has only six. Political orientation variables (political ideology has eight statistically significant total effects and party identification has twelve) are more consistent predictors, with self-identified liberals and Democrats reporting greater worry about environmental problems than their conservative and Republican counterparts. Finally, environmental movement identity is the strongest predictor of all the control variables, with all twelve total effects positive and statistically significant.

## Conclusion

Combining insights on gendered risk perceptions from Bord and O'Connor (1997) with other theoretical arguments summarized by Davidson and Freudenburg (1996) and Blocker and Eckberg (1997), our study identified and tested six substantive hypotheses (with their corresponding sub-hypotheses) about gender differences in environmental concern: (1) safety concerns; (2) religiosity; (3) economic salience; (4) family roles; (5) parenthood; and (6) gendered risk perceptions. We utilized six years of nationally representative Gallup survey data that include multi-item measures of (1) worry about health-related environmental problems, (2) worry about global environmental problems, and (3) generalized risk perception, as well as single-item measures of key theoretically relevant variables. This data set offers the advantage of examining the performance of key predictors across multiple years. We employed structural equation modelling to appropriately model the theoretically expected direct and indirect effects of gender and other key variables.

We found weak but somewhat consistent support for the safety concerns hypothesis. While there is virtually no gender difference in worry about global environmental problems, women are indeed slightly more worried than are men about health-related environmental problems, even while controlling for key social roles variables. The religiosity hypothesis expects that religiosity has a negative influence on environmental concern and that religiosity greatly mediates the effect of gender on environmental concern. Our results indicated only weak support for the first part of this hypothesis and no support for the second part of this hypothesis.

In addition, our results offer no support for the social roles arguments that men's and women's differential performance of key social roles in society account for gender differences in environmental concern. Full-time employment, homemaker status, and parenthood do not influence environmental concern, contrary to theoretical expectations. These results largely support Mohai's (1997:166) claim from nearly fifteen years ago, which McCright (2010) more recently confirmed, that gender differences in environmental concern are most likely due to 'the differing socialization experiences of men and women . . . rather than the roles they occupy or other structural factors' (see also Zelezny et al. 2000).

Finally, our results provide consistent support for the gendered risk perception hypothesis, argued most clearly by Bord and O'Connor (1997). According to this argument, risk perception largely mediates the direct effect of gender on environmental concern. We found that gender has a consistent effect on risk perception, risk perception has a strong influence on environmental concern, and risk perception indeed mediates the effect of gender on environmental concern. When environmental concern is operationalized as worry about specific environmental problems (arguably health-related or not), it seems that the gender difference in environmental concern is due to differentially perceived vulnerability to risk.

Our findings suggest that concern for health and safety and perceptions of social and economic risks among the general public are two robust predictors of environmental concern. Risk perception is particularly influential judging by the size of its effects and its contribution to explained variance in environmental concern measures. Thus communicating through a frame of risk will likely prove effective in promoting public concern for the environment and increasing public support for environmental protection.

Given the results of our study, we suggest five ideas for future research. First, future work should expand the scope of the gendered risk perception hypothesis. In their initial explication of this argument, Bord and O'Connor (1997) claim that gender differences in risk perception will explain gender differences in environmental concern when the latter is operationalized in ways that trigger women's heightened sensitivity to risk, such as survey questions about environmental issues widely perceived as risks and question formats that ask for levels of 'worry', 'concern', or 'seriousness'. Our study offers confirmation of this argument within this specific scope condition. Yet, future research should also examine the gendered risk perception hypothesis with environmental concern operationalized as environment/economic tradeoffs, pro-environmental behaviours, and pro-environmental attitudes or ecological worldviews.

Second, future research should simultaneously test key socialization hypotheses, including the gendered risk perception hypothesis. Given the lack of empirical support for the various social roles arguments over the years, we suggest that scholars worry less about these poor-performing hypotheses and instead focus on adjudicating among important socialization hypotheses. To simultaneously test socialization arguments and the gendered risk perceptions argument will likely require scholars to design new survey instruments to model latent factor measures of these key variables (e.g., trust in science and technology, value orientations, and risk perceptions).

Third, in these new survey instruments, scholars should employ refined measures of gender. Continued use of survey items measuring gender as demographically male or female is less than optimal. We argue for the use of single-item or multi-item indicators of gender identity, which measure individuals' masculinity and femininity along a continuum, such as Bem's (1993) Sex Role Inventory. Fourth, future work should employ CFA and SEM, where possible, due to their superior ability for modelling complex variables as latent factors and estimating theory-driven structural models that are crucial for the examination of mediating effects. Finally, it is also worth noting that most explanations we examined in this chapter originate from Western societies, particularly the United States. Future research should aim to analyze the cross-cultural applicability of these explanations by testing them in different settings, such as China (see Xiao and Hong 2010, 2012).

## Acknowledgements

The authors thank the Gallup Organization and Riley Dunlap for making the data available for analysis.

## Notes

This chapter has been adapted, with permission and with the assistance and approval of the authors, from the article 'Explaining Gender Differences in Concern about Environmental Problems in the United States', published in 2012 in *Society & Natural Resources* 25(11): 1067–1084.

1 The other three include (1) the 'Environmental Knowledge' hypothesis (Blocker and Eckberg 1997) or 'Knowledgeable Support Hypothesis' (Davidson and Freudenburg 1996); (2) the 'Trust in Science and Technology Hypothesis' (Blocker and Eckberg 1997) or the 'Institutional Trust Hypothesis' (Davidson and Freudenburg 1996); and (3) the argument (Stern et al. 1993) that differences in men's and women's value orientations explain gender differences in environmental concern (see also Dietz et al. 2002).

2 Structural equation modelling is an advanced multivariate analysis tool, primarily designed to simultaneously test multiple structural relations (i.e., regression models) that are specified according to a theoretical

framework. Such a technique is capable of providing statistical significance tests not only for individual regression coefficients but also for how the entire model fits the empirical data, which then gives a fuller examination of the mentioned theoretical framework than simple regression analyses.

3　We initially also controlled for respondents' residence (rural vs. suburban vs. urban) due to its potential differential effects on certain risks (e.g., crime and violence) and environmental problems (e.g., air pollution) but found no statistically significant residence difference. To save space, we decided to exclude residence from our final analyses.

4　This measure of environmental movement identity predicts membership in environmental movement organizations, assessment of environmental organizations and the overall movement, and performance of pro-environmental behaviours (Dunlap and McCright 2008; see also McCright and Dunlap 2008).

# References

Batson, C. D., Schoenrade, P. and Ventis, W. L. (1993) *Religion and the Individual*. New York: Oxford University Press.

Bem, S. L. (1993) *The Lenses of Gender*. New Haven, CT: Yale University Press.

Blocker, T. J. and Eckberg, D. L. (1989) 'Environmental issues as women's issues', *Social Science Quarterly* 70: 586–593.

Blocker, T. J. and Eckberg, D. L. (1997) 'Gender and environmentalism', *Social Science Quarterly* 78: 841–858.

Bollen, K. A. (1989) *Structural Equations With Latent Variables*. New York: Wiley.

Bord, R. J. and O'Connor, R. E. (1997) 'The gender gap in environmental attitudes', *Social Science Quarterly* 78: 830–840.

Chodorow, N. J. (1978) *The Reproduction of Mothering*. Berkeley, CA: University of California Press.

Davidson, D. J. and Freudenburg, W. R. (1996) 'Gender and environmental risk concerns', *Environment and Behavior* 28: 302–339.

Dietz, T., Dan, A. and Shwom, R. (2007) 'Support for climate change policy: Social psychological and social structural influences', *Rural Sociology* 72: 185–214.

Dietz, T., Kalof, L. and Stern, P. C. (2002) 'Gender, values, and environmentalism', *Social Science Quarterly* 83: 353–364.

Duckworth, L. T., Frank-Stromborg, M., Oleckno, W. A., Duffy, P. and Burns, K. (2002) 'Relationship of perception of radon as a health risk and willingness to engage in radon testing and mitigation', *Oncology Nursing Forum* 29: 1099–1107.

Dunlap, R. E. and McCright, A. M. (2008) 'Social movement identity: Validating a measure of identification with the environmental movement', *Social Science Quarterly* 89(5): 1045–1065.

Eckberg, D. L. and Blocker, T. J. (1989) 'Varieties of religious involvement and environmental concerns', *Journal for the Scientific Study of Religion* 28: 509–517.

Eckberg, D. L. and Blocker, T. J. (1996) 'Christianity, environmentalism, and the theoretical problem of fundamentalism', *Journal for the Scientific Study of Religion* 35: 343–355.

Finucane, M. L., Slovic, P., Mertz, C. K., Flynn, J. and Satterfield, T. A. (2000) 'Gender, race, and perceived risk: The "white male" effect', *Health, Risk, and Society* 2(2): 159–172.

Freudenburg, W. R. (1993) 'Risk and recreancy', *Social Forces* 71: 909–932.

Freudenburg, W. R. and Davidson, D. J. (2007) 'Nuclear families and nuclear risks', *Rural Sociology* 72(2): 215–243.

Gilligan, C. (1982) *In a Different Voice*. Cambridge, MA: Harvard University Press.

Greenbaum, A. (1995) 'Taking stock of two decades of research on the social bases of environmental concern', in Mehta, M. D. and Ouellet, E. (eds) *Environmental Sociology*. North York, Ontario: Captus Press, 125–152.

Greene, W. H. (2000) *Econometric Analysis*. Upper Saddle River, NJ: Prentice Hall.

Hayes, B. C. (2001) 'Gender, scientific knowledge, and attitudes toward the environment', *Political Research Quarterly* 54: 657–671.

Hillman, J. (2008) 'Knowledge, attitudes, and experience regarding HIV/AIDS among older adult inner-city Latinos', *International Journal of Aging and Human Development* 66: 243–257.

Keller, E. F. (1985) *Reflections on Gender and Science*. New Haven, CT: Yale University Press.

Kimmel, M. (2009) *Manhood in America: A Cultural History* (third edition). New York: The Free Press.

Lundborg, P. and Andersson, H. (2008) 'Gender, risk perceptions, and smoking behavior', *Journal of Health Economics* 27: 1299–1311.

McCright, A. M. (2010) 'The effects of gender on climate change knowledge and concern in the American public', *Population and Environment* 32: 66–87.

McCright, A. M. and Dunlap, R. E. (2008) 'Belief systems and social movement identity: An examination of the consistency of beliefs about environmental problems within the American public', *Public Opinion Quarterly* 72(4): 651–676.

May, D. C., Rader, N. E. and Goodrum, S. (2010) 'A gendered assessment of the "threat of victimization": Examining gender differences in fear of crime, perceived risk, avoidance, and defensive behaviors', *Criminal Justice Review* 35: 159–182.

Mohai, P. (1992) 'Men, women, and the environment', *Society and Natural Resources* 5: 1–19.

Mohai, P. (1997) 'Gender differences in the perceptions of most important environmental problems', *Race, Gender, and Class* 5: 153–169.

Robertson, A. A., Stein, J. A. and Baird-Thomas, J. (2006) 'Gender differences in the prediction of condom use among incarcerated juvenile offenders: Testing the information-motivation-behavior skills (IMB) model', *Journal of Adolescent Health* 38: 18–25.

Siegrist, M., Gutscher, H. and Earle, T. C. (2005) 'Perception of risk: The influence of general trust, and general confidence', *Journal of Risk Research* 8: 145–156.

Slovic, P. (1999) 'Trust, emotion, sex, politics, and science: Surveying the risk-assessment battlefield', *Risk Analysis* 19: 689–701.

Slovic, P. (ed) (2001) *The Perception of Risk*. London: Earthscan.

Smith, S. E., Smiley, H., Hosgood, D., Michelson, E. S. and Stowe, M. H. (2008) 'Americans' nanotechnology risk perception', *Journal of Industrial Ecology* 12: 459–473.

Stern, P. C., Dietz, T. and Kalof, L. (1993) 'Value orientations, gender, and environmental concern', *Environment and Behavior* 25: 322–348.

Stern, P. C., Young, O. R. and Druckman, D. (1992) *Global Environmental Change: Understanding the Human Dimensions*. Washington, DC: National Academy Press.

Xiao, C. and Hong, D. (2010) 'Gender differences in environmental behaviors in China', *Population and Environment* 32(1): 88–104.

Xiao, C. and Hong, D. (2012) 'Gender and concern for environmental issues in urban China', *Society and Natural Resources* 25(5): 468–482.

Zelezny, L. C., Chua, P. and Aldrich, C. (2000) 'Elaborating on gender differences in environmentalism', *Journal of Social Issues* 56: 443–457.

# 12

# SOCIAL ECOLOGY

## A transdisciplinary approach to gender and environment research

*Diana Hummel and Immanuel Stieß*

### Introduction

This chapter provides an overview of social ecology, an approach to social-ecological research that applies transdisciplinary methods to the analysis of social relations to nature in life sustaining practices. Gender relations are central to this analysis, not only because they shape the life situations of men and women, but also because policies and strategies for promoting sustainable development that do not take gender norms and asymmetries into account will fail. Analyzing how gender shapes people's lives allows for a better understanding of the consumption practices and patterns of decision-making that contribute to or thwart progress to sustainability.

Our discussion outlines key theoretical and methodological dimensions of social ecology that have been developed at Institute for Social-Ecological Research (ISOE) in Frankfurt am Main, which is one of the leading independent research institutes engaged in sustainability research in Germany. Its research in the areas of food, water, energy consumption, and mobility follows a transdisciplinary approach that integrates findings from the natural and social sciences, as well as extra-scientific practical knowledge. We draw extensively on the body of scholarship that has been produced over the past twenty-five years at ISOE. Since much of the research we discuss is published in German only, this chapter offers unique insight into this approach, to which many in the English-speaking world will not have had access.

In the first sections of the chapter, we explain the link between the concept of societal relations to nature and the scientific principle of transdisciplinarity, and demonstrate how the category of gender is conceptualized in this approach. By exploring the model of the transdisciplinary research process we use in ISOE projects, we will then illustrate how gender perspectives can be taken into consideration in research practice. We present three examples from the areas of food consumption, energy use, and waste to show how transdisciplinary research in the field of gender and environment can be operationalized, how we approach gender-sensitive research in transdisciplinary research projects, and how this problem-oriented research can generate knowledge that can be transferred into policy.

### What is social ecology?

For some readers, social ecology may be associated with the school of eco-political thought developed by the late American anarchist philosopher Murray Bookchin and his followers. However, in the German-speaking world, it means something different. For scholars working in such places as the Institute of Social Ecology in Vienna and the ISOE in Frankfurt/Main, *Soziale Ökologie* is conceived of as the science of societal relations to nature. This emerging field of research is part of sustainability science, and investigates complex problems at the intersections of nature and society, thereby intervening reflexively in social-ecological problem situations. On the one hand, social ecology as a science follows a theoretical program. On the other hand, it follows a transdisciplinary research approach to develop solutions that can be implemented in everyday life (Becker et al. 2006). Social ecology does not represent a genuine gender-theoretical science, even though feminist scholars have been involved in it since the mid-1980s with the formulation of conceptual and epistemological foundations for this new scientific field in Germany (Scheich and Schultz 1991; Schultz and Weller 1995; Schultz et al. 2006; Schultz et al. 2010). From the eighties until today, the epistemological approaches and concepts concerning nature, matter, and gender have been extensively developed, particularly under the influence of dominant discourses in science and alternating guiding principles both in feminist research and environmental research.

In the first decade of the new millennium, the German Federal Ministry of Education and Research (BMBF) established 'Social-Ecological Research' (SOEF) as a funding priority and declared the consideration of gender issues in research projects a major issue. The SOEF funding program provoked considerable advances in developing innovative inter- and transdisciplinary concepts and approaches. Different feminist concepts such as *Vorsorgendes Wirtschaften* (in English, 'provident economy'), which stresses the satisfaction of needs rather than abstract values (Biesecker et al. 2000; Biesecker and Hofmeister 2006), the feminist political economy analyses of social reproduction/reproductivity (see Mellor, this volume; Mellor 1997; Mellor 2006), and the deconstructivist approaches of feminist political ecology (Nightingale 2006) have been linked to natural scientific, social scientific, and techno-scientific epistemologies in a number of research projects, depending on the respective problems and research questions of the funded projects (Schäfer et al. 2006; Schultz et al. 2015).

In the search for a comprehensive framework linking different conceptual and methodological approaches, the term 'societal relations to nature' came out on top and has made a remarkable career within the ongoing debate, at least in German-speaking countries. Often, it is merely used as a metaphor for relations between nature and society. As a *scientific* concept that is subject to different interpretations by scholars, the term is used in environmental sociology, human ecology, political ecology, and social ecology (Becker et al. 2011).

## Societal relations to nature, gender relations, and transdisciplinarity

The term 'societal relations to nature' designates an object of cognition as well as a theoretical framework for the analysis and better comprehension of relationships between nature and society in terms of their empirical characteristics (Becker et al. 2006; Becker et al. 2011). Generally speaking, 'societal relations to nature' refers to the patterns of relations between humans, society, and nature. They emerge from the culturally specific and historically variable forms and practices by which individuals, groups, and societies shape and regulate their relations to nature. The focus is directed systematically to *relations* between society and nature. On the one hand, the concept helps analyze how societal and natural elements, structures, and processes are linked to one another by identifiable practices and mechanisms; on the other hand, existing interactions between natural and societal processes are considered.

An important issue is the question as to which forms of relations are to be emphasized, and how to define and classify these relations according to their content. The concept therefore distinguishes between the physical-material and the cultural-symbolic aspects of relations. This distinction emphasizes the materiality of all the relations between nature and society, while at the same time taking into account their embedding in symbolic orders, interpretive contexts, and social constructions. Other research approaches use similar distinctions, such as the Viennese approach of social ecology (Fischer-Kowalski and Weisz 1999), the actor-network theory (Latour 2005) or Donna Haraway's concepts of material semiotics and naturecultures (Haraway 1989; Haraway 2008; see also Merrick in this volume). 'Nature' and 'society' are thus poles within an interrelationship which cannot be reduced to one side or another. The Frankfurt approach of social ecology claims that neither society nor nature can be seen as undifferentiated entities. Rather, they are related to each other, and the distinction between nature and society is applied to specific phenomena such as mobility, food or water supply, consumption, and energy use. That way, it is possible to analyze how different societal and natural elements, structures, and processes are selectively and dynamically linked to each other. It is therefore important to differentiate between a plurality of societal relationships to nature.

Similar to other approaches of critical and post-modern reflections on science in the twentieth century, social ecology takes the nature-culture dichotomy in the sciences as the starting point for scientific epistemological deconstructions and reconstructions. Social ecology considers the dualistic juxtaposition of the natural sciences and social sciences that developed during the nineteenth century as epistemologically and methodologically distinguishable scientific fields. The belief that they are two entirely separate scientific perspectives has been reproduced in dominant interpretations of 'ecological crisis' since the 1960s. Thus we can detect a 'naturalization' of social-ecological crisis phenomena, which is often combined with the naïve assumption that society's treatment of the natural resource base would be assignable to the (natural) sciences. A 'culturalization', on the other hand, can be found in radical constructivist approaches of semiotic fabrication of nature and of society, which see the world and reality as something linguistically 'produced' (and hence only accessible by language). These approaches tend to disregard material aspects of nature-society interactions that are not arising from language and symbolic systems (Schultz 2006).[1]

Societal practices of distinction that draw a line between the natural sphere and the societal sphere can be analyzed in dualistic descriptions of the natural and engineering sciences on the one hand and the social sciences and humanities on the other. A critique can illustrate dichotomizing practices such as categorical distinctions between body and mind, and nature and culture, as familiar from the European Cartesian tradition. Such a critique, however, presumes that nature and society are discriminable, so that their mutual relationship can be identified. In social ecology, the distinguishability of society and nature does not constitute a metaphysical-ontological presupposition but a historical-cultural one (Becker et al. 2011). The central hypothesis of 'crisis-prone societal relations to nature' is thus associated with a double-sided critique of naturalization and culturalization of societal relations to nature, since both perspectives include naturalist and culturalist reductionisms. This double-sided critique is thus a constitutive element of the concept of societal relations to nature. Using this kind of appraisal, one-sided naturalist or culturalist descriptions and evaluations of social-ecological problems in research approaches can be identified and related to one another, thus revealing the blind spots and limited claims of validity (Bergmann et al. 2012:70ff.). The prerequisite therefore is a critical inter- and transdisciplinarity that enables the identification of reciprocal connections and thus the application of natural scientific as well as social scientific concepts and methods. This is a premise for social-ecological descriptions. Here the term 'social-ecological' does not designate independent subject matter, but rather a type of connection. 'Thinking in terms of relations' in this way implies important methodological consequences: the focus is on relations rather than on substances, and includes a shift from the focus on 'elements' to the processes in which these elements and structures develop (Janowicz 2011:28).

The social-ecological understanding of *gender relations* is based on this epistemological framework (Hummel and Schultz 2011). It emphasizes relations instead of a substantially and ontologically conceived nature-culture difference, and reflects the 'handling of dichotomies' (Becker-Schmidt 1998). The social-ecological understanding of gender is related more to the scientific practice of distinguishing between nature and society than to an essentialist understanding of nature and society (Schultz et al. 2006). In contrast to the latter, it seeks to transcend the opposition of essentialism and constructivism by critically reflecting the two perspectives in their extremes as naturalization and culturalization of the gender difference, and as the difference between 'social gender' and 'biological sex' (Schultz 2006). The two sides of the double-sided critique (against the naturalization of gender relations on the one hand, and against the culturalization of gender relations, on the other) can be joined together by situating and re-contextualizing knowledge through problem-oriented research. According to the theoretical concept of societal relations to nature, these practices of critique result in a new understanding of the difference between sex and gender:

> 'Sex' is seen in a constructive way, but nevertheless remains different from 'gender'. 'Sex' implies the descriptions of gender relations by medical, technical, and natural sciences, while 'gender' means the descriptions of the same gender relations from cultural, social, and economic perspectives. In this perception of gender relations, both sides are understood from a (de)constructive and reconstructive perspective.
>
> *(Schultz 2006:382)*

With respect to an understanding of gender, the concept of societal relations to nature includes the strong theoretical assumption that the interconnections of the natural sciences with the social sciences are grounded in symbolic, abstract, and fragmented inventories of knowledge about gender relations. This assumption can be proved by considering the history of sciences (Schultz 2001). Ever since the academic disciplines of sociology and economy were developed in the eighteenth and nineteenth centuries, and since the formation of disciplines such as evolutionary biology, physiology, medicine, and psychology in the nineteenth and twentieth centuries, an ongoing transfer of knowledge about gender issues between the two scientific cultures can be traced, which is combined with strong normative implications for gender-specific attributes and social roles. As Irmgard Schultz observes,

> this 'gender knowledge' was basic for the construction of gendered relations in different societal and scientific fields. As a result of this dynamic knowledge transfer, gender can be reconstructed only through interdisciplinary research and cooperation between the two scientific cultures.
>
> *(Schultz 2006:382)*

## Gendering basic societal relations to nature

Social-ecological research aims to generate knowledge with respect to specific problem situations. The intention is that this knowledge should permit practical interventions within the world, following the threefold claim of sustainability research: 'understanding, evaluating, shaping' (BMBF 2012). Correspondingly, the concept of societal relations to nature does not claim to give a universal explanation of the world, but aims to generate contextualized knowledge for enabling and supporting transformations toward more sustainable development.

A peculiarity of the Frankfurt approach to social ecology is its focus on *basic societal relations to nature*. They are called 'basic' because they are indispensable for both individual and societal reproduction, and for the capacity of individuals and societies to develop. If their regulation fails, temporally, spatially, and socially, then far-reaching crises can result. Examples of such basic societal relations to nature include work and production, land use and nutrition, sexuality and reproduction, and mobility and transport. These relations are vital for the intergenerational continuation of societal life processes in every society. At the same time, they constitute the context for those intricate processes in which the basic needs of human beings are satisfied and access to life-supporting goods and services is regulated. Vital, life-supporting basic needs such as breathing, eating, and drinking, and shelter from heat and cold, are also profoundly shaped culturally and economically; they always have both a physical and a cultural-symbolic side. To satisfy their vital needs, people need oxygen-rich air that is low in pollutants in order to breathe, clean drinking water, enough water for agriculture, food in sufficient quantity and quality, housing and shelter from heat and cold, and means of mobility and transportation, and so on. Meeting these needs requires resources and ecosystem services which are limited in supply. A significant percentage of the world population is not able to satisfy these vital, life-supporting basic needs, as data on the global water crisis and widespread food insecurity dramatically indicate (Becker et al. 2011).

In defining basic societal relations to nature, a particular anthropological assumption is made. Human beings are defined as natural and cultural beings whose vital life-supporting needs exist only as formed through cultural processes and practices such as diets and eating habits, or mobility patterns and therefore only in subjectively and societally interpreted) configurations. These socialized needs cannot be satisfied without work and production or without appropriate means of transportation and communication systems. Therefore, basic societal relations to nature should be regarded as entities whose material and symbolic characteristics are not to be arbitrarily separated from one another.

Here, it has proved indispensable to reflect on the category of gender, since societal relations to nature are structured by gender relations and vice versa. A basic assumption is that crisis-prone gender relations (e.g., gender-specific asymmetries and power relations) are at the core of the 'social-ecological crises' (e.g., climate change, loss of biodiversity, or food insecurity) and that both are mutually enforcing one another (Schultz et al. 2006:225). Gender represents a primary pattern of societal order, one which shapes individual and collective perceptions, interpretations, distinctions, and evaluations. Needs and everyday practices, for example, are always oriented toward people as gendered beings. Within the concept of societal relations to nature, gender is understood *relationally*: gender relations in the sense of a plural understanding of relationships between the genders. Here, the gender category serves as a kind of 'eye opener' which allows us to focus our analytic view on gender-specific and other social differentiations and inequalities such as age, class, ethnicity, sexual orientation, and so on (Schultz et al. 2006), a topic that is also subject of feminist debates about intersectionality (Winker and Degele 2011).

Similar to 'transition studies' in sustainability research, social ecology follows a multi-level perspective of societal regulation (cf. Geels 2010). Culturally determined patterns of regulation for societal relations to nature are formed at three levels: the micro, the meso, and the macro level (Hummel and Kluge 2006). At the *micro level* of individual actions and individual needs satisfaction, patterns of regulation are closely linked to the corporeality of human beings and their psycho-physical processes (e.g., motivations, modes of perception). At the *meso level* of societal organization and institutions, patterns of regulation are closely linked to societal demands, and are determined by societal supply systems (e.g., water and energy supply systems) as well as by technical structures (e.g., for transport or communication). At the *macro level* of society-wide structures and processes, patterns of regulation governing societal reproduction and social integration intensify and stabilize in terms of relations of production, gender relations, and power relations. At this level, the ways are shaped in which societal relations to nature can be regulated at the micro and meso levels, and the limits are set within which regulation is possible.

At all levels, the regulation patterns of societal relations to nature are significantly structured by gender relations. For example, gender asymmetries in a specific region, combined with gender-specific forms of labour division and unequal access to resources, have immediate influence on patterns of land use and food security. As an abstract, generalizable category, gender relations can be related to societal relations to nature. Empirically, however, the linkages between these concepts can only be investigated on the level of specific contextualized social-ecological problems. If research aims at generating 'better knowledge for society', it needs to develop knowledge for understanding and intervening in specific social-ecological problem situations. Hence, social-ecological research is committed to a transdisciplinary research mode. The development of practical knowledge for societal actors is integrated in the knowledge generation process. In this context, concepts of societal transformation and regulation, and concepts from gender studies such as empowerment, shaping power, and citizenship are of crucial importance.

The plural concept of gender *relations* emphasizes their contextuality and situatedness. Scientific analysis at the intersection of nature and society requires *interdisciplinarity* between the disciplines of the social sciences, natural sciences, and techno-sciences. In addition, *transdisciplinarity* calls for the combination of scientific knowledge and everyday life knowledge – including the development of appropriate concepts and methods. In social ecology, the concept of gender relations is developed as inter- and transdisciplinary category (Hofmeister and Mölders 2006; Schultz et al. 2006).

The inter- and transdisciplinary content of gender relations can be historically reconstructed. As historical gender research has elaborated in great detail, the prevailing notion of gender and gender differences has been described and developed by modern scientific disciplines (biology, sociology, medicine, etc.) based on mutual knowledge transfer (Scheich 1993); in exchange with society, the idea has been fixed in common understanding and everyday practices. Moreover, the transdisciplinary concept of gender relations in theory refers to the interrelation between scientific knowledge and society. This implies a strong claim of transdisciplinary sustainability research for intervening in societal processes of designing and implementing solutions and strategies for sustainability problems (Weller 1999; Schultz et al. 2010).

## *Transdisciplinary research*

Transdisciplinarity describes a specific principle of science and research rather than a method (Mittelstraß 2005). The core of transdisciplinary research is its reference to real-world problems such as sustainable development or resource management (Klein et al. 2001). It is carried out at the interface of society and science and seeks to develop solutions for societal problems (Bergmann et al. 2012:14). As Jahn et al. have explained:

> Transdisciplinarity is a reflexive research approach that addresses societal problems by means of interdisciplinary collaboration as well as the collaboration between researchers and extra-scientific actors; its aim is to enable mutual learning processes between science and society; integration is the main cognitive challenge of the research process.
>
> *(Jahn et al. 2012:4)*

In transdisciplinary research, it is important to integrate different bodies of knowledge: insights, theories, and methods from different scientific disciplines, as well as the extra-scientific, practical knowledge of various stakeholders. Furthermore, the actors involved in the research processes have distinct interests, roles, and communication practices that must be brought together. At the ISOE, a conceptual model for an integrative, transdisciplinary research approach has been developed that can serve as a hands-on tool for research (Jahn 2008; Jahn et al. 2012). It takes into account the specific structure of social-ecological problems and, as such, constitutes a practical guide and instrument for analyzing different empirical research projects. The model distinguishes three phases of an ideal transdisciplinary research process.

In the *first phase* (A), a common research object must be determined and an adequate research team established. During this phase, the focus lies on a 'problem transformation', in which, ideally, all parties involved participate in order to promote cohesion and commitment throughout the research process: the given societal, real-world problem is transformed into an 'epistemic object' as the basis from which research questions are derived.

In the *second phase* (B) of the ideal transdisciplinary research process, the main priority is to generate new disciplinary and interdisciplinary knowledge. Since transdisciplinary research is based on disciplinary practice, this phase is characterized by the interplay between specialists working in sub-teams (see the vertical pillars at the centre of Figure 12.1), which include researchers from different natural-scientific and social-scientific disciplines. In this phase, the challenge is to guarantee the transferability of the newly generated knowledge. This means that an explicit interdisciplinary integration concept is required, which helps to connect the various bases of knowledge generated in the sub-teams during this phase (see the horizontal beams in Figure 12.1).

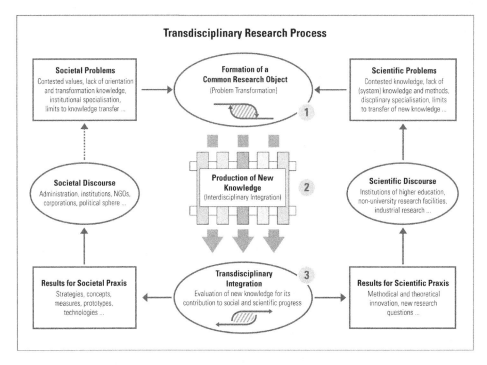

*Figure 12.1* The transdisciplinary research process

*Source*: Jahn et al. (2012:83)

In the *third and final phase* of the research process (C), the research results are brought together and assessed with respect to their potential contribution to societal as well as scientific progress. Ideally, the newly generated knowledge can be combined in such a way that practical, actor-specific knowledge, useful for solving the original real-world problem, can be linked with scientific innovation.

As illustrated in the model, transdisciplinarity ideally intervenes both in the societal and scientific discourses on the issue at hand by means of knowledge transfer carried out by scientists and societal actors (see centre left and right in Figure 12.1). The possible impacts of these interventions (e.g., in terms of implementation of strategies, legislation or new scientific methods) might give rise to a new transdisciplinary research process with modified research questions and understanding of the research object (Bergmann et al. 2012:36ff; Jahn et al. 2012:5ff.).

Social-ecological research on gender and environment draws on disciplinary and interdisciplinary gender perspectives, which are linked with other disciplinary perspectives for analyzing environment and sustainability problems. In the following section, we will illustrate how this model can be used to structure this operationalization and integration of gender issues in the transdisciplinary research process.

## Operationalizing gender relations in transdisciplinary research: three examples from ISOE

In the ideal transdisciplinary research process, as sketched in Figure 12.1, two epistemic paths are pursued simultaneously: on the left side there is the societal path, which generates new options for action on societal problems and 'knowledge for practice' such as integrated strategies for resource management. On the right side, there is the science path, developing new scientific concepts and methods and thus creating 'knowledge for science' (Bergmann et al. 2012:35). In transdisciplinary research practice, different forms of knowledge from various scientific disciplines and stakeholders must be related to each other and connected. As already mentioned, integration is the main challenge for transdisciplinarity (Jahn 2008:32f.). At the *cognitive* level, expert and disciplinary knowledge must be differentiated and linked; the same goes for scientific and practical real-world knowledge. At the *social* level, the different disciplinary cultures and interests of the participating researchers and non-scientific actors must be differentiated and correlated. At the *communicative* level, different linguistic expressions and communicative practices must be linked in order to develop a common discursive practice that allows mutual understanding (Bergmann et al. 2012:45). These different problems of integration require particular attention when gender issues come to the fore of research, since their integration in the research process touches the cognitive as well as social and communicative dimensions.

## *Problem transformation: the 'Ernährungswende' (food change) research project*

As described previously, a transdisciplinary research project must begin by defining a common research object. In other words, the given real-world problem must be localized and translated into a scientific research question. A good example for such a 'translation' is the overall research question of the collaborative research project 'Ernährungswende' (food change), funded by the German Federal Ministry of Education and Research (BMBF) from 2002–2005. At the centre of the project was the real-world problem of 'overconsumption of food', which includes various issues such as increasing adiposity among children, food scandals, or the huge impact of agricultural production on climate change. The aim of the project was to generate knowledge that opens up new vistas for solutions to the problem of over-nutrition. This everyday life problem was translated into a scientific issue by reframing the problem of 'wrong nutrition' within the social field of action 'environment–nutrition–health'. The latter placed everyday nutritional practice at the fore of the epistemic object of research, which was then ready for cross-disciplinary analysis. Insights from hitherto unrelated scientific fields had to be explored and connected in innovative ways.

By means of a synopsis of the different approaches from environmental sciences, nutrition and health research, and social sciences, the scientific correlate to the real-world problem 'wrong nutrition' was defined as 'overburdening in everyday life', resulting from inappropriate daily nutritional supplies and misdirected allocation of nutrition competencies. This overburdening related to nutrition practices in everyday life in Germany was investigated by a triangulation of quantitative and qualitative social-empirical studies. Gender research was applied in the analysis by means of theoretical assumptions on gender-specific differences in orientations and practices. The interview guideline included both physical aspects such as the body mass index and symbolic aspects such as food related orientations and attitudes, as well as food-related practices. The results of the social-empirical analysis revealed gender-specific distributions of nutrition responsibility and food related practices. They show that women are key decision makers and actors throughout the different stages of the nutrition related feeding practices (e.g., planning and organization of nutrition related housework, purchasing groceries, meal preparation, or cooking for guests; Stieß and Hayn 2005).

These differences are mirrored in a typology of 'nutrition styles' (Schultz and Stieß 2008). The nutrition style approach explores the interplay between food-related orientations and the way people manage their diet in everyday life. Based on a representative survey, the typology of nutrition styles illustrates the broad diversity of nutrition practices in Germany, ranging from 'uninterested fast fooders' to highly sophisticated nutrition-conscious practices (Schultz and Stieß 2008). Together with estimates about the emissions of carbon dioxide of each specific nutrition style, these gender-specific differences provide new insights about nutrition practices with respect to the dimensions environment and health.

## Integration through interdisciplinary conceptual work: the 'demons' research project

The second project phase is dedicated to the production of new knowledge for specific issues in sub-projects and a corresponding integration of the specialized pluralistic knowledge. In the social-ecological junior research project 'Demographic trends, needs and supply systems (*demons*)', interdisciplinary conceptual work was applied as one major integration method. A key challenge for transdisciplinary research projects is reaching a shared understanding of key concepts and terms that transcends the boundaries of the individual disciplines involved in the project (Bergmann et al. 2012:53f.). The *demons* project investigated interactions between demographic changes and transformations of water and food supply systems in different regions of the world (Hummel 2008). In the project, these supply systems were conceptualized as social-ecological systems that comprise material-energetic and cultural-symbolic dimensions. Specific theoretical terms and concepts relevant in all participating disciplines (biology, geography, political science, economics, and sociology) had to be integrated into the interdisciplinary context. During the project it became clear for the researchers that they could not simply refer to and combine the individual understandings of key concepts in the respective scientific fields and disciplines. Instead, the different disciplinary terminologies (with concepts such as 'population', 'resources', 'needs', or 'regulation') and approaches had to be reworked within the problem-oriented setting (social-ecological problems of water and food supply) and related in a fresh light in order to meet the challenge of transferability to the disciplines involved in the project.

An illustrative example of this challenge is the concept of 'population' as a key concept in biology, demography, and ecology. For studying human populations, the biological concept of population cannot simply be extended by adding one or more social dimensions. In *demons*, 'population' was reconstructed theoretically by referring to the concept of basic societal relations to nature, and enriched by bringing into play societal factors (e.g., provisioning practices, which are ignored in the biological concept). This interdisciplinary reworking and re-contextualization of the population concept in turn had a theoretical impact on the disciplinary concepts of 'population' and 'species' in biology. 'Population' could no longer be understood as merely referring to reproductive communities in the biological sense of a propagating community but had to be conceptualized also as 'provisioning communities', whose members acquire food in common and thereby create the conditions necessary for their survival and growth. This rendered a conceptual extension possible for biology and allowed for an inclusion of societal and social factors such as reproductive work (e.g., care work), education, income, and so on, thus opening up a perspective on social differences and inequalities, including gender impacts.

## Gender relations and gender responsiveness of policy instruments: the EUPOPP project

In the following section, we want to demonstrate how a gender perspective can be integrated systematically into the transdisciplinary generation of knowledge. This implies the stages of a problem transformation, empirical analysis, and the development of policy recommendations. Conceptually, this approach draws on the distinction between symbolization and interpretation of gender relations on the one hand, and effects of social-ecological problems and solutions on gender relations on the other (Schultz et al. 2006:235f.). The underlying idea is that gender relations shape the life situation of women and men at various levels. They appear on the level of values, role models, personal identity, and expectations as well as on the level of the rules, practices, and institutional arrangements that structure social relations and everyday life. In order to assess gender impacts of policies and instruments, gender researchers have elaborated an analytical framework encompassing the following three dimensions:

*   the gendered division of labour;
*   body, health, and the societal organization of intimacy; and
*   empowerment and access to decision-making.

*(see Verloo and Roggeband 1996; Schultz et al. 2001, 2003)*

In addition to these three dimensions, access to resources and ecosystem services can be added as a further dimension of gender analysis. This framework represents a generalized model of gender dimensions in societal relations to nature. It provides an analytical tool that can be applied to explore gender relations in different fields of investigation.

The approach was applied in the collaborative research project EUPOPP – European Policies to Promote Sustainable Consumption Patterns (www.eupopp.net) – in order to integrate a gender perspective into the analysis of sustainability impacts of strategies and policy instruments for sustainable consumption in the European Union. EUPOPP was focusing on policy instruments that target the demand side (i.e., private or organizational consumption, and respective products), giving particular attention to food consumption and domestic energy use (Heiskanen et al. 2010; Brohmann and Barth 2011). Linking gender analysis to the study of sustainable consumption policies had some critical implications for framing the research object and the research questions of EUPOPP (Schultz and Stieß 2009).

On a *conceptual level*, a gender perspective allowed for a better understanding of consumption practices, stressing the active role (or agency) of women and men in 'producing everyday life'. Gender debates and gender policies link the question of sustainable consumption to the question of livelihood rights, good livelihood, and everyday life. A gender approach toward everyday life stresses the importance of consumption practices that are social rather than individual processes and that are embedded in a social context such as household, family, and community life. Using a 'gender lens', which puts the focus on gender relations and gendered differences in consumption patterns, the different agency of women and men in 'doing sustainable consumption' becomes visible, leading to a better understanding of behavioural mechanisms related to the goals of sustainable consumption.

On the *level of policy analysis*, a normative concern with gender equity, which is acknowledged as an urgent concern of sustainable development strategies (Council of the European Union 2006), could be translated into an object for empirical investigation. Introducing gender as an analytical category, the overall research question of EUPOPP could be reformulated, placing a strong focus on how the implementation and the effects of political instruments are shaped by gender relations, and how gender relations are affected by these policies and instruments. This question opened up a new research perspective that can be termed as 'gender responsiveness to sustainable consumption instruments' (Schultz and Stieß 2009). This research perspective is exploring how gender aspects promote or hinder intended effects of sustainable consumption instruments (see Weller in this volume).

The three gender dimensions mentioned previously helped structure further analysis of the different agency of women and men in consumption practices. As part of the project, a comprehensive literature review on gender and consumption showed that with respect to the gendered division of labour, there is evidence that women are more often in charge of consumption decisions related to food, clothing, and household articles, and they are key decision-makers in the fields of food, washing, and cleaning. Women and men have different consumption-related competencies, with women tending to be more food-literate, and men tending to be more knowledgeable about technical aspects of household energy consumption (see Weller in this volume). From an overall perspective, time budget studies reveal different patterns of time use by gender and show that the core household work is still left up to women (Eurostat 2004; FSO 2006). As a result, women find it less easy to reconcile obligations from professional work and housework when organizing their everyday lives. Compared to men, they suffer more from time scarcity and have less generous access to leisure time (Schultz and Stieß 2009). With respect to the issue of body, health, and societal intimacy, women tend to be more concerned about health issues because of their responsibility for care duties. Physical vulnerability to harmful substances in everyday products differs greatly depending on sex/gender as well as age (e.g., children and older people can be more vulnerable).

The third gender dimension, empowerment and access to decision-making of women and men, is of particular importance for changing consumer behaviour – that is, the design of policy instruments to promote sustainable consumption. Empirical data on gender responsiveness to sustainable consumption-related instruments and policies are scarce and mainly available in the context of product labels (Stolle and Micheletti 2005). With respect to labels, women tend to respond more often to ethical, social, and environmental criteria of goods and services than men. With respect to other sustainable consumption instruments, one can draw on the findings from gender impact assessments on environmental laws and regulations (Hayn and Schultz 2002; Weller 2004). With respect to market instruments such as environmental subsidies or product charges, insights from gender budgets (Rake 2000, 2002; Sharp and Broomhill 2002) provide useful insights. Both types of instrument seem to work more effectively if women and men are not addressed in general but in intersection with other aspects of cultural diversity and social differences. Furthermore, regulative and financial instruments can be made more effective when they are accompanied by communication measures which are directed to the target groups affected.

The focus on empowerment and decision-making has another important implication on a procedural level. Consumption, long believed to be the domain of women, has largely been viewed as a private and apolitical sphere of life. The notion of political consumerism, which includes practices such as boycotting and 'buycotting' (i.e., purchasing according to social and environmental criteria and labels), challenges this view of consumption as a purely private matter. When consumers are conceived of as political actors, they are part of a collective movement that aims to change the framework conditions via individual (and collectively coordinated) action. In this case, consumers need to be addressed and empowered as consumer-citizens (i.e., not only private but also political actors; Micheletti 2003, 2004; Boström et al. 2005; Micheletti and Stolle 2005). By designing instruments to promote sustainable consumption, a gender approach suggests that women and men, female and male citizen-consumers, need to participate in all stages of the policy cycle, which in turn requires access to decision-making and the development of suitable institutional settings.

In EUPOPP, these considerations were linked to the empirical policy analysis in order to develop recommendations for improving sustainable consumption-related policies (Wolff and Schönherr 2011). The findings of the EUPOPP project demonstrate that sustainable consumption-related policies can be more effective if they tie in with consumers' daily routines and are sensitive to the different consumption-related responsibilities and competencies of woman and men (Brohmann and Barth 2011; Schönherr et al. 2011). For example, the responsibility for energy saving and the use of sustainable energy in the household does not appear to follow gender differences (Schultz and Stieß 2009). However, women are more prone to changing everyday life practices in order to reduce their carbon footprint, while men more frequently state that they would rather invest in green technology. Consequently, women tend to initiate energy conservation in households (Clancy and Röhr 2003). On the other hand, information on energy use is usually targeted to men, because they are still seen as the more technologically oriented addressees.

Sustainable consumption policies should respond to gendered differences in consumption patterns when attempting to strengthen consumer knowledge and capacities. At the same time, it is important that neither women nor men should be addressed as homogeneous gender groups. Instead, communication instruments and campaigns should be designed with caution in order to avoid gendered stereotypes such as the 'male breadwinner' or the 'female carer and consumer', and to resist 'feminization' of the responsibility for consumption (see Weller, this volume). Moreover, sustainable consumption policies should account for the fact that the agency of consumers emerges at the intersection of gender with other aspects of cultural diversity and social difference such as class, 'race', and age. For example, growing concern with healthy nutrition, food quality, and nutrition related risks is particularly likely to arise in households with newborn children. In this vein, the birth of a child may be a biographical 'window of opportunity' where parents are more accessible for issues of sustainable consumption, because it is a key event where the organization of nutrition-related work within a household is frequently renegotiated and new competences are developed. Sustainable consumption policies can support this reorientation providing access to appropriate information and services.

## Conclusion and outlook

A transdisciplinary approach to gender and environment introduces new and promising perspectives to the Frankfurt tradition of social-ecological research called social ecology. On a conceptual level, a gender perspective helps translate societal problems into more accurate research objects and questions. On an empirical level, the awareness of differences among gender and other social groups is sharpened. The model of the transdisciplinary research process can structure the integration of a gender perspective at all stages of the research process, including problem analysis, empirical investigation, and the development of policy recommendations. Including a gender perspective in policy analysis can render environmental policy-making more gender responsive. Moreover, a transdisciplinary approach highlights the fact that solutions to real-life problems can only be found when the situated practical knowledge of stakeholders is taken into account. This knowledge is enmeshed in specific contexts. A rich understanding of how societal relations to nature are inferred and structured by gender relations and environment cannot be achieved by theoretical generalizations, but needs a careful investigation of these problem situations and a translation between different types of knowledge. In this way, the social-ecological approach provides a basis for a move from practice to policy and contributes to gender justice and sustainable development.

## Acknowledgement

We express our sincere thanks to Irmgard Schultz for her inspiration, which was an essential source of this article.

## Note

1 A closer look to the current debates about new materialisms would be worthwhile here, but goes beyond the scope of this chapter (see, for example, Barad 2007; Braidotti 2007; Haraway 2008; Coole and Frost 2010).

## References

Barad, K. (2007) *Meeting the Universe Halfway: Quantum Physics and the Entanglement of Matter and Meaning.* Durham: Duke University Press.

Becker, E., Hummel, D. and Jahn, T. (2011) 'Gesellschaftliche Naturverhältnisse als Rahmenkonzept', in Groß, M. (ed) *Handbuch Umweltsoziologie.* Wiesbaden: VS Verlag, 75–96.

Becker, E., Jahn, T. and Hummel, D. (2006) 'Gesellschaftliche Naturverhältnisse', in Becker, E. and Jahn, T. (eds) *Soziale Ökologie. Grundzüge einer Wissenschaft von den gesellschaftlichen Naturverhältnissen.* Frankfurt and New York: Campus, 174–197.

Becker-Schmidt, R. (1998) 'Trennung, Verknüpfung, Vermittlung: Zum feministischen Umgang mit Dichotomien', in Knapp, G.-A. (ed) *Kurskorrekturen: Feminismus Zwischen Kritischer Theorie und Postmoderne.* Frankfurt and New York: Campus, 84–125.

Bergmann, M., Jahn, T., Knobloch, T., Krohn, W., Pohl, C. and Schramm, E. (2012) *Methods for Transdisciplinary Research: A Primer for Practice.* Frankfurt/Main: Campus.

Biesecker, A. and Hofmeister, S. (2006) *Die Neuerfindung des Ökonomischen. Ein (re)produktionstheoretischer Beitrag zur sozial-ökologischen Forschung.* München: oekom.

Biesecker, A., Matthes, M., Schön, S. and Scurrell, B. (eds) (2000) *Vorsorgendes Wirtschaften. Auf dem Weg zu einer Ökonomie des guten Lebens.* Bielefeld: Kleine.

BMBF – Bundesministerium für Bildung und Forschung (2012) *Understanding – Evaluating – Shaping Transdisciplinary Knowledge for a Sustainable Society.* Bonn: Author.

Boström, M., Føllesdal, A., Klintman, M., Micheletti, M. and Sørensen, M. P. (eds) (2005) *Political Consumerism: Its Motivations, Power, and Conditions in the Nordic Countries and Elsewhere.* TemaNord 2005: 517.

Online. Available at: http://www.norden.org/pub/velfaerd/konsument/sk/TN2005517.asp (accessed 14 December 2008).

Braidotti, R. (2007) *Metamorphoses: Towards a Materialist Theory of Becoming*. Cambridge: Polity Press.

Brohmann, B. and Barth, R. (eds) (2011) *Policies to Promote Sustainable Consumption Patterns in Europe: How Effective Are Sustainable Consumption Policies in the EU-27?* Oeko-Institute Darmstadt. Online. Available at: http://www.eupopp.net/docs/eupopp_brochure_110621.pdf (accessed 6 October 2014).

Clancy, J. and Röhr, U. (2003) 'Gender and energy: Is there a northern perspective?', *Energy for Sustainable Development* 7(3): 16–22.

Coole, D. and Frost, S. (eds) (2010) *New Materialisms: Ontology, Agency, and Politics*. Durham, NC: Duke University Press.

Council of the European Union (2006) *Review of the EU Sustainable Development Strategy (EU SDS) – Renewed Strategy, Brussels*. 10117/06 from 9 June 2006.

Eurostat (2004) *How Europeans Spend Their Time – Everyday Life of Women and Men – Data 1998–2002*. Luxembourg: Office for Official Publications of the European Communities.

Fischer-Kowalski, M. and Weisz, H. (1999) 'Society as hybrid between material and symbolic realms: Towards a theoretical framework of society-nature interaction', *Advances in Human Ecology* 8: 215–251.

FSO – Federal Statistical Office (2006) *In the Spotlight: Women in Germany*. Wiesbaden: Author.

Geels, F. W. (2010) 'Ontologies, socio-technical transitions (to sustainability), and the multi-level perspective', *Research Policy* 39: 495–510.

Haraway, D. (1989) *Primate Visions: Gender, Race and Nature in the World of Modern Science*. New York and London: Routledge.

Haraway, D. (2008) *When Species Meet*. Minneapolis, MN: University of Minnesota Press.

Hayn, D. and Schultz, I. (2002) *Gender Impact Assessment in the Field of Radiation Protection and the Environment – Concluding Report* (Engl. version). With expertise by: Simone Mohr, Regine Barth, Christan Küppers and Anja Ruf. Frankfurt/Main.

Heiskanen, E., Brohmann, B., Schönherr, N., Fritsche, U. and Aalto, K. (2010) 'Policies to promote sustainable consumption: Framework for a future-oriented evaluation', *Progress in Industrial Ecology* 6(4): 387–403.

Hofmeister, S. and Mölders, T. (2006) 'Geschlecht als Basiskategorie der Nachhaltigkeitsforschung', in Schäfer, M., Schultz, I. and Wendorf, G. (eds) *Gender-Perspektiven in der Sozial-ökologischen Forschung*. München: oekom, 17–37.

Hummel, D. (ed) (2008) *Population Dynamics and Supply Systems: A Transdisciplinary Approach*. Frankfurt and New York: Campus.

Hummel, D. and Kluge, T. (2006) 'Regulationen', in Becker. E. and Jahn, T. (eds) *Soziale Ökologie. Grundzüge einer Wissenschaft von den gesellschaftlichen Naturverhältnissen*. Frankfurt am Main: Campus Verlag, 248–258.

Hummel, D. and Schultz, I. (2011) 'Geschlechterverhältnisse und gesellschaftliche Naturverhältnisse – Perspektiven Sozialer Ökologie in der transdisziplinären Wissensproduktion', in Scheich, E. and Wagels, K. (eds) *Körper Raum Transformation. gender-Dimensionen von Natur und Materie*. Münster: Westfälisches Dampfboot, 218–233.

Jahn, T. (2008) 'Transdisciplinarity in the research practice: Translation of the article', in Bergmann, M. and Schramm, E. (eds) *Transdisziplinäre Forschung. Integrative Forschungsprozesse verstehen und bewerten*. Frankfurt am Main and New York: Campus, 21–37. Online. Available at: http://www.isoe.de/fileadmin/redaktion/Downloads/Transdisziplinaritaet/jahn-transdisziplinaritaet-2008.pdf (accessed 2 September 2014).

Jahn, T., Bergmann, M. and Keil, F. (2012) 'Transdisciplinarity: Between mainstreaming and marginalization', *Ecological Economics* 79: 1–10.

Janowicz, C. (2011) 'Das Konzept der gesellschaftlichen Naturverhältnisse und seine Bedeutung für die Umweltsoziologie', in Kruse, S. and Baerlocher, E. (eds) *Natur und Gesellschaft. Sozialwissenschaftliche Perspektiven auf die Regulation und Gestaltung einer Wechselbeziehung*. Basel: Edition Gesowip, 21–43.

Klein, J. T., Grossenbacher-Mansuy, W., Häberli, R., Bill, A., Scholz, R. W. and Welti, M. (eds) (2001) *Transdisciplinarity: Joint Problem Solving Among Science, Technology, and Society*. Basel: Birkhäuser.

Latour, B. (2005) *Reassembling the Social: An Introduction to Actor-Network-Theory*. Oxford Oxford University Press.

Mellor, M. (1997) 'Women, nature and the social construction of "economic man"', *Ecological Economics* 20(2): 129–140.

Mellor, M. (2006) 'Ecofeminist political economy', *International Journal of Green Economics* 1(1–2): 139–150.

Micheletti, M. (2003) *Political Virtue and Shopping: Individuals, Consumerism, and Collective Action*. New York: Palgrave.

Micheletti, M. (2004) 'Put your money where your mouth is! Political consumerism as political participation: The market as an arena for politics', in Garsten, C. and Lindh de Montoya, M. (eds) *Market Matters Exploring Cultural Processes in the Global Market*. London: Palgrave.

Micheletti, M. and Stolle, D. (2005) 'Swedish political consumers: Who they are and why they use the market as an arena for politics', in Boström et al. (eds) *Political Consumerism: Its Motivations, Power, and Conditions in the Nordic Countries and Elsewhere*. TemaNord 2005: 517, 146–164. Online. Available at: www.norden.org/pub/velfaerd/konsument/sk/TN2005517.asp (accessed 14 December 2008).

Mittelstraß, J. (2005) 'Methodische Transdisziplinarität', *TATuP – Zeitschrift des ITAS zur Technikfolgenabschätzung* 14(2): 18–23.

Nightingale, A. (2006) 'The nature of gender: Work, gender, and environment', *Environment and Planning D: Society and Space* 24(2): 165–185.

Rake, K. (2000) 'Into the mainstream? Why gender audit is an essential tool for policymakers', *New Economy* 7(2): 107–110.

Rake, K. (2002) *Gender Budgets: The Experience of the UK's Women's Budget Group*. A paper prepared for the conference 'Gender Balance – Equal Finance'. Basel, Switzerland, March 2002.

Schäfer, M., Schultz, I. and Wendorf, G. (eds) (2006) *Gender-Perspektiven in der Sozial-ökologischen Forschung*. München: oekom.

Scheich, E. (1993) *Naturbeherrschung und Weiblichkeit. Denkformen und Phantasmen der Naturwissenschaften*. Pfaffenweiler: Centaurus-Verlag.

Scheich, E. and Schultz, I. (1991) *Soziale Ökologie und Feminismus*. Frankfurt/Main: IKO.

Schönherr, N., Wolff, F. and Brunn, C. (2011) *Synthesis Report: In-depth Analysis of the Effects of Sustainable Consumption Instruments on Consumption Patterns and Examination of Conditions of Success or Failure*. With contributions from Eva Heiskanen, Kristiina Aalto, Ana Alcantud, Dafne Mazo, Denise Leung and Ingrida Bremere. Oeko-Institute Darmstadt. Online. Available at: www.eupopp.net/docs/deliverable%203_2_1_%20110730_abbrev.pdf (accessed 7 October 2012).

Schultz, I. (2001) 'Umwelt- und Geschlechterforschung: eine notwendige Übersetzungsarbeit', in Nebelung, A., Poferl, A. and Schultz, I. (eds) *Geschlechterverhältnisse – Naturverhältnisse*. Opladen: Leske und Budrich, 25–51.

Schultz, I. (2006) 'The natural world and the nature of gender', in Davis, K., Evans, M. and Lorber, J. (eds) *Handbook of Gender and Women's Studies*. London, Thousand Oaks and New Delhi: Sage Publications, 376–396.

Schultz, I., Hummel, D. and Hayn, D. (2006) 'Geschlechterverhältnisse', in Becker, E. and Jahn, T. (eds) *Soziale Ökologie. Grundzüge einer Wissenschaft von den gesellschaftlichen Naturverhältnissen*. Frankfurt and New York: Campus, 224–235.

Schultz, I., Hummel, D., Empacher, C. et al. (2003) 'Research on gender, the environment and sustainable development (state of the art)', Studies on Gender Impact Assessment of the Programmes of the Fifth Framework Programme. European Commission, Luxembourg (EUR 20313).

Schultz, I., Hummel, D., Hayn, D. et al. (2001) 'Gender impact assessment of the specific programmes of the Fifth Framework Programme', Environment and Sustainable Development sub-programme. Final report. European Commission. Brussels.

Schultz, I., Hummel, D. and Padmanabhan, M. (2010) 'Feministische Perspektiven auf Nachhaltigkeitspolitik', *Femina Politica. Zeitschrift für Feministische Politikwissenschaften* 19(1): 9–21.

Schultz, I., Schramm, E. and Hummel, D. (2015) 'Gender als Integrationsdimension in der transdisziplinären sozial-ökologischen Forschung', in Katz, C. et al. (eds) *Nachhaltigkeit anders denken. Veränderungspotentiale durch Geschlechterperspektiven*. Berlin: Springer, 5–17.

Schultz, I. and Stieß, I. (2008) 'Linking sustainable consumption to everyday life. A social-ecological approach to consumption research', in Tukker, A., Charter, M. and Vezzoli, C. (eds) *Perspectives on Radical Changes to Sustainable Consumption and Production: System Innovation for Sustainability 1*. Sheffield, UK: Greenleaf Publishing Ltd, 288–300.

Schultz, I. and Stieß, I. (2009) 'Gender aspects of sustainable consumption strategies and instruments', *EUPOPP Working Paper 1*. Institute for Social-Ecological Research (ISOE), Frankfurt/Main.

Schultz, I. and Weller, I. (1995) *Gender and Environment: Ökologie und die Gestaltungsmacht der Frauen*. Frankfurt/Main: IKO.

Sharp, R. and Broomhill, R. (2002) 'Budgeting for equality: The Australian experience', *Feminist Economics* 8(1): 25–47.

Stieß, I. and Hayn, D. (2005) 'Ernährungsstile im Alltag. Ergebnisse einer repräsentativen Untersuchung' [Nutrition styles in everyday life. Results from a representative survey]. In collaboration with Konrad

Götz, Steffi Schubert, Gudrun Seltmann and Barbara Birzle-Harder. ISOE-discussion Paper, No. 24. Frankfurt/Main.

Stolle, D. and Micheletti, M. (2005) 'What motivates political consumers?', First draft for the Special Issue on '*The Underestimated Consumer-Power – Prospects for the New Consumer Movement*' in 'Forschungsjournal Neue Soziale Bewegungen' (No. 4, 2005).

Verloo, M. and Roggeband, C. (1996) 'Gender impact assessment: The development of a new instrument in the Netherlands', *Impact Assessment* 14(March): 3–20.

Weller, I. (1999) 'Gestaltungsmacht von Frauen in neuen Ansätzen der Umweltforschung zur Produktentwicklung', in Collmer, S., Döge, P. and Fenner, B. (eds) *Technik – Politik – Geschlecht. Zum Verhältnis von Politik und Geschlecht in der politischen Techniksteuerung.* Bielefeld: Kleine Verlag, 77–98.

Weller, I. (ed) (2004) 'Gender Impact Assessment – Review of the Hanseatic City of Bremen's Support Program for Applied Environmental Research (1996–2001)', Final Report, Bremen.

Winker, G. and Degele, N. (2011) 'Intersectionality as multi-level analysis: Dealing with social inequality', *European Journal of Women's Studies* 18(1): 51–66.

Wolff, F. and Schönherr, N. (2011) 'The impact evaluation of sustainable consumption policy instruments', *Journal of Consumer Policy* 34(1): 43–66.

# 13

# GENDER AND ENVIRONMENTAL (IN)SECURITY

## From climate conflict to ecosystem instability

*Nicole Detraz*

## Introduction

For decades, scholars, policy makers, and the media have discussed the connections between security and climate change. These actors have utilized various discourses and narratives to reflect on the negative impacts that a changing climate will have and is currently having on state security, human security, and the security of ecosystems (Detraz 2013).[1] Climate change has been discussed by the defense and military establishments of several states, it has been the subject of multiple sessions before the United Nations (UN) Security Council, and its security implications have been the subject of media profiles as well as numerous academic outlets such as special journal issues and book series.

To date, gender is a missing feature of most securitized climate change narratives. Actors typically discuss climate change and security links as though they are gender neutral. Gender refers to a set of socially constructed ideas about what men and women *ought* to be. This conceptualization of gender stresses that societal understandings of appropriate and acceptable behaviour for both men and women shapes their experiences in various ways. Security issues and environmental issues have each been the subject of feminist analysis, which highlights how gendered assumptions often result in various sources and manifestations of insecurity for women around the world (Enloe 1990, 2000; Seager 1993; Sjoberg and Gentry 2007; Oswald Spring 2008). This is not to suggest that all women experience insecurity in the same ways or that men do not experience insecurity – far from it. Rather, it suggests that regularized patterns of experience can be seen in the ways that gender intersects with marginalization and insecurity. Feminist scholars have not yet written a great deal about gender and environmental security specifically; however this is a growing area of feminist scholarship.[2]

In this chapter I use discourse analysis to explore how existing security and climate change discourses are gendered, and I provide a blueprint for how gender can be fruitfully included in the ways that we understand the concepts of threat, risk, and vulnerability in particular. I argue that while there are possible negative implications of securitizing climate change, a gender-sensitive, feminist environmental security discourse highlights issues of human insecurity and environmental instability in ways that are useful for policy-making. The chapter speaks to multiple areas of the international relations field, including the sub-fields of security studies and global environmental politics.

## Climate security debate

Discourse analysis of key texts reveals that there are several narratives that have been used to indicate a connection between climate change and various conceptualizations of 'security'. Global environmental politics scholars have used discourse analysis to explore a variety of questions about environmental issues in recent years (Hajer 1997; Andrée 2005; Bäckstrand and Lövbrand 2006; Barry et al. 2008; Epstein 2008; McDonald 2013). I understand discourse analysis to be a process of identifying regularized ways of understanding or discussing certain issues.[3] The process of discourse analysis involves tracing the storylines or narratives that make up a larger discourse. A narrative is a set of concepts, ideas, or themes that are repeated and combined to form a discourse (Hajer 2006). Narratives structure the terms of debate as well as set limits on the kinds of policies regarded as suitable and reasonable to address the issue at hand (Bäckstrand and Lövbrand 2006; Lovell et al. 2009). Discourses shape our understanding of the terms of a debate, and are therefore powerful aspects of environmental policy-making.

Included in each of the climate security narratives is the argument that climate change impacts will result in certain significant negatives for a variety of actors – including states, individuals, and ecosystems. There are several key concepts that are recurring in debates about whether and how climate change is a security issue. Discourse analysis of high profile documents which have linked climate change and security illustrate the prevalence of the concepts of threat, risk, and vulnerability in particular. Feminist security scholars like Cynthia Enloe (1990, 2000) and J. Ann Tickner (1992) have long challenged the international relations community to critically engage with security-related concepts in order to reveal the myriad ways in which they are gendered. In the following sections I address the concepts of threat, risk, and vulnerability in turn, and offer an assessment of how all intersect with gender.

### *Threat*

In 1983, Richard Ullman argued that

> a threat to national security is an action or sequence of events that 1) threatens drastically and over a relatively brief span of time to degrade the quality of life for inhabitants of a state, or 2) threatens significantly to narrow the range of policy choices available to government of a state or to private, nongovernmental agencies (persons, groups, corporations) within the state.
>
> *(quoted in Liotta and Shearer 2007:5)*

Within the field of security studies, threats are often discussed in connection to discussions of state stability and security, but threats also relate to the security of individuals and groups. Essentially, a threat is that which is understood to directly undermine security.

In 2006 former UN Secretary General Kofi Annan referred to climate change as a 'threat to peace and security'. In his opening address to the 12th Conference of the Parties to the UN Framework Convention on Climate Change (UNFCCC), Annan stressed that the international community must devote the same attention to climate change as it does to preventing war and the proliferation of weapons of mass destruction. Climate change has routinely been referred to as a 'threat multiplier' (CNA 2007; Brown and Crawford 2009; Parthemore and Rogers 2010; National Research Council 2012). This means that the negative impacts of climate change will likely exacerbate existing sources of insecurity. Climate change is predicted to result in multiple, overlapping 'chronic conditions', which adds 'a new hostile and stressing factor into the national and international security environment' (CNA 2007:6, 44). This suggests that climate change increases the likelihood of instability in multiple ways. When climate change is deemed a threat multiplier, it typically refers to threats to state security (McDonald 2013).

There is often an implicit distinction made between climate-related threats to state security in the Global North and the Global South.[4] Many sources link climate change impacts to 'poverty, environmental degradation, and the further weakening of fragile governments. Climate change will contribute to food and water scarcity, will increase the spread of disease, and may spur or exacerbate mass migration' (US Department of Defense 2010:84). Climate change is not typically understood to be a sole cause of conflict, but rather an accelerant of conflict and/or instability. This outcome is understood to place a burden to respond upon militaries and civilian institutions, primarily militarized institutions in the Global North acting in the Global South. For example, the German Advisory Council on Global Change warns that if the international community fails to come together to address it:

> [C]limate change will draw ever-deeper lines of division and conflict in international relations, triggering numerous conflicts between and within countries over the distribution of resources, especially water and land, over the management of migration, or over compensation payments between the countries mainly responsible for climate change and those countries most affected by its destructive effects.
>
> *(WBGU 2007:1)*

This threat narrative is extremely common within climate security debates.[5]

Another threat narrative that appears in several scholarly and policy sources is the notion that migrating people are a threat. This notion relates to debates about climate migration fueling resource shortage, overwhelming infrastructure, exacerbating ethnic tensions, and so on (Schwartz and Randall 2003; Brown et al. 2007; CNA 2007; Raleigh and Urdal 2007; WBGU 2007; Hartmann 2010; Detraz and Windsor 2014). Again, ecological migration is typically discussed as something that will happen in the Global South and will create instability and potential insecurity for Southern states that will pull the Global North into tensions (White 2011).

Each of these narratives of threats reflect a connection between the concepts of 'threat', 'uncertainty', and 'fear'. Mike Hulme (2008) explains that discourses of fear related to climate change go back centuries. He traces more recent discourses of 'danger' and 'catastrophe' to the rise of environmentalism in the 1960s.[6] These fear-based discourses centre around fear of the unknown – including unknown causes, places, and futures. The unpredictability of climate change is frequently discussed in ways linked to insecurity. For example, a US Center for Naval Analyses report cites Retired Air Force General Charles F. Wald as saying:

> A stable global climate is what shaped our civilizations. An unstable climate, which is what we're creating now with global warming, will make for unstable civilizations. It will involve more surprises. It will involve more people needing to move or make huge changes in their lives. It pushes us into a period of non-linear change. That is hugely destabilizing.
>
> *(CNA 2009:2)*

The link between instability and uncertainty or unpredictability is clearly made in this statement.

In sum, threats linked to climate change are frequently discussed with reference to state security, with occasional exceptions. Climate change has repeatedly been identified as a potential 'threat multiplier', which can undermine the stability of states in the Global South in particular.

States in the Global North are also expected to have to address climate change impacts on things like military infrastructure, but climate change is infrequently associated with a direct threat to state stability in the North. Climate change has also been associated with instability stemming from climate migration. Each of these threat narratives connects to ideas of fear and uncertainty over the ability to maintain stability in the future.

## Risk

The second central concept in discourses linking climate change and security is risk. Sociologist Ulrich Beck is one of the most well-known scholars to tackle the concept of risk. Inspired a great deal by his reflections on environmental change, Beck (1992) discusses the idea of a 'risk society' in which we are exposed to a great number of risks, many of which are produced by more complex and dangerous technologies than we have seen in the past. These contemporary risks have new characteristics, such as being unbound by place, and potentially catastrophic. These kinds of risks can result in insecurity at individual levels, but they can also result in political instability. Beck argues that we see the political potential of catastrophes in risk society: 'Averting and managing these can include a *reorganization of power and authority*. Risk society is a *catastrophic* society. In it the exceptional condition threatens to become the norm' (1992:24). As the notion of risk has become more frequently discussed, themes like preventive approaches and risk management have become more relevant in security discussions (Trombetta 2008).

We can think of risks, therefore, as centred mainly on the component of time and likelihood of effects occurring. The difference between threats and risks is not about size or scale, but more so about timing. According to many risk scholars, a risk is an event or scenario located in the future which is linked to policy proposals offering a method of prevention (Corry 2012; von Lucke et al. 2014). Olaf Corry explains the difference between climate change as a risk and climate change as a threat thusly: 'the *risk* of climate change concerns the way it makes harmful events possible (or more likely) whereas climate change as a *threat* involves propositions about direct causation of harm' (2012:246–247). The policy options that will most likely stem from each narrative differ significantly. Risk narratives are liable to lead to a focus on ensuring resilience. In global environmental politics language, resilience refers to the ability to recover after a disruption.

Many texts within climate security debates specifically discuss climate risks. For example, Schwartz and Randall explain that 'because of the potentially dire consequences, the risk of abrupt climate change, although uncertain and quite possibly small, should be elevated beyond a scientific debate to a US national security concern' (2003:3). Likewise, in its treatment of uncertainty and climate change, the US National Research Council explains that

> security analysts are focused on risk, which is usually understood to be the likelihood of an event multiplied by the seriousness of the consequences if it should occur. Thus security analysts become seriously concerned about very high-consequence negative events even if scientists cannot estimate the probability of their occurrence with confidence and, indeed, sometimes even if they are fairly confident that the probability is quite low.
> (US National Research Council 2012:26)

## Vulnerability

Risk is a concept that cannot be understood without reflecting on the idea of vulnerability. How likely it is that a set of negative impacts stemming from climate change will occur has direct ties to how susceptible communities are to those impacts. Much has been written about the concept of vulnerability within the literature on environmental politics in general (Liotta and Shearer 2007; McLaughlin and Dietz 2008; Soroos 2010). Typical ideas of vulnerability focus on the 'characteristics of a person or group in terms of their capacity to anticipate, cope with, resist and recover from the impact of a natural hazard' (Blaikie et al. 1994:9). This definition has several pieces, the first being the idea of anticipating a natural hazard. This would include having access to early warnings of disasters. Second, the idea of coping with natural hazards and/or resisting them is likely the most common association people have with the notion of vulnerability. It relates to the ability to adequately address the instances of insecurity that accompany natural hazards, or avoid them altogether. Finally, recovering from natural hazards has a time component. Natural hazards frequently have adverse impacts on the livelihoods of those who are most vulnerable. This concept of livelihood refers to a degree of command that individuals or groups have over income or resources (Blaikie et al. 1994:9). Vulnerability, then, is that which makes one more susceptible to threats or makes it difficult to overcome threats to their security. The concept of vulnerability in climate security discussions follows a similar narrative structure to general discussions of vulnerability (Raleigh 2010; Cuomo 2011). Vulnerability is understood to result in human insecurity.[7] These sorts of mentions of vulnerability are pervasive in climate security discussions; however they often appear in the literature with little reflection on where both threats and vulnerabilities come from.

In sum, vulnerability refers to that which makes actors more susceptible to threats or makes it difficult to overcome security threats. This narrative typically has ties to notions of human security; however there are occasional discussions of state vulnerability to climate change impacts. As it relates to human security, for example, climate change is discussed as undermining people's livelihoods and thus exacerbating poverty. This vulnerability increases the risk that people will experience insecurity.

## A feminist approach to climate security

Gender has not been widely included within most mainstream discussions of environmental security in general, and climate security in particular (Detraz 2014). Despite the important shifts in security and environment scholarship over the past few years, there is still a noticeable silence on the ways these topics intersect with gender. For example, in nearly each of the texts that were assessed in the discourse analysis for this chapter, only a very few contained any mention of gender. When gender is included in discussions of security and environment linkages, it has tended to be brief and at times essentialist in nature, meaning that when gender is present in securitized environmental debates it is typically confined to depictions of women as a vulnerable group. This is problematic because it essentializes both men's and women's experiences, when it pays attention to them at all.

Revealing gender in climate security debates requires rethinking terms and concepts, problematizing power relations, and asking new questions. One way of thinking about the links between gender and climate security is through the use of a *feminist environmental security* discourse that builds on existing elements of security-environment narratives and goes beyond them. Elsewhere I have outlined such a counter-discourse, and explained that it has the protection of human security, gender emancipation, and environmental sustainability as three central, overlapping goals (Detraz 2014). Important components of the discourse include engaging multilevel and multiple perspectives of security and the environment, utilizing broad and critical conceptualizations of key terms, engaging in critical reflection on potential causes of environmental insecurity, and entertaining and promoting inclusive and just solutions to environmental insecurity (Detraz 2014). The discourse allows us to assess the concepts of threat, risk, and vulnerability as having important connections to gender.

## Gendered threats

A feminist environmental security discourse focuses attention on the specific threats to human security that stem from climate change. This marks a shift away from the state-centrism that appears to dominate much of the climate security discussions by scholars and policy makers. Rather than assume that the presence of threats is objective fact, a feminist environmental security discourse conceptualizes threats as rooted in perception. This is in line with much feminist security scholarship as well as other critical approaches to security (Campbell 1998; Wibben 2011).

The focus on humans as the primary referent object of security is consistent with feminist environmental security discourse's overall goal of the protection of human security. The discourse contains some room to consider threats to state security, insofar as there are ties to policy choices and human security, but the focus is very different. A feminist environmental security discourse would also question the reasons for the continued dominant position of state security narratives in climate change debates. The fact that powerful actors, such as representatives from state militaries, often utilize these narratives is an important subject for feminist enquiry. Consider, for example, the narrative about climate migration threatening state security/stability. A feminist environmental security discourse is critical of the focus on people as threats, which is typically devoid of much critical analysis of the circumstances that make migration a likely action. Betsy Hartmann, a key scholar who warns of the dangers of simplistic narratives on population and migration, has been vocal about the potential negatives associated with climate refugee narratives. Hartmann (2010) claims that these narratives oversimplify an extremely complex story about the processes of migration to the point of obscuring our understanding of power relations, systems of marginalization, and uneven experiences of discrimination within society. One necessary component of climate change scholarship is understanding the gendered patterns of migration that stem from climate change impacts (Detraz and Windsor 2014). To date there are not many in-depth studies that examine the ways that gender intersects with environmental motivations to migrate and experiences during environmental migration. Research in this area is necessary in order to highlight the complexity of a process which receives a large amount of attention in the scholarly community, and could increasingly become the subject of security policy-making.

The narratives of the climate refugee debate echo many other discourses of threats associated with climate change – discourses that appear to be closely associated with fear of the unknown and fear of instability. These fears can be critically assessed for how they are portrayed as 'natural' or 'normal'. While threats to security obviously do exist, many fears discussed within climate security debates are historically contingent. They are the product of 'particular historical intersections and political, cultural, and technological conjunctures' (Hartmann et al. 2005:3). For those oriented toward the status quo, uncertainty and instability of existing structures and processes is concerning. Reorienting our understanding of (in)security and climate change in ways that take gender seriously requires reflecting on that which is uncomfortable (Wibben 2011).

## Gendered risks

Like the previous discussion of threat, gender and risk intersect in complex ways. Feminist theorists and other critical scholars have criticized much risk analysis for assuming that an objective reality exists. Critical approaches to risk see it as 'strongly influenced by socially constructed categories – e.g., gender, class and racial categories – that are taken-for-granted as "natural"'

(McLaughlin and Dietz 2008:103). Additionally, many studies have found that women frequently have different perceptions of risk when compared to men (Newman 1992; Norgaard and York 2005; Arora-Jonsson 2011). Previous work indicates that women perceive various hazards as more risky than do men (Flynn et al. 1994) and that women are less willing than men to impose health and environmental risks on others (Barke et al. 1997). For example, in a study of American evangelical Christians, Smith and Leiserowitz (2013) found that while Evangelicals in general tended to perceive climate change as less of a risk than non-Evangelicals, Evangelical women tended to assess climate change as a risk more frequently than men, along with individuals with lower incomes over individuals with higher incomes. These findings suggest that people who have experienced some form of marginalization, be it based on gender or class, may be more cautious in their assessment of risk.

Giovanna Di Chiro (1997) explains that women environmental justice activists have long engaged in a critique of science and risk calculation. In particular, the notion of 'acceptable risk' has been critiqued as authorizing circumstances where it is acceptable for individuals to knowingly be put in harm's way as long as corporate, scientific, and policy-making bodies have weighed in first (Newman 1992). While a lengthy treatment of feminist critiques of science is beyond the scope of this chapter, this critique of the science of risk calculation is consistent with feminist contributions to debates about expertise and power more broadly (Seager 2003). Power relations in a society determine who has the authority to speak about risks and whose perception of risk influences policy-making. The perceived legitimacy of the scientific community has resulted in its central place within discussions of risk and how it should be managed (Keller 2009), but what are the gendered implications of this relationship? Women activists or volunteers 'are less likely to receive credit as experts, even though they have important insights and analyses to offer' (MacGregor 2006:195). It is essential that these gendered perceptions of authority are critically analyzed and problematized if we are to achieve a multifaceted understanding of climate risks.

Risks are typically conceptualized as something that cannot be eliminated, but only managed. Differing perceptions of risk may be tied to differing expectations about how well potential insecurity will be managed in the future. Members of groups that tend to be marginalized, including women, may have lower expectations about the likelihood that a risk that will result in their insecurity will be met with adequate policy responses; therefore they view the risk as 'real'.

A feminist environmental security discourse likewise approaches the concept of risk as something to be assessed in order to ensure gender emancipation and protect human security through promoting environmental sustainability. The concept of resilience, which has been associated with both risk and vulnerability, can potentially aid our understanding of approaches to climate security oriented toward these goals. There is a good deal of debate over the meaning of the term resilience as the ability to recover after a disruption. Systems that are dynamic and/or adaptable will be much more likely to rebound quickly. Systems that lack these flexibilities will likely fail to rebound or else take a longer time to do so (Steinberg 2009; Dalby 2013).[8] It goes without saying that those most at risk of experiencing the negative impacts of climate change are those that are most vulnerable to them. In order to understand where risks lie, it is essential to reflect on questions about the processes of marginalization and vulnerability, as well as assessments of specific policy options geared toward improving resilience and security, for example, evaluating the impacts of adaptation finance on climate risk reduction (Barrett 2013) and engaging in gender-sensitive risk mapping in areas predicted to be particularly hard-hit by climate change impacts (Khosla and Masaud 2010). Each of these is in line with a feminist environmental security approach to gender emancipation and human security.

## *Gendered vulnerabilities*

Connections between gender and vulnerability have received scant attention in most of the debates about environmental security in general, and climate security in particular (Denton 2002). The Intergovernmental Panel on Climate Change defines vulnerability as

> the degree to which a system is susceptible to, and unable to cope with, adverse effects of climate change, including climate variability and extremes. Vulnerability is a function of the character, magnitude and rate of climate change and variation to which a system is exposed, its sensitivity, and its adaptive capacity.
>
> *(IPCC 2007:6)*

This definition emphasizes extreme events and dependence on climate features, especially the magnitude of change to be experienced, which are both characteristics of a hazard paradigm or approach to vulnerability (Gaillard 2010). An alternative way to think about the gendered nature of vulnerability is through an approach which recognizes and assesses the socially constructed nature of susceptibility to climate change impacts and adaptive capacity. Many frameworks view vulnerability as having both biophysical and human factors (Ribot 2010). Along these lines, Justina Demetriades and Emily Esplen stress that

> where women and girls have less access to and control over resources (material, financial, and human), and have fewer capabilities than men, these impediments undermine their capacity to adapt to existing and predicted impacts of climate change, and to contribute important knowledge and insights to adaptation and mitigation decision-making processes.
>
> *(Demetriades and Esplen 2010:133)*

One aspect of gender and vulnerability that has received a significant degree of attention from scholars and some policy makers is discussions of vulnerability to increased natural disasters (Dankelman 2010; Demetriades and Esplen 2010; Arora-Jonsson 2011; Enarson 2012). Neumayer and Plümper (2007) analyzed a sample of up to 141 countries between 1981 and 2002 and found an adverse impact of disasters on female compared to male life expectancy. They link this finding to the extent of socially constructed vulnerability by showing that women died more where they were socio-economically disadvantaged. They conclude that 'it is the socially constructed gender-specific vulnerability of females built into everyday socioeconomic patterns that lead to the relatively higher female disaster mortality rates compared to men' (Neumayer and Plümper 2007:551). Because men tend to be taught certain skills which can be lifesaving (swimming, climbing trees), have more access to early warning systems, and be more heavily represented among stable economic classes, their levels of vulnerability can differ substantially from women's (Arora-Jonsson 2011; Enarson 2012).

While studies like these are important, feminist environmental scholars frequently express concern about the use of essentialized ideas of women as a vulnerable category of actors who lack agency (Denton 2002; MacGregor 2009; Arora-Jonsson 2011; Cuomo 2011). In many climate policy documents, gender is only mentioned when tied to the idea that women need special protection due to poverty. Seema Arora-Jonsson argues that women are often simplistically portrayed as either vulnerable or virtuous in discussions about climate change. There are three main elements to these characterizations: 'Firstly, that women need special attention because they are the poorest of the poor; secondly, because they have a higher mortality rate during natural calamities caused by climate change and thirdly because women are more environmentally conscious' (Arora-Jonsson 2011:745). The first two elements tend to refer mainly to the women in the South, while the third is often linked to women in the North. She claims that both of these portrayals can result in policy-making that leads to an increase in women's responsibilities without corresponding rewards.

The varying patterns of women's vulnerability to climate change impacts are not a 'natural' phenomenon. Rather, they are the product of a socially constructed understanding of the appropriate or acceptable roles and responsibilities for men and women in society (Cuomo 2011). It is essential, therefore, to encourage critical and inclusive analyses of the gendered experiences of climate change. While several studies have documented gendered aspects of women's climate vulnerability, these must be assessed with an eye toward understanding the social processes and power relations that make these vulnerabilities persist (McLaughlin and Dietz 2008). Also needed are studies that examine how male privilege and masculine roles make men – even where they are poor and marginalized – relatively less vulnerable and less responsible than women for coping with the impacts of climate change. It is unhelpful to lump all marginalized individuals into the same category and expect the same policy solutions to address what amounts to quite different social problems. Along these same lines, there has been much criticism of the concept of the 'feminization of poverty' as a concept that masks the complex relationships between gender and poverty. Rather than calling attention to the gendered nature of poverty, it can just as easily cause policy makers to assume that all poverty reduction strategies will automatically lead to gender equity (Chant 2008).

For example, Ajibade et al. (2013) conducted interviews and focus groups about the 2011 flooding in Lagos, Nigeria. They found that women typically expressed no concern about gendered vulnerability to flooding. Most believed that flood impacts were gender neutral. Despite these perceptions, evidence indicates that impacts varied among income groups and neighborhoods, and gender differences were apparent. Women in the low-income neighborhood within their study recorded higher impacts and slower recovery compared to other social categories of women and men. This suggests that gendered and classed patterns of vulnerability *do* exist, but that our perceptions of these phenomena require careful, intersectional analysis. More of these detailed examinations of vulnerability are necessary if the policy-making and scholarly community are to fully grasp the security implications of climate change.[9]

## Into the future

A feminist environmental security analysis appraises threat, risk, and vulnerability as multifaceted, complex concepts with various ties to insecurity. It acknowledges that threats and risks are not purely objective realities, but rather are socially conditioned understandings of events which connect to the identities of states and individuals (Dalby 2002). It is a normative discourse with the goals of gender emancipation, the protection of human security, and environmental sustainability. It sees environmental degradation as a driver of human insecurity. It is primarily concerned with how individuals and groups experience the negative impacts associated with climate change over being concerned with insecurity of states. The discourse calls into question the power relations and societal expectations that contribute to some members of society being more susceptible to climate insecurity than others. It also has a normative commitment to identifying options for removing sources of vulnerability that negatively impact the security of individuals and ecosystems.

A feminist environmental security discourse focuses on policy options explicitly aimed at reducing vulnerability. It identifies non-militarized solutions to climate change to be the most appropriate for tackling a complex environmental problem.[10] This approach can obviously relate to climate change adaptation measures in general, but more specifically it means identifying gendered patterns of vulnerability and working to empower those who are marginalized. Studies from India suggest that ensuring women's access to health care, literacy, and other components tied to well-being can reduce environmental vulnerability (Roy and Venema 2002; Dankelman 2010). Irene Dankelman argues that there are several factors that affect people's ability to adapt to climate change, including 'access to assets, protection of their economic livelihood, access to services, political participation in decision-making, access to information and enhanced leadership' (2010:68). Each of these factors are gendered, meaning socially constructed ideas about the appropriate and acceptable roles and responsibilities of men and women influence where people are located with respect to aspects of empowerment and marginalization. The challenge for scholars and policy makers is to understand how these gendered social processes contribute to threats to human security. In order to ensure that decision-making is truly gender-responsive, it is essential that women who represent diverse experiences have a voice in policy-making (Khosla and Masaud 2010; see also chapters by Arora-Jonsson, Morrow, and Buckingham in this volume).

Finally, a feminist environmental security discourse encourages an approach to risk that acknowledges that climate change impacts are likely to have observable negative effects on the stability and well-being of individuals in many countries across the globe. At the same time, risk cannot be understood in isolation from positions of power and marginalization, which influence aspects of resilience and vulnerability. Risk assessment must acknowledge those factors which make communities more or less at risk of security threats, and understandings of risk must reflect on the social processes which make certain segments of society more concerned about risk than others.

## Conclusion

Most of the scholarly voices who weigh in on climate change and security connections do so out of a genuine commitment to identifying what they perceive as serious challenges to the well-being of states and/or individuals. There are many reasons why actors in policy, academic, and activist arenas would use securitized narratives to discuss climate change; however there are also some serious pitfalls associated with using these discourses. These include encouraging militarized solutions to the problem of climate change; making vulnerable people targets of policy solutions due to their perceived role in increasing population and engaging in migration; and spreading 'climate change fatigue', or a sense of hopelessness and resignation in the face of a huge challenge.

Climate change discussions have had a tendency to highlight worst-case scenarios because they get the most attention. The unintended side-effect of this tendency is that climate change ends up being portrayed as 'a fifth horseman of the apocalypse that will inevitably usher in conflict regardless of the specific context or the international community's response' (Brown et al. 2007:1153). This apocalyptic portrayal can result in citizens and policy makers becoming resigned to climate change being an inevitable force that cannot be stopped (Swyngedouw 2010). Viewing climate security through a feminist environmental security lens on the other hand focuses attention on potential pathways to addressing threats, risks, and vulnerabilities, rather than suggesting that the climate apocalypse is upon us. While utilizing security narratives can always, unfortunately, run the risk of being understood as the militarization of an issue, I argue that putting forward alternative security discourses which shift our focus to issues of human security remains a worthwhile endeavor.

Climate change has been referred to as 'one of the greatest risks we face in the 21st century' and a factor that 'will cripple the security environment' (Carrington 2013; Graves 2013). It is essential that we understand both the sources of climate change and the processes that make some communities particularly susceptible to its negative impacts. Gender is an important part of the story about how climate change is researched, experienced, and addressed. Rather than understanding climate change as a horseman of the apocalypse, we should instead view it as a significant policy challenge that will only be addressed justly and fairly if we assess the complex and overlapping ways that threats, risks, and vulnerabilities contribute to gendered insecurity at multiple levels.

# Notes

1 Elsewhere I argue that the anthropocentric discourses centred around state security and human security have been far more prominent than ecocentric discourses within climate security debates (Detraz 2013).
2 Exceptions include Oswald Spring (2008), Goldsworthy (2010), and Detraz (2013).
3 My conceptualization of discourse analysis follows from the work of Hajer (1997) in particular.
4 The discussion of threats in connection to states in the Global North typically do not portray them as existential threats. On the other hand, several sources also discuss sea level rise threatening the very existence of states, most of which are located in the Global South (Barnett and Adger 2010).
5 There is also a discussion in some texts of issues such as sea level rise 'threatening' military infrastructure of the US military, like coastal bases and other defense installations (CNA 2007; Carmen et al. 2010; Department of Defense 2010; National Research Council 2012).
6 Similarly, Angela Oels (2014) outlines a shift in discourse from one assessing 'tolerable levels of climate change', which characterized discussions of the 1990s and early 2000s, to a discourse of 'climate apocalypse'.
7 Vulnerability is typically discussed in ways connected to human security, but there are times when it has also been linked to state security (Schwartz and Randall 2003; WBGU 2007; CNA 2009).
8 For example, in discussing the resilience of governing institutions, Paul Steinberg (2009:65) explains that 'an institution is resilient to the extent that it maintains its effectiveness over time despite changing external conditions'.
9 One important obstacle to reflecting on the gendered nature of vulnerability is a lack of these site-specific studies.
10 This perspective is echoed in much of the climate security literature. For this reason, a feminist environmental security discourse is compatible with several existing environmental security discourses which focus on human security.

# References

Ajibade, I., McBean, G. and Bezner-Kerr, R. (2013) 'Urban flooding in Lagos, Nigeria: Patterns of vulnerability and resilience among women', *Global Environmental Change* 23: 1714–1725.
Andrée, P. (2005) 'The Cartagena Protocol on biosafety and shifts in the discourse of precaution', *Global Environmental Politics* 5(4): 25–46.
Arora-Jonsson, S. (2011) 'Virtue and vulnerability: Discourses on women, gender and climate change', *Global Environmental Change* 21: 744–751.
Bäckstrand, K. and Lövbrand, E. (2006) 'Planting trees to mitigate climate change: Contested discourses of ecological modernization, green governmentality and civic environmentalism', *Global Environmental Politics* 6(1): 50–75.
Barke, R. P., Jenkins-Smith, H. and Slovic, P. (1997) 'Risk perception of men and women scientists', *Social Science Quarterly* 78: 167–176.
Barnett, J. and Adger, W. N. (2010) 'Environmental change, human security, and violent conflict', in Matthew, R. A., Barnett, J., McDonald, B. and O'Brien, K. L. (eds) *Global Environmental Change and Human Security*. Cambridge, MA: The MIT Press, 119–136.
Barrett, S. (2013) 'Local level climate justice? Adaptation finance and vulnerability reduction', *Global Environmental Change* 23: 1819–1829.
Barry, J., Ellis, G. and Robinson, C. (2008) 'Cool rationalities and hot air: A rhetorical approach to understanding debates on renewable energy', *Global Environmental Politics* 8(2): 67–98.
Beck, U. (1992) *Risk Society: Towards a New Modernity*. London: Sage Publications.

Blaikie, P., Cannon, T., Davis, I. and Wisner. B. (1994) *At Risk: Natural Hazards, People's Vulnerability and Disasters.* New York: Routledge.

Brown, O. and Crawford, A. (eds.) (2009) 'Battling the elements: The security threat of climate change', *International Institute for Sustainable Development.* Online. Available at: www.iisd.org/sites/default/files/publications/COP15_Commentary_Battling_the_Elements_Oli_Alec.pdf (accessed 3 July 2011).

Brown, O., Hammill, A. and McLeman, R. (2007) 'Climate change as the "new" security threat: Implications for Africa', *International Affairs* 83(6): 1141–1154.

Campbell, D. (1998) *Writing Security: United States Foreign Policy and the Politics of Identity.* Minneapolis: University of Minnesota Press.

Carmen, H. E., Parthemore, C. and Rogers, W. (2010) 'Broadening horizons: Climate change and the U.S. Armed Forces', *Center for a New American Security.* Online. Available at: www.cnas.org/sites/default/files/publications-pdf/CNAS_Broadening%20Horizons_Carmen%20Parthemore%20Rogers.pdf (accessed 17 July 2012).

Carrington, D. (2013) 'Climate change poses grave threat to security, says UK envoy', *The Guardian.* Online. Available at: www.theguardian.com/environment/2013/jun/30/climate-change-security-threat-envoy (accessed 30 June 2013).

Center for Naval Analyses (CNA) (2007) 'National security and the threat of climate change', *The CNA Corporation.*

Center for Naval Analyses (CNA) (2009) 'Powering America's defense: Energy and the risks to national security', *The CNA Corporation.*

Chant, S. (2008) 'The "feminisation of poverty" and the "feminisation" of anti-poverty programmes: Room for revision?', *Journal of Development Studies* 44(2): 165–197.

Corry, O. (2012) 'Securitisation and "riskification": Second-order security and the politics of climate change', *Millennium: Journal of International Studies* 40(2): 235–258.

Cuomo, C. J. (2011) 'Climate change, vulnerability, and responsibility', *Hypatia* 26(4): 690–714.

Dalby, S. (2002) *Environmental Security.* Minneapolis: University of Minnesota Press.

Dalby, S. (2013) 'Environmental dimensions of human security', in Floyd, R. and Matthew, R. A. (eds) *Environmental Security: Approaches and Issues.* New York: Routledge, 121–138.

Dankelman, I. (2010) *Gender and Climate Change: An Introduction.* Sterling, VA: Earthscan.

Demetriades, J. and Esplen, E. (2010) 'The gender dimensions of poverty and climate change adaptation', in Mearns, R. and Norton, A. (eds) *Social Dimensions of Climate Change: Equity and Vulnerability in a Warming World.* Washington, DC: The World Bank, 133–144.

Denton, F. (2002) 'Climate change vulnerability, impacts, and adaptation: Why does gender matter?', *Gender and Development* 10(2): 10–20.

Detraz, N. (2013) 'Gender and environmental security', in Floyd, R. and Matthew, R. A. (eds) *Environmental Security: Approaches and Issues.* New York: Routledge, 154–168.

Detraz, N. (2014) *Environmental Security and Gender.* New York: Routledge.

Detraz, N. and Windsor, L. (2014) 'Evaluating climate migration: Population movement, insecurity and gender', *International Feminist Journal of Politics* 16(1): 127–146.

Di Chiro, G. (1997) 'Local actions, global visions: Remaking environmental expertise', *Frontiers: A Journal of Women Studies* 18(2): 203–231.

Enarson, E. (2012) *Women Confronting Natural Disaster: From Vulnerability to Resilience.* Boulder: Lynne Reiner Publishers.

Enloe, C. (1990) *Bananas, Beaches and Bases: Making Feminist Sense of International Politics.* Berkeley: University of California Press.

Enloe, C. (2000) *Maneuvers: The International Politics of Militarizing Women's Lives.* Berkeley: University of California Press.

Epstein, C. (2008) *The Power of Words in International Relations: Birth of an Anti-Whaling Discourse.* Cambridge, MA: The MIT Press.

Flynn, J., Slovic, P. and Mertz, C. K. (1994) 'Gender, race, and perception of environmental health risks', *Risk Analysis* 14(6): 1101–1108.

Gaillard, J.-C. (2010) 'Vulnerability, capacity and resilience: Perspectives for climate and development policy', *Journal of International Development* 22(2): 218–232.

Goldsworthy, H. (2010) 'Women, global environmental change, and human security', in Matthew, R. A., Barnett, J., McDonald, B. and O'Brien, K. L. (eds) *Global Environmental Change and Human Security.* Cambridge, MA: The MIT Press, 215–236.

Graves, L. (2013) 'Top U.S. Admiral: Climate change biggest threat', *The Huffington Post*. Online. Available at: www.huffingtonpost.com/2013/03/11/climate-change_n_2855007.html (accessed 11 March 2013).

Hajer, M. (1997) *The Politics of Environmental Discourse: Ecological Modernization and the Policy Process*. London: Oxford University Press.

Hajer, M. (2006) 'Doing discourse analysis: Coalitions, practices, meaning', in van den Brink, M. and Metze, T. (eds) *Words Matter in Policy and Planning: Discourse Theory and Method in the Social Sciences*. Utrecht: Labor Grafimedia, 65–74.

Hartmann, B. (2010) 'Rethinking climate refugees and climate conflict: Rhetoric, reality and the politics of policy discourse', *Journal of International Development* 22(2): 233–246.

Hartmann, B., Subramaniam, B. and Zerner, C. (eds) (2005) *Making Threats: Biofears and Environmental Anxieties*. New York: Rowman & Littlefield Publishers, Inc.

Hulme, M. (2008) 'The conquering of climate: Discourses of fear and their dissolution', *The Geographical Journal* 174(1): 5–16.

Intergovernmental Panel on Climate Change (IPCC) (2007) 'Climate Change 2007: Synthesis report', *IPCC*. Online. Available at: www.ipcc.ch/pdf/assessment-report/ar4/syr/ar4_syr.pdf (accessed 16 January 2010).

Keller, A. C. (2009) *Science in Environmental Policy: The Politics of Objective Advice*. Cambridge, MA: MIT Press.

Khosla, P. and Masaud, A. (2010) 'Cities, climate change and gender: A brief overview', in Dankelman, I. (ed) *Gender and Climate Change: An Introduction*. Sterling, VA: Earthscan Publications Ltd, 78–96.

Liotta, P. H. and Shearer, A. W. (2007) *Gaia's Revenge: Climate Change and Humanity's Loss*. Westport, CT: Praeger.

Lovell, H., Bulkeley, H. and Owens, S. (2009) 'Converging agendas? Energy and climate change policies in the UK', *Environment and Planning C: Government and Policy* 27: 90–109.

McDonald, M. (2013) 'Discourses of climate security', *Political Geography* 33: 42–51.

MacGregor, S. (2006) *Beyond Mothering Earth: Ecological Citizenship and the Politics of Care*. Vancouver: UBC Press.

MacGregor, S. (2009) 'A stranger silence still: The need for feminist social research on climate change', *The Sociological Review* 57(2): 124–140.

McLaughlin, P. and Dietz, T. (2008) 'Structure, agency and environment: Toward an integrated perspective on vulnerability', *Global Environmental Change* 18: 99–111.

National Research Council (2012) 'Climate and social stress: Implications for security analysis', *The National Academies Press*. Online. Available at: www.nap.edu/catalog.php?record_id=14682 (accessed 12 March 2014).

Neumayer, E. and Plümper, T. (2007) 'The gendered nature of natural disasters: The impact of catastrophic events on the gender gap in life expectance, 1981–2002', *Annals of the Association of American Geographers* 97(3): 551–566.

Newman, P. (1992) 'The environment: An issue of health, safety and social justice', *Action-Gram Riverside County Department of Community Action* 8(1).

Norgaard, K. and York, R. (2005) 'Gender equality and state environmentalism', *Gender and Society* 19(4): 506–522.

Oels, A. (2014) 'Climate security as governmentality: From precaution to preparedness', in Stripple, J. and Bulkeley, H. (eds) *Governing the Climate: New Approaches to Rationality, Power and Politics*. New York: Cambridge University Press, 198–218.

Oswald Spring, Ú. (2008) *Human, Gender and Environmental Security: A HUGE Challenge*. Bonn, Germany: UNU Institute for Environment and Human Security.

Parthemore, C. and Rogers, W. (2010) 'Sustaining security: How natural resources influence national security', *Center for a New American Security*. Online. Available at: www.cnas.org/files/documents/publications/CNAS_Sustaining%20Security_Parthemore%20Rogers.pdf (accessed 22 July 2012).

Raleigh, C. (2010) 'Political marginalization, climate change, and conflict in African Sahel states', *International Studies Review* 12(1): 69–86.

Raleigh, C. and Urdal, H. (2007) 'Climate change, environmental degradation and armed conflict', *Political Geography* 26: 674–694.

Ribot, J. (2010) 'Vulnerability does not fall from the sky: Toward multiscale, pro-poor climate policy', in Mearns, R. and Norton, A. (eds) *Social Dimensions of Climate Change: Equity and Vulnerability in a Warming World*. Washington, DC: The World Bank, 47–74.

Roy, M. and Venema, H. D. (2002) 'Reducing risk and vulnerability to climate change in India: The capabilities approach', in Masika, R. (ed) *Gender, Development, and Climate Change*. Oxford: Oxfam GB, 78–83.

Schwartz, P. and Randall. D. (2003) 'An abrupt climate change scenario and its implications for United States national security', *Environmental Media Services*.

Seager, J. (1993) *Earth Follies: Coming to Feminist Terms With the Global Environmental Crisis*. New York: Routledge.

Seager, J. (2003) 'Pepperoni or broccoli? On the cutting wedge of feminist environmentalism', *Gender, Place and Culture* 10(2): 167–174.

Sjoberg, L. and Gentry, C. E. (2007) *Mothers, Monsters, Whores: Women's Violence in Global Politics*. London: Zed Books.

Smith, N. and Leiserowitz, A. (2013) 'American evangelicals and global warming', *Global Environmental Change* 23: 1009–1017.

Soroos, M. S. (2010) 'Approaches to enhancing human security', in Matthew, R., Barnett, J., McDonald, B. and O'Brien, K. (eds) *Global Environmental Change and Human Security*. Cambridge, MA: The MIT Press, 199–192.

Steinberg, P. F. (2009) 'Institutional resilience amid political change: The case of biodiversity conservation', *Global Environmental Politics* 9(3): 61–81.

Swyngedouw, E. (2010) 'Apocalypse forever? Post-political populism and the spectre of climate change', *Theory, Culture and Society* 27(2): 213–232.

Tickner, J. A. (1992) *Gender in International Relations: Feminist Perspectives on Achieving Global Security*. New York: Columbia University Press.

Trombetta, M. J. (2008) 'Environmental security and climate change: Analysing the discourse', *Cambridge Review of International Affairs* 21(4): 585–602.

Ullman, R. H. (1983) 'Redefining security', *International Security* 8(1): 129–153.

United States Department of Defense (2010) *Quadrennial Defense Review Report*. Washington, DC: United States Government. Online. Available at: www.defense.gov/qdr/qdr%20as%20of%2029jan10%201600. PDF (accessed 16 October 2010).

von Lucke, F., Wellmann, Z. and Diez, T. (2014) 'What's at stake in securitising climate change? Towards a differentiated approach', *Geopolitics* 19(4): 857–884.

WBGU (German Advisory Council on Global Change) (2007) *Climate Change as a Security Risk*. London: Earthscan.

White, G. (2011) *Climate Change and Migration: Security and Borders in a Warming World*. New York: Oxford University Press.

Wibben, A. T. R. (2011) *Feminist Security Studies: A Narrative Approach*. New York: Routledge.

# 14

# GENDER, ENVIRONMENTAL GOVERNMENTALITY, AND THE DISCOURSES OF SUSTAINABLE DEVELOPMENT

*Emma A. Foster*

## Introduction

The story of international environmental politics tends to be narrated through a catalogue of international and United Nations (UN) summits that have 'become firmly established as land-mark moments of environmental governance' (Death 2011:1). Not only have these summits marked changes to the discursive field for understanding environmental problems and policy solutions, most notably with the launch of the concept of sustainable development in the early 1990s; they have simultaneously integrated and constructed particular understandings of *gendered ecological subjects* (as empirical bodies) alongside symbolic gender norms (Bretherton 1998, 2003; Foster 2011, 2014). For example, assumptions about women having a natural capacity to care and nurture, and the interrelated construction of the Earth as symbolically feminine (or more importantly maternal), have at points been reflected in the discourses of sustainable development during various summits (Foster 2011). This is only one example of the gender norms and assumptions that have been emphasized in UN sustainable development discourses. The promulgation of gender norms and assumptions has at least two outcomes: first, it works to legitimize various environmental policy 'solutions', and second, it works to entrench heteronormative gender expectations.

Indeed, in this chapter I argue that the governmental rationalities underpinning environmental decision-making and subjectification are gendered. Moreover, it is important to note that the constructions of gender (empirically and symbolically) that are (re)constructed and (re)configured in the UN's sustainable development discourses are not ahistorical, and it is, in part, my aim in this chapter is to demonstrate how this complicated matrix of gender assumptions and symbolic gender incarnations underpinning these summits has changed over time. To do so, I explore the discourses associated with two key environmental summits – namely the Rio Earth Summit of 1992 and the Rio+20 Conference held in 2012.[1] I have selected these two mega conferences because they are milestones in how the international community understands sustainable development. I explore the reception for both conferences along with each conference's main policy informing document; the Rio Earth Summit's *Agenda 21* (1992) and Rio+20's *The Future We Want* (2012).

Through an exploration of these two conferences and their accompanying documents, I argue that there has been a marked shift in the international consensus on sustainable development, from one which (at least ostensibly) engaged in a discourse of governance and citizen decision-making to one that is almost solely fixated on the market and technology. This shift in the discourses surrounding the two Rio Summits also marks a transformation in how citizens are *instructed* to be 'good' ecological subjects (or citizens), and this has implications for how gender is *constructed* in service of so-called environmental sustainability. In order to make sense of this shift in instruction/construction, a Foucauldian approach is helpful. Most notably, Michel Foucault's conceptualization of governmentality (1991) works well as a lens through which to understand international environmental governance, gender, and sustainable development. To this end, this chapter is separated into five sections. The first discusses gender scholarship in relation to the field of global environmental politics. The second section briefly outlines Foucault's concept of governmentality. The third section explores how governmentality has been utilized as a framework for analysing gender and environmental politics. The final two sections then discuss how gender is constructed in the context of the Rio Earth Summit and Rio+20 respectively.

## Gender and global environmental politics

The field of global environmental politics has far from embraced gender and feminist analyses (MacGregor 2010). That is not to say that there has been a blanket ignorance of gender within the field of global environmental politics, but that work that does make references to gender often reduces the term to mean women and subsequently discusses those women as an empirical category (as bodies that can be identified, counted and processed into metrics). What has been less common, and maybe less accepted, within the field has been the feminist work that investigates global environmental politics through a gendered lens, understanding gender as an analytical category. In other words, this means looking at 'how masculinity and femininity – gender understood as a meaning system – produce and are produced by' (Peterson 2005:499), in this case, global environmental politics and governance.

The handful of feminist scholars who have considered global environmental politics through the application of 'analytical gender' have made a series of important contributions (see Braidotti et al. 1994; Bretherton 1998, 2003; Agrawal 2005; MacGregor 2010). For example, discussing the preparatory processes leading up to the 1992 Rio Earth Summit, as well as the event itself, in *Women, the Environment and Sustainable Development* Rosi Braidotti and colleagues (1994) offered a robust critique of the ways in which femininity was essentialized to fulfil the strategic aims of the women's lobby seeking to influence proceedings and how this essentialized form of femininity was reproduced in the outcomes of 1992 Rio. This outcome is not surprising, because these discourses of femininity did not challenge or disrupt prevailing gender norms or the gender order.

Braidotti et al.'s book was in direct response to the 1992 Rio summit, offering a series of reflections. More broadly related to global environmental politics and governance, Charlotte Bretherton's (1998) article 'Global Environmental Politics: Putting Gender on the Agenda?' discusses international politics to argue that while the rhetoric of gender may be well rehearsed in relation to the environment, actually this inclusion of gender continues to treat women as an addendum. Moreover, she argues that women are constructed in problematic ways within global environmental governance (something I will discuss in more detail later). Since Bretherton's appeal to put 'gender on the agenda', subsequent feminist scholars who have analyzed global environmental politics (for example, see Agrawal 2005; MacGregor 2010; Foster 2011, 2014) have sought to integrate a 'gender analytic' into global environmental politics and governance, but this important project has yet to be given appropriate attention in the mainstream of the field.

Nonetheless, speaking to and extending the gender analytical scholarship, I want to provide a gender analysis of global environmental politics by focusing on the discourses produced at 1992 Rio and 2012 Rio+20. Central to this analysis is an understanding of gender constructions and international efforts toward sustainable development that is informed by the Foucauldian concept of governmentality, which I discuss in the following section.

## Gender and governmentality

Governmentality, a term coined by Michel Foucault during his lectures at Collège de France in 1978 and 1979, has been of interest to feminist and gender studies scholars in part because the concept relates to government beyond but including the state. In other words, for Foucault, government (or governing) is not something restricted to formal (and traditionally masculine) political institutions, but rather something that exceeds arena politics and occurs between, for example, peers, kin, colleagues, and over one's self (in the form of self-government or self-regulation). As such, for feminists influenced by the work of Foucault (such as Sandilands 1999, 2004, 2005), the concept works as a framework for understanding how one is governed and self-governs in relation to gendered expectations whereby particular ideals of masculinity and femininity are rendered as the standard to aspire to. Moreover, governmentality works to shed light on the ways in which gendered bodies are produced and regulated through the conduit of the broader governing-mentality. In this sense, governmentality refers to the particular political rationality, such as liberalism or neoliberalism for instance, which underpins governing across spatial domains (the state, the house, the self). To paraphrase Thomas Lemke (2001), governmentality as a concept seeks to address the question of why people behave in ways which perpetuate socio-political and economic norms in the absence of a disciplinary sovereign power. Therefore governmentality relates to 'the discursive field in which exercising power is "rationalised"' (Lemke 2001:191) and the processes of subjectification that create appropriate citizens to be governed and to self-govern within a particular rationality. This, I argue, is a gendered process.

More relevant to examining contemporary understandings of sustainable development and gender constructions is the scholarship on neoliberal governmentality (see, for example, Lemke 2001; Ferguson and Gupta 2002; Schinkel and Van Houdt 2008). Neoliberal governmentality, as a political rationality, operates through the façade of a reduced state in favour of the market, while simultaneously producing 'individuals [who] are mechanised, in congruence with market logic, to behave as rational and autonomous actors imbued with a capacity to weigh up the costs and benefits of their behaviour' (Foster et al. 2014:233). As I demonstrate in more detail later in the chapter, the centrality of market logics is crucial to the operation of neoliberal environmental governmentality and to the construction of gendered ecological subjects. As such, at this juncture it is important briefly to visit the literature on environmental governmentality and the gender(ing) of good green citizens or what I call 'eco-citizens'.

## Environmental governmentality and the construction of gendered eco-citizens

There has been a diverse body of scholarship applying the concept of governmentality, or rather the 'Foucauldian analytics of government' (for example, see Lövbrand et al. 2009; Methmann 2013), as a way to explore the governing rationalities behind different approaches to the environment. This work is collectively understood as the literature on environmental governmentality or 'environmentality' (Agrawal 2005), and its purpose is to investigate the governing rationalities that underpin environmental decision-making or environmental behaviours among individuals. With regard to the former, the main concern is with the discursive field in which decisions on the environment are made. The concept of neoliberal governmentality is often used to make sense of the ways in which environmental problems are framed to privilege market-based solutions. As such, the governmentality literature tends to focus on how the environment is shoehorned into neoliberal rationality by presenting nature as a series of goods and services, for instance by constructing biodiversity management (Fletcher 2010) or pollution and carbon (Methmann 2013) as quantifiable and therefore tradeable objects. This construction works to produce market-based solutions that ultimately maintain the dominant governing rationality underpinning both the construction of environmental problems and solutions, making for a self-perpetuating process which has more to do with economy than ecology (Hajer 1995). With regard to the latter, it is of key concern to many theorists of environmental governmentality (for example, see Darier ed. 1999; Sandilands 1999, 2004; Agrawal 2005) to understand how environmental subjects are produced and what it means to be an environmental subject or 'eco-citizen'. In other words, they ask how political rationalities underpinning the understanding of human-human/human-nature relations 'work through the establishment of particular codes of conduct, standards of responsible behaviour and the production of particular kinds of subjects' (Death 2011:4).

The way that particular governmental rationalities are rendered 'rational' and the construction of good eco-citizens is one that, as I have argued elsewhere (Foster 2011), works to organize – and is organized by – constructions of gender and sexual identity. In other words, the environmental governmentality informing and proliferated through discourses of sustainable development set the parameters of what it means to be a good eco-citizen. Or as Catriona Sandilands notes:

> In order to be a good environmental citizen, one must willingly organize one's life according to the contained dictates of environmental knowledge regimes, much of which signals little more than a slightly greener shade of capitalist accumulation.
>
> *(Sandilands 2003:19)*

For example, the construction of women as victims of environmental degradation (Bretherton 1998), alongside a notion that economic development helps individuals to adapt to environmental damage, works to perpetuate a governing rationality that suggests that women's economic empowerment offers a solution to environmental problems (Foster 2008). In this instance, a good eco-citizen is a woman 'empowered' through education and wage work who subsequently 'chooses' a smaller family (thereby reducing the pressures of population growth on the Earth's limited resources) and becomes more resilient to natural 'threats' (Sandilands 1999; see also Sasser in this volume). Even better would be for that woman to become economically empowered enough to make green consumer choices, 'voting' with her money to provide environmentally friendly goods for her 'modestly sized' family. The female eco-citizen here is rooted in the ideals of capitalism and hetero-patriarchy, with her role in the family as wife and mother remaining unchallenged (of which more in the next section). In other words, governmental rationalities underpinning environmental decision-making and subjectification are gendered as well as racialized and heterosexualized (Sandilands 1999, 2004, 2005).

Indeed, a consideration of both the political rationality that underpins the construction of environmental problems and solutions, and the subsequent instruction that shapes the subjects to (be) govern(ed) within this neoliberal environmental governmentality is of crucial importance in exploring the changes in sustainable development discourses between 1992 and 2012 – along with the gendered implications of subjectification that run parallel to said transformations. As such, informed by Foucault's work on governmentality, in the following sections I discuss the discourses of the 1992 Rio Earth Summit and 2012 Rio+20. The remainder of this chapter is based on my previous research (Foster 2011, 2014) identifying trends in the use of symbolically masculinized terms (such as technology, science, and economy) and symbolically feminized terms (e.g., risk, limitations, and vulnerability), alongside quantifying the frequency of terminology related to empirical gender categories (men, women, boy, girl) within key UN sustainable development documents.

## Rio Earth Summit 1992: empowering women to save 'Mother Earth'

Most sources agree that 1992 was the year when the international community adopted the concept of 'sustainable development' as a way to mitigate environmental problems while maintaining a steady level of economic development (Chichilnisky 1999). The term 'sustainable development' had been defined and discussed prior to 1992, most notably by the World Commission on Environment and Development (WCED) in their report *Our Common Future*. Here sustainable development was defined as 'development that meets the needs of the present without compromising the ability of future generations to meet their own needs' (1987:43), and it is this definition that was generally accepted at the Rio Summit. Moreover, the nascent emphasis within the 1992 construction of sustainable development was one that ostensibly recognized the importance of governance, and devolving power to citizens in making environmental decisions (Kapoor 2001). As such, this incarnation of sustainable development was concerned with, at least on the surface, ensuring the participation of hitherto excluded groups: youths, women, and indigenous communities. These communities were considered to be instrumental to pursuing environmental sustainability because they are constructed as living/being closer to the natural environment, and as such, they represent a 'cheap, effective way of ensuring that [sustainable development] policies are implemented' (Bretherton 2003:104). Within the main and most extensive accompanying document to the Rio Earth Summit, namely *Agenda 21* (1992), the importance of these communities in solving environmental problems is clearly stated (UNCED 1992: chapter 3).

*Agenda 21*'s sustainable development plan of action promotes advocacy for groups, not least women, who are often overlooked in elite male-dominated environmental decision-making. Amid its 351 pages of recommendations on how regions, states, and multilateral institutions could work toward a more sustainable future, there is a special chapter (titled 'Global Action for Women toward Sustainable and Equitable Development') dedicated to the role of women in relation to the environment and environmental management. This focus on governance and the inclusion of women (along with indigenous communities and youths) demonstrated that women were pivotal to the notion of good (and bad) eco-citizenship, that women (along with their other 'vulnerable' allies) were central to the process of environmental governmentality at this historical moment. The way women were constructed throughout *Agenda 21* rendered governmentality operational. As I have argued elsewhere (Foster 2008, 2011, 2014) 'constructions of gender are a crucial organising factor in the operation of environmental governmentality' (Foster 2011:137). Bretherton (1998) makes the related point that, in the discourses of *Agenda 21*, it is the construction of women as *victims* of environmental degradation, superior environmental *managers* and reproductive *mothers* that creates and sustains the conditions for this particular flavour of political rationality.[2]

Drawing on Bretherton's useful framework, it is important to note that *Agenda 21*'s special chapter on women focuses on how women are particularly affected by environmental degradation. For example, it is noted that

> Countries should take urgent measures to avert the ongoing rapid environmental and economic degradation in developing countries that generally affects the lives of women and children in rural areas.
>
> *(UNCED 1992: chapter 24)*

How environmental threats are constructed can be regarded as a technology of government. Within *Agenda 21*, for example, environmental threats are marked by the frequent emphasis on resource scarcity and limits, which particularly affect women and children. Here, the idea that women are particular victims of environmental and economic insecurity works to encourage support for environmental and economic action. Indeed, this technique has been noted in the field of feminist security studies where the representation of oppressed women, usually in non-Western countries, is used as a way to rally support for military intervention (see Shepherd 2006). With regard to sustainable development, representations of women threatened by environmental damage and poverty, work not only to rally military support, but also to legitimize economic intervention. In other words, representations of women (and children) as victims of environmental and economic problems work to promote particular policy solutions.

When considered critically, however, these solutions have more to do with economic development than environmental sustainability. The solution presented in *Agenda 21* is one whereby market intervention is constructed as the panacea to address women's disempowerment and, conveniently, environmental unsustainability (UNCED 1992: Chapter 24). The construction of positive-sum games within the 1992 rhetoric of sustainable development, whereby women's (largely economic) empowerment is intertwined with both economic growth and environmental sustainability, is demonstrative of neoliberal environmental governmentality. It is unsurprising that, within an environmentalism underpinned by the governing rationality of neoliberalism, the good eco-subject would be encouraged to be proficient in economics and market-based mechanisms, given that the 'key feature of the neoliberal rationality is the congruence it endeavours to achieve between a responsible and moral individual and an economic-rational actor' (Lemke 2001:201). What was perhaps more surprising in the 1992 discourse was that the concept of sustainable development represented was one whereby good eco-citizenship was tied to female and indigenous political empowerment. Women and indigenous groups were constructed as important decision makers in terms of environmentalism. There were a couple of reasons for this construction.

First, there was a wider concern for female empowerment at the international level, most notably marked by the UN Decade for Women (1976–1985). Again, this series of UN events tied women's empowerment to neoliberal Western models, prompting heavy criticism from authors such as postcolonial feminist Gayatri Spivak (1996). Indeed, Spivak problematized how, in an era typified by globalization, or rather neoliberal expansionism, the UN was correlating women's empowerment globally to Western ideals of economic autonomy. What we see with the documents supporting the Rio Earth Summit in 1992 is an extension of this ideal to promote environmental sustainability.

Second, the feminization of good eco-citizens was one that drew on discursive legacies derived from Cartesian thought that binarized and stratified the mind over the body, men over women, culture over nature, and so on (Plumwood 1993). Indeed, this point of critique remains a central 'feminist challenge to Western metaphysics, the foundation of which is the equivalence of the mind with the masculine and the privileging of the mind over the body – the devalued realm associated with the feminine' (Budgeon 2003:37). It is this logic that permeates the discourses of sustainable development in 1992. Women are constructed as closer to nature and the body – and separate from men, culture, and the mind – and therefore it follows that the environment is an obvious policy domain for women's decision-making 'abilities'. In 1992 solutions to environmental problems were seen as requiring a more 'naturally caring' individual who had a greater investment in saving the planet for future generations due to her investment in child-bearing and child-rearing. This assumption draws on essentialist and naturalized constructions of womanhood which equates femininity to motherhood and regards women as closer to nature – as 'earth mothers', if you like, who are most able to make good decisions about the environment (see MacGregor 2006 for an in depth critique).

A third construction of women presented in *Agenda 21* is the idea that women are problems for the environment, a construction that very much rests on women's roles in reproduction (Bretherton 1998). The argument is that in a world with limited resources (a theme consistently noted in 1992) population growth works to exacerbate environmental problems (more people means more pollution and fewer resources). The solution outlined in *Agenda 21*, and in subsequent summits focusing on population and development, is for women (especially those in the Global South) to manage their family size in line with Western (nuclear) family models. This proposition was and remains to be seen as good for the environment and, incidentally, recognized as good for economic development (as women can more readily engage in wage labour with fewer children) and women's empowerment. The subjectification of women as rational actors within this particular political rationality means that the notion of choice has to be presented as paramount, given that liberalism and neoliberalism rely on the notion that individuals are autonomous. However, through systems of marginalization and exclusion, the discourses of *Agenda 21* 'whisper a common articulatory thread: "You will enjoy your smaller family, you will enjoy your new found economic prosperity, you will enjoy the process of controlling your fertility"' (Sandilands 1999:83). As such, the choice to manage family size is already somewhat determined via systems of governmentality – creating the conditions for the 'correct' choice to be made (see also Sasser in this volume).

Overall, *Agenda 21* and the discourses surrounding the first Rio Earth Summit presented a central role for women in environmental management. Backdropped by the UN Decade for Women and amid growing concerns over the environment internationally, Rio 1992 proposed a series of policy recommendations that rendered the environment governable through the empowerment of women (based on Western neoliberal ideals of empowered femininity) and through economic growth. This focus on women worked to legitimize expansion of neoliberal governmental rationalities globally under the guise of environmentalism and women's rights.

## Rio+20: green economy boomers to the rescue

If the 1992 Rio Earth Summit was characterized by a zeitgeist of economic confidence, globalization, and women's empowerment, then the 2012 Rio+20 Summit was characterized by economic uncertainty and a betrayal of gender aims. Rio+20 and its accompanying document *The Future We Want* were met with, at best, a lukewarm response from the international community and environmental groups. This stands in contrast to their responses to the Rio Earth Summit and *Agenda 21*, despite Rio+20 being hailed as a success by UN Secretary General Ban Ki-moon. Indeed, the document was criticized by political commentators, international relations and environment scholars, and UN major groups, among others, for offering '283 paragraphs of fluff' (Bigg 2012), only reiterating 'promises made elsewhere' (Clémençon 2012), being limited in scope (Brand 2012) and, perhaps most notably in relation to my discussion of gender and sustainable development, a failure to both 'women and future generations' (UN Women's Major Group 2012).

Generally speaking, *The Future We Want* document restates, underscores, and recommits to many of the policy recommendations that were highlighted in *Agenda 21*. The main exception to this observation is the insertion of the concept of the 'green economy'. However, even though it appears that *The Future We Want* is largely consistent with *Agenda 21*, there has been a shift in emphasis within sustainable development discourses in relation to both gender and the balance between sustainability and development. This shift can be understood as an outcome of two different eras of neoliberal governmentality: the first is one where eco-citizens were constructed and instructed within the context of neoliberalism buoyed by rationalities successfully linked to expansion in the guise of globalization; the latter is underpinned by a neoliberal governmentality that has to forcefully, even violently, reassert itself within a context of a rationality where economic growth is necessary to the survival of populations, of individuals, and of neoliberalism itself. In other words, 1992 was marked by expansionism and 2012 was marked by survivalism provoked by the 2008 financial crash. Indeed, it is within the context of what some international political economy scholars (for example, Brenner et al. 2010; Fine 2009; Peck 2010) are calling a 'zombie' neoliberalism that a reconfigured form of sustainable development has emerged. To extend the zombie metaphor, neoliberalism – 'having nothing new to offer other than [a] parasitic extension of its principles to new applications' (Fine 2009:888) – has voraciously attached itself to sustainable development to a degree not witnessed before. I will return to this broader contextual argument at the end of the chapter; however, for now I will outline how normative constructions of gender and gendered domains of knowledge have transformed, alongside changes to the eco-citizen more broadly, within the 2012 discourses of sustainable development backdropped by zombie neoliberal governmentality.

In *The Future We Want* document (as in *Agenda 21*) there is considerable emphasis on how technologies and modernization offer solutions to environmental problems. Both documents demonstrate a commitment to forms of eco-modernization, where eco-modernization relates to 'a technology-based and innovation-oriented approach to environmental policy' (Jänicke 2008:557). However, one of the most notable differences between the two documents relates not to the technical and market-based solutions presented to ameliorate environmental problems, but rather that the 2012 document places much less emphasis on environmental limits, dangers, and the need for precautions. In fact, words like 'limits', as related to future ways to act to mitigate environmental degradation, are completely absent in *The Future We Want*. Rather, 'limits' are only discussed in relation to the capacity to deal with waste and the notion that the Sustainable Development Goals, which are the successors to the Millennium Development Goals, should be limited in number (UNSD 2012:39, 43).

Similarly, resource depletion is not discussed at all in *The Future We Want*, and precaution is only mentioned under the heading of 'Seas and Oceans'. This is in stark contrast to *Agenda 21*, which discussed 'limits' and 'depletion' frequently. Moreover, 'precaution', most often framed within the *Agenda 21* document as 'precautionary and anticipatory approaches', is also mentioned more frequently and across a range of 'environmental topics' beyond 'Seas and Oceans'. As such, it could be said that while *Agenda 21* presented a mixture of 'boomer and doomer' narratives, where 'boomer' links to capacities for solving environmental issues and 'doomer' links to limits to environmental goods and services (see Booth 1991), *The Future We Want* only presents a boomer narrative. *Agenda 21* proposed that, alongside eco-modernization, humans (individuals, businesses, governments) needed to act in response to resource limits/depletion through a variety of governance strategies by limiting human impact and employing the precautionary principle. However, *The Future We Want* primarily 'highlighted the central role of technological cooperation for the achievement of sustainable development' (UN Division for Sustainable Development 2014) and largely omitted the 'doomer' narrative.

As such, the maintenance of the eco-modernization rhetoric, left unchecked and unbalanced, has resulted in an almost cornucopian discourse, whereby technology, modernization, and economic changes become the key drivers toward sustainable development. What is more, these drivers are presented as inevitable given the economic situation post-2008. This has led some authors, notably the ecofeminist theorist Ariel Salleh, to argue in relation to Rio+20 that '[t]he UN, together with the transnational capitalist class, looks to technology and new institutional architectures to push against the limits of living ecologies, and these measures are given legitimation as "economic necessity"' (2012:141; see also Littig in this volume). Here an emphasis on economic and technological development supersedes the environmental security narratives of limits and depletion, marking a change of tone to environmental governmentality whereby human bodies, particularly those bodies culturally intelligible as women, are dislocated from roles as subjects of environmental policy and 'literally become objects of technocratic management efforts' (Sandilands 2004:20). In the 2012 sustainable development narratives, limits (to behaviour) and precaution are rendered unnecessary in relation to environmental problems. A good eco-citizen, then, is no longer someone who modifies their behaviour in line with resource scarcity as was the case, at least in part, in 1992; instead a good eco-citizen is a good consumer (Sandilands 1993), pumping money into the economy to revive it while conveniently, and simultaneously, saving the environment. This altered process of subjectification has been a gendered one. In other words, a move from the eco-citizen instructed to appreciate limits alongside economic empowerment to the eco-citizen as consumer buying into eco-technological innovations links to a number of gendered consequences and implications detailed as follows.

Women's special relationship with nature as outlined in *Agenda 21*, a feature of the document that has admittedly been much criticized by feminist scholars (myself included), has been largely overlooked in *The Future We Want*. In fact, decision-making citizens become secondary within a document that invests a great deal of promise in technology and economy, in scientists and consumers. In *Agenda 21* women's supposed special relationship with the natural world, albeit problematic due to its essentialist and universalizing undertones (Braidotti 1994), demonstrated a particularly feminized version of eco-citizenship. However, the more pronounced move toward technology and economy in 2012 places sustainable development within symbolically masculinized domains (relating to science and wage labour) as opposed to the symbolically feminine domain of the 'natural world'. The movement from doomer/boomer, whereby broadly speaking doomer is linked with a form of risk aversion and pessimism traditionally associated with femininity, to boomer alone, has led to women's relegation within sustainable development governance. This has been replaced by a more masculinized technologically and economically oriented boomer version of sustainable development.

This shift in emphasis from feminized nature-knowers to masculine technology-shapers is well illustrated in the film used to open the Rio+20 Conference, entitled *Welcome to the Anthropocene* (2012, http://vimeo.com/39048998). The concept of the Anthropocene relates to a planet transformed (note not degraded or exploited) by humanity – a humanity that is represented as unified and whose environmental responsibilities are not differentiated in relation to the privileges associated with gender, class, geographical location, and ethnicity (among other intersections; see chapter by Di Chiro in this handbook). In this video the eerie female cyborg voice states that 'We have shaped our past, we shape our present and we can shape our future' and that 'we must find a safe operating space for humanity'. There is no discussion of limiting production or reproduction; instead adapting to environmental challenges through human innovation and ingenuity is the key emphasis in the opening script. Examining the now-widely used discourse of the Anthropocene, Eileen Crist notes:

> The Anthropocene discourse veers away from environmentalism's dark idiom of destruction, depredation, rape, loss, devastation, deterioration and so forth of the natural world into the tame vocabulary that humans are changing, shaping, transforming, or altering the biosphere, and, in the process, creating novel ecosystems and anthropogenic biomes.
>
> *(Crist 2013:133)*

A gendered lens demonstrates how constructions of life giving yet vulnerable Mother Earth implicitly, and sometimes explicitly, present in the 1992 Earth Summit, have been replaced by a feminine but disembodied female voice hailing for adaptation and techno-fixes to environmental problems in line with the new emphasis on the Anthropocene.

The symbolic construction of the Earth as feminine (most commonly as a mother) informed environmental debates pre-Rio (for example, Lovelock's Gaia Hypothesis) as well as post-1992. Moreover, this feminized personification worked to complement the 'Earth from space' epiphany, where it was argued that seeing the Earth from space in the first space missions of the 1960s produced a common realization within the public imaginary that the Earth was fragile and, potentially, in need of saving (see Hajer 1995). This idea filtered into the original 1987 Brundtland report on sustainable development:

> In the middle of the twentieth century, we saw our planet from space for the first time . . . From space we see a small fragile ball dominated not by human activity and edifice but by a pattern of clouds, oceans, greenery and soils.
>
> *(WCED 1987:1)*

Unsurprisingly, this vision of the fragile and feminized Earth filtered into the 1992 Rio negotiations and textual outputs. The Earth was constructed as an entity that needed to be protected and cared for. On the other hand, although displaying a visual image of the Earth from Space (fully alight with human activity), the *Welcome to the Anthropocene* video does not highlight an Earth that needs protecting, but rather an Earth that needs to be modified to accommodate human life. Indeed, drawing on Foucault's work on governmentality and panopticism, Eva Lövbrand et al. (2009) discuss differing rationalities that underpin environmental politics through the construction of the Anthropocene as a governable entity. The presentation of the Anthropocene in this instance would be one considered 'management first' within Lövbrand et al.'s typology, whereby 'such a "global gaze" may become a totalizing perspective that omits human agency and privileges the vantage point of a technical elite. It is only the view from space that the illusion of planetary management becomes possible' (2009:11–12). Whereas the Rio Earth Summit discussed limits (to resources and human activity in response), the female sci-fi voiceover in *Welcome to the Anthropocene* anticipates the use of technology to correct the shortcomings of 'Mother Earth' – because she cannot provide for human needs and the growing population. As such, sustainable development rhetoric moves from a discourse of motherly protection to a discourse of technological modification.

So the planet remains feminized in the contemporary sustainable development discourse, but: is there a discussion of gender in *The Future We Want*? Interestingly, relative to *Agenda 21*, where men understood as empirical bodies were largely absent, the word 'men' makes many appearances in *The Future We Want*. Arguably, the focus placed on men in *The Future We Want* is consistent with the Rio+20 'boomer' emphasis on the traditional masculine domains of economics and technoscience. In other words, as Rio+20 has shifted toward finding environmental solutions within the historically masculine fields of science and economics, references to men and men's roles have simultaneously increased. In addition, in *The Future We Want*, the word 'women' is more often than not post-fixed with the word empowerment, indicative that 'women's' participation in (green) markets and (green) jobs is desirable. In other words, empowerment in this context relates primarily to economic empowerment (as noted previously). This focus on women's empowerment is consistent between the 1992 and 2012 documents and is an aspect of neoliberal governmentality whereby 'the empowerment and equality outlined, when analyzed, in fact works to create and uphold the self-regulation appropriate for capitalism' (Foster 2008:551; also see Bretherton 1998; Sandilands 1999).

As well as being post-fixed by the word 'empowerment', women are also mentioned alongside men in relation to health, education, employment, and technology. This signposts an aspiration toward rendering women and men economically viable within a neoliberal system. What is missing from *The Future We Want*, as opposed to *Agenda 21*, is the idea that women's privileged episteme in relation to environmental matters makes them crucial to decision-making within a framework of sustainable development. In *The Future We Want* the masculinized domains of technology and economy become key to achieving sustainable development. As such, environmental problems that were to some extent considered political problems in 1992 have been constructed, almost entirely, as economic concerns in 2012. Within this shift, women's position in ameliorating environmental issues is no longer presented within governance networks, and instead it is the traditionally masculine wage labourer and technological innovator who can help to adapt the environment to provide for humankind through eco-modernization strategies.

## Conclusion

Good environmental citizenship, since the sustainable development rhetoric of 1992, has been continually constructed through the wider discursive field of neoliberalism. This neoliberal mentality/rationality has in different ways worked to promote gendered processes of subjectification. However, the 2008 financial crisis changed the character of neoliberalism, from an expansionist project to a survivalist one. Arguably, this in turn has changed the way in which environmental problems and solutions are constructed and gendered citizens and narratives are rendered operational. Post 2008, in the 2012 Rio+20 Summit and its accompanying document, *The Future We Want*, global environmental politics is marked by a more aggressive assertion of the primacy of markets. As such, the good eco-citizen is one who equates to an ethical consumer. The sustainable development of 2012, unlike that of 1992, does not undermine the consumer by presenting a variety of resource limits – after all, the economic 'recovery' is very much based on the consumer fuelling the markets through spending (Gough 2010). Therefore a good eco-citizen in this instance should rely on the market, buying in to 'ethical' goods and relying on technocrats and the techno-fixes they produce. Moreover, this move toward a more technocentric model of sustainable development, from one that at least paid lip service to governance, is saturated with gendered symbols and inscriptions. A move away from the ecological governance (albeit superficial governance in the first place), limits, and citizen engagement and toward technocentrism, cornucopianism, and expert professionals is in itself inherently gendered. The former marks a more feminized arena, whereas the latter marks a more masculine model for good environmental citizenship.

## Notes

1 The 1992 Rio Earth Summit is also known as the United Nations Conference on Environment and Development or UNCED. The Rio+20 Conference held in 2012 marked the twentieth anniversary of the Rio Earth Summit and is also known as the United Nations Conference on Sustainable Development or UNCSD.
2 It is perhaps surprising to note that few gender scholars, perhaps with the exception of R.W. Connell (2014), have considered how masculine subjectivities have been constructed in UN (sustainable) development discourses. This may, to a certain extent, be because gender is often read as a synonym for women, rendering men invisible except when positioned in relation to women as 'relatively less vulnerable and more culpable' (MacGregor 2010:228).

## References

Agrawal, A. (2005) *Environmentality: Technologies of Government and the Making of Subjects.* Durham, NC: Duke University Press.

Bigg, T. (2012) 'Five things we've learnt from Rio+ 20', *Governance.* Online. Available at: www.iied.org/five-things-we-ve-learnt-rio20 (accessed 22 April 2015).

Booth, W. (1991) 'With twice as many people on earth, planet could expect boom – Or doom', *Washington Post.* Online. Available at: https://news.google.com/newspapers?nid=1957&dat=19910119&id=UmxGAAAAIBAJ&sjid=7ugMAAAAIBAJ&pg=1494,4315853&hl=en (accessed 22 April 2015).

Braidotti, R., Chatkiewicz, E., Hausler, S. and Wieringa, S. (1994) *Women, the Environment and Sustainable Development: Towards a Theoretical Synthesis.* London: Zed Books.

Brand, U. (2012) 'Green economy–the next oxymoron? No lessons learned from failures of implementing sustainable development', *GAIA-Ecological Perspectives for Science and Society* 21(1): 28–32.

Brenner, N., Peck, J. and Theodore, N. (2010) 'After neoliberalization?', *Globalizations* 7(3): 327–345.

Bretherton, C. (1998) 'Global environmental politics: Putting gender on the agenda?', *Review of International Studies* 24(1): 85–100.

Bretherton, C. (2003) 'Movements, networks, hierarchies: A gender perspective on global environmental governance', *Global Environmental Politics* 3(2): 103–119.

Budgeon, S. (2003) 'Identity as an embodied event', *Body and Society* 9(1): 35–55.

Chichilnisky, G. (1999) 'What is sustainable development?', *Man-Made Climate Change* 1: 42–82.

Clémençon, R. (2012) 'Welcome to the Anthropocene: Rio+ 20 and the meaning of sustainable development', *The Journal of Environment and Development* 21(3): 311–338.

Connell, R. W. (2014) 'Change among the gatekeepers: Men, masculinities, and gender equality in the global arena', *Signs* 40(1): 1801–1805.

Crist, E. (2013) 'On the poverty of nomenclature', *Environmental Humanities* 3: 129–147.

Darier, E. (ed) (1999) *Discourses of the Environment.* Oxford: Blackwell.

Death, C. (2011) 'Summit theatre: Exemplary governmentality and environmental diplomacy in Johannesburg and Copenhagen', *Environmental Politics* 20(1): 1–19.

Ferguson, J. and Gupta, A. (2002) 'Spatializing states: Toward an ethnography of neoliberal governmentality', *American Ethnologist* 29(4): 981–1002.

Fine, B. (2009) 'Development as zombieconomics in the age of neoliberalism', *Third World Quarterly* 30(5): 885–904.

Fletcher, R. (2010) 'Neoliberal environmentality: Towards a poststructuralist political ecology of the conservation debate', *Conservation and Society* 8(3): 171.

Foster, E. A. (2008) 'Sustainable development policy in Britain: Shaping conduct through global governmentality', *British Politics* 3(4): 535–555.

Foster, E. A. (2011) 'Sustainable development: Problematising normative constructions of gender within global environmental governmentality', *Globalizations* 8(2): 135–149.

Foster, E. A. (2014) 'International sustainable development policy: (Re) producing sexual norms through eco-discipline', *Gender, Place and Culture* 21(8): 1029–1044.

Foster, E. A., Kerr, P. and Byrne, C. (2014) 'Rolling back to roll forward: Depoliticisation and the extension of government', *Policy and Politics* 42(2): 225–241.

Foucault, M., Burchell, G., Gordon, C. and Miller, P. (eds) (1991) *The Foucault Effect: Studies in Governmentality.* Chicago: University of Chicago Press.

Gough, I. (2010) 'Economic crisis, climate change and the future of welfare states', *21st Century Society* 5(1): 51–64.

Hajer, M. A. (1995) *The Politics of Environmental Discourse: Ecological Modernisation and the Policy Process.* Oxford: Oxford University Press.

Jänicke, M. (2008) 'Ecological modernisation: New perspectives', *Journal of Cleaner Production* 16(5): 557–565.

Kapoor, I. (2001) 'Towards participatory environmental management?', *Journal of Environmental Management* 63(3): 269–279.

Lemke, T. (2001) '"The birth of bio-politics": Michel Foucault's lecture at the Collège de France on neoliberal governmentality', *Economy and Society* 30(2): 190–207.

Lövbrand, E., Stripple, J. and Wiman, B. (2009) 'Earth system governmentality: Reflections on science in the Anthropocene', *Global Environmental Change* 19(1): 7–13.

MacGregor, S. (2006) *Beyond Mothering Earth: Ecological Citizenship and the Politics of Care.* Vancouver: University of British Columbia Press.

MacGregor, S. (2010) '"Gender and climate change": From impacts to discourses', *Journal of the Indian Ocean Region* 6(2): 223–238.

Methmann, C. P. (2013) 'The sky is the limit: Global warming as global governmentality', *European Journal of International Relations* (October 27): 1–23.

Peck, J. (2010) 'Zombie neoliberalism and the ambidextrous state', *Theoretical Criminology* 14(1): 104–110.

Peterson, V. S. (2005) 'How (the meaning of) gender matters in political economy', *New Political Economy* 10(4): 499–521.

Plumwood, V. (1993) *Feminism and the Mastery of Nature.* London: Routledge.

Salleh, A. (2012) '"Green economy or green utopia?" Rio+20 and the reproductive labour class', *American Sociological Association* 18(2): 141–145c.

Sandilands, C. (1993) 'On "green" consumerism: Environmental privatization and "family values"', *Canadian Woman Studies* 13(3): 45–47.

Sandilands, C. (1999) 'Sex at the limits', in Darier, E. (ed) *Discourses of the Environment.* Oxford: Blackwell, 79–94.

Sandilands, C. (2003) 'Eco-Homo: Queering the ecological body politic', *Social Philosophy Today* 19: 17–39.

Sandilands, C. (2004) 'Eco-Homo: Queering the ecological body politic', *Social Philosophy Today* 19: 17–39.

Sandilands, C. (2005) 'Unnatural passions? Notes toward a queer ecology', *Invisible Culture* 9. Online. Available at: www.rochester.edu/in_visible_culture/Issue_9/sandilands.html (accessed 22 April 2015).

Schinkel, W. and Van Houdt, F. (2010) 'The double helix of cultural assimilationism and neo-liberalism: Citizenship in contemporary governmentality', *The British Journal of Sociology* 61(4): 696–715.

Shepherd, L. J. (2006) 'Veiled references: Constructions of gender in the Bush administration discourse on the attacks on Afghanistan post-9/11', *International Feminist Journal of Politics* 8(1): 19–41.

Spivak, G. C. (1996) '"Woman" as theatre–United Nations conference on women', *Beijing 1995-Commentary, Radical Philosophy* 75: 2–4.

UN Division for Sustainable Development (2012) *The Future We Want.* Online. Available at: http://sustainabledevelopment.un.org/futurewewant.html (accessed 17 August 2014).

UN Division for Sustainable Development (2014) *Sustainable Development Knowledge Platform.* Online. Available at: http://sustainabledevelopment.un.org/index.html (accessed 30 August 2014).

United Nations Commission in Environment and Development (UNCED) (1992) *Agenda 21.* Online. Available at: sustainabledevelopment.un.org/content/documents/Agenda21.pdf (accessed 15 August 2014).

UN Women's Major Group (2012) *Final Statement on Rio+20.* Online. Available at: www.uncsd2012.org/index.php?page=view&nr=1307&type=230&menu=38 (accessed 17 August 2014).

Welcome to the Anthropocene (2012) Online. Available at: http://vimeo.com/39048998 (accessed 30 August 2014).

World Commission on Environment and Development (WCED) (1987) *Our Common Future.* Oxford: Oxford University Press.

# 15

# FEMINISM AND BIOPOLITICS

## A cyborg account

*Catriona Sandilands*

## Introduction

Both within and outside environmental thought, most thinkers working with the influential concept of *biopolitics* – the intensifying organization of power, in modernity, through bodies and corporeal relations – have done so without attention to gender: the genealogy of the concept largely proceeds without the *many* feminist thinkers who have engaged in broadly biopolitical thinking since at least the 1980s, under the rubrics, for example, of ecological feminism (or ecofeminism) and feminist science studies. Perhaps more surprisingly, several recent writings under the umbrella of 'new' *feminist* materialisms also disavow this older feminist work in their claims that 1990s feminist theory actively and only turned *away* from nature and biology.

I begin this chapter, then, with a consideration of the nature of feminist absence in biopolitical and new feminist materialist discourses: in the rush to embrace certain trajectories of thought (often those associated with Continental philosophy and thinkers such as Foucault, Agamben, Derrida, Deleuze, and Latour), feminist traditions addressing very similar questions of power, knowledge, bodies, and ecologies are systematically overlooked. As a very partial corrective to these intellectual lacunae, I will then consider the centrality of Donna Haraway's 1985 'Cyborg Manifesto' to the development of biopolitical and materialist thinking: at the same time as the figure of the cyborg revolutionized understanding of the human political subject in the context of increasingly disruptive bio- and techno-politics, it also attended centrally to gender, race, and class as key vectors. Although not without problems, the 'Cyborg Manifesto' is thus a strong reminder that feminism is at the historical centre of biopolitical theorizing, and vice versa.

## Biopolitics, feminism, and 'new' materialism

Timothy Campbell and Adam Sitze begin their edited collection *Biopolitics: A Reader* with the observation that the concept of biopolitics does not have a singular origin:

> no defining interval offers itself as the lens able to superimpose the past and the future, allowing us to look back and say 'ah, yes, it was precisely then that biopolitics was born,

exactly then that politics gave way to biopolitics, and life to *bios*, *zoē*, and the forms of life that characterize our present'.

(Campbell and Sitze 2013:1)

And then they name one:

the reactivation of an account of life and politics offered some thirty years ago by a French philosopher named Michel Foucault [whose] first analysis of 'biopolitics' appeared in a short piece . . . titled ominously 'Right of Death and Power over Life', which forms the final part of his 1976 book *La Volonté de Savoir*.

(Campbell and Sitze 2013:3)

This essay was first published in English as part of *The History of Sexuality, Volume 1*. There is no question that Foucault's understanding of biopolitics has been extraordinarily influential in contemporary thought about the ways in which matters of life are, increasingly, subjects of political concern: despite disagreements about the historical divide he proffers between ancient and modern, it's fairly safe to agree with his statement that

a society's 'threshold of modernity' has been reached when the life of the species is wagered on its own political strategies. For millennia, man remained what he was for Aristotle: a living animal with the additional capacity for a political existence; modern man is an animal whose politics places his existence as a living being in question.

(Foucault 1978:143)

Despite the influence of his formulation, however, Foucault was hardly the first or only thinker to consider the ways in which life is, in modernity especially, increasingly, invasively, and terrifyingly the subject of politics, a fact that Campbell and Sitze tacitly acknowledge in their inclusion of selections from Hannah Arendt's The *Origins of Totalitarianism* (1951) and *The Human Condition* (1958) in the collection. Although there are other arguments to be had about the particular contents of this collection, the one that most concerns me is the jump that the editors then make between *La Volonté de Savoir* (*The History of Sexuality* without the specifically queer parts) and the 1998 English translation of Giorgio Agamben's *Homo Sacer: Sovereign Power and Bare Life*, which they credit with *reactivating* 'Foucault's long-dormant text . . . in its current form' (Campbell and Sitze 2013:4, my emphasis). They then jump to Michael Hardt and Antonio Negri's *Empire* (2000): with these texts, they argue, 'the concept of "Biopolitics" *began* to migrate from philosophy to not-so-distant shores, including but not limited to the fields of anthropology, geography, sociology, political science, theology, legal studies, bioethics, digital media, art history, and architecture' (4, my emphasis).

Really? There were no thinkers responding to Foucault between 1978 and the late 1990s? There were no works concerning 'the entry of life into politics' that might be worthy of inclusion in the history of a concept as ultimately influential as *biopolitics*? There was no talk about the fact that Foucault's biopolitics made it into English in the context of a book about *sexuality*? And there we approach the heart of the matter: even editors of a collection so intensely focused on Euro-white-male theorists as this one are forced to admit that

certainly, feminist readings of Foucault's biopolitics, especially Donna Haraway's 1989 essay on postmodern bodies [included in the anthology], played an early and important role in pushing forward biopolitics as a central category in post-modernity [and that]

Étienne Balibar, Paul Gilroy, Agnes Heller, and Anne Laura Stoler [not included in the anthology] . . . singled out the term in the 1990s as a decisive horizon for studies in the politics of race.

*(Campbell and Sitze 2013:4)*

But these crucial texts are read as peripheral rather than core: other than the one essay by Haraway (in addition to Mbembe's 'Necropolitics'), the anthology proceeds to assemble an understanding of biopolitics with no particular grounding in relations of gender, race, or sexuality.

Why am I so infuriated by this editorial genealogy (it's just one collection)? Because it is *ubiquitous*: feminist, anti-racist, queer, disability, and other specifically located formulations of life, bodies, and politics are systematically left out of most standard intellectual histories. As if feminist, anti-racist, queer, disability, and other formulations of life, politics, bodies, and history are particular afterthoughts to the 'real' work of conceptualization. As if there weren't heated discussions about biopolitics from well before the 1990s to the present moment about the ways in which bodies and lives are *specifically* rendered objects and subjects of politics. As if *any* understanding of biopolitics can proceed without particular bodies, lives, institutional and neoliberal incorporations, and micro/macropolitical relationships at the centre of discussion (one of Foucault's major insights, no?).

Campbell and Sitze are not alone in their marginalization of these particularities, of course. A 2015 essay by Claire Colebrook (who has elsewhere [2014] claimed kinship with ecofeminist thought even if she has not much relied on it) on 'What Is It Like to Be a Human?' (a fundamental question of biopolitics, according to Agamben) also unapologetically bypasses feminist thought to focus on Heidegger: 'while there are, of course, other major twentieth-century works on animality (Donna Haraway's *Companion Species* [2003] among them), I focus here on the peculiarly post-Heideggerian dimension of Agamben, Derrida, and Deleuze' (Colebrook 2015:227). Very smart essays by Susan Fraiman (2012) and Greta Gaard (2011) have analyzed the overwhelming trend to privilege the male and the Continental over the feminist and the grassroots in discussions of animality, life, and bio/eco-politics: in both the fixation of critical animal studies on Derridean thought over feminist animal rights praxis, and in the theoretical rejection/forgetting of ecofeminism by ecocritics and others in favour of perspectives more clearly grounded in poststructuralism (and not even the feminist ones), there has been a distinct tendency to privilege the thought of white, male, universalizing philosophers at the expense of thinkers who are more willing to locate their work in particular gendered, racialized, corporeal, biopolitical, and otherwise socially situated relationships. As if that weren't enough, Ewa Płonowska Ziarek's essay 'Bare Life on Strike' points out the considerable flaws of any version of biopolitical thinking that does not take into consideration crucial questions of race, class, sex, and gender:

bare life cannot be regarded in complete isolation from all cultural and political characteristics. If bare life emerges as the remnant of a destroyed form of life, then, according to Agamben's own emphasis on its inclusive exclusion in the political, its formulation has to refer, in a negative way, to the racial, sexual, ethnic, and class differences that [are] used to characterize its form of life.

*(Ziarek 2008:103)*

At the same time as we take note of the considerable tendency to marginalize feminism in histories of biopolitics, we should also consider that Sarah Ahmed (2008) and others have remarked on the more surprising tendency of so-called new materialist feminist thought to disavow the history of biopolitics in feminism. Several texts published in this field (e.g., Stacy Alaimo and Susan Hekman's 2009 *Material Feminisms* and Diana Coole and Samantha Frost's 2010 *New Materialisms*) have been premised on the idea that feminism, in its extensive 1990s and early millennial engagements with poststructuralist theory, has forgotten, ignored, or turned away from questions of matter, biology, and nature. The feminist focus on 'social constructivism', in this argument, has led to a repudiation of the material body, a failure to engage with the earthly and fleshy world in and of itself, and even a hostile 'antibiologism' in which a 'routinized antiessentialism' (often blamed on Judith Butler) dictates that 'the body . . . is pursued in its socially, experientially, or psychically constituted forms, but rarely in its physiologically, biochemically, or microbiologically constituted form, the idea of biological construction having been rendered either unintelligible or naïve' (Wilson 1998:14–15). While with Ahmed I find much that is excellent in these so-called new materialist feminist explorations (indeed, I have a chapter in Alaimo and Hekman's collection), I also share Ahmed's concern with the gesture of 'newness' that underscores the founding rhetoric of this position, in which feminists are called to a *discovery* of the body, of matter, of science, and of the natural world as if we had somehow forgotten they mattered (or even existed) while we were busily focusing on questions of discourse, power, and intersectionality. As Ahmed writes, 'this gesture has itself been taken for granted, and . . . in turn . . . both offers a false and reductive history of feminist engagement with biology, science and materialism, and shapes the contours of a field' around a very specific set of claims, traditions, and theoretical/political engagements (2008:21).

Here, Gaard (2011) would point to the persistence of ecofeminist thought during this period. Indeed, one can note that some new materialist feminists (e.g., Elizabeth Grosz) simultaneously decry the feminist renunciation of the body ('we have forgotten where we come from', [2004:2]) and then proceed to deploy the works of French feminists such as Luce Irigaray and Hélène Cixous, who have been actively *and continuously* exploring the intersections of matter, body, and language since the 1970s. (It is no accident that the term 'ecofeminism' was coined by French feminist Françoise d'Eaubonne in 1974.)[1]

Ahmed also raises the important history of feminist science studies scholarship, both historically and (again, quite continuously) into the present – Linda Birke, Sandra Harding, Evelyn Fox Keller, Emily Martin, and of course Haraway – a tradition that cannot be accused of forgetting the mattering of bodies and natures. Singling out Grosz's failure to engage in any significant way with this tradition, Ahmed remarks pointedly that 'you can only argue for a return to biology by forgetting the feminist work on the biological, including the work of feminists trained in the biological sciences. In other words, you can only claim that feminism has forgotten the biological if you forget this feminist work' (2008:27). It is crucial to point out: in all of these traditions of feminist biological/ecological engagement, there is a clear distinction drawn between an *interest in biological/corporeal processes* and an acquiescence to *biological determinism*. For most ecofeminists, French feminists, and feminist scholars of science, that distinction is very much the point of engaging with bodies and environments in a feminist mode in the first place. They seek to sort through the ways in which corporeal and ecological processes are organized in and through intersecting power relations, especially but not only sex and gender, and made to do certain kinds of political work in different historical and cultural contexts; they also seek to sort through the ways in which these power relations are precisely organized and manifest in and through tangible bodies and material relationships (what Butler meant by 'materialization', and also echoing ongoing materialist feminist traditions practicing in a more socialist mode; see, for example, Hennessey [1993], neither of which I am able to discuss here). In other words, the question of *biopolitics* lies at the centre of feminist histories of corporeal and ecological engagement: the 'entry of life into politics' means looking at the dynamic interplay between bio/eco-logical bodies and the multiple and intersecting power relations in which they are always already located (and vice versa).

When I first planned this essay, I thought I would go on from my infuriation to write a brief feminist history of biopolitics in order to restore gender to its proper place in the history of the concept, and in order to remember publicly a distinct tradition of biopolitical thinking within feminism against the bifurcation of so-called social constructivism from corporeal and material concerns. Because this history turns out to be so very rich (ironic, no?) – as explored, for example, by the works by Ahmed, Fraiman, Gaard, and Ziarek mentioned previously – I will, instead, turn to the travels of one especially influential feminist biopolitical text in order to suggest that *feminism has neither been far from biopolitics nor biopolitics from feminism*, really, ever. Although what follows does not aspire toward totality, it nevertheless illustrates the fact that, for research in the field of gender and environment, feminist and other thinkers don't need to go too far afield in order to find a rich and nuanced biopolitical trajectory to take to questions of bodies, ecologies, and gender/intersectional politics: for all of the lacunae of the field, at least since the mid-1980s, we have had a pretty good story at our disposal with which to begin.

## 'Cyborg Manifesto': a feminist biopolitics

Although it was not an unreasonable choice for Campbell and Sitze to include Haraway's 1989 essay 'The Biopolitics of Postmodern Bodies: Constitutions of Self in Immune System Discourses' in a genealogical anthology of writings about the concept of biopolitics, the work that really catapulted Haraway's biopolitical thinking as such into a feminist (and wider) imaginary was her earlier essay, 'A Manifesto for Cyborgs: Science, Technology, and Socialist Feminism in the 1980s', published originally in *Socialist Review* in 1985 in response to a call to Left thinkers to consider the future of socialist and feminist politics in the Reagan era.

The 'Cyborg Manifesto' (hereafter CM), multiply republished and reinterpreted, has had many lives since then. It was, in a revised version, an anchor essay in Haraway's landmark collection *Simians, Cyborgs, and Women* (1991). It was widely taken up – and hotly debated – in feminist circles in the late 1980s and throughout the 1990s for its challenges to eco- and other feminist politics (see, for example, commentaries by Christina Crosby, Mary Ann Doane, and Joan W. Scott in Weed 1989; also Alaimo 1994; Sturgeon 1997; Cuomo 1998). It has been a lightning rod for very diverse conversations about gender, bodies, power, labour, identity/affinity, politics, science, technology, and nature well into the millennial conversations about the complex intersections of nature and culture ('naturecultures') that eventually became the 'new materialism' (see Merrick and Grebowicz 2013 and the chapter by Merrick in this handbook for a fuller assessment of Haraway's influence). And it appears again, in 2016, in *Manifestly Haraway*: 'Haraway's "Cyborg Manifesto"', says the University of Minnesota Press blurb, 'is even more relevant today, when the divisions that she so eloquently challenges – of human and machine but also of gender, class, race, ethnicity, sexuality, and location – are increasingly complex' (2016:n.p.). As commentators such as Carla Lam have noted, CM can thus be considered a watershed between a 'modern' feminist trajectory emphasizing 'women as agential self-directed subjects of feminist politics' and a 'postmodern' one focused on 'querying women's subjectivity as constitutive of power' (2015:103), challenging the coherence of the idea of 'women's experience' and asking tough questions about the ways in which bodies – including animal, human, and cybernetic ones (the boundaries between them being far from clear) – are both physically and sociopolitically organized through new technologies and relations of domination, an '"integrated circuit" . . . unhindered by boundaries and specifically the dualisms of Western enlightenment narratives' (104).

In arguing that 'Haraway's work on cyborgs not only influenced a whole body of writing in the 1990s but still provides the cornerstone of *any theoretical work into the posthuman today*' (2013:109, my emphasis), Heather Latimer also squarely acknowledges the centrality of CM to the conceptualization of biopolitics, even as Haraway herself dismisses the term itself as inadequate (for the record, she also rejects the term posthuman). In one of my favourite scholarly zingers ever, Haraway writes in CM that 'Michel Foucault's biopolitics is a *flaccid premonition* of cyborg politics' (1991:150, my emphasis). Working with but moving beyond his understandings of the biopolitical relations of discipline and subjectivation, Haraway's cyborg politics rests on the understanding that, 'by the late twentieth century, our time, a mythic time, we are all chimeras, theorized and fabricated hybrids of machine and organism' (1991:150), in which the deep corporeality of our politics is very much an 'open field' as a result of technological interventions that not only act upon/organize our animality but also call into question the very nature of our individual bodies and species being. For Haraway, then, we are not merely 'animal[s] whose politics places [our] existence as . . . living being[s] in question', but also living beings whose existence as (only) animals is entirely questionable, especially at the current techno-historical conjuncture. Our bodies – and the countless other bodies that are interpenetrated with ours – are sites of control and contestation in the midst of an 'informatics of domination' in which power relations of gender, race, and class are multiple, microscopic, networked, invasive, totalizing, and inscribed and experienced through bodies that are neither integral nor autonomous. Moreover – and here's the watershed point – a socialist feminist politics that aims to engage, challenge, and interrupt these relations must not do so through recourse to narratives of nature, unity, unalienated labour, innocence, or purity. Instead, it is the cyborg (famously, not 'the goddess') that 'is our ontology and gives us our politics'; we need to abandon a search for authenticity in favour of '*pleasure* in the confusion of boundaries and . . . *responsibility* in their construction' (1991:150, my emphases), the cyborg being both a product of technocapitalist modernity and a sensuously potent figure, both metaphor and lived reality, with which to understand and resist the biological, economic, political, and cultural relations of a world in which the line around the concept of human is thoroughly breached.

Here I would like to highlight two ways in which CM should be understood as a key text in the genealogy of biopolitical thought. First, as Latimer notes, the initial section of CM 'describing what the cyborg "is", is the one most often taken up by other theorists' (2013:111). In this section, Haraway outlines the ways in which the primary biopolitical subject of Western modernity, the 'human', is both ontologically and historically/politically questionable; from her perspective, 'three crucial boundary breakdowns' (1991:152) demand a rethinking of biopolitical agency on top of the questioning of the 'human' that has always been the task of feminist thought (Colebrook 2014). In the first, as a result of extensive research across the sciences, 'the boundary between human and animal is thoroughly breached . . . language, tool use, social behavior, mental events, nothing really convincingly settles the separation of human and animal' (Haraway 1991:151–152): although the line between human and nonhuman animal has always been questionable (which Haraway acknowledges), it is especially tenuous now as a result of burgeoning research that demonstrates how animals (and, I will add, also plants) display the kinds of intelligence, for example, that were once considered the sole purview of *homo sapiens*. In the second, as a result of cybernetic, genetic, and other technologies, the line between organism and *machine* is 'thoroughly ambiguous [, and] the line between natural and artificial, mind and body, self-developing and externally designed' (Haraway 1991:152) is entirely confused: even for organisms that are not obviously fused with cybernetic technologies in the manner of *Blade*

*Runner*, the line between life and 'artificial' life is increasingly complex, including everything from pacemakers and wearable monitors to genetically modified organisms. In the third, 'the boundary between physical and non-physical is very imprecise for us', in which 'the silicon chip is a surface for writing; it is etched in molecular scales disturbed only by atomic noise, the ultimate interference for nuclear scores' (153). Here, Haraway emphasizes the fact that techno-biological politics are as much about invisible modes of communication as they are about tangible machinic interventions: miniaturization has irrevocably shattered any boundary that may have been thought to exist between mind and body. Emphasizing the historical conditions of technocapitalist corporeality, the power of the cyborg figure inheres in both its dramatic capture of a techno- and bio-political regime that includes 'the final imposition of a grid of control on the planet' and in its radical call to *embrace* these conditions of our corporeal implication in this regime, to imagine 'lived social and bodily realities in which people are not afraid of their joint kinship with animals and machines, not afraid of permanently partial identities and contradictory standpoints' (154).

Second, as a text committed to the reanimation of a specifically socialist feminism, CM rightfully places questions of gender, race, and class at the heart of its biopolitical understanding. Although there are also many ways in which CM has been taken up by feminist thinkers to theorize the biopolitical stakes of new reproductive technologies and relations (e.g., Lam 2015), the key focus of CM is on the ways in which the 'homework economy', enabled and organized by cyborgian technologies and boundary-breaches, not only reorganizes labour relations but also produces 'new sexualities and ethnicities' – and new bodies and intimacies – along the way. It is, for Haraway, not simply that women in the Global South

> are the preferred labour force for the science-based multinationals in the export-processing sectors, particularly in electronics. The picture is more systematic and involved reproduction, sexuality, culture, consumption, and production. . . . Many women's lives have been structured around employment in electronics-dependent jobs, and their intimate realities include serial heterosexual monogamy, negotiating childcare, distance from extended kin or most other forms of traditional community, a high likelihood of loneliness and extreme economic vulnerability as they age.
>
> *(Haraway 1991:166)*

Here, CM clearly emphasizes that one cannot understand the dynamics of biopolitics without attending to the particular social inequalities that are both harnessed and reorganized in new, globalizing capitalist technologies and relations of production. The feminization of labour is attached, in the context of the decline of the welfare state (where one had existed) and the reorganization of labour and property (under what we would now call neoliberalism), to the feminization of poverty and the rearticulation of family life; the concomitant and increasingly globalized technologized organization of family life – for example, through the consumption of video games (smart phones had not yet been invented) – likewise produces 'high-tech, gendered imaginations . . . that can contemplate destruction of the planet and a sci-fi escape from its consequences' (168). The reorganization of the cyborg body is also not gender neutral: 'the close ties of sexuality and instrumentality, of views of the body as a kind of private satisfaction- and utility-generating machine, are described nicely in sociobiological origin stories that stress a genetic calculus and explain the inevitable dialectic of domination of male and female gender roles' (169). In short, the 'massive intensification of insecurity and cultural impoverishment' (172) that is the informatics of domination cannot be adequately understood *without attending to gender, race, and class* and, at the same time, these intersecting relations cannot be understood *without attending to the biological, technological, corporeal, and species politics* that are integral to global capitalism. This combined insight, I think, makes CM a truly revolutionary text in the history biopolitical thought.

## Conclusion

The Cyborg Manifesto is not without flaws. Disability scholars have rightly taken issue with Haraway's very passing comment that 'perhaps paraplegics and other severely handicapped people can (and sometimes do) have the most intense experiences of complex hybridization with other communication devices' (1991:178). Here, her deployment of the cyborg as metaphor – and of the person with a disability as exemplary cyborg – does not sufficiently attend to the diverse and concrete experiences of people with disabilities that involve, for example, some form of complex experience of corporeal hybridity: 'the wheelchair user, the person with a cochlear implant, artificial leg or pacemaker, someone who uses an assistance dog' (Reeve 2012:94). To raise the figure of the disabled-cyborg, here, without attending precisely to the relations in which people with disabilities are marginalized, impoverished, and physically/socially (re)organized according to late capitalist normative corporeal logics, shows a lack of specific thought about the ways in which notions of individual bodily *productivity* are very much at the heart of the biopolitics of neoliberal capitalism.

In a similar vein, anti-racist feminist scholars have criticized Haraway's understanding that organizing by 'women of colour' represents a cyborg politics *par excellence,* centred on the fact that the political category 'women of colour' is always already an oppositional-hybrid fiction that collects a diverse coalition of racialized and gendered biopolitical experiences. Critics note, for example, that the 'incorporation by analogy' of racialized women's experiences into cyborg biopolitics, and especially Haraway's argument that the term 'women of colour' is less a reflection of particular racialized experience than it is a performative utopian hybrid collectivity, 'denies primacy to the voices of the colonized that have proclaimed the preeminence of . . . racial difference' (Schueller 2005:65). Again, the metaphorical power of the cyborg as universalizing figure falls apart in the midst of experiences that, perhaps ironically, demonstrate precisely the micropolitically specifying powers of the biopolitical conjuncture that Haraway sought to theorize in CM toward a politics of affinity rather than identity. As Schueller concludes, Haraway's analogy of woman of colour as cyborg eventually 'functions like a colonial fetish enabling the white feminist theorist to displace racial difference onto a safer notion of similarity . . . . Racial analogy within (white) feminist theory helps whiteness retain its privilege by being uninterrogated' (2005:82).

These criticisms are inescapably important: to what extent does Haraway's socialist feminist cyborg end up practically *erasing* exactly the specifying power relations it purports to highlight in theory? Is there a fatal tension between the universalizing desires of cyborgian ontology and the lived particularities of women of colour, people with disabilities, and LGBTQ (lesbian, gay, bisexual, transgender, and queer) folks who might also want to say something about corporeality, identity, and technology (see Felski 2006)?

Jasbir Puar suggests that, perhaps, Haraway does not go far enough in her understanding of boundary-rupture, and puts forward an understanding of *intersectionality as assemblage* in order to better get at the complex interpenetrations of bodies, identities, and representations that comprise late capitalist 'control' societies: here, assemblages – complex, moving collections of things and relations –

> are interesting because they de-privilege the human body as a discrete organic thing.
> As Haraway notes, the body does not end at the skin. We leave traces of our DNA

everywhere we go, we live with other bodies within us, microbes and bacteria, we are enmeshed in forces, affects, energies, we are composites of information. Assemblages do not privilege bodies as human, nor as residing within a human animal/nonhuman animal binary.

*(Puar 2012:57)*

In this posthuman framework of assemblage, 'categories – race, gender, sexuality – are considered events, actions, and encounters between bodies, rather than simply entities and attributes of subjects' (58).

Despite its weaknesses, however, there is no question of the importance of CM to histories of biopolitical scholarship, and there is also no question of Haraway's lasting impact on current work such as Puar's that attempts, like CM, to theorize the very complicated operations of bodies (including nonhuman ones), technologies, identities, and politics. Non-feminist genealogies would do well to remember both the key role of cyborgs, and the creative impact of their 'exceedingly unfaithful' relationships to their theoretical origins: 'their fathers, after all, are inessential' (Haraway 1991:151).

## Note

1 There is not space in this essay to rehearse the complex history of ecofeminism. There are many solid accounts available; of course, there are also *different* versions depending on the many lively differences among ecofeminists. See, for example, my *The Good Natured Feminist: Ecofeminism and Democracy* (1999), and Sherilyn MacGregor's *Beyond Mothering Earth: Ecological Citizenship and the Politics of Care* (2006): both texts are careful to demonstrate the polyvocality of ecofeminism in opposition to those critics that dismiss the movement as inherently and irrevocably essentialist. See also Sturgeon (1997), Gaard (2011), and chapters in this handbook by Thompson and MacGregor and Gaard.

## References

Agamben, G. (1998) *Homo Sacer: Sovereign Power and Bare Life*. Stanford, CA: Stanford University Press.

Ahmed, S. (2008) 'Imaginary prohibitions: Some preliminary remarks on the founding gestures of the "New Materialism"', *European Journal of Women's Studies* 15(1): 23–39.

Alaimo, S. (1994) 'Cyborg and ecofeminist interventions: Challenges for an environmental feminism', *Feminist Studies* 20(1): 133–152.

Alaimo, S. and Hekman, S. (eds) (2009) *Material Feminisms*. Bloomington: Indiana University Press.

Arendt, H. (1951) *The Origins of Totalitarianism*. New York: Houghton Mifflin.

Arendt, H. (1958) *The Human Condition*. Chicago: University of Chicago Press.

Campbell, T. and Sitze, A. (eds) (2013) *Biopolitics: A Reader*. Durham, NC: Duke University Press.

Colebrook, C. (2014) *Sex After Life: Essays on Extinction, Volume 2*. Ann Arbor, MI: University of Michigan, Open Humanities Press.

Colebrook, C. (2015) 'What is it like to be a human?', *TSQ: Transgender Studies Quarterly* 2(2): 227–243.

Coole, D. and Frost, S. (eds) (2010) *New Materialisms: Ontology, Agency, and Politics*. Durham, NC: Duke University Press.

Cuomo, C. J. (1998) *Feminism and Ecological Communities: An Ethic of Flourishing*. London: Routledge.

Felski, R. (2006) 'Fin de Siècle, Fin du Sexe: Transsexuality, postmodernism, and the death of history', in Stryker, S. and Whittle, S. (eds) *The Transgender Studies Reader*. New York: Routledge, 565–573.

Foucault, M. (1978) *The History of Sexuality, Volume I: The Will to Knowledge*. New York: Pantheon.

Fraiman, S. (2012) 'Pussy panic versus liking animals: Tracking gender in animal studies', *Critical Inquiry* 39: 89–115.

Gaard, G. (2011) 'Ecofeminism revisited: Rejecting essentialism and re-placing species in a material feminist environmentalism', *Feminist Formations* 23(2): 26–53.

Grosz, E. (2004) *The Nick of Time: Politics, Evolution and the Untimely*. Durham, NC: Duke University Press.

Haraway, D. (1991) 'A cyborg manifesto: Science, technology, and socialist feminism in the late twentieth century', in Haraway, D. (ed) *Simians, Cyborgs, and Women: The Reinvention of Nature.* New York: Routledge, 149–181.

Haraway, D. (2003) *The Companion Species Manifesto: Dogs, People, and Significant Otherness.* Chicago: Prickly Paradigm Press.

Haraway, D. (2016) *Manifestly Haraway.* Minneapolis: University of Minnesota Press.

Hardt, M. and Negri, A. (2000) *Empire.* Cambridge, MA: Harvard University Press.

Hennessy, R. (1993) *Materialist Feminism and the Politics of Discourse.* New York: Routledge.

Lam, C. (2015) *New Reproductive Technologies and Disembodiment: Feminist and Material Resolutions.* London: Ashgate Publishing.

Latimer, H. (2013) *Reproductive Acts: Sexual Politics in North American Fiction and Film.* Montreal: McGill-Queen's University Press.

MacGregor, S. (2006) *Beyond Mothering Earth: Ecological Citizenship and the Politics of Care.* Vancouver: University of British Columbia Press.

Merrick, H. and Grebowicz, M. (2013) *Beyond the Cyborg: Adventures With Donna Haraway.* New York: Columbia University Press.

Puar, J. (2012) 'I would rather be a cyborg than a goddess: Becoming-intersectional in assemblage theory', *PhiloSOPHIA* 2(1): 49–66.

Reeve, D. (2012) 'Cyborgs, cripples, and iCrip: Reflections on the contribution of Haraway to disability studies', in Goodley, D., Hughes, B. and Davis, L. J. (eds) *Disability and Social Theory: New Developments and Directions.* London: Palgrave, 91–111.

Sandilands, C. (1999) *The Good-Natured Feminist: Ecofeminism and Democracy.* Minneapolis: University of Minnesota Press.

Schueller, M. J. (2005) 'Analogy and (white) feminist theory: Thinking race and the color of the cyborg body', *Signs: Journal of Women in Culture and Society* 30(1): 63–92.

Sturgeon, N. (1997) *Ecofeminist Natures: Race, Gender, Feminist Theory, and Political Action.* New York: Routledge.

Weed, E. (ed) (1989) *Coming to Terms: Feminism, Theory, Politics.* London: Routledge.

Wilson, E. (1998) *Neural Geographies: Feminism and the Microstructure of Cognition.* New York: Routledge.

Ziarek, E. P. (2008) 'Bare life on strike: Notes on the biopolitics of race and gender', *South Atlantic Quarterly* 107(1): 89–105.

# 16

# EXPLORING INDUSTRIAL, ECOMODERN, AND ECOLOGICAL MASCULINITIES

*Martin Hultman*

## Introduction

Gender analysis in the field of environmental studies has become increasingly important in recent years, even though some 'strange silences' remain (MacGregor 2009). It has opened up new and different perspectives and has demonstrated the need for, among other things, interdisciplinary research on intersectionality (Kaijser and Kronsel 2014), transcorporeality (Alaimo 2010), and 'naturecultures' (Haraway 2008). Feminist political ecology and ecofeminism have become prominent approaches to understanding a range of different phenomena, from the feminization of nature to women's environmental activism. Of less interest within environmental studies have been the roles and experiences of men-*qua*-men and how different forms of masculinities influence environmental problems. This gap is a curious one, because men have dominated all aspects of environmental research, policy, and politics for much longer than there has been a field called environmental studies.

This chapter introduces, and endeavours to situate historically, the study of masculinities in environmental politics. I discuss three concepts – 'industrial masculinities', 'ecomodern masculinities', and 'ecological masculinities' – and illustrate them by drawing on findings from empirical research that I have developed at length elsewhere (Hultman 2013, 2014b, 2015; Anshelm and Hultman 2014a; Hultman and Pulé forthcoming). Examples from the discourse of climate change scepticism in the United States and Sweden, from mainstream American politics, and from sustainable transitions in New Zealand provide insights into how different forms of masculinities are performed against the backdrop of political, social, and environmental change. This empirical research enables me to theorize how three distinct discourses have been co-constructed with figurations (or types) of masculinities that have developed within environmental politics. Exploring these different figurations and their discursive construction opens up space for further research on how masculinities shape and are shaped by environmental politics.

## Masculinities in environmental scholarship

The absence of research on men and masculinities in the environmental humanities and social sciences should be viewed in the context of the development of gender and environment scholarship more broadly. Feminist scholarship on gender has tended to avoid environment and nature

(Alaimo 2000), leaving this focus to a smaller and often marginalized body of work by ecological feminists. Since the 1980s ecofeminism has been concerned to understand how humans (most often women) and the natural world are affected by capitalism, science, industrialization, and colonialism, and to identify the roots of exploitation and domination (Plumwood 1993). Another linked tradition, feminist political ecology has had a similar focus on the connections between social and ecological injustice, with special attention to development processes in the Global South (e.g., Rocheleau et al. 1996; Nightingale 2006; Arora-Jonsson 2013). Added to these approaches, the field of feminist science studies has made important analyses of the gender-technoscience-environment nexus (e.g., Haraway 1988; Braidotti 2002).

Ecofeminism deserves to be recognized for pioneering the analysis of masculinities and environment and for making entanglements of masculinity, power, and environmental destruction visible. In her classic book *The Death of Nature: Women, Ecology, and the Scientific Revolution*, environmental historian Carolyn Merchant (1980) tells a story of how a once lively natural world came to be regarded as dead matter and how once productive, active women became passive pieces of property (see Thompson and MacGregor in this handbook). The driving force behind these changes from ancient to modern times, she explains, are men – as philosophers, theologians, and scientists. Merchant provides ample evidence of nature-destructive masculinities. Men such as Francis Bacon (father of the scientific method), Rene Descartes (father of the mind-body dualism), and Robert Boyle (father of modern chemistry) are discussed in detail, with examples of their writings to illustrate the deep connections they made between inert nature and subhuman women, all to their own great advantage.

Looking at the rise of modern science in Western Europe, Merchant (1980) identifies a kind of masculinity that accuses others of religious fervour at the same time that it uses Christian faith as a basis for its embrace of a modern industrial society. She also documents a shift from organic metaphors of nature, dominant up until the sixteenth century in Europe, to mechanical metaphors: eventually nature was regarded as dead but possible to make use of – as if a machine – when proposing a human-made Eden on Earth in the shape of Nuclear Society (Anshelm 2010). This shift coincided with the rise of a new capitalist class who viewed nature as a resource to be extracted, for example, in the mining and timber industries. The paramount example of the early masculine scientific project discussed in Merchant's book is Francis Bacon's utopian novel published in 1627, *The New Atlantis*, in which a small group of male scientists with the aid of mechanical skills 'extract secrets' from a feminized, dead nature in order to transform them into commodities. Central to Enlightenment thought, Merchant shows, was a separation of man/woman and culture/nature that lead to the domination of men/culture over women/nature. This separation played a pivotal role in pushing European society toward industrialization, mechanization, and capitalism.

Given the importance of Merchant's book, it is curious that her focus on men and masculinities has been almost lost in ecofeminist scholarship since then (Gaard 2014). Ecofeminism tends to focus on women's experiences and, in recent years, to theorize femininities and feminization in ways that are sensitive to differences and intersections and careful to avoid 'essentialism'. To the extent that they appear in ecofeminist writing, elite men tend to be portrayed as 'the bad guys' (i.e., the people with too much power), but without much sustained analysis of why they come to think and act as they do (Connell and Pearse 2014). This lacunae is problematic, not only because of the powerful impact that men as individuals, and men's ideas and enterprises, have had on humanity and the rest of nature, but also because of the urgent need to change existing power relations.

An interdisciplinary field called masculinity studies (also known as men's studies and men and masculinities), has been evolving since the early 1980s, mostly as part of gender studies programmes in universities in Anglo-European/American countries. This body of scholarship has traditionally had a focus on issues such as class, sexualities, violence, crime, education, family, popular media, militarism, and gender justice (Kimmel et al. 2004; Connell and Pearse 2014). Sociologist R.W./Raewyn Connell, who can be considered the leading figure within the field of masculinities research lead the important theoretical change, in the 1990s, from hegemonic masculinity to hegemonic masculinities in order to make the argument about multiplicity, diversity, and plurality. Connell's (1995) work established that masculinities are not the same thing as men; they are patterns of practice that people engage in, practices which place them within a gender order and in a set of gender relations. Certain patterns of masculine practice are associated with norms and privilege, marking them out as dominant or hegemonic. The concept of hegemonic masculinity has played a central, even though sometimes contested role, in men and masculinities studies for more than thirty years (Barrett 1996; Bird 1996; Connell and Messerschmidt 2005; Connell and Wood 2005).

It is interesting to note that one of the first publications ever to use the concept of 'hegemonic masculinity' was an article by Connell (1990) titled 'A Whole New World: Remaking Masculinity in the Context of the Environmental Movement' published in the journal *Gender and Society*. Based on life-history interviews with six men involved in the Australian environmental and counter-cultural movements, the paper explores the extent to which engaging with feminism has an impact on men's practices of and attitudes toward masculinity. The men interviewed in Connell's study explained how a structural change away from an industrial society toward an ecologically sound one needed to go hand in hand with a change in masculinities. The overall findings of the paper are, first, that trying to be counter-sexist and to reconstruct masculinity in response to encounters with feminism can be an extremely fraught, stressful process for men and, second, that progressive gender politics should be built on 'the solidarities – always partial but nevertheless real – that exist between particular men and particular women as kin or as workers or as targets of racial oppression' (Connell 1990:477). The 'ultimate goal' should be 'a recomposition' (Connell 1987:289–291) rather than 'an obliteration of the social elements of gender' (Connell 1990:477). Connell also seems to suggest that there is a need to raise the level of understanding of feminist political issues and principles among men in the environmental movement; the men interviewed had very little knowledge of 'the nature and problems of feminism as a political movement' (465).

Even if there are relatively solid academic foundations for connecting research on gender, feminism, and environmentalism, few scholars have been interested in continuing the theoretical and empirical analyses of the masculinities-environment nexus that Merchant and Connell started more than three decades ago. A review of the academic literature looking beyond the texts that are explicitly interested in issues of masculinities and environmental politics suggests that there are only very small amounts of relevant research in six humanities and social science disciplines: environmental history, rural sociology, occupational studies, environmental sociology, eco-philosophy, and ecocriticism. The following is a brief sketch of the kinds of topics covered in this work.

In environmental history there has been discussion of men and nature as early as in the late 1970s, with research on the mythologies behind the 'Green Man' motif found carved in wood or stone, thought to symbolize the cycle of rebirth in ancient cultures (Basford 1978). Environmental historians more recently have given much attention to issues such as hunting and masculinities (e.g., Loo 2001; Sramek 2006) as well as men's involvement in the environmental movement of the 1960s (Melosi 1987; Rome 2003; Hazlett 2004). Within rural sociology, there are studies focusing on activities such as hunting, fishing and farming (e.g., Brandth 1995; Saugeres 2002) as well as studies of changing masculine identities in relation to economic change (e.g., Brandth and Haugen 2000). Studies of rural life appear to be a relatively strong field for discussions of the intersection of masculinities and various understandings of nature or the environment (e.g., Bell 2000; Campbell and Mayerfield Bell 2000; Ní Laoire 2001). Similar types of research can be found in occupational studies, especially those studies with a focus on extractive industries within sectors such as mining. This field has some similarities with rural sociology since the spaces researched are often rural, but the focus is more on the internal dynamics of workplaces and occupations. One issue that has been the focus of recent research in occupational studies is the masculine workforce within the energy sector (e.g., shale gas extraction; see Filteau 2014).

The broad field of environmental sociology has made some notable contributions to the study of masculinities and environment. Here we find quantitative, comparative, and cross-national research into the attitudes and practices of men and women. For example, studies have found that because they earn more and consume more, men tend to have a larger ecological footprint than women (e.g., Hanson 2010). They also report lower levels of concern for environmental issues and are less involved than women in pro-environmental actions (e.g., Mohai 1992; Grasswick 2014). While white men occupy the leadership positions of the majority of environmental organizations, women outnumber them in rank and file membership (Buckingham and Kulcur 2009; Stoddardt and Tindall 2011; Taylor 2014). There is also a fair amount of science and technology research revealing men's higher level of belief in the potential of new and better end-of-pipe technologies to solve environmental problems (e.g., Alaimo 2010; Hultman 2013). Recent research by environmental sociologists has been able to connect global environmental issues with masculinities by establishing a link between right-wing, elite male attitudes and climate change scepticism (McCright and Dunlap 2011; Anshelm and Hultman 2014b) and between gender mainstreaming (i.e., a policy approach that seek to reduce male domination by improving women's status) and national environmental policies (Norgaard and York 2005).

Within the more theory-based fields of environmental philosophy and eco-literary criticism (or ecocriticism), there have been relatively few publications that interrogate the intersections of masculinities and environment (Gaard 2014). Environmental philosophy arguably has been gender blind, dominated for most of its evolution by male philosophers writing about male philosophers who have not considered the relevance of masculine identities or experiences. One new contribution is made by Paul Pulé (2013), who develops what he calls 'ecological masculinism'. Offering an analysis of the place of masculinity in eco-political thought (deep ecology, ecofeminism, and social ecology), he argues that the masculine 'ethics of daring' should be replaced by an 'ethics of caring' for self, society, and environment with associated values of trust, compassion, reciprocity, and cooperation. A notable text in the field of ecocriticism is Mark Allister's (2004) interdisciplinary anthology *Eco-man: New Perspectives on Masculinities and Nature*. This edited collection of essays brings together the normally disconnected fields of ecocriticism and men's studies to interrogate the social construction of nature in relation to masculinities. More specifically it attempts to develop an 'ecomasculine lens' through which to view different cultural forms and norms of masculine practice. It also explores the potential of 'construct[ing] a manhood around ecological principles and practice' (Allister 2004:7).

What is obvious from this brief literature review is that although there has been research about men and nature, most studies (perhaps with the exception of those in environmental sociology) focus on a specific case study or at the micro-level, with few trying to understand contemporary masculinities in relation to broader environmental-political trends. Even fewer include normative content about how critical analysis of men and masculinities might contribute to changing gender relations or reducing the negative impacts of male domination on cultures or the biophysical world. Connell (2005) discusses how 'ecological masculinities' is a concept that could offer resistance to traditional, industrial forms of masculinities, if only scholars were committed to understanding it better. Similar ideas are put forward by ecofeminist scholar Greta Gaard (2014) who argues that neither ecocriticism, nor men's studies, nor queer ecologies, nor (to date) ecofeminism has offered a theoretically sophisticated foray into the potentials for understanding the entanglements of natures and masculinities. The potential for change is there, but so far remains largely underexplored and untapped.

## Understanding the men-environment nexus: three types of masculinities

In this section, I draw on more than a decade of my own empirical research to explain three types of masculinities that I have developed as a contribution to the environmental humanities and social sciences (Hultman 2016).

### *Industrial masculinities*

The first type or concept – 'industrial masculinities' – comes out of an extensive study of debates over global climate change that was published in the book *Discourses of Global Climate Change*, co-authored with Jonas Anshelm (2014a). The research involved analyzing a set of approximately 3,500 letters to the editor and signed contributions found in the database Artikelsök using keywords (e.g., climate change). This study brought to life the concept of industrial masculinities. I use this term to mark the central role elite masculinity has played in shaping human-nature relations in industrialized societies. The term has been used in previous research to describe how changes in masculinities from an industrial to a post-industrial society influence educational possibilities (e.g., Nayak 2003). Connell (1990) argues that the men who dominated and ran industrial modernization performed a hegemonic form of masculinity. With its roots in modern science and Enlightenment reason (described so vividly by Merchant [1980]), and later in engineering and neoclassical economics, industrial masculinities embrace the superiority of 'Man' and values nature only as a resource for human extraction.

Until the mid-1960s, there was a strong belief that industrial modernity, with its centralized management and engineering capabilities, would clean up its own environmental mess. When a number of environmental problems (such as chemical and air pollution and resource scarcity) were highlighted in the 1960s, the dominant political parties and most environmental groups agreed that it was possible to resolve these problems with the help of industrial modern technological solutions (McNeill 2003). There was almost complete faith that economic growth and a rationalization of production could fulfil both energy and environmental policy requirements. Industrial modernization was simultaneously presented as a cause of environmental problems and as a tool for overcoming them (Anshelm 2010).

It was this hegemonic form of industrial masculinities that men and women in the environmental movements of the 1970s and 1980s attempted to challenge as they tried to create another world (Connell 1990). Their challenge did not change the system, however: a new form of environmental politics called 'ecological modernization' (discussed later) emerged to enable the continuation of industrial modernity but with a green veneer. Throughout the decades since the rise of the environmental movement, carbon dioxide emissions from the burning of fossil fuels have continued to grow. When industrial modernization once again was challenged in the wake of the now dominant agenda on climate change, industrial masculinities re-appeared on the environmental political scene in the form of climate scepticism (Anshelm and Hultman 2014a).

## *Male climate sceptics*

Scepticism about the existence and causes of climate change exists in many parts of the industrialized world. It has been found to be strongest in the United States and the United Kingdom, but there is evidence of its hold in other countries as well, such as Sweden and Australia (Dunlap 2013; Capstick and Pidgeon 2014; Capstick et al. 2015; Tranter and Booth 2015). It is well recognized that in order to maintain an illusion of intense controversy, industries, special interest groups, and public relations firms have manipulated climate science in a similar way as tobacco companies have exploited the US media (Oreskes and Conway 2010).

Climate scepticism is not a social movement; it is a project of a few influential men. These men have successful careers in academia and/or private industry, strong beliefs in a market society, and a great mistrust of government regulation. A few voices return again and again with virtually the same dystopian predictions (Anshelm and Hultman 2014b). Even though it is readily apparent that the vast majority of climate sceptics are men, there is a dearth of academic research on this phenomenon. Sociologists Aaron McCright and Riley Dunlap (2011) are two of a very small number of academics who have analyzed the relationship between hegemonic masculinities and climate change scepticism in the United States. They have used Gallup polling data to demonstrate a correlation between self-reported understanding of global warming and climate change denial among conservative white men. They find that white conservative (or right-wing, Republican Party–political) men are more likely than any other group to be sceptical of climate change. Drawing on a body of social psychological literature on risk perception, they call this the 'white male effect' (McCright and Dunlap 2011). Climate change denial can be understood as a form of 'identity protective cognition', meaning that the envisioned change needed to deal with an extractivist mind-set and practises making up the dominance by the countries of Global North, are at odds with the industrial masculinities enacted by these men.

For the purposes of developing an understanding of industrial masculinities, climate scepticism can be theorized as consistent with the Enlightenment worldview that sees nature as dead, Rational Man as the rightful dominator, and engineering as the method of creating wealth for humanity. The sceptics' arguments are strengthened by references to ostensibly authoritative titles found in a variety of academic disciplines and thereby demonstrate a general belief in positivistic industrial modern science. In relation to climate science, however, these sceptics adopt a constructivist position. They dismiss climate-science as a mix of science and politics so entwined that they can no longer be distinguished. This claim can be supported with evidence from climate scepticism in Sweden.

Swedish climate sceptics have connections to associations where representatives of business, science, and technology meet. One clear example is Per-Olof Eriksson, a former board member of Volvo and former president of Sandvik, who wrote an article in the leading Swedish business paper *Dagens Industri* declaring his doubts that carbon emissions affect the climate. He said the Earth's average temperature has risen due to natural variations. Eriksson (2008) added that many in the business world and academia share his opinion but dare not admit it publicly for fear of reprisals. Another example is Ingemar Nordin, professor of philosophy of science, who has argued that the Intergovernmental Panel on Climate Change's (IPCC) selection and review of scientific evidence are consistent with what politicians wanted. Nordin (2008) claims that politics shapes scientific research on the climate and only scientists who produce politically acceptable truths are awarded funding. Economics professors Marian Radetzki and Nils Lundgren (2009) further claim that the IPCC deliberately construct their models 'in an alarmist direction' using feedback mechanisms that give the impression that significant climate change is taking place.

Fifteen Swedish professors, all men, have publically proclaimed themselves to be climate sceptics (Einarsson et al. 2008).

The sceptics describe themselves as marginalized and oppressed dissidents who are forced to speak up against a faith-like belief in climate science. They appeal to citizens' mistrust of the state and the establishment in a populist, and at the same time patriarchal, manner. Terms such as 'elite' or 'the fancy people' create an image that climate change proponents are an exclusive group out of touch with ordinary people's everyday lives. In this way, climate sceptics – quite paradoxically since they are themselves part of the elites – have tried to shape a conflict between citizens and decision makers and between concrete, short-term, and individual everyday problems and long-term, abstract, and global issues. This is a common strategy in heavily contested political areas (Boykoff and Boykoff 2004). It is paradoxical because these men themselves hold prominent positions and have been part of the dominant class. In their arguments, climate sceptics defend the scientific rationality, instrumentality, economic growth, and domination over nature that have been hegemonic throughout the modern era (Merchant 1980). For climate sceptics, industrial progress is intrinsically connected to rationality and positivistic scientific values, and this leads them to see climate science and pro-environmental policies as threats. Rather conveniently, they believe that the world's problems can only be solved through continuing modernization and economic growth – processes that elite white men have embraced and benefitted from their whole lives.

## Ecomodern masculinities

The second type of masculinities that plays a role in shaping environmental politics is what I call 'ecomodern masculinities', which I see as a continuation of industrial masculinities but with the addition of a green tinge. The ambition of letting go of destructive behaviour is there, as well as the knowledge regarding environmental issues, but it is not fully adopted in a transformative way. This type emerges out of my empirical research on energy politics between 1978 and 2005, which was grounded in extensive reading of over 2,000 journal articles, archive studies, and interviews (Hult-man 2010). In addition, the 'ecomodern masculinities' configuration is underpinned by the analysis of an archive study published as the book *Den inställda omställningen* (Hultman 2015).

Ecomodern discourse emerged out of the intense clash between an industrial modern, pro-growth agenda on one hand and environmental movement discourses criticizing economic growth as a measure of prosperity on the other. The apparent resolution of this conflict was found in the concept of ecological modernization, an 'ecomodern' discourse that now dominates international policies on energy and sustainable development. Ecological modernization blends two seemingly contradictory agendas by claiming economic growth as the basis for a post-carbon energy transition and development toward a sustainable future (Mol 2001).

This ecomodern discourse brought major changes to environmental and energy policies in the early 1990s. The descriptions of environmental problems changed from being threats to civilization – which demanded radical system-wide changes – to being characterized as mostly under control and soon to be solved (Hajer 1995). Economic growth was placed squarely at the centre of the environmental debate, and it was now claimed that there was no conflict between economic growth and environmental problems. In fact, it was declared that environmental problems actually fostered growth, innovation, and competitiveness (Lundqvist 2000). Conservative politicians and industry actors pushed this discourse to pave the way for market solutions and a belief that unfettered competition would create 'green jobs'. The electricity grid was privatized in many countries, and research money was increasingly directed to private-public collaborations. Environmental organizations participated in this shift by running several campaigns favouring eco-friendly consumption patterns without questioning the total volume of the products consumed. These changes meant that the focus shifted away from small-scale 'alternative' technologies with potential for more democratic control toward $CO_2$ emission reduction technologies and that leading polluters created collaborative organizations with environmental groups (Anshelm and Hansson 2011).

As I have argued elsewhere (Hultman 2013), ecological modernization brought about a shift from industrial modern masculinities to ecomodern masculinities in which toughness and determination are mixed with appropriate amounts of compassion and care. Ecomodern masculinities demonstrate a keen recognition of environmental problems, not least climate change, while at the same time supporting policies and technologies that conserve the structures of climate-destroying systems. A perfect example of this particular configuration is Arnold Schwarzenegger when, as Governor of California, he promoted policies supporting the development of fuel cells and hydrogen technology as part of a 'green' agenda.

## Mr. Green Governator

In 2003 Arnold Schwarzenegger ran for the governorship of California on a promise to 'terminate' his opponents and say 'hasta la vista' to the state's budget problems. Before then he had been involved in high profile relationships with (the scandal-ridden) energy corporation Enron and with the Hummer sport utility vehicle (SUV). The Hummer symbolized a combination of violence and boundless technological progress. These affiliations gave him an image problem as far as environmental and energy policies were concerned. The suitable solution he found was to promote a 'green' Hummer with fuel cell and hydrogen technology. Later, as governor, Schwarzenegger aligned himself with the high expectations for clean technology in the form of fuel cells and hydrogen.

With his hydrogen-powered car, Schwarzenegger could describe himself as an ecomodern man. His performance of ecomodern masculinities contains a recognition of environmental problems, especially climate change. (Here it is worth noting that Schwarzenegger did not follow the lead of his fellow Republican climate sceptics.) The energy-inefficient Hummer was no longer a problem when the fuel consisted of hydrogen and the exhaust from the car was only water. Ecomodern 'greenwash' made it possible to brand these giant cars with an image of care and affection for the environment. Both the ecological modernization discourse and such performances of ecomodern masculinities can be understood as attempts to incorporate and deflect criticism in order to perpetuate hegemony – in other words, to ensure 'business as usual'. Schwarzenegger presented himself as a symbol of the 'green economy': someone who made a serious effort for the environment while not forsaking economic growth. He constantly used ecomodern discourse and expressed win–win situations, such as when he launched his so-called hydrogen highway.

Ecomodern masculinities are presented as a symmetrical amalgamation of care for the environment and commitment to economic growth. However, they can instead be understood as highly asymmetrical in that they conserve and favour existing system solutions. The focus of the ecomodern discourse is on emissions (symptom), not on the production of fuel (root cause). For example, arguments for a pollution-free fuel cell technology legitimize the continued expansion of private cars and visions of alternative transport systems become redundant. Car use, it must be noted, is and has historically been highly masculinized (Carlsson-Kanyama et al. 1999). Ecomodern masculinities – where toughness and determination go hand in hand with well-chosen moments of compassion, vulnerability and eco-friendly technology – appear to be a cover up for continuing down the same modern industrial path that created the problems in the first place.

Whereas industrial masculinities portray nature as dead and work with it accordingly, ecomodern masculinities are able to depict nature as alive and in need of care. In both cases nature becomes something 'out there', which is possible to dominate with masculine practices.

## *Ecological masculinities*

We have looked at the anti-nature qualities of industrial masculinities and the caring-violent tendencies of the ecomodern man. It remains now to ask: What would a truly pro-ecological type of masculinities look like? The third figuration in my tripartite framework for understanding masculinities and environment is ecological masculinities. It emerges from my work on ecological discourse (Hultman 2014a, 2015) and from a study of ecological sustainable entrepreneurship – so-called 'ecopreneurship' – based on over forty interviews and field work in New Zealand and Sweden (Hultman 2014b; Hultman et al. 2016; Hultman and Pulé forthcoming). As I noted earlier, there is a small amount of existing research on masculinities that has used similar terminology, such as 'ecological masculinism' (Pulé 2013), 'eco-masculinities' (Gaard 2014), and 'eco-man' (Allister 2004). 'Ecological masculinities' has been used by Wendy Woodward (2009) in an edited text on ecocriticism, which looks at how a set of authors position themselves in connection to ecological discourses through their constructions of masculine identities. Connell (2005) has written about how more pro-environmental masculinities might offer resistance to traditional, industrial forms of masculinity. I understand 'ecological masculinities' as being connected to the theoretical traditions of ecofeminism and posthumanism that question how to create collaborative rather than abusive relationships with the non-human world.

In the late 1960s, in Western countries, ecological masculinities were enacted in antagonism to industrial masculinities. The localization of economies, use of small-scale technologies, creation of renewable energy, and decentralization of power structures were seen as necessary components of an ecological society. In opposition to large segments of the political and scientific elite, initiatives such as ecovillages, ecolabelling requirements, and cooperative wind and solar projects were established. Existing traditional knowledge was translated into practical projects and arranged in new kinds of communities. Initiatives were part of and supported by the growing environmental movement that, together with concerned scientists, questioned consumer waste, urban smog, deforestation, and declining seal and fish populations. During this period, a changed form of masculinities of a more caring, humble, and sharing sort was presented as being more appropriate in an ecologically-sound society. As change agents, ecological masculine subjects do not shut themselves off from society, but create alternative projects amidst the dominant model. Their models and experiments were in the mid-1980s part of an international peak in environmental consciousness and are today connected to a plethora of movements across the globe recognizing that the era of extractive industries needs to end so that more sustainable alternatives may flourish.

### *Male ecopreneurs*

Research on this third figure of masculinity is still under development. I will give three preliminary examples of individuals who appear to embody ecological masculinities from my research on ecopreneurship in New Zealand. With a degree of similarity to Connell's work in the 1990s, I conducted in depth life history interviews with a sample of men involved in various forms of pro-sustainability professions and businesses.

The first man is the architect and Māori entrepreneur Rau Hoskins who is the CEO of designTRIBE. Hoskins is well-known in New Zealand as a prominent Māori spokesperson and functions as a catalyst for an emerging Māori group of architects. Hoskins' architectural practice is connected to a holistic perspective on how to integrate new technologies with old traditions. In interviews, he talked about the importance of caring for common land and sharing resources. For Hoskins, Eurocentric architecture alienates humans from the environment. One of his primary goals with architecture is 'making people spend more time outdoors. Our ancestors only retreated inside when it was dark'.

A second example is Paul Geraet, a builder of rammed earth houses, who is re-creating the oldest and most common building technique in the world in the midst of industrialized New Zealand. For him the idea of sustainable housing developed as a reaction to construction development which is taking wrong paths in regards to the public good. According to Paul the construction community is failing to provide shelter that is affordable, functional, healthy and durable; it is therefore not *sustainable*. His approach to building was shaped by a permaculture design course that he took in the early 1980s at the same time as he studied political philosophy of anarchism. He came to the conclusion that 'we need to take responsibility for ourselves'. For him anarchy is part of how a community can make decisions from the bottom up.

The third example of ecological masculinities is Pete Russell who lives in an ecovillage on Waiheke Island, New Zealand, and runs a distribution network of organically grown food called Ooooby. The business was established to address the 'myopia of globalized food system'. His eyes were opened when he became a father and started to realize that he was part of something that he would never sign up to. Having an 'airplane lifestyle', moving from one place to another, never allows relationships to evolve, he said. Instead 'as human animals, we need to fulfil a sense of place, familiar with the space, relationships you evolve'. Pete says that 'real sense of fulfilment is about having a meaningful role to play within a group of people, a community of people that really matter'.

These are, admittedly, very small glimpses of how ecological masculinities can be enacted by three men who are not representative of dominant entrepreneurialism and nor do their stories provide evidence of a trend toward ecological masculinities. But there may be many more possible examples to be considered and further research might help to understand them. Research into how people have tried to make positive, 'green' change in their everyday lives, workplaces, and communities needs to be far more aware of different forms of environmental masculinities (such as destructive, show off, or transformative) than it has been to date. It is worth noting that to date there exists no research on how masculinities (or gender more generally, for that matter) have shaped Transition Town movements or the various new forms of political consumption and 'new domesticity' that are emerging in affluent Western societies (Schlosberg and Coles 2016). Bringing a gender lens that is fine-tuned to see the role played by femininities and masculinities may give us the possibility of conducting more in-depth, critical studies, as well as finding positive examples for the future.

## Conclusion

Gender configurations matter. But research on gender in the environmental fields has mainly considered how women are affected by and try to resist environmental destruction, with little or no interest in men-*qua*-men. The foregoing discussion has explored historically situated forms of masculinities and has introduced the concepts of industrial, ecomodern, and ecological masculinities with reference to some empirical examples. My overall aim in this chapter has been to show how three distinct discourses are enacted from figurations developed within the environmental political arena.

The concepts outlined previously might provide inspiration, not only for historical studies, but also for contemporary case studies of how masculinities shape and are shaped by environmental politics. There is a need for more exploration of the values and practises of men, not least because of the large importance they play in shaping, formulating, and deciding environmental issues globally. A first step might be to understand why there is such oversight. It is important to remember that the majority of the gatekeepers of academic disciplines, including in the environmental fields, are elite white men who may well be unwilling to shed light on their own identities, practices, and privilege. Hegemonic masculinity is thus *an unmarked category*. Similarly, research funding decisions remain in the hands of male gatekeepers who might not be reflexive enough to promote masculinities research at a time when economic growth dominates a neoliberal academic agenda. The clue to overcoming these barriers to studying masculinities and environment more systematically is to make better use of the spaces within academia that allow for such inquiries to thrive. The field of environmental humanities might be such a space that allows these investigations to be done in an intra-, supra- or even 'undisciplined' way. This is a space gaining a lot of attention in the 2010s, and has at its core an open and innovative approach to these issues (Rose et al. 2012; Hutchings 2014). Since destructive masculinities have taken us to the point where we are today, the future of our common earth depends on understanding and changing masculinities for the better.

## Acknowledgements

I am grateful for all the support, critical comments, inspiration, suggestions, and motivation that others have shared with me during the last couple of years. Especially Anna Lundberg (who encouraged me to carefully carve out the concept of ecomodern masculinity), Raewyn Connell (who motivates me with support both in written form and in spiritual presence), Susan Buckingham (who is a source of great inspiration), Sherilyn MacGregor (who in dialogue has made many great suggestions to my work as well as been an organizer of amazing scholarly venues of much importance for me), Ulf Mellström (who handed me the responsibility of the master course in gender and technology way back), and Paul Pulé (who made me realize the missing final tweak to this chapter) are all such a big part of how this text has come about and why you just have read this piece. Thank you.

## References

Alaimo, S. (2000) *Undomesticated Ground: Recasting Nature as Feminist Space*. Ithaca: Cornell University Press.

Alaimo, S. (2010) *Bodily Natures: Science, Environment and the Material*. Bloomington: Indiana University Press.

Allister, M. (ed) (2004) *Eco-man: New Perspectives on Masculinity and Nature*. Charlottesville: University of Virginia Press.

Anshelm, J. (2010) 'Among demons and wizards: The nuclear energy discourse in Sweden and the re-enchantment of the world', *Bulletin of Science, Technology and Society* 30(1): 43–53.

Anshelm, J. and Hansson, A. (2011) 'Climate change and the convergence between ENGOs and business: On the loss of utopian energies', *Environmental Values* 20(1): 75–94.

Anshelm, J. and Hultman, M. (2014a) *Discourses of Global Climate Change*. London: Routledge.

Anshelm, J. and Hultman, M. (2014b) 'A green fatwā? Climate change as a threat to the masculinity of industrial modernity', *NORMA: International Journal for Masculinity Studies* 9(2): 84–96.

Arora-Jonsson, S. (2013) *Gender, Development and Environmental Governance: Theorizing Connections*. London: Routledge.

Barrett, F. J. (1996) 'The organizational construction of hegemonic masculinity: The case of the U.S. Navy', *Gender, Work and Organization* 3(3): 129–142.

Basford, K. (1978) *The Green Man*. Cambridge: DS Brewer.

Bell, D. (2000) 'Farm boys and wild men: Rurality, masculinity, and homosexuality', *Rural Sociology* 65(4): 547–561.

Bird, S. R. (1996) 'Welcome to the men's club: Homosociality and the maintenance of hegemonic masculinity', *Gender and Society* 10(2): 120–132.

Boykoff, M. and Boykoff, J. (2004) 'Balance as bias: Global warming and the US prestige press', *Global Environmental Change* 14(2): 125–136.

Braidotti, R. (2002) *Metamorphoses: Towards a Materialist Theory of Becoming.* Cambridge and Malden: Polity Press.

Brandth, B. (1995) 'Rural masculinity in transition: Gender images in tractor advertisements', *Journal of Rural Studies* 11(2): 123–133.

Brandth, B. and Haugen, M. S. (2000) 'From lumberjack to business manager: Masculinity in the Norwegian forestry press', *Journal of Rural studies* 16(3): 343–355.

Buckingham, S. and Kulcur, R. (2009) 'Gendered geographies of environmental injustice', *Antipode* 41(4): 659–683.

Campbell, H. and Mayerfeld Bell, M. (2000) 'The question of rural masculinities', *Rural Sociology* 65(4): 532–546.

Capstick, S. B. and Pidgeon, N. F. (2014) 'What is climate change skepticism? Examination of the concept using a mixed methods study of the UK public', *Global Environmental Change* 24: 389–401.

Capstick, S., Whitmarsh, L., Poortinga, W., Pidgeon, N. and Upham, P. (2015) 'International trends in public perceptions of climate change over the past quarter century', *Wiley Interdisciplinary Reviews: Climate Change* 6(1): 35–61.

Carlsson-Kanyama, A., Linden, A. and Thelander, Å. (1999) 'Insights and applications: Gender differences in environmental impacts from patterns of transportation – A case study from Sweden', *Society and Natural Resources* 12(4): 355–369.

Connell, R. W. (1987) *Gender and Power: Society, the Person and Sexual Politics.* Cambridge: Polity Press.

Connell, R. W. (1990) 'A whole new world: Remaking masculinity in the context of the environmental movement', *Gender and Society* 4: 452–478.

Connell, R. W. (1995) *Masculinities.* Cambridge: Polity Press.

Connell, R. W. (2005) *Masculinities* (second edition). Berkeley and Los Angeles: University of California Press.

Connell, R. W. and Messerschmidt, J. W. (2005) 'Hegemonic masculinity: Rethinking the concept', *Gender and Society* 19: 829–858.

Connell, R. W. and Pearse, R. (2014) *Gender: In World Perspective* (third edition). Cambridge: Polity Press.

Connell, R. W. and Wood, J. (2005) 'Globalization and business masculinities', *Men and Masculinities* (4): 347–364.

Dunlap, R. E. (2013) 'Climate change skepticism and denial: An introduction', *American Behavioral Scientist* 57(6): 691–698.

Einarsson, G., Franzén, L. G., Gee, D., Holmberg, K., Jönsson, B., Kaijser, S., Karlén, W., Liljenzin, J., Norin, T., Nydén, M., Petersson, G., Ribbing, C. G., Stigebrandt, A., Stilbs, P., Ulfvarson, A., Walin, G., Andersson, T., Gustafsson, S. G., Einarsson, O. and Hellström, T. (2008) '20 toppforskare i unikt upprop: Koldioxiden påverkar inte klimatet', *Newsmill*, 17 December 2008.

Eriksson, P. (2008) 'Jorden går inte under av utsläpp och uppvärmning', *Dagens Industri* 4/6.

Filteau, M. R. (2014) 'Who are those guys? Constructing the oilfield's new dominant masculinity', *Men and Masculinities* 17(4): 396–416.

Gaard, G. (2014) 'Towards new ecomasculinities, ecogenders, and ecosexualities', in Adams, C. J. and Gruen, L. (eds) *Ecofeminism: Feminist Intersections With Other Animals and the Earth.* New York: Bloomsbury Publishing, 225–239.

Grasswick, H. (2014) 'Climate change science and responsible trust: A situated approach', *Hypatia* 29(3): 541–557.

Hajer, M. A. (1995) *The Politics of Environmental Discourse: Ecological Modernization and the Policy Process.* Oxford: Clarendon.

Hanson, S. (2010) 'Gender and mobility: New approaches for informing sustainability', *Gender, Place and Culture* 17(1): 5–23.

Haraway, D. (1988) 'Situated knowledges: The science question in feminism and the privilege of partial perspective', *Feminist Studies* 3: 575–599.

Haraway, D. (2008) *When Species Meet* (Vol. 224). Minneapolis: University of Minnesota Press.

Hazlett, M. (2004) '"Woman vs. man vs. bugs": Gender and popular ecology in early reactions to *Silent Spring*', *Environmental History* 9: 701–729.

Hultman, M. (2010) *Full gas mot en (o) hållbar framtid: Förväntningar på bränsleceller och vätgas 1978–2005 i relation till svensk energi-och miljöpolitik*. Dissertation.

Hultman, M. (2013) 'The making of an environmental hero: A history of ecomodern masculinity, fuel cells and Arnold Schwarzenegger', *Environmental Humanities* 2: 83–103.

Hultman, M. (2014a) 'Transition delayed: The 1980s ecotopia of decentralized renewable energy systems', in Bradley, K. and Hedrén, J. (eds) *Green Utopianism: Perspectives, Politics and Micro Practices*. London: Routledge, 243–258.

Hultman, M. (2014b), 'Ecopreneurship within planetary boundaries: Innovative practice, transitional territorialisation's and green-green values', Paper at Transitional Green Entrepreneurs: Re-thinking Ecopreneurship for the 21st Century Symposium, 3–5 June 2014, Umeå University.

Hultman, M. (2015) *Den inställda omställningen: svensk energi- och miljöpolitik i möjligheternas tid 1980–1991*. Möklinta: Gidlund.

Hultman, M. (2016) 'Gröna män? Konceptualisering av industrimodern, ekomodern och ekologisk maskulinitet', Special Issue Environmental Humanities in *Kulturella Perspekiv* 25(1): 28–39.

Hultman, M., Bonnedahl, K. J. and O'Neill, K. J. (2016) 'Unsustainable societies–sustainable businesses? Introduction to special issue of small enterprise research on transitional Ecopreneurs', *Small Enterprise Research* 23(1): 1–9.

Hultman, M. and Pulé, P. (forthcoming) *Ecological Masculinities: Re-conceptualising Modern Western Men and Masculinities in the Anthropocene*. London: Routledge.

Hutchings, R. (2014) 'Understanding of, and vision for, the environmental humanities', *Environmental Humanities* 4: 213–220.

Kaijser, A. and Kronsell, A. (2014) 'Climate change through the lens of intersectionality', *Environmental Politics* 23(3): 417–433.

Kimmel, M. S., Hearn, J. and Connell, R. W. (eds) (2004) *Handbook of Studies on Men and Masculinities*. London: Sage Publications.

Loo, T. (2001) 'Of moose and men: Hunting for masculinities in British Columbia, 1880–1939', *Western Historical Quarterly* 32(3): 296–319.

Lundqvist, L. J. (2000) 'Capacity-building or social construction? Explaining Sweden's shift towards ecological modernization', *Geoforum* 31(1): 21–32.

McCright, A. and Dunlap, R. (2011) 'Cool dudes: The denial of climate change among conservative white males in the United States', *Global Environmental Change* 21(4): 1163–1172.

MacGregor, S. (2009) 'A stranger silence still: The need for feminist social research on climate change', *Sociological Review* 57: 124–140.

McNeill, J. (2003) *Någonting är nytt under solen – Nittonhundratalets miljöhistoria*. Stockholm: SNS förlag.

Melosi, M. V. (1987) 'Lyndon Johnson and environmental policy', in Divine, R. A. (ed) *The Johnson Years: Vietnam, the Environment, and Science*. Lawrence: University Press of Kansas, 119–120.

Merchant, C. (1980) *The Death of Nature: Women, Ecology, and the Scientific Revolution* (first edition). San Francisco: Harper and Row.

Mohai, P. (1992) 'Men, women and the environment: An examination of the gender gap in environmental concern and activism', *Society and Natural Resources* 5: 1–9.

Mol, A. P. J. (2001) *Globalization and Environmental Reform: The Ecological Modernization of the Global Economy*. Cambridge, MA: MIT Press.

Nayak, A. (2003) '"Boyz to men": Masculinities, schooling and labour transitions in de industrial times', *Educational Review* 55(2): 147–159.

Nightingale, A. (2006) 'The nature of gender: Work, gender, and environment', *Environment and Planning D: Society and Space* 24(2): 165–185.

Ní Laoire, C. (2001) 'A matter of life and death? Men, masculinities, and staying "behind" in rural Ireland', *Sociologia Ruralis* 41(2): 220–236.

Nordin, I. (2008) 'Klimatdebatten – en röra', *Östgöta Correspondenten*, 9 June 2008.

Norgaard, K. and York, R. (2005) 'Gender equality and state environmentalism', *Gender and Society* 19(4): 506–522.

Oreskes, N. and Conway, E. (2010) *Merchants of Doubt: How a Handful of Scientists Obscured the Truth on Issues From Tobacco Smoke to Global Warming*. New York: Bloomsbury Press.

Plumwood, V. (1993) 'The politics of reason: Towards a feminist logic', *Australasian Journal of Philosophy* 71(4): 436–462.

Pulé, P. (2013) *A Declaration of Caring: Towards Ecological Masculinism*. PhD thesis, Murdoch University.

Radetzki, M. and Lundgren, N. (2009) 'En grön fatwa har utfärdats', *Ekonomisk debatt* 5: 58–61.

Rocheleau, D., Thomas-Slayter, B. and Wangari, E. (eds) (1996) *Feminist Political Ecology: Global Issues and Local Experiences*. London and New York: Routledge.

Rome, A. (2003) '"Give earth a chance": The environmental movement and the sixties', *Journal of American History* 90(September): 534–541.

Rose, B. D., van Dooren, T., Chrulew, M., Cooke, S., Kearnes, M. and O'Gorman, E. (2012) 'Thinking through the environment, unsettling the humanities', *Environmental Humanities* 1(1): 1–5.

Saugeres, L. (2002) 'The cultural representation of the farming landscape: Masculinity, power and nature', *Journal of Rural Studies* 18(4): 373–384.

Schlosberg, D. and Coles, R. (2016) 'The new environmentalism of everyday life: Sustainability, material flows and movements', *Contemporary Political Theory* 15: 160–181.

Sramek, J. (2006) '"Face him like a Briton:" Tiger hunting, imperialism, and British masculinity in colonial India, 1800–1875', *Victorian Studies* 48(4): 659–680.

Stoddart, M. C. and Tindall, D. B. (2011) 'Ecofeminism, hegemonic masculinity and environmental movement participation in British Columbia, Canada, 1998–2007: "Women always clean up the mess"', *Sociological Spectrum* 31(3): 342–368.

Taylor, D. (2014) 'The state of diversity in environmental organizations: Mainstream NGOs, foundations, government agencies', *Green 2.0*. Online. Available at: www.diversegreen.org/the-challenge/ (accessed 12 August 2016).

Tranter, B. and Booth, K. (2015) 'Skepticism in a changing climate: A cross-national study', *Global Environmental Change* 33: 154–164.

Woodward, W. (2009) 'The nature feeling: Ecological masculinities in some recent popular texts', in Wylie, D. (ed) *Toxic Belonging? Identity and Ecology in Southern Africa*. Cambridge: Cambridge Scholars Publishing, 143–157.

# 17

# TRANSGENDER ENVIRONMENTS

*Nicole Seymour*

Are you tired of those damned anti-oppression articles that keep crowding out stories about hardcore lockdowns and monkeywrenching in the [*Earth First! The Radical Environmental*] *Journal?* Bored by incessant ramblings about 'privilege', 'gender', 'race', 'analysis' and so on? Me neither! And that's why I want to discuss transgender awareness.

*(Trouble! 2007:28)*

## Introduction

Queer theorist and disability studies scholar Robert McRuer recently observed that there are 'queer ways of being or living in harmony with the environment that are yet to be envisioned' (2013:77). This chapter proceeds from the idea that there are also specifically *transgender* ways of being or living in harmony – or disharmony – with the environment, but that these ways have yet to be fully addressed in scholarly circles.[1] I thus insist that the environmental humanities consider the category of transgender, and that inquiries around gender and environment – the charge of this volume – go beyond static and normative conceptions of gender and sex.[2]

In what follows, I draw on my background as a literature and culture scholar engaged with questions of gender and environment to provide a wide-ranging view of where and how that work might take place. In the first section, I survey the frameworks of environmental justice, material ecocriticism/feminism, and queer ecology, outlining what I see as each framework's current engagement (or lack thereof) with transgender concerns and phenomena, and potential for future engagement. In the second, I demonstrate how scientific-oriented environmental inquiry has foreclosed ethical, justice-oriented conversations around transgender issues. In the third, I consider recent US young adult fiction that engages with the counter-discourse of *organic transgenderism*. I show how literature can model a capacious queer ecological consciousness, one that takes the 'T' in LGBTQ (lesbian, gay, bisexual, transgender, and queer) as more than mere window dressing. I thus offer this third section as a counterpoint to the critiques that I make in the previous sections. Overall, I offer this essay as a potential model for further work on the relationship between transgenderism and environment – and even for a new theoretical framework that we might call 'trans ecology'.[3]

## Environmental justice, material ecocriticism/feminism, and queer ecology: gaps and possibilities

Despite recent legal gains and increased public awareness of transgender issues in some parts of the world, including the United States,[4] statistics on trans health and safety are rather bleak. As the Trans Women's Anti-Violence Project reports, drawing on 2010 US figures from the National Coalition of Anti-Violence Programs, '44 per cent of LGBTQH [lesbian, gay, bisexual, transgender, queer, and HIV-positive] . . . murder victims were trans women, and in 2009 trans women were 50 per cent of [all] murder victims. Yet trans people as a whole are only about 1 per cent of the LGBTQH population', and as few as 0.1 per cent of the general population.[5] This bleak picture extends to employment, housing, and health care. As transgender urban/regional planning scholar Petra Doan observes, 'the trans community faces a kind of "double whammy" consisting of lower incomes resulting from employment discrimination combined with overt discrimination in the housing market' (2011:103); the homelessness that many trans people subsequently experience leaves them further vulnerable to discrimination and violence.[6] And according to a joint 2011 study conducted by the US National Center for Transgender Equality and the US National Gay and Lesbian Task Force,

> 19 per cent [of transgender adults] reported having been refused treatment by a health care provider because of their gender identity, and 28 per cent said they had postponed medical care because of discrimination. For those who had visited a doctor's office or hospital, 24 per cent said they had been denied equal treatment, [and] 25 per cent reported having been harassed.
>
> *(Richards 2014:n.p.)*

The international statistics gathered by projects such as the Transgender Day of Remembrance and Trans Murder Monitoring paint a no-less distressing picture across the globe.[7]

While this reality is clearly an issue of social injustice, I propose that we also understand it as one of environmental injustice. After all, environmental justice scholars and activists are concerned with health and safety wherever people 'live, work, and play' (or, as the case may be, *don't get to* live, work, or play), and they have recently called for expanded conceptions of justice (Sandler and Pezzulo 2007; see also Sze in this volume). As David Schlosberg states, drawing on feminist political theorist Iris Young, equal 'distribution (of resources, goods, and benefits) is not the only problem; a concept of justice needs to focus more on the elimination of institutionalized domination and oppression, particularly of those who represent difference and remain un-, mis-, or malrecognized' (2007:15). But while environmental justice scholars have indicated their readiness to attend to 'new' oppressed populations, they have not, as far as I can see, done so when it comes to transgender people. For instance, in *New Perspectives on Environmental Justice*, Rachel Stein observes that

> because divergent *sexual identities and practices* have historically been condemned and punished as 'unnatural' expressions of desire, environmental justice theory and perspectives offer us a useful set of principles to adopt for struggles for *sexual justice*. . . . By reframing *sexuality issues* as environmental justice concerns, we can argue that people of *differing sexualities* have the human right to bodily sovereignty and the right to live safely as *sexual bodies* within our social and physical environments.
>
> *(Stein 2004:7, my emphasis)*

Stein clearly has non-normative *sexuality* in mind here, not non-normative *gender* – though her points are equally, if not more, applicable to the latter.[8] After all, trans people have historically experienced extreme unsafety in 'social and physical environments', as noted previously. And they have unique experiences of having their 'bodily sovereignty' disciplined, thanks to the medical construction of and gatekeeping around transsexuality.[9] Moreover, public discourses regularly frame trans people as particularly 'unnatural' – not just generally against 'Mother Nature's' plan, as lesbian, gay, and bisexual people are often considered, but also literally, physically constructed through medicine, technology, or even toxicity, as I discuss in the following section. Thus, while a major gap exists in the literature of environmental justice when it comes to transgender issues, this literature seems to offer a promising path for further inquiry.

Another area, the so-called new materialisms, likewise has potential, but also some sticking points. While that designation encompasses an immense, and diverse, body of recent humanities scholarship, I will focus here on recent work in material ecocriticism and material feminisms – work that aims '[t]o bring the material, specifically the materiality of the human body and the natural world, into the forefront of feminist theory and practice' and that insists we 'tak[e] matter seriously' (Alaimo and Hekman 2008:1, 6). We might begin with the fact that this work has engaged with the concept of 'trans', broadly construed. For example, in her co-edited collection *Material Feminisms* (2008, with Susan J. Hekman) and her monograph *Bodily Natures: Science, Environment, and the Material Self* (2010), feminist ecocritic Stacy Alaimo has developed her influential concept of 'trans-corporeality' – 'in which the human is always intermeshed with the more-than-human world, underlin[ing] the extent to which the substance of the human is ultimately inseparable from "the environment"' (2010:2). Here, the 'trans' in 'trans-corporeality' does not seem to have any implied resonance with 'trans' as in transgender; the only gloss Alaimo offers is that '*trans* indicates movement across different sites' (2010:2). However, her thinking seems conceptually aligned with recent transgender studies scholarship, specifically that which proposes an expanded conception of transgender phenomena and which has demonstrated similar interest in interconnectivity and interrelationship. In their introductory essay for the special 'Trans-' issue of *Women's Studies Quarterly*, for example, Susan Stryker, Paisley Currah, and Lisa Jean Moore explain their choice of terminology, arguing that the hyphen therein 'marks the difference between the implied nominalism of "trans" and the explicit *relationality* of "trans-", which . . . resists premature foreclosure by attachment to any single suffix [including gender]' (2008:11). In this particular sense, material ecocriticism and feminism might prove hospitable to inquiries around 'transgender' and 'environment'.

However, this work tends to criticize poststructuralism, the linguistic and discursive turns in the humanities, and theories of social construction more broadly, for having 'forgotten' or 'bracketed' the material body. For example, Alaimo reports that, 'despite the tremendous outpouring of feminist theory and cultural studies of "the body", much of this work tends to focus exclusively on how various bodies have been discursively produced, *which casts the body as passive, plastic matter*' (2010:3, my emphasis). She also sees a 'troubling parallel between the immateriality of contemporary social theory and a widespread, popular disregard for nonhuman nature' and thus seeks to 'address the dematerializing networks that cross through academic theory, popular culture, [and] contemporary discourse' (Alaimo 2010:2). Especially considering that this work does not cite specific examples of this 'immaterial' or 'dematerializing' theory, such comments potentially draw what Sara Ahmed, in her critique of the 'new materialisms' and material feminism in particular, calls a 'caricature of poststructuralism as matter-phobic' (2008:34).[10]

But more to the point of this essay, poststructuralism, the linguistic and discursive turns, and theories of social construction have been crucial to much, though certainly not all, transgender studies scholarship and movements. For one thing, those theories have criticized how cisgender[11] and heterosexual identities have long been implicitly positioned as 'natural', to the detriment of transgender and queer identities. Further, as Stryker tells us, the new ways 'of thinking about sex, gender, and reality' offered by poststructuralist feminists such as Judith Butler 'opened up for theorists within the new transgender movement the prospect that new "truths" of transgender experience, new ways of narrating the relationship between gendered sense of self, social role, and embodiment, could begin to be told' (Stryker 2008:132).[12] Such theories also prove relevant when we consider that many trans bodies are in fact *not* material, not 'real' – because they are instead imagined, hoped-for, discursively constructed, or simply irrelevant ('immaterial', we might even say) to one's gender identity. Here, we might think of the powerful speech delivered by Harry/Harriet, an assigned-male-at-birth trans character in Michelle Cliff's novel *No Telephone to Heaven* (discussed as follows): 'Cyann [can't] afford [sex-reassignment surgery]. . . . [B]ut *the choice is mine, man, is made.* Harriet live and Harry be no more . . . you know, darling, *castration ain't de main t'ing* . . . not a-tall' (1987:168, my emphasis). Considering these points, I believe that material ecocritics and feminist theorists need to grapple with what is potentially lost in their reactions to poststructuralism and in their interest in the 'body "as such"' (Alaimo 2010:7) – and with what those reactions imply for transgender movements and scholarship.

I want to turn here to transgender studies scholar Gayle Salamon, who has mounted her own critique of materialist approaches, though specifically within transgender studies movements and scholarship – such as in the work of figures like Jamison 'James' Green. This critique, as I will show, resonates very closely with Ahmed's and my own responses to material ecocriticism/feminism. First, Salamon argues that the 'call for a return to "real" gender, as opposed to gender as it is merely "theorized" . . . posits the materiality of the body as a stable ground against the wild proliferations of a supposedly disembodied and disengaged theorizing'; like Ahmed, Salamon finds that these calls 'flatte[n] out "theory" to the point of caricature' (2006:578). Moreover, she tells us, 'a return to the "real" of the body' has 'troubling consequences . . . [that] can be seen in the work of several *critics* of transgenderism' (Salamon 2006:578, my emphasis). That is to say, Salamon identifies a surprising overlap between trans scholars, activists, and individuals and their own critics, an overlap that she believes casts much doubt on materialist approaches. As she explains, for example, opponents of sex-reassignment surgery 'see the phenomenon as evidence that the real of the body is resistant to ideologies of gender' (587). The stubborn materiality of one's 'truly' female or 'truly' male body and its biological apparatuses will resist any claims one might make to a different gender identity. Salamon (2006) counts feminist scholar Berenice L. Hausman – who has infamously referred to transsexuals as 'the dupes of gender' (1995:140) – as one of these 'critics of transgenderism'; we should therefore note that both material ecocriticism and material feminism have relied on scholars such as Hausman, and other problematic figures such as Elizabeth Grosz, whose academic writings contain transphobic commentary.[13] For example, Grosz has argued that

[m]en . . . can never, even with surgical intervention, feel or experience what it is like to be, to live, as women. At best the transsexual can live out his [*sic*] fantasy of femininity – a fantasy that . . . is usually disappointed with the rather crude transformations effected by surgical and chemical intervention.

*(Grosz 1994:207)*

As we can see here, one consequence of a framework that insists on the 'realities' of the body is that it tends to dismiss trans bodies and the people to whom they are attached. They become nefarious, artificial interlopers, if they are counted at all.

Moving forward, then, material ecocritics and feminist theorists might directly address the transphobia of figures such as Grosz and Hausman, or of other feminists such as Elinor

Burkett and Germaine Greer,[14] in addition to exploring the implications for trans people of their calls to return to the 'material body'. In the meantime, we might ask how something like 'trans-corporeality' might look different when we gloss the 'trans-' more specifically in terms of transgenderism, or, at least, in terms of Stryker, Currah, and Moore's version of 'trans-'. And we might build on material ecocritical/feminist theorizing by asking questions such as: How might trans identities or experiences be adopted, prompted, or conceived through moves across species or other ontological borders? How might our sensibilities be 'trans-ed' through our recognition of interconnectivity with the nonhuman, nature, and environment? What are the limits to those processes?

The final framework I want to survey in this section is queer ecology. Queer ecology scholars have asked, 'How might a clearer [or queerer!] attention to issues of nature and environment – as discourse, as space, as ideal, as practice, as relationship, as potential – inform and enrich queer theory, lgbtq politics, and research into sexuality and society?' (Mortimer-Sandilands and Erickson 2010:5; see also Butler in this handbook). As such questions indicate, this emerging framework is implicitly concerned with the category of trans. In my own queer ecology work, I have paid particular attention to this category. In *Strange Natures: Futurity, Empathy, and the Queer Ecological Imagination*, I identify a counter-discourse that I term 'organic transgenderism' (Seymour 2013:36) circulating in contemporary trans-themed novels from the Americas. These novels include Jamaican-American writer Cliff's *No Telephone to Heaven*, US writer and activist Leslie Feinberg's *Stone Butch Blues* (1993), and Canadian-Trinidadian-Irish writer and artist Shani Mootoo's *Cereus Blooms at Night* (1998). Organic transgenderism, as I see it, is a way of conceiving of gender transitioning outside of the Western medical-industrial complex that has historically fetishized the 'correct' body as a commodity to be obtained from or created by others. Organic transgenderism, instead, focuses on gender transitioning as a self-directed, even spontaneous phenomenon akin to the life-cycle changes of plants or animals. I maintain that this counter-discourse is not a cynical or purely self-serving attempt at legitimizing transgenderism by framing it as 'natural', but, rather, something that emerges from an expanded ecological consciousness and environmental ethics. The characters in the aforementioned novels come to understand themselves as at least partly 'natural' and worthy of patience and care, as they come to understand their connection to the nonhuman natural world and learn to approach it with patience, care, and even empathy.

On the whole, though, queer ecology has not attended much to the specificity of trans experiences and perspectives. In the few instances when the terms 'transgender' or 'transsexual' appear within such scholarship, it is usually within the context of a list, as with 'LGBTQ'. For example, Catriona Mortimer-Sandilands and Bruce Erickson's groundbreaking edited volume *Queer Ecologies: Sex, Politics, Nature, Desire* (2010), which consists of an introduction and thirteen essays, contains only six unique mentions of 'transgender' or 'transsexual' issues. Robert Azzarello's *Queer Environmentality: Ecology, Evolution, and Sexuality in American Literature* contains only two, the first an ironic recitation of various theories on Willa Cather's identity – 'Was [she] a self-hating lesbian? A resentful proto-transsexual?' (Azzarello 2012:90) – and the second a reference to the elision of trans people, lesbians, bisexuals, and other 'queer beings' in popular science writing (104). Indeed, while the 'queer' in queer ecology *theoretically* encompasses transgenderism, it does not seem to do so in practice; more often than not, 'queer' means non-normative in a sexual or affiliational sense (say, gay cruising in a park, being polyamorous, or finding nature erotic) but not in a gendered one. In the next section, I demonstrate more explicitly why this matters – why we need a theory of trans ecologies or, at least, environmental frameworks attuned to the category of 'trans'.

## Transphobia and cisnormativity in environmental research and discourse

Several scholars have recently shown that contemporary environmental science and discourse reflect the biases of homophobia, heteronormativity, and heterosexism. Azzarello's (2012) *Queer Environmentality*, for instance, traces how the long-standing conceptual connections between heterosexuality and health on the one hand, and queerness and sickness on the other, have made environmental discourse particularly queer-unfriendly. One potential path for ethically thinking of the connection between transgender issues and environmental issues, then, is to consider how *trans*phobia, *cis*normativity, and *cis*sexism[15] inform our views of, and work on, the environment. Mortimer-Sandilands and Erickson allude to such a path. As they report,

> In one case, well-meaning ecologists, convinced of the evolutionary pathology of same-sex sexual behaviour, argued that the widespread presence of female homoerotic activity among seagulls in a particular location must be evidence of some major environmental catastrophe (Silverstone 2000). As it turns out, it wasn't. . . . But this kind of 'repro-centric' environmental position remains dominant; it has even been used to argue that the increasing prominence of transgendered individuals (human and other) is clear evidence of environmental contamination.
>
> *(Mortimer-Sandilands and Erickson 2010:11)*

The latter research to which Mortimer-Sandilands and Erickson refer appears spotty, not to mention potentially problematic from an ideological standpoint. As they conclude:

> Although the effect of endocrine disruption on human (and other animal) health is a serious issue, the line of research is profoundly flawed in several ways, not least its reduction of transgender identities to biological questions and its equation of sexual health with sexual difference.
>
> *(Mortimer-Sandilands and Erickson 2010:41)*

Here, the latter presumably means 'dimorphism'. But I would propose that it is not (just) 'repro-centri[sm]' but, specifically, transphobia, cissexism, and cisnormativity that inform some of this research and its attendant discourses. Indeed, I would submit that, in many if not most Western contexts, non-reproductive cisgender women such as myself experience vastly less stigma than do transgender women of any reproductive status. After all, while many cisgender women can certainly be stigmatized for not reproducing, that stigma does not necessarily produce conditions of injustice such as unemployment or homelessness.

I want to explore these propositions through a critique of acclaimed environmental memoirist Janisse Ray's essay 'Changing Sex', published in the 2007 anthology *Courage for the Earth* in honour of Rachel Carson. Ray opens her essay with a direct invocation of the first page of Carson's groundbreaking environmental work *Silent Spring*, which reads, 'There was once a town in the heart of America where all life seemed to live in harmony with its surroundings' (Carson 1962:1):

> There was once a town at the edge of America where plastics had been banned, as had all chemicals of dubious safety. Children ran around playing with wooden toys and leather balls, eating homemade cookies. The baker served steamed organic milk in earthenware mugs.
>
> *(Ray 2007:109)*

While this homage appears at first to be to be a parody – reading like a *Portlandia* sketch mocking yuppie Whole Foods culture – the sentimental reproductive futurism[16] we see here continues throughout the chapter. Ray goes on to claim that chemicals, in addition to being lethal in high doses, and carcinogenic in other cases, 'may be affecting us in other life-threatening ways' (112). But it turns out that she does not have *mortality* in mind here, as the average reader would at first assume, but rather *reproductive normality* – specifically, the possession of normal genitals, normally functioning reproductive organs, and the ability to produce another generation of offspring with normal genitals and normally functioning reproductive organs. In Ray's formulation, then, 'life' is defined in a very narrow, normative, and heteroreproductive sense.

But as I have been hinting, there is more than heteronormative reproductivism at work here. After Ray meets two transgender people within one month – and having been pondering what effect all that plastic has on human beings and their reproductive capabilities – she begins to suspect that transgenderism may be caused by 'environmental toxins and endocrine disruption' (Ray 2007:124). Transgenderism is clearly so perplexing to Ray that she looks for an external environmental cause, and a nefarious, meddlesome one at that – thus further stigmatizing an identity and embodiment already long derided as 'unnatural'. While I would hesitate to label such thinking transphobic (especially as Ray reports in this essay her acceptance of a trans family member), it is clearly cisnormative and cissexist. It re-entrenches cisgenderism's status as superior by leaving it unquestioned, unquestionable.

Equally as troubling, when Ray anxiously reports on research about nonhuman animals and their sex or gender changes, intersex statuses, and other 'abnormalities', she does not acknowledge the vast array of species that 'naturally' change sex or gender and/or have both male and female reproductive organs (that is, not as the result of toxic chemicals or other outside interference).[17] Much as it does with transgender humans, then, Ray's essay frames by omission these nonhuman life forms as tragic accidents. It also thereby participates in the 'suppress[ion] and den[ial] [of] diversity' that transgender evolutionary biologist Joan Roughgarden sees as rampant in environmental and scientific research (2004:3). Indeed, only recently has the existence of 'trans', 'intersex', and 'homosexual' flora and fauna begun to enter the public consciousness, thanks in part to works such as Bruce Bagemihl's *Biological Exuberance: Animal Homosexuality and Natural Diversity* (1999) and Roughgarden's *Evolution's Rainbow: Diversity, Gender, and Sexuality in Nature and People* (2004). David Bell calls such work a 'new science of sexuality, in all its exuberant rainbows, [that] challenges the natural history equation of procreative heterosexuality, sex selection, and nature' (2010:140). But this science is not all new: Charles Darwin, for instance, understood long ago that most invertebrates do not have distinct sexes, and are thus hermaphroditic or intersex.[18] But even this 'old', basic information is not widely known to the average person, many of whom would consider sex/gender indeterminacy or instability definitively unnatural.

For all its problems, however, Ray's essay thus offers us the opportunity to ask some difficult, potentially paradigm-shifting questions. First, to paraphrase Giovanna Di Chiro's critique of Ray, we might ask: Why are 'social-bodily "ambiguities"' . . . easier attributed to a poisoned environment than to normal human sexual difference' (2010:221)? Malin Ah-King and Eva Hayward's work on the same general topic asks a similarly incisive question: 'Why is sex more central than cancer, autoimmune disease, and even death [in conversations around toxic exposure]?' (2014:4). And why do scientists and environmentalists look for the environmental origins of intersex or transgender/transsexual conditions, but not of cisgender conditions? Further, why assume that people suffer from transgender *ontologies*, rather than from *transphobia*, such that we have to get to the root of transgenderism, but not to the root of transphobia – or, say, corporate pollution?[19] Why shift the burden of self-justification to the transgender person, rather than to the transphobic person? And, more broadly, to what extent have transphobia, cisnormativity, and cissexism informed our past and present understandings of the nonhuman natural world? A trans ecologies framework could and should address such questions.

This framework could also meet one particular challenge: how to acknowledge problems such as environmental toxins while avoiding the pathologization of transgenderism or transsexuality, and of sex, gender, and reproductive variance more broadly. Ah-King and Hayward's work is exemplary in this sense: they remind us that we are *all* endocrine-disrupted creatures, and call for an understanding of sex as 'a dynamic emergence with environment, habitat, and ecosystem, and made toxically so within the context of pollution' (2014:1).[20] We might then imagine a complete shift from Ray's 'Changing Sex': focusing on the environmental/health risks that threaten *actually existing trans people*, as well as actually existing cis people, not on the environmental/health risks that might produce *imagined or hypothetical trans people*. Indeed, while overwhelming amounts of evidence link human conditions such as cancer or asthma to environmental contamination, currently only a miniscule amount links transgenderism in humans to environmental contamination, and much of that work is contested, as noted previously. Thus, to focus on transgenderism as a *result* of environmental injustice, rather than on the extensively documented environmental injustices *perpetrated against* transgender people, seems like a major ethical and political misstep. A more justice-oriented perspective on transgenderism and environment might also prompt us to shift from a ciscentric and anthropocentric viewpoint (*most humans are cisgender and therefore cisgenderism must be natural across all life*) to an inclusive, ecocentric viewpoint (*many animals are transgender, transsexual, or intersex; how might that change how we think of ourselves as human animals?*).

Several queer ecologists and animal studies scholars have, however, warned of the potential dangers in thinking across species. For example, Bell argues that

> research on queer animals stages a troubling re-essentialization or renaturalization of same-sex acts, often mobilized as part of the political project of staking rights claims for sexual minorities on the grounds that, because this is a natural phenomenon, denying rights is discriminatory.
>
> *(Bell 2010:138)*

He believes that such moves put too much faith in science as the arbiter of truth, and observes, further, that

> [T]he call upon science to explain the nature of sex[uality] sits at odds . . . with the powerful anti-essentialism of queer theory and politics . . . . Wary of the uses of scientific discourses of sexuality, and equally wary of the problematic fixity of identity categories, queer theory and politics have proven resistant to claims to biological or natural explanation of sexuality.
>
> *(Bell 2010:139)*

We might reasonably extrapolate Bell's points about queer sexuality to queer gender (transgenderism). But while I believe such caveats are crucial to keep in mind, I also believe that we are obliged to at least engage with discourses that position gender transitioning as partly 'natural' or, at least*, no less unnatural than cisgenderism*. After all, it is one thing to express our scepticism around science as an authority, or to acknowledge the essentialist, normative, and biopolitical implications of the very category of 'transgender'. But it is quite another to say that we do not care about how homophobia or transphobia shape environmental and scientific knowledge, or how such knowledge affects people's daily lives. In the next section, I consider a site at which transgenderism, environment, science, and 'nature' meet more amiably.

## 'Natural' histories and domestic environments in post-post-transsexual fiction

I consider the transnational counter-discourse of organic transgenderism, as found in the 1980s and 1990s novels of Cliff, Feinberg, and Mootoo, to be a 'post-transsexual' one (Seymour 2013:40–41), insofar as it coincides with a move away from medicalized conceptions of 'transsexuality' and toward the umbrella concept of 'transgender' – which includes individuals who, for example, choose not to undergo surgery. Since the publication of the aforementioned novels, it seems that a new generation – what we might even call *post*-post-transsexual novels – has appeared. At least two of these novels, like the earlier three, engage explicitly with environmental and natural themes: Julie Anne Peters' *Luna* (2004) and Ellen Wittlinger's *Parrotfish* (2007). Both novels, set in the contemporary United States and from US authors, are intended for young adult audiences.

While these novels lack the aesthetic and political complexity of 'adult' novels such as those of Cliff, Feinberg, and Mootoo, I will propose that the category of young adult fiction is a particularly promising site for considering the relationship between transgender and environment. First, these fictional texts have emerged at a time when the medical model that, as I have argued, organic transgenderism labours against has been widely criticized and increasingly rejected. Second, trans people are coming out and transitioning at increasingly younger ages, thus making for new, complex relationships to 'the natural' and thus different cultural narratives. These novels, then, offer insight into how contemporary experiences of transgenderism intersect with shifting concepts of nature, environment, medicine, and health.

*Luna* is narrated by a cisgender female teenager named Reagan whose older sibling, named Liam at birth, dresses as a girl only under cover of night in Reagan's room. The novel, which is set in a present-day American suburb, thereby offers an interesting parallel to Mootoo's Caribbean-set *Cereus Blooms at Night*, in which the narrator Tyler transitions clandestinely with the help of sympathetic others (Seymour 2013:51) – just as the titular plant for which ze[21] cares blooms on rare occasion. But whereas *Cereus* celebrates Tyler's feelings of release, *Luna* details the dissatisfactions of such an undercover existence. As Reagan describes one night, 'The moon cast an eerie glow through my basement window. A spotlight. A spray of luminescent beams "Luna," she repeated softly, more to herself than me. "Appropriate, wouldn't you say? A girl who can only be seen by moonlight?"' (Peters 2004: Kindle Locations 35–36).

Like Cliff, Feinberg, and Mootoo's characters, Reagan turns to natural processes to explain her sibling's struggle to herself (and, presumably, to the novel's real-life youth audience). Examining 'before and after' photographs of Luna's adult transgender mentor, whom Luna met online, Reagan reflects,

> Teri Lynn, the male, seemed to be another person altogether. A dead person, the way Liam appeared sometimes. . . . The other Teri Lynn . . . had blossomed and sprung to life. The way Liam broke free when he morphed into Luna. Like a butterfly emerging from a chrysalis, I thought. . . . Except in Luna's case, the butterfly is forced to rein in her wings and reinsert herself into the cocoon every day.
>
> *(Peters 2004: Kindle Locations 1763–1767)*

The metaphor extends to the novel's cover, which features a butterfly perching on the shoulder of a slim white figure whose face is obscured. This linking of larval metamorphosis to human gender transitioning is not unique to *Luna*; consider, for example, the long-running US transgender publication *Chrysalis Quarterly*, the UK-based Chrysalis trans support centres, or even the Chrysalis line of lingerie aimed specifically at trans women. The enduring popularity of this link would be worth investigating in and of itself – but suffice to say here that in *Luna* it serves to naturalize not just transgender ontology but the process of coming out as transgender.

Compared to *Luna*, Wittlinger's *Parrotfish* more explicitly connects transgenderism to the nonhuman natural world. When the novel's protagonist and narrator Grady, once 'Angela', first comes out to a short, nerdy cisgender male classmate named Sebastian, the latter's reaction is positive and affirming: 'Wow! . . . You're just like the stoplight parrotfish! . . . I'm doing a report on them for Environmental Science!' (Wittlinger 2007:43–44). As Sebastian explains, 'I picked the stoplight parrotfish for my report because they're so pretty, and because they change colour when they go from female to male – from dull grey to bright green with a yellow stripe' (Wittlinger 2007:70). He then continues with a dizzying catalog reminiscent of Bagemihl or Roughgarden: 'And the two-banded anemonefish can change either way. Slipper limpets can change back and forth, and so can hamlets and small-eyed goby and water fleas and slime mold –' 'Fleas and slime mold', Grady interrupts. 'Wow, I'm in good company' (Wittlinger 2007:70–71). Grady's reaction here could be read as anthropocentric superiority, though it might also indicate how 'understanding . . . one's self as interconnected with the wider environment marks a profound shift in subjectivity' (Alaimo 2010:20) – but a shift that is often uncomfortable for humans, especially minority humans, to embrace. Of course, this reaction might also be plain old disaffected teenage irony.

It is not until the end of the novel that Grady takes any of this information seriously, reading the final report draft that Sebastian has given hir under the pretense of needing proofreading help. The novel's general narrative trajectory could thus be said to move not (just) from closetedness to outness, from individual trans isolation to community acceptance, but also from human ignorance of connections to the nonhuman, to greater awareness. Wittlinger excerpts Sebastian's report at length (given in italics below), along with Grady's still-sometimes-sardonic reactions:

> *Nature creates many variations, and gender ambiguity is not unusual . . . . Particularly among fish, gender can be quite flexible. In fact, reef fish that do not change gender are in the minority.* Okay, that is pretty cool. If only I were a better swimmer. *Gender shifting occurs only when it's necessary for survival.* Now, that I can relate to. It's necessary that I no longer live as a female. Necessary for my mental survival, if not actually all that great for my day-to-day physical life.
>
> *(Wittlinger 2007:209)*

But Grady soon learns that Sebastian means survival *of the species,* not of the individual organism; parrotfish change to male when there are not enough females with which to reproduce. 'So what's my excuse [for transitioning]?' Grady asks himself. 'Having babies has nothing to do with my reasons for wanting to live as a male. In fact, [transitioning] may – probably will – hinder my chances of ever reproducing. Sebastian meant well, but alas, I am just not a fish' (Wittlinger 2007:210).

This discussion is important in several senses when it comes to a transgender/environment perspective. First, it indicates the protagonist's (and, perhaps, the author's) recognition of the diversity of all life, human and nonhuman, *as well as* the limits to cross-species generalizations. Second, it draws the distinction that Ray (2007) fails to draw in 'Changing Sex': that between 'life-threatening' as in threatening an individual life and 'life-threatening' as in threatening the possibility of normative reproduction. The novel, in this small way, thus demonstrates an environmental justice mind-set oriented toward transgenderism: coming out and transitioning, *not* hiding in the closet or living in one's assigned gender, are identified as survival mechanisms. Transphobia, rather than transgender appearance or ontology, is thus positioned as the real problem.

While *Luna* and *Parrotfish*'s engagements with 'the natural' likens them to Cliff, Feinberg, and Mootoo's novels – and thereby indicates that the concept of organic transgenderism continues to circulate in transgender literature – they differ from those earlier works in several ways. One is in their focus on the private, domestic environments in which gender transitioning is negotiated – which, in turn, leads to a focus on relationships with immediate family members. These differences result from *Luna* and *Parrotfish*'s focus on relatively early transitioning, but they are also a result of their protagonists' relatively more stable, privileged lives. Whereas Luna and Grady have intact, nuclear biological families, the poor and/or working-class adult protagonists of *No Telephone to Heaven*, *Stone Butch Blues*, and *Cereus Blooms at Night* are estranged from their (largely abusive) families; their character development, then, is centred on self-instantiation in adulthood, not coming out to others as youths.

This new focus on domesticity and family allows Peters and Wittlinger to detail their characters' growing awareness of how gender regimes affect *all* humans, not just transgender ones. This anti-cisnormative perspective thus avoids pathologizing trans existence as anomalous. In *Luna*, for instance, we find the following exchange between Reagan and Luna:

> 'I think [Mom] feels her talents are wasted on perfecting the art of homemaking', [Luna said]. 'What's wrong with homemaking?' I said. . . . 'It's the most important job in the world when you have kids.' Liam [Luna] gunned the engine at the green light . . . . 'With that kind of attitude, you could set the women's movement back a hundred years'.
>
> *(Peters 2004: Kindle Locations 848–852)*

Gendered division of household labour is an issue in *Parrotfish* as well, though Wittlinger takes it on more humorously. Near the end of the novel, Grady gives hir mother a Christmas coupon that reads, 'I, your son Grady, promise to help you cook dinner two nights a week, thereby saving several nights for other persons in my family who might also want to learn the non-gender-specific ritual of preparing the evening meal' (Wittlinger 2007:272). Relatedly, Peters and Wittlinger use the biological family to question the cissexist assumption that only transgender people modify their bodies or perform identity. At one point, for example, *Luna*'s Reagan reports that she heard her mother 'on the wall phone in the kitchen. "Will you please have Dr. Rosell call me?" she said. "I need an early refill on my estrogen"' (Peters 2004:1799–1800) – presumably, for menopause.[22]

As might be clear at this point, these novels lack critical awareness of class, racial, and sociopolitical positionality – which is central to Cliff, Feinberg, and Mootoo's novels and the vision of environmental ethics they offer. Indeed, as I show in *Strange Natures*, the organic transgenderism and environmental ethics of these earlier novels are directly tied to the trans protagonists' positions as poor, working-class, and/or postcolonial subjects (Seymour 2013). *Luna* and *Parrotfish* prompt us to ask, only by omission: What is it like to be trans when you can't retreat into your own private bedroom, as both Luna and Grady can and do? What if you don't have a car and can't escape your family or community, as Luna and Grady can and do? What is it like to come out or transition when you don't have disposable income, as Luna does, with the lucrative after-school job of building computers? In short, neither novel acknowledges how Luna's and Grady's respective transitions are eased by their positions as white, middle-to-upper-class US youth with intact nuclear families.[23] Thus these novels do not address the realities of social and environmental injustice, including homelessness and unemployment, faced by so many trans youth, not to mention trans adults.

Moreover, despite their engagement with discourses of the natural and with environmental science research, neither *Luna* nor *Parrotfish* fully achieve what we might call ecological consciousness or a vision of environmental ethics – though *Parrotfish* comes closer. Their young characters do learn to empathize with others, but the novels are largely concerned with insular human issues such as dating, school dances, and family celebrations. In fact, in *Luna* and *Parrotfish*, the characters' understanding of their transitioning in relation to the natural world threatens to become a self-serving articulation – which, as I argue, Cliff, Feinberg, and Mootoo's novels pointedly avoid. Whereas, for instance, Tyler lovingly tends the plant that helps hir understand hir transition in Mootoo's *Cereus Blooms at Night*, *Parrotfish*'s Grady never shows any particular interest in the stoplight parrotfish itself or its environment beyond its similarity to hir; the creature is merely a point of reference, a citation on a page. And aside from a few references to weather and region, geographical environment is treated as negligible in both novels; *Luna* and *Parrotfish* take place in bland, unspecified suburban locations that could be easily exchanged with countless others throughout the Western world. In Cliff, Feinberg, and Mootoo's novels, on the other hand, the protagonists' awareness of their specific physical environments informs their understanding of their own transitioning and their development of environmental ethics. Of course, one could argue that these are necessary features for young adult fiction. A generic setting, for example, may allow a wider swath of readers to identify with the story in question and thus to find transgender figures relatable. But we may nonetheless find these features a bit disappointing, considering the ongoing need for perspectives invested in both transgender and environmental issues.

## Conclusion

Overall, Peters's *Luna* and Wittlinger's *Parrotfish* offer sensitive, empathetic portraits of both trans people and their family and friends. Such portraits are rare in a contemporary Western climate still hostile to gender variance in humans, not to mention hostile to nonhuman nature. In further developing the counter-discourse of organic transgenderism, these novels allude to the connections among transgenderism, 'nature', and environment – connections that, I am suggesting, environmental humanities scholars should investigate more thoroughly.

I want to conclude with one last modelling of such investigation, drawing on recent real-world incidents. After controversy broke out over the trans-exclusive policies of radical US environmental group Deep Green Resistance (DGR), a spirited debate unspooled on the Earth First! newswire. On 14 May 2013, a poster with the moniker 'Brother, can you spare some bread?' declared, 'the world is burning, people. Lets [*sic*] all take a deep breath and let it go. No disrespect to trans folk at all, but in the total scheme of things, since the planet is, you know, burning, it might be good to focus on that instead of who has what parts'. Though this reaction was relatively mild compared to others, its invocation of the 'rearranging the deck chairs on the Titanic' concept is typical of how certain environmental movements have discounted questions of social injustice, framing the concerns of oppressed groups as pesky distractions from pro-environmental efforts. (The epigraph for this essay, from an activist writing in *Earth First! The Radical Environmental Journal* [Trouble! 2007], directly critiques such framing.) In this particular case, 'Brother' condescendingly – and, I would argue, quite inaccurately – portrays *trans* people, rather than *transphobic* people, as obsessively focusing on 'who has what parts' (see Houlberg, this volume, for a discussion of DGR).

Four months later, at the We Are Power Shift climate-change activism conference held in Pittsburgh, Pennsylvania, one could find a compelling (indirect) response. Washington, D.C.–based transgender activist Ruby Corado and climate activist Lauren Wood led a panel titled 'Critical Transitions, Common Ground: Lessons from Transgender Activism for the Climate Justice Movement'. As the panel description reads,

> Trans* communities fight challenges *that are often even more life and death* than conventional environmental issues. If the climate movement cannot embrace people who embody courageous transition, how can we call for a transformation of society? Come and learn how to better support . . . *trans* people already active in the fight against climate change* . . . *as well as* how to link to the broader movements for people's rights.
>
> *('We Are Power Shift' conference panel description 2013:n.p.; my emphasis)*

This description rejects the idea that daily injustices can be placed on the back burner, while ultimately refusing the binary of the environmental *or* the social. It indicts disregard for trans issues, if not transphobia, within environmental movements, while clearly identifying trans concern for environmental issues and pointing to grounds for coalitional activism.

But perhaps more important in terms of thinking forward, the question posed in the second sentence of this description raises another compelling question: In what ways might transgender identities, experiences, or frameworks uniquely lend themselves to recognizing or addressing environmental problems, including shifting away from the systems and status quos with which we are all so familiar? While some of the discourses surveyed previously would foreclose such a question altogether, I would like to propose it here as the basis for future work. Perhaps such work might begin with the remarks of Anohni, the British-American transgender musician, artist, and activist who, after several projects centred around environmental crisis (as Antony and the Johnsons), told interviewer Lawrence Ferber:

> [E]specially in regards to this body of work I like the idea of a kind of feral, empathic connection with the world around you. It's the nature of the transgender person just on account of their increased sensitivity to their environment.
>
> *(Anohni, interview 2010:n.p.)*

## Acknowledgements

I began developing this essay during a 2013–2014 fellowship at the Rachel Carson Center (RCC) for Environment and Society. I was lucky to be in residence at the RCC at the same time as Sherilyn MacGregor; I'm thankful for her invitation to contribute to this volume and for our many chats over *Weissweinschorle* in the biergartens of Munich. I am also grateful to Cate Sandilands, who continually pushes my thinking forward.

## Notes

1 A note on terminology: 'transgender' functions as an umbrella term for gender-non-conforming and gender-variant people, including those who do not undergo sex reassignment surgery, and those who do not identify with either side of the strict male-female binary. 'Transgender' is frequently shortened to 'trans', as I will occasionally do here. (Some activists have also recently proposed 'trans*' to indicate the diversity that might be found under this umbrella.) 'Transgender' and 'trans' have largely supplanted 'transsexual', which is currently considered by many to be too clinical and outdated – though some people continue to self-identify as such, and the term still is used in a scientific sense to refer to nonhuman organisms.

2 I thus align myself with scholars and writers including, but certainly not limited to, Oliver Bendorf, Mel Y. Chen, Eli Clare, Eva Hayward, Bailey Kier, Michael Mlekoday, Ely Shipley, Jeanne Vaccaro, and Cleo Woefle-Erskine, who have begun to think through the links between transgender or 'trans' and environment.

3 The phrase 'trans ecologies' has appeared here and there in scholarly channels, such as in a January 2014 Call for Papers for a conference organized by Harlan Weaver and Veronica Sanz, and in Bendorf's May 2014 keyword article for *Transgender Studies Quarterly*, 'Nature'. However, I have not found any substantial related work, nor any attempts to define the phrase or outline what it might entail. To my knowledge, this essay and my 2016 essay, 'Trans Ecology and the Transgender Road Narrative' (*The Oxford Handbook of Ecocriticism*) constitute the first such work.

4 For example, on 9 June 2014, trans actress and activist Laverne Cox (*Orange Is the New Black*) made history as the first out trans person to appear on the cover of *Time* magazine, with an article by Katy Steinmetz titled 'The Transgender Tipping Point: America's Next Civil Rights Frontier'.

5 This number might be larger depending on how broadly 'transgender' or 'trans' is being conceived. See the Williams Institute report authored by Gary J. Gates at http://williamsinstitute.law.ucla.edu/wp-content/uploads/Gates-How-Many-People-LGBT-Apr-2011.pdf for a discussion of the difficulties of measuring trans populations. The report includes state, national, and international statistics that put the transgender-identified population anywhere from .1 to 2 per cent of the total population.

6 According to Doan, drawing on Grant et al., 'for transgender respondents who attempted to access a homeless shelter, "29 per cent were turned away altogether, 42 per cent were forced to stay in facilities designated for the wrong gender, and others encountered a hostile environment"' (2011:103).

7 See www.tgeu.org/node/53 and www.transgenderdor.org/.

8 In Stein's (2004) collection, 'gender' seems to refer primarily to cisgender women or men, and 'sexual diversity' does not seem to include gender diversity. The first makes statistical sense and the second conceptual sense, but perhaps both are worth noting, considering how the collection otherwise strives for – and, I believe, largely achieves – inclusivity.

9 To offer two concrete examples: first, as Sandy Stone (2006) and others have described, medical requirements often stipulate that trans people satisfactorily pass psychiatric evaluations before they can receive hormone prescriptions. Second, as Doan observes, drawing on Moulton and Seaton, 'A transgendered person who has transitioned but has not yet been able to afford the expensive surgery required in most states for a legal sex change is in most cases considered by the authorities as their birth gender' – thus, if incarcerated or housed in a homeless shelter, for example, 'a male to female transgendered person would be housed with men' and vulnerable to violence and abuse (Doan 2011:103).

10 The introductions to Alaimo's *Bodily Natures* and Alaimo and Hekman's *Material Feminisms* repeat the idea of theoretical work that rejects or ignores the material, but do not cite a single example of such work. Here, I am reminded of Gayle Salamon's critique of materialist approaches in transgender studies scholarship and activism: 'One wonders exactly what it is that is passing for social construction in these conversations' (2006:581). I should acknowledge here that several scholars have produced materialist-ecocritical and -feminist work that is informed by poststructuralism (Catriona Sandilands, for example), and that other scholars have taken materialist approaches to questions of 'trans' (Chen and Hayward, for example). My goal in this section of the essay is simply to think through the implications of certain materialist approaches.

11 'Cisgender' refers to people who, unlike transgender individuals, identify with the gender assigned to them at birth. The term is usually deployed in an attempt to illuminate cisgender privilege and avoid singling transgender people out terminologically.

12 Similarly, as Julie L. Nagoshi and Stephan/ie Brzuzy write, 'Queer theory developed from feminist and deconstructivist theories that posited that "normative" and "deviant" sexual behaviors and cognitions are social constructs. . . . Queer . . . rebels against . . . these kinds of essentialist views by proposing that gender roles, gender identity, and sexual orientations are social constructs and, therefore, open to questioning, subversion, and self-construction' (2010:434).

13 Problematically, Alaimo positions Hausman as a representative of 'transgender theory' (2010:7), despite the fact that many transgender activists and scholars have criticized her work. See, for example, Jacob Hale's 'Suggested rules for non-transsexuals writing about transsexuals, transsexuality, transsexualism, or trans ____' or Susan Stryker and Stephen Whittle's introductory commentary on Hausman in *The Transgender Studies Reader*.

Grosz contributed to, and is widely cited in, *Material Feminisms*. And, indeed, queer ecology scholars such as Myra Hird, author of 'Animal Trans' (2008), also (somewhat curiously, in my opinion) rely on

Grosz despite her transphobic stance. To be clear, none of the citations of Hausman and Grosz in *Bodily Natures* or *Material Feminisms* are related to transgenderism at all – though perhaps it's worth pointing out that these two scholars' transphobia thereby goes unacknowledged.

14 See, for example, Burkett's *New York Times* essay 'What makes a woman?' or Cleis Abeni's coverage of Greer's anti-trans position in *The Advocate*. See the references for links.

15 'Cisnormativity', following the definition of 'heteronormativity' established by Lauren Berlant and Michael Warner, would be 'institutions, structures of understanding and practical orientations' that position cisgenderism as 'unmarked, as the basic idiom of the personal and the social; or marked as a natural state; or projected as an ideal' (1998:548). 'Cissexism', following accepted definitions of 'heterosexism', would entail bias against transgender individuals that thereby privileges cisgender individuals.

16 Here, I borrow terminology from Lee Edelman's (2004) *No Future: Queer Theory and the Death Drive*.

17 There are several other problems here that I don't have room to discuss fully. For example, Ray conflates disparate terms, dubbing transgenderism an issue of 'sexuality' (2007:123) when it is clearly an issue of gender and/or sex.

18 'Hermaphrodite' is considered politically incorrect and outdated when it comes to humans; the term 'intersex' is largely favored instead. However, 'hermaphrodite' is still used in scientific contexts to refer to nonhuman organisms.

19 Similarly, in an article on public anxiety over so-called transgender fish, Bailey Kier asks 'why the idea of transgenderedness is being used to represent toxicity and eco-catastrophe, instead of the various economic and political aspects of "development" that create toxic endocrine disrupting conditions in the Potomac River. Stated simply, why is "transgender" the signifier and not "Merck & Co, Inc.," or "Perdue, Inc."?' (2010:314).

20 See Kier (2010) again, and Heather Davis's 2015 article, 'Toxic Progeny: The Plastisphere and Other Queer Futures'.

21 I use the gender-neutral pronouns 'hir' (rather than 'her' or 'his') and 'ze' (rather than 'she' or 'he'), proposed by transgender author and activist Leslie Feinberg, in reference to both Mootoo's character Tyler and Wittlinger's character Grady. I do so, respectively, because Tyler transitions throughout the narrative and because Grady emphasizes hir gender queerness, not (just) hir male identity; born Angela, ze chooses the new, 'neutral' (Wittlinger 2007:38) name of Grady, enthusing, 'It's a name that could belong to either gender . . . Also, I like the gray part of it – you know, not black, not white. Somewhere in the middle' (Wittlinger 2007:6). In contrast, because *Luna* unambiguously employs female pronouns for its titular character, I use those here.

22 We might read even further into this scene, considering how scholars such as Kier and Hayward have shown how humans and nonhumans are linked within the 'hormonal prism' (Kier 2010:310). For example, Hayward's (2014) short essay 'Transxenoestrogenesis' reminds us that progesterone, which is made from pregnant mares' urine, is used by both transgender and postmenopausal women.

23 Race is not actually mentioned in either novel, but the characters are thereby marked as white, especially considering their middle-class suburban existence. Moreover, both novels' covers feature white figures.

# References

Abeni, C. (2015) 'Feminist Germaine Greer goes on anti-trans rant over Caitlyn Jenner', *The Advocate*. Online. Available at: www.advocate.com/caitlyn-jenner/2015/10/26/feminist-germaine-greer-goes-anti-trans-rant-over-caitlyn-jenner (accessed 29 July 2016).

Ah-King, M. and Hayward, E. (2014) 'Toxic sexes: Perverting pollution and queering hormone disruption', *O-Zone: The Journal of Object-Oriented Studies* 1: 1–12.

Ahmed, S. (2008) 'Imaginary prohibitions: Some preliminary remarks on the founding gestures of the "New Materialism"', *European Journal of Women's Studies* 15(1): 23–39.

Alaimo, S. (2010) *Bodily Natures: Science, Environment, and the Material Self*. Bloomington: Indiana University Press.

Alaimo, S. and Hekman, S. (eds) (2008) *Material Feminisms*. Bloomington: Indiana University Press.

Azzarello, R. (2012) *Queer Environmentality: Ecology, Evolution, and Sexuality in American Literature*. Farnham, UK: Ashgate.

Bagemihl, B. (1999) *Biological Exuberance: Animal Homosexuality and Natural Diversity*. New York: St. Martin's Press.

Bell, D. (2010) 'Queernaturecultures', in Mortimer-Sandilands, C. and Erickson, B. (eds) *Queer Ecologies: Sex, Nature, Politics, Desire*. Bloomington: Indiana University Press, 134–145.

Berlant, L. and Warner, M. (1998) 'Sex in public', *Critical Inquiry* 24(2): 547–567.

Brother, can you spare some bread? (pseud.) (2013) Comment on 'DGR Meets Resistance at the Law and Disorder Conference', *Earth First! Journal Newswire*. Online. Available at: http://earthfirstjournal.org/newswire/2013/05/13/dgr-meets-resistance-at-the-law-and-disorder-conference/ (accessed 6 June 2014).

Burkett, E. (2015) 'What makes a woman?', *The New York Times*. Online. Available at: www.nytimes.com/2015/06/07/opinion/sunday/what-makes-a-woman.html?_r=1 (accessed 29 July 2016).

Carson, R. (1962) *Silent Spring*. New York: Houghton Mifflin Company.

Cliff, M. (1987) *No Telephone to Heaven*. New York: Vintage International.

Davis, H. (2015) 'Toxic progeny: The plastisphere and other queer futures', *PhiloSOPHIA* 5(2): 231–250.

Di Chiro, G. (2010) 'Polluted politics? Confronting toxic discourse, sex panic, and economativity', in Mortimer-Sandilands, C. and Erickson, B. (eds) *Queer Ecologies: Sex, Nature, Politics, Desire*. Bloomington: Indiana University Press, 199–230.

Doan, P. (ed) (2011) *Queerying Planning: Challenging Heteronormative Assumptions and Reframing Planning Practice*. Farnham, UK: Ashgate.

Edelman, L. (2004) *No Future: Queer Theory and the Death Drive*. Durham: NC: Duke University Press.

Feinberg, L. (1993) *Stone Butch Blues*. Ithaca, NY: Firebrand Books.

Ferber, L. (2010) 'Two spirits', *Dallas Voice*. Online. Available at: www.dallasvoice.com/spirits-1049945.html (accessed 1 June 2014).

Gates, G. J. (2011) 'How many people are lesbian, gay, bisexual, and transgender?', *The Williams Institute, UCLA*. Online. Available at: http://williamsinstitute.law.ucla.edu/wp-content/uploads/Gates-How-Many-People-LGBT-Apr-2011.pdf (accessed 3 June 2014).

Grosz, E. (1994) *Volatile Bodies: Toward a Corporeal Feminism*. Bloomington: Indiana University Press.

Hale, Jacob. 'Suggested Rules for Non-Transsexuals Writing About Transsexuals, Transsexuality, Transsexualism, or Trans ____'. Online. Available at: http://sandystone.com/hale.rules.html (accessed 3 June 2014).

Hausman, B. (1995) *Changing Sex: Transsexualism, Technology, and the Idea of Gender*. Durham, NC: Duke University Press.

Hausman, B. (2006) 'Body, technology, and gender in transsexual autobiographies', in Stryker, S. and Whittle, S. (eds) *The Transgender Studies Reader*. New York: Routledge, 335–361.

Hayward, E. (2014) 'Transxenoestrogenesis', *TSQ: Transgender Studies Quarterly* 1(1–2): 255–258.

Hird, M. J. (2008) 'Animal trans', in Giffney, N. and Hird, M. J. (eds) *Queering the Non/Human*. Farnham, UK: Ashgate, 227–247.

Kier, B. (2010) 'Interdependent ecological transsex: Notes on re/production, "transgender" fish, and the management of populations, species, and resources', *Women and Performance: A Journal of Feminist Theory* 20(3): 299–319.

McRuer, R. (2013) 'Pink', in Cohen, J. J. (ed) *Prismatic Ecology: Ecotheory Beyond Green*. Minneapolis, MN: University of Minnesota Press, 63–82.

Mootoo, S. (1998) *Cereus Blooms at Night*. New York: Grove.

Mortimer-Sandilands, C. and Erickson, B. (2010) 'Introduction: A genealogy of queer ecologies', in Mortimer-Sandilands, C. and Erickson, B. (eds) *Queer Ecologies: Sex, Nature, Politics, Desire*. Bloomington: Indiana University Press, 1–48.

Nagoshi, J. and Brzuzy, S. (2010) 'Transgender theory: Embodying research and practice', *Journal of Women and Social Work* 25(4): 431–443.

Peters, J. A. (2004) *Luna*. New York: Little, Brown, Kindle Edition.

Ray, J. (2007) 'Changing sex', in Matthiessen, P. (ed) *Courage for the Earth: Writers, Scientists, and Activists Celebrate the Life and Writing of Rachel Carson*. New York: Houghton Mifflin, 109–128.

Richards, S. E. (2014) 'The next frontier in fertility treatment', *New York Times*. Online. Available at: www.nytimes.com/2014/01/13/opinion/the-next-frontier-in-fertility-treatment.html (accessed 16 April 2016).

Roughgarden, J. (2004) *Evolution's Rainbow: Diversity, Gender, and Sexuality in Nature and People*. Berkeley, CA: University of California Press.

Salamon, G. (2006) 'Boys of the Lex: Transgenderism and rhetorics of materiality', *GLQ* 12(4): 575–597.

Sandilands, C. and Erickson, B. (eds) (2010) *Queer Ecologies: Sex, Nature, Politics, Desire*. Bloomington: Indiana University Press.

Sandler, R. and Pezzulo, P. C. (eds) (2007) *Environmental Justice and Environmentalism: The Social Justice Challenge to the Environmental Movement*. Cambridge, MA: MIT Press.

Schlosberg, D. (2007) *Defining Environmental Justice: Theories, Movements, and Nature*. Oxford, UK: Oxford University Press.

Seymour, N. (2013) *Strange Natures: Futurity, Empathy, and the Queer Ecological Imagination*. Urbana, IL: University of Illinois Press.

Seymour, N. (2016) 'Trans ecology and the transgender road narrative', in Garrard, G. (ed) *Oxford Handbook of Ecocriticism*. Oxford, UK: Oxford University Press. Ebook version.

Stein, R. (2004) 'Introduction', in Stein, R. (ed) *New Perspectives on Environmental Justice: Gender, Sexuality, and Activism*. New Brunswick, NJ: Rutgers University Press, 1–18.

Steinmetz, K. (2014) 'The transgender tipping point: America's next civil rights frontier', *Time*. Online. Available at: http://time.com/135480/transgender-tipping-point/ (accessed 16 April 2016).

Stone, S. (2006) 'The empire strikes back: A posttranssexual manifesto', in Stryker, S. and Whittle, S. (eds) *The Transgender Studies Reader*. New York: Routledge, 221–235.

Stryker, S. (2008) *Transgender History*. Berkeley, CA: Seal Press.

Stryker, S., Currah, P. and Moore, L. J. (2008) 'Introduction: Trans-, trans, or transgender?', *Women's Studies Quarterly* 36(4): 11–22.

Trouble! (2007) 'Trannies are taking over', *Earth First! The Radical Environmental Journal* 27(2): 28–29.

We Are Power Shift (2013) 'Power Shift 2013' conference website. Online at http://powershift.org/conference/powershift2013 (accessed 05-05-17).

Wittlinger, E. (2007) *Parrotfish*. New York: Simon and Schuster.

# 18

# A FRUITLESS ENDEAVOUR

## Confronting the heteronormativity of environmentalism

*Cameron Butler*

## Introduction

With its focus on saving the planet for 'our' children and grandchildren, sustainability is arguably about as 'straight' a political project as one can imagine. Emotional appeals to save future generations from ecological catastrophe are commonplace in high-level environmental conferences. In the opening ceremonies of the annual COPs to the UNFCC, for example, videos portraying pleading children regularly serve to underscore the notion that taking urgent action to stop the climate crisis is a non-optional moral duty. The assembled policy makers are focused on a family-oriented future almost as narrowly as a closeted man denying his homosexual urges. Of course they are motivated to tackle climate change out of concern for their own lives and families, but it is important to consider the implications of this broader framing. What ideological work does this child- and future-centric rhetoric do for the green cause? Upon what assumptions is it based, and whom does it include or exclude from its frame?

Dominant environmental understandings of sustainability have been at best exclusive of, and at worst at odds with, the realities of LGBTQ2SIA (lesbian, gay, bisexual, trans, questioning, two-spirit, intersex, and asexual; herein referred to as *queer*) people and communities. Environmentalists frequently raise concerns about the effects of synthetic chemicals on fertility and links between toxic pollution and 'genetic abnormalities' (be they related to physical impairments or sex characteristics); rarely do environmentalists express outrage at the HIV/AIDS crisis or the high rates of poverty and violence experienced by queer and trans people (trans people of colour in particular). Sustainable development strategies in mainstream environmental policy simply do not acknowledge, let alone address, the harms that queer people experience in societies around the world.

Critical race theorists, ecofeminist scholars, and environmental justice activists have posed important challenges to mainstream environmentalism, creating in response radical conceptions of, and actions to achieve, sustainability that are based on social and ecological justice (cf. Martinez-Alier 2002; Pezzullo and Sanders 2007; see also chapters by Sze and Di Chiro in this handbook). In contrast, queer theorists who work to understand 'the extensive range of ways in which notions of sexuality and gender impact – at times implicitly – on everyday life' (Sullivan 2003) have been slower to engage with sustainability and environmentalism, due in part to the way persistent deployments of the notion of the 'natural' (or perhaps more accurately the 'unnatural') have been used to justify the oppression of queer people (Azzarello 2012:17). As a result, sustainability has rarely been approached from a queer perspective, nor have advocates of sustainability considered queerness in their future-building work. This lack of engagement has meant that while what might be called the 'mainstream sustainability movement' (MSM) has sought to address a number of harmful societal practices, it has left others unchallenged and unchanged, namely:

1   *heteronormativity* – the positioning of heterosexuality as natural and normal;
2   *cissexism* – the conflating of gender and sex and positioning of cisgender people as natural and normal; and
3   *reprocentricity* – the positioning of reproduction (or procreation) as being central to all people's lives.

These tendencies in mainstream environmentalism raise a number of important questions for those interested in the study of gender and environment, such as how are gender roles defined and reinforced in relation to the heterosexual family unit in environmental rhetoric? When so-called traditional family units are the basis for eco-political discussion and policy initiatives, what happens to the people who don't follow those familial narratives? And how do heteronormativity and reprocentricity contribute to current ecological disasters?

To pursue this line of inquiry, in this chapter I present a review of the academic field of *queer ecology* and the important role it can play in re-shaping views of environment and nature and of human and nonhuman species. Queer ecology brings queer theory and method into the realm of environmental discourse, disrupting categorical boundaries and heteronormative values that are projected onto nature. In the first part of the chapter I give an overview of queer ecology, exploring its major works, concepts, and evolution over time. This review will provide readers with an understanding of what it is to think in a queer ecological way and what a queer ecological perspective brings to environmental discourse. Following this discussion, I go on to apply a queer ecological lens to aspects of the MSM, focusing on the underlying heteronormativity in its discourses and policies that, I argue, remains largely unchecked. Finally, I make a case for what a 'queer sustainability' might look like and how it might lead to different kinds of policies, actions, and outcomes.

## Follow the rainbow-brick road: the evolution of queer ecology

Queer ecology as a field started roughly two decades ago. One of the earliest writings was Greta Gaard's 'Towards a Queer Ecofeminism' published in 1997. It was a powerful and influential essay that argues 'that liberating the erotic requires reconceptualising humans as equal participants in culture and in nature, able to explore the eroticism of reason and the unique rationality of the erotic' (1997:126). It was a challenge for ecofeminists to expand their analysis to engage with queerness and heterosexism. In the article, Gaard traces the history of homosexuality being viewed as a 'crime against nature' and argues that procreation is central to the categorizing of natural versus unnatural, and that that focus on procreation is used to oppress women and queer people. Soon thereafter, Bruce Bagemihl and Joan Roughgarden published groundbreaking books arguing that *nature is queer*. They explore, among other things, the wealth of empirical evidence, often denied by biologists and environmental scientists, that nonhuman animals engage in all manner of non-heterosexual relationships and non-reproductive sexual acts for pleasure.

In *Biological Exuberance: Animal Homosexuality and Natural Diversity* (1999), Bagemihl gives a number of examples of 'same-sex' interactions and relationships between nonhuman species such as bottlenose dolphins, where the lives of males are 'characterized by extensive bisexuality, combined with periods of exclusive homosexuality' (751). He also uses examples to illustrate the kaleidoscopic nature of gender and sexuality, including female grizzly bears forming non-sexual partnerships (for travelling and raising cubs) and female bonobos using branches and leaves as sex toys for masturbation. All of the examples he gives are woven together to support his argument that

> Phenomena such as homosexuality or gender mixing are never seen as neutral or expected variations along a sexual and gender continuum (or continua), but rather as abnormal or exceptional conditions that require explanation. At the root of this perception is the idea that homosexuality and transgender are dysfunctional behaviours or conditions because they do not lead to reproduction.
>
> *(Bagemihl 1999:221)*

Importantly, Bagemihl argues that homophobia shapes the supposed objectivity of scientists in their surveying of nonhuman animal behaviour; scientists therefore ignore or dismiss homosexual activity among the nonhuman animals they study. This view not only has negative impacts on the broader expanse of scientific knowledge, but it in turn feeds into the homophobic rhetoric that queerness is a uniquely human experience that is unnatural and therefore immoral.

Roughgarden's invocation of the rainbow, in her book *Evolution's Rainbow: Diversity, Gender and Sexuality in Nature and People* (2004), is a direct reference to the symbol of queer pride and diversity since the late 1970s. She presents evidence of a wide range of different forms of sexual activity and gender roles that exist outside of a cissexist male/female binary among nonhuman animals. She gives examples of species with more than two biological sexes, as well as other species whose members change their sexes and genders at times. For example, the bluehead wrasse fish has three genders, one which consists of individuals who are males for their entire lives, one which consists of individuals who are females for their entire lives, and one which consists of individuals who begin as females and later change into males based on changes in social organization. She also discusses the existence of multiple-gender 'family' organizations that can be observed among human and nonhuman species. These examples provide a wealth of evidence that heteronormativity and reprocentricity are social constructs, not biological truths: animals do not live solely to procreate. *Evolution's Rainbow* shows that all sorts of intimate interactions can be considered natural and normal, that diversity is the default position in nature.

Alongside this work of cataloguing queerness in nature, other scholars have developed important theoretical frameworks for analyzing heteronormativity in societal beliefs and institutions. Two books that have been influential in building a queer ecological lens are Donna Haraway's *The Companion Species Manifesto* (2003) and Lee Edelman's *No Future: Queer Theory and the Death Drive* (2004). In her book, Haraway presents the notion of 'natureculture', the idea that 'the very idea of nature itself is not natural; *nature is cultural*', though that is not to say that nature is subsumed within culture (emphasis in original, quoted in Bell 2010:143). Rather, it means that our notions of nature are formed through a cultural lens, shaped by our perspectives, held beliefs, and positionalities. As such, interrogating the frameworks through which nature is conceived and discussed reveals what is included and excluded; with humans and anything humans create usually being in the excluded column. This is a foundational concept within queer ecology and provides a theoretical tool for understanding how societal logics like heteronormativity or misogyny become transposed upon nature, or rather what is considered to be nature/natural.

Edelman, while not a queer ecologist himself, explores themes of reprocentricity and anti-futurity that are important to queer ecology. Anti-futurity is a position that 'a future-oriented politics informed by a positive, hopeful conception of the future is necessarily opposed to and exclusionary of queerness', and therefore queerness must always disturb and threaten the stability that that future-oriented politics aims for (in Hall 2014:207–208). He argues in *No Future* that the oppression of marginalized groups in the present is justified by claims that it is for the sake of a theorized future Child (his capitalization); queer people are subjected to violence in the present in order to protect an imagined Child-yet-to-be-born. For example, the state of North Carolina in the United States recently passed bill HB2, which, among other things, seeks to prevent trans people from using any public toilet/restroom besides the one that corresponded to the gender listed on their birth certificate (changing the gender marker is a difficult task due to other state laws), supposedly to protect children from being assaulted in these places. It received international condemnation, and even led to Britain's Foreign and Commonwealth Office issuing a travel advisory for queer people travelling to the United States. In the face of public outcry, the Lieutenant Governor Dan Forest issued a press release stating that 'If our action in keeping men out of women's bathrooms and showers protected the life of just one child or one woman from being molested or assaulted, then it was worth it . . . They are precious and priceless' (April 5, 2016). It is rare to see so explicitly how the protection of some imagined 'precious and priceless' Child is used to justify blatant discrimination. It is particularly striking for how much it diverges with reality. Whereas there is a lack of evidence that men claim to be trans in order to sneak into restrooms to assault children, there is a wealth of evidence documenting that trans people regularly experience violence when using public toilets/restrooms (Steinmetz 2016:website).

Inspired by such 'real life' events, there are a growing number of books and articles that seek to develop the political potential of queer ecology. Noël Sturgeon's *Environmentalism in Popular Culture: Gender, Race, Sexuality, and the Politics of the Natural* (2008) was followed by Catriona Mortimer-Sandilands' and Bruce Erickson's edited collection *Queer Ecologies: Sex, Nature, Politics, Desire* (2010) and Robert Azzarello's *Queer Environmentality: Ecology, Evolution, and Sexuality in American Literature* (2012). These texts are predominantly, though not exclusively, engaged with fiction, films, and art, applying queer ecology frameworks in order to draw insights about social conceptions of nature. Individual chapters in these volumes ask such questions as: What does *Brokeback Mountain* reveal about the need to control queer eroticism and nonhuman animals' reproduction? How does Thoreau's *Walden* create space for queerness within nature? As a whole, this work forms an intricate spider's web, connecting distant points of inquiry but also revealing the large gaps that have yet to be filled.

In her book Sturgeon breaks down common environmental narratives and tropes to expose how they reify societal oppressions. She focuses on the need to build broad coalitions and engage in intersectional social justice in order to achieve long-term environmental and social sustainability. *Queer Ecologies* provides a clear articulation of the goals of queer ecology, which, according to the editors' introduction, are to create

> a sexual politics that more clearly includes considerations of the natural world and its biosocial constitution, and an environmental politics that demonstrates an understanding of the ways in which sexual relations organize and influence both the material world of nature and our perceptions, experiences, and constitutions of that world.
>
> *(Mortimer-Sandilands and Erickson 2010:5)*

In his chapter in *Queer Ecologies*, Andil Gosine explores how queer eroticism, which emphasizes pleasure rather than utility or productive potential, challenges the erotophobia that limits understandings of non-(re)productive nature (such as the dismissal of queer nonhuman animal activity) and instead presents new ways of forming or valuing relationships (2010:165–166). In another chapter, Giovanna Di Chiro highlights how public responses to reports of environmental toxins and pollution are overly focused on the effects on reproductivity and sex characteristics because of how they threaten gender divisions (2010:202). While much of his book is focused on analyzing the works of American authors, Azzarello also provides a detailed account of the history of queer ecology, as well as the historical tension between queer theory and ecocriticism.

A major effort within queer ecological scholarship has been tracing the history of queer people's displacement from nature, and understanding how it manifests in the twenty-first century. Historical accounts identify two important trends that occurred simultaneously from the mid-1700s following the urbanization of Western Europe and North America, brought on by the Industrial Revolution. The first was that urban centres rapidly degraded due to increased, and increasingly concentrated, consumption and pollution. The second trend was the transformation of the social mix of urban centres due to an influx of immigrants, the participation of women in the market and politics, and the visibility of queer people in the public sphere (Mortimer-Sandilands and Erickson 2010:3–4). To observers at the time, these trends appeared to be linked, as if marginalized people's improved social conditions were tied to ecological degradation. This meant that straight white men – until then those with an exclusive claim to public space – believed they were being exposed to environmental and social pollution (Sbicca 2012). As a result, those straight white men needed an escape from the smog and the social deviance of urban life. From a queer ecology perspective, the conservation movement emerged in the mid-nineteenth century to provide that escape, with 'the creation of remote recreational wild spaces and the demarcation of "healthy" green spaces inside cities' for the purpose of being 'a therapeutic antidote to the social ravages of effeminate homosexuality' (Mortimer-Sandilands 2005:10). In other words, preserving nature was not for the sake of nature itself, but rather to ensure that straight white men had a space to go to reclaim their masculinity. For example, the US National Parks Service was created by a group of white men, a number of whom were deeply xenophobic and racist and wanted the parks as a natural sanctuary from poor people and people of colour (Mock 2016).

Other important texts have moved the field of queer ecology out of the realm of literary and cultural studies into new areas for critical analysis. For example, Mel Y. Chen's *Animacies: Biopolitics, Racial Mattering and Queer Affect* (2012) brings queer-of-colour scholarship to queer ecology and critical animal studies, tracing the interlacing influences of heteropatriarchy and white supremacy onto animacy. Animacy, as Chen describes it, 'bears no single standard definition' but rather 'has been described variously as a quality of agency, awareness, mobility, and liveness' (2012:2). Chen turns to the field of linguistics to explore histories of dehumanizing insults, and embodiment, and environmental illness. She explores the way animacy can be seen on a scale, such that objects like rocks and metals can have near-zero-but-not-zero position on the animacy hierarchy, and how 'animacy is implicated in political questions of power and the recognition of different subjects, as well as ostensible objects' (9).

Another important book is Nicole Seymour's *Strange Natures: Futurity, Empathy, and the Queer Ecological Imagination* (2013), which continues in the vein of literary criticism but adds explicit analysis of connections between literary texts/films and political activism. She ties together heteronormativity and capitalism, to further the argument that queer non-reproductivity and economic non-productivity are intertwined. This comes through in her analysis of *Brokeback Mountain*, where she shows that the two male protagonists are not merely queer sexually, as they commence a sexual relationship, but also economically, as they fail to do their job and do not produce the profits demanded by their employer. By connecting the productive goals of capitalism to heteronormativity and futurity, Seymour underscores how anti-capitalism becomes a key feature of queer ecological analysis and action. Building off these connections, Seymour presents a queer empathy and care that is detached from reprocentric criteria of earning care via demonstrated usefulness and (re)productive potential.

In 2015, the Canadian student environmental studies journal, *Undercurrents: Journal of Critical Environmental Studies*, published a special issue titled 'From Queer/Nature to Queer Ecologies', marking the twentieth anniversary of its pioneering 'Queer/Nature' issue (published in 1994), which was also one of the earliest collections of essays that brought together environmental discourse and queer theory. As part of the special issue, the editors held a round-table with important queer ecology writers including Catriona Sandilands, Peter Hobbs, and Gordon Brent Brochu-Ingram, on the history, present, and future of queer ecology. An edited transcript of the roundtable, along with the full recording, is available with the journal and highly recommended as a thoughtful snapshot of the field as it stands. Some of the major points they raise are about the bridges being formed between queer ecology, decolonial and Indigenous theorizing around environment, and queer-of-colour theory. They look at those connections as being the promising future of queer ecology. They also speak to how queer ecology has been successful in building a diverse set of scholarly and creative practices, but has been slow to shape activism and action. Queer ecology has been creating a catalogue of theory and ideas that, for the most part, have yet to be put into practice. My aim here is to demonstrate how queer ecology can reorient activism, efforts, and policies in more inclusive and system-changing directions.

## But how does it work? Outlining a queer ecological lens

Queer ecology provides critical analysis of how heteronormativity and reprocentricity shape expectations and ideas around gender, gender roles, sexuality, and nature/environment. By now it should be clear that heteronormative futurity, characterized as 'the governing compulsion, the singular imperative, that affords us no meaningful choice . . . the compulsion to embrace our own futurity in the privileged form of the Child' (Edelman 2004:15) is a central theme. Alongside sexual reproduction, a queer ecological lens focuses on how economic (re)production dictates and leads sustainability policies and, as a result, criticism of capitalist production and its treatment of humans and nature is a key feature of work in this field.

Beyond these two lines of questioning, there is a third important aspect of the queer eco-logical lens. Queer ecology thinkers use the word 'queer' as an adjective to describe sexuality and gender, but they also use it as a verb, as in 'to queer', to engage in the act of queering. *To queer* is to question the categories, definitions, divisions, distinctions, and dualities that exist and that usually go unchallenged within society. A queer ecological lens focuses, in particular, on destabilizing the identities and categories of nature, pushing against the way ecosystems are defined, or how value is ascribed to a landscape. As Sandilands has asserted, 'to queer nature is to question its normative use, to interrogate relations of knowledge and power by which certain "truths" about ourselves have been allowed to pass, unnoticed, without question' (Sandilands 1994). Importantly, the approach is 'anti-essentialist, anti-assimilationist, and het-erogeneous' (Seymour 2013:25).

A fourth aspect of a queer ecological lens that I want to highlight here is the use of irony discursively to subvert environmental degradation and illuminate oppressive logics. The use of irony has often been seen as incompatible with the (stereo)typical seriousness, sincerity, and self-righteousness of environmentalism (Seymour 2013:149). However, Seymour argues that it is deeply ironic (yet still necessary) to act on firm beliefs of environmental ethics and social justice while maintaining a critical scepticism of the categories, boundaries, and distinctions employed in those ethics. Working in solidarity with an Other that we cannot so easily communicate with (i.e., the nonhuman), while recognizing our limited capacity to 'know' the world and the relationship between living things, is an ironic act. She practices irony by pointing to the care shown by characters in the book *Cereus Blooms at Night*. Tyler, a trans person of colour nurse, cares similarly for hir patient, Mala, as to the cereus plant. Ze acts 'ethically and even lovingly . . . not because [ze] want[s], or expect[s] to get anything back, but because it is fulfilling in and of itself to do so' (57). Seymour outlines such a queer ecological irony as one that is not 'cruel or dismissive' but rather 'simultaneously compassionate, introspective, and good-humoured' (172). It is an irony that aims to support ethics of care by showing where none exists. Irony thus can be a tool used to highlight the gaps of hypocrisy wherein oppression manifests.

I use irony throughout this chapter as part of a queer ecological critique of sustainability. Note that the section titles involve word plays, which serve to underscore my criticisms, while also lightening the tone. What better way to ease the tension of a harsh criticism than to make a silly joke? My chapter title 'A Fruitless Endeavour' is a play on words. In one aspect, 'fruitless' is meant to refer to the homophobic slang of 'fruit' (to refer to a gay man) in order to highlight the lack of consideration toward queer people within the MSM, and the lack of engagement with the environment by queer theorists. It is also meant to assert that the MSM will fail to achieve its goal of creating a sustainable society if the issues raised by queer ecology are not properly engaged with and addressed. In a similarly ironic move, I use 'MSM' to emphasize the lack of queer people in the sustainability imagination. The acronym 'MSM' historically has referred to 'men who have sex with men' and was created by epidemiologists in the 1990s because many of those who engaged in cruising (i.e., having anonymous sex in public places) did not identify as gay or bisexual, so a behaviourally-based term was needed (United States Centers for Disease Control 1995). It has been most notably used by the police in their surveilling and arresting of men cruising in parks, particularly in North America and parts of Europe (Maynard 1994). There is a long history of public officials (in cities in the United States, Canada, Australia, and across Europe) claiming that cruising men ruin the parks and harm the environment through littering, despite a lack of evidence (Gosine 2010:155). Officials commonly resort to removing undergrowth and bushes as a means of discouraging cruising; ironically destroying the very environment they are trying to protect (Gosine 2010:160). In this chapter, therefore, I re-appropriate the acronym MSM for 'mainstream sustainability movement' in order to highlight the ironies that arise when oppressing marginalized people is so important that it is worth sacrificing the environment to do it.[1]

## You can't paint a rainbow only with green: queer critiques of the MSM

Having explained the key elements of a queer ecological lens, I now use this lens to offer a critique of the discourse and policies of the mainstream sustainability movement. I will consider and then deconstruct the binaries of nature/culture, productive/unproductive, and beauty/ugly, because each one plays a significant role in shaping MSM discourse. After that, I take a deeper look at the problematic Child, specifically how it demands the attention and (in)action of environmental activists and policy makers. Finally, I attempt to ground these more abstract critiques in actually existing sustainable development policies, showing how heteronormativity, futurity, and capitalist (re)productivity have shaped key documents such as *Agenda 21*.

## *Green thumbs in a petrified garden: deconstructing binaries*

As mentioned previously, queer ecology takes particular aim at dismantling the nature/culture binary that is pervasive throughout MSM rhetoric and efforts. Sturgeon argues that

> mainstream environmentalists, in their emphasis on wilderness, species extinction, and in general seeing the environment as excluding human beings, often fall into service to this dominant Western logic of seeing the natural as pure, unchanging, untainted by social influence and without history.
>
> *(Sturgeon 2010:263)*

One effect of the nature/culture binary within the MSM is that humans are placed outside of nature, and human bodies are subsequently not viewed as spaces for environmental action or concern (Falek 2015). Or human bodies can be used as means to achieving environmental ends, such as when the campaign group PETA uses sexist images of women to promote their cause (Glasser 2011). As environmental justice activists and authors have demonstrated, social justice concerns have not been sufficiently integrated into the MSM (Pezzullo and Sanders 2007; Soltys 2012). MSM organizations have been criticized for disregarding social justice questions, either dismissing them outright or arguing that they are distractions from the more important issues of environmental and climate catastrophe (Bardos 2016). As Di Chiro has persuasively argued, the popular green concept of the Anthropocene papers over the fact that the poorest people are hurt the most by a global ecological crisis that they have had very little role in creating (see her chapter in this handbook). Further, marginalized communities, particularly Indigenous communities, have at times been directly harmed by MSM efforts. For example, Greenpeace activists literally trampled on the cultural heritage of Peruvian people in order to put a banner protesting climate change on the Nazca Lines (McGrath 2014: website). The creation of wildlife preserves globally has often involved forcibly removing Indigenous peoples from land in order to 'protect' it from human influence (Gosine 2010:152). It is not uncommon for environmentalists to show blatant disrespect for those communities' sovereignty and rights, and a silencing of their voices, in the effort to 'return' land to a human-less, and therefore 'natural', state.

Closely related to the nature/culture binary within the MSM is the distinction between pristine and polluted environments. Conservation and preservation efforts arguably have developed out of an ahistorical human-less construction of nature as 'wilderness'. They have worked to protect unspoiled nature and reduce the (assumed) negative impact that the human presence has on the environment. Conservation ethics, as articulated in the early twentieth century by Gifford Pinchot, strives to use nature 'for the greatest good for the greatest number of people for the longest time' (quoted in Hunter Jr. 1993:119). Humans are viewed in this framework as being separate from nature, and as having only damaging effects on nature, which must be mitigated and minimized. This pristine/polluted binary results in ecosystems being forced into a strange state of petrification. It becomes impossible to differentiate between 'natural' changes that come out of evolution and 'typical' environmental shifts, and 'unnatural' changes that are caused by destructive humans, because any change reflects a failure to control nature. This attempt to distinguish the origins of ecological changes, and to control supposedly 'unnatural' ones, is a misguided one that fails properly to place humans as part of the broader environment and ecological community.

From a queer ecology perspective, the management and supervision of nature through conservation work runs parallel to the handling of sexuality in Western culture, as both are regulations of desire (Seymour 2013:107–108). Both socially and environmentally, the pristine/polluted binary is crossed via uncontrolled and unrestricted desire and (re)production. Without proper management, unwanted species will crop up and 'ruin' a space, similar to how allowing queer people to live and thrive supposedly leads to social decay. The happy white suburban family is threatened by both poisonous toxins and corrupting queer influences on their children. In response to the potential threat of shifting from pristine to polluted, there is a rhetorical and material move toward 'constant monitoring and restrictions to access, so [as to] be free of undesirable elements' (Seymour 2013:144). Population discourse within the MSM demonstrates this. Sexuality is reduced to heteronormative production of children, which must be limited through family planning efforts, in order to protect the environment from human impact (Sandilands 1999:84). Pristine ecosystems must be protected from human-induced harm, just as non-white families must be protected from having too many children.

Two further binaries worth highlighting in this section are closely tied together: productive/unproductive and beauty/ugly. Heteronormative capitalist goals of (re)productivity fundamentally drive the ways ecosystems are (de)valued. An ecosystem's worth is dependent on its perceived capacity to be productive in economically quantifiable ways. The MSM relies on what Judith Butler (1993) describes as 'citational legitimacy', the drawing of power and authority by referencing a powerful institution, in this case the economy and market value. It deploys the notion of services rendered with the concept of ecosystem services and other attempts to valourize and monetize, such as The Economics of Ecosystems and Biodiversity (TEEB) initiative; moral value and worth are drawn from proving a financial worth as if each tree or pond could be reduced to a price tag. In effect, the erotic potential of nature, its capacity to exist, flourish, and (re)produce in ways that are not economically useful, aesthetically pleasing, or desirable must be stamped out and crushed, just as queerness is targeted for its refusal to participate in heteronormative (re)productivity. This can be seen in historical shift in farming, with incredible movements toward genetically homogeneous monocultures due to their increased harvesting and planting efficiency, and therefore greater economic benefit, despite drastically reducing biodiversity and creating potential risks for diseases and pests (Marshall 1977:1–2).

Ideally, to be worth protecting, an ecosystem needs to be either aesthetically pleasing, economically productive, or both. The capacity to be beautiful counts as a kind of productivity. And the Western construction of an ugly/beauty binary is deeply mired in racist and sexist tones. There is a wealth of research on how Western beauty standards are intensely racialized and gendered (see Patton 2006; Hall 2007; Swami et al. 2010). These conceptions of what is beautiful or ugly are also projected onto the environment and landscapes. As Seymour explains, Western constructions of 'ugly' landscapes have historically been those populated by Indigenous, racialized, and poor people – the politics of beauty are inextricably tied to racism, classism, colonialism, and sexism (2013:164). This includes crowded urban areas, often seen as 'dirty' and 'ugly', and which are typically more populated by people of colour, as well as desert regions – seen as 'barren', 'empty', and 'useless' – which historically have been populated by Indigenous peoples (Seymour 2013:164).

## *Won't somebody please think of the children?*
## *Questioning futurity*

Stated simply, sustainability is fundamentally a project of futurity. As defined in the Brundtland report, *Our Common Future,* sustainable development is 'the development that meets the needs of the present without compromising the ability of future generations to meet their own needs' (WCED 1987:43). Viewed through a queer ecological lens, this definition connects environmental concern with heteronormative reproduction. The MSM often relies on a sentimentalized rhetoric of creating a better world for 'our children', suggesting that 'concern for the future qua the planet *can only emerge, or emerges most effectively,* from white, heterosexual, familial reproductivity' (Seymour 2013:7; emphasis in original).

This strategy is particularly at odds with queer theorists who champion anti-futurity, such as Edelman. When the fundamental explanation for why people should care for the environment is 'for the sake of the kids', the strategy can fall flat with people who don't identify with the heteronormative narrative. The reliance on protecting future generations as a moral foundation for sustainability has, unsurprisingly, turned queer theorists off environmentalism until relatively recently. It has also shaped which causes are given attention and which are ignored. Shifting the focus of motivation to the future and to impending disasters, such as climate change (which tends to be discussed in the future tense even though it is happening now and its effects are being felt in many parts of the planet), shifts attention away from ecological problems that are hurting people today, such as toxic pollution and biodiversity loss (MacGregor 2010). As noted previously, this is a major reason that ecofeminist, critical race and environmental justice theorists have worked to challenge environmental thought, because the unique harms their communities experience are lost in the generalized, future-focused rhetoric of the MSM.

## *Straight plays on the global stage: problematizing policy*

Moving away from theoretical critiques of the MSM, I now want to explore how these queer ecological critiques can highlight the unchallenged heteronormativity that shapes actually existing environmental policies. Institutions and policies can be viewed for how they are shaped by systems of oppression; institutions reconfigure themselves to maintain power imbalances (Foucault 1990:92). The outcome document from the 1992 Rio Earth Summit – *Agenda 21* – remains an important international policy document for the MSM. While aiming to promote global sustainability, it arguably is embedded within oppressive logics of heteronormativity and reprocentricity. And while the document aims to improve the quality of the environment for all, it has the effect of reinforcing existing hierarchies and power dynamics.

Aspects of *Agenda 21* can be interpreted through a Foucauldian lens as being consistent with neoliberal governmentality because the effect is to regulate bodies and (re)produce normalized gender identities in a non-coercive way in the service of environmental protection (Foster 2011).

Emma A. Foster argues that the positioning of non-Western women in *Agenda 21*, as childlike victims in need of aid, 'works to legitimize the operation of a neo-colonizing Western economic project, further projecting Western hegemonic ideals of "development" and framed through a green (in)security narrative' (Foster 2011:143; see also her chapter in this handbook). This economic development project ascribes a state of poverty to individuals for their lack of participation in the market economy, regardless of whether their needs are met or not (Foster 2011). Active participation in capitalism is the metric for measuring human well-being. In doing so, *Agenda 21* not only fails to criticize global capitalism for its role in human exploitation and ecological degradation; it also makes capitalism a key dimension of its effort to achieve sustainability.

As noted earlier, fear of overpopulation is ubiquitous within MSM discourse, and is especially evident in *Agenda 21*. In decrying population growth in the Global South, the bodies of poor brown women are demonized for their potential to give birth and threaten the lifestyles of traditional white families in the Global North. This focus on how many people exist distracts from the issue of how those people live and consume; it often ignores the fact that smaller populations in the Global North have a far greater impact on the planet than larger numbers of people living in the South (Sturgeon 2010:124–125). MSM organizations in the Global North have a long history of promoting xenophobia domestically and racist sexual regulation globally (Gosine 2010:157). It is unsurprising that MSM organizations in North America such as the Sierra Club have played a role in promoting anti-immigration policies domestically and the regulation of sexual reproduction in the Global South, repackaging their racism as concern for the environment. Betsy Hartmann has famously called this 'the greening of hate' (Hartmann 2010; see also Aufrecht 2013). In *Agenda 21*, overpopulation is addressed through the promotion of education and resource provision. These efforts link family planning to women's education and economic opportunities, presenting a capitalist feminist liberation that pushes for the 'rational' choice to have fewer children (Sandilands 1999:89). This education is limited to one of abstinence in countries with anti-contraception and anti-abortion beliefs, thus reducing sexual relations to solely reproduction and directly tying (hetero)sexuality to acceptable, heteronormative familial structures (Foster 2011). Principle 9, which declares that 'the family is the basic unit of society and as such should be strengthened' (UNCED 1992), exemplifies the unquestioned naturalization of heter-onormativity in MSM rhetoric. This narrow focus on family as the all-encompassing soci-etal relation erases the notion of communities, and of broader networks of support and solidarity. MSM solutions are located within families, and the state is there to push people into them.

*Agenda 21* does emphasize the importance of addressing gender inequality in a number of ways, but its reason for doing so is not ideal from either a feminist or queer perspective. The most pertinent portion is point 5.12, which states that

> awareness should be increased of the fundamental linkages between improving the state of women and demographic dynamics, particularly through women's access to educa-tion, primary and reproductive health care programmes, economic independence and their effective, equitable participation in all levels of decision-making.
>
> *(UNCED 1992:24)*

All of these goals are valuable and could have positive impacts. However, the moral justification for them is problematic: the efforts are not ends in and of themselves; they are a means to the 'greater' end of slowing population growth. Women's economic opportunities are only promoted *because* the opportunity cost of having children is greater when a woman is making an income and so a family may choose to have fewer children. There are approximately forty-five mentions of women in *Agenda 21* that are directly linked to children, children's health, and care, while there are only four mentions of men in relation to children, specifically referring to the need for 'measures to ensure that women and men have the same right to decide . . . the number and spacing of their children' (UNCED 1992). In fact, there are four points that raise the need to 'fully support women's productive and reproductive roles'.

It seems that in the eyes of the MSM women matter only in that they become wives who bear their husbands' children and fulfil their roles as mothers. What of the women who can't, or chose not to, reproduce? What about infertile women, or queer women, or trans women? Are their needs not important? Are they undeserving of justice and action because they are unlikely to have children? The centring of reproduction in the environmentalist framing of and concern for gender inequality means that women who do not have children do not matter; there is effectively no space for them in the conversations. The goals rely upon and reinforce the notion that women should be responsible for housework and raising children; there is only a single mention of men taking on household tasks in the 351-page document, and even that only pushes for an 'equal distribution of household tasks'. The framing and focus of the points reduce women's lives, experiences, goals, and aspirations to childbearing. So long as discussions in the MSM of women's struggles begin and end with reproduction, gendered oppression will not be dismantled.

## Acid raining on your pride parade: queering sustainability

The foregoing discussion of the major criticisms queer ecology can direct toward the MSM leads to a process of mapping out what a sustainability politics grounded in queer ecology might be. What might an environmental policy look like if it was grounded in a rejection of heteronormative and reproductive futurity, a destabilization of categories, and a sense of irony? This last section begins the work of answering that question, thereby delving into a realm that queer ecology does not tend to occupy, at least at the time of writing. Drawing on Seymour, whose work is at the forefront of politicized queer ecological theorizing, I aim to demonstrate some potential contributions of queer ecology as it expands beyond literary analysis and into the realm of activism and action. In my view, a deep commitment to environmental activism and sustainability efforts must be coupled with intense self-criticism and reflection on the flaws of motivations, discourse, and tactics. A queer ecological sustainability holds a deep sense of care for the environment while simultaneously interrogating how 'the environment' is conceptualized.

The rejection of heteronormative futurity has been outlined in depth previously. However, in rejecting (re)productive futurity, it is important to recognize where queer theorists can overextend their critiques as (predominately) white scholars. Edelman's casting of futurity as inherently heteronormative and worthless is questionable in the face of post- and decolonial and critical race theory work. For example, Indigenous activist Winona LaDuke explores the careful futurity of the Six Nations Iroquois Confederacy, which is based on potential harm of a decision, 'consider[ing] the impact on the seventh generation from now' (quoted in Seymour 2013:9). This futurity, attuned to social justice issues, provides one example of a futurity that is not based in heteronormative (re)productivity. A queer ecological futurity would be one that situates our actions as meaningfully connected to possible imagined futures, but does not use those futures to justify harm in the present.

A queer sustainability always challenges and works to dismantle binaries, pushing against the lines of categories to reveal their artificial nature. In the collapsing of Western binaries of nature/culture, us/them, self/other, and so on, the interconnectivity of humans, other members of ecological communities, and landscapes can be revealed. According to Seymour, the result of breaking down these binaries is a queer sustainability 'not rooted in stable or essentialized identity categories', but instead is founded on 'a care that is not just a means of solving human-specific problems, a care that does not operate out of expectation for recompense' (2013:184). Tearing down the nature/culture binary shifts the discussion away from how to minimize human impact on the environment, and instead to where and how humans fit as a member of the broader ecological community that supports its fellow members. This shift can drastically change the way problems are conceptualized or solved. One example that could have a huge impact is construction and building design. The building envelope (i.e., the physical outer shell, including walls, roof, and foundation, that allows for controlling heat, light, and air flow into and out of the building) separates the interior human space from the external environment. It is, in many ways, a literal manifestation of the nature/culture binary. If the design goal shifted away from creating a static, hard envelope to instead a more dynamic, fluid, and adaptable envelope, it would lead to hugely different buildings (Butler and Adamowski

2015:15). This might mean that buildings are more integrated into the environment, such as being built into the ground or hills and reducing required materials, or having internal conditions respond to external conditions, such as lighting being affected by the weather. Additionally, by focusing on the goal of supporting the broader ecological community, buildings would be designed more to create 'homes' for nonhuman species, both flora and fauna (Butler and Adamowski 2015:18). With regard to global climate policies, as outlined previously, a queer sustainability would reject the global carbon balance sheet method of handling GHG emissions. Instead, processes would be developed to address emission sources throughout the life cycle of a product, resource, or industry at the point of emission. This approach would come out of recognition that the impacts of waste and pollution have immediate impacts on the local level, and on local communities, that are not remedied by global-level emission credit trading. Communities affected by smog in one region are not helped or healed by carbon sequestration projects in another.

A queer ecological imagination requires an explicit engagement with, and support for, the ugly. As mentioned previously, Western constructions of 'ugly' landscapes have historically tended to be those populated by people of colour, Indigenous people, and/or poor people. Community educator and organizer Mia Mingus challenges the politics of beauty and calls for activists to 'mov[e] beyond a politic of desirability to loving the ugly . . . [see] its power and magic, [see] the reasons it has been feared. [See] it for what it is: some of our greatest strength' (2011: website). A queer ecological sustainability extends this respect of 'Ugly for how it has shaped us and been exiled' to all bodies and landscapes, finding magnificence in the unwanted, revelling in the ugly. As one example, it means not disproportionately directing research money toward species that are 'cute', to the neglect of 'uglier' species (Metrick and Weitzman 1996:14–15; Biber 2002:165). It finds wonder in a world seen as strange (Sandilands 1994).

At its core, a queer ecological sustainability rejects the privatization and commodification of bodies and land and focuses on care instead of profit or compensation (Seymour 2013:109). Rejecting the privatization of nature allows ecosystems and people to be supported as unmanaged and uncontrolled, building a broader (re)imagining of how humans and nonhumans can live in unproductive and exciting ways. It means creating a system to support their flourishing in unpredictable and unique ways, not based on rehabilitating to, or achieving, an idealized conception of existence. This is a queer ethics of care, defined by its rejection of usefulness and (re)production as prerequisites to 'earning' care, which focuses on the emotional dimensions of interpersonal relationships and shared Otherness (Perpich 2006). It is one that works to sustain and improve the well-being of bodies and landscapes, while being critical of how spatial and temporal conceptions of well-being are constructed and embedded within broader politics. Different bodies and beings need and/or want different relations with spaces (Sbicca 2012). Collective value-creation provides both spaces for coalition-building and radical restructuring of engagements within nature (Seymour 2013:11). Lesbian separatist farm communes help point to a form of sustainable living that engages with this environmental ethic, in their treatment of the land as a partner and guide to live with and learn from, as opposed to a commodity to consume and manage (Unger 2010:181–182). It is important to acknowledge that these understandings of care are indebted to Indigenous peoples and so a queer sustainability must position anti-colonial and anti-racist solidarity as central features (Seymour 2013:168).

Again looking to Seymour, an important political dimension of a queer ecological sustainability is its prioritization of coalition building across forms of oppression, taking demands for justice outside of the realm of personal affronts and into the general discourse of solidarity and mutual support (Seymour 2013:97). It does not lead to systemic change or liberation on its own, but rather through connection and supplementation with other marginalized communities, particularly communities of colour. For example, the challenging of categorical boundaries can help expand analysis of environmental racism and classism by complicating spatial and temporal scopes (Seymour 2013:74). Environmental harm tends to be described simplistically, such that particular spaces or sites are seen as uniformly harmful to all who move through them; instead analysis can be pushed to look at how different people engage with a site and thus experience different levels of harm. As Seymour points out, a suburban home can be safe for the family that lives there, while domestic workers who clean the house are exposed to cleaning chemicals and experience much greater harm in that same environment (2013:77). Additionally, a queer sustainability recognizes the body as a site of ecological (in)justice, as in the works of Eli Clare, who situates the body as home and uses the body as a scale to explores ecological violence (Di Chiro 2010:199–200). Breaking down these binaries allows us to shift the focus, temporally and spatially, from bodies to landscapes in ways that allow more thoughtful explorations of well-being and care.

## Conclusion: goodbye to the circus

To conclude, I have argued that the MSM, in its narrow focus on protecting a pristine and untouched nature for future generations, has built itself upon oppressive politics and heteronormative capitalist logics, which (ironically!) prevent it from achieving its goals. In response, I have asserted that these political underpinnings must be challenged and destabilized as part of the queering of sustainability. The tent of the MSM circus must be taken down; it is time for the cages to be opened, the nonhuman animals freed, and the tightly choreographed act replaced with a messier and more unpredictable improv. Queer ecology can bring unique contributions to ecological and social action, but it can only be part of liberatory projects when engaging in solidarity with communities of colour, poor communities, communities in the Global South, disabled communities, landscapes, ecosystems, and all communities that are devalued and Othered. Particularly with regards to studies of gender and environment, queer ecology provides a basis for criticizing the reprocentricity that shapes how the MSM engages, or fails to engage, with gendered experiences and the liberation of all those who experience patriarchal oppression.

Queer ecology is a piece of the sustainability puzzle that refuses to let its edges be clearly defined. A queer sustainability is one that is deeply sceptical of categorizations of nature and yet still works to support ecological communities through care, solidarity, and communal valuation. It maps out new connections between members of an expansive ecological community, imagining and creating possible futures where the needs of all, human and nonhuman alike, are supported. Importantly, the rejection of heteronormativity and capitalist drive for (re)productivity creates space for bodies and landscapes to flourish in unique, weird, and unpredictable ways, rather than being managed into idealized conceptions of what will be useful or beautiful. Queer ecology asks just who and what are 'nature' and refuses to allow easy answers to go unchallenged.

## Note

A much shorter and substantially different version of this chapter was published in 2015 in *Convergence: A Journal of Undergraduate and Community Research*, with the title 'Seeing the Forest for the Fags: Reimagining Sustainability as a Queer Project'. It was adapted for this Handbook with the permission of the journal editors.

1  Anticipating likely objections, it is important here to explain that my use of 'MSM' is not meant to encompass a fixed collection of specific environmental groups or perspectives. Rather I use it as a provocative rhetorical device to call attention to a set of common traits that can be seen within environmentalism, environmental activism, sustainability, ecological preservation, and so on. It is meant to provoke self-reflection among readers as to whether their own efforts have been guilty of these features at one time or another. The features I have in mind include divorcing people from nature, disregarding people's interests in the name of 'saving the environment', and considering people only insofar as they hurt or can help the environment. These misanthropic traits rely on, and perpetuate, societal oppression, and tend to lack an analysis of capitalism as a system that is antithetical to ecological and social justice (Stevens 2013: website).

# References

Aufrecht, M. (2013) 'Rethinking "greening of hate": Climate emissions, immigration, and the last frontier', *Ethics & the Environment* 17(2): 51–74.

Azzarello, R. (2012) *Queer Environmentality: Ecology, Evolution, and Sexuality in American Literature*. Burlington, VT: Ashgate Publishing.

Bagemihl, B. (1999) *Biological Exuberance: Animal Homosexuality and Natural Diversity*. New York: St. Martin's Press.

Bardos, L. (2016) 'Is sustainability only for the privileged?', *degrowth*. Online. Available at: www.degrowth. de/en/2016/05/is-sustainability-only-for-the-privileged/ (accessed 17 July 2016).

Bell, D. (2010) 'Queernaturecultures', in Mortimer-Sandilands, C. and Erickson, B. (eds) *Queer Ecologies: Sex, Nature, Politics, Desire*. Bloomington, IN: Indiana University Press, 134–145.

Biber, E. (2002) 'The application of the Endangered Species Act to the protection of freshwater mussels: A case study', *Environmental Law* 32(91): 92–174.

Butler, C. and Adamowski, J. (2015) 'Home in the garden: Developing an eco-queer framework for sustainable housing design', *Journal of Undergraduate Research and Scholarly Excellence* 5: 14–20.

Butler, J. (1993) 'Critically queer', *GLQ: A Journal of Lesbian and Gay Studies* 1(1): 17–32.

Chen, M. Y. (2012) *Animacies: Biopolitics, Racial Mattering, and Queer Affect*. Durham, NC: Duke University Press.

Di Chiro, G. (2010) 'Polluted politics? Confronting toxic discourse, sex panic, and co-normativity', in Mortimer-Sandilands, C. and Erickson, B. (eds) *Queer Ecologies: Sex, Nature, Politics, Desire*. Bloomington, IN: Indiana University Press, 199–230.

Edelman, L. (2004) *No Future: Queer Theory and the Death Drive*. Durham, NC: Duke University Press.

Falek, J. (2015) 'Monumental erections: UnCovering Jewish identity and communal memory', *Canons: Undergraduate Journal of Religious Studies* 6: 73–84.

Forest, D. (2016) 'Lt. Governor Forest responds to PayPal decision', *North Carolina Government*. Online. Available at: http://ltgov.nc.gov/content/lt-governor-forest-responds-paypal-decision (accessed 12 October 2016).

Foster, E. A. (2011) 'Sustainable development: Problematising normative constructs of gender within global environmental governmentality', *Globalizations* 8(2): 135–149.

Foucault, M. (1990) *The History of Sexuality: An Introduction* (Vol. 1). Translated by R. Hurley. New York: Vintage Books.

Gaard, G. (1997) 'Toward a queer ecofeminism', *Hypatia* 12(1): 114–137.

Glasser, C. L. (2011) 'Tied oppressions: An analysis of how sexist imagery reinforces speciesist sentiment', *The Brock Review* 12(1): 51–68.

Gosine, A. (2010) 'Non-white reproduction and same-sex eroticism: Queer acts against nature', in Mortimer-Sandilands, C. and Erickson, B. (eds) *Queer Ecologies: Sex, Nature, Politics, Desire*. Bloomington, IN: Indiana University Press, 149–172.

Hall, C. C. I. (2007) 'Asian eyes: Body image and eating disorders of Asian and Asian American women', *Eating Disorders: The Journal of Treatment & Prevention* 3(1): 8–19.

Hall, K. (2014) 'No failure: Climate change, radical hope, and queer crip feminist eco-futures', *Radical Philosophy Review* 17(1): 203–225.

Haraway, D. (2003) *The Companion Species Manifesto: Dogs, People, and Significant Otherness*. Chicago, IL: Prickly Paradigm Press.

Hartmann, B. (2010) 'The greening of hate: An environmental essay', in Potok, M. (ed) *Greenwash: Nativists, Environmentalism and the Hypocracy of Hate*. Southern Poverty Law Center, 13–15. Online. Available at: http://climateandcapitalism.com/2010/08/31/the-greening-of-hate-an-environmentalists-essay/ (accessed 31 October 2016).

Hunter Jr., M. L. (1993) 'Natural fire regimes as spatial models for managing boreal forests', *Biological Conservation* 65: 115–120.

McGrath, M. (2014) 'Greenpeace sorry for Nazca lines stunt in Peru', *BBC News*. Online. Available at: www. bbc.com/news/science-environment-30422994 (accessed 16 July 2016).

MacGregor, S. (2010) 'Plus ça (climate) change, plus c'est la même (masculinist) chose: Gender politics and discourses of climate change', in Lee, Y. (ed) *The Politics of Gender*. London: Routledge, 83–101.

Marshall, D. R. (1977) 'The advantages and hazards of genetic homogeneity', *The Genetic Basis of Epidemics in Agriculture* 287: 1–20.

Martinez-Alier, J. (2002) *The Environmentalism of the Poor: A Study of Ecological Conflicts and Valuation*. Northampton: Edward Elgar Publishing.

Maynard, S. (1994) 'Through a hole in the lavatory wall: Homosexual subcultures, police surveillance, and the dialectics of discovery, Toronto, 1890–1930', *Journal of the History of Sexuality* 5(2): 207–242.

Metrick, A. and Weitzman, M. L. (1996) 'Patterns of behaviour in endangered species preservation', *Land Economics* 72(1): 1–16.

Mingus, M. (2011) 'Moving toward the ugly: A politic beyond desirability', *Leaving Evidence*. Online. Available at: https://leavingevidence.wordpress.com/2011/08/22/moving-toward-the-ugly-a-politic-beyond-desirability/ (accessed 21 May 2015).

Mock, B. (2016) 'The US national park service grapples with its racist origins', *CityLab*. Online. Available at: www. citylab.com/politics/2016/08/the-us-national-park-system-grapples-with-its-racist-origins/497615/?utm_source=atlfb (accessed 3 September 2016).

Mortimer-Sandilands, C. (2005) 'Unnatural passions? Notes towards a queer ecology', *Invisible Culture: An Electronic Journal for Visual Cultures* 9.

Mortimer-Sandilands, C. and Erickson, B. (2010) 'Introduction: A genealogy of queer ecologies', in Mortimer-Sandilands, C. and Erickson, B. (eds) *Queer Ecologies: Sex, Nature, Politics, Desire*. Bloomington, IN: Indiana University Press, 1–47.

Patton, T. O. (2006) 'Hey girl, am I more than my hair? African American women and their struggles with beauty, body image, and hair', *NWSA Journal* 18(2): 24–51.

Perpich, D. (2006) 'Review of connected lives: Human nature and an ethics of care', *Hypatia* 21(4): 224–227.

Pezzullo, P. C. and Sandlers, R. (ed) (2007) *Environmental Justice and Environmentalism: The Social Justice Challenge to the Environmental Movement*. Cambridge, MA: MIT Press.

Roughgarden, J. (2004) *Evolution's Rainbow: Diversity, Gender, and Sexuality in Nature and People*. Berkeley and Los Angeles, CA: University of California Press.

Sandilands, C. (1994) 'Lavender's green? Some thoughts on queer(y)ing environmental politics', *Undercurrents* 6: 20–25.

Sandilands, C. (1999) 'Sex at the limits', in Darier, E. (ed) *Discourses of the Environment*. Oxford: Wiley-Blackwell, 79–94.

Sbicca, J. (2012) 'Eco-queer movement(s): Challenging heteronormative space through (re)imagining nature and food', *European Journal of Ecopsychology* 3: 33–52.

Seymour, N. (2013) *Strange Nature: Futurity, Empathy, and the Queer Ecological Imagination*. Urbana, IL: University of Illinois Press.

Soltys, M. (2012) *Tangled Roots: Dialogues Exploring Ecological Justice, Healing, and Decolonization*. Guelph, ON: Heal the Earth Press.

Steinmetz, K. (2016) 'Why LGBT advocates say bathroom "predators" argument is a red herring', *Time Magazine*. Online. Available at: http://time.com/4314896/transgender-bathroom-bill-male-predators-argument/ (accessed 12 October 2016).

Stevens, K. (2013) 'Are mainstream environmental groups keeping racism alive?', *The Wrong Kind of Green*. Online. Available at: www.wrongkindofgreen.org/2013/07/29/are-mainstream-environmental-groups-keeping-racism-alive/ (accessed 16 July 2016).

Sturgeon, N. (2008) *Environmentalism in Popular Culture: Gender, Race, Sexuality, and the Politics of the Natural*. Tuscon, AZ: University of Arizona Press.

Sturgeon, N. (2010) 'Penguin family values: The nature of planetary environmental reproductive justice', in Mortimer-Sandilands, C. and Erickson, B. (eds) *Queer Ecologies: Sex, Nature, Politics, Desire*. Bloomington, IN: Indiana University Press, 102–133.

Sullivan, N. (2003) *A Critical Introduction to Queer Theory*. New York: New York University Press.

Swami, V., Coles, R., Wilson, E., Salem, N. and Furnham, A. (2010) 'Oppressive beliefs at play: Associations among beauty ideals and practices and individual differences in sexism, objectification of others, and media exposure', *Psychology of Women Quarterly* 34(3): 365–379.

Unger, N. C. (2010) 'From jook joints to sisterpace: The role of nature in lesbian alternative environments in the United States', in Mortimer-Sandilands, C. and Erickson, B. (eds) *Queer Ecologies: Sex, Nature, Politics, Desire*. Bloomington, IN: Indiana University Press, 173–198.

United Nations Conference on Environment and Development (UNCED) (1992) *Agenda 21*. Rio de Janeiro, Brazil: United Nations. Online. Available at: https://sustainabledevelopment.un.org/content/documents/Agenda21.pdf (accessed 15 November 2013).

United States Centers for Disease Control (1995) 'Update: Trends in AIDS among men who have sex with men–United States, 1989–1994', *Morbidity and Mortality Weekly Report*. Online. Available at: www.cdc.gov/mmwr/preview/mmwrhtml/00037153.htm (accessed 13 November 2013).

World Commission on Environment and Development (WCED) (1987) *Our Common Future*. London: Oxford University Press.

# PART III

# Politics, policy, and practice

# 19

# GENDER AND ENVIRONMENTAL POLICY

*Seema Arora-Jonsson*

## Introduction

'Gender' gained ground in the 1970s in environmental policy and practice when scholars first brought up questions of women's unequal positions vis-à-vis development interventions and focused on the critical roles that women play in environmental management. From the eighties onward, researchers have used gender as an analytic category to probe how power relations organize all systems and interventions and how gender relations are implicit in environmental outcomes. Drawing on the work of a range of feminist theorists (e.g., Scott 1988; Butler 1990; Haraway 1991), gender and environment scholars have asserted that gender analysis involves critical examination of power relationships and the practices through which definitions of masculinity and femininity are naturalized in different environmental contexts.

In environmental policy, 'gender' has most often been used as shorthand for 'women'. As opposed to social policy, environmental policy has conventionally been about the biophysical world and not necessarily about people. Yet as policy makers, especially those in the Global South, have come to acknowledge, the social and political are inextricably linked to the biophysical, and impossible to separate in practice. The intersection of development and environmental policy-making has been difficult to avoid. More recently, there has been corresponding acknowledgement of gender issues in environmental policy-making in countries in the Global North, especially in Europe. Although there are vast differences in each national context, whether in North or South, the aim of this chapter is to provide broad brush strokes of global trends in environmental policy-making vis-à-vis gender. Research by gender and environment scholars has had an important role to play in these developments. As is evident in what follows, much of the literature on environment and gender is based in countries in the Global South, although there is now a growing literature on the North.

In this chapter, I examine gender and environment debates in relation to shifts in the policy and practice of environmental work over the past four decades. This is not a comprehensive review of all the literature on gender and environmental policy initiatives over time; rather it is a review of themes that I believe have been important in environmental policy in relation to gender. I draw on my research experiences, along with the work of other gender and environment scholars, to examine some major strands in research. I analyze the uptake of some gender research in policy, effects on the ground, and indications for the future. The discussion is driven by these questions: (1) What can we claim to know after forty years of gender research and how has some of the early gender research been put into practice in environmental policy; (2) What has moved on, what appears to be standing still, and what effect has such gender research had in policy and practice?; and (3) Where are we today and what is the future of gender-sensitive environmental policy and practice?

## Decentring the subject of environmental management and policy

Scholars working on gender and environment in the 1980s showed how women and men often fare differently due to their socially ascribed roles, status, types of work, and their different relationships to their environments. This research brought attention to women's work that was largely invisible in mainstream studies on the environment. Feminist scholars in the Global North described how women's environmental skills and knowledges were eroded with the establishment of modern science (see, for example, Merchant 1980). In the Global South, under the broad 'women, environment, and development' (WED) banner, scholars did the important work of bringing women into environmental study and policy by foregrounding the value of women's work (e.g., Mies and Shiva 1993; Wickramasinghe and Momsen 1993; Bryceson 1995; Navarro and Korrol 1999). They highlighted the extensive, hands-on knowledge about their environments that women continue to bring to everyday life.

While this research helped to decentre the male subject of environmental policy, some strands of this research have been criticized for assigning essentialist attributes to women as a homogeneous group. Critics drew attention to the need to understand women's actions in relation to the political economy of their everyday environments and the division of property and labour (Agarwal 1992; Jackson 1996). Also, the category of the 'victimized woman' of the Global South in use in much 'Western' gender research of the 1980s and 1990s was criticized by Chandra Mohanty (2003) and other postcolonial and 'Third World feminists' who called for a fine tuned analysis of the contexts and gender relations that were being studied (e.g., Grewal and Kaplan 1994; Narayan and Harding 2000; Shohat 2001; Chaudhuri 2004). As a result, by the mid-nineties there was a conscious turning away from the emphasis on women as victims of patriarchy and environmental hazards, to focus instead on women's agency in relation to environmental issues and their differentiated struggles for emancipation. Feminist research highlighted the importance of collective action and how women came together in groups and took action in protecting their environments in many parts of the world (Shiva 1989; Odoul and Kabira 1995; Rocheleau et al. 1996). On the other hand, in some contexts women also organized to protect working class men's employment in environmentally damaging resource sectors such as conventional forestry. Reed argues that such collective action by women tended to be ignored in feminist research on the environment (Reed 2000). Such contradictions that affirmed existing gendered rural ideologies called for deeper discussion and debate.

As approaches to environment and gender changed in the academy, policy initiatives also took varied forms. For example, policy-making on forests came to acknowledge that forests were not simply a source of timber but complex ecosystems that sustained livelihoods and provided a range of products and environmental services. It has since been widely recognized that forests contribute to rural development and poverty alleviation. In the 1980s and 1990s debates about sustainable development brought social and economic concerns to bear on biological diversity, conservation, and natural resource management. As a result, '[c]onservation-with-development' programs began to pay attention to a mix of state/commercial and local livelihood interests in buffer zones outside of core reserve areas (Green et al. 1998:261). International institutions promoting environment and development programs in the Global South came to appreciate that women played an essential role in the management of natural resources and that, without their support, programs were difficult to implement (e.g., World Bank 1992).

In the 2010s, national governments and international organizations are increasingly concerned to understand how policy issues take shape across scales. They are also prompted by the desire to 'scale-up' or 'scale-out' and model best practices and policies in relation to gender. There is an attempt to eschew past sector-based approaches, although it has been difficult not to slip into old routines.[1] One approach being promoted by some organizations within the Consultative Group on International Agricultural Research (CGIAR) is the 'Landscape Approach'.[2] While it is difficult to pin down, it is an attempt at looking for solutions to environmental problems across disciplines and sectors. Such a perspective promises the hope of analyzing geographical, material, and social relations as interrelated and indivisible in policy, but there is also a danger that such an approach subsumes gender and power in all-encompassing concepts about the landscape as the example of policy-making on resilience demonstrates (see Harrison 2012).[3]

It is undeniable that, at the time writing, 'gender' is acknowledged in its many different forms as an important consideration in environmental governance and resource management, in local, national, and international policies. But for the most part, gender continues to signify women. It is accepted that effective forest and water management is impossible without women's involvement in community-based organizations, or that disaster relief and risk reduction approaches get nowhere unless women are part of programs. The tangible effects of including women, or how much change has resulted from participatory and gender-sensitive language in documents and strategies, is of course a different story depending on context. In the following section, I examine where this history of gender and environmental policy appears to leave us and to what effect.

## What has moved on? What appears to be standing still?

In the past, gender research has challenged mainstream academic theorizing on the environment, often disrupting taken-for-granted categories and pointing to their androcentric bias. When development practitioners and policy makers have leaned toward answers or models based on conventional research, they automatically and perhaps unintentionally have undermined the possibilities for incorporating gender and power in their work. And yet, in significant ways, gender research has contributed to how we think about our environments. Initiatives related to gender have coalesced around three main rubrics that recur in different ways in response to insights from research. These have included (1) efforts to mainstream gender in environmental programs; (2) attempts to delineate property rights and to increase women's economic empowerment by promoting income generation activities and establishing micro-credit programs; and (3) efforts to involve women in environmental governance. In this section, I analyze the consequences of some of these approaches.

### *Gender mainstreaming in environmental programs*

Gender mainstreaming is an important concept in the gender and environmental policy field. Referring to the inclusion of a gendered analysis and concerns at all stages of the policy process, it was adopted by many governments in the 1990s and included in policies and programs at national and international levels. However, this practice did not reach environmental policy to the same extent as it did social policy. At the time feminists criticized many large-scale environmental projects for lacking attention to gender issues and thus for compromising women's resource interests (e.g., Green et al. 1998). Nonetheless, the early period can be looked back on as a time when the idea of 'gender' (taken to be synonymous with women) did, in fact, make its way onto the environmental policy agenda. Over the years, from instrumentalist justifications about greater efficiency (cf. Moser 1989) to it being 'smart economics' to invest in women (World Bank 2011) and alongside discourses on rights-based approaches,[4] gender has become an important ingredient of environment and development policy, 'a must' in policy documents, in applications for research grants, and in development projects. Whether or not this inclusion served the purpose of removing discrimination is a moot point. Different understandings of gender, both in policy and research, lie at the root of disjunctures that I discuss further later in the chapter.

Efforts to mainstream gender in environmental policy and practice have been uneven. The transposition of feminist research into non-feminist governmental machinery has worked both ways: while gender concerns have been appropriated into formalistic machinery, bureaucrats and practitioners could not totally ignore gendered issues and thus have been forced to acknowledge women's networks and other activist groups. Since the mid-1990s, women's groups have been able to lobby for gender perspectives, funds for environmental programs, and for women's inclusion at all levels. Institutional networks, feminists within bureaucracies, and individual activists have succeeded in building capacities and changing institutions and ideologies (see Basu and McGrory 1995; Keck and Sikkink 1998). But mainstreaming became a formalistic ritual and at times had opposite effects than those envisaged by its proponents. For example, Baden and Goetz (1998) argue that as gender perspectives were included in policy documents and programs or projects, its political focus was diluted. In the years following the 1995 UN Conference on Women in Beijing, where gender mainstreaming was adopted as a major strategy, women's groups, especially in the Global South, began to raise critical voices. Night Khan from Pakistan was one among others who asserted that the focus that had been on women previously, shifted to women and men (due to the idea of 'gender') and conveniently back to men, for example, by prompting discussions on 'men at risk' (Baden and Goetz 1998). The point here is that 'gender' became important but women disappeared – or that 'women's liberation' was replaced by 'gender equality' (Brush 2002).

Gender mainstreaming became a technocratic exercise, evident, for example, in the quantitative expertise of economists expected to think about differences in women and men's involvement in environmental management. Baden and Goetz (1998) point out that although such information is important, by not simultaneously taking into account issues of power and gender relations, gender and women's interests were reduced to a set of needs or gaps amenable to administrative decisions about the allocation of resources. Technocratic attempts to mainstream gender and their negative consequences are equally evident in the academy. I have reviewed papers from environmental scientists who tabulate gender-disaggregated data and make far-reaching conclusions, often as is clear, without much basis for their analysis and without reading the literature on gender to which they allude. Although this criticism cannot be said to apply to all researchers, my observation goes beyond questioning the quality of their research. It is a recurring issue of misusing gender research to say that women are vulnerable or marginalized to legitimize the promotion of new technologies or preconceived ideas about development that have nothing to do with gender or relationships of power.

Gender-sensitive language and generalizations about including gender aspects in program documents have not necessarily meant concrete change on the ground. In Europe, Elizabeth Prugl (2010) shows that in the EU's Leader programs in most places, despite lip service to mainstreaming, nothing was done. In Sweden, resource centres for women were shut down in favour of mainstreaming gender, 'a strategy that was unclear to those who were meant to implement it' (Tollin 2000). Critiques of gender mainstreaming have also pointed to its heteronormative assumptions about the family where women and men are always coupled and always in unequal positions, thus failing to challenge gender norms (see Davids, Francien Van, and Parren 2014 for an overview of critiques of gender mainstreaming).

Scholars also point to a more insidious side of mainstreaming in relation to policy. They criticize development initiatives for taking on board certain ideas about gender when they tended to serve larger agendas. For example, Melissa Leach (2007) argues that ideas about women's close relationships to the environment were picked up by policy makers and bureaucrats in the 1990s to make use of women's labour in conservation and tree protection. By appealing to women's altruism and closeness to nature, responsibility for various environmental programs as well as the eradication of poverty was given to women regardless of whether they had the resources or time to be able to carry them out (Leach 2007). This resulted in a 'feminization of responsibility' in development programs (Chant 2008). Environmental chores got added to women's already long list of caring roles. It was convenient to assume that women's participation is good for women in general. As Green et al. write:

> the poor performance of . . . such project interventions was especially unfortunate . . . such projects may have stoked up expectations that women as environmental managers have the ability to 'fix' environmental problems. The failure of the environmental sector projects that have attempted to address gender issues to deliver such a result may lead to disillusionment among policy makers in their attempts to take account of gender concerns.
>
> *(Green et al. 1998:275)*

## Property rights and economic empowerment

Gender and environment researchers have demonstrated that gender asymmetries in property rights affect the efficiency, environmental sustainability, equity, and empowerment outcomes of natural resource use. They have endorsed the idea that women should be given legal rights to land and water to be able to enhance their bargaining position and to improve their status in the household and community. Notable examples of these discussions can be found in articles calling for 'a field of one's own' (Agarwal 1994), 'a plot of one's own' (Zwarteveen 1996), and a 'well of one's own' (Jordans and Zwarteveen 1997). However, in many places where land tenure reforms have been enacted in the Global South, the gap between law and practice has persisted (Agarwal 1994; Basu 1999). The near impossibility of transferring the 'bundle of rights' and social relations attached to land and water in legal transfers continues to haunt such reforms. While collective ownership is increasingly acknowledged in tenure reforms in many countries, the focus has been on individual ownership and privatization. Customary land law for example is seen as moving steadily, even if in a chaotic and problematic way, toward individualized tenure and land markets (Whitehead and Tsikat 2003:94). In many ways, this has also led to undermining cooperation around resource use, epitomizing a broader trend of individualizing interventions within development and environmental legislation.

Though the granting of tenure rights has been an important step in securing women's rights to property, scholars have been critical of attempts to grant tenure to women that have disregarded their social position. Studies from South Asia show how women choose not to contest patriarchal inheritance norms in order to preserve their positions within society, despite the existence of legislation to the contrary (Rankin 2003; Rao 2007). In sub-Saharan Africa, recourse to social norms is crucial in building up women's claims (Whitehead and Tsikat 2003:97). An example of the granting of tenure to poor women in disregard of social position is Rhodante Ahlers's (2002) study of the land and water reforms in Mexico in the early 1990s. Despite acquiring formal rights, women were effectively disenfranchised, losing customary access and often selling their rights off at prices markedly less than those their male counterparts received.

The current focus on markets and privatization of tenure seems to be reemphasizing this trend. Women's rights over land have been an important ingredient in pushing through other policy objectives. For example, Sagari Ramdas (2009) describes the repercussions for women in Andhra Pradesh, India, who were awarded individual titles under the Forests Rights Act of 2006. The women were paid wages through a government scheme (the NREGA) if they cooperated by planting cash crops on their land. Ramdas writes that these crops made the women vulnerable to irrigation problems, volatile markets, and agricultural chemicals, and resulted in a total change in their livelihoods. In some districts women were 'encouraged' to grow biodiesel plants (*Pongamia pinnata*) as part of climate programs that would enable them to earn carbon credits. The degraded forests, which they would have regenerated with indigenous species, and agriculture lands that supported food crops were replaced with mono-cultural plantations. After receiving one payment from the World Bank for neutralizing carbon emissions, a few years down the line, 80 per cent of the trees perished. Most families were then forced to sell their cattle, became increasingly dependent on chemicals, and ended up ruining their land in the process. What also emerged was that the women were completely unaware of the reason they had received the money and had no idea about the ramifications of the carbon trade or the relationship of their self-help group activities to climate change (Ramdas 2009).

The privatizing, neoliberal moment in land and water policies appears to offer possibilities for realizing feminist ambitions. However, as the examples from Mexico and India demonstrate, neoliberal policy language and concepts tend to hide precisely those issues that much feminist research questions – policy frameworks that invisibilize, naturalize, and objectify the politics and powers involved in resource re-allocation (Ahlers and Zwarteveen 2009; also see Harris 2009 for review on gender and neoliberalized water governance). It is clear that while law and legal rights to land and resources remain an important basis of environmental governance, social praxis, and the social contexts in which policies are enacted determine outcomes. So what appears as lack of change despite legal reform in many contexts comes from the social embeddedness of law and the relational aspects of gender and power that are largely ignored by statutory codes and development schemes.

On the one hand, women's inclusion in markets, in some places and to some extent, has increased their options and power in the family. On the other hand, it has led to women being drawn into a system over which they have little control (Harriss-White 1998; Arora-Jonsson 2013; Elias and Saussey 2013). Policies advocating market-based solutions have promoted the idea that economic grants and income generation programs or women's involvement in commodity/value chains would solve all women's problems, problems that in fact arise from unequal power relations. Several decades of research has shown that there is no direct correlation between economic growth and gender equality (e.g., Jackson 1996). On the contrary, researchers have argued that economic programs for women, focusing on individual women, seek to dull resistance and depoliticize poverty (Keating et al. 2010). For example, micro-credit programs have been accompanied by discourses about women's conscientious and responsible behaviour in saving for their families as compared to men. But the widespread micro-credit programs for women have mixed results. Advocated as a progressive strategy for challenging existing distributions of wealth and power, they have been subjected to considerable feminist critique. Scholars have argued that these programs dilute collective action as individual women monitor each other to check defaulting on loans and take each other to task. In their study of micro-credit programs, Christine Keating et al. (2010) argue that micro-credit programs are a mechanism of gendered 'accumulation by dispossession' (cf. Hartsock 2006) and are in fact a set of processes by which poor women are brought into the structure of capitalism in exploitative ways.

Prescriptions on the importance of market-based programs often disregard women's own preferences and understanding of their livelihoods. For example, in my discussions with women's 'self-help' groups in Odisha in India, several women complained that they were never consulted on decisions regarding programs selected for them. Many remained unaware, long after a micro-credit program had been accepted, of what exactly was expected of them, or what the program entailed. I was told by a women's group that they had been 'taken for a picnic' to the neighbouring state of Andhra Pradesh, when the NGO representatives later informed me that it was actually an introductory workshop on micro-credit. The women were dismissive of the time and money spent on the picnic/workshop in which they had little interest and insisted that they would rather use their resources for different ends. Such programs, much like gender mainstreaming, have replaced previous welfare measures with investments in small-scale female entrepreneurs. Employment or entrepreneurship and saving and not welfare are policy leitmotifs, in disregard of the relations that perpetuate unequal social positions to begin with (Arora-Jonsson 2013).

Some feminist criticisms have been taken on board within policy-making. Chant and Sweetman (2012) cite the example of the World Bank's 'Applying Gender Action Plan's Lessons 2010–2013' report as a welcome shift in approach with comprehensive plans for women's gendered concerns in their programs. Similarly, the World Bank's flagship World Development Report of 2012, which was dedicated to gender issues, recognizes gender as politics, the intrinsic value of gender equality and women's unpaid labour, and that gender equality does not automatically come with growth. Yet, as several scholars point out, the focus of current policy remains on the instrumentality of gender to ensure economic returns. Investing in women, or 'fixing' women for economic growth, remain the core of policy messages, exacting a heavy toll on the lives of poor women (Chant and Sweetman 2012; Razavi 2012). These processes are contingent on the labour of women but without accompanying social safeguards or taking account of 'structures of constraint' (Folbre 1994) that poor women often face in local and global markets. Social and environmental policy that would ensure security has still considerable catching up to do.

## Gender and environmental governance

While not writing specifically about environmental governance, sociologist Lisa Brush (2003) makes a classification that is useful for thinking about environmental policy and gender. She points to the distinction between the 'governance of gender' and the 'gender of governance'. The governance of gender refers to how states and social policies produce and police the boundaries between masculinity and femininity and thus enforce or undermine male privilege in everyday life. Like others before her (e.g., Pateman 1988), Brush defines 'the gender of governance' as the ways in which practices and assumptions of gender difference and dominance organize the institutions, capacities, and ideologies of governance – that policies and political theories of the state depart from an androcentric bias while purporting to be universal or neutral.

In environmental governance, the governance of gender has often meant adding women to existing structures and organizations that continue to be dominated by certain groups of men. But research shows that it is not enough to 'add women and stir'. The singular focus on institutions and organizations in disregard of the social context has been criticized by scholars who have studied the everyday practices (outside of mainstream organizations) that are actually responsible for the management of natural resources (e.g., Cleaver 1998). Women have often been expected to join organizations and accommodate themselves to existing norms and structures, rather than try to change the structures to accommodate their needs and ideas or to redress disadvantage (Arora-Jonsson 2013).

Environmental policy initiatives have promoted women's self-help groups especially in relation to water. This has not meant that all such groups irrespective of how they come together (especially those that are set up as a response to programs and grants) necessarily bring about more equitable gender relationships in environmental management. In many cases the inclusion of women, both in the Global North and the South, has played the role of rubberstamping male dominated organizations by legitimizing them as peoples' organizations. It is often when women have been able to carve out separate and alternative spaces for themselves through collective environmental action in relation that it has led to their empowerment as well as of their communities (Arora-Jonsson 2013).

On the other hand, inclusion of women's collectives in governance mechanisms because program policies prescribed it and it was enforced, has in several places resulted in synergies among women's groups. As I elaborate in my book, *Gender, Development and Environmental Governance: Theorizing Connections,* discourses on participation and the rights of 'all' villagers in local management brought with them subversive openings in villages in Odisha in India and in Dalarna in Sweden (Arora-Jonsson 2013). Women's groups in both places were able to open up a space for themselves in environmental governance. Women's micro-credit programs in Odisha enabled them to organize themselves and take a place in public spaces. They had legitimate reasons to meet in public space and make demands. Some women's groups used this space and language to resist oppression in other spheres as well – such as violence by men. They spoke about 'women's rights' within the family, sometimes using terminology and language that had so far been alien for them.

On a similar theme, Aradhana Sharma (2006), who studies a women's empowerment program in the state of Uttar Pradesh, India, concludes that empowerment (like gender mainstreaming) has emerged as a key modality of neoliberal self-government. She writes that 'empowerment is increasingly becoming mainstreamed and packaged into government-sponsored development programs' – it has, in other words, become what Partha Chatterjee (2004) calls 'a category of governance'. However, her analysis of the program echoes Chatterjee's claim that governmental programs do not just produce bureaucratized and passive state subjects. In postcolonial contexts, these programs produce active, sometimes dissident, political actors who can provide the ground for mobilizations in which marginalized subjects make claims on the state, negotiate entitlements, and contest social hierarchies (Sharma 2006). As Lakshmi Lingam (2002) writes, in some places in India, state funded programs have ended up in the peculiar position of sponsoring women's struggles against the state itself.

To sum up, despite overarching national and international imperatives that environmental policy and practice must not ignore diversity, the impulse has been toward using singular and naturalized categories such as men, women, and/or gender. This assumption of coherence makes them acceptable in policy discourse, but difficult to act upon on the ground. The thrust of much environmental policy-making vis-à-vis gender has been to equate gender with women or with assumed universal differences between men and women, thus bureaucratizing the very idea of gender.

## Where are we now?

A variety of definitions of gender lie at the heart of the contradictions that I described previously. As I show in this section, these tensions become evident – as static interpretations of gender become a part of the official machinery, when women are regarded as a collective but addressed as individuals in programs and when the focus is on the governance of gender with little attention to the gender of neoliberal governance.

Gender has become relatively institutionalized in environmental policy, at least in policy rhetoric. One tangible reason for this attention to gender is that gender research has built up a whole body of work in relation to environmental issues especially in relation to countries in the Global South. Over the years, research has shown conclusively that environmental policy and practice ignores gendered concerns at its peril. Now that extensive budgets for gender expertise are being allocated in environmental and development organizations, what are the implications for gender research?

Paradoxically, in some ways the ubiquitous talk of gender may be seen as the stumbling block to recognition of gender inequalities on the ground. A major push for change, for example, gender mainstreaming, has come due to the work of feminist researchers and practitioners who are active in international arenas. But it has also given rise to what Janet Halley and others within the spheres of law and policy call 'governance feminism' – where some things are taken up in disregard of other forms of gendered discrimination (Halley et al. 2006). This can work in both ways as they point out – while it highlights some issues, it can also be used as a tool in the hands of powerful players in local contexts. In the case of current environmental initiatives that I discuss further later in this chapter, it is recognizable in stereotypes about women and men and what they do, in the empowered individual woman as object of policy, and in the need to include women in existing structures and especially into markets.

Women as a group often serve as a 'conduit for policy' (Molyneux 2006 in Chant and Sweetman 2012), legitimizing development interventions and environmental initiatives such as non-timber forest produce markets, infrastructural projects, or climate instruments. In current policy thinking then, hopes for the environment rest on individual women becoming entrepreneurs and selling non-timber forest products. These hopes do not extend to demands for an end to discrimination and violence that the women in Sweden and India tried to bring into the environmental forums as a condition for women to be able to work at all (cf. Arora-Jonsson 2013). Strangely enough, while stereotypes about women as a social group abound in policy, redress for inequalities is directed mainly at individuals. Significant about environmental policy initiatives and programs, especially those associated with income generation and micro-credit, are their focus on the individual, especially individual women. The vulnerable or virtuous woman, the privileged subject of policy has a new badge of honour: the conscientious female saver and small-scale entrepreneur. The examples of land reforms cited earlier show how well-intentioned reforms and granting individual property rights, in the absence of a sensitivity to context and an infrastructure that supports those rights, can put women in precarious positions and compound women's disadvantage. As Chant and Sweetman (2012) observe, universal understanding of women's empowerment based on neoliberal models of self-determination conflates the empowerment of women as individuals with the feminist goal of removing structural discrimination that women face as a constituency.

One solution to gender inequalities and an effort to 'govern gender' has been the focus on inclusion – of women's work in the body of knowledge on the environment, women's inclusion in committees and local organizations, and most importantly the inclusion of women's labour in markets. However, treating gender as a problem of individual women's inclusion is counterproductive if not seen in relation to other women and to men. Gender is taken up as if men and male privilege have nothing to do with gender and as if all women are interchangeable. Different women's relations to different groups of men in particular contexts are ignored. As research has shown, the inclusion of a few women in structures of governance or the allocation of grants and loans to women for community activities has depoliticized 'gender' away from a struggle for change. This has a parallel in the kind of data that policy makers look for. Gender disaggregated data has been extremely important in seeing patterns of discrimination in specific places but also over larger scales. At the same time, as Brush writes:

> The bad news is that comparative research on gender seldom assesses women in social relation to men. In particular, analyses of women's subordination (rather than mere underrepresentation) are virtually impossible with the types of data at the centre of equality gap comparisons. The cultural, sexual, physical and emotional enforcement of male dominance goes unmeasured, unremarked, and unchallenged.
>
> *(Brush 2002:176)*

Images of vulnerable women threatened by environmental hazards or of environmentally conscious women trying to save the planet abound in current environmental policy discussions on climate change (Arora-Jonsson 2011). Despite decades of gender research and advocacy to the contrary, policy makers continue to operate with the notion of the 'male breadwinner'. Efforts to promote productivity are largely targeted at men, while women are expected to carry on contributing to household livelihoods and caring for the family with little recognition of or support for their efforts (Kabeer 2003). Writing on welfare regimes in Europe, Jane Lewis points out that even where policy-making has opted for greater individualization, in an 'adult-worker' model, without social provisions for the complexity of gendered family behaviour, the unpaid care work performed mainly by women and the constraints in the labour market, is fraught with danger for women (Lewis 2001). References to gender, framed as already-known truisms about men and women and the environment promote the status quo as structures and unequal relations that cause disadvantages are not questioned and continue to persist (Arora-Jonsson 2011).

Furthermore, as several have pointed out (e.g., Larner 1998; Fraser 2009; Dahl 2012) governmental rhetoric has co-opted notions of participation, local responsibility, and women's agency as part of a process of dismantling of welfare measures to be replaced by neoliberal discourses on innovation and entrepreneurship. The World Bank believes in promoting gender equality as part of smart economics (World Bank 2011), or what critical observers have called a tool for legitimacy and for 'soft governance' (Arnfred 2012). There is increased faith among policy makers that inclusion of populations hitherto outside of formal economies would solve the crisis of sustainability. It does appear then that the ubiquitous mention of gender today has something to do with the desire to engage women into formal economies just as 'natural resources are being increasingly brought into the realm of global markets' (McAfee 1999). In the light of these trends, how may we think of gender research in relation to environmental policy and practice in the future? Where does it appear to be going and what can we do? And what of the future?

At the heart of the contradictions outlined here, between the current widespread use of gender and lack of change on the ground, is the tension about what 'gender' means and how it is put into practice. The meaning of gender, theorized extensively as relationships of power, tends sometimes in research and almost always in policy to slip instead into a descriptive category meaning women or at best differences between men and women. More often than not, 'gender' is reduced to stereotypes about men and women.

The current focus on gender in environmental policy is due in part to the work of feminist scholars and activists to bring it on to the agenda and the accumulated body of knowledge that now exists on this issue. Some feminists use this opening and work within the official language – of 'smart economics' or 'mainstreaming' or the 'win-win' motto (with carbon sequestration, biodiversity and poverty eradication goals) of climate instruments – in coalition with organizations and bureaucracies that might have very different aims. Others warn of the dangers of the 'governance feminism' approach (Halley et al. 2006), calling for caution in such engagements (cf. Chant and Sweetman 2012). They want to stop the second wave of feminism from being an inadvertent handmaiden to neoliberalism (Fraser 2009). The settling of these terms – of gender equality, of women's empowerment, of smart economics or mainstreaming – can become a bureaucratic exercise that limits substantive change. Is the current resurgence of attention to gender then a stumbling block for real change and an instrument for other ends? While some argue for jettisoning terms such as gender equality and mainstreaming altogether,[5] others argue for more comprehensive gender mainstreaming and empowerment. According to Tine Davids et al. (2014), we need to let go of the idea of a transformative change. They argue for breaking down mainstreaming into its many components and away from its utopian vision of women's empowerment, believing that it is then that gender mainstreaming can be considered a slow revolution.

Government programs and calls for the governance of gender cannot be underestimated. Discourses and ideas about participation and rights have enabled space for claim making and for demands for democratic and gender equitable governance. Policy-making and the work of NGOs have opened up spaces in unexpected places – giving rise to networks and links that go beyond 'gender' issues and take up questions of distribution and privilege (see discussion of my work and that of Sharma in a previous section). 'Mainstreaming' of women in governance, though fraught, has made a difference.[6] Looking back, it was often practitioners of development in the Global South who looked to (and often funded) gender research in the 1980s when confronted with the complex realities and uncertainties of environmental work. However, women's collective mobilization and struggle that are empowering have often come about as unintended effects of environmental and development programs, rather than with their support. Women's collective action and carving out of alternative spaces for themselves in local struggles have been empowering (e.g., Ivesen 2010; Arora-Jonsson 2013). Yet such attempts have not had the same kind of policy support as those directed toward individual women. There have been few policy interventions where women's groups have been supported to take up their political struggles – struggles that contribute not only to their emancipation but potentially also to better environmental governance. Surely there must be better ways of supporting such movements?

## Conclusion

As the examples given demonstrate, what gender means in each context is far from settled. The ubiquitous use of the word 'gender' in development and environmental contexts can be seen as an attempt to settle the unsettlable meanings of gender. For those looking to gender research for guidance on how to deal with inequalities, gender research has sometimes provided settled answers – about women and men. However, 'gender analysis' constitutes a critical engagement with disputed meanings and is an attempt to reveal their contradictions and instabilities as they are manifest in the lives of those we study, as well as our own. As an analytical lens, gender is about asking questions (Scott 2012:20). Posing gender as a set of questions requires us to think critically about what makes 'men' men and 'women' women, and how conceptions of men and women's work are produced in different situations. At the same time, it is about challenging the structures and connections that seek to settle these terms. While theoretical knowledge is privileged in the academy, the practical work of environment and development projects is not only about 'practice' but practice is at the heart of theories that many researchers espouse. There is a need to go beyond and reconstruct in specific contexts the categories that have been assigned especially to women – as vulnerable, as resilient, mothers, as skilled savers or small-scale entrepreneurs. And as Ahlers and Zwarteveen (2009) argue, there is a need to challenge the individualization and marketization and the consumer/client focus of the neoliberal paradigm. Neither can there be one final answer. Judith Butler puts it this way: 'Sexual difference is the site where a question concerning the relation of the biological to the cultural is posed and reposed, where it must and can be posed, but where it cannot strictly speaking, be answered' (Butler 2004:16).

Such questions need to be asked of policy-making, practice, and research, all of which are social processes. There needs to be a tactical understanding of social relationships, building on locally situated criticism and action as the basis for development and environmental governance. These are not novel approaches, but require focused and long-term involvement. Participatory research, especially feminist participatory research that has sought to collaborate with local communities, has brought about meeting spaces that have been shown to make a difference and have given rise to new questions (see Fortmann 2008). The problem is not only that fine sounding policies result in apolitical and technocratic measures or are not implemented. How policy is formulated is also important. Issues of social equity are rarely included in evaluations of ongoing shifts in current environmental policy. Policy and programs can offer leverage against male dominance, class hierarchy, and other types of asymmetry. Laws and social policies can promote women's economic welfare, personhood, and participation. We know that is not enough. We also need to remedy the 'invisibility' of privilege (cf. Brush 2003) – whether of men, the rich, or privileged castes. The structures and unequal relations that cause disadvantage to persist need to be challenged.

## Notes

This chapter has been adapted by the editor with the assistance and approval of the author from the article 'Forty years of gender research and environmental policy: Where do we stand?' published in *Women's Studies International Forum* 47(2014): 295–308. Reprinted with permission.

1  Personal communication with people working in development organizations.
2  See www.landscapes.org.
3  There is always a danger of cementing such constructs into policy. In her study in the UK, Elizabeth Harrison (2012) shows how the focus on resilience as an antithesis of vulnerability among researchers and policy makers has lent itself to an overemphasis on the ability of those at the sharp end of economic downturn to bounce back, where resilience becomes a euphemistic way of talking about increased unpaid work of social reproduction that comes at considerable costs in terms of time. As with domestic labour itself, evidence suggests that the burden of this falls disproportionately to women.
4  See a review on the topic by Cornwall and Nyamu-Musembi (2004).
5  For example, the debate in the Swedish media after two researchers suggested doing away with the term 'gender equality' (and mainstreaming) in Swedish politics which they see as depoliticized and a bureaucratic exercise – http://feministisktperspektiv.se/2012/10/26/framat-ar-vagen/. See also Arora-Jonsson (2013:233–234) for the tensions of working with established gender categories that pull you back and yet the problems of giving them up completely.
6  Examples from Sweden and Pakistan demonstrate that the inclusion of women has led to important legislation protecting women's rights.

## References

Agarwal, B. (1992) 'The gender and environment debate: Lessons from India', *Feminist Studies* 18(1): 119–158.

Agarwal, B. (1994) *A Field of One's Own: Gender and Land Rights in South Asia.* Cambridge and New Delhi: Cambridge University Press.

Ahlers, R. (2002) 'Moving in or staying out: Gender dimensions of water markets', in Whiteford, S. and Melville, R. (eds) *Protecting a Sacred Gift: Water and Social Change in Mexico.* San Diego: Center for US–Mexico Studies at UC–San Diego, 65–86.

Ahlers, R. and Zwarteveen, M. (2009) 'The water question in feminism: Water control and gender inequities in a neo-liberal era', *Gender, Place and Culture* 16(4): 409–426.

Arnfred, S. (2012) *Gender Equality has Become a Central Part of World Bank Politics: On Gender in Development Discourse and in African Societies*. Online. Available at: http://naiforum.org/2012/03/gender-equalityhas-become-a-central-part-of-world-bank-politics/ (accessed 7 January 2013).

Arora-Jonsson, S. (2011) 'Virtue and vulnerability: Discourses on women, gender and climate change', *Global Environmental Change* 21: 744–751.

Arora-Jonsson, S. (2013) *Gender, Development and Environmental Governance: Theorizing Connections*. London and New York: Routledge.

Baden, S. and Goetz, A. M. (1998) 'Who needs [sex] when you can have [gender]? Conflicting discourses on gender at Beijing', in Jackson, C. and Pearson, R. (eds) *Feminist Visions of Development: Gender Analysis and Policy*. London: Routledge, 3–25.

Basu, A. and McGrory, E. (eds) (1995) *The Challenge of Local Feminisms: Women's Movements in Global Perspective*. Boulder: Westview Press.

Basu, S. (1999) 'Cutting to size: Property and gendered identity in the Indian higher courts', in Sunder Rajan, R. (ed) *Signposts: Gender Issues in Post-Independence India*. New Delhi: Kali for Women, 249–292.

Brush, L. D. (2002) 'Changing the subject: Gender and welfare regime studies', *Social Politics: International Studies in Gender, State and Society* 9(2): 161–186.

Brush, L. D. (2003) *Gender and Governance*. AltaMira: Walton Creek.

Bryceson, D. (ed) (1995) *Women Wielding the Hoe: Lessons From Rural Africa for Feminist Theory and Development Practice*. Oxford: Berg.

Butler, J. (1990) *Gender Trouble: Feminism and the Subversion of Identity*. New York: Routledge.

Butler, J. (2004) *Undoing Gender*. New York: Routledge.

Chant, S. (2008) 'The "feminisation of poverty" and the "feminisation" of anti-poverty programmes: Room for revision?', *Journal of Development Studies* 44(2): 165–197.

Chant, S. and Sweetman, C. (2012) 'Fixing women or fixing the world? "Smart economics", efficiency approaches, and gender equality in development', *Gender and Development* 20(3): 517–529.

Chatterjee, P. (2004) *The Politics of the Governed: Reflections on Popular Politics in Most of the World*. New York: Columbia University Press.

Chaudhuri, M. (ed) (2004) *Feminism in India*. New Delhi: Kali for Women.

Cleaver, F. (1998) 'Incentives and informal institutions: Gender and the management of water', *Agriculture and Human Values* 15(4): 347–360.

Cornwall, A. and Nyamu-Musembi, C. (2004) 'Putting the "rights-based approach" to development into perspective', *Third World Quarterly* 25(8): 1415–1437.

Dahl, H. M. (2012) 'Neo-liberalism meets the Nordic welfare state – Gaps and silences', *NORA* 20(4): 283–288.

Davids, T., Francien Van, D. and Parren, F. (2014) 'Feminist change revisited: Gendermainstreaming as slow-revolution', *Journal of International Development* 26(3): 396–408.

Elias, M. and Saussey, M. (2013) '"The gift that keeps on giving": Unveiling the paradoxes of fair trade Shea butter', *Sociologia Ruralis* 53(2): 158–179.

Folbre, N. (1994) *Who Pays for the Kids? Gender and the Structures of Constraint*. London and New York: Routledge.

Fortmann, L. (ed) (2008) *Participatory Research in Conservation and Rural Livelihoods: Doing Science Together*. London: Wiley-Blackwell.

Fraser, N. (2009) 'Feminism, capitalism and the cunning of history', *New Left Review* 56: 97–117.

Green, C., Joekes, S. and Leach, M. (1998) 'Questionable links: Approaches to gender in environmental research and policy', in Jackson, C. and Pearson, R. (ed) *Feminist Visions of Development*. London and New York: Routledge, 259–283.

Grewal, I. and Kaplan, C. (eds) (1994) *Scattered Hegemonies: Postmodernity and Transnational Feminist Practices*. Minneapolis: University of Minnesota Press.

Halley, J., Kotiswaran, P., Shamir, H. and Thomas, C. (2006) 'From the international to the local in feminist legal responses to rape, prostitution/sex work and sex trafficking: Four studies in contemporary governance feminism', *Harvard Journal of Law and Gender* 29: 226–424.

Haraway, D. (1991) *Simians, Cyborgs, and Women: The Reinvention of Nature*. London: Free Association Books.

Harris, L. M. (2009) 'Gender and emergent water governance: Comparative overview of neoliberalized natures and gender dimensions of privatization, devolution and marketization', *Gender, Place and Culture* 16(4): 387–408.

Harrison, E. (2012) 'Bouncing back? Recession, resilience and everyday lives', *Critical Social Policy* 33(1): 97–113.

Harriss-White, B. (1998) 'Female and male grain marketing systems: Analytical and policy issues for West Africa and India', in Jackson, C. and Pearson, R. (eds) *Feminist Visions of Development*. London and New York: Routledge, 189–213.

Hartsock, N. (2006) 'Globalization and primitive accumulation: The contributions of David Harvey's dialectical Marxism', in Castree, N. and Gregory, D. (eds) *David Harvey: A Critical Reader*. Malden and Oxford: Blackwell, 166–190.

Ivesen, K. (2010) 'Justifying exclusion: The politics of public space and the dispute over access to McIvers ladies' baths, Sydney', *Gender, Place and Culture* 10(3): 215–228.

Jackson, C. (1996) 'Rescuing gender from the poverty trap', *World Development* 24(3): 489–504.

Jordans, E. and Zwarteveen, M. (1997) *A Well of One's Own: Gender Analysis of An Irrigation Program in Bangladesh*. Colombo, Sri Lanka: IIMI.

Kabeer, N. (2003) *Gender Mainstreaming in Poverty Eradication and the Millennium Development Goals: A Handbook for Policy Makers and Other Stakeholders*. London: Commonwealth Secretariat.

Keating, C., Rasmussen, C. and Rishi, P. (2010) 'The rationality of empowerment: Microcredit, accumulation by dispossession, and the gendered economy', *Signs* 36(1): 153–176.

Keck, M. E. and Sikkink, K. (1998) *Activists Beyond Borders: Advocacy Networks in International Politics*. Ithaca and London: Cornell University Press.

Larner, W. (1998) 'Post-welfare state governance: Towards a code of social and family responsibility', Paper presented at the Refashioning Sociology: Responses to a New World Order. Brisbane: Queensland, University of Technology.

Leach, M. (2007) 'Earth mother myths and other ecofeminist fables: How a strategic notion rose and fell', *Development and Change* 38(1): 67–85.

Lewis, J. (2001) 'The decline of the male breadwinner model: Implications for work and care', *Social Politics* (Summer): 152–169.

Lingam, L. (2002) 'Taking stock: Women's movement and the State', in Shah, G. (ed) *Social Movements and the State* (Vol. 4). New Delhi, Thousand Oaks and London: Sage Publications, 310–334.

McAfee, K. (1999) 'Selling nature to save it? Biodiversity and green developmentalism', *Environment and Planning D: Society and Space* 17: 133–154.

Merchant, C. (1980) *The Death of Nature: Women, Ecology and the Scientific Revolution*. New York: Harper One.

Mies, M. and Shiva, V. (1993) *Ecofeminism*. London: Zed Books.

Mohanty, C. T. (2003) *Feminism Without Borders: Decolonizing Theory, Practicing Solidarity*. New Delhi: Zubaan.

Moser, C. (1989) 'Gender planning in the Third World: Meeting practical and strategic gender needs', *World Development* 17(11): 1799–1825.

Narayan, U. and Harding, S. (eds) (2000) *Decentering the Center: Philosophy for a Multicultural, Postcolonial, and Feminist World*. Bloomington: Indiana University Press.

Navarro, M. and Korrol, V. S. (1999) *Latin America and the Caribbean*. Bloomington: Indiana University Press.

Odoul, W. and Kabira, W. M. (1995) 'The mothers of warriors and her daughters: The women's movement in Kenya', in Basu, A. (ed) *The Challenge of Local Feminisms*. Boulder: Westview Press, 187–208.

Pateman, C. (1988) *The Sexual Contract*. Stanford, CA: Stanford University Press.

Prugl, E. (2010) 'Feminism and the postmodern state: Gender mainstreaming in European rural development', *Signs* 35(2): 447–475.

Ramdas, S. R. (2009) 'Women, forestspaces and the law: Transgressing the boundaries', *Economic and Political Weekly* XLIV(44): 65–73.

Rankin, K. N. (2003) 'Cultures of economies: Gender and socio-spatial change in Nepal', *Gender, Place and Culture* 10(2): 111–129.

Rao, N. (2007) 'Custom and the courts: Ensuring women's rights to land, Jharkhand, India', *Development and Change* 2: 299–319.

Razavi, S. (2012) 'World development report 2012: Gender equality and development – A commentary', *World Development* 43(1): 423–437.

Reed, M. G. (2000) 'Taking stands: A feminist perspective on "other" women's activism in forestry communities of northern Vancouver Island', *Gender, Place and Culture* 7(4): 363–387.

Rocheleau, D., Thomas-Slayter, B. and Wangari, E. (eds) (1996) *Feminist Political Ecology: Global Issues and Local Experiences*. London: Routledge.

Scott, J. W. (1988) *Gender and the Politics of History*. New York: Colombia University Press.

Scott, J. W. (2012) 'The uses and abuses of gender', *Södertörn Lectures* 8. Stockholm: Södertörn University.

Sharma, A. (2006) 'Crossbreeding institutions, breeding struggle: Women's empowerment, neoliberal governmentality, and state (re)formation in India', *Cultural Anthropology* 21(1): 60–95.

Shiva, V. (1989) *Staying Alive: Women, Ecology and Development*. London: Zed.

Shohat, E. (ed) (2001) *Talking Visions: Multicultural Feminism in a Transnationalage* (Vol. 5). New York: New Museum of Contemporary Art/MIT Press.

Tollin, K. (2000) *Det måste finnas män med för att det skall bli jämställt: En utvärdering av Mainstreamingprojektet inom Arbetsmarknadsverket Västerbotten*. Umeå: Statsvetenskapliga institutionen, Umeå universitet.

Whitehead, A. and Tsikata, D. (2003) 'Policy discourses on women's land rights in sub-Saharan Africa: The implications of the re-turn to the customary', *Journal of Agrarian Change* 3(1 and 2): 67–112.

Wickramasinghe, A. and Momsen, J. (1993) 'Women's roles in rural Sri Lanka', in Momsen, J. and Kinnaird, V. (eds) *Different Places, Different Voices: Gender and Development in Africa, Asia and Latin America*. London: Routledge, 159–175.

World Bank (1992) *World Development Report 1992: Development and the Environment*. New York: Author.

World Bank (2011) *World Development Report 2012: Gender Equality and Development*. Washington, DC: Author.

Zwarteveen, M. (1996) *A Plot of One's Own: Gender Relations and Irrigated Land Allocation Policies in Burkina Faso*. Colombo, Sri Lanka: International Irrigation Management Institute.

# 20

# GENDER POLITICS IN GREEN PARTIES

*Stewart Jackson*

## Introduction

Green parties are a political phenomenon of the late twentieth century. Growing out of the dissatisfaction of youth in the post-war economic boom period, and harnessing a burgeoning interest in the environment, Green parties have surfed on the wave of post-material expansion. They have participated in government across Europe, including the core democracies of France and Germany, and have helped shape politics into the twenty-first century. Yet beneath this rosy picture, Green parties have struggled with sometimes bitter internal debates, at times not dissimilar to those in more traditional parties on the left and right. From the beginning, the Green party philosophy has been an uneasy amalgam of competing foci; the parties themselves often an uneasy alliance of different social and political movements – and too often being seen as 'just' representing the environment. While prominent early members could claim long histories in social movements, especially the peace and women's movements, those movement ties have weakened over the years. A signal moment came in 1998 when then leader of *Die Grünen* (the German Greens) and German Foreign Minister, Joschka Fisher, pushed the Greens to agree to German involvement in North Atlantic Treaty Organization's (NATO) intervention into Kosovo, against the cries of internal critics and external peace activists. At that time the question could be asked whether the Greens had betrayed their movement origins or had simply matured.

The purpose of this chapter is to examine Green parties' sometimes ambivalent attitude toward gender politics. Greens will argue that they have the best record among all political parties in preselecting and electing women into parliament and into leader positions. The parties can point to relatively healthier gender ratios than other parties among their rank and file membership and elected members of parliament (MPs). They can also argue that internal processes promote women into leadership, and can equally point to a string of high profile female leaders. Yet the success of the Greens in promoting gender equity within the party does not extend to challenging key institutions as gendered (read: male dominated) organizations in both form and function. While the Greens might argue for greater participation of women in parliaments, this claim does not address ongoing complaints about the structure, operation, and language of parliamentary politics, particularly the aggressive adversarial nature of parliamentary debate.

So, in looking at gender politics within Green parties, it is important to consider a number of elements, from the shifts in participation and forms of electoral and community campaigning from the parties' earliest days to their role in shaping – or not – existing institutions and processes within big 'p' Politics in the countries in which they operate. Parties are themselves embedded in political structures, even those that might seek to undermine existing political paradigms. The question is, have Green parties been successful in challenging more traditional conceptions of the role of individuals (as members and leaders), and women in particular, in these institutions?

I will begin with an overview of the development of Green parties before examining their attitudes to gender issues. While participation rates and leadership structures within the Greens would suggest a feminized party, a closer inspection of internal party processes reveals the continuation of behavioural patterns noted in other left wing parties and trade unions. I conclude the discussion with some reflections on the negative role that party structures can have on women's participation in politics.

## Green parties in context

Green parties arose in the context of the cultural and social revolutions that swept across the Western world in the 1960s. A phenomenon clearly linked to the various social movements that found expression during that period, in their earliest incarnations the parties mirrored the diverse and often fractured debates on how a post-capitalist, post-materialist world might be structured. Appearing in the mid to late 1970s, the first national Green parties, in Aotearoa-New Zealand, Switzerland, Germany, and the United Kingdom managed to bring together these at times quite divergent elements into single electoral vehicles. Green parties in other Western countries, such as in Australia, Canada, the United States (US), Italy, and France, took longer to weld the disparate groups together, often suffering splits and reformulations until an acceptable structure could be agreed.

That the genesis of Green parties was in the counter-cultural movements of the sixties also meant an increased focus on individual identity and empowerment. This appeared to play out well for members of the expanding post-war middle classes. The long post-war boom had brought economic development, and successive European governments developed the key welfare state institutions. As Inglehart (1990) has explained, as previous political demands for material access were being met, there was a shift toward post-material values, with individual empowerment, participatory decision-making, and environmental health now being emphasized. An emergent environmental awareness, a renewed vigour among feminists, and increasing concern with Western nations' military activities in developing nations – particularly around the Vietnam War – forged new alliances between previously disparate groups. When the small groups of activists who formed two of the earliest proto Green parties, the United Tasmania Group in Australia and the Values Party in Aotearoa-New Zealand, announced their political platforms they included elements from all these movements (Dann 2008). Thus Greens can be said to have their roots in social movements, and early iterations of the Greens to be what Kitschelt (2006) calls 'movement parties'.

The emerging Green parties themselves were aided by more assertive news media prepared and able to report on emerging environmental problems; the scientific explorations of Rachel Carson (see Seager, this volume) and the Club of Rome into the disaster for the environment of exponential growth; and the growing awareness among academics and citizens alike of the intersection of social and environmental issues. Equally, an emerging strand of feminism, ecofeminism, sought to link patriarchy and capitalist exploitation to environmental destruction (Salleh 1997; Gaard 1998). The traditionally structured and focused parties, both conservative and social democratic, built upon existing social and class cleavages, struggled to adapt to the new pressures. Nonetheless, the majority of voters continued to support mainstream parties to the extent that they could take on the fig-leaf of regulation while continuing to promote an economic model still based on environmental exploitation. US President Richard Nixon's establishment of the US Environmental Protection Agency and the adoption of environmental regulation such as the Clean Air Act of 1963 was certainly one important such action.

These early Green parties clearly drew upon their social movement bases to argue against hierarchies and formal power structures and for equality of representation. This initially translated into mechanisms for ensuring equal representation of men and women, sometimes expressed as affirmative action rules and at other times as 'shared positions' – that is, co-leader positions jointly held by women and men. Leadership roles, such as Party Convenors and Secretaries, were seen – and structured – as functionary roles, generally subordinate to councils comprised of local representatives. The first MPs were often term-limited, in part to undermine entrenched power and to force the subordination of parliamentary representatives to the party branches.

## Gender in political parties

Although studies of gender in Green parties are almost non-existent, the study of political representation and gender in politics are wide and relatively well established fields. While research on gender in politics (or more accurately *women* in politics) is fairly extensive, it tends to be more focused on systemic issues across political institutions as opposed to specific organizations, often taking the form of examining perspectives such as the aggregate number of women in parliaments or overall female membership numbers within parties.[1] So, there is an extensive literature built up around the issue of parliamentary quotas for women to increase the number of women parliamentarians, whether at the national level, including designated seats for women, or internal party representation, including legislatively stipulated or party-imposed quotas (Dahlerup and Freidenvall 2005; Kittilson 2005).

To consider the work of parties, though, we need to consider the context in which parties operate. Parties themselves operate within a political and social context, as well as being structured organizations. Acker (1990) points toward the potential for organizations to be gendered, whether through the social construction of roles or the creation and re-creation of internal hierarchies. Lovenduski (1996) clearly shows the gendered nature of politics generally, which Crawford and Pini (2010) demonstrate leads to the creation of gendered (i.e., male dominated) parliamentary institutions, in part through the creation and maintenance of men's advantage.

The academic literature on political parties as gendered organizations is less wide, however. Party-specific research is limited except as part of general investigations of party internal workings, such as by Cross and Katz (2013), although Lovenduski and Norris (1993) show clearly that party organization can have a critical impact on women's participation and inclination to vote for parties, typically through entrenching processes and hierarchies that favour men, in terms of policy, candidate selection, and leadership. Female participation as party members or activists is often reduced to a variable against which other forms of participation can be tested, except where it directly affects leadership and representation, such as through the application of quotas. Moreover, while feminist political scientists such as Weldon (2002) point to the impact non-legislative actors can have on policy directly on women (in this case, policies on domestic violence), this might be seen as referring to movements and policy entrepreneurs. What is the role of the party in such a schema, given that the party is generally the nominator of the legislator: are they just an extension of the individual legislator or an actor in their own right?

While parties might be seen as separate beasts, the role of the individual political actor or leader is often cast as being of critical importance. However, as Childs and Webb (2011) demonstrate, the role of the political leader can be critical in changing the internal dynamics of the party in relation to the promotion of women and women's policy interests, as much as the public perception of the party. This is particularly important as the discussion is of David Cameron as leader of UK Conservative Party, and follows from these researchers' previous examinations of women in politics.

The many scholarly works evaluating gender quotas for parties indicate that a key element for increasing women's participation in politics is improving the number of female political representatives, and that candidate selection is the key to representation. While many of these studies point to supply-side factors (i.e., availability of qualified female candidates) or demand-side (i.e., the role of political elites in selection) factors, there is an argument for a broader acknowledgement of the party-as-institution, and to place candidate selection within this context requires an understanding of a range of institutional factors (Krook 2010). Thus Lovenduski (2002) points to a range of other factors that influence the selection of women as candidates, irrespective of whether the seat they are selected for is 'winnable' or not. In contrast to the positive effect, Childs and Webb (2011) were able to show, where a party does *not* have a strong impetus to promote or select women, then it will not do so. If this is linked to particular conceptions of politics as being masculine by nature – that is, as 'men's work' – then a party might equally be inimical to women's interests or representation. Thus while social democratic parties can point to positive aspects of using quotas to raise women's participation and representation,[2] without some impetus to promote women, more negative norms of behaviour would re-assert themselves, as demonstrated by Lovenduski (2002).

When we consider the non-conservative parties, the issue of the linkages between the party and affiliated organizations also becomes increasingly important. Social democratic parties with strong links to trade unions – such as between Australian and UK Labour Parties and their affiliated unions – will be influenced by the established union-based norms of behaviour toward women. Trade unions, particularly those covering manual industries, remain male dominated, but unions have perhaps always been thus. Even where progress has been made toward gender equity (see Kirton 2015), the question remains regarding other forms of discrimination within organizations. As Healy and Kirton (2000) powerfully demonstrate, even where union structures incorporate quotas and women's officers, more subtle forms of discrimination affect women's participation. These subtler forms, such as verbal and visual harassment, belittling of reserved position holders, and a perceived need to de-gender issues to win support, work to undermine the expansion of women past reserved positions, and are similar to those that can be identified within parties generally.

While Green parties do not tend to have the same affiliations with extra-parliamentary groupings as social democratic parties have traditionally had, they do have some close relationships with individuals in the external movements, particularly environmental and conservation organizations. Certainly, Green parties were most often formed around environmental campaigns, and MPs have often previously been high profile members of environmental organizations. However, as Salleh (1987) notes, the groups supporting these politicians also exhibit the characteristics of gendered organizations, adopting hierarchical campaign structures, sometimes with women in clearly subordinate roles, and often with men as dominant leaders (see also Taylor 2014; Buckingham in this handbook). At least some of this behaviour might be expected to transfer through to the party itself. Conversely, the Greens also have historical links to peace movement groups, at least some of which could be argued to be feminist. From those groups a number of core internal party practices were derived.

## Gender dynamics in Green parties

As noted earlier, within this broader research, a focus on the gender dynamics in Green parties is fairly limited. This is due to several factors, including: the relatively small size of Green parties (except in a handful of European/Western nations); the assumption that as the parties have adopted pro-active policies for women there is no 'gender issue' to discuss; and a primary focus on the parties' environmental credentials, as if that is their sole motivation or alignment. While the Greens are indeed relatively small in many countries, when compared to larger conservative, Christian democratic or social democratic parties, since they have had some electoral success and several have been involved in governing coalitions, greater scrutiny might be expected. Because Green parties have been seen to promote women into positions of power, have effective nominated and elected representatives, and have policies that while not radical can be seen as solidly feminist, the question of whether the Greens are a pro-gender equality or even a *feminist party* has been less well researched. Certainly with high profile current and former leaders such as Natalie Bennett, Caroline Lucas (both UK), Elizabeth May (Canada), Christine Milne (Australia), and Dominique Voynet (France), Greens might appear to have successfully 'dealt with' the issue of women in representative politics. But have they?

Where some research has been conducted on gender dynamics in Green parties, it has tended to be confined to either descriptive studies of party histories or as anecdotal evidence collected in party surveys. While Gaard (1998) certainly offers a telling, in depth exploration of the interaction of ecofeminists and the US Greens, other writings on North American Greens, such as by Hawkins (2006), have elided the issue altogether. Gaard (1998) in particular, in picking apart the 1996 US Presidential campaign by Green party candidate Ralph Nader, highlights a key gap in Green theorizing around democracy – that it tends to sit within already existing paradigms and amounts to 'trickle down democracy', akin to 'trickle down economics'. An interesting exception is Chamberlayne's (1990) dissection of the debates within Germany surrounding the Mother's Manifesto promoted by women within the German Greens. The Mother's Manifesto challenged assumptions about policy aimed at the public sphere, such as employment and political representation quotas, at the expense of ignoring issues of justice in the private sphere. However, the debates themselves became entangled in arguments about essentialism and maternalism (or conceptualizing women-as-mothers in political rhetoric) and the role of women as nationalist symbols (see MacGregor 2006 for an examination of maternalism in environmental politics).

While green political theorists such as Eckersley (2004) have sought to promote different models of the state and democratic practices, these alternative models do not appear to have made any inroads into Green parties themselves, leaving existing conceptions of the worth of liberal democratic practices untouched. This acceptance of existing practices links back to the debates discussed previously regarding the role of women as mothers. As Ferree makes clear, 'Once the state recognises women's motherhood, the state's inability to see women as anything but mothers makes "mommy politics" problematic' (1993:109). MacGregor goes further, noting the result is that women replace 'lost state-provided services with their own unpaid, caring labour in private households and through volunteer work in communities' (2006:68).

What we might take from the existing research is the notion that Green parties are feminized organizations. Martin (1990) provides an overview of feminist organizations as ones that share a feminist ideology, values, goals, and seek feminist outcomes. Political parties such as the Greens operate with far broader agendas, yet may retain elements that promote feminist values and goals, and might therefore be considered a *feminized party*. Childs (2013a) provides at least some direction in what a feminized party might look like, as one that, if not explicitly feminist, certainly responds to feminist demands. She argues that when we think about party responses to feminist agendas, there should also be consideration given to the internal organization of the party in respect of women's status and male-female gender balance. This extends from women's participation in the political process, through access to political leadership and policy-making, to whether feminist critiques are accepted or acted upon by the party. Table 20.1 shows the most relevant party models for Green parties. Childs argues for other models to cover the full range of party structures, but those discussed here are the closest to what we might assume are Green party structures and approaches.

We might consider legislative means to enforce quotas, representation, or policy inclusivity. However, more fully regulating parties' internal structures would require a significant shift in the way in which parties are currently regulated, except where parties engage in voluntary regulation. The introduction of quotas could be mandated through legislation, but this further changes the nature of parties as voluntary associations. Equally, and given the gendered nature of the parliamentary context, we should not be surprised when parties do not adopt voluntary regulatory measures, or apply them in a general and mechanistic manner. An example sometimes used is that of the Australian Labour Party (ALP), which introduced a quota system for candidate selection in 2002 (Gauga and Cross 2015). While this quota has enjoyed some success, the quality of seats (e.g., is it likely to be won) has at times been questionable, and the system remains open to manipulation by party factions. Thus measures to ensure such internal action that are both substantive and practical can be delineated, but implementation remains problematic (see, for instance, Childs 2013b; Krook and Norris 2014).

*Table 20.1* Feminized party models

| | First dimension | | Second dimension |
| --- | --- | --- | --- |
| | *Integration of women parliamentary elites* | *Integration of women party members* | *Integration of women's concerns* |
| *Responsive party I (feminist both dimensions)* | High/moderate representation; well designed and fully implemented quotas; or absence of obstacles to women's representation | Parity of members; women's organizations are fully integrated into party policy-making | Positive and in feminist direction |
| *Responsive party II (feminist second dimension)* | Low representation; absent or poorly designed/ implemented quotas | Fewer women members; integrated women's organizations | Positive and feminist |
| *Co-optive party (feminist on first dimension, neutral on second)* | High/moderate representation; may have quotas | Parity of members; auxiliary women's organizations | Negative (women's concerns are not addressed) or positive (women's concerns are addressed but in a neutral direction) |

Amended from Childs (2013a)

What we perhaps should be taking from the structures described previously is the importance of both participation and representation in any discussion of feminized parties. Green parties have higher rates of participation and representation than existing parties that developed from cleavage structures associated with class or religion (Cross 2013). Even then, Green parties in Western Europe have not achieved complete gender parity in the membership, even while their representation of women in parliament remains relatively high compared to other parliamentary parties. Feminist policy concerns regarding issues that directly affect women – such as reproductive rights, male violence against women, affordable childcare, equal access to health care and education – are all addressed by Green party policies. More broadly, women are known to be more concerned about environmental issues than men, particularly those that are associated with risks from toxic chemicals and nuclear radiation (Bord and O'Connor 1997; Franzten and Vogel 2013) and climate change (McCright 2010).

## *Leadership*

One of the more striking elements in the development of Green parties has been the shift in leadership structures. Whereas most Green parties began with collective, rotational, or multiple-person leadership structures, the move over time has been to dual positions – usually one male and one female co-leader (see Table 20.2) – or even to the more conventional one leader system. This change in leadership structure has also been generally accompanied by a streamlining of internal party structures and processes. A number of parties, such as the French and Australian Greens, originally had structures designed to frustrate the central concentration of power, and to empower branches, regions, and states. The streamlining of structures principally involves

*Table 20.2* Change in Green party leadership structures

| Country | Party structure | Early leadership structure | Most recent structure |
| --- | --- | --- | --- |
| Germany | Federal | Three co-speakers (rotational) | Co-chairs (non-rotational) |
| Finland | Unitary | Collective (Green commission) | Leader |
| England and Wales | Unitary | Three co-chairs | Co-leaders |
| Ireland | Unitary | Collective | Leader |
| France | Unitary | Collective (national council) | National secretary |
| Austria | Federal | Collective (national executive) | Leader |
| Switzerland | Federal | Shared – executive board and president | President |
| Sweden | Unitary | Shared – annual Congress and Parl. party (each with two co-speakers) | Two co-spokespersons |
| Belgium | Federal | Two separate parties: *Écolo* – federal secretariat; *Agalev* – steering committee | Two separate parties: *Écolo* – co-leaders; *Groen* (formerly *Agalev*) – leader |
| Australia | Federal | Collective (national council) | Parliamentary leader |
| Canada | Federal | Three co-spokespersons | Leader |
| New Zealand | Unitary | Collective (national council) | Co-leaders |

Adapted from *Cunningham and Jackson* (2014)

reducing the power of the regions and states, and a collapsing of directly subordinate bodies such as administrative and finance committees (Miragliotta 2015). While those in the leadership positions may not gain a direct increase in their positional power, there is a significant increase in the perception that their words, instructions, and statements carry the weight of the party. So, for instance, a statement from former Australian Greens Leader Bob Brown regarding the sale of the national public telecommunications corporation in 2001 was widely seen as indicating a change in party policy, even though Brown could not enforce such a policy internally within the party, and in any case the party policy stated the opposite.

The reason cited most often by Green parties for these changes in leadership structure is that it is for organizational and parliamentary efficiency. An ability to respond to media enquiries is seen as important, as well as being able to move quickly when legislation is brought forward or votes are called. The debate that has occurred in various parties is interesting insofar as the repeated refrain is that if the party does not select a leader, then the media will choose a person to go to for comments – a person who will thus become the de facto party leader – or that other parties in parliament will be confused about who to deal with and may ignore or exclude the Greens from discussions. Because these outcomes are seen as unprofessional and potentially damaging, several Green parties have made the shift to a more conventional (i.e., single leader) approach to leadership.

The demand to be able to respond rapidly to events within national parliaments points to two effects: the subordination of party structures to parliamentary demands, and the acceptance of existing political structures as appropriate. The role of the extra-parliamentary party is then downplayed in favour of the parliamentary party, and parliament appears to be where the principal activity of the party should lie. While this has not necessarily been harmful to gender parity, it does mean that parliamentary norms in respect of decision-making, leader selection, and policy negotiation become those of the party.

## Gender differences in membership and participation

While a number of high profile female leaders may have emerged from within Green parties, whether women members participate equally within the parties is less clear. Participation rates by women in parties generally is already known to be lower than for men, whether as party members

*Table 20.3* Female membership rates in Green parties, 2010–2015

| Country | Green party | F:M ratio |
| --- | --- | --- |
| Belgium | Écologistes (Écolo) | 36:64 |
| Denmark | Socialistisk Folkeparti | 49:51 |
| France | Les Verts | 30:70 |
| Germany | Die Grünen | 38:62 |
| Netherlands | Groen Links | 43:57 |
| Spain | Iniciativa Catalunya Verde | 32:68 |
| United Kingdom | Green Party of England and Wales | 42:58 |
| Australia[†] | The Australian Greens | 50:50 |
| New Zealand[††] | Green Party of Aotearoa New Zealand | 47:53 |

*Source*: Van Haute and Gauja (2015), except [†]Jackson (2016) and [††] and see note[3]

or as activists and functionaries (van Haute and Gauja 2015). Green parties outperform many other traditionally structured and organized parties, but not to the extent that their participation is equal with men. As can be seen from Table 20.3, female participation rates within Green parties are still far less than equal, with the exception of a small handful of parties.

For the Australian Greens and Green Party of Aotearoa-New Zealand, the equal participation of men and women can be seen within the roots of both parties in the combining of movements within both countries. The UK Greens were previously reported to have a higher percentage of women within the party (Lovenduski and Norris 1993), at 47 per cent, but this appears to have fallen to 42 per cent (Bennie 2015), even as the party has increased its representation.

When the predominance of men as Green party members is seen in the light of the even higher levels of male party membership within the traditional parties, it might be argued that this is in fact a positive outcome as women are being drawn to joining the party when they might not otherwise be engaged in politics. Unfortunately, however, the Greens are also found to have a skew toward women in terms of their voter base (see, for instance, Bean and McAllister 2015:414). This means that there still remains a participation gap between those voting for the party and those participating within the party. Just as the Greens have been seen to attract a predominantly youthful voter base while their membership base is considerably older, a gap exists in gender participation – women vote more than men for a party whose membership base is male dominated.

What we can begin to see is how Green parties might fit within the models shown in Table 20.1. When we consider that Greens are often capable of electing women into legislatures, and some of the parties (such as in Denmark and Australia) begin to approach parity in membership ratios, this is most often achieved without quotas. Women's concerns regarding policy are broadly considered, although policy is still officially cast as gender neutral. Women are generally fully contained within the party, with limited numbers of separate women's organizing spaces, such as Women's Committees – although this is not clearly reported in the research described previously – and leadership roles may be taken on by women. This fact would suggest that Green parties fall well within the limits of Childs's (2013a) 'responsive party' model for a feminized party, but vary in the details between them. However, while Green parties may appear to be feminized parties, do they necessarily operate that way?

## Gender and internal party processes

While an overview of the various Green parties can be derived from their membership and representation rates, deeper markers of change must be sought to properly examine the internal party processes and whether these internal workings can be considered feminized or whether they replicate other, gendered, structures. One example might be the Australian Greens, upon which some research has been done, where the change in internal processes is tracked and the attitudes of male and female party members – including whether practices are discriminatory or exclusionary – is noted (see, for instance, Miragliotta 2006, 2012; Jackson 2012, 2016; Gauja and Jackson 2015). Australian Greens' processes owe something to the variety of social movements to which they are connected, and key elements of feminist and peace activist distrust of hierarchy and concentration of power were incorporated into the early party structures. At the same time, party processes were modelled along cooperative and consensual lines. However, just as more conventional positions have been adopted to replace collective leadership, internal processes have changed to allow for non-consensual decision-making.

Equally, while the Australian Greens might argue that they have achieved equality in the nomination and election of MPs, and gender parity in membership, does this extend to the practicalities of how meetings operate or decisions are made? While the earliest elements of the party attempted to control who spoke and for how long in meetings, this practice has fallen away as the party has become more embedded in national and state legislatures. Early party processes attempted to provide a reflective space for both meeting facilitators and participants. Designated participants watching for the domination of meeting space and talking time by individuals, and monitored for tensions between meeting participants, while separate training was provided in facilitation skills (Lange 1994). National meetings of the Australian Greens are now perceived as work spaces for decision-making, not discursive arenas. While this shift may well be thought appropriate for a political party engaged in state and national affairs, it has also meant that men are able to (and do) occupy the available time and space for decision-making at meetings. Dahlerup (1988) discusses the notion of a 'critical mass' of women in politics (even while still in a minority), and the expected effect of this criticality on political and institutional activities: less formality, shorter speeches, and meetings to the point. Yet even where a commitment to equality of participation exists, this does not extend to equal speaking time, perhaps as the ability to control conversations (or debates) is associated with power (Lakoff 2003). The issue of domination within meetings by particular participants, whether male or female, remains largely unaddressed, and indeed largely unacknowledged in the Australian Green party. Where it is recognized, such as in the New South Wales (NSW) state party, instigation of an annual state meeting with a preference for female delegates and speakers – so designated as a 'Women's State Delegates Council' – has simply served to provide equal participation of women at that meeting, rather than improve women's participation at state meetings generally. In other state meetings, men continue to dominate discussion both in speaking more often and for longer, serving to highlight that even where party organizations designate a space were women are to be dominant, in reality they still only receive 50 per cent of the available meeting space.[4]

Interestingly, within the Australian Green party generally, male domination has not been seen as a significant problem, at least when party members were surveyed in 2012 (Jackson 2016). At that time 94 per cent of male party members and 84 per cent of women in the party stated that there was no discrimination against women internally. The difference in the two results perhaps points to a clear difference in perception about internal discrimination between women and men in the party, but not to a significant level. Yet women in the Australian Greens are more supportive of quotas than men, indicating at least some understanding of systemic failings within the party in terms of women's participation.

Returning to Childs and Webb's (2011) description of a feminized party model, the Australian Greens have appeared to be a highly responsive party based on female membership of the party, the election of women as MPs and women's ability to occupy leadership positions. But there are also reasons to suspect that the party may be less advanced down the path toward feminization, including a lack of awareness of exclusionary or non-participatory practices (such as scheduling meetings at times when children need parental care) and the general lack of open acknowledgement of women's committees. These missing elements may, however, also be a result of the aging of the party's membership. As with most parties, Greens have noted the increasing age of their membership, even as their membership remains strongest among younger people. Aging members are less likely than young members to have children requiring active care and so might not have the pressure to provide childcare, make provisions for children at meetings or adjust meeting times to suit parents. These issues, although faced by all parents, still remain significantly the responsibility of women, reinforcing the notion of politics as 'men's business', where 'unencumbered' men are free to attend meetings and engage in party activities.

## Conclusion

The gender dynamics of party politics is a topic that has been well covered over the past forty years, with critiques of political parties and their key players emphasizing the gendered nature of the party as an institution, and its existence within the parliamentary sphere. Class affiliations and the structure of extra-parliamentary organizations such as trade unions and political clubs have come under scrutiny from feminist political scholars (see, for instance, Ledwith and Hansen 2013). The role of women in relation to the environment has been debated for more than thirty years, yielding important contributions to our understanding of human-environment and human-animal interactions. Yet Green parties appear to have been largely ignored in this scholarship, in part because of an assumption that, due to their history and early structural debates, they must have some special insight into women in politics, that they have solved the problem of gender inequality, or (perhaps most likely) because they have simply not been important enough to discuss. To some extent, the lack of attention to gender politics within Green parties can also be attributed to what has been observed as the gender-blind nature of mainstream political science, including the sub-field of environmental politics (cf. MacGregor 2009).

The record thus far indicates that women have been drawn to join Green parties because of the parties' clear policies to address discrimination, equality of representation in members and MPs, and they apparently take concerns about male-dominated political processes quite seriously. As politicians, women have fared far better in Green parties than in most other traditional parties. This success means that they may be in the position to serve in government when Greens make electoral gain, as they have done in a few European countries (e.g., Germany, Ireland, and France). But if Green parties are going to be part of governing coalitions, then feminists need to consider whether they are really are vehicles for social change, or whether they will provide little more than superficial gains in representation, even while the mechanisms and structures of politics goes on unchanged. Should women and feminists then stick with Green parties or start/join their own explicitly feminist parties, such as the Feminist Initiative in Sweden and the Women's Equality party in the UK?

What is also not extant in any of the literature on Green parties, on this avowedly global political movement, is the role of women in non-Western Green parties.[5] The paucity of research on Green parties in South America, Africa, and the Asia Pacific may be blamed on the small size of Green parties, where they even exist at all. But especially in the case of the South American parties, they have had candidates who have done surprisingly well in presidential elections, have polled and elected parliamentarians in numbers at times similar to a number of European Green parties, and have also provided government ministers. A good example is the career of Marina Silva of Brazil who, having previously been environment minister as part of the Workers' Party, joined the Greens and ran for the presidency under the Greens' banner in 2010, polling almost 20 per cent. Silva subsequently ran under the banner of the Brazilian Socialist Party, and although appearing for a time to be a serious challenger to President Dilma Rousseff, eventually finished with 21 per cent of the vote (Hochstetler and Oliveira 2015).

Yet an investigation of how gender plays a role in these parties might also provide some genuine insights into the universality of some of the Green broader messages surrounding gender, equity, and human rights. One of the key concerns to conclude with, therefore, must be this lack of research. While major analyses of the largest parties, particularly in European countries, has taken place over the past two decades, these all too often omit Green parties, and where they do the issue of gender is non-existent or poorly addressed. While women may appear to have reached the top in some of these parties, there is still a pressing need to investigate whether the rhetoric matches the reality of intra-party activities. If anecdotal evidence is correct, then there still exists a distinct failing in the performance of Green parties. What might then be concluded is that parties themselves, as political structures, remain a significant barrier to the full participation, on their own terms, of women in big 'p' Politics.

## Notes

1   Previous examinations of gender in political science have tended to be approached in quantitative terms (e.g., how many women, what positions?), rather than qualitative (e.g., what is their experience, what are the process used to exclude?). Mainstream political science rarely studies the roles and actions of men *as men* in politics, such that discussion of gender in political science research can be assumed to focus on women.
2   Gauja and Cross (2015) show that in Australia centralized candidate selections have had an impact, but only for the Australian Labour Party (ALP). In the case of the ALP, centrally introduced quotas have lifted women's selection as candidates and election as MPs, whereas in the conservative Liberal Party, centralized selection has maintained and even increased the number of male candidates and MPs.
3   Tim Bale conducted the first academic survey of the Aotearoa-New Zealand Greens in 2002, and these figures are drawn from the unpublished data set.
4   This research is unpublished. The figures are derived from speaking lists for each Greens NSW State Delegates Council kept by the state party co-convenor. These were provided to the author by the co-convenor, and corroborate the author's previous observations and recording of the gender of speakers at such meetings.
5   There is an equal lack of extant research on LGBTQ membership in Green parties, even as these parties draw heavily on these communities for support.

## References

Acker, J. (1990) 'Hierarchies, jobs, bodies: A theory of gendered organizations', *Gender and Society* 4(2): 139–158.

Bean, C. and McAllister, I. (2015) 'Documenting the inevitable: Voting behaviour at the 2013 Australian election', in Johnson, C., Wanna, J. and Lee, H.-S. (eds) *Abbott's Gambit: The 2013 Australian Federal Election.* Canberra: ANU Press, 411–424.

Bennie, L. (2015) 'Party membership in Britain: A minority pursuit', in van Haute, E. and Gauja, A. (eds) *Party Members and Activists.* London: Routledge, 169–185.

Bord, R. and O'Connor, R. (1997) 'The gender gap in environmental attitudes: The case of perceived vulnerability to risk', *Social Science Quarterly* 78(4): 830–840.

Chamberlayne, P. (1990) 'The mother's manifesto and disputes over "Mutterlichkeit"', *Feminist Review* 35: 9–23.

Childs, S. (2013a) 'In the absence of electoral sex quotas: Regulating political parties for women's representation', *Representation* 49(4): 401–423.

Childs, S. (2013b) 'Intra party democracy: a gendered critique and a feminist agenda', in Cross, W. and Katz, R. (eds) *The Challenges of Intra-party Democracy.* Oxford: Oxford University Press, 81–99.

Childs, S. and Webb, P. (2011) *Sex, Gender and the Conservative Party: From Iron Lady to Kitten Heels.* New York: Palgrave Macmillan.

Crawford, M. and Pini, B. (2010) 'The Australian parliament: A gendered organization', *Parliamentary Affairs* 64(1): 82–105.

Cross, W. (2013) 'Party leadership selection and intra-party democracy', in Cross, W. and Katz, R. (eds) *The Challenges of Intra-party Democracy.* Oxford: Oxford University Press, 100–115.

Cross, W. and Katz, R. (eds) (2013) *The Challenges of Intra-party Democracy.* Oxford: Oxford University Press.

Cunningham, C. and Jackson, S. (2014) 'Leadership and the Australian Greens', *Leadership* 10(4): 496–511.

Dahlerup, D. (1988) 'From a small to a large minority: Women in Scandinavian politics', *Scandinavian Political Studies* 11(4): 275–298.

Dahlerup, D. and Freidenvall, L. (2005) 'Quotas as a "fast track" to equal representation for women', *International Feminist Journal of Politics* 7(1): 26–48.

Dann, C. (2008) 'Experimental evolution down under: Thirty years of Green party development in Australian and New Zealand', in Gene Frankland, E., Lucardie, P. and Rihoux, B. (eds) *Green Parties in Transition: The End of Grassroots Democracy?* Farnham, UK: Ashgate, 177–198.

Eckersley, R. (2004) *The Green State: Rethinking Democracy and Sovereignty.* Cambridge, MA: MIT Press.

Ferree, M. (1993) 'The rise and fall of "mommy politics": Feminism and unification in (East) Germany', *Feminist Studies* 19(1): 89–115.

Franzen, A. and Vogel, D. (2013) 'Two decades of measuring environmental attitudes: A comparative analysis of 33 countries', *Global Environmental Change* 23(5): 1001–1008.

Gaard, G. (1998) *Ecological Politics: Ecofeminists and the Greens.* Philadelphia: Temple University.

Gauja, A. and Cross, W. (2015) 'The influence of party candidate selection methods on candidate diversity', *Representation* 51(3): 287–298.

Gauja, A. and Jackson, S. (2015) 'Australian Greens party members and supporters: Their profiles and activities', *Environmental Politics* 25(2): 359–379.

Haute, van E. and Gauja, A. (eds) (2015) *Party Members and Activists.* London: Routledge.

Hawkins, H. (ed) (2006) *Independent Politics: The Green Party Strategy Debates.* Chicago: Haymarket Books.

Healy, G. and Kirton, G. (2000) 'Women, power and trade union government in the UK', *British Journal of Industrial Relations* 38(3): 343–360.

Hochstetler, K. and Oliveira, M. (2015) 'Old ways and new alternatives in Brazilian politics', *Current History* 114(769): 62–67.

Inglehart, R. (1990) *Culture Shift in Advanced Industrial Society.* Princeton: Princeton University Press.

Jackson, S. (2012) 'Thinking activists: Australian Greens party activists and their responses to leadership', *Australian Journal of Political Science* 47(4): 593–607.

Jackson, S. (2016) *The Australian Greens: From Activism to Australia's Third Party.* Melbourne: Melbourne University Press.

Kirton, G. (2015) 'Progress towards gender democracy in UK unions 1987–2012', *British Journal of Industrial Relations* 53(3): 484–507.

Kitschelt, H. (2006) 'Movement parties', in Katz, R. and Crotty, W. (eds) *Handbook of Party Politics.* London: Sage Publications, 278–290.

Kittilson, M. (2005) 'In support of gender quotas: Setting new standards, bringing visible gains', *Politics & Gender* 1(4): 622–638.

Krook, M. (2010) 'Beyond supply and demand: A feminist-institutionalist theory of candidate selection', *Political Research Quarterly* 63(4): 707–720.

Krook, M. and Norris, P. (2014) 'Beyond quotas: Strategies to promote gender equality in elected office', *Political Studies* 62(1): 2–20.

Lakoff, R. (2003) 'Language, gender, and politics: Putting "women" and "power" in the same sentence', in Holmes, J. and Meyerhoff, M. (eds) *The Handbook of Language and Gender.* Carlton South: Blackwell Publishing, 161–178.

Lange, C. (1994) *Being Green: The Making of Collective Identity in the Greens (WA).* Unpublished doctoral thesis, University of Western Australia.

Ledwith, S. and Hansen, L. L. (eds) (2013) *Gendering and Diversifying Union Leadership.* Abingdon: Routledge.

Lovenduski, J. (1996) 'Sex, gender and British politics', *Parliamentary Affairs* 49(1): 1–16.

Lovenduski, J. (2002) 'Feminizing politics', *Women: A Cultural Review* 13(2): 207–220.

Lovenduski, J. and Norris, P. (eds) (1993) *Gender and Party Politics.* London: Sage Publications.

McCright, A. M. (2010) 'The effects of gender on climate change knowledge and concern in the American public', *Population and Environment* 32(1): 66–87.

MacGregor, S. (2006) *Beyond Mothering Earth: Ecological Citizenship and the Politics of Care.* Vancouver: UBC Press.

MacGregor, S. (2009) 'Natural allies, perennial foes? On the trajectories of feminist and green political thought', *Contemporary Political Theory* 8(3): 329–339.

Martin, P. Y. (1990) 'Rethinking feminist organizations', *Gender & Society* 4(2): 182–206.

Miragliotta, N. (2006) 'One party, two traditions: Radicalism and pragmatism in the Australian Greens', *Australian Journal of Political Science* 41(4): 585–596.

Miragliotta, N. (2012) 'From local to national: Explaining the formation of the Australian Green party', *Party Politics* 18(3): 409–425.

Miragliotta, N. (2015) 'Minor organizational change in Green parties An Australian case study', *Party Politics* 21(5): 699–711.

Salleh, A. (1987) 'A green party: Can the boys do without one?', in Hutton, D. (ed) *Green Politics in Australia: Working Towards a Peaceful, Sustainable and Achievable Future*. North Ryde, NSW: Angus and Robertson, 67–90.

Salleh, A. (1997) *Ecofeminism a Politics: Nature, Marx and the Postmodern*. London: Zed Books.

Taylor, D. (2014) 'The state of diversity in environmental organizations: Mainstream NGOs, foundations, government agencies', *Report prepared for Green 2.0*. Online. Available at: http://orgs.law.harvard.edu/els/files/2014/02/FullReport_Green2.0_FINALReducedSize.pdf (accessed 13 August 2016).

Weldon, S. L. (2002) 'Beyond bodies: Institutional sources of representation for women in democratic policymaking', *The Journal of Politics* 64(4): 1153–1174.

# 21

# GOOD GREEN JOBS FOR WHOM?

## A feminist critique of the green economy

*Beate Littig*

## Introduction

'Green economy' and 'green jobs' have become new buzzwords in the international sustainable development discourse. Since 2008, after about twenty years' debate, important supra- and international political actors have tried to steer heterogeneous and vague notions of what 'sustainable development' means in a particular direction. That direction is green growth via intensified investments into eco-efficient technologies and the economization of ecosystem services; in short, the global greening of capitalist economies is presented as the promising 'way out' of the global crisis. The promises of the green economy include the reconciliation of economy and ecology, the creation of new green jobs, and the reduction of social inequalities on a global scale.

This international credo about a brave new green world, which was unveiled at the UN Rio+20 Conference in 2012, has provoked a long list of gender-related concerns. For example, to what extent does the green economy actually take gender differences into consideration? Can it contribute to removing social inequality between the sexes? The green economy is intended as a means of reducing poverty, which affects women (and children) to a far higher extent than men. How does the green economy address and handle this issue from a gender perspective? And finally, what are feminist alternatives to a capitalist green growth economy?

This chapter looks at the ongoing debate about the green economy from a feminist perspective. It starts with a brief outline of the discourse of sustainable development (SD) and its relationship to gender issues. This historical recapitulation shows a growing gender fatigue within the SD discourse. Contrary to the beginning of the debate in the early 1990s, gender issues are (again) marginalized in the supranational arenas; women's rights and gender equity seem to be declining in importance on the political agenda. I will underline this judgment by examining so-called green jobs, which are officially promoted as a potential success story within the greened economy. Empirical findings about the working conditions of green jobs reveal their limited socio-ecological promise as well as the potential gender-blindness of the official debate. In the concluding part of the chapter, I will present feminist alternatives that advocate socially equitable and ecologically sustainable development. Feminist approaches include pleas for a fundamental change of the dominant model of the capitalist economy, which should be led by the principle of, and inevitable human need for, *care*. The reassessment and redistribution of work, the preservation and equal sharing of common goods, and the escape from the Northern growth-driven economic imperative are basic strands of the international feminist contribution to the green economy debate.

## From sustainable development to the green economy

June 2012 saw Rio de Janeiro host its second UN conference on sustainable development. The choice of date and venue for the Rio+20 event was symbolic, since the first Rio conference in 1992 had marked the official start of the global sustainability debate. Despite its critics, the first Rio conference was accompanied by a sense of great hope that global justice could be brought about by policies that were both redistributive and environmentally friendly at the same time. The optimism at this so-called global summit was shared both by the official delegates and by the participants at the non-governmental organization (NGO) forum, who worked together to deliberate policy. Persistent lobbying by international feminist NGOs also ensured the successful inclusion of women's issues in the official conference documents: Chapter 24 of the UN's *Agenda 21* plan of action recognizes women as key players in the implementation of SD and emphasizes the need to empower women (Littig 2001; Schultz et al. 2010).

Yet twenty years later, the overall balance of achievements is essentially negative. The global environmental situation has worsened in many respects, including biodiversity loss, climate change, marine pollution, and overuse of resources and sinks (see Haberl et al. 2011; UNEP 2012; IPCC 2014). Global poverty is on the rise, and wealth is no longer unevenly distributed just in the Global South, but also increasingly in the Global North (UNDP 2014). Women and children remain particularly affected by poverty (UNDP 2011). Critics conclude that sustainability policies have failed (Brand 2012a). Nonetheless, the Rio+20 Conference – as befits such an anniversary event – was all about renewed commitment to sustainable development. Its outcome document, entitled *The Future We Want*, refers repeatedly to the twenty-year-old documents (e.g., *Agenda 21*) and also contains a section (no. 8) on 'gender equality and the empowerment of women' (UN Division of Sustainable Development 2012). This has more recently been affirmed with the declaration of the Sustainable Development Goals (UN 2015).

The lead-up to the conference in 2012 included a longer discussion process on how to eradicate the weak points in the proclaimed sustainable development concept. UN Environmental Programme (UNEP) experts had already pointed to a need to improve this concept back in 2008. This was also the year in which the UNEP-led Green Economy Initiative was launched, with its demands for a 'green new deal' as a solution to the looming global economic crisis and the ongoing environmental crisis (UNEP 2008). UNEP also successfully called for Rio+20 to focus on the so-called green economy, which it views as a more precise concept than its broad and altogether vague sustainable development counterpart. Indeed, proponents of the green economy view it as an enhancement of SD. A green economy builds on technical innovation and the efficient use of energy and resources, not least as drivers of growth, new jobs, and thus a reduction in poverty:

> UNEP has developed a working definition of a green economy as one that results in *improved human well-being and social equity, while significantly reducing environmental risks and ecological scarcities.* . . . Practically speaking, a green economy is one whose growth in income and employment is driven by public and private investments that reduce carbon emissions and pollution, enhance energy and resource efficiency, and prevent the loss of biodiversity and ecosystem services.
>
> *(UNEP 2011:1; emphasis in original)*

The notion of a green economy is clearly popular. It has replaced its forerunner (sustainable development) and meanwhile is the model for what seems politically conceivable and reasonable (Brand and Wissen 2015). In addition to UNEP, the Organization for Economic Cooperation and Development (OECD), some ecology and Green parties, various NGOs, and a growing number of economists and ecologists are all promoting this approach to addressing the global economic crisis. The current EU growth strategy also embraces the green economy concept: *Europe 2020* sees itself as a 'new strategy for jobs and smart, sustainable and inclusive growth' and assigns priority to the efficient use of resources, the creation of new jobs, and the reduction of poverty (European Commission 2010). However, if we look beyond the common concerns regarding the foreseeable depletion of natural resources or the consequences of climate change or the consensus concerning the need to abandon fossil fuels, understandings vary with regard to what constitutes a green economy and, in particular, how it should be realized (Heinrich-Böll-Stiftung 2012). The demarcation line runs between those approaches that focus primarily on technological solutions and green growth, without essentially questioning economic growth as an indicator of prosperity (e.g., UNEP 2009; European Commission 2010; OECD 2011), and those that also demand a fundamental reformulation of social prosperity, which also extends to the prevailing high resource and energy consuming lifestyles practiced in the Global North (e.g., Green parties; WBGU 2011; Heinrich-Böll-Stiftung 2012; Paech 2014). In the latter case, criticism of growth goes hand-in-hand with a critical attitude to the consumer society and is accompanied by talk of the need for transformation (WBGU 2011) from an affluent society to a new culture of prosperity (Denkwerk Zukunft 2011) and an 'economy of sufficiency' (Paech 2014; Schneidewind and Zahrnt 2014). Most of these approaches do not refer systematically to gender issues, despite the fact that gender differences are relevant in the various strategies of greening the economy.

## Gender in/and the green economy

There are many specific references to gender in the international documents on the green economy mentioned above. Yet even if the UN's *The Future We Want* declaration calls for gender equality and the empowerment of women, its actual wording simply repeats the well-known, general gender mainstreaming objectives (an increase in the number of women in decision-making bodies and positions, equal access to education, health care, and so on) without specifying any concrete measures. Petitions submitted in the run-up to its publication by various feminist organizations clearly did not find their way into the document. The submission by the Global Women's Major Group network, which essentially summarized the debate, focused above all on the demand that '[s]ocial equity, gender equality and environmental justice must form the heart of sustainable development' as had already been negotiated at the first Rio conference in 1992. It listed and sought the launch of concrete bundles of measures to address this demand and provide 'gender equality in all spheres of our societies', 'respect for human rights and social justice', and 'environmental conservation and protection of human health'. It also advocated the use of the term 'sustainable and equitable economy' instead of 'green economy' to tie in directly with and strengthen the decisions made in 1992 (Women's Major Group 2011). But the hard-fought political acknowledgement achieved twenty years earlier – namely, that sustainable development is not gender neutral, that society's relationships to nature cannot be sustainably transformed without giving due consideration to the gender situation, and that gender equality is an integrative component of a sustainable world – was accorded at best a marginal role at Rio+20. Needless to say, subsequent statements issued by international women's groups reflected their disappointment and outrage, as the following comment from the Development Alternatives with Women for a New Era (DAWN) network demonstrates:

> In sharp contrast to twenty years ago at the historic Earth Summit when linkages between gender and all three pillars of sustainable development were substantively acknowledged, the Rio+20 outcome document has relegated women's rights and gender equality to the periphery without recognition of a wider structural analysis.
>
> *(Genanet 2012:n.p.)*

Since feminist expert groups had been working in those twenty years to substantiate the topic on both the scientific and the political level, this relegation of gender issues to the sidelines requires explanation. However, there had also already been signs of a political exclusion of feminist positions at the Rio+10 Conference in Johannesburg (Schultz et al. 2010). The German feminist Christa Wichterich (2012) suggests a number of plausible causes for the disappearance of the topic of sustainability and women from the public debate. Firstly, during the last major UN conferences on human rights, population, social change, women, habitat, and nutrition the political interest has focused directly on these specific topics. The core points of the *Agenda 21* pertaining to 'women and the environment' were included in the Declaration and Platform for Action which was adopted at the Fourth World Conference on Women (held in Beijing in 1995). This inclusion might have meant that they were recognized as being part of the domain of women's rights and gender equality, but – since it is not formally binding – without further consequences. In the years that followed, international women's movements had protested against new global developments such as neoliberalism or the privatization of public goods and, in the process, lost sight of the linkages that had been established between sustainability and economic, ecological, and social factors. Last but not least, Wichterich points to a kind of evaporation effect in development, environmental, and sustainability policy: even when gender aspects are considered in policy statements in line with gender mainstreaming demands – as is the case in *The Future We Want* – they tend to volatilize when it comes to implementation. She also identifies a general sense of 'gender fatigue' in all participants: on the part of the women involved, out of frustration at the lack of progress, in the institutions involved, because they had felt progress would be made through (discursive) mainstreaming, and in the NGOs, where the feminist approaches had also left no major mark and a stereotypification and simplification of the relationship between women and nature dominated discussion. This was frequently echoed in the media, where the anticipated global growth in population as the key ecological problem was highlighted.

Yet even if the focus on the green economy in the current sustainability debate appears blind to gender issues, it does have a number of implications for gender policy. These will be outlined as follows using the example of one of the core ingredients of the green economy: the creation of green jobs designed to further the so-called de-carbonization of the economy.

## Green jobs, good jobs – and women?

The promotion of green jobs should serve several purposes simultaneously, namely to protect natural resources and means of livelihood, to raise the quality of life, and to create secure, highly qualified jobs.

The UNEP-funded report on 'Green Jobs: Towards Decent Work in a Sustainable, Low Carbon World' (UNEP et al. 2008), which was published in 2008 by the Worldwatch Institute, constitutes a milestone in the international green jobs initiative at a number of UN organizations. It provides estimates of the expected global increase in green jobs in those sectors viewed as particularly relevant from an environmental perspective; it uses a broad definition of what constitutes a 'green job'[1]:

> We define green jobs as work in agricultural, manufacturing, research and development (R&D), administrative, and service activities that contribute substantially to preserving or restoring environmental quality. Specifically, but not exclusively, this includes jobs that help to protect ecosystems and biodiversity; reduce energy, materials, and water consumption through high efficiency strategies; de-carbonize the economy; and minimize or altogether avoid generation of all forms of waste and pollution.
>
> *(UNEP et al. 2008:3)*

The UNEP's Green Jobs report also refers to the working conditions for so-called decent jobs outlined by the International Labour Organization (ILO), which include commensurate pay, a safe workplace, job security, career prospects, and respect for employee rights (ILO 2008a; UNEP et al. 2008). The ILO's paper on green jobs points explicitly to the extremely diverse range of profiles for green jobs, which stretch from highly skilled jobs in research and development to low skilled sorting functions in the recycling sector (ILO 2008a). It also notes that many such low skilled jobs are performed on an informal basis, particularly in the Global South, and are thus not covered by employment regulations. In addition, it identifies potential for the violation of employment regulations or the use of child or slave labour in the production of biofuels or the handling of hazardous chemicals. According to the report, however, the transformation to a green economy and the creation of green jobs has still strong potential to provide decent work – even though this will not be easy or automatic (ILO 2008a:35). Another ILO paper addresses explicitly the great promise of green jobs for women: 'Women, with their unique knowledge and capabilities of natural resource management and use of energy sources are strong change agents and key contributors to climate change mitigation and adaptation programmes at local, regional and international levels' (ILO 2008b:1). The green job potential, especially for women in the Global South, reaches from waste collection, separation, and recycling to micro-enterprises of female solar technicians in rural areas financed by micro loans to disaster mitigation. Women are presented as more vulnerable to ecological damages and climate change than men on the one hand, but as winners of a greening economy on the other hand. Their growing inclusion into the formal economy is judged as a means of female empowerment and at the same time as a way to overcome traditional patriarchal (family) structures. But there is also an economic rationale linked with micro-credits for women: they tend to more reliable with regard to paying back the credit rates than men (Littig 2016).

Yet, with few exceptions, the quality of green jobs remains of little relevance in either the political debate or in research (UNEP et al. 2008; Kuhl 2012).[2] This situation has not changed since the 1970s, when the discourse about the reconciliation of ecology and economy and green jobs started with the first 'oil crisis' (Littig 2012). In many cases, the debate simply holds to the (unqualified) blanket assumption that green jobs equal higher quality work.

There are just a few empirical studies about the work quality of green jobs. The available studies concentrate on the labour market situation in the Global North and paint an ambivalent picture of green jobs.[3] In a study carried out for the US government, researchers used case studies (from the manufacturing, construction, waste management, and goods transport sectors) to identify areas in which low incomes dominated and no employee representation bodies were active as well as areas in which people held the expected 'good, middle-class jobs' (Mattera et al. 2009). Their findings led them to the conclusion that '[g]reen jobs are not automatically good jobs. We have to make them so' (6). A comparable study, that deals with the working conditions and employment potential of green jobs, analyzes the situation in Austria and reports similar findings (Leitner et al. 2012): an unclear net growth potential of green jobs, a great heterogeneity of the working conditions and just a small ratio of publicly advertised good green jobs for technical experts with (additional) environmental qualifications, whose working conditions are not considered precarious:

> The sector that corresponds most to this image is the energy supply sector, but with a share of only 6 per cent of all green jobs, this sector only plays a limited quantitative role. In contrast, the public debate makes no mention of the fact that the majority of Green Jobs are in fact found in sectors with poor working conditions, such as agriculture, forestry, construction and trade.
>
> *(Leitner et al. 2012:82; my translation)*

These findings have gender implications too. The good green jobs (i.e., those that usually require some form of technical or scientific training) are not only fewer in number, but they are also primarily occupied by men. The share of women in these sectors of education still remains relatively low. Women are employed above all in those purportedly green sectors of the labour market where working conditions are poor and qualification requirements and income possibilities are low: trade, tourism, and to some extent, agriculture. A general improvement in the quality of work is required (not only) in these sectors, even if the political approaches to defining and implementing improved working conditions that were under discussion at the turn of the millennium have now clearly taken a back seat since the start of the global economic and financial crises. Given the increasing economic uncertainty and growing unemployment figures, the emphasis has shifted to quantity not quality. Contrary to this general trend, some trade unions have launched initiatives to strengthen qualitative aspects of paid work.[4] For example in Germany, the IG Metall metalworkers union continues to use its '*Gute Arbeit*' (good work) media campaign to promote the need to take quality criteria into consideration and thus force a normative debate (Schröder and Urban 2010). Particular emphasis is placed in the trade union-based discussion of good work on the different living and working conditions facing men and women (Pickshaus 2007:18). Key themes in this respect include the multiple burdens placed on women as a result of their commitments at work and at home, the large number of women working in the emotionally and physically stressful services sector and at low levels in the employment hierarchy, the lack of flexibility in such jobs, and the frequent lack of continuity in women's employment histories.[5]

A number of accompanying measures are needed to make green jobs, and in particular high quality green jobs, attractive to women. These range from efforts to increase the number of girls and women studying or choosing a career in science or technology through to gender mainstreaming in this segment of the job market, the establishment of gender equality in decision-making functions, the promotion of the work–life balance, as well as a change in the male-dominated work culture (for details, see Kuhl 2012:12ff; DGB 2011). Yet, with only a few exceptions, green job propaganda almost entirely fails to address such gender issues – in the Global North and in the Global South (Bauhardt 2014).[6] In addition, the growing (global) labour market of women in the Global South via green jobs has been fundamentally criticized as another imperialistic project that undermines autonomous approaches in the countries of the Global South (ILO 2015; Shiva 1990; see also Isla in this handbook).

Another factor that must be added to the sceptical assessments of green jobs is the fact that their growth potential – and that of the green economy as a whole – depends to a considerable extent on favourable legislation and corresponding public subsidies, with the latter far from certain in times of cut-backs and stringent austerity packages. In the context of a comprehensive debate on sustainability that seeks to address ecological demands, the need for the efficient use of resources and energy as well as social justice criteria, green jobs are at best a small building block in a larger social and ecological transition (Fischer-Kowalski and Haberl 2007; WBGU 2011; Brand and Daiber 2012). Since a high percentage of the green jobs are in the end-of-the-pipe segment of the green economy (e.g., waste and sewage management, filter technologies), their contribution to the prevention of environmental damage and resource depletion is limited. Even if the so-called green economy does have the potential to create a limited number of new, high quality jobs – for women as well, if appropriate measures are taken (particularly in knowledge-intensive sectors) – it is still a long way away from being able to solve the multiple crises. And if these measures will affect women's labour market positions at all, they will predominantly be favourable for a limited number of women in the Global North and in the emerging economies (Littig 2016).

## Feminist critiques of the green economy

The assumption that the green economy falls short of the mark is echoed in feminist proposals to resolve the current crises. These also add the *care crisis* to the economic/financial and environmental crises that have already been diagnosed. Thus feminist economists theorized it as a triple crisis (Bauhardt 2014). In this regard, a discussion paper published by a network of different German women's organizations presents an extended definition of the green economy concept:

> Our understanding of a green economy means prioritizing a socially and environmentally just society and a corresponding economic system that will facilitate a 'good life for all'. . . . Thus, it is essential to acknowledge the multifaceted and productive care work that is overwhelmingly performed by women, as well as the productivity of the natural environment, as the basis of any economic activity.
>
> *(Genanet 2011:1)*

This feminist understanding of a green economy has explicit, normative implications, since it seeks to make care – in the 'taking care of' and 'providing for' senses – the maxim of all economic activity (Schildberg 2014). It also has conceptual implications for the definition of work: (productive) work should no longer just include paid work, but also the work of providing for and taking care of others that is carried out in the home mainly by women. The concept of the 'caring economy' (*Vorsorgendes Wirtschaften*) has been promoted since the 1990s by a group of German-speaking feminist political economists as the quasi-antithesis to the prevailing understanding of the economy. Like other feminist economic critics, the advocates of the 'caring economy' accuse economics of excluding reproductive activities in the home from the economy (Biesecker and Hofmeister 2010; Tronto 2013; see also Mellor in this handbook): The capitalist view of economics focuses on the money-based market economy, not the economy as a whole. It appears to all intents and purposes autonomous from its natural surroundings and social environment. In line with the prevailing economic rationale, the market economy only caters to abstract value creation and not the satisfaction of needs. In this respect, the purpose and means of economics have been reversed. In contrast, the caring economy concept focuses on practical and natural values, with money-based exchange processes serving to realize the purposes of life and not abstract value creation. *Vorsorgendes Wirtschaften* takes a critical view on gendered power relations and relates these to the capitalist domination of nature.

The concept of a care-based economy is echoed in many of the feminist critiques of the capitalist system, which were discussed in Rio in 1992 and where feminist groups from the Global South in particular demanded an economy of livelihood (survival).[7] All of these approaches call the profit-based market economy into question. They also advocate the preservation of reproduction and the integrity of nature. To summarize, there are three main strands to the international feminist debate:

1   The reassessment and redistribution of the work that needs to be done in society;
2   A united approach to common goods like education, social security, health, mobility, and an undamaged environment (far removed from neoliberal privatization and marketization); and
3   The escape from the growth paradigms of the capitalist economy at the expense of nature and based on an unjust North-South divide.

These feminist demands require not only an economics of sufficiency, but also a visionary model of society. They are reflected in the alternative final document of the Peoples' Summit, which took place in opposition to the official Rio+20 summit with participation of feminist activists (Salleh 2012). The statement, which is entitled 'Another future is possible', puts forward the notion of a bio-civilization (Peoples' Summit 2012). The document does not state quantitative limits, but qualitative transformation: There is no limit to 'being more' through a 'sustainable economy . . . based on care and on use that neither destroys nor generates waste, but renews and regenerates' (2012:10). The 'bio-civilisation' is presented as a 'possible utopia' grounded in the idea of 'living well' based on existing practices (11). It is an alternative plan of development, which is directed against the dominant neoliberal model and its green economy, characterized as an attempt at 'full control of the entire biosphere' (7).

## Conclusion

The jury appears to be out on the green economy's chances of becoming a reality. The most recent sustainability conference in Rio in 2012, in any case, took few concrete steps in this direction. The Sustainable Development Goals from 2015 (UN 2015) affirmed this general pathway, and the Human Development Report on work (UNDP 2015) in the end also follows this line.[8] The green economy, as conceptualized by the UN and other international organizations, aims primarily to thoroughly modernize the (capitalist) economy and sees green technologies as new investment opportunities for surplus capital. It might give way to a green capitalism (Brand and Wissen 2015). But no matter how welcome the promise of a green economy might be, scepticism remains – not only from a gender perspective, but also with regard to the inconsistencies in the concept. Included in these inconsistencies are, for example, the rebound effect (Brand 2012b), the rise of a global consumer middle class (Brand and Wissen 2012), the global production of regenerative energy and forced evictions and the expropriation of land (Heinrich-Böll-Stiftung 2012), and the economization of ecosystem services (Unmüßig 2014).

On the whole, it can be presumed that the green economy is, as Wissen contends, an 'exclusive modernization project restricted to the Global North and the emerging areas of the Global South, which spawns new national and international forms of exclusion and is secured through imperialistic relationships to other parts of the world' (2012:34; my translation). There is much to support the notion that a green economy does not resolve the social and ecological contradictions of capitalism, but at best makes them workable in a temporary and geographically limited context.

As far as the feminist gender perspective is concerned, the green economy concept must give explicit consideration to gender inequalities and establish concrete objectives and measures to overcome them (Röhr 2011). It is also difficult to predict what chances alternative concepts like the feminist approaches mentioned previously will have. They are, however, reflected to a certain extent in some social ecology experiments, like the Global Ecovillage network, urban gardening (i.e., the shared use of public spaces as gardens), and initiatives within the Solidarity Economy (see Altvater and Sekler 2006). While it might be easy to question the generalizability of such projects, they are still significant because they represent the kind of social innovation that is needed more than ever in times of crisis.

With regard to the demands (not only) from feminists to expand the concept of labour, there are options to connect to a new line of discussion in the current sustainability debate, which questions in particular the prevailing focus on growth for ecological and economic reasons (Martínez-Alier 2009; Paech 2014; Barth, Jochum, and Littig 2016). In this post- and de-growth perspective, the reorganization of current working societies and the achievement of more sustainable ways of living go hand in hand (Schneidewind and Zahrnt 2014; Muraca 2013; Schor 2010). Proponents of a sustainable de-growth strategy call for an enlarged understanding of work: mixed work – including paid work, reproductive (care) work, volunteering, and self-provision as the social ideal-type of work (Littig 2012). The concept of mixed work refers to ongoing changes within the sphere of paid work, primarily to the erosion of the standardized work time frames, the feminization of male (work-)life patterns (i.e., the interruption of careers throughout the work-life due to unemployment, further training, or care), and an increasing desire for a better work-life balance, which provide starting points for its implementation (HBS 2001). The furtherance of the envisaged socio-ecological transformation toward a sustainable working society with mixed work, mixed qualifications, and mixed income as a general mode of work needs a redistribution of work, less working hours, and the flexibility of work-time combined with a re-organization of the social security system. In addition to that, the cost relations between the different production factors need to be reorganized (for an overview see Littig and Spitzer 2011).

The mixed work approach has been criticized by feminists – especially from the previously mentioned 'care economy' (*Vorsorgendes Wirtschaften*) perspective – who find the concept of mixed work too reformist, not tackling the basic bearings of the capitalist economy. Instead these feminist authors working in the field of a sustainable transformation argue for a fundamental change within the economic paradigm – namely, the (re)orientation of the economy according to care as the basis of human existence and well-being. Yet it remains to be seen whether or to what extent critical voices who demand fundamental socio-ecological transformations will find an ear in the current array of crises (Brand and Daiber 2012). After all, it is economic growth that takes precedence on the political centre stage. However, a new political bottom-up movement, heterogeneous but unified under the umbrella of 'degrowth', has started to grow. This became evident in the fourth international conference on 'Degrowth for Ecological Sustainability and Social Equity' in Leipzig, Germany, in 2014 and again at the follow-up conference in Budapest in 2016.[9] Feminist concepts of a sustainable, equitable, and caring society have been discussed there, too, if not in a systematically integrated way, but nevertheless they are often implicitly – and sometimes explicitly – present.

## Notes

1 The promising potential of green jobs for the employment sector is reflected in the EU 'Agenda 2020' strategy, which states that efforts based on environmental, economic, and employment policy considerations should be taken to create an additional three million green jobs within the EU by 2020.

2  Instead of looking at working conditions in the broad sense, several studies focus specifically on the profiles of green jobs, but do not take gender differences into consideration (e.g., OECD 2011).

3  The UNEP et al. report on green jobs problematizes the precarious situation of the mainly female waste collectors in Brazil. Although this work belongs to the informal sector and little firm data are available, the report states that many of the existing recycling-related jobs cannot be considered green. They cause both pollution and health hazards and do not represent decent work, even if improvement initiatives are launched (UNEP et al. 2008:21).

4  Such as the international 'Integration, Security, Innovation (INSITO) – European Answers to the Worldwide Financial and Economic Crisis' project with 41 partners from academia and the trade unions. Available at: www.kooperationsstelle.uni-goettingen.de/koop_2_6.html (accessed 31 August 2014).

5  The DGB's 'Good Work' Index, for example, reflects these topics and is intended as a representative tool for assessing the quality of work in Germany. Available at: www.dgb-index-gute-arbeit.de (accessed 31 August 2014).

6  Exceptions include the European Greens (cf. Kuhl 2012) and the DGB's (German Confederation of Trade Unions) 'Renewable Energies – a Job Market for Women' project in Brandenburg. Available at: http://berlin-brandenburg.dgb.de/ueber-uns/projekte/erneuerbare-energien-ein-arbeitsmarkt-fuer-frauen (accessed 31 August 2014).

7  These also include subsistence-based approaches like those proposed by Veronika Bennholdt-Thomsen and Maria Mies (1997) and Vandana Shiva 1990, Genevieve Vaughan's 'Gift Economy' approach (2007), general movements criticizing globalized growth based capitalism like the Solidary Economy (Altvater and Sekler 2006), and the degrowth economy (Martínez-Alier 2009; Muraca 2013). However, the latter approaches have been criticized for not including gender issues systematically (Bauhardt 2014).

8  The last Human Development Report, 'Work for Human Development', presents an enlarged and revised understanding of work including paid work as well as all forms of unpaid care, community, or creative work (UNDP 2015). The report argues that the (ecological) non-sustainability of current ways of life and work threatens to undermine the future potential of human development, since it endangers the possibility to work at all (ibid. 155). Thus sustainable work has to reconcile environmental and development issues: it needs to foster the potential of human development while at the same time minimizing the ecologically harmful side effects of work, to finally ensure future work. The centre of this argumentation is to safeguard the sustainability of work itself. Green growth is a central means to achieve these goals.

9  4th Degrowth, Conference Leipzig, 2014. Online. Available at: http://leipzig.degrowth.org/en/ (accessed 28 August 2016); 5th Conference in Budapest 2016. Online. Available at: http://budapest.degrowth.org/?page_id=107 http://leipzig.degrowth.org/en/ (accessed 28 August 2016).

# References

Altvater, E. and Sekler, N. (eds) (2006) *Solidarische Ökonomie. Reader des Wissenschaftlichen Beirats von Attac.* Hamburg: VSA Verlag.

Barth, T., Jochum, G. and Littig, B. (eds) (2016) 'Nachhaltige Arbeit und gesellschaftliche Naturverhältnisse. Theoretische Perspektiven und Forschungsperspektiven', in Barth, T., Jochum, G. and Littig, B. (eds) *Nachhaltige Arbeit. Soziologische Beiträge zur Neubestimmung der gesellschaftlichen Naturverhältnisse.* Frankfurt: Campus, 312–354.

Bauhardt, C. (2014) 'Solutions to the crisis? The green new deal, degrowth, and the solidarity economy: Alternatives to the capitalist growth economy from an ecofeminist economics perspective', *Ecological Economics* 102(2014): 60–68.

Bennholdt-Thomsen, V. and Mies, M. (1997) *Eine Kuh für Hillary. Die Subsistenzperspektive.* München: Verlag Frauenoffensive.

Biesecker, A. and Hofmeister, S. (2010) 'Focus: (re)productivity: Sustainable relations both between society and nature and between genders', *Ecological Economics* 69(8): 1703–1711.

Brand, U. (2012a) 'Green economy – The next oxymoron? No lessons learned from failures of implementing sustainable development', *GAIA* 21: 28–32.

Brand, U. (2012b) *Beautiful Green World: On the Myths of a Green Economy.* Luxemburg argumente 2(3), Rosa Luxemburg Foundation, Berlin.

Brand, U. and Daiber, B. (eds) (2012) 'Special issue socio-ecological transformation', *Journal für Entwicklungspolitik* 28(3).

Brand, U. and Wissen, M. (2012) 'Global environmental politics and the imperial mode of living: Articulations of state-capital relations in the multiple crisis', *Globalizations* 9(4): 547–560.

Brand, U. and Wissen, M. (2015) 'Strategies for a green economy, contours of a green capitalism', in van der Pijl, K. (ed) *The International Political Economy of Production: Handbook of Research on International Political Economy Series*. Cheltenham: Edward Elgar, 508–523.

Denkwerk Zukunft. Stiftung kulturelle Erneuerung (ed.) (2011) *Altering Attitudes: From a Culture of Consumerism to a Culture of Prosperity*. Online. Available at: www.denkwerkzukunft.de/downloads/Altering_attitudes.PDF (accessed 31 August 2014).

DGB Bezirk Berlin-Brandenburg (2011) *Handlungsleitfaden: Frauen in die erneuerbaren Energien!* Online. Available at: http://berlin-brandenburg.dgb.de/themen/++co++36d7643a-4c15–11e1–456d-00188b4dc422 (accessed 31 March 2014).

European Commission (2010) 'EUROPE 2020 – A strategy for smart, sustainable and inclusive growth', *COM(2010) 2020 final*. Online. Available at: http://eurlex.europa.eu/LexUriServ/LexUriServ.do?uri=COM:2010:2020:FIN:EN:PDF (accessed 31 March 2014).

Fischer-Kowalski, M. and Haberl, H. (eds) (2007) *Socio-ecological Transitions and Global Change*. Cheltenham: Edward Elgar.

Genanet – Leitstelle Gender, Umwelt, Nachhaltigkeit (2011) *Green Economy: Gender_Just! Towards a Resource-Light and Gender-Just Future*. Online. Available at: www.genanet.de/fileadmin/user_upload/dokumente/Care_Gender_Green_Economy/G3_discussion_paper_en.pdf (accessed 31 August 2016).

Genanet – Leitstelle Gender, Umwelt, Nachhaltigkeit (2012) *Governments Gamble With Our Future. South Feminists Demand Responsible Action Now*. Online. Available at: www.dawnnet.org/feminist-resources/content/dawnrio20-governments-gamble-our-future-south-feminists-demand-responsible-action-now (accessed 28 August 2016).

Global Ecovillage Website. Online. Available at: http://gen.ecovillage.org/ (accessed 31 March 2014).

Haberl, H. et al. (2011) 'A socio-metabolic transition towards sustainability? Challenges for another great transformation', *Sustainable Development* 19: 1–14.

HBS (Hans Boeckler Stiftung) (ed) (2001) *Pathways to a Sustainable Future: Results From the Work and Employment Interdisciplinary Project*. Düsseldorf: Setzkasten GmbH.

Heinrich-Böll-Stiftung (ed) (2012) *Critique of the Green Economy – Toward Social and Environmental Equity*. Barbara U., Wolfgang S. and Thomas F., Band 22 der Schriftenreihe Ökologie. Heinrich-Böll Stiftung (ed), Berlin. Online. Available at: http://www.boell.de/en/content/critique-green-economy-toward-social-and-environmental-equity (accessed 31 March 2014).

Intergovernmental Panel on Climate Change (IPCC) (2014) 'Summary for policymakers', in Edenhofer, O. et al. (eds) *Climate Change 2014, Mitigation of Climate Change: Contribution of Working Group III to the Fifth Assessment Report of the Intergovernmental Panel on Climate Change*. Cambridge and New York: Cambridge University Press. Online. Available at: http://www.ipcc.ch/ (accessed 31 August 2014).

International Labour Organization (ILO) (2008a) 'Global challenges for sustainable development: Strategies for green jobs ILO background note', G8 Labour and Employment Ministers Conference, 11–13 May 2008 Niigata, Japan. Online. Available at: www.ilo.org/public/english/bureau/dgo/speeches/somavia/2008/g8paper.pdf (accessed 31 March 2014).

International Labour Organization (ILO) (2008b) *Green Jobs: Improving the Climate Equality, Too!* Online. Available at: www.ilo.org/wcmsp5/groups/public/---dgreports/--gender/documents/publication/wcms_101505.pdf (accessed 31 March 2014).

International Labour Organization (ILO) (2015) 'Gender equality and green jobs', Policy Brief. Online. Available at: www.ilo.org/wcmsp5/groups/public/---ed_emp/---emp_ent/documents/publication/wcms_360572.pdf (accessed 17 August 2016).

Kuhl, M. (2012) 'Geschlechteraspekte des Green New Deal eine Analyse der Strategiepapiere der Grünen/EFA Green-New-Deal-Arbeitsgruppe', *Studie im Auftrag der Fraktion der Grünen/Freie Europäische Allianz auf Initiative von Elisabeth Schroedter*. Online. Available at: www.elisabeth-schroedter.de/themen/green-jobs/green-jobs/GenderAspectsGNDfinal.pdf (accessed 31 March 2014).

Leitner, A., Wroblewski, A. and Littig, B. (2012) *Green Jobs. Diskussion von Arbeitsbedingungen und Beschäftigungspotenzialen*. Projektbericht des Instituts für Höhere Studien, Wien an die Arbeiterkammer Wien.

Littig, B. (2001) *Feminist Perspectives on Environment and Society*. London: Pearson Education.

Littig, B. (2012) 'Von Rio 1992 zu Rio+20. Arbeit im Kontext der aktuellen Nachhaltigkeitsdiskussion', *WSI-Mitteilungen* 2012(8): 581–588.

Littig, B. (2016): 'Nachhaltige Zukünftige von Arbeit? Geschlechterpolitische Perspektiven', in Barth, T., Jochum, G. and Littig, B. (eds) *Nachhaltige Arbeit: Soziologische Beiträge zur Neubestimmung der gesellschaftlichen Naturverhältnisse*. Frankfurt: Campus, 75–98.

Littig, B. and Spitzer, M. (2011) *Arbeit neu. Erweiterte Arbeitskonzepte im Vergleich.* Arbeitspapier 229. Düsseldorf: Hans Böckler Stiftung.

Martínez-Alier, J. (2009) 'Socially sustainable economic degrowth', *Development and Change* 40(6): 1099–1119.

Mattera, P. et al. (2009) *High Road or Low Road? Job Quality in the New Green Economy.* Washington: Good Jobs First. Online. Available at: http://www.goodjobsfirst.org/publications/high-road-or-low-road-job-quality-new-green-economy (accessed 31 August 2014).

Muraca, B. (2013) 'Décroissance: A project for a radical transformation of society', *Environmental Values* 22(2013): 147–169.

Organisation for Economic Co-operation and Development (OECD) (2011) *Towards Green Growth.* Paris: OECD.

Paech, N. (2014) *Liberation From Excess: The Road to a Post-Growth Economy.* München: Oekom Verlag.

Peoples Summit (2012) *Another Future Is Possible.* Rio de Janeiro: World Social Forum. Online. Available at: http://rio20.net/wp-content/uploads/2012/02/Another-Future-is-Possible_english_web.pdf (accessed 31 August 2014).

Pickshaus, K. (2007) 'Was ist gute Arbeit?', in IG Metall Projekt Gute Arbeit (ed) *Handbuch 'Gute Arbeit'. Handlungshilfen und Materialien für die betriebliche Praxis.* Hamburg: Verlag, 16–31.

Röhr, U. (2011) 'Green economy: Die Wirtschaft soll grüner werden – aber wird sie damit auch gerechter?', *FrauenRat* 5: 2–4.

Salleh, A. (2012) 'Green economy or green utopia? Rio+20 and the reproductive labor class', *Journal of World Systems Research* 18(2): 141–145.

Schildberg, C. (ed.) (2014) *A Caring and Sustainable Economy: A Concept Note from a Feminist Perspective.* Online. Available at: http://library.fes.de/pdf-files/iez/10809.pdf. (accessed 31 March 2014).

Schneidewind, U. and Zahrnt, A. (2014) *The Politics of Sufficiency: Making It Easier to Live the Good Life.* München: oekom Verlag.

Schor, J. (2010) *Plenitude: The New Economics of True Wealth.* Berkeley: The Penguin Press.

Schröder, L. and Urban, H.-J. (2010) *Gute Arbeit. Handlungsfelder für Betriebe, Politik und Gewerkschaften.* Issue 2010, Frankfurt am Main: Bund Verlag.

Schultz, I., Hummel, D. and Padmanabhan, M. (2010) 'Feministische Perspektiven auf Nachhaltigkeitspolitik', *Femina Politica* 1: 9–22.

Shiva, V. (1990) 'Development as a new project of western patriarchy', in Diamond, I. and Orenstein, G. F. (eds) *Reweaving the World: The Emergence of Ecofeminism.* San Francisco: Sierra Club Books, 189–200.

Tronto, J. (2013) *Caring Democracy: Markets, Equality and Justice.* New York: New York University Press.

UN (United Nations) (2015) *Transforming Our World: The 2030 Agenda for Sustainable Development.* New York: Author.

UNDP (United Nations Development Programme) (2011) *Gender Inequality Index and Related Indicators.* Online. Available at: http://hdr.undp.org/en/media/HDR_2011_EN_Table4.pdf (accessed 31 March 2014).

UNDP (United Nations Development Programme) (2014) *Human Development Index 2014.* Online. Available at: http://hdr.undp.org/en/2014-report/ (accessed 31 August 2014).

UNDP (United Nations Development Programme) (2015) *Human Development Report 2015. Work for Human Development.* Online. Available at: http://hdr.undp.org/sites/default/files/2015_human_development_report.pdf (accessed 23 August 2016).

UNEP (United Nations Environment Programme) (2008) *Global Green New Deal – Environmentally-Focused Investment Historic Opportunity for 21st Century Prosperity and Job Generation.* Online. Available at: www.unep.org/Documents.Multilingual/Default.asp?DocumentID=548&ArticleID=5957&l=en (accessed 31 August 2014).

UNEP (United Nations Environment Programme) (2009) *Rethinking the Economic Recovery: A Global Green New Deal.* Online. Available at: www.unep.org/greeneconomy (accessed 31 March 2014).

UNEP (United Nations Environment Programme) (2011) *Towards a Green Economy: Pathways to Sustainable Development and Poverty Eradication: A Synthesis for Policy Makers.* Online. Available at: www.unep.org/greeneconomy (accessed August 2014).

UNEP (United Nations Environment Programme), ILO (International Labour Organization), IOE (International Organisation of Employers), ITUC (International Trade Union Confederation) (eds.) (2008) *Green Jobs: Towards Decent Work in a Sustainable, Low Carbon World.* Online. Available at: www.unep.org/PDF/UNEPGreenJobs_report08.pdf (accessed 31 March 2014).

United Nations Division for Sustainable Development (2012). *The Future We Want.* Online. Available at: http://sustainabledevelopment.un.org/futurewewant.html (accessed 31 August 2014).

Unmüßig, B. (2014) *Vom Wert der Natur – Sinn und Unsinn einer Neuen Ökonomie der Natur.* Heinrich-Böll-Stiftung, Berlin. Online. Available at: www.boell.de/de/2014/02/25/vom-wert-der-natur (accessed 31 August 2014).

Vaughan, G. (ed) (2007) *Women and the Gift Economy.* Toronto: Inanna Publications.

WBGU (Wissenschaftlicher Beirat der Bundesregierung Globale Umweltveränderungen) (2011) *Welt im Wandel. Gesellschaftsvertrag für eine Große Transformation.* Berlin: WBGU. Online. Available at: www.wbgu.de/fileadmin/templates/dateien/veroeffentlichungen/hauptgutachten/jg2011/wbgu_jg2011_ZfE.pdf (accessed 31 March 2014).

Wichterich, C. (2012) *The Future We Want: A Feminist Perspective.* Berlin: Heinrich-Böll-Stiftung.

Wissen, M. (2012) 'Post-neoliberale Hegemonie? Zur Rolle des Green-Economy Konzepts in der Vielfachkrise', *Kurswechsel* 2: 28–36.

Women's Major Group Summary (2011) *Input to 'Zero Draft' Outcome Document UN Conference on Sustainable Development (Rio+20).* Online. Available at: www.uncsd2012.org/content/documents/514Womens%20Major%20Group%20Submission_with%20Annex_1%20Nov%202011.pdf (accessed 31 March 2014).

# 22

# GENDER DIMENSIONS OF SUSTAINABLE CONSUMPTION

*Ines Weller*

## Introduction

Sustainable consumption and production patterns have been prominent issues from the very start of the sustainable development debate. In fact, *Agenda 21*, the plan of action adopted at the 1992 United Nations Conference on Environment and Development (UNCED) held in Rio de Janeiro stated that 'the major cause of the continued deterioration of the global environment is the unsustainable pattern of consumption and production, particularly in industrialized countries . . .' (UN 1992:31). Although the urgent need for fundamental changes in consumption and production patterns, which would transform societies and push them in the direction of sustainable development, has been recognized since that time, particularly in the Global North, there are still very few signs that any such transformation is taking place. World energy consumption grows unabated as global carbon emissions continue to rise. The fundamental inequalities between the Global North and South also remain, despite very high rates of growth in the newly industrialized and developing countries of the Global South in particular (IEA 2013). In this context, and especially in the context of sustainable patterns of consumption and production, the attitudes and behaviours of private citizens and consumers, their perceptions of environmental problems, and associated use of resources all play an important role. Hitherto, however, these debates have neglected the significance of gender, gender relations, and gender justice for sustainable consumption.

In this chapter, I will focus on debates and research in Germany/Western Europe. I begin by introducing the definitions, objectives, and areas of responsibility of various actors for sustainable consumption. This compact overview focuses in particular on the relationship between production and consumption as gendered societal spheres. I then move on to consider the tension that exists between the theory of privatized environmental responsibility, on the one hand, which criticizes tendencies to overstate and moralize the power of private consumers to shape change and, on the other, women as change agents for more sustainable consumption. The next part of the chapter is organized around the distinction, which is useful for analyzing the gender aspects of sustainable consumption, between *explicit and implicit gender dimensions*. With reference to feminist theorist Sandra Harding (1986), I draw together the individual and structural levels of gender as explicit gender dimensions. Both of these are for the most part based on statistical data and empirical findings, particularly concerning gender differences and, in this respect, link to ambivalence between the analysis of gender and gender hierarchies, on the one hand, and the reproduction of traditional gender images and dichotomies on the other. The discussion focuses in particular on the symbolic conceptual level of gender, which I consider in detail in relation to a specific example. The background is the feminist critique of the claim of the natural sciences to objectivity (Orland and Scheich 1995). Drawing on the example of a study on the volume of food waste, I draw attention to several gender-related 'blank spaces' and gaps in the data that have been produced in this field. This emerges more clearly from closer consideration of the treatment given to male-coded production and female-coded consumption.

## Sustainable consumption: definitions, objectives, and actors

### *Definitions and objectives*

A concise definition of sustainable consumption, which draws on the 1987 Brundtland definition of sustainable development, is 'The use of goods and services that respond to basic needs and bring a better quality of life, while minimizing the use of natural resources, toxic materials and emissions of waste and pollutants over the life cycle, so as not to jeopardize the needs of future generations' (Jackson 2006:5). So sustainable consumption should minimize or reduce the ecological and social problems associated with the production and use of goods. But because this definition is very abstract, the specific ways in which various aspects of consumption, such as food, mobility, or housing can be made more sustainable need to be identified. The concept of 'sustainable consumption and production' underlines the inextricable links and mutual relationships that apply within an overall system of consumption and production. Here, however, and in line with usage in Europe, I use 'sustainable consumption' to refer to both aspects (i.e., to include production). It must also be borne in mind that consumption encompasses much more than just buying. It includes other activities, such as obtaining information, using, and disposing of goods and the connected transports (Schultz and Stieß 2009).

The objectives of sustainable consumption are ecological, economic, and social. The overall ecological aims of sustainable consumption are to reduce the use of natural resources ('quantitative perspective') and to avoid adverse impacts on the environment over the course of the entire life cycle of products and services ('qualitative perspective'). Social criteria typically include health aspects, in particular, often relating to production-based occupational health and safety, as well as social justice and gender justice – although gender justice is not always included. Economic objectives tend to be defined rather more vaguely as, for example, fair prices or stable relations along the value chain. The sustainable consumption debate has so far concentrated on ecological objectives and much greater progress has been made in quantifying and specifying these objectives, in the form of indicators, for example, than social and economic objectives (see, for example, Fischer et al. 2012).

In the process of spelling out further what exactly is meant by sustainable consumption, three different components can be distinguished. The first involves redirecting demand and purchasing decisions toward resource-efficient and ecological products (i.e., consuming differently). Second, consumption decisions must take account of issues of social justice, especially the working conditions under which products are manufactured (i.e., consuming responsibly). Third, absolute levels of consumption must be reduced (consuming less). In other words, fewer goods should be purchased and fewer resources should be exploited in the process of using the goods that are bought (Jackson 2006; Weller 2008). These three components of sustainable consumption are also reflected in the three strategies of efficiency, sufficiency, and consistency. The efficiency strategy focuses on resource productivity (i.e., reducing resource throughput and optimizing use). The consistency strategy focuses on qualitative changes in the resource base of production and consumption while the sufficiency strategy concentrates specifically on reducing levels of consumption and emphasizes new values in the handling of material goods in the sense of 'less is more'. Between the lines, discussions of these strategies are often based on the assumption – sometimes implicit, sometimes explicit – that different agents are responsible for different tasks. Producers are assigned primary responsibility for achieving efficiency and consistency; sufficiency, on the other hand, is something which consumers are expected to achieve by, for instance, bringing their behaviour into line with values such as moderation and restraint.

The way that responsibilities are assigned in the sustainable consumption literature has been widely criticized from a feminist perspective. An important line of criticism is that it cements the distinction between, on the one hand, the public sphere and the ascription of maleness to production and related resource efficiency, and the private sphere and the ascription of femaleness to consumption and linked issues of restraint on the other. This dichotomy, and the assignment of responsibilities implicit within it, has been criticized from the earliest days of feminist discussion of sustainability concepts (Weller et al. 1999). In fact, all three strategies are critically important for both production and consumption. In terms of sufficiency, it is reasonable, even at the production stage, to call into question the sheer volume of goods that are manufactured.

## Actors and their responsibility for sustainable consumption

The most relevant actors in the project of achieving sustainable levels of consumption are, first, the economic players who, in their capacity as producers, decide which products will be introduced to the market and how they will be manufactured and designed. The next group of actors are retailers, the 'gatekeepers' who exercise considerable influence at the interface between production and consumption on the range of products that is offered to consumers. The state is seen as being responsible for creating a general framework that supports sustainable patterns of consumption and production. Consumers have only indirect influence, which comes from their decision to buy or not to buy certain goods. While this assignment of responsibilities is largely uncontroversial, there is still considerable disagreement about the degree of responsibility, which ordinary consumers have for their own sustainable consumption.

On the one hand consumers are regarded as important 'change agents' in modifying behaviour in the direction of sustainable consumption and are treated accordingly by environmental policy makers (Heidbrink et al. 2011). Proponents of the 'moralization of the markets' argument also work on the assumption that consumers have a high level of responsibility for the environment and that they are increasingly able to live up to this responsibility. This assumption can be traced back to a shift in values in society as a whole, as well as the increasing importance of post-material values in affluent capitalist countries (Stehr 2007). One of the factors underlying this position is the share of resources that societies use in the form of consumption; private consumption, for example, accounted for just over 50 per cent of GDP in Germany in 2014 and for 56.9 per cent in the Eurozone (Eurostat 2015).[1] Arguments also draw on the results of life cycle assessments,[2] according to which products use up more resources during their consumption than during their manufacture. Others take the view that private consumers generally have very little influence and, for this reason, warn against further privatization of sustainability (Grunwald 2012). Arguments along these lines point to factors such as the integration of patterns of consumption in supply systems that significantly constrain consumers' own ability to shape change (e.g., Southerton et al. 2004).

The proponents of this position also stress that the decisions that ultimately determine what impact products have on the environment are mainly taken at the beginning of the life cycle – that is, during production processes and in the course of product design, rather than when goods are consumed (Huber 2011).

The hypothesis of the 'feminization of environmental responsibility' was developed before, and largely in parallel to, these discussions. Drawing on the example of Germany's waste management policies in the 1980s, Schultz and Weiland (1991) showed how the extra burden of work involved in the separate collection of waste in households was overwhelmingly placed on the shoulders of women.[3] Bearing in mind the – perhaps modest – changes that have taken place in the traditional gender-specific division of labour in private households since the nineties, this hypothesis may now be referred to as the 'feminization or privatization of environmental responsibility'. Its basic assumption is that debates about sustainable patterns of consumption and production tend to inflate private consumers' scope of influence and turn their conduct into a private moral issue for individuals (Weller 2004). The hypothesis of the feminization of environmental responsibility was not only conceived for the countries of the Global North, but also for countries of the Global South, where it makes reference to the tendency to transfer more and more responsibility for the conservation of natural resources to women (Wichterich 1992; see also Arora-Jonsson in this volume). This imbalance is also problematic because it distracts attention from, and fails to take adequate account of, the other actors who are as relevant, and perhaps even more influential, in the development of strategies and concepts for promoting sustainable patterns of consumption and production than individuals. As a result the implementation of policies may fall far short of expectations, and objectives may only be partially met.

New research now appears to show that the influence of private consumers on sustainable consumption is rather limited. That consumers are limited both in the choices they can make and in their ability to shape change is attributed to the integration of patterns and everyday practices of consumption in complex systems of supply, values, lifestyles, and collective consumption practices. This means, for example, that consumers can only opt to use local public transport or electricity from renewable energy sources if such services are actually on offer and if they are compatible with their values and orientations. Practice theory[4] also emphasizes that most everyday activities take the form of (often unconscious) habits and routines. From this perspective the difficulty in shifting existing patterns of consumption toward greater sustainability arises from the close interdependence of consumption practices and socio-material structures (Shove and Spurling 2013; Jaeger-Erben and Offenberger 2014). Strategies and steering instruments that take into account the interplay between business, consumers, and policy (the triangle of change) are therefore needed in order to bring about the necessary transformation.

My point is not to dismiss fundamentally and entirely the influence of private consumers. What is more important, however, is to consider in what ways, to what degree, and under what conditions private consumers or various groups of consumers are able to exercise influence. The expectation that private purchase decisions may offer a way of exercising political influence was also one of the fundamental ideas of the women's movement in Germany after 1968. At that time, the idea that 'the personal is political' turned supposedly private consumption and private day-to-day behaviour into political issues. In more recent discussions, this idea has been expressed in the concept of 'political consumerism' that points out the dual role of consumers and citizens (or the 'consumer citizen'; Micheletti and Stolle 2005; quoted in Schultz and Stieß 2009). One striking feature of this way of exercising influence, such as boycotts of genetically modified food, is the very high proportion of women taking part in these types of political consumption (Schultz and Stieß 2009). The significance of women as initiators of sustainable innovations is also illustrated by the role played by two Dutch women in establishing the recycling of waste glass. In the 1970s these women, who were concerned about the increasing amounts of waste visibly accumulating in the world around them every day, introduced glass recycling containers in their communities. These containers caught on very quickly and are now regarded as the source of successful waste glass recycling in Europe (Oldenziel and Hård 2013).

## Gender dimensions of sustainable consumption: conceptual framework

The relationships between the environment, sustainability, and gender have been studied and conceptualized in a number of different ways since the earliest days of the sustainability debate (see, for example, Braidotti et al. 1994; Katz 2006; Hofmeister et al. 2013). More recently the state of the art in research has been the subject of increasingly critical and controversial scholarly debate (see, for example, Arora-Jonsson 2011; Hawkins and Ojeda 2011). There is not a great deal of research in this area, but links between gender and sustainable consumption have attracted greater attention in recent years. Today, there is a growing number of gender analyses of sustainable consumption, even if these remain relatively few and far between (Vinz 2009). The first general surveys of this topic have also begun to emerge. At the European level, for instance, a review of the gender aspects of research and of policies to promote sustainable consumption in particular has now appeared (Schultz and Stieß 2009). A comprehensive analysis of these gender-related issues has also been produced at the national level for a priority funded study of sustainable consumption in Germany (Jaeger-Erben et al. 2012).

In my view, these various gender analyses and their findings can be categorized using the following three levels at which gender norms and relations can be observed[5] (Harding 1986; Weller 2004):

- The individual level: These are studies and data that focus on potential differences in male and female (or men's and women's) consumption and sustainability-related attitudes, consumption behaviour, and the associated use of resources.
- The structural level: These studies primarily analyze the gender-specific division of labour and power, and their significance for sustainable consumption.
- The symbolic-conceptual level: These studies focus on perceptions and evaluations of the areas and spheres of society that were assigned and allocated by gender categories with the emergence of modern (natural) sciences and market economics (see, for example, Biesecker and Hofmeister 2010; Hofmeister et al. 2013). The treatment of such areas that have strong gender connotations, such as production (male) and reproduction or consumption (female), is especially relevant in connection with sustainable consumption. Cultural and historical studies of consumption in particular have shown that 'production and consumption are gendered'.

*(Lubar 1998: 7)*

I combine these three levels of gender analysis and refer to them as having an 'explicit' or 'implicit' gender dimension; the first two encompass individual and structural gender dimensions, the last one the symbolic-conceptual level (Harding 1986; Weller 2004). The analysis of explicit gender dimensions is geared to the determination of gender differences on the basis of gender-specific disaggregated data at the individual and structural level. At the same time the importance of intersectional links between gender and other influencing factors, such as class, race/ethnicity, age, income, and life situation is growing in importance (see Winker and Degele

2009 for a discussion of intersectionality in feminist research). The analysis of implicit gender dimensions is geared to the symbolic-conceptual level of gender, and studies the ascription of gender in research on sustainable consumption and associated blind spots or imbalances. The analysis takes a critical look at the assumptions on which the findings are based. Also included are analyses of metaphors or the representations of masculinity and femininity on which debates about sustainable consumption draw.

Having provided a framework for understanding the gender dimensions of sustainable consumption, I will now discuss the findings of a selection of empirical studies that have focused on each of the three levels of analysis.

### *Explicit gender dimensions: the individual level*

Attitudes about, and the willingness to take action on, sustainable consumption have been matters of study in research on the environment and sustainability in the social sciences for several decades. Summarizing the findings of a number of such empirical studies of gender differences, Schultz and Stieß conclude that '[w]omen tend to have a higher environmental awareness than men . . ., but they tend to feel less informed about environmental risks' (2009:30). This tendency is not, however, confirmed by all studies. The Eurobarometer surveys of attitudes of European citizens have produced conflicting findings on gender differences in attitudes toward the environment (e.g., EU 2008; EU 2009; EU 2014). In contrast, empirical findings on people's sustainability-related willingness to act and consumption behaviour are relatively consistent: As a rule, more women than men express a willingness to make sustainable consumption choices (BMU 2008; EU 2008; EU 2009; EU 2014). Significantly more women than men say they would be willing to take action in their day-to-day lives to protect the climate and environment (EU 2008). More women still express an interest in products that have eco-labels (BMU 2008), they purchase more organic foods, eat less meat, use local public transport more often, and drive cars less often than men (Johnsson-Latham 2007). A study by Johnsson-Latham (2007) aims to identify real gender differences in the environmental impacts of male and female consumption and distinguishes the ecological footprint of consumption according to gender in Sweden. It concludes that

> Men on average consume more than women in a handful of major areas: eating out, alcohol, tobacco/snuff, transport and sport. Women for their part consume more on average than men in terms of consumer goods, including medical care and health, clothing and shoes, books and culture.
>
> *(Johnsson-Latham 2007:39)*

Other studies of gender differences in the consumption-driven use of resources show, in particular, that the persistence of a traditional, gender-based division of labour has an impact on the use of resources, for example in terms of dietary styles and time patterns. On average, for example, men's diets contain more meat and are consequently associated with higher carbon emissions, whereas in contrast women's greater consumption of fruit and vegetables is associated with higher levels of water consumption (Meier and Christen 2012). A similar study finds that, on average, women spend more time on carbon intensive housework-related activities, whereas men engage in more carbon intensive leisure and transport activities outside of the home (Druckman et al. 2012). These and similar results have been summed up by Schultz and Stieß in their overview of sustainable consumption and gender as follows: 'Women consume in a more environmentally friendly manner' than men (2009:30).

However, these studies and their results are properly criticized for treating men and women as homogeneous groups and for inappropriately generalizing about 'women' and 'men' as a whole (Arora-Jonsson 2011). There is also a danger that focusing on 'women' and 'men' as homogeneous groups might reinvigorate traditional gender stereotypes in the context of sustainable consumption. Schultz and Stieß (2009) are also critical of this generalization and point to initial studies of the influence of gender with other factors that have arrived at differentiated findings on the differences and similarities between various groups of men and women. As far as diet is concerned, for example, some ways of life and lifestyles clearly attach greater importance to ecological and sustainable consumption than do others. These differences are also apparent in their relevant gender composition (Stieß and Hayn 2005; Schultz and Stieß 2009). Fischer has also shown that, when seeking advice on the insulation of buildings, there are marked differences in the information which men who have a technical background (and may also know about insulation) expect to be given and the information which men and women with no such previous knowledge wish to receive (Fischer 2011). As far as the integration of users in the development of sustainable products is concerned, it has been shown that it is not only important to achieve the right balanced gender composition, but also to ensure a sufficiently diverse range of participating user groups (Jaeger-Erben et al. 2012). The individual dimension of gender in intersectional connections with other categories of difference provides further and differentiated insights for research on sustainable consumption.

Most empirical (single) findings on gender and sustainable consumption are available at the individual level. These suggest that a sensitive awareness of environmental issues and of sustainability-related behavioural changes fit better into 'female' than into 'male' gender constructions. However, the significance of these findings for sustainable consumption is ambiguous. On the one hand, they reveal the still largely untapped and socially disregarded potential for moving consumption behaviour toward greater sustainability offered by people with 'female' life experience and background. They also reveal gender differences that are of relevance for research on sustainable consumption and especially on the development of strategies to support sustainable consumption, such as concerning patterns of consumption and the resources such patterns use up. On the other hand, there is a danger that the development of related gender-specific strategies may be used to maintain traditional notions of gender roles and to continue feminizing responsibility for the environment. Initial suggestions on how to deal with this tension advise addressing 'specific gendered groups' or 'addressing the in fact existing gendered behaviours of men in private household and family contexts by putting them into a sustainability context (that means to search for sustainable consumption behaviours of men in household contexts and highlighting them)' in order to escape the implicit assumption of and orientation toward responsibility of women for (sustainable) consumption (Schultz and Stieß 2009:63).

## Explicit gender dimensions: the structural level

The background here consists of continuing gender inequalities, particularly in terms of income and access to resources such as time, the distribution of paid and unpaid work, and in the power to shape change in the context of sustainable consumption and production patterns. Even if gender roles have shifted in the past, particularly as regards childcare and certain aspects of household work, the basic pattern of gender-specific divisions of labour and power has not radically changed. Very little study has thus far been done on the consequences of this for sustainable consumption. For example, research on sustainable consumption has shown that the income levels of consumers are key factors influencing consumption and the use of resources in two different ways. Current analyses show that more resources are consumed when incomes rise and that, conversely, fewer resources are consumed when incomes fall (UNEP 2010). This then also relativizes the influence of attitudes toward the environment and sustainable consumption values when it comes to making significant reductions in the consumption of resources. On the other hand, higher incomes also go hand-in-hand with a willingness to purchase more sustainable alternative products. The central importance of income levels for sustainable consumption raises the so far unanswered question as to what impact, on average, the higher incomes of men and the lower incomes of women have on sustainable consumption. While initial findings suggest that some women set ecological priorities despite having lower incomes, this claim still needs to be verified (Weller et al. 2010). More problematic for those groups in society who live in poverty, or are at risk of poverty, is their limited access to goods such as mobility or energy. These groups often include single mothers or older women who, as an 'involuntary ecological avant-garde' use considerably fewer resources but, from the perspective of social justice, can hardly be regarded as being sustainable (Weller et al. 2010).

Time is another scarce resource that is relevant to sustainable consumption. It is still very unclear how gender inequalities in the distribution of time budgets for paid and unpaid work affects sustainable consumption or in which ways sustainable consumption either saves or costs time. The importance of this aspect does, however, underlie the need for strategies that are designed to promote sustainable consumption to recognize and take account of the lack of time available to women, particularly in child-rearing phases, and of the precarious economic situations and time budgets of vulnerable groups (Schultz and Stieß 2009).

Studies of negotiation and decision processes relating to (sustainable) consumption in private households also belong at this, the structural, level of gender and sustainable consumption. There are some initial indications here that more egalitarian family roles can support sustainable consumption, but at the same time that negotiation processes in certain phases of life, such as after the birth of a child, can reinforce a traditional gender-specific allocation of tasks (i.e., in which responsibility for sustainable consumption is assigned to women; Empacher et al. 2002; Jaeger-Erben et al. 2012). On the other hand, there is evidence that biographical transitions and life events, such as the birth of children, illness or relocation, can offer significant 'windows of opportunity', which may support the perception and acceptance of more sustainable forms of consumption (Schäfer and Jaeger-Erben 2012).

The structural level also includes gender-specific analyses of participation and power to shape change in the context of sustainable development, both in terms of the design of (sustainable) products and as regards the development of concepts and instruments to promote sustainable consumption. To date, however, there are very few indications of direct influence being exercised by consumers and citizens. According to Franz-Balsen, there is an overall gender gap in participation throughout the EU and in the United States (Franz-Balsen 2014). In Germany, for example, several research projects have now examined the impact of new forms of participative product development and design, which take explicit account of gender, on patterns of sustainable consumption (Jaeger-Erben et al. 2012). Over the last ten years the significance of participation and new forms of governance has come increasingly to the fore in the sustainability debate. Nonetheless, there is still a very definite need for further research on the way in which gender relations are reflected in these participative approaches.

## *Implicit gender dimensions: the symbolic-conceptual level*

Symbolic-conceptual gender dimensions include the feminist critique of the division of consumption and production: While in modern economic thought, consumption is constructed as a private activity of no economic value of its own and as a 'female' (feminized) task, production is regarded as a highly relevant economic and public activity that carries 'male' (masculinized) connotations (Schultz and Stieß 2009; Biesecker and Hofmeister 2010). Against this background, consumption and reproduction appear to be private and 'female' matters that are overshadowed by and in many respects are the complete opposite of production. In the context of feminist economics the concept of (re)productivity has been developed as a feminist alternative that regards production and reproduction/consumption as parts of a single entity. From this theoretical perspective the focus is squarely on the (re)productive qualities of production and consumption processes (see the chapter by Mellor in this handbook). A conception of production and reproduction/consumption as part and parcel of the same thing highlights the invisibility and undervaluing of 'social female and natural (re)productivity' and also shifts attention to the economy in its 'entirety' and, in particular, to the relatively neglected area of care work (Biesecker and Hofmeister 2010). These theoretical considerations are linked to a paradigm shift in debates on and research into sustainable consumption and patterns of production. The focus moves to requirements and problems from the perspective of reproduction. This poses a huge challenge for research: to identify which products and services, in what quantities, are needed for a good and sustainable way of life.

Production and consumption can also be critically studied in terms of the relative impact they both have on the environment. In this context, criticism is concentrated on the way in which the resources and emissions resulting from production and consumption are accounted for. This must be seen against the background of the life cycle assessments that have grown in importance in recent years. While the original purpose of life cycle assessments was to compare the environmental impact of two or more product alternatives, they are now also used to determine resource intensity, carbon emissions, and environmental impacts along the entire life cycle of products. They are also used to determine how much of each of these inputs and releases are related to production, consumption, or the use of products. In this context, the life cycle assessments of products such as food and clothes have been shown to differ considerably in terms of the relative impact on the environment of production, consumption, and use. These differences can be ascribed in particular to the differing assumptions about user behaviour that find their way into life cycle assessments. The use phase is treated paradoxically, however, in what is otherwise supposedly objective, scientifically derived economic data. On the one hand, the significance of the use phase is played down by falling back on simplified and apparently plausible assumptions about average patterns of use without verifying these empirically. On the other hand, there is a tendency to overstate the environmental impact of the consumption phase (Weller 2004; Weller 2012).

I will use the example of a German study of food waste to illustrate how supposedly objective figures can implicitly gloss over certain aspects or present an unbalanced picture. This becomes especially obvious when a critical approach is adopted to their use as a means of perceiving the use phase and, in comparison, the production sphere. This study was undertaken against the backdrop of recent policy debates concerning the growing quantity of food waste. The study was commissioned by Germany's Federal Ministry of Food, Agriculture and Consumer Protection (BMELV) to determine the volume of such waste in Germany more accurately and to develop measures to reduce it. The study found that 61 per cent of food waste comes from private households, while only 5 per cent comes from wholesale and retail trade, and 17 per cent comes both from large-scale consumers and the food industry (Kranert et al. 2012). According to this calculation, private consumers generate 81.6 kilos of food waste per person each year on average. Of this total, around 53 kilos of food per person and year is considered to be entirely or at least partly avoidable. In this context, private households appear to be places in which food is wasted. The figures appear unambiguous: the lion's share of waste is shown to be the responsibility of private consumers. But it is worth looking at how these figures – which are taken for granted in public discussions of the study findings – are worked out in a little more detail.

First, it must be noted that the figures do not include agriculture. For pragmatic reasons, only the amount of food waste generated by the food industry, large-scale consumers, wholesale and retail trade, and private households was determined. The importance that agricultural production plays in the amount of food waste has been shown by a study by the UN Food and Agriculture Organisation (FAO). According to this study, relevant waste streams do indeed come from this sector, depending on the food group. The agricultural sector's shares of food waste vary from 2 per cent (grains) and 9.4 per cent (fish and seafood) up to 20 per cent (fruit and vegetables; FAO 2011). If this phase was included in the total amount of food waste, the percentage of waste generated by private households (as well as that of the other three sectors) would decrease significantly.

Second, with regard to life cycle assessment, it is important to note that the quality of the data for the four phases varies considerably and that the lack of reliable data has meant that extrapolated figures have been used with all the associated variation that goes with them. The authors of this study took this into account by, among other things, calculating minimum values, the median and maximum values for waste volumes in each of the four phases. However, only the median values were used to determine the share of food waste produced in each of the different phases. The following 'numbers game' illustrates the influence of the underlying data: If the maximum value is taken instead of the median for the data for the four areas, then the share of household-related food waste falls from 61 per cent to 50.3 per cent and the share of food industry-related waste rises from 17 per cent to 30.6 per cent. If, on the other hand, the minimum value is assumed for all four phases, the share assigned to households goes up to 70 per cent while the share of the food industry drops to below 5 per cent (our own calculations based on data derived from Kranert et al. 2012).

Third, there are grounds for looking critically at the differentiation between avoidable, partly avoidable, and unavoidable food waste. Avoidable food waste is defined as discarded food that 'was still fully fit for human consumption at the time of discarding or would have been edible if [it] had been eaten in time' (Kranert et al. 2012:13). Partly avoidable food waste results from 'different consumer habits', with bread crusts and apple skins are mentioned as examples (Kranert et al. 2012:13). Unavoidable food waste is defined as food that is inedible, such as bones, banana skins, or potato peelings. At any rate, this definition involves considerable room for interpretation, which in turn allows space for implicit moral judgements. This is reinforced by the fact that the distinctions between avoidable, partly avoidable and unavoidable food waste are usually only applied to private households (Kranert et al. 2012:151). This differentiation does not seem to be important and/or workable in the other sectors, that is, the food industry, wholesale and retail trade, and for large-scale consumers. In this respect, this study and the publication of its findings carry with them the risk that moral judgements and exaggerated claims will be made about private households' waste conduct. This detailed example is intended to illustrate symbolic-conceptual level gender dimensions and to demonstrate how critical analysis, particularly of the way in which gendered spheres of production and consumption are handled, can reveal 'blank spaces' and gaps in allegedly objective data.

A quite different perspective on implicit gender dimensions can be found in media analyses, which study how the social construction of gender is reflected in the way issues relating to sustainable development in general, and about sustainable or unsustainable consumption in particular, are communicated. For example, in her review of gender and (un)sustainability, Franz-Balsen refers to a gender study undertaken by Rogers that analyzed three advertisements to work out the complex interrelations between gender and consumption using the example of meat: 'as a code for masculinity, sustainability as a threat to hegemonic masculinity, and masculinity as a threat to sustainability' (2014:1976). At the same time, she emphasizes the need to distinguish between individual men and women and hegemonic masculinity: 'when hegemonic masculinity is described, we are not talking about individual men or the male part of the population, but about an idealization of masculinity' (2014:1981).

Implicit gender dimensions have attracted less attention to date than explicit gender relations. They have also evoked little interest in the context of sustainable consumption. This is partly to do with the fact that they shed light on possible blind spots and imbalances in research on sustainable consumption. This means that they adopt a critical perspective which requires considerable explanation ('what's that got to do with gender?'). Nor are such findings very easy to translate into specific policy recommendations or strategies for action and therefore they do not correspond with the highly applied focus and ambition of research and debates on sustainable consumption.

## Conclusion

The findings I have discussed in this chapter are still little more than a 'hotchpotch' of isolated insights into gender and sustainable consumption. No consistent view of the importance of gender perspectives for sustainable consumption has yet emerged. What is more, ambivalence about how to treat gender is also apparent. At the same time, gender dimensions clearly offer considerable potential for research and for policy or steering instruments for promoting sustainable consumption. The data and studies on explicit gender dimensions underline, for example, that it makes sense to consider the relevance of gender in intersectional connection ('intersectionality') with other social categories such as class, age, income, or ethnic background. This approach makes it easier to take account of an increasingly differentiated society and the preconditions, possibilities, and barriers that exist for various groups in society with regard to sustainable consumption and, consequently, to develop concepts that are better focused on specific target groups.

In addition, structural gender dimensions draw attention to the social and gender inequalities that are associated with sustainable or unsustainable consumption. What policy makers must do is design instruments and strategies in such a way as not to reinforce these inequalities but in a way that leads to more justice between men and women and between more and less privileged groups in society. A central prerequisite in this context is knowledge and awareness of these relationships. This in turn depends on empirically and theoretically sound gender analyses, and on the integration and inclusion of gender-analytic competence in environmental policy. Instruments that have already been introduced, such as gender impact assessments, may be useful in such analyses (Schultz and Stieß 2009). Little attention has so far been given in this connection to the interests that different actors and groups in society have in the transformation or the continuation of unsustainable patterns of consumption and production. The next immediate issue is how the various actors differ in terms of their power and ability to influence and shape the transformation or continuation of existing relationships, and how these reflect gender inequalities. At the symbolic-conceptual level, the close linkages between the social construction of gender ('doing gender') and consumer behaviour ('doing consumption') become apparent. Policies and strategies for promoting sustainable consumption thus face the challenge of understanding and reflecting patterns of behaviour and consumption in the context of social and individual notions of 'masculinity' and 'femininity'.

## Notes

Parts of this chapter were previously published in Weller, I. (2013), 'Nachhaltiger Konsum, Lebensstile und Geschlechterverhältnisse', in Hofmeister, S., Katz, C. and Mölders, T. (eds), *Geschlechterverhältnisse und Nachhaltigkeit. Die Kategorie Geschlecht in den Nachhaltigkeitswissenschaften.* Berlin and Toronto: Opladen, 286–295.

1 The other half of GDP expenditure is due to government and investment.
2 Life cycle assessment (LCA) is a tool for the systematic evaluation of the environmental aspects of a product or service system through all stages of its life cycle.
3 A more recent study has shown that this has changed to the extent that couples are now more likely to perceive the separation of waste as a task that needs to be organized together, even if women are still more likely to take the initiative in these activities (Oates and McDonald 2006).
4 Practice theory is a sociological approach that is popular within research on sustainable consumption and driven by particular scholars like Elizabeth Shove, Alan Warde, and Gert Spaargaren (see, for example, Shove and Spurling 2013; Jaeger-Erben and Offenberger 2014).
5 This three-levels framework is based on an understanding of gender as a social construct rather than a biological condition – 'doing gender', not being a gender (see West and Zimmerman 1987). For the purpose of analysing gender, it is useful to distinguish three levels at which the processes of socially constructing gender can be observed.

## References

Arora-Jonsson, S. (2011) 'Virtue and vulnerability: Discourses on women, gender and climate change', *Global Environmental Change* 21: 744–751.

Biesecker, A. and Hofmeister, S. (2010) 'Focus: (re)productivity: Sustainable relations both between society and nature and between the genders', *Ecological Economics* 69(8): 1703–1711.

BMU and UBA (2008) *Umweltbewusstsein in Deutschland 2008. Ergebnisse einer repräsentativen Bevölkerungsumfrage.* Berlin, Bundesministerium für Umwelt, Naturschutz und Reaktorsicherheit.

Braidotti, R., Charkiewicz, E., Häusler, S. and Wieringa, S. (eds) (1994) *Women, the Environment and Sustainable Development: Towards a Theoretical Synthesis.* London: Zed Books.

Druckman, A., Buck, I., Hayward, B. and Jackson, T. (2012) 'Time, gender and carbon: A study of the carbon implications of British adults' use of time', *Ecological Economics* 84: 153–163.

Empacher, C., Schultz, I., Hayn, D. and Schubert, St. (2002) 'Die Bedeutung des Geschlechtsrollenwandels', in Umweltbundesamt (ed) *Nachhaltige Konsummuster. Ein neues umweltpolitisches Handlungsfeld als Herausforderung für die Umweltkommunikation. Mit einer Zielgruppenanalyse des Frankfurter Instituts für sozial-ökologische Forschung.* Berlin: Erich Schmidt Verlag, 182–214.

EU (2008) *Special Eurobarometer 300. Europeans' Attitudes Towards Climate Change.* Brussels. Online. Available at: http://ec.europa.eu/public_opinion/archives/ebs/ebs_300_full_en.pdf (accessed 30 September 2014).

EU (2009) *Climate Change: Special Eurobarometer 372.* Brussels. Online. Available at: http://www.ec.europa.eu/public_opinion/archives/ebs/ebs_322_en.pdf (accessed 30 September 2014).

EU (2014) *Special Eurobarometer 416: Attitudes of European Citizens Towards the Environment.* Brussels. Online. Available at: http://ec.europa.eu/public_opinion/archives/eb_special_419_400_en.htm#416 (accessed 12 July 2015).

Eurostat (2015): *National Accounts and GDP.* Brussels. Online. Available at: www.ec.europa.eu/eurostat/statistics-explained/index.php/National_accounts_and_GDP (accessed 12 July 2015).

Fischer, D., Michelsen, G., Blättel-Mink, B. and Di Guilio, A. (2012) 'Sustainable consumption: How to evaluate sustainability in consumption acts', in Defila, R., Di Giulio, A. and Kaufmann-Hayoz, R. (eds) *The Nature of Sustainable Consumption and How to Achieve It.* München: oekom, 67–80.

Fischer, K. (2011) 'Genderaspekte der Gebäudekerndämmung aus wiederverwerteten Rohstoffen', *Artec-Paper*, Nr. 176. Bremen.

Food and Agriculture Organization (FAO) of the United Nations (2011) *Global Food Losses and Food Waste: Extent, Causes and Prevention.* Rome: Author.

Franz-Balsen, A. (2014) 'Gender and (un)sustainability: Can communication solve a conflict of norms?', *Sustainability* 6: 1973–1991.

Grunwald, A. (2012) *Ende einer Illusion. Warum ökologisch korrekter Konsum die Umwelt nicht retten kann.* München: oekom.

Harding, S. (1986) *The Science Question in Feminism.* Ithaca: Cornell University Press.

Hawkins, R. and Ojeda, D. (2011) 'Gender and environment: Critical tradition and new challenges', *Environment and Planning D: Society and Space* 29: 237–253.

Heidbrink, L., Schmidt, I. and Ahaus, B. (eds) (2011) *Die Verantwortung des Konsumenten. Über das Verhältnis von Markt, Moral und Konsum.* Frankfurt/Main and New York: Campus.

Hofmeister, S., Katz, C. and Mölders, T. (2013) *Geschlechterverhältnisse und Nachhaltigkeit. Die Kategorie Geschlecht in den Nachhaltigkeitswissenschaften.* Opladen, Berlin and Toronto: Verlag Barbara Budrich.

Huber, J. (2011) *Allgemeine Umweltsoziologie.* 2., vollständig überarbeitete Auflage. Wiesbaden: VS Verlag für Sozialwissenschaften.

International Energy Agency (IEA) (2013) *World Energy Outlook 2013.* Paris: Author.

Jackson, T. (ed) (2006) *The Earthscan Reader in Sustainable Consumption.* London: Earthscan.

Jaeger-Erben, M. and Offenberger, U. (2014) 'A practice theory approach to sustainable consumption', *GAIA* 23(S1): 166–174.

Jaeger-Erben, M., Offenberger, U., Nentwich, J., Schäfer, M. and Weller, I. (2012) 'Gender in the focal topic "From knowledge to action – New paths towards sustainable consumption": Finding and perspectives', in Defila, R., Di Guilio, A. and Kaufmann-Hayoz, R. (eds) *The Nature of Sustainable Consumption and How to Achieve It.* München: oekom, 263–276.

Johnsson-Latham, G. (2007) 'A study on gender equality as a prerequisite for sustainable development', *Report to the Environment Advisory Council*, Sweden.

Katz, N. (2006) 'Gender und Nachhaltigkeit. Neue Forschungsperspektiven', *GAIA* 15(3): 206–214.

Kranert, M., Hafner, G., Barabosz, J., Schuller, H., Leverenz, D. and Kölbig, A. (2012) *Ermittlung der weggeworfenen Lebensmittelmengen und Vorschläge zur Verminderung der Wegwerfrate bei Lebensmitteln in Deutschland.* Stuttgart.

Lubar, S. (1998) 'Men/women/production/consumption', in Horowitz, R. and Mohun, A. (eds) *His and Hers: Gender, Consumption, and Technology.* Charlottesville and London: The University Press of Virginia, 7–38.

Meier, T. and Christen, O. (2012) 'Gender as a factor in an environmental assessment of the consumption of animal and plant-based foods in Germany', *International Journal of Life Cycle Assessment.* Published online 21 February 2012. Available at: www.nutrition-impacts.org/media/2012%20Gender%20in%20 LCA.pdf (accessed 30 September 2014).

Micheletti, M. and Stolle, D. (2005) 'Swedish political consumers: Who they are and why they use the market as an arena for politics', in Boström, M. et al. (eds) *Political Consumerism: Its Motivation, Power, and Conditions in the Nordic Countries and Elsewhere.* Proceedings from the 2nd International Seminar on Political Consumerism. TemaNord 2005: 517, Kobenhaven, 146–164.

Oates, C. J. and McDonald, S. (2006) 'Recycling and the domestic division of labour: Is green pink or blue?', *Sociology* 40(3): 417–433.

Oldenziel, R. and Hård, M. (2013) *Consumers, Tinkerers, Rebels: The People Who Shaped Europe.* New York: Palgrave Macmillan, 235–271.

Orland, B. and Scheich, E. (1995) *Das Geschlecht der Natur.* Frankfurt am Main: Suhrkamp.

Schäfer, M. and Jaeger-Erben, M. (2012) 'Life events as windows of opportunity for changing towards sustainable consumption patterns? The change in everyday routines in life-course transition', in Defila, R., Di Guilio, A. and Kaufmann-Hayoz, R. (eds) *The Nature of Sustainable Consumption and How to Achieve It.* München: oekom, 195–210.

Schultz, I. and Stieß, I. (2009) *Gender Aspects of Sustainable Consumption Strategies and Instruments.* Frankfurt/ Main. Online. Available at: www.eupopp.net/docs/isoe-gender_wp1_20090426-endlv.pdf (accessed 30 September 2014).

Schultz, I. and Weiland, M. (1991) *Frauen und Müll. Frauen als Handelnde in der kommunalen Abfallwirtschaft.* Frankfurt am Main: IKO-Verlag für interkulturelle Kommunikation.

Shove, E. and Spurling, N. (2013) *Sustainable Practices: Social Theory and Climate Change.* London: Routledge.

Southerton, D., Warde, A. and Hand, M. (2004) 'The limited autonomy of the consumer: Implications for sustainable consumption', in Southerton, D., Chappells, H. and Vliet, B. (ed) *Sustainable Consumption: The Implications of Changing Infrastructures of Provision.* Cheltenham: Edward Elgar, 32–48.

Stehr, N. (2007) *Moralisierung der Märkte.* Frankfurt/Main: Suhrkamp.

Stieß, I. and Hayn, D. (2005) 'Ernährungsstile im Alltag. Ergebnisse einer repräsentativen Untersuchung', *ISOE-Diskussionspapier*, Nr. 24. Frankfurt am Main.

United Nations (1992) 'Agenda 21: Programme of Action for Sustainable Development. Rio Declaration on Environment and Development', The final text of agreements negotiated by Governments at the

United Nations Conference on Environment and Development (UNCED), 3–14 June 1992, Rio de Janeiro, Brazil.

United Nations Environmental Programme (UNEP) (2010) 'Assessing the environmental impacts of consumption and production', *Priority Products and Materials*. Online. Available at: www.unep.fr/shared/publications/pdf/DTIx1262xPA-PriorityProductsAndMaterials_Report.pdf (accessed 30 September 2014).

Vinz, D. (2009) 'Gender and sustainable consumption: A German environmental perspective', *European Journal of Women's Studies* 16: 159–179.

Weller, I. (2004) *Nachhaltigkeit und Gender. Neue Perspektiven für die Gestaltung und Nutzung von Produkten.* München: oekom.

Weller, I. (2008) 'Konsum im Wandel in Richtung Nachhaltigkeit? Forschungsstand und Perspektiven', in Lange, H. (ed) *Nachhaltigkeit als radikaler Wandel. Die Quadratur des Kreises?* Wiesbaden: VS Verlag für Sozialwissenschaften, 43–70.

Weller, I. (2012) 'Klimawandel, Konsum und Gender', in Çaglar, C., do Mar Castro Varela, M. and Schwenken, H. (eds) *Geschlecht – Macht – Klima. Feministische Perspektiven auf Klima, gesellschaftliche Naturverhältnisse und Gerechtigkeit.* Opladen: Verlag Barbara Budrich, 177–191.

Weller, I. (2013) 'Nachhaltiger Konsum, Lebensstile und Geschlechterverhältnisse', in Hofmeister, S., Katz, C. and Mölders, T. (eds) *Geschlechterverhältnisse und Nachhaltigkeit. Die Kategorie Geschlecht in den Nachhaltigkeitswissenschaften.* Berlin and Toronto: Opladen, 286–295.

Weller, I., Hoffmann, E. and Hofmeister, S. (eds) (1999) *Nachhaltigkeit und Feminismus: Neue Perspektiven – Alte Blockaden.* Bielefeld: Kleine Verlag.

Weller, I., Krapf, H., Wehlau, D. and Fischer, K. (2010) 'Untersuchung der Wahrnehmung des Klimawandels im Alltag und seiner Folgen für Konsumverhalten und Vulnerabilität in der Nordwest-Region. Eine explorative Studie', *Artec-Paper*, Nr. 166. Bremen.

West, C. and Zimmerman, D. H. (1987) 'Doing gender', *Gender & Society* 1(2): 125–151.

Wichterich, Ch. (1992) *Die Erde bemuttern. Frauen und Ökologie nach dem Erdgipfel in Rio. Berichte, Analysen, Dokumente.* Köln: Heinrich-Böll-Stiftung.

Winker, G. and Degele, N. (2009) *Intersektionalität. Zur Analyse sozialer Ungleichheiten.* Bielefeld: Transcript.

# 23

# SEXUAL STEWARDSHIP

## Environment, development, and the gendered politics of population

*Jade Sasser*

To achieve a sustainable future, we must address the root causes of environmental degradation – including population growth and overconsumption of natural resources – and ensure women and families can voluntarily determine the number, timing, and spacing of their children.

('The Fate of the World Is in Your Hands and in Your Pants',
*Sierra Club Global Population and Environment Program Brochure*)

## Introduction

This opening statement illustrates the paradoxical nature of current narratives on population, environment, and development. Drawing on neo-Malthusian logic, which asserts that population growth is a primary cause of environmental problems, it describes women's access to voluntary family planning as key to environmental sustainability. In other words, contraceptives are the necessary antidote to impending planetary doom. As the Sierra Club's Global Population and Environment Program slogan states on program materials, t-shirts, buttons, and branded condom wrappers, 'the fate of the world is in your hands and in your pants'. Given the suggestion of moral duty to make reproductive decisions in the interest of the greater environmental good, perhaps a better phrasing would be that the weight of the world is in women's wombs.

Other environmental organizations have also recently carried forth the banner of a revitalized approach to population, emphasizing family planning as a key tool in the fight against climate change. For example, a Worldwatch Institute report argues, 'Through slowing growth and other benefits, supporting women's efforts to manage their own lives and improving their status will in turn elevate the well-being of all of the world's population – with Earth's climate representing one aspect of this' (Engelman 2010:14). A population and climate change webpage sponsored by the US Center for Biological Diversity, creators of the Endangered Species Condoms campaign directly linking human sexual activity with species loss (condom slogans include 'Wear a Jimmy Hat—Save the Big Cat'), skips the emphasis on voluntary family planning, stating: 'we not only need smaller footprints, but fewer feet' (US Center for Biological Diversity: online).

In many ways, these narratives are deeply familiar. The relationship between population growth and environmental degradation is one of the oldest and most contentious debates within environmental circles. Since the eighteenth century, when Malthus argued that exponential population growth outpaced the earth's ability to produce adequate food for human sustenance, scholars and activists from a range of fields have debated the impacts of population growth. Neo-Malthusians took up the charge in the twentieth century, drawing connections between global population growth and deforestation, soil erosion, poor air quality, and a range of other problems. The common twentieth century mainstream narrative described population growth as an attribute of poor, rural communities in the Global South, locating environmental degradation as the inevitable outcome. In the twenty-first century, the emphasis is increasingly on climate change and impending global catastrophe, but with a twist: the problems wrought by population growth are to be solved, not through top-down, coercive population control, but via an emphasis on women's empowerment and voluntary access to family planning.

How did the narrative shift from controlling population growth to empowering women? I argue that late twentieth century shifts in international population gave rise to the construction of a development model – that I refer to as *sexual stewardship* – in which women are expected to act as responsible environmental actors through managing their fertility and reproduction. When non-governmental organizations (NGOs) discursively link population growth, environmental problems, and family planning to women's empowerment, they construct a model of an ideal sustainable development subject: a moral agent who manages her fertility and the environment responsibly through contraceptive use for the greater good. I refer to this model subject as a sexual steward.

This chapter tracks the origins and current use of this narrative in population and development programs, in three sections. First, I delve into the origins of sexual stewardship, tracing it to mid-1990s rhetorical shifts that de-centred state-based population control in favour of an emphasis on women's reproductive health and rights. While these shifts were widely hailed as empowering to women, they also reflected a new emphasis – and new responsibility – on women's voluntary reproductive control as a key component of development. Next, I demonstrate the ways sexual stewardship discourses are brought to life by environment and development NGOs, both through advocacy messages and community-level interventions. I conclude with a discussion of the return of neo-Malthusian arguments in contemporary climate change discourse, and the renewed need for critical feminist perspective on the issue.

## The making of sexual stewardship

The population-pressure-on-resources narrative has dominated the framing of environmental degradation among mainstream environmental NGOs for decades. This approach characterizes environmental threats as originating in communities that are poor, lack knowledge and resources, and who have large families:

> A great deal of the pressures on biodiversity comes [sic] from large, poor families. The search for fuelwood, water, and other basic needs creates the direct threats that drive environmental change . . . community residents who rely on resource harvesting, such as hunting or fishing, contribute to destructive environmental practices as they lack the knowledge of alternative practices and access to other employment opportunities. They therefore continue to exert pressures on already threatened resources.
>
> *(Edmond et al. 2009:3–4)*

While these 'degradation narratives' (Hartmann 2006) continued to circulate, beginning in the 1990s, a parallel narrative emerged in the population, environment, and development sector.

While still identifying population growth as a key environmental threat, this narrative focused on the reasons why rapid population growth occurs – through a global focus on gender inequality and women's restricted access to education, income generating opportunities, and contraceptives. Proponents of this approach argue that environmental benefits result from improving women's reproductive autonomy and social status as a whole, as exemplified in a statement made at a 2010 event celebrating the launch of a book titled *A Pivotal Moment: Population, Justice, and the Environmental Challenge*, by Lori Mazur:

> Fewer children means slower population growth, which often means more resources for education and other social programs, so more girls will get educated. There are many other things we can do to reduce inequality, slow population growth and improve people's lives, like reducing maternal and child mortality, enforcing child marriage laws and advancing women's rights. Each is vitally important in its own right. Each will help slow population growth, and reduce pressure on natural systems.
>
> *(Mazur 2009, personal communication)*

How do two starkly different approaches to the same set of questions arise and circulate within the population and development community? More importantly, what did the second narrative accomplish that the first does not? I argue that the shift to a focus on gender inequality and contraceptives derives from negotiations and agreements in the mid-1990s that sought to integrate family planning into population and environment discourses through the language of women's reproductive health and rights. As a result, the focus of population policies and programs shifted away from state responsibility for maintaining population targets, and toward an emphasis on the individual responsibility of women and couples to manage their fertility and reproduction. This shift was productive; it led to new development networks, new community-level programs, and changes in the funding landscape in the population sector. It also produced a new kind of subject: the sexual steward.

## From Rio to Cairo

In 1992, the UN Conference on Environment and Development (UNCED), also known as the Earth Summit, was convened in Rio to report progress toward achievement of the goals of the Brundtland Report, titled *Our Common Future* (1987), a document which laid out a vision for international cooperation toward defining and achieving sustainable development. One significant component of the conference was the role of population debates, held off-site in a separate NGO forum at the 'Women's Tent'. In intense, often heated discussions, NGO representatives, population control advocates, feminist activists, members of women's health organizations, and representatives of the Vatican negotiated the role that population would play in the official proceedings of the conference (Campbell 1998; Cohen 1993). A particularly strong argument emerged from radical feminists and other anti-Malthusians, who asserted that a framework that protects reproductive rights and gender autonomy would be compromised if it also prioritized population reductions.

The more critical voices prevailed. The document that emerged from the debates, known as the 'Treaty on Population, Environment and Development', asserted that 'women's empowerment to control their own lives is the foundation for all action linking population, environment and development' (1992: paragraph 1), and explicitly rejected all forms of control over women's bodies by governments and international institutions, including coerced sterilization, experimental contraceptive development, and denial of access to abortion. The document identified militarism, debt, structural adjustment, inequitable trade policies, and patterns of consumption and production in the industrialized North as the predominant causes of global environmental problems, rather than population growth. Notably, this mention was in sharp contrast to prevailing demographic arguments at the time, by focusing much of its critique on consumption in the industrialized North, rather than population growth in the Global South. It was also the first document included in an international development conference's proceedings in which a broad women's empowerment agenda was articulated in the context of family planning. The preamble to the treaty states that its authors 'affirm and support women's health and reproductive rights and their freedom to control their own bodies', an approach which demands 'the empowerment of women, half of the world's population, to exercise free choice and the right to control their fertility and to plan their families' (1992: paragraph 3).

Not everyone was happy with the Rio Treaty. American members of the population establishment, the environmental lobby, and mainstream women's reproductive health advocates viewed it as a threat to future funding for international population and family planning policies and programs – and worried that it would play into the interests of religious conservatives, despite the treaty authors' stated opposition to the Vatican (Hartmann 1987). In preparation for the 1994 International Conference on Population and Development (ICPD) at Cairo, Adrienne Germain and Joan Dunlop of the International Women's Health Coalition worked with leaders of the Women's Environment and Development Organization (WEDO), as well as mainstream members of the population-environment lobby and a broad group of women's rights supporters, to create a shared platform for policy negotiations. This transnational coalition designed what would eventually form the basis of the Cairo conference's Program of Action, also known as the Cairo Consensus. The document declared reproductive rights to be universal and asked all nations of the world to foreground women's empowerment as a central component of population and development programs. It enshrined principles such as advancing gender equality, elimination of male violence against women, prioritizing women's ability to control their own fertility, and the abandonment of demographic targets and quotas (UNFPA 2004). However, it rested fundamentally on neo-Malthusian thought, rooting environmental problems in demographic trends:

> Demographic factors, combined with poverty and lack of access to resources in some areas, and excessive consumption and wasteful production patterns in others, cause or exacerbate problems of environmental degradation and resource depletion and thus inhibit sustainable development.
>
> *(UNFPA 2004:25)*

At the same time, the Consensus framed population interventions through the lens of women's empowerment and contraceptive access:

> Advancing gender equality and equity and the empowerment of women, and the elimination of all kinds of violence against women, and ensuring women's ability to control their own fertility, are cornerstones of population and development-related programmes.
>
> *(UNFPA 2004:9)*

The language in the Cairo Consensus also articulated a new responsibility for individuals to manage their fertility in the service of broader sustainable development goals. While it states clearly that 'any form of coercion has no part to play', the document nevertheless offers a clear message that successful population programs are predicated on the responsibility of individuals: 'the success of population education and family-planning programmes in a variety of settings demonstrates that informed individuals everywhere can and will *act responsibly* in the light of their own needs and those of their families and communities' (2004:64; emphasis added). The document also argues that governments should formulate population policies and programs that integrate demographic data into environmental assessments and planning, promoting sustainable resource management, and reducing unsustainable patterns of production and consumption. What had previously been seen as a policy issue to be managed through demographically driven population targets, quotas, and other state-based forms of population control now became articulated as a matter of individual reproductive choice *and* responsibility to broader social and environmental goals.

While the ICPD negotiations that produced the document were racked by fractures, bitter struggles, philosophical and political debates, and ultimately a struggle over the future direction of global population policies, including the role of women's reproductive health and rights, the Cairo Consensus ultimately united the perspectives of neo-Malthusians, environmental activists, feminists, and others in a pragmatic policy compromise (Hodgson and Watkins 1997; Cohen 1993). In top-down, demographically driven programs, 'the underlying philosophy driving this approach is the urgency of slowing population growth for the sake of the planet and only secondarily for the benefit of individuals' (Cohen 1993:64). After Cairo, the top-down emphasis was transformed into a bottom-up perspective. The language of birth quotas and other references to potentially involuntary fertility control became taboo following feminist organizing for a strong women-centred approach. In NGO programs, the language of women-centredness became aligned with neo-Malthusian approaches, creating a new narrative in which slowing population growth achieves planetary benefits, and individual women's voluntary reproductive control becomes the vehicle for doing so.

This emphasis on the role of individual women's responsibility is the cornerstone of what I refer to as sexual stewardship: it is predicated on women's central responsibility for morally engaged, responsible management of resources, whether those resources are environmental or within their own bodies. Feminist scholars have critiqued the multiple positions of women in gender, environment, and development discourse as sources of blame, victims, and as solvers of problems (Bretherton 2003; Arora-Jonsson 2010). In the case of sexual stewardship, what is happening is an extension of the problem solvers narrative, in which environmental problem-solving is extended to the feminized reproductive body.

## Making sexual stewardship

The concept of sexual stewardship begins with the idea of the environmental steward: deriving from the Judeo-Christian concept of a moral obligation to serve as good stewards of God's creation; it refers to one who carefully manages natural or environmental resources held in common. I expand this common notion of stewardship to capture how contemporary activists understand the relationships between sex, fertility, population, and environmental change in the current moment. Sexual stewardship asserts that when population and environment are linked through neo-Malthusian arguments, it is not only the natural resources of land, water, and air, but also women's sexuality and its associated effects – fertility and reproduction – which must be responsibly managed for the common good. Women's responsibility is compounded through the need to manage sex, reproduction, and the environment.

Who is a sexual steward? In my conceptualization, she is the following:

1    a fertile woman;
2    who consciously chooses to manage her fertility by using Western contraceptives;

3    who either does not bear children, or who delays childbearing and has no more than two (replacement fertility);
4    who is empowered;
5    who is aware of the environment and sees herself as playing a positive role in conserving and sustaining it;
6    who is a moral, responsible, ethical actor;
7    who has, and utilizes, access to education and income generation opportunities; and
8    whose actions are only constrained by issues of access (to Western contraceptives).

In reality, the sexual steward does not exist: she is an ideal-type subject, constructed within the offices of international (sustainable) development professionals. She exists conceptually as a model of the good population-environment-development subject: she uses contraceptives consistently and correctly, she values the environment and is motivated to protect its resources, and she views her own childbearing as having direct potential consequences for the environment. As a result, she adopts an intentional and responsible approach to managing her sexuality, reproduction, and childbearing – one that is oriented toward the common good.

The remainder of the chapter demonstrates how the sexual stewardship model is embedded in discourses and programs focused on population, environment, and development projects. First I explore the discourses increasingly used by NGO-based global population advocates who promote support for international family planning policy. The following section analyzes development projects that have operationalized these discourses through community-based population interventions.

## Linking population, health, and environment through sexual stewardship

Population, health, environment (PHE) programs are rural development projects that integrate family planning and other health services into environment and conservation projects. They originated in the 1950s, when the Northern-based development NGO World Neighbors initiated a program in Nepal. While implementing a food and agriculture project, program administrators found that local community members frequently approached them for information on health issues, specifically reproductive health and family planning. Over time, World Neighbors staff began to explicitly incorporate family planning information into project activities.

Over the decades, PHE projects have evolved into a service delivery model in which international conservation, population, and public health NGOs partner to integrate family planning services integrated with conservation, agriculture, and other environmental management strategies. PHE has been defined as the 'linkage, within a community or group of communities, of natural resource management or similar environmental activities and the improvement of reproductive health, always including but not limited to provision of family planning services' (Engelman 2005:14). At a minimum, these projects provide contraceptives, but they often provide additional health services as well, including sexually transmitted infection (STI) prevention and treatment, childhood immunizations, nutritional interventions, and water, hygiene, and sanitation interventions. The central goal of PHE programs is to 'simultaneously improve access to FP [family planning] and health services, while helping communities manage natural resources in ways that improve health and livelihoods, and also conserving the critical ecosystems on which they depend' (Pielemeier et al. 2007:6). Taking a human and ecosystem health perspective, the approach 'recognizes the interconnections between people and their environment and supports cross-sectoral collaboration and coordination' (Patterson 2007:1).

Specifically, PHE projects are predicated on a Cairo-based model in which family planning and population stabilization are crucial components of achieving environmental conservation aims. They evolved based on feedback early practitioners received in rural communities, where they found that the most effective way to ensure community participation in resource steward-ship was to provide health services, particularly to rural communities living in poverty (Piele-meier et al. 2007; D'Agnes and Margolius 2007). By providing access to Western medicine, contraceptives, and other basic health services, PHE program managers seek to enroll broader segments of rural communities, particularly women, in resource conservation and management projects. At the same time, they attract men to participate in family planning and health activ-ities. Traversing multiple development sectors, they are designed to be 'cost efficient, generate added value and . . . create synergies not found in vertical programs and projects' (D'Agnes and Margoluis 2007).

One program in particular, a coastal resources conservation project, demonstrates the Cairo-led framing of population and environment in the project's philosophy:

> The rapidly growing coastal population of the southwest region poses a serious threat
> to the sustainability of the region's coral reefs and other marine resources, upon which
> the livelihoods and economic wellbeing of the Vezo communities depend. Ensuring
> adequate provision of family planning services is recognised as being an important
> component of environmental management efforts focused on promoting more sus-
> tainable resource use.
>
> *(Mohan 2009:4)*

The project, and others like it, views contraceptives as not just a tool of public health, but as an environmental tool, one that is integral to both human and ecological health in the region. Communities come to matter in these projects through their compliance with project objec-tives, blurring the lines between projects that are truly generated by community demand and those whose aims include community acceptance of outside agendas (Oldham 2006). Project successes and failures are measured by whether and how many women accept and use contra-ceptives. As a result, women's compliance with contraceptive program objectives is the measure by which communities will continue to receive services or not, with potentially disastrous consequences.

Janice Harper's (2002) analysis of a disastrous PHE project at a national park in Madagascar demonstrates the potential effects of these projects for local communities. The rural commu-nity she studied forged an agreement with a national park project in which they agreed to stop using local forests to access their traditional medicines, in exchange for Western medical services including doctor visits, basic medicine, and contraceptives. However, when women in the community later refused the contraceptives, the project withdrew all medical support while continuing to restrict and surveil locals' use of forest resources. Given the conditions of poverty, limited transportation access and road infrastructure, and high incidence of infectious diseases, 10 per cent of community members died within several years of the withdrawal.

This example raises the question of how gender is embedded more broadly in PHE program objectives. While it is not defined as a specific objective in PHE programming literature, there are some indications that projects aim to ensure increased gender equity in different sectors of devel-opment work. For example, women are often underrepresented as participants in environment and conservation projects; PHE projects aim to increase their participation by offering health care. At the same time, many projects aim to increase men's knowledge of, and participation in, family planning services. Through integrating these otherwise separate and siloed sectors of development, planners aim to decrease some of the gender barriers to community involvement in projects. As a result, gender is rendered technical, measured through uptake and participation in events or technologies, and surveilled through statistical data and other apparatuses of tracking. Regulation and management are present through the ever-present possibility of removing services. More importantly, women bear an unequal responsibility for compliance. They must comply with contraceptive uptake in order to be good citizens of the project, but also in order to be good stewards of the environment. The long term effects PHE managers are looking for are reductions in population growth; measurements of contraceptive use focus almost exclusively on those methods controlled by women (as opposed to condoms, for example). As a result, women become sexual stewards, responsible for the potential results of their fertility and reproduction on the environment. By stewarding their reproduction, they become compliant environmental actors, thus solving larger problems for communities and the planet.

## Donors and discourses

PHE programs have been in financial crisis for a number of years now, due to waning donor interest and an overall shortfall of funds in the family planning sector. Initially, donor interest in these programs was high: the early 1990s saw an increasing number of NGOs developing PHE programs at the behest of a range of donors, mainly at private philanthropies (Sasser 2009; Hartmann 2006). Over time, however, the ability to identify and translate tangible program outcomes as successes was lacking. Funding constraints in the early 2000s led private donors to only fund programs that offered 'low hanging fruit' – easily measurable outcomes that could quickly indicate project success (Sasser 2009). Although extensive program documents and tools have been developed to show program managers how to better monitor and evaluate PHE projects, gather success stories, and represent program achievements to donors, support has continued to wane.

Waning private support for PHE dovetailed with increasing public donor participation. In 2002, the US Agency for International Development (USAID) officially began to fund PHE programs in the field as a result of new language included in the FY02 Foreign Operations Appropriations bill. This and subsequent bills have stated that 'under the Child Survival and Health Programs Fund some portion of the funds for family planning/reproductive health [should be allocated] in areas where population growth threatens biodiversity or endangered species' (USAID 2009). It provided stop-gap support for the continuation of PHE programming as other funders reduced or eliminated their grant-making in this area. As a result, USAID became the most significant funder of PHE programming, funding over a dozen programs in countries including Madagascar, Democratic Republic of Congo, Cambodia, and the Philippines (Anderson 2010:25; USAID EH Project 2016).

The sources of donor funds are significant in that public and private donors vary in their ability to be flexible and to support new ways of conceptualizing the links between population, environment, and development. USAID, for example, is beholden to the priorities of individual members of US Congress who fund their family planning programs, many of whom are more likely to support family planning programs focused on population stabilization than programs focused solely on women's reproductive health. At the same time, private population donors have also prioritized alarmist discourses, particularly the environmental security approach that links Global South population growth to uncontrolled migration and international political instability (Hartmann 2006). Regardless of funding sources, the Cairo agenda has come to dominate international approaches to population and development, particularly because of its emphasis on women's empowerment and human rights. As a result, advocacy projects that would have previously been described as population control are now reclassified as 'progressive' and 'women-centred' under the Cairo banner (Sasser 2014a), rendering efforts to criticize these projects much more complicated. The increasing emphasis on climate change in environmental and development circles increases the challenge, as the crisis narratives underlying much of the global climate debate feeds further into neo-Malthusian paradigms and revives them for a new generation of activists (Sasser 2014b).

## The responsibility of 'autonomy'

We all create emissions. More people = more emissions. Rapid population growth is a major contributor to global warming.

*(2009 website for Pop Offsets, a program offering carbon offsets as in return for investments in contraceptive projects)*

As attention and concern about global climate change increase, so do public debates about population growth. Magazine and journal articles wonder whether population growth accelerates greenhouse gas emissions globally, while prominent feminists argue that universal contraceptive access would help protect communities from the future impacts of a warming planet (Sasser 2016). Somewhat more dramatically, a Chinese government official argued in 2007 that the millions of lives averted through China's notorious one child policy could be understood as averted carbon emissions. Citing the estimate that China's population has approximately 300 million fewer people than projected without the policy being in place, he stated that this 'means we averted 1.3 billion tonnes of carbon dioxide in 2005' (Doyle 2007).

Given that the one-child policy is widely viewed as draconian (and since 2015 is being phased out in China), it might be tempting to dismiss the idea that averted-life-as-averted-emissions would be taken seriously. However, a recent study sponsored by British charity and think tank Population Matters suggests otherwise. The report, titled 'Fewer Emitters, Lower Emissions, Less Cost' (Wire 2009) states that for every $7 (USD) invested in contraceptive access programs, carbon emissions would be reduced by one ton, compared with an average $32 required to achieve the same reductions via low carbon technology. It then concludes that 'the total cost of stabilising carbon emissions in family planning is four times more effective than investing the same money in conventional solutions', a claim that is grounded through the slogan, 'smaller families, less carbon', which Population Matters promotes on its Pop Offsets website (2016).

While technical in tone, these approaches rest on an assumption that women are both victimized by, and potential solvers of, environmental problems, and thus uniquely positioned to adopt particular forms of environmental responsibility. These ideas are not new; as noted earlier, feminist scholars working in the gender and environment field have long critiqued the enduring environmental narratives that cast women in dual roles of victims and problem solvers (Leach 2007; Arora-Jonsson 2010; MacGregor 2010; Resurrección 2013; see also Arora-Jonsson in this volume). Similar narratives shape the ways women are characterized in population and development advocacy documents. Reports frequently describe women, both in isolation and in relationship to men, through the twinned lenses of vulnerability and potential as problem solvers, as exemplified in a Worldwatch Institute report:

Women and children in poverty are among the most vulnerable to the impacts of climate change, despite their disproportionately low contribution to the problem. Removing the obstacles that hold back more than 3 billion potential agents of change – women and girls – is both pragmatic and necessary.

*(Engelman 2010:5)*

It goes on to state that 'the importance of women and the autonomy they exercise may be far greater to the climate's future than most experts and negotiators on climate change – who have been until recently overwhelmingly male – have realized' (2010:5).

The autonomy that is described here is actually the freedom to behave in the way that development actors prefer, which is to have fewer children. And the ability to exercise so-called autonomy comes with a price: the expectation, nay *obligation*, to act as sexual stewards in the service of climate change priorities. This perspective was echoed in a 2008 policy brief produced by the Population-Health-Environment Policy and Practice Group, a network that included Worldwatch Institute, Izaak Walton League, Conservation International, World Wildlife Fund, Sierra Club, Population Action International, Population Connection, Population Reference Bureau, and National Audubon Society. Its authors argued that empowering women by investing in global population and family planning programs should be considered as a long-term strategy to mitigate climate change, describing it as 'easy to implement', 'already in demand', and 'inexpensive' (PHE Policy and Practice Group 2008:2).

Drawing on language from the Cairo Program of Action, as well as narratives from Gender and Development (GAD) research, these documents suggest three things: that population growth is a direct cause of climate change; that gendered inequality is a principal cause of population growth; and that empowering women is a pragmatic way of solving individual, environmental, and social problems. They encapsulate the sexual stewardship model: women are assumed to be fertile, reproducing beings, whose improved status will ideally lead to making responsible family choices – choices that include the *proper* spacing, timing, and number of children that will slow global population growth. Linking these decisions and behaviours to climate change not only reasserts the neo-Malthusian link, but places women's individual reproductive lives in global context. Women's childbearing decisions are thus never individual, never free from the weight of potential environmental catastrophe, and thus never free from a duty to reproduce (or not) responsibly.

While these discourses are found primarily in advocacy documents and are used to support calls for increased funding for international family planning policies, they have an indirect impact on intervention programs. NGOs engaged in population, environment, and development work are linked through formal and informal professional networks and the donors who support them. They are increasingly being made to channel their efforts toward climate change mitigation and adaptation programs. Despite different strategies, policy and program approaches stem from a shared perspective on population and development – the Cairo Program perspective – which drives how these ideas are made manifest, both in the halls of policy-making institutions, and in community-level interventions with the women they are intended to target.

## Conclusion

In this chapter I have demonstrated how population-environment narratives persist and are given new life, particularly in the context of climate change. The symbolic figure of the sexual steward is key to this persistence, given that she grounds sustainable development notions of women's vulnerability, responsibility, and individual moral action. At the same time, the discursive presence of sexual stewards highlights what is absent from the discussion – namely, the roles of men, male domination, and masculinist values in population programs and policies, as well as climate change rhetorics and strategies.

While there has been sustained feminist critique of population-environment narratives, and increasingly of population-climate narratives, there remains a need for feminist analyses of gendered bodies and the environment in terms of questions of positive/negative framings and discourses of justice/injustice. The work of Barajas-Roman and Hartmann (2009), Di Chiro

(2008), and the PopDev DifferenTakes series demonstrate the need for analyses that integrate environmental justice, climate justice, and reproductive justice. Building frameworks linked through justice approaches helps us pay attention to how the fertile and reproductive bodies of marginalized women are often produced and shaped in the context of environmental narratives, politics, and inequalities. They also offer a blueprint for new forms of activist organizing and alliance-building across progressive communities, a necessary counterpoint to the increasing narratives encapsulating population fears, environmental crises, and their solutions in women's wombs.

# References

Anderson, M. (2010) *History and Future of Population-Health-Environment Programs: Evolution of Funding and Programming.* Master's thesis, University of Minnesota.

Arora-Jonsson, S. (2010) 'Virtue and vulnerability: Discourses on women, gender and climate change', *Global Environmental Change* 21: 744–751.

Barajas-Roman, E. and Hartmann, B. (2009) 'Reproductive justice, not population control: Breaking the wrong links and making the right ones in the movement for climate justice', Paper prepared for the WE ACT for Environmental Justice conference on Advancing Climate Justice: Transforming the Economy, Public Health and Our Environment, New York.

Bretherton, C. (2003) 'Movements, networks, hierarchies: A gender perspective on global environmental governance', *Global Environmental Politics* 3(2): 103–119.

Campbell, M. (1998) 'Schools of thought: An analysis of interest groups influential in international population policy', *Population and Environment: A Journal of Interdisciplinary Studies* 19(6): 487–512.

Cohen, S. (1993) 'The road from Rio to Cairo: Toward a common agenda', *International Family Planning Perspectives* 19(2): 61–66.

D'Agnes, L. and Margoluis, C. (2007) *Integrating Population, Health, and Environment (PHE) Projects: A Programming Manual.* Washington, DC: United States Agency for International Development.

Di Chiro, G. (2008) 'Living environmentalisms: Coalition politics, social reproduction, and environmental justice', *Environmental Politics* 17(2): 276–298.

Doyle, A. (2007) 'China says one-child policy helps protect climate', *Reuters.* Online. Available at: www.reuters.com/article/us-climate-population-correction-idUSL3047203920070830 (accessed 5 December 2015).

Edmond, J. et al. (2009) *Healthy Families, Healthy Forests: Improving Human Health and Biodiversity Conservation.* Arlington, VA: Conservation International Foundation.

Engelman, R. (2005) *Fertile Soil: A Guide to Linking Reproductive Health, Environment, and Livelihood in Communities.* Washington, DC: Population Action International.

Engelman, R. (2010) *Worldwatch Report 183, 'Population, Climate Change, and Women's Lives'.* Washington, DC: Worldwatch Institute.

Harper, J. (2002) *Endangered Species: Health, Illness and Death Among Madagascar's People of the Forest.* Durham, NC: Carolina Academic Press.

Hartmann, B. (1995/1987) *Reproductive Rights and Wrongs: The Global Politics of Population Control.* Cambridge, MA: South End Press.

Hartmann, B. (2006) 'Liberal ends, illiberal means: National security, "environmental conflict", and the making of the Cairo Consensus', *Indian Journal of Gender Studies* 13(2): 195–218.

Hodgson, D. and Cotts Watkins, S. (1997) 'Feminists and neo-Malthusians: Past and present alliances', *Population and Development Review* 23(3): 469–523.

Leach, M. (2007) 'Earth mother myths and other ecofeminist fables: How a strategic notion rose and fell', *Development and Change* 38(1): 67–85.

MacGregor, S. (2010) 'A stranger silence still: The need for feminist social research on climate change', *The Sociological Review* 57(s2): 124–140.

Mazur, L. (2009) *A Pivotal Moment: Population, Justice, and the Environmental Challenge.* Washington, DC: Island Press.

Mohan, V. (2009) *Providing Sexual and Reproductive Health Services for Communities in Velondriake, Southwest Madagascar: Project Development Plan 2009–2011.* London, UK: Blue Ventures.

Oldham, J. (2006) *Rethinking the Link: A Critical Review of Population-Environment Programs.* Amherst, MA: Political Economy Research Institute.

Patterson, K. P. (2007) *Integrating Population, Health, and Environment in Ethiopia*. Washington, DC: Population Reference Bureau.

PHE Policy and Practice Group (2008) *Human Population Growth and Greenhouse Gas Emissions*. Washington, DC. Online. Available at: www.wilsoncenter.org/sites/default/files/Human%20Population%20Growth%20and%20Greenhouse%20Gas%20Emissions.pdf (accessed 30 August 2015).

Pielemeier, J., Hunter, L. and Layng, R. (2007) *Assessment of USAID's Population and Environment Projects and Programming Options*. Washington, DC: United States Agency for International Development.

*PopOffsets*. Online. Available at: www.popoffsets.org (accessed 15 December 2009).

Population Matters. *PopOffsets*. Online. Available at: www.popoffsets.org/ (accessed 15 January 2016).

Resurrección, B. (2013) 'Persistent women and environment linkages in climate change and sustainable development agendas', *Women's Studies International Forum* 40: 33–43.

Sasser, J. (2009) *Environmental Organizations and Population Programs: A Preliminary Analysis*. Berkeley, CA: Venture Strategies for Health and Development.

Sasser, J. (2014a) 'From darkness into light: Race, population, and environmental advocacy', *Antipode* 46(5): 1240–1257.

Sasser, J. (2014b) 'The wave of the future? Youth advocacy at the nexus of population and climate change', *The Geographical Journal* 180(2): 102–110.

Sasser, J. (2016) 'Population, climate change, and the embodiment of environmental crisis', in Godfrey, P. and Torres, D. (eds) *Systemic Crises of Climate Change: Intersections of Race, Class, and Gender*. New York: Routledge, 57–70.

Sierra Club Global Population Environment Program, *Program Brochure*. Washington, DC: Sierra Club. Online. Available at: www.sierraclub.org/population/advocacy-resources (accessed 15 January 2016).

United Nations Population Fund (UNFPA) 2004 (1994) Programme of Action: Adopted at the International Conference on Population and Development, 5–13 September 1994, Cairo. New York: UNFPA.

United States Agency for International Development (USAID) (2009) *Population and Environment*. Online. Available at: www.usaid.gov/our_work/global_health/pop/techareas/environment/index.html.

USAID Environmental Health Project (EH Project) *Population, Health, and Environment (PHE) Projects by Country*. Online. Available at: http://ehproject.org/phe/phe_projects.html (accessed 10 January 2016).

US Center for Biological Diversity, *Human Population Growth and Climate Change*. Online. Available at: www.biologicaldiversity.org/programs/population_and_sustainability/climate/ (accessed 15 January 2016).

Various authors (1992) 'Treaty on population, environment, and development', Produced at the United Nations Conference on Environment and Development (UNCED), Rio, Brazil. Online. Available at: www.stakeholderforum.org/fileadmin/files/Earth_Summit_2012/1992_treaties/Treaty_on_Population_Environment_and_Development.pdf (accessed June 2015).

Wire, T. (2009) *Fewer Emitters, Lower Emissions, Less Cost: Reducing Future Carbon Emissions by Investing in Family Planning*. London: Optimum Population Trust.

World Commission on Environment and Development (1987) 'Our common future, report of the World Commission on Environment and Development', Published as Annex to General Assembly document A/42/427 (also known as the Brundtland Report 1987).

# 24

# GENDER EQUALITY, SUSTAINABLE AGRICULTURAL DEVELOPMENT, AND FOOD SECURITY

*Agnes A. Babugura*

## Introduction

Gender equality, sustainable agricultural development, and food security are interconnected and critically important to sustainable development. Agriculture is a major sector in many developing countries with potential to influence food security, economic growth, and human development (FAO 2011). In spite of its potential, the sector is also known to have significant impacts on the natural resource base on which farming systems depend. It is a major contributor to greenhouse gas emissions – responsible for about 17 per cent of global greenhouse emissions – and a major driver of both deforestation and land-use change. Given its dependency on the earth's climate, the agricultural sector is significantly vulnerable to the threats of climate change, affecting, for example, crop and livestock production. Such impacts, already evident in several regions of the world, often result in decreased crop production, high food prices, negative consequences on livelihoods, increased malnourishment, and reduced supply and availability of animal protein (FAO 2009; Lobell and Field 2011; Skoufias et al. 2011). Ultimately the consequences manifest in a food crisis that plunges many people into deeper poverty, threatening national security and economic growth (Conforti 2011).

It is within this context that integrating the three principles of sustainable development – economic growth, social equity, and protection of the environment – into the ethos of agricultural development became vital (see, for example, the discussion on *Agenda 21* in Chapter 14). Harmonizing these three principles to achieve 'sustainable agricultural development' means managing and conserving the natural resource base and directing technological and institutional change toward the attainment and continued satisfaction of human needs, now and into the future (Jackson 1978; Francis and Youngberg 1990; Ongley 1996). The point of Sustainable Development Goal (SDG) no. 2 is to 'end hunger, achieve food security and improve nutrition, and promote sustainable agriculture'. Without a strong and sustainable agricultural sector, achieving this goal will be a significant challenge.

Food security and sustainable agricultural development are inextricably linked: agriculture is the only source of food for both direct consumption and as raw material for refined foods. As an issue of international and national responsibility, food security has been one of the most debated of the basic human rights. Coined in the mid-1970s in the wake of a global food crisis, the food security concept encompasses a number of definitions depending on its usage (see FAO 2003; FAO 2006) and strategies used to secure food. Following the World Food Summit in 1996, the concept is widely defined as: 'Food security exists when all people at all times, have physical and economic access to sufficient, safe and nutritious food to meet their dietary needs and food preferences for an active and healthy life'. It is built on the three pillars of: (1) food availability (with elements related to agricultural production, distribution, and exchange); (2) food access (with elements related to affordability, allocation, and preference); and (3) food utilization (with elements related to nutritional value, social value, and food safety; FAO 2003). These pillars are important for the technical analysis that underpins policy recommendations.

One of the most important challenges facing the world today is how to feed a population of nine billion by 2050. At the 2012 UN Conference on Sustainable Development (also known as 'Rio+20'), world leaders reaffirmed the right of everyone to have access to safe and nutritious food, consistent with the right to adequate food and the fundamental right to be free from hunger. Guaranteeing that all people have access to the food they need for an active and healthy life is a concern for developing countries in particular. Almost all the hungry people on the planet – 780 million out of 795 million – live in developing countries. In the sub-Saharan region, more than one in four people are said to be undernourished – the highest prevalence of any region in the world (FAO 2014; Rosen et al. 2014; IFPRI 2015).

Closely linked to sustainable agricultural development and food security is the concept of gender equality. This concept refers to women and men having equal conditions for realizing their full human rights and for contributing to, and benefiting from, economic, social, cultural, and political development. Previously represented by Millennium Development Goal (MDG) no. 3, and currently represented by SDG no. 5, gender equality is both a right and an end in itself. Attaining gender equality is acknowledged globally as a key prerequisite for sustainable development (OEDC 2010; Stevens 2010; UNDP 2011; UN 2012; UN Women 2014). This point is clearly reiterated in a significant number of international declarations and frameworks, including the Millennium Declaration, *Agenda 21*, Rio+20 Outcome, the Rio Conventions and the Hyogo Framework for Action, the 1995 the Beijing Declaration and Platform, The Rome Declaration on World Food Security, General Assembly resolution 68/139, and the current 2030 development agenda. Despite such acknowledgments, however, and the inseparable linkages to sustainable agricultural development and food security, gender aspects are often a neglected piece of the puzzle when tackling development issues. Analyses of deep-rooted gender inequality indicate that women are at the core of sustainable agricultural development and food security, and hence key drivers of sustainable development. Understanding the gender dimensions in their complexity, however, has been a low priority on the development agenda. The neglect of gender concerns in agricultural development and food security is reflected in failure to reinforce and translate existing gender policy commitments into actions.

Framed by this context, this chapter explores the gender dimensions of agriculture and food security, as they intersect with the goals of sustainable development. One aim of this chapter is to provide an overview of the main themes that have been studied in the gender, environment, and development field for over four decades. Another aim is to provide the necessary knowledge to inform public debates, with the hope of influencing decision-making processes, policy development, and planning. Having set the context, in the next section I present a brief historical overview of the gender equality debate in agriculture. This is followed by a discussion of the role of women and their contributions to sustainable agricultural development and food security.

I then explain the barriers that hinder gender equality in sustainable agricultural development and food security. I conclude with key issues emerging from the chapter, as well as some policy recommendations.

## Gender equality and agriculture: a brief overview

The policy ideal of gender equality can be traced back to 1945, when the UN acknowledged the need to respect 'human rights and fundamental freedoms for all without distinction as to race, sex, language, or religion' (UN Charter-Article 1.3, 1945). The UN Commission on the Status of Women (CSW) was soon thereafter established to monitor and promote gender equality and women's empowerment. By the 1950s and 1960s evidence was accumulating that raised concerns regarding the exclusion of women from development policies and processes (Parpart et al. 2000). In the early 1970s the concept of women in development (WID) came into use (Rathgeber 1989). Since then, a series of high profile international conferences and seminars have been held to debate various gender concerns. Several international and national agreements have been ratified and frameworks developed to facilitate the advancement of gender equality.

Within the agricultural context, analyses of gender interests were shaped by the Danish economist Esther Boserup, who first drew attention to the role of women in agricultural production. In her book *Woman's Role in Economic Development*, Boserup (1970) presented evidence from her investigation of African farming systems to show how the role of women in food production was overlooked and largely unrepresented. She concluded by stating that the economic survival and development of the Third World (as it was called at the time) would depend heavily on efforts to integrate women fully into the development process, and this included agricultural development. Boserup's work increased the attention paid to women's issues within the UN, as well as in development agencies and non-governmental organizations (NGOs). Her analysis shaped the debates at the International Women's Conference held in Mexico in 1975. Prior to Boserup's interventions, development resources were channelled to women in their roles as mothers and homemakers. Their roles as economic producers – farmers as well as wage labourers – had been ignored (Buvinic and Mehra 1990). Therefore Boserup's findings opened a window of opportunity for challenging traditional gender norms in the context of agricultural development and development in general. It enabled people working under the WID banner to strengthen their claims that women are highly productive members of society, hence ignoring their central role was to waste a valuable resource. The WID approach was instrumental in ensuring that women's issues made it on the agenda of development agencies, and it played an important role in establishing national women's policy machineries worldwide (Parpart et al. 2000).

The WID approach was not without weaknesses, however. The concept of women and development (WAD) emerged in the late 1970s to contest the WID assumption that the exclusion of women from earlier development strategies had been an unintentional oversight. Scholars who adopted the WAD approach argued that women have always been integrated into development processes, as the work they undertook both inside and outside the household was vital to the survival and continuance of society (Rathgeber 1989; Moyoyetta 2004; Duffy 2006). The analysis drew on insights from political economy to argue that this integration served primarily to sustain existing international structures of inequality (Rathgeber 1989; Duffy 2006) and that non-elite Third World men were also adversely affected by the structure of inequality within the international system. In other words, what WID lacked was a critical analysis of social relations of gender within classes (Rathgeber 1989; Moyoyetta 2004). But while the WAD approach acknowledged the impact of class in practical project design and implementation, like WID, it tended to group women together without paying sufficient attention to intersections of class, race, or ethnicity that influence women's actual social status (Rathgeber 1989). Even though WAD offered a more critical view of women's position than WID, it failed to undertake a full-scale analysis of relationships between patriarchy, differing modes of production, and the complex causes of women's subordination and oppression (Rathgeber 1989). What is more, both WID and WAD intervention strategies focused mainly on the development of income-generating activities without taking into account the time burdens that the strategies placed on women (Rathgeber 1989).

Realizing that efforts to empower and uplift women through the WID and WAD approaches had done little to change the customs, beliefs, and power structures that contributed to women's subordination in the first place, new thinking began to emerge in the late 1980s and early 1990s. The new thinking was shaped by earlier research by feminists whose work had focused on the concept of gender. For example in her book, *Sex, Gender and Society*, sociologist Ann Oakley (1972) pointed out how differences between women and men were being considered in terms of biology (sex), yet in reality most differences emanated from the cultural concept of gender: the distinction between masculinity and femininity, which determines the social roles of men and women and the relationships between them. The research also highlighted that gender is not a rigid concept, but a flexible one shaped through a variety of social, historical, religious, and economic factors. Gender was therefore viewed as a concept that is dynamic and socially constructed (Oakley 1972). This shift in understanding away from the focus on women as a biologically determined group resulted in a new approach called gender and development (GAD), which focused on gender relations and the various experiences of women and men. The GAD approach transformed the debate on women's rights and gender equality and later resulted in the gender mainstreaming strategy.[1] However, GAD advocates did not completely abandon the WID strategy as women-targeted initiatives were found to be necessary given the sociocultural norms that dictate what women can and can't do. In some cases, women also preferred acquiring new knowledge and skills in the company of other women (Chant and Gutmann 2000).

Boserup's work also prompted some scholars, notably rural sociologists and agricultural geographers (e.g., Sachs 1983; Reimer 1986; Burg and Endeveld 1994; Whatmore et al. 1994), to expand their research to better understand the gender relations between men and women in the agricultural sector. Scholars such as Friedmann (1986), Whatmore (1990), and Shortall (1992) further expanded rural gender research to explore power relations within the family, ownership of land, capital transfer, and women's unpaid household and agricultural work. These studies revealed how the marginalization of women and their exclusion from agricultural property had sustained male domination in agricultural production. With a better understanding of gendered social relations, it also became clear that women are not just victims but also key agents of change, hence supporting the need to improve the development model to redress gender disparities.

New development ideas that were being debated within the academic, social, economic, and political spheres, at both national and international levels, pointed to the birth of sustainable development in the late 1980s. Understanding women's and men's roles and responsibilities in all spheres of development was acknowledged as key to achieving sustainable development. The challenges of achieving sustainable development and gender equality together became a pressing issue. The two were also seen to reinforce each other in powerful ways (Agarwal 2002; Buckingham-Hatfield 2002; Johnsson-Latham 2007). Gender analysis became a significant factor in all spheres of sustainable development, including sustainable agricultural development. It was seen as an instrument for studying relations between women and men by examining the activities, responsibilities, opportunities, and constraints regarding resources, decisions, and the execution of activities. Essential questions in this type of analysis were: Who does what? When? Why and for whom? The argument was that when applied to sustainable agricultural development and food security, gender analysis should examine the roles played by women and men in relation to the spheres of production (FAO 2005).

From this historical viewpoint, it is clear that active and meaningful engagement of both women and men is critical to sustainable agricultural development and food security. Disregarding women's contributions is not only costly in terms of development but also undermines their rights, dignity, and abilities to be agents of change. While mainstream agricultural development once ignored women, treating them as invisible and dismissing them as unimportant, within the spaces of sustainable agricultural development women are now legitimatized and recognized as key players. Sustainable agricultural development offers a platform for valuing and remunerating women's agricultural work, affirming their contributions and market development from women's perspective. Today there is a greater appreciation for women-led initiatives promoting sustainable agricultural development and food security.

It is important to note, however, that despite recent gains, scholars working in the field of gender and development agree that much more work remains to be done to advance gender equality in sustainable agricultural development and all other spheres of development. While gender integration and analysis have been emphasized as key to sustainable development, and despite all efforts to promote gender equality, girls and women continue to be disadvantaged and marginalized in all spheres of development. Hence girls and women – especially in developing countries – are restricted from enjoying their economic and social rights (UNDP 1993; UNDP 1995; Lincoln 1997; UN Department of Economic and Social Affairs 2010; Ponge 2013). In agriculture, despite women constituting an average of 43 per cent of the labour force, and despite the appreciation of their role and contributions in the sector, they continue to be marginalized and disadvantaged, as discussed in the sections that follow. It is for this reason that there is still a heavy focus on uplifting and empowering women. This also explains and justifies the tendency for literature to be more focused on women than men. The sections that follow highlight the role and contributions of women and their barriers in agriculture, as acknowledged in the literature. In the next section, I reflect on women's role and contributions to sustainable agriculture and food security. This reflection strengthens the case for promoting gender equality and presents a case for why women's contributions to sustainable agricultural development and food security must not be disregarded.

## Women's contributions to sustainable agricultural development and food security

There is now no doubt that women make important contributions to sustainable agricultural development and food security in all regions of the world. Women work as farmers in their own right, as unpaid workers on family farms, and as paid or unpaid labourers on other farms and agricultural enterprises (FAO 2011). Their roles and contributions vary considerably between and within regions, as follows.

### *Women in the agricultural labour force*

On average, women make up 43 per cent of the agricultural labour force in developing countries. The female share of the agricultural labour force is reported to range from about 20 per cent in Latin America to almost 50 per cent in Eastern and South-eastern Asia and sub-Saharan Africa (Doss 2011; FAO 2011). However, women in sub-Saharan Africa are reported to have relatively higher overall labour-force participation rates, as well as the highest average agricultural labour-force participation rates in the world (FAO 2011). The averages in Africa range from just over 40 per cent in Southern and Northern Africa to just over 50 per cent in Eastern Africa. The Asian average is dominated by China, where the female share of the agricultural labour force is reported to have increased slightly during the past three decades (Doss 2011). Countries of the Americas have a much lower average: just over 20 per cent of the female agricultural labour force compared to other developing country regions.

## Women's roles in agricultural production

Research shows that, in comparison to men, women in the developing world perform most of the agricultural and food security activities (e.g., Jacoby 1992; FAO et al. 2010; Doss 2011; FAO 2011). While men are often responsible for land clearing and burning, and polishing, women's activities typically include producing agricultural crops, tending animals, processing and preparing food, and working for wages in agricultural enterprises (FAO, IFAD and ILO 2010; Doss 2011). In sub-Saharan Africa, women in household animal-production enterprises tend to have the primary responsibility for the husbandry of small animals and ruminants. Their role in tending to large-animal systems includes: herding, providing water and feed, cleaning stalls, and milking. Women have a predominant role in processing milk products and are usually responsible for their marketing (FAO 2010).

## Women's environmental knowledge

Critical to sustainable agricultural development and food security are environmental knowledge and management. Due to gender differentiated roles, men and women interact differently with the environment resulting in different opportunities to protect it as well as unique perspectives, which take into account knowledge and awareness of the environment (Agarwal 2010, 2016; Milgroom et al. 2015). Women possess the knowledge, capabilities, and networks needed to drive real solutions for achieving sustainable agricultural development and food security (World Bank 2015). For example, women living in villages of the Deccan Plateau in India took the lead in the global movement toward sustainable agricultural practices. These women shifted away from growing genetically modified seeds, which caused devastating crop failure and resulted in farmers having high debt as they were forced to purchase the non-regenerative seeds after each harvest. To address these unsustainable practices, the women have returned to traditional indigenous agricultural practices. They teach each other the ritual of seed banking and sharing, they use a diversity of cropping methods, and they work to create safety nets for their villages. Although the women are among the poorest in the world, they have taken on leadership roles within the sustainable food movement.

## Women farmers promote sustainable agricultural practices

Based on the case study of women living in villages of the Deccan Plateau, Satheesh and Pimbert (1999) and Kumbamu (2011) provide detailed narratives of the success of women's sustainable farming practices. The practices utilized by the women farmers in the Deccan Plateau include the use of organic manure to enrich soil fertility and mixed crop farming. The women reintroduced a variety of crop species which offered food, shelter, and new niches for an array of naturally occurring insects, spiders, fungi, birds, and small mammals. The complex plant architectures included mixes of pigeon pea, amaranth, Dollicos bean, Niger, cowpea, horsegram, pearl millet, greengram, little millet, dry sown paddy, and groundnut. The agroecosystem components include various edible wild vegetable plants that are highly nutritious and are important for local food security throughout the year. The farmers make use of non-pesticidal management options (NPM), most of which are based on farmers' traditional knowledge systems. The adopted NPM options include deep summer ploughing, use of pest tolerant crop variety, crop rotation, trap cropping with marigold, castor and sunflower, enhancement of soil fertility to build stronger and richer soil (which can be the first antidote to the pest attack), and enhancing the biodiversity on farms as the first defence against insect pests.

## Women farmers as innovators and change agents

Satheesh and Pimbert's (1999) research further highlights the critical contributions of women farmers to bringing about change through sustainable agricultural initiatives. They have found that women farmers in dryland India have brought about remarkable changes through highly successful decentralized and community-managed systems for producing, storing, and distributing coarse grains at the local level. The women set up the Deccan Development Society (DDS), with the aim of reaching the poorest of the poor through innovative and equitable agricultural rural development. Through the project, the DDS has also set out to attain gender equality within their own families and communities. They have established women's affinity groups called 'sanghams' in around forty villages. Within two years of implementation, the project dramatically enhanced local food security, community resilience, and biodiversity. More than 2,500 acres of fallow land were brought under the plough. Within the first year of the project, an extra 800,000 kg of sorghum was produced in several villages. Communities were able to produce nearly three million extra meals in thirty villages – 1,000 extra meals per family. Fodder generated from the newly cultivated fields sustained more than 6,000 head of cattle in thirty villages. Most importantly, in the first two years, the project generated a total employment of 4,830 person days, earning the communities in thirty-two villages a total wage income of Rs 72,450 (US$1,685). Project evaluations have confirmed the remarkable results that have been achieved in terms of gender equity, food security, autonomy and capacity of local groups, recovery of agricultural biodiversity and degraded lands, and sustained increases in agricultural productivity.

The DDS now works in seventy-five villages with about 5,000 women's self-help groups. The women farmers continue to learn how to develop eco-friendly enterprises. They are taking up seed banking, learning how to use homemade manure, and adopting other simple technologies to boost growth. Seed banking has made women more self-reliant. Hundreds of backyard bio-fertilizer units behind their homes are improving the productivity of soils and generating income. They have knowledge of different types of soil and exactly what kind of crops are best adapted to grow on each, when, and how to plant them. They understand the adaptability and drought-resistant properties of crops (DDS 2015; Prabu 2015). Marginalized women who were once landless now plough more than twenty acres of their own land (DDS 2015). Despite being marginalized and working on marginalized lands, they have courageously preserved and conserved agricultural biodiversity in the Deccan, and they have elevated agricultural biodiversity from the concern of small farmer groups to become a national concern. They have provided a new path and vision for the National Biodiversity Action Plan of India. They have redefined ecology, agriculture, biodiversity, and governance.

The DDS case study is not an isolated one. Women farmers around the world are taking the lead in crop and varietal diversification as an effective adaptation strategy to respond to changing farming conditions, including the changing climate (Vernooy 2015). Against the odds, women are reorienting farming knowledge, practices, and the social relationships of sustainable agricultural production. They are successfully organizing themselves to strengthen their food security systems, their livelihoods, and their autonomy (see Milgroom et al. 2015; Vernooy 2015). Women's movements in Asia and Africa are making land ownership a priority for women. They are working with officials to get land titles in their names as well as to register their land for agriculture cooperatives (see, for example, Milgroom et al. 2015).

There is sufficient evidence to support the importance of advancing gender equality to achieve sustainable agricultural development and food security and in turn a ripple effect on other sustainable development goals. There is a clear indication that the knowledge that rural and indigenous women farmers possess, and the different ways they interact with ecologies, is valuable and vital for sustainable agricultural development and food security. It is clear that the contributions women make to agricultural production are vital, not only for the sector, but also for achieving other sustainable development goals. However, their contributions are not being 'harnessed' to full potential due to the persistence of obstacles they face. The next section addresses some key barriers that hinder the advancement of gender equality in agricultural development and food security.

## Barriers to gender equality in sustainable agricultural development and food security

Despite increased attention and commitments to promote gender equality, inequalities in agricultural and food security systems prevail. Women continue to be marginalized and regarded as home producers or assistants ('farmers' wives') on the farm, and not as farmers and economic agents in their own right (FAO 2011; IFAD 2011). They continue to experience gender-specific barriers that undermine their abilities to contribute effectively to sustainable agricultural development and food security (FAO 2011; Silva and Nansen 2011; Tandon and Wegerif 2013; Busto et al. 2015; Chiweshe 2015). Lack of information and knowledge, inadequate or discriminatory policies and laws, and weak governance also contribute to the observed gender inequalities in sustainable agricultural development and food security systems.

Empirical evidence generated from the Food and Agriculture Organization's study – *The State of Food and Agriculture 2010–2011, Women in Agriculture: Closing the Gender Gap for Development* – reveals several barriers that women across regions face as farmers (FAO 2011). Compared to men, women have less access to critical productive resources and opportunities. Gender specific barriers are identified across a range of assets, inputs, and services, including land, livestock, farm labour, education, extension services, financial services, and technology. These barriers as noted here are also acknowledged in the academic literature (see, for example, Agarwal 2012, 2016; Mare and Girmay 2015; Ragassa 2014; Peterman et al 2011).

## *Lack of access to land*

Access to land is a basic requirement for farming. Access to and control over land continues to be a major stumbling block for rural women (FAO 2011). In general, women own less land than men (Mason and Carlsson 2004; Doss 2006; FAO 2011; SOFA Team 2011). This is mainly attributed to statutory and customary land tenure systems resulting in weak property and contractual rights to land (Agarwal 2011; FAO 2011). In cases where legislation exists to protect women's property rights, lack of legal knowledge and weak implementation are reported to limit women's ability to exercise these rights (Quisumbing and Pandolfelli 2010; Amanor 2012). Based on available data in some developing countries, the percentage of women who own land varies between 3 and 20 per cent. For example, in Kenya, only 5 per cent of registered landowners are women

(Agarwal 2012). In Uganda only about 16 per cent of the women own land in their own right. Their ownership of registered land is reported to be even lower – 7 per cent (Rugadya 2010). In Ethiopia a study found that only 21.19 per cent of women owned land, while the percentage for men who owned land was 78.81 per cent (Mare and Girmay 2015).

In Ghana, another study revealed that uncertain access to land and a history of losing land rights discouraged women's long-term investment in agriculture (García 2006). Furthermore, the land owned by women is usually of lower quality and smaller in size compared to that owned by men (Mason and Carlsson 2004; Doss 2006; FAO 2011; SOFA Team 2011; Agarwal 2012). For instance, in Ghana, the study highlighted that women's access to land was further restricted to less fertile land. As a result women were only able to cultivate cassava and other food crops destined for immediate consumption in the household (known as subsistence crops), while men cultivated the more fertile land for cash crops (García 2006).

Like land, livestock is one of the most valuable agricultural assets. While evidence regarding the extent of women's ownership of livestock is scant, the available data point to systematic gender inequalities, not only in terms of ownership but also in the types of livestock men and women own. FAO (2011) found that male-headed households have larger livestock holdings, on average, than female-headed households. Inequality in livestock holdings was found to be particularly acute in Bangladesh, Ghana, and Nigeria, where male holdings are more than three times larger than those of female-headed households. It has been noted that livestock holdings of female farmers tend to be much smaller than those of men (FAO 2011; Njuki and Sanginga 2013); hence women are much less likely to own large animals, such as cattle and oxen, which are useful as draught animals (FAO 2011). In north-eastern Uganda a study found significant gender disparities in cattle ownership, with 62 per cent of men and only 14 per cent of women reporting ownership (Oluka et al. 2005). Another study revealed that in Kenya, men owned ten times more cattle than women, while in Tanzania men owned eighteen times more cattle than women. The lowest gender disparity in cattle ownership was found in Mozambique, with women owning 0.8 head for every one head of cattle that men owned. The study found that women usually own smaller animals, such as goats and poultry, which are kept near the house (Njuki and Sanginga 2013). However, ownership patterns of livestock were said to be more complex and strongly related to the livestock production system as well as social and cultural factors (Njuki and Sanginga 2013).

## Lack of extension services

Extension services encompass the wide range of services provided by experts in the areas of agriculture (FAO 2011). Van Walsum (2015) highlights that globally female farmers still receive only 5 per cent of all extension services, yet they do 75 per cent of the work in agriculture and produce 75 per cent of the world's food. In South-east Asia women provide up to 90 per cent of the labour used in rice cultivation. In sub-Saharan Africa, they produce up to 80 per cent of basic foodstuffs for both household use and sale. They have primary responsibility for the husbandry of small and large animals (FAO 2009; Peterman et al. 2010; FAO 2011). Despite women's significant engagement in agriculture, FAO (2011) notes that extension service agents tend to approach male farmers more often than female farmers. This is said to be due to a general misperception that women do not farm and that extension advice will eventually 'trickle down' from the male household head to all other household members. It has also been reported that the way in which extension services are delivered constrain women farmers from receiving information on innovations. Furthermore, women tend to have lower levels of education than men, which is likely to limit their active participation in training that uses a lot of written material. In addition, time constraints and cultural reservations may hinder women from participating in extension activities, such as field days outside their village or within mixed groups (FAO 2011).

## Lack of financial services

Capital resources, such as savings, credit, and insurance services, also tend to heavily favour male farmers. These services provide opportunities for improving agricultural output, food security, and economic vitality at the household, community, and national levels (FAO 2011). In Ethiopia, for example, Mare and Girmay (2015) have established that rural women with access to different types of financial resources account for only 2.5 per cent, while the men accounted for 97.5 per cent. In many cases, women are also excluded from the services offered by agricultural cooperatives (FAO 2011; Majurin 2012). Evidence shows that credit markets are not gender-neutral. Legal barriers and cultural norms have been found to sometimes bar women from holding bank accounts or entering into financial contracts in their own right. FAO (2011) highlights several examples to support these findings. A study in Nigeria, for example, shows that 14 per cent of men obtained formal credit compared to only 5 per cent of women. In Kenya the numbers are 14 per cent for males and 4 per cent for females, respectively, and in Uganda, women entrepreneurs receive just 1 per cent of available credit in rural areas.

## Farm labour constraints

Often the availability of farm labour depends on how much family labour a household can mobilize as well as how much labour can be hired in local labour markets (FAO 2011). Compared to men and male-headed households, labour constraints are known to be more acute for women and female-headed households. This is because female-headed households are usually smaller and have fewer working-age adult members. Women also have heavy and unpaid household duties (such as cooking and childcare) that take them away from more 'productive' (i.e., income earning) activities (FAO 2011). Male out-migration is also seen as a contributing factor that heightens the already existing constraints.

FAO (2011) further notes that due to household and community responsibilities and gender-specific labour requirements, women farmers cannot farm as productively as male farmers. In some communities, depending on cultural norms, certain farming activities – ploughing and spraying, for instance – rely on access to male labour. This has been the case in Ethiopia, according to research by Holden et al. (2001). Therefore, without male labour, women farmers experience delays that are likely to result in output losses (FAO 2011).

## Lack of access to agricultural technology

Access to new agricultural technology is critical for maintaining and improving agricultural productivity and food security. As noted by FAO (2011), gender disparities exist for a wide range of agricultural technologies. These include machines and tools, improved plant varieties and animal breeds, fertilizers, pest control measures, and management techniques. Kilic et al. (2014) attribute gender disparities in access, use, and adoption of agricultural technologies to four main reasons. First, insecure land tenure lowers investments in improved technologies. Second, structural factors, such as lack of financial products, influence technology adoption; collateral requirements, mobility constraints, significant transaction costs, and cultural barriers have been found to prevent women from accessing financial products and credit. Third, due to a lack of access to agricultural technologies, women farmers typically tend to use lower levels of purchased technological inputs such as fertilizer and high-yielding seed varieties. And fourth, low human capital and women's non-wage household production work prevents them from using technologies. A study in Ethiopia found that adoption of sustainable agricultural practices depend on household size and labour as adoption of such techniques increases women's workload (Teklewold et al. 2013). Research by Peterman et al (2014) and Gilbert et al (2013) offer more details regarding gender disparities and agricultural technologies.

Addressing gender inequality has great potential to improve and promote sustainable agricultural development and food security. As noted by FAO (2011), giving women equal access to agricultural productive resources could increase production by 20 to 30 per cent on women's farms in developing countries. This could raise total agricultural production in developing countries by 2.5 to 4 per cent, which could in turn reduce the number of hungry people in the world by 12 to 17 per cent, or 100 to 150 million people. Hence enhancing women's access and control over land and other agricultural productive resources are crucial to the successful development of any program or policy ultimately concerned with sustainable agricultural development and food security.

## Conclusion

As I have discussed in this chapter, despite national and international commitments to promoting gender equality, inequalities in agricultural development and food security systems prevail. Women continue to be marginalized and regarded as small-scale home producers or assistants on the farm, and not as farmers and economic agents in their own right (FAO 2011). What seems to be lacking is the reinforcement of existing gender equality commitments, which require strong and sustained good governance systems, gender responsive policies and institutions, sufficient resources, and societal and political will. Failure to translate gender equality commitments into action is a significant hindrance for sustainable agricultural development and food security. I have put forth the argument, based on several decades of empirical research, that men and women have equally important roles to play in advancing sustainable agricultural development and food security. In spite of this well-supported claim, there remain tendencies to marginalize women and exclude them from contributing effectively in the growth of their nations, communities, and households. Factors that are well known to influence women's marginalization include sociocultural norms and traditions, unequal positions in society, and discriminatory laws. Evidence strongly suggests that closing the gender gap in agricultural development has the potential to lead to several positive development outcomes, including better management of natural resources, improved household food security and nutritional well-being, and more inclusive community development. Recommendations, frameworks, and strategies to advance gender equality in sustainable agricultural development and food security have been numerous and well-documented. Mainstreaming gender into the agricultural sector remains a key strategy for promoting gender equality. In their *Closing the Gender Gap* report, the FAO (2011) highlights recommendations focused on three key areas:

1   Eliminating discrimination against women in access to agricultural resources, education, extension and financial services, and labour markets. A major requirement for achieving this goal is legal reform in all national legislation that perpetuates gender biases. For example, statutory laws that prohibit women from owning land and accessing natural resources need to be changed.
2   Investing in labour-saving and productivity-enhancing technologies and infrastructure to free women's time for productive farming activities. For instance, the construction of water

sources such as bore holes in villages can significantly reduce the time women and girls spend on fetching water. The time saved on these activities can be used for more productive farming activities.

3    Facilitating the participation of women in flexible, efficient, and fair rural labour markets.

Given that agriculture is an important source of self- and wage-employment, particularly for women, promoting equitable and productive employment in agriculture is critical. As highlighted by FAO (2011), this would mean, among other things, generating better jobs that benefit men and women equally; closing the gender gap in labour standards by raising awareness of workers' rights among governments, employers', and workers' organizations, as well as individual women and men workers; and promoting rural institutions that represent – accurately and equally – women's and men's interests.

There is no need to reinvent the wheel but to recommend and challenge state leaders and all other stakeholders to honour their commitments to gender equality so as to ensure sustainable agricultural development and food security. There is a need, however, to review and reflect on previous commitments so as to better strategize on action plans to ensure concrete results are achieved. Unless commitments to gender equality are translated into action, and supported by effective monitoring and evaluation, they are likely to remain words on paper.

## Note

1    According to the UN, gender mainstreaming is 'a process of assessing the implications for women and men of any planned action, including legislation, policies or programmes, in all areas and at all levels. It is a strategy for making women's as well as men's concerns and experiences an integral dimension of the design, implementation, monitoring and evaluation of policies and programmes in all political, economic and societal spheres so that women and men benefit equally and inequality is not perpetuated. The ultimate goal is to achieve gender equality' (UN 2002:1).

## References

Agarwal, B. (2002) 'Gender inequality, cooperation and environmental sustainability', *SFI Working Paper*. Santa Fe, New Mexico: Santa Fe Institute.

Agarwal, B. (2010) *Gender and Green Governance: The Political Economy: The Political Economy of Women's Presence Within and Beyond Community Forestry*. Oxford and New Delhi: Oxford University Press.

Agarwal, B. (2011) 'Food crises and gender inequality', *Working Paper*, No 107. New York: United Nations Department of Economic and Social Affairs.

Agarwal, B. (2012) 'Food security, productivity, and gender inequality', *IEG Working Paper*, No. 320. New Delhi: Institute of Economic Growth.

Agarwal, B. (2016) *Gender Challenges*. Oxford and New Delhi: Oxford University Press.

Amanor, K. S. (2012) *Land Governance in Africa: How Historical Context Has Shaped Key Contemporary Issues Relating to Policy on Land*. Framing the Debate Series, 1. Rome: International Land Coalition.

Boserup, E. (1970) *Women's Role in Economic Development*. New York: St. Martin's Press.

Buckingham-Hatfield, S. (2002) 'Gender equality: A prerequisite for sustainable development', *Geography* 87(3): 227–233.

Burg, M. van der. and Endeveld, M. (eds) (1994) Women on family farms. Gender research – gender research, EU policies and new perspectives. Wageningen, the Netherlands: Circle for Rural European Studies.

Busto, M., Mercado, N. G. P., Rengam, S. V., Zita, D., Castillo, M., Acosta, K., Lopez, T. K. and Covero, L. (2015) *Our Stories, One Journey: Empowering Rural Women in Asia on Food Sovereignty*. Penang, Malaysia: Pesticide Action Network Asia and the Pacific.

Buvinic, M. and Mehra, R. (1990) *Women in Agriculture: What Development Can Do*. Washington, DC: International Center for Research on Women.

Chant, S. and Gutmann, M. (2000) *Mainstreaming Men Into Gender and Development: Debates, Reflections, and Experiences*. Oxford: Oxfam Great Britain.

Chiweshe, M. K. (2015) 'Women and the emergence of grassroots institutions on post-fast track farms in Zimbabwe', *Journal of Gender, Agriculture and Food Security* 1(1): 40–53.

Conforti, P. (2011) *Looking Ahead in World Food and Agriculture*. Rome: FAO.

Deccan Development Society (2015) *Tales of Ecological Heroism*. Online. Available at: http://ddsindia.com/publications.htm (accessed 1 March 2016).

Doss, C. R. (2006) 'The effects of intra-household property ownership on expenditure patterns in Ghana', *Journal of African Economy* 15(1): 149–180.

Doss, C. R. (2011) *The Gender Asset and Wealth Gaps: Evidence From Ecuador, Ghana, and Karnataka*. Bangalore: Indian Institute of Management.

Duffy, V. (2006) 'Gender and development', in Regan, C. and Borg, B. (eds) *80:20 Development in an Unequal World*. 80:20 Educating and Acting for a Better World, Ireland, pages 159–174. Online. Available at: http://www.developmenteducation.ie/teachers-and-educators/transition-year/extra-resources/Resources/8020-additional-resources/10.PDF (accessed 21st July 2016).

FAO (2003) Trade Reforms and Food Security: Conceptualizing the Linkages. Rome: FAO.

FAO (2005) *Gender and Farming Systems: Lessons From Nicaragua*. Rome: FAO.

FAO (2006) *The Double Burden of Malnutrition: Case Studies From Six Developing Countries*. FAO Food and Nutrition Paper 84, Rome: FAO.

FAO (2009) *The State of Food Insecurity in the World*. Rome: FAO.

FAO (2011) *The State of Food and Agriculture 2010–2011: Women in Agriculture – Closing the Gender Gap for Development*. Rome: FAO.

FAO (2014) *The State of Food and Agriculture Report 2014*. Online. Available at: http://www.fao.org/3/a-i4040e.pdf (accessed 28th February 2016).

FAO, IFAD and ILO (2010) *Gender Dimensions of Agricultural and Rural Employment: Differentiated Pathways Out of Poverty (Status, Trends and Gaps)*. Rome: FAO.

Francis, C. and Youngberg, G. (1990) 'Sustainable agriculture: An overview', in Francis, C., Flora, C. B. and King, L. D. (eds) *Sustainable Agriculture in Temperate Zones*. New York: Wiley, 1–12.

Friedmann, H. (1986) 'Family enterprises in agriculture: Structural limits and political possibilities', in Cox, G., Lowe, P. and Winter, M. (eds) *Agriculture, People and Policies*. London: Allen and Unwin, 41–60.

García. Z. (2006) 'Agriculture, trade negotiations and gender', Food and Agriculture Organization (FAO). Online. Available at: ftp://ftp.fao.org/docrep/fao/009/a0493e/a0493e.pdf (accessed 20 February 2016).

Gilbert, R. A., Sakala, W. D. and Benson, T. D. (2013) 'Gender analysis of a nationwide cropping system trial survey in Malawi', International Food Policy Research Institute (IFPRI), 2015 Global Hunger Index. Online. Available at: www.ifpri.org/publication/2015-global-hunger-index-armed-conflict-and-challenge-hunger (accessed 28 February 2016).

Holden.S. T., Deininger, K. and Ghebru, H. (2011) 'Tenure insecurity, gender, low-cost land certification and land rental market participation in Ethiopia', *The Journal of Development Studies* 47(1): 31–47.

IFAD (2011) 'Rural poverty report 2011', International Fund for Agricultural Development (IFAD). Online. Available at: https://www.ifad.org/documents/10180/c47f2607-3fb9-4736-8e6a-a7ccf3dc7c5b (accessed 20 February 2016).

International Food Policy Research Institute (IFPRI) (2015) *2015 Global Hunger Index*. Online. Available at: https://www.ifpri.org/publication/2015-global-hunger-index-armed-conflict-and-challenge-hunger (accessed 28 February 2016).

Jackson, W. (1978) 'Toward a sustainable agriculture', *Not Man Apart*. Mid-November/December, 4–6.

Jacoby, H. (1992) 'Productivity of men and women and the sexual division of labour in peasant agriculture of the Peruvian Sierra', *Journal of Development Economics* 37: 265–287.

Jonsson-Latham, G. (2007) *A Study on Gender Equality as a Prerequisite for Sustainable Development*. Stockholm: Environment Advisory Council.

Kilic, T., Lopez, P. A. and Goldstein, M. (2014) Caught in a productivity trap: A distributional perspective on gender differences in Malawian agriculture. World Development. Online. Available at: http://dx.doi.org/10.1016/j.worlddev.2014.06.017 (accessed 28th February 2016).

Kumbamu, A. (2011) 'How does localized social economy sustain in a globalizing world?', Paper presented at the UNRISD conference Green Economy and Sustainable Development: Bringing Back the Social Dimension, 10–11 October 2011, Geneva. UNRISD. Online. Available at: www.unrisd.org/80256B42004CCC77/(httpInfoFiles)/A3104491EF62144DC12579210034D7A4/$file/4–3%20Kumbamu.pdf (accessed 28 February 2016).

Lincoln, K. (1997) 'To bear any burden: Asia's women pay a disproportionately high price for the region's economic boom', *Far Eastern Economic Review* 158: 42–43.

Lobell, D. B. and Field, C. B. (2011) 'California perennial crops in a changing climate', *Climatic Change* 109(1 suppl): S317–S333.

Majurin. E. (2012) How women fare in East African cooperatives: The case of Kenya, Tanzania and Uganda International Labour Organization (ILO). Online. Available at: http://www.ilo.org/public/english/employment/ent/coop/africa/download/woman_eastafrica.pdf (accessed 18 February 2016).

Mare, Y. and Girmay, G. (2015) 'Rural women's access to productive resources: Implications for poverty reduction—The case of Gamo Gofa Zone, Southern Nations, Nationalities, and Peoples' Region', *African Journal of Agricultural Research* 11(4): 221–227.

Mason, K. O. and Carlsson, H. M. (2004) *The Impact of Gender Equality in Land Rights on Development.* Washington, DC: World Bank.

Milgroom, J., Laats, H., Bruil, J., Van Walsum, E., Berg van den, L. and Peterson, D. (eds) (2015) *Farming Matters: Women Forging Change With Agroecology.* Wageningen, the Netherlands: ILEIA Centre for Learning on Sustainable Agriculture.

Moyoyetta, L. (2004) 'Women, gender and development', *Women for Change, Zambia and 80:20. Educating and Acting for a Better World, Ireland.* Online. Available at: www.developmenteducation.ie/media/documents/women_gender_dev.pdf (accessed 1 August 2016).

Njuki, J. and Sanginga, P. C. (eds) (2013) 'Gender and ownership of livestock assets', in Njuki, J. and Sanginga, P. C. (eds) *Women, Livestock Ownership and Markets: Bridging the Gender Gap in Eastern and Southern Africa.* International Livestock Research Institute and the International Development Research Centre. New York: Routledge, 21–38.

Oakley, A. (1972) *Sex, Gender and Society.* London: Temple Smith.

OECD (2010) *Investing in Women and Girls: The Breakthrough Strategy for Achieving all the MDGs.* Online. Available at: www.oecd.org/dataoecd/45/55/45704694.pdf (accessed 1 August 2016).

Oluka, J., Owoyesigire, B., Esenu, B. and Ssewannyana, E. (2005) 'Small stock and women in livestock production in the Teso Farming System region of Uganda', *Small Stock in Development.* National Agricultural Research Organisation.

Ongley. E. D (1996) 'Control of water pollution from agriculture', *FAO Irrigation and Drainage Paper 55.* Rome: FAO.

Parpart, J. L., Connelly, M. P. and Barriteau, V. E. (2000) *Theoretical Perspectives on Gender and Development.* Ottawa, Canada: International Development Research Centre.

Peterman, A., Behrman, J. A. and Quisumbing, A. R. (2014) 'A review of empirical evidence on gender differences in nonland agricultural inputs, technology, and services in developing countries', *IFPRI Discussion Paper 00975.*

Peterman, A., Quisumbing, A., Behrman, J. and Nkonya, E. (2011) 'Understanding the complexities surrounding gender differences in agricultural productivity in Nigeria and Uganda', *Journal of Development Studies* 47(10): 1482–1509.

Ponge, A. (2013) 'Gender mainstreaming and women's empowerment in political party processes in Kenya: Implementing the new constitution in earnest', *International Journal of Humanities and Social Science* 3(3): 63–71. Online. Available at: www.ijhssnet.com/journals/Vol_3_No_3_February_2013/6.pdf (accessed 28 July 2016).

Prabu, M. J. (2015) 'Banking on millet magic', *The Hindu*, India. Online. Available at: www.thehindu.com/todays-paper/tp-in-school/banking-on-millet-magic/article7004592.ece (accessed 1 March 2016).

Quisumbing, A. R. and Pandolfelli, L. (2010) 'Promising approaches to address the needs of poor female farmers: Resources, constraints, and interventions', *World Development* 38(4): 581–592.

Ragassa, C. (2014) 'Improving gender responsiveness of agricultural extension', in Quisumbing, A., Meinzen-Dick, R., Raney, T., Croppenstedt, A., Behrman, J. and Peterman, A. (eds) *Gender in Agriculture and Food Security: Closing the Knowledge Gap.* Dordrecht, the Netherlands: Springer and FAO, 411–430.

Rathgeber, E. M. (1989) 'WID, WAD, GAD: Trends in research and practice', *International Development Research Centre,* Ottawa, Canada. Online. Available at: https://idl-bnc.idrc.ca/dspace/bitstream/10625/5225/1/34345.pdf (accessed 18 July 2016).

Reimer, B. (1986) 'Women as farm labor', *Rural Sociology* 51(2): 143–155.

Rosen, S., Meade, B., Fuglie, K. and Rada, N. (2014) *International Food Security Assessment, 2014–24.* Economic Research Service, United States Department of Agriculture.

Rugadya, M. (2010) *Women's Land Rights in Uganda: Status of Implementation of Policy and Law on Women's Land Rights for ECA, ACGS Addis Ababa.* Maastricht University.

Sachs, C. E. (1983) *The Invisible Farmers*. Totowa, NJ: Rowan and Allanheld.

Satheesh, P. V. and Pimbert, M. (1999) *Affirming Life and Diversity: Rural Images and Voices on Food Sovereignty in South India*. London: International Institute for Environment and Development (IIED).

Shortall, S. (1992) 'Power analysis and farm wives: An empirical study of the power relationships affecting women on Irish farms, *Sociologia Ruralis* 32(4): 431–452.

Silva, L. and Nansen, K. (eds) (2011) *Women and Food Sovereignty: Voices of Rural Women of the South*. Amsterdam, the Netherlands: Friends of the Earth International.

Skoufias, E., Rabassa M., Olivieri S. and Brahmbhatt, M. (2011) 'The poverty impacts of climate change', *The World Bank Economic Premise No 51*.

SOFA Team (2011) *Gender Differences in Assets*. Rome: FAO.

Stevens, C. (2010) 'Are women the key to sustainable development?', *Boston University Frederick Pardee Center for the Study of the Longer-Range Future*. Online. Available at: www.bu.edu/pardee/files/2010/04/UNsd-kp003fsingle.pdf (accessed 20 July 2016).

Tandon, N. and Wegerif, M. (2013) *Promises, Power and Poverty: Corporate Land Deals and Rural Women in Africa*. Oxford, UK: OXFAM International.

Teklewold, H., Kassie, M. and Shiferaw, B. (2013) 'Adoption of multiple sustainable agricultural practices in rural Ethiopia', *Journal of Agricultural Economics* 64(3): 597–623.

United Nations (1945) Charter of the United Nations, 1 UNTS XVI. Online. Available at: http://www.refworld.org/docid/3ae6b3930.html (accessed 28 February 2017).

United Nations (2002) *Gender Mainstreaming: An Overview*. Office of the Special Adviser on Gender Issues Department of Economic and Social Affairs. New York, New York, USA.

United Nations (2012) 'The empowerment of rural women and their role in poverty and hunger eradication, development and current challenges', *Report of the Secretary-General*. Online. Available at: www.un.org/womenwatch/daw/csw/csw56/documentation.htm (accessed 28 February 2016).

United Nations Department of Economic and Social Affairs (2010) *Achieving Gender Equality, Women's Empowerment and Strengthening Development Cooperation*. New York: United Nations. Online. Available at: www.un.org/en/ecosoc/docs/pdfs/10–50143_(e)_(desa)dialogues_ecosoc_achieving_gender_equality_women_empowerment.pdf (accessed 28 July 2016).

United Nations Development Programme (UNDP) (1993) *Human Development Report*. New York: Oxford University Press.

United Nations Development Programme (UNDP) (1995) *Human Development Report*. New York: Oxford University Press.

United Nations Development Programme (UNDP) (2011) *Human Development Report: Sustainability and Equity: A Better Future for All*. Online. Available at: http://hdr.undp.org/en/reports/global/hdr2011/ (accessed 28 July 2016).

UN Women (2014) *World Survey on the Role of Women in Development 2014: Gender Equality and Sustainable Development*. Online. Available at: www.unwomen.org/en/digital-library/publications/2014/10/world-survey-2014 (accessed 20 July 2016).

Vernooy, R. (2015) 'Seeds of adaptation: Climate change, crop diversification and the role of women farmers', *Center for International Forestry Research* (CIFOR), Bogor, Indonesia. Online. Available at: www.cifor.org/publications/pdf_files/Brief/5896-GenderClimateBrief.pdf (accessed 5 March 2016).

Walsum, van E. (2015) 'Women showing the way with agroecology', in Milgroom, J., Laats, H., Bruil, J., Van Walsum, E., Berg van den, L., and Peterson, D. (eds) *Farming Matters: Women Forging Change With Agroecology* 31(4): 6–9, ILEIA Centre for Learning on Sustainable Agriculture.

Whatmore, S. (1990) *Farming Women: Gender, Work and Family Enterprise*. London: Macmillan.

Whatmore, S., Marsden, T. and Lowe, P. (eds) (1994) *Gender and Rurality*. London: David Fulton.

World Bank (2015) 'The cost of the gender gap in agricultural productivity in Malawi, Tanzania, and Uganda', *World Bank Group*, Washington, DC. Online. Available at: http://documents.worldbank.org/curated/en/2015/10/25155021/cost-gender-gap-agricultural-productivity-malawi-tanzania-uganda (accessed 10 March 2016).

# 25

# WHOSE DEBT FOR WHOSE NATURE?

## Gender and nature in neoliberalism's war against subsistence

*Ana Isla*

### Introduction

Since the official recognition of the planetary crisis, which was launched at the Rio Earth Summit in 1992, the concept of sustainable development (SD) has been a driving force behind global environmental and development policy. A key concept in SD is 'natural capital', which is used to refer to the goods and services that the planet's stock of water, land, air, and renewable and non-renewable resources provides (Fenech et al. 1999). As a result of nature being defined as natural capital in the SD discourse, all areas of the earth have been opened up to global intervention. The past two decades have seen a steady process of monetizing nature, where most parts of the ecosystem have been turned into goods and services to be traded on financial markets. At the same time, the UN, its agencies, and various non-governmental organizations (NGOs) present economic growth as the solution to poverty and inequality across the globe. The twin goals of ecological sustainability and poverty reduction are present in the 'green economy', a concept that framed the 2012 Earth Summit (Rio+20). It is defined by the United Nations Environment Programme (UNEP) as a vision for 'improved human well-being and social equity, while significantly reducing environmental risks and ecological scarcities' (UNEP n.d.).

In this chapter, I draw on ecofeminist theory to challenge claims that SD and the green economy will create social and gender equality, reduce poverty, confront ecological destruction, and combat climate change. In the first part, I present ecofeminist critiques of capitalism and SD that offer valuable insights into the processes of enclosure and appropriation on which capitalism is based and which have led to the exploitation of nature and women. I then apply these insights to analyze a case study of the debt-for-nature exchanges between Canada and Costa Rica that were delivered from 1995 to 1999 by two environmental non-governmental organizations (ENGOs) operating in the Arenal-Tilaran Conservation Area (ACA-Tilaran). I document 'a war against subsistence', by examining the triple crisis brought about by the debt-for-nature exchanges: crises with extremely negative effects on the lives of women and children, on peasants and Indigenous peoples, and on nature itself. I conclude by naming 'green capitalism' as another phase of capital accumulation and arguing that its real war is not against poverty and unsustainability but against subsistence.

## Ecofeminist critiques of capitalism and sustainable development

An important theme for gender and environment scholars is the connection between the treatment of human and non-human lives under capitalism. They argue that the illusion that economic growth is positive and benign has been sustained because the costs have been borne primarily by that which has been *devalued and feminized*: Indigenous and racialized peoples, peasants, women, children, the so-called underdeveloped world, and nature. Gender analysis plays a central role in this argument by deconstructing the meanings, practices, and relations of femininity and masculinity that people create as they go about their daily lives in different settings. It examines how gender differences are implicated in systems of exploitation. Ecofeminist theorists have contributed particularly valuable theoretical insights into the complex interrelationships between the oppression of women and the domination of nature under patriarchal capitalism.

Ecofeminist scholars working in the field of political economy, political ecology, development, and globalization studies are critical of SD politics that operate within the framework of capitalist economic growth (see Mellor's chapter in this handbook). The evolution of the gender and environment field in general, and ecofeminism in particular, has been driven in large part by theoretical analyses of, and political stands against, mainstream 'green' agendas that fail to address the root causes of poverty, violence, and ecological destruction, thereby sustaining the status quo. Attempts to make capitalism green are exposed as a form of green-washing. My analysis in this chapter is informed by the work of scholars who have developed radical critiques of capitalism and SD, namely Silvia Federici, Maria Mies, and Vandana Shiva. These theorists argue that programs associated with SD have tended to result in enclosure of the commons and the appropriation of unpaid, feminized labour, which have put the practices and knowledge of everyday subsistence under threat.

The concept of 'the commons', meaning simply resources held in common, has always been central to the study of political economy and has been important to environmental theorizing since the 1970s (cf. Ostrom 1990). For some, the privatization of once-commonly held resources – land, water, fuel – is the root cause of ecological ruin. The enclosure movement began in England in the sixteenth century and entailed both the closing off of common land and the appropriation of the common wealth of workers through the elimination of customary right. From a Marxist perspective, this process paved the way from feudalism to capitalism; it was the 'original' or primitive form of accumulation whereby some people were able to amass profit and others had to sell their labour power. The Marxist-feminist philosopher Silvia Federici (2004) argues, contra Marx, that that primitive accumulation was not just a precondition for, but is an essential and enduring quality of capitalism. In order to sustain itself, capitalism requires a constant supply of expropriated capital. In *Caliban and the Witch: Women, the Body and Primitive Accumulation* (2004), she observes that the privatization of the commons happened in the same historical period as the European witch trials that lead to the devaluation of women. With the enclosure of the commons, she argues, the social aspects of a community and its autonomy were eliminated. In time this produced a new gendered division of labour, in which women's position in society as providers and producers was redefined in relation to men, to become wives, daughters, mothers, and widows, all of whom 'hid their status as workers, while giving men free access to [their] bodies, their labour, and the bodies and labour of their children' (Federici 2004:97). Federici draws a long historical line from the witch trials and enclosure movement of the sixteenth century to modern day prostitution and the monetization of nature (from trees to genes) in her theorizing of the systematic subjugation and appropriation of women and nature, bodies and labour, under capitalism.

Ecofeminist political economists are critical of the Eurocentric assumption that unpaid work has no value. Like Federici, the feminist sociologist Maria Mies locates the origins of women's oppression in the co-evolving and interconnected systems of capitalism, patriarchy, and colonialism. In *Patriarchy and Accumulation on a World Scale* (1986), she argues that when women, peasants, and Indigenous people are described as 'closer to nature', they are made exploitable – their bodies and labour power are free for the taking. Mies uses the term 'housewifization' to capture the process whereby hitherto productive (life sustaining) work is captured, confined, devalued, and put to use in support of 'real' (monetized) production, in effect as a free subsidy. The division of labour into reproductive (subsistence, supplemental, housewife) labour and productive (income-earning, breadwinning) labour is necessary for capitalism to function. Mies presents a detailed case for understanding this division as existing on a world scale via colonialism, in much the same way that it exists in families and households. The labour and bodies of racialized peasants in the Global South are appropriated and objectified by white industrialists by means of violence and forced dependency. She writes:

> Violence against women and extracting women's labour through coercive labour relations are . . . part and parcel of capitalism. They are necessary for the capitalist accumulation process and not peripheral to it. In other words, capitalism has to use, to strengthen, or even to invent, patriarchal men-women relations if it wants to maintain its accumulation model. If all women in the world had become 'free' wage earners, 'free' subjects, the extraction of surplus would, to say the lease, be severely hampered. That is what women as housewives, workers, peasants, prostitutes, from Third World and First World countries, have in common.
>
> *(Mies 1986:170–171)*

In response to their criticisms of capitalist patriarchy, some ecofeminist scholars see subsistence economies as an alternative model of social, economic, gender, and environmental justice. For example, Mies and Shiva (1993) and Bennholdt-Thomsen and Mies (1999) argue for what they call 'the subsistence perspective', which is based on production that includes all work expended in the creation and maintenance of immediate life and which has no other purpose: 'subsistence production . . . stands in contrast to commodity and surplus value production for profit' (1999:20). Bennholdt-Thomsen and Mies present it as a form of resistance to the effects of global capitalism and colonialism by acknowledging that 'life comes from women and food comes from the land' (1999:80). Subsistence producers all over the world – the majority of whom are women and/or feminized – should be seen as experts who can lead the way to recovering autonomous ways of living, starting from territorial autonomy, food security in small farms, and energy efficiency.

The ecofeminist activist-academic Vandana Shiva uncovers an important Western cultural bias in the myth of the subsistence livelihood as akin to living in poverty. In *Staying Alive: Women, Ecology and Development* she argues that 'subsistence economies, which satisfy basic needs through self-provisioning are not poor in the sense of being deprived' (1989:10). After the Second World War these economies could be universally labelled as 'poor' because the gross national product (GNP) – which counts only goods and services that pass through the market – was introduced as the international standard to measure a nation's wealth (Waring 1988). Gauging value and wealth by money alone leaves the wealth of nature and the everyday skills and production of women, peasants, and Indigenous peoples invisible under the cost-benefit theory. It opens the door for the imposition of policies designed to 'develop' the hitherto underdeveloped, to help the poor sell, work, and spend their way out of poverty. Shiva calls this process 'maldevelopment', as it 'allows the violation of the integrity of organic, interconnected, and interdependent systems, that sets in motion a process of exploitation, inequality, injustice and violence' (1989:6–7).

Shiva has long been a critic of the efforts of global institutions such as the UN and the World Bank to impose environmental policies and plans on people of the Global South. She argues that when problems like ozone depletion and biodiversity loss are defined as 'global crises' not only are the power relations created by the international division of labour masked, but 'the North gains a new political space in which to control the South. Claims about the "global" thus create a moral base for green imperialism' (Shiva 1994:198). The sustainable development of the 1990s and the neoliberal 'green economy' of the 2010s, with their shared vision of making economic growth compatible with ecological integrity and human dignity, are arguably no different. The local needs, practices, and knowledge that enable subsistence livelihoods are reduced in value and/or commoditized, along with the natural environments on which they depend. It is for this reason that projects and policies that have been imposed by the World Bank and the UN under the banner of SD are especially ripe for critical ecofeminist analyses.

## Neoliberalism's war against subsistence: the case of Costa Rica

At the 1992 Rio Earth Summit, participating governments negotiated a plan of action called *Agenda 21*, which officially linked development and environment in the concept of SD. Neo-liberal economists of the World Bank articulated, under the concept of SD, a set of prescriptions designed to manage the so-called natural capital on which markets and the entire global economic system depends. These prescriptions demonstrate the highly politicized nature of the environment, where economic policy and ecological policy are intertwined. Nature must be protected to ensure the steady supply of capital.

Since its inception, SD has been equated with economic growth that would rescue poor countries from their poverty, even in the most remote areas of the world (Pearce and Warford 1993). In this frame, the ecosystem must be embedded in the economic system through the price system. In other words, the environment requires a fully monetized world in order to be protected. This means that ecological commons, such as the atmosphere, oceans and seas, land, forest, mountains, biological diversity, ecosystems, freshwater, and so on, need to be priced as natural capital (Hamilton 2001), thus legitimizing the privatization of the ecological commons. The idea of SD is that there must be an exchange process between those with money to buy and those with natural capital to sell (Hamilton 2001). According to the World Bank, 'there is a considerable willingness worldwide to pay to preserve nature and the critical functions that ecosystems provide' (1997:20). This point of view assumes that the well-being of human agents is of primary importance for economics, in terms of maximizing the satisfaction of human wants.

The prescriptions formulated by the World Bank were first applied in Costa Rica with the following results. The 1981 debt crisis brought the International Monetary Fund (IMF) and the World Bank, as well as the Reagan Administration, to Costa Rica's doorstep (Sojo 1992). During the debt crisis, the Costa Rican government agreed to move away from a publically administered economy and to embark on a process of privatization that depended on large capital investments. This process created a policy of land expropriation that accelerated the concentration of land into large commercial farms and was responsible for changes in rural activities from subsistence agriculture to export-oriented agriculture and service work (Costa Rica, Ministerio de Economía, Industria y Comercio 1998).

The debt was also used as a reason by the United States to impose USAID as a direct agent to take control of Costa Rica's economy (Petch 1988). During USAID's tenure, plans to implement the World Bank's policies were assembled by the World Wildlife Fund United States (WWF-US) at the Estrategia de Conservación para el Desarrollo Sostenible (ECODES) conference in 1988. While discussing Costa Rica's sustainable development programs, the head of the WWF-US at the time, biologist Christopher Vaughan, emphasized the role of population growth and peasant communities in hastening environmental degradation (Quesada 1990). He argued that local biodiversity would be seriously threatened if the ecological and social landscapes were not transformed into conservation areas. Participants of ECODES recognized that the pursuit of development as economic growth, capital accumulation, and technology was the cause of the debt crisis, poverty, dispossession, and deforestation in Costa Rica. Nevertheless, economic growth, capital accumulation, and technology based on the country's ecology were offered as a cure by the USAID and WWF-US in the form of sustainable development (Quesada 1990). SD, by using debt-for-nature exchange, was supposed to bring wealth, progress, social achievements, and environmental protection standards, while also enabling debt repayments. At ECODES the ideology was promoted that debt-for-nature exchange is a conservation instrument to develop a model of environmental management in conservation areas that can be applied to all indebted countries in the world.

*Agenda 21* established that SD was a government responsibility. Costa Rica received an award for being an example of SD in the periphery. The role of Costa Rica has been to establish in the indebted world the concept of conservation areas using debt-for-nature swaps as a way to connect the new nature and the new labour to the international power relations of creditors. In effect, Costa Rica became the first green neoliberal project. A megaproject – the Sistema Nacional de Areas de Conservación or SINAC (the National System of Conservation Areas) – was implemented to manage the country. SINAC divided the country into eleven conservation areas, and created a Ministerio de Ambiente y Energia – MINAE (Ministry of Environment and Energy). One of these areas is the Arenal Conservation Area (ACA-Tilaran), which later changed into Arenal-Tempisque Conservation Area. ACA-Tilaran is a telling case that highlights several key aspects of neoliberalism's greenwashing of its war on subsistence, or what I call 'greening'.

## The Canada-Costa Rica debt-for-nature exchange

From the late 1980s, many debt-for-nature exchange agreements were made between national governments as a means of turning local natural landscapes in the indebted periphery into globally significant conservation areas (Sheikh 2007, 2010). My Canada-Costa Rica case study is useful for illustrating how debt-for-nature exchanges are used as a mechanism for reducing poverty and environmental degradation in the name of SD. The analysis in this section uncovers the logic behind the structural changes to land governance and the gendered class relations that create the conditions, not for greater sustainability and justice, but for increased capital accumulation.

The Canada-Costa Rica debt-for-nature exchange was a bilateral initiative that implemented so-called sustainable development programs in ACA-Tilaran. As part of international rules created by the creditors, the Canadian and Costa Rican governments were not allowed to receive debt titles directly. Instead, they donated to the World Wild Life Fund Canada (WWF-C) and Instituto Nacional de Biodiversidad (INBio), which became the government's creditors (Government of Canada and Government of Costa Rica 1995). In ACA-Tilaran the Ministerio de Recursos Naturales, Energia y Minas (MIRENEM), the Canadian International Development Agency (CIDA), and the WWF-C developed the Plan General de Uso de la Tierra (the Land Plan; Costa Rica. Ministerio de Recursos Naturales, Energía y Minas. Area de Conservación Arenal 1993). The Land Plan disassembled the natural commons and enclosed 250,000 hectares of land on which people depended for their livelihood.

In the Canada-Costa Rica debt-for-nature exchange there are several types of enclosures involved. I will discuss three types of enclosure before explaining how these have resulted in a war against nature, peasants and Indigenous people, and women and children in Costa Rica.

First, the debt-for nature swap has resulted in the enclosure of Costa Rica's biodiversity for use in biotechnological production. The 1992 Convention on Biological Diversity gave access to genetic resources to NGOs and corporations. The convention established rules and regulations to benefit the 'whole humanity', a euphemism for technologically advanced countries being able to expropriate the biochemical components from biodiversity through biotechnology. Biotechnology is the use of biological processes in industrial production. As a result of the patent system, the laboratories of large multinational seed companies and genetic banks are allowed to accumulate and preserve biodiversity, and to enjoy a monopoly over its commercial exploitation. In Costa Rica, since 1998 the Biodiversity Law (Number 7788, Article 6) has been the judicial instrument for the application of the Biological Diversity Covenant. Signed in 1992 and ratified in 1994, it determined that biochemical and genetic properties of wildlife and domestic biodiversity are in the public domain. Therefore the government authorizes exploration, investigation, and bioprospecting, which is the process of the 'discovery' and exploitation of biodiversity elements, such as genes. Since then, access to wildlife species has been regulated by licenses, permits and auctions, and the government has created the National Commission for the Management of Biodiversity to develop and coordinate policies on biodiversity.

In 2004 intellectual property rights were expanded by the implementation of the Free Trade Agreement (FTA) between the United States and Costa Rica. In the FTA bioprospecting permits are defined as 'investment accords' in order to conclude that investment ought to be protected by intellectual property rights, that is, the privatization and monopolization of the results (Rodriguez 1995). This means that the resources and knowledge of peasants and Indigenous people, which generated sustenance and survival, were brought into global trade. Bioprospecting, genetic engineering, and other approaches that classify and research biodiversity for commercial ends involve the search for new and potentially profitable biological samples by corporations, NGOs, and aid organizations. These organizations look for new uses for biodiversity and their products, monopolize the information gathered, and create barriers that limit the use of biodiversity by local communities.

Second, there has been a process of enclosing Costa Rica's rainforests to use as carbon sinks. Governments first agreed to tackle climate change at the 1992 Rio Earth Summit. Scientific theories have highlighted the fact that forest vegetation absorbs and stores carbon that might otherwise trap heat in the atmosphere, driving up temperatures and speeding up climate change (Lohmann 2005). At the Climate Change Convention held in Kyoto in 1997, industrial countries proposed the creation of mechanisms to reduce greenhouse gas emissions. Absorbing carbon dioxide ($CO_2$) from the overflowing waste of industrial countries to reduce the greenhouse effect has become part of the SD agenda. The Kyoto Protocol set a non-binding goal of stabilizing emissions at 1990 levels by the year 2000. Among the six kinds of targeted gases is $CO_2$, which is discharged disproportionately by the industrial world. However, reducing emissions implies high costs for industries. So the major emitting corporations, with the backing of their governments, proposed a self-interested solution: the creation of a global market in carbon dioxide, focused on the forests of indebted countries.

Since Kyoto, rainforests have been valued economically in terms of the amount of carbon they sequester. As carbon emissions became subject to trading on the open market, the rainforest in Costa Rica became valued as a carbon sink. Costa Rica was the first country to take part in the Joint Implementation Program (JIP) organized by the UN (UNFCCC 2005). JIP allows an industrialized country to earn emission reduction credits by buying them from another country. Costa Rica was one of the first countries to voluntarily sell carbon credits to the industrial world to achieve emission reductions. Since then numerous payments for ecosystem services, such as Reduction of Emissions from Deforestation and Forest (REDD+) and the European Emissions Trading Systems (ETS) emissions certificates, have been developed (see Tovar-Restrepo in this handbook for a discussion of REDD+).

Third, the Canada-Costa Rica debt-for-nature exchange has led to the enclosure of wild spaces for a new industry: ecotourism. New areas of intervention for ENGOs became 'wild areas', which they propose to 'sell' to mostly Northern consumers for recreation. Ecotourism is promoted as an activity that contributes toward economic growth and generates income for local communities while purportedly protecting the environment. It is endorsed as an environmentally friendly activity that promotes visits to relatively undisturbed natural areas to study, admire, and appreciate the scenery, wild plants and animals, and other cultural aspects such as medicinal plants (Ulloa 1996). It offers rainforests, parks, sunshine, beaches, mountains, and Indigenous knowledge. Ecotourism promoters promise aesthetic and recreational benefits that will restore a visitor's physical, emotional and spiritual health – a world of leisure, freedom, and good taste, risk-free for those with money to spend. Simultaneously it is supposed to be politically empowering and economically advantageous for some of the most disadvantaged groups of society – namely poor peasants, rural women, and Indigenous peoples.

For national governments and international lenders, ecotourism enjoys a generally positive reputation in the nature conservation industry. By the early 1990s, under pressure from the IMF and the World Bank, indebted Costa Rica had become the most important ecotourism destination in Latin America, adopting travel and ecotourism as a strategy of SD and as an employment priority in the hope that it would bring foreign exchange and investment to repay its foreign debt.

## Sustainable development's triple crisis

From an ecofeminist perceptive, informed by the concepts and arguments presented earlier, the past practices of enclosure and appropriation and the current day practices of sustainable development have been used by patriarchal capitalism to commit violence against feminized bodies and nature (Bennholdt-Thomsen and Mies 1999; Federici 2004). If nature is violated for capitalist gain, then peasant and Indigenous women and men, who have been feminized and defined as being closer to nature than any other group, can be equally violated. In this section, I explain how the three types of enclosure that have come with the 'greening' agenda of SD in general, and debt-for-nature swaps in particular, have resulted in a war against nature, peasants, and Indigenous people, and women in Costa Rica. I thereby paint a stark picture of sustainable development's triple crisis.

### *The crisis of nature: the 'greening' of forests*

One of the worst effects of 'greening' is the crisis of nature. The Costa Rican government, through its Ministry of Environment and Energy (MINAE), appraises the ability of private forest farms to sell carbon credits. However, selling carbon credits is particularly promoted among large-scale agricultural entrepreneurs in association with international capital. Lands categorized as forest reserves, which receive payments for environmental services, are exempted from property taxes. This tax relief, under a scheme called Fiscal Forestry Incentives, subsidizes plantations owned by international corporations to promote forest species of high yield and great market value, such as gmelina (*Gmelina arborea*) and teak (*Tectona grand*), which are native to South and Southeast Asia. Mono-arboriculture has been defined in this system as 'reforestation' even though these plantations constitute artificial ecosystems, and corporations are allowed to cut the trees down after fifteen years of growth and transform them into wood for floors or paper, boxes for fruit export or furniture. With credits provided by the World Bank, the Costa Rican government enthusiastically promoted the conversion of forest ecosystems into sterile monocultures by planting homogeneous forests (Baltodano 2004; Figuerola 2005).

The monoculture of tree species has become a time bomb for biodiversity in Costa Rica. As Vandana Shiva (1989) has explained so clearly, a monoculture is not a forest because it does not reproduce itself but rather needs external inputs such as agrochemicals to grow to maturity. Moreover, the natural forest of the humid tropics is a highly productive ecosystem. For instance, a hectare of tropical forest has more than three hundred species of trees. Biodiversity means that a forest will have a great number of *leguminosae* (trees, shrubs, plants) with leaves of different sizes, which lessen the impact of rainfall and prevent erosion. Sonia Torres, a forestry engineer, explains how teak plantations have resulted in the erosion of flatlands:

> Since the planting of these foreign species, I have observed that teak has a root system that grows deep into the soil, but in the rainforest the systems of nutrient and water absorption are at the surface. In general, nutrients and water are concentrated at a depth of between 70 and 100 centimeters. As a result, teak trees are encircled by flaked soil. In addition, when it rains, the large-sized leaf accumulates great amounts of water that then pours violently onto the soil. A drop of water, at a microscopic level, forms a crater; when water falls from 15 meters or more it forms holes. Water descending on soft soil destroys the soil. The far-reaching spread of the roots and the shade produced by the leaves obstruct the vegetative growth on the lower forest layer, which could prevent the soil damage from the violent cascades.
>
> *(Sonia Torres, interview, August 2000)*

Ecologists from Costa Rica oppose the payment of environmental services for arboreal monoculture. Many are not against selling so-called environmental services in general, but instead they promote reforestation through the natural and simple regeneration of secondary forests, which conserve biodiversity and regulate hydrology (Figuerola 2003; Franceschi 2006). They argue that the conservation of forests with native wood species and associated plants and fauna should be a priority, that restoration and natural regeneration, with its own ecological complexity, is a legitimate goal, and that local peasants must be taken into consideration to avoid irreconcilable conflicts.

## The crisis of dispossession: the 'greening' of Indigenous people and peasants

The Convention on Biodiversity and the Costa Rican government have devalued the commons of Indigenous peoples' knowledge because official economic measures only count production for the market. Treating nature as a well-stocked laboratory for biotechnology ignores Indigenous peoples' collective property, culture, and knowledge, and the fact that they have been enjoying and using biological diversity for millennia. It also ignores peasants' contributions to the creation of biodiversity. Consequently, the practice of biotechnological development in 'wild' areas of the Global South (such as the Costa Rican rainforests) has become known as bioprospecting and even 'biopiracy'. Biopiracy amounts to the appropriation of the traditional knowledge and biogenetic resources of Indigenous peoples and peasants to feed the knowledge systems of global corporations (Shiva 1989). For Indigenous peoples, biopiracy brings with it the most offensive and dangerous forms of dispossession and expropriation because it touches the very core of their lives, identities, and ultimately their survival.

In 1996, to comply with the Letter of Intent for Sustainable Development, Cooperation, and Joint Implementation of the Kyoto Protocol, Costa Rican President José Maria Figueres signed a decree known as the Forestry Law (no. 7575) and put into effect article no. 2 on land expropriation. Since then, acts of dispossession and plunder are reframed as an initiative to advance conservation. The state's project of selling carbon credits meant expropriating land from small- and medium-sized landholders in most cases without compensation to the owners. In 2001, the Costa Rican Minister of the Environment Elizabeth Odio openly admitted not paying for land expropriation:

> A symbol of pride of Costa Ricans, the national parks constitute a unique model in the world, which offer innumerable benefits to society in particular and the planet in general, but they are in a critical situation due to the lack of resources to give them sustainability and cancel the debt to the former property owners whose lands were expropriated or frozen for the sake of conservation.
>
> *(Odio 2001:3)*

The Forestry Law left thousands of peasants without land and without money, because they were not paid for their expropriated land. Communities that used to live in the forest were declared enemies of the rainforest. Peasants understand that land has been expropriated by the government in exchange for crumbs of money from international markets, while they have been abandoned. The eviction of rainforest dwellers (Indigenous people and peasants) was also justified by claims that displaced people would find employment in the cities. As they leave rural areas and join the unemployed in the cities, they are ignored by the national government, because the social and economic crises created by the debt crisis are managed by the IMF stabilization and World Bank structural adjustment programs.

## The gender crisis: the 'greening' of women and children

Women and children who are also peasants and Indigenous people are affected in an especially acute way by the processes and enclosures that come with 'greening'. For peasant women, the disappearance of forests is an issue of survival, forcing many to migrate to the large cities, such as the capital city of San José, in the hope of earning an income for themselves and their dispossessed families. But Costa Rican women know that the ideology where cities purportedly offer rich opportunities for well-paid jobs and upward mobility is a myth. For instance, IndexMundi shows that for the last twenty years, the highest level of unemployment has been among female labour force between fifteen- to twenty-four years old (IndexMundi n.d).

Many other women migrate to ecotourism areas in search of jobs. In ACA-Tilaran, for example, the building of hotels, cabins, bed and breakfasts, and ecotourist lodges has meant that not only have volcanoes, mountains, rivers, and forests been marketed and sold as recreation products, but the resident community has also been turned into a branded product for sale to customers (tourists) in a variety of forms. Some male community members have become ecotourism specialists as bird-watching and adventure-tour guides, while women tend to become waitresses serving liquor or servants making beds. Some impoverished women have little option but compromise their dignity in order to earn all or part of their living as prostitutes.

Hidden beneath the veneer of ecotourism, sex tourism offers women's and children's feminized bodies as commodities that are pure, exotic, and erotic. This image of Costa Rica entangles two aspects of capitalist patriarchal economics: the domination of creditors (core countries) over debtors (the periphery), and the domination of men over women. The two are related: as Costa Rica is increasingly impoverished by foreign debt and the enclosure of the commons, the mark of international gender power relations is stamped on the bodies of Costa Rican women and children. Most of the pimps who profit from the organization of sex tourism are men from countries of the Global North, such as the United States, Canada, Spain, Germany, Italy, among others. Jacobo Schifter estimates that there are between 10,000 and 20,000 sex workers in Costa Rica, and between 25,000 and 50,000 sex tourists. He calls them 'whoremongers', meaning regular clients who visit each year. The vast majority – 80 per cent – of them are US citizens (Schifter 2007:43). Rogers (2009) reports that the United States has become Costa Rica's pimp, as crack cocaine and sex with prostitutes helps male tourists and old retirees affirm their masculinity and 'escape reality' from their dissatisfied financial and social decline back home. At *Tico Times*, an English language weekly newspaper in Costa Rica, agencies advertise various types of prostitution, such as mail order brides, and dating and escort agencies, specifically to tourists and expatriates. On the Internet there are hundreds of websites selling Costa Rican women and children. Schifter concludes:

> Obviously, globalization has linked us to an international economy in which each country finds their specialization. In the Latin countries, it is increasingly concentrated in our genitalia. If in agriculture and industry our hands and feet had given us food before, now penises and vaginas do. In the case of Costa Rica, whether we like it or not, sex tourism is a strong component of our Gross National Product.
>
> *(Schifter 2007:265)*

As Costa Rica slides into a subordinated position internationally, the country becomes a paradise for sexual trafficking, paedophilia, and child pornography. In this way, just as nature has been commodified, the bodies of women and children are turned into another form of human capital so they can to contribute to the global tourism industry, to the wealth of businesses, and to state coffers to pay its debt.

## Conclusion

I will conclude by briefly emphasizing my point that policies associated with sustainable development and the green economy can be seen as part of a neoliberal 'greening' process. Green capitalism can be understood as a new phase of capital accumulation that entails four aspects. First, it entails the expansion of credit instruments, such as debt-for-nature exchanges by financial capital to create economic growth. In this frame, the debtor's obligation is to allocate domestic resources for financing ecological projects in exchange for extinguishing a limited portion of the country's foreign debt. Second, it involves the World Bank licensing big ENGOs to broker the indebted countries' resources with large corporations involved in economic restructuring and globalization. The role of ENGOs is to establish the monetary values of the 'global commons' of the indebted periphery such as biodiversity, air, and scenery, and to export these values in stock exchanges. I gave the example of the Canada-Costa Rica debt-for-nature exchange that channelled funds to WWF-Canada and the Costa Rican INBio. Third, there are new types of markets – biodiversity for biotechnology and intellectual property rights, forests, for carbon credits, and scenery for ecotourism – located in conservation areas. A conservation area is a designated domain where private and public activities are interrelated in order to manage and conserve a region's nature for capital accumulation. Finally the 'greening' process results in peasants and Indigenous people acquiring new roles as service providers in new industries such as ecotourism. These roles are gendered in that they reproduce existing gender roles: men work as tour guides while women work in hotels and resorts or as prostitutes. Viewed through the lens of ecofeminism, these aspects of 'greening' come together to wage war on women and subsistence.

At the end of this analysis, my conclusion is that the UN, through the World Bank's neoliberal approach to sustainable development, promotes rather than redresses poverty and unsustainability. The enacting of monetary value into the commons requires the devaluing of other forms of social existence: transforming skills into deficiencies; commons into resources; knowledge into ignorance; autonomy into dependency; self-sufficiency into loss of dignity for women and children. In opposition to this destructive agenda, ecofeminist theorists, and the activists they inspire, propose a subsistence perspective that entails fundamental transformation of the economy before capitalist accumulation reaches the last ecological limit.

# References

Baltodano, J. (2004) 'Bosques en reservas del Ida: Biodiversidad y manejo', *Ambien-Tico* 133: 14–17.

Bennholdt-Thomsen, V. and Mies, M. (1999) *The Subsistence Perspective: Beyond the Globalized Economy*. New York: Zed Books.

Costa Rica Ministerio de Economía, Industria y Comercio, Area de Integración Económica y Desarrollo Regional (1998) *Cuadro No 1: Costa Rica Importaciones de Frijol: Enero–Abril, 1998*. San José: Costa Rica.

Costa Rica Ministerio de Recursos Naturales, Energía y Minas. Area de Conservación Arenal (1993) *Plan General de Uso de la Tierra* (Vols. I–IV). San José. MIRENEM, Agencia Canadiense de Desarrollo Internacional, and Fondo Mundial para la Naturaleza de Canadá.

Federici, S. (2004) *Caliban and the Witch: Women, the Body and Primitive Accumulation*. Brooklyn, NY: Autonomedia.

Fenech, A., Hansell, R., Isla, A. and Thompson, S. (eds) (1999) *Report of an April 23, 1999 Workshop on Natural Capital: Views From Many Perspectives*. Toronto, ON: University of Toronto, Institute for Environmental Studies.

Figuerola, J. (2003) 'Pago de servicios ambientales a la tala rasa', *Ambien-Tico* 123: 10–11.

Figuerola, J. (2005) 'Nativos y exóticos pero conservando la biodiversidad', *Ambien-Tico* 141: 16–17.

Franceschi, H. (2006) 'Conflictos socio ambientales intercampesinos por los recursos naturales', *Revista de Ciencias Sociales* 111–12: 37–56.

Government of Canada and Government of Costa Rica (1995) *Memorandum of Understanding Between the Government of Canada and the Government of the Republic of Costa Rica concerning the Canadian Debt Conversion Initiative for the Environment* (n.p.).

Hamilton, K. (2001, September) 'Genuine savings, population growth and sustaining economic welfare'. Paper presented at Conference on Natural Capital, Poverty and Development, Toronto, Ontario, Canada.

Index-Mundi (n.d.) *Unemployment, Youth Female (% of Female Labour Force Ages 15–24)*. Online. Available at: www.indexmundi.com/facts/costa-rica/unemployment (accessed 15 October 2015).

Lohmann, L. (2005) 'Marketing and making carbon dumps: Commodification, calculation and counterfactuals in climate change mitigation', *Science as Culture* 14(3): 203–235.

Mies, M. (1986) *Patriarchy and Accumulation on a World Scale: Women in the International Division of Labour*. London: Zed Books.

Mies, M. and Shiva, V. (1993) *Ecofeminism*. London: Zed Books.

Odio, E. (2001, August 24) 'Modelo unico en el mundo', *Al Dia*, op-ed column, p. 3.

Ostrom, E. (1990) *Governing the Commons: The Evolution of Institutions for Collective Action*. Cambridge: Cambridge University Press.

Pearce, W. D. and Warford, J. J. (1993) *World Without End: Economics, Environment and Sustainable Development*. New York: Oxford University Press.

Petch, T. (1988) 'Costa Rica', in Roddick, J. (ed) *The Dance of the Millions: Latin America and the Debt Crisis*. London: Latin America Bureau, 191–215.

Quesada, C. (1990) *Estrategia de Conservación para el Desarrollo Sostenible de Costa Rica*. San José, Costa Rica: Ministerio de Recursos Naturales, Energía y Minas, República de Costa Rica.

Rodriguez, S. (1995) 'Los determinismos mercantiles y tecnocráticos en el "modelo" de funcionamiento del INBio', *Ambien-Tico* 32: 11–16.

Rogers, T. (2009) *Costa Rica's Sex-Tourism Is Growing*. Online. Available at: http://ticotimes.com/costa-rica/sex-prostitution-growing (accessed 15 October 2015).

Schifter, J. (2007) *Viejos Verdes en el Paraiso: Turismo Sexual en Costa Rica*. San José, Costa Rica: Editorial Universidad Estatal a Distancia.

Sheikh, P. A. (1994) 'Conflicts of global ecology: Environmental activism in a period of global reach', *Alternatives* 19: 195–207.

Sheikh, P. A. (1999) *Biopiracy: The Plunder of Nature and Knowledge*. Boston, MA: South End Press.

Sheikh, P. A. (2007) *Debt-for-Nature Initiatives and the Tropical Forest Conservation Act: Status and Implementation (CRS Report for Congress RL31286)*. Washington, DC: Congressional Research Service, Library of Congress.

Sheikh, P. A. (2010) *Debt-for-Nature Initiatives and the Tropical Forest Conservation Act: Status and Implementation (CRS Report for Congress RL31286)*. Online. Available at: www.cnie.org/NLE/CRSreports/10Apr/RL31286.pdf (accessed 15 October 2015).

Shiva, V. (1989) *Staying Alive: Women, Ecology and Development*. London: Zed Books.

Sojo, C. (1992) *La Mano Visible del Mercado: La Asistencia de Estados Unidos al Sector Privado Costarricense en la Década de los Ochenta*. San José, Costa Rica: Ediciones CRIES.

Ulloa, C. (1996) *Diagnostico socioambiental de la unidad territorial priorizada*. La Fortuna, San Carlos: Proyecto de Conservación y Desarrollo Arenal, Tilaran, Costa Rica.

United Nations Environment Programme (n.d.) *What Is the Green Economy?* Online. Available at: www.unep.org/greeneconomy/AboutGEI/WhatisGEI/tabid/29784/Default.aspx (accessed 15 October 2015).

United Nations Framework Convention on Climate Change (2005) 'Joint Implementation (JI)', *The Kyoto Protocol*. Online. Available at: http://unfccc.int/kyoto_protocol/mechanisms/joint_implementation/items/1674.php (accessed 15 October 2015).

Waring, M. (1988) *If Women Counted: A New Feminist Economics*. San Francisco, CA: Harper and Row.

World Bank (1997) *Expanding the measure of wealth: indicators of environmentally sustainable development*. Environmentally sustainable development studies and monographs series; no. 17*ESSD Environmentally & Socially Sustainable Development Work in Progress. Washington, DC: The World Bank. http://documents.worldbank.org/curated/en/555261468765258502/Expanding-the-measure-of-wealth-indicators-of-environmentally-sustainable-development.

# 26

# GENDER AND CLIMATE CHANGE POLITICS

*Susan Buckingham*

## Introduction

*The Women's Manifesto on Climate Change*, published on 15 May 2007, emerged from a collaboration between the Women's Environmental Network (WEN) and the National Federation of Women's Institutes (NFWI), forged at the UK party political conferences in Autumn 2006. Stemming from awareness that environmental politics can be 'gender-blind', both organizations support women to voice and take action on their environmental concerns, and to campaign on local and global issues, including climate change (see Bond and Cleevely 2010; Metcalf et al. 2015; WEN 2010, n.d.). The NFWI's remit goes beyond environmental issues, although it is not always easy, or appropriate, to establish where the boundaries lie between these issues and those of broader social justice (Di Chiro 2008). Interestingly, WEN's incursion into climate change campaigning had been energetically discussed at its trustees' meetings. WEN had historically campaigned on a range of environmental issues as they specifically affected women's lives. Its past campaigns included those against lindane in chocolate, as well as how chocolate manufacturers target women consumers; chemicals in sanitary products which can cause the potentially lethal adverse reaction 'toxic shock syndrome'; and disposable nappies, which, by 2007 were contributing 3 to 4 per cent to the UK's non-recyclable waste stream (The Nappy Alliance 2007; Metcalf et al. 2015). Campaigning to address climate change in ways that empowered and benefited women would be a departure in WEN's style and scope and was, in part, occasioned by the changes in a funding environment in which climate change-related activity was being prioritized. Eventually, WEN trustees and employees agreed, with a degree of reluctance, to reframe its work to take advantage of these changes.

As one of the participants at these party conferences, and one of the originators of the manifesto, I will reflect, from an insider perspective, on the genesis of the document. This chapter presents a narrative of how the manifesto emerged, and uses it as a basis for critically examining the gender politics in the environmental movement(s), particularly in the United Kingdom. My focus is on the position of women in women-focused organizations such as WEN and in more mainstream (or, perhaps more accurately, 'malestream') environmental non-governmental organizations (ENGOs). I argue that ENGOs operate in a gendered institutional and political milieu that they reflect as much as challenge and that, as such, their power to create change is limited. Nevertheless, I am encouraged by what I perceive as a renewed interest in and commitment to feminism in many parts of the world, which may yet generate some potential for systemic change.

To make sense of these phenomena, I draw on two feminist theories that I have found useful for understanding the context and potential of women's climate change action: feminist political theorist Nancy Fraser's 'status model', in which 'recognition' is seen as a corollary of redistribution in the domain of justice, and the epistemic privilege of 'standpoint theory', whereby structural change can only be created by those with least to benefit from prevailing systems of power.

## The birth of the *Women's Manifesto on Climate Change*

In the late summer of 2006, the editor of *The Independent* newspaper invited WEN to participate in the 'Climate Clinic' fringe event the newspaper was organizing at the UK party political conferences that autumn.[1] These conferences are increasingly seen by businesses and other organizations as opportunities for lobbying the governing party and its main opposition (Harris and Lock 2002). At the conferences, the influence of lobbyists is signified by their relative proximity to the decision makers. Fringe participants do not have the right to enter the main conference and will only, therefore, have access to those politicians and their advisors who agree to join a fringe panel or are interested enough to attend. Participants at the Climate Clinic ranged from the giants of the ENGO world such as World Wide Fund for Nature (WWF), the Royal Society for the Protection of Birds (RSPB), Friends of the Earth (FoE), and Greenpeace; quasi-autonomous non-governmental organizations (NGOs, or 'quangos') such as Natural England; academic institutes such as the Tyndall Centre; and businesses keen to present their green credentials, such as Saab and the Co-operative Bank. A handful of smaller NGOs were also invited in a gesture toward inclusiveness. Speakers across the programme included journalists, business representatives, a few MP and ministers sympathetic to (or at least wanting to be associated with) environmental issues, and spokespeople from participating organizations. The panels, as advertised in the programme for the Labour Conference, were overwhelmingly male, with the 101 male presenters vastly outnumbering the nineteen females (the one exception was WEN's all-female panel). Of the thirty-five panels, only three were chaired by women. Notably twelve panels, including a number of high profile ENGOs, had no women contributors at all. The Climate Clinic at the Conservative Party conference was smaller, but no more gender balanced. Of the twenty-five panels, one was chaired by a woman; participants included sixty men and six women. So few women were there that it is easier to count those panels with women (four) than those without.

*The Independent* published a special conference edition newspaper featuring the programme and sixteen commissioned articles, of which only two were written by women: one by WEN (Sutton 2006a, b) about the role women can and do play in mitigating climate change, and one on making it easier for consumers to buy products with low environmental impact written for the retailer B&Q (Kenrick 2006a). The front covers of the Labour and Conservative special editions featured, respectively, a close up of then prime minister Tony Blair and, more strikingly, a Gore-Tex clad Tory party leader David Cameron striding out across the Arctic snow with a team of huskies in his now legendary bid for the green vote.

At the Labour fringe conference, WEN's panel 'Climate Change Is a Gendered Issue' featured Susan Buckingham (me) speaking for WEN; Ruth Bond, then Chair of the NFWI; and Emily Thornberry, Labour MP for South Islington. It was chaired by Baroness Uddin (Member of the House of Lords). The panel for the Conservative Party event comprised Joanne Bowlt (the regional coordinator of 'Women2Win', an organization supporting women to stand as parliamentary candidates for the Conservative Party); Baroness Byford (then Shadow Minister for Environment, Food and Rural Affairs [DEFRA]); Juliet Davenport, the Founder and CEO of Good Energy, a renewable energy power distributor; Ruth Bond; and myself. It was chaired by Lucy Siegle, ethical living journalist with *The Observer*. We had been allocated rather low profile time slots at both events (8:30 and 9:30 in the mornings), and attracted a (not entirely unexpectedly) small audience, mostly women.

Unsurprisingly, our experience of participating in these fringe events was of being overwhelmed by a hyper-(white)-masculinity, which reflected our experience of government and ENGOs more generally (with more on this later). It was our perceived exclusion from the political and organizational 'boys' clubs' of environmental politics, the clear but unacknowledged masculine gender bias that manifested in the 'out of hours' social arrangements at both conferences (among other things), which prompted the initial drafting of a specifically *women's* manifesto on climate change. Only able to afford a modest hotel in the inflated accommodation market of conference season, we four women, the chairs and press and public affairs officers of WEN and NFWI, retired to our quiet, darkly upholstered and veneered hotel bar to ponder what this manifesto might include, and how it might differ from the climate change campaigning of mainstream ENGOs. As a result of these discussions, the two organizations commissioned a survey of five hundred women to identify 'what women wanted' regarding climate change, and the data generated provided the basis of the manifesto (see Box 26.1 and WEN/NFWI 2007).

The broad categories that encompassed the findings of the survey were that much more action was necessary to tackle climate change; more help and guidance was needed to enable women to take decisions to minimize carbon impact; and greater involvement and representation of women in climate change action and decision-making was required. The manifesto was officially endorsed by Green Party MP and WEN ambassador Caroline Lucas, and collected signatories, including ActionAid, Oxfam, Breast Cancer UK, Women's Environment and Development Organisation (WEDO), and World Wide Fund for Nature (WWF). With this support, the manifesto was used in campaigning for the UK government to do more at both national and international levels to enable women and others to live and act in ways that reduce their carbon emissions.[2] Box 26.1 reproduces the main points of the manifesto, which can be seen as covering the areas of home, travel, shopping, energy, children and family responsibilities, jobs and education, and developing countries. What comes through, also, is women's desire to have some recognition by government for their concerns and the work they are already doing, a concern which Nancy Fraser (2000) considers, alongside redistribution, to be a key dimension of justice.

Fraser's (2000) 'status model', in which recognition is understood as 'a question of status', and where a lack of access to resources (economic) impedes participation (political), is helpful to understand the potential of social action and protest. The model identifies 'struggles for recognition [properly conceived]' as an aid to redistributing 'power and wealth and can promote interaction and co-operation across gulfs of difference' (Fraser 2000:109). With this in mind, I will next review how recognition of women has been addressed in the broader institutional context of environmental politics before considering women's experiences in ENGOs, as the latter are more embedded in masculinist institutional structures than might, at first glance, be expected.

---

## Box 26.1   Women's Manifesto on Climate Change

### 1. In our homes

- More clear guidance, advice and practical support to enable women to switch to a low-carbon lifestyle;
- More government grants and incentives to make green energy choices, including energy conservation, cheaper and more easily available;

- More help to prevent waste and consistent and comprehensive recycling facilities in all local authority areas;
- Stronger environmental standards for both new builds and refurbishments, to make all housing stock carbon neutral.

## 2.   In our travel

- Efficient, affordable and safe public transport, which women are more likely to use than men;
- Safe and comprehensive cycling and walking options, including car-free school runs for women and children;
- Introduction of a tax on aviation fuel and/or other fiscal measures to ensure the true environmental and social costs of air travel are accounted for.

## 3.   In the marketplace

- Lower prices for environmentally friendly goods;
- Clear labelling so consumers know the food miles and carbon footprint of the goods they buy;
- Legislation to ban products which are unsustainable or contribute heavily to climate change;
- Legislation to encourage product durability and re-use, reduce excess packaging and waste;
- Much stronger support for local food production and supply.

## 4.   In our use of energy

- Investment in renewable energy which matches or exceeds that in non- renewable sources, to make it a viable industry;
- More government grants and incentives to reduce carbon emissions through greater energy efficiency and lower energy demand;
- More support for microgeneration as an alternative to fossil-fuel based electricity generation;
- Greater transparency so that women know where the energy they use is coming from, allowing them to make greener choices.

## 5.   For us and our children

- More information about the best ways to reduce the environmental impact of the first years of a child's life, for example, support for real nappy promotion schemes;
- More education about climate change, its causes and ways to avoid it – for all age groups;
- More help, support and encouragement for women to enable them to take climate change action at home and with their family.

## 6.   For the future

- Equal involvement of women and men in environmental decision-making in industry, government, and civil society;
- Measures to increase the number of girls and women studying science subjects and working in science related jobs;
- Recognition that most women are concerned with the expansion of nuclear power. A survey for WEN found 72 per cent against; other surveys have recorded more than 50 per cent of women against;

- The inclusion of air and sea freight $CO_2$ emissions in the UK's carbon footprint so the true scale of emissions from food and product miles can be measured and action can be taken to reduce them;
- Greater promotion to UK residents of holidays in the UK, without flying;
- Greater government recognition of the contribution that women are already making in reducing personal and domestic carbon emissions, which account for the majority of the nation's carbon footprint.

### 7. For developing countries

- Recognition by the UK Government that climate change is a matter of social justice, affecting the poor in developing countries, and especially women, the most;
- More government funding of initiatives which will help women and their families to adapt to climate change, focusing on the need for sufficient food, water and renewable clean energy, cooking fuels, a climate-proof asset base to prevent poverty, protection against climate-induced floods, famine, drought and conflict, and the provision of climate change related education and information;
- Support for appropriate climate offsetting schemes which will help to support poor women in mitigating and adapting to the effects of climate change;
- More knowledge transfer of low carbon technologies to develop sustainable solutions in both developed and developing countries;
- Respect for indigenous cultures and values and avoidance of exporting western values and consumerism.

## *Stop Climate Chaos*

As member organizations of the Stop Climate Chaos coalition, both WEN and NFWI support demands on the UK Government to:

- Negotiate internationally for global warming to peak at no more than 2°C above pre-industrial levels. This will mean global greenhouse gas emissions must peak by 2015 and then decline irreversibly thereafter;
- Institute a Carbon Budget to reduce UK greenhouse gas emissions by an average of at least 3 per cent p.a.;
- Give all necessary support to developing countries to help them adapt to climate change.

## *Conclusion*

The women of this country have the will to tackle climate change. What we need now is the way – which is currently made difficult by government inaction. With our concern for the environment, we are your single biggest constituency to the cause and an important part of the solution.

## The role of gender in environmental policy-making

Since 1996, and following the European Union's adoption of it as a policy approach, the UK has made a legal commitment to *gender mainstreaming*, which the EU defines as 'the integration of the gender perspective into every stage of policy processes – design, implementation, monitoring and evaluation – with a view to promoting equality between women and men'

(European Commission 2016). In pilot research for the EU's Environment Directorate, I explored how effectively waste management was gender mainstreamed, and found little evidence of success six years after the legislation was introduced (Buckingham et al. 2005). Angela McRobbie (2009) calls into question how just gender mainstreaming is, suggesting that it bolsters neoliberal managerialism by focusing on how decision-making can benefit from women's skills and knowledge, rather than on the gender justice of equal opportunities (and outcomes) for women. Within the context of climate change, Röhr et al. (2008) argue that gender mainstreaming has been institutionalized very tenuously, and attributes this weakness to the androcentricism of governmental institutions. They go on to state that while it is necessary to have an equal number of male and female decision makers, alone it will not guarantee '(gender) justice in institutional orientation'. This view informs Magnusdottir and Kronsell's (2014) conclusions about the lack of impact on the drafting of gender sensitive climate change policy in Scandinavian countries, despite gender balance, and in some cases, greater proportions of women, in climate policy-making. Röhr et al. (2008) argue the need to go beyond a consideration of gender differences to understand and question gender relationships which are underpinned by differential power. Without dismantling these structural dimensions of gender inequality, it is impossible to make any fundamental changes, which may explain the limited success of gender mainstreaming.

It is useful to bear this claim in mind when considering efforts to increase the proportion of women on company boards. Since the publication of the 2011 Davies Report, the UK government has, at least superficially, acknowledged that businesses would do better if their boards were more gender balanced, and has agreed a voluntary target of 25 per cent of board members to be women for the Financial Times Stock Exchange (FTSE) one hundred listed companies (Davies 2011). By 2014, 20.7 per cent of FTSE100 board members were women. Of course, this assumes that what Röhr et al. (2008) would term the androcentrism of these organizations remains intact, and the inclusion of more women enables better performance within existing structures. Better gender balanced boards (40 per cent minimum of either men or women) are also the subject of an EU directive which was agreed upon by the European Parliament in November 2013. Contradictorily, however, there is no similar requirement for government departments to follow this practice, and these are weighted toward men. At the time of writing, the departments with greatest responsibility for climate change related matters have between 25 per cent of senior managers who are women (Department of Transport) and 40 per cent (DEFRA). The UK Department of Energy and Climate Change (DECC) has 30 per cent of their most senior management posts held by women.[3]

Equality Impact Assessments (EIAs) can be carried out by policy-making bodies to determine how potential policies are likely to affect 'protected groups' identified by the UK's Public Sector Equality Duty (PSED). While not a legal requirement, EIAs can be used to provide evidence of complying with the PSED, which is a requirement. This could be seen as an attempt to 'gender mainstream' and has led to the practice of reviewing policies for their likely impact on vulnerable populations. In reality, however, these assessments are often inexpertly made after the policies have been drafted, by staff who lack the training to undertake a rigorous analysis (Buckingham and Kulcur 2017). There is no evidence of equality concerns informing policy design at its inception, which suggests (after Röhr et al. [2008]) that the gendering of institutions and institutional practices are preserved intact.

Feminist campaigners are caught in a paradox here: while supporting any move, such as gender mainstreaming or the gender equality duty, which encourages greater equality of opportunity to achieve decision-making status for (some) women, we recognize that this is not, in itself, likely to change fundamentally the way in which business is done, or how climate change continues to be produced, analyzed, framed, and addressed.

## *Male domination of climate change policy-making*

Often claimed as the pre-eminent environmental issue of our time,[4] climate change is both the result and reinforcer of deep-seated social and political divisions. It is the result of a 'long durée' drive for economic and material growth which itself is predicated on inequalities: between countries, communities, ethnicities, classes, and genders. No system built on these inequalities can address climate change, as the past twenty years of superficial attempts have made clear. Joni Seager (2009) reflects on the genesis of the target of holding climate change to two degrees above what was the average global temperature when climate change began to be considered as an international problem. She cites William Nordhaus as proposing this as the tipping point, or 'trade-off between economic growth and environmental policy' (Nordhaus 1979 in Seager 2009:13), and thereby what has become understood as a scientific 'desideratum' had its origin in the mind of 'economic man'.

The fields that dominate climate change decision-making, whether as an entirety (economists, politicians, civil servants, climate change scientists) or in its component parts (transport, energy, water, waste management) are heavily dominated by professional men who, by virtue of their status in society, are precisely those most able to evade its impacts (see MacGregor 2010; Nelson 2012). Feminist standpoint theory, most often attributed to philosopher Sandra Harding (ed) (2003), argues that those so embedded in, and benefiting from, positions of power cannot readily see the consequences of this power and as such lack the epistemic privilege required to understand and therefore properly address this. It argues that the most authentic epistemic privilege is available to those who are most likely to be affected. However, as those who monitor gender (im)balances in the international climate change negotiations consistently point out, these are dominated by men. As Figure 26.1 shows, from data

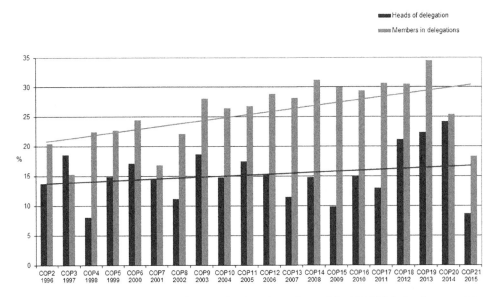

*Figure 26.1*  Percentage of women delegation heads and members of the UNFCCC Conference of the
Parties, 1996–2015

*Source*: GenderCC (2015)

compiled by GenderCC, the proportion of women members of negotiating teams rarely (and for women leads never) exceeds 30 per cent. More salutary is the lack of what might be seen as steady progress, with the data for the UNFCCC conference of the parties – COP21 – in 2015 revealing one of the lower participation rates for women since 1996 (GenderCC 2015; see also Morrow in this volume).

A most striking illustration of the masculinism – machismo, even – of climate change decision-making is provided by the international negotiations which take place every year. By their detailed account of COP 6 in 2000 at The Hague, Grubb and Yamin (2001) identify the brinkmanship, lack of transparency, and dominance of English language speaking elites as contributing to the breakdown of talks, and particularly the failure of the European Union and United States to agree on elements of the Kyoto Protocol. Particularly inflammatory was the dispute between the UK and French delegations occasioned by then UK Deputy Prime Minister John Prescott's decision to negotiate a deal 'backstage' with the Americans, which was heavily challenged by a number of EU member states, including the Nordic countries, Germany, and France, whose chief negotiator was a woman: then French environment minister (and founding member of the French Green Party), Dominique Voynet. According to a UK newspaper report at the time:

> [T]he Deputy Prime Minister blamed [Dominique Voynet] for the collapse of the environment summit in The Hague. . . . Mr Prescott had stormed out of the summit in the early hours of Saturday, complaining that Mme Voynet had scuppered a deal on climate control because she had 'cold feet' and was 'tired and exhausted'.
>
> *(McSmith 2000:n.p.)*

In response, she

> accused him of behaving like an 'inveterate macho' . . . With the backing of Downing Street, Mr Prescott sought to make a joke out of her rebuke, despite concern that the row could damage relations with France . . . 'Macho man – moi?' he said in the Commons. 'I must say that remark leaves me most gutted'. Voynet retaliated by describing Mr Prescott's reaction as 'really pathetic'. His comments, she said, were 'unacceptable, both in form and content . . . mediocre and shabby'. Later she told a news conference: 'He does no service either to his image or mine; nor does he do any service to the cause of the EU'. Mme Voynet added with heavy irony: 'Of course a woman is tired, is frightened and doesn't understand things'.
>
> *(McSmith 2000:n.p.)*

Voynet's admission 'that she was (by the end of the final night) too exhausted to understand the issues and explain them properly to the full EU group of Ministers' (Grubb and Yamin 2001) is probably more reflective of the conditions of negotiating (the hours of which would surely contravene any international labour law) than of her ability, and bespeaks the machismo of international climate change negotiations commented on by participants and observers in these conferences. For example, one observer notes that responses from women's organizations involved in COP9 in 2003 'showed that the group who felt uncomfortable with both the mode and content of negotiations was bigger than expected' (Röhr 2009). Since this gendered 'showdown', there have been calls for more women to be involved in, as well as gendered concerns to be addressed by, the international climate change negotiations (Röhr and Hemmati 2008), although there appears to have been limited development in either regard (see Buckingham 2010 and Figure

26.1). In addition, there is very little attention to these issues by non-feminist scholars of global environmental politics and policy-making.

It is interesting that research indicates a connection, which may or not be causal, between governments with higher than average proportions of women in them, and those which have stronger climate change related legislation (Buckingham 2010). The relationship between countries in which women have higher political status and those which had lower per capita $CO_2$ emissions has been tested statistically in a cross-national study by Ergas and York (2012). Even when controlling for variables such as countries' level of 'modernization', 'world-system position' and 'democracy', the relationship between women's status and per capita $CO_2$ emissions appears to be robust. In 2012 the COP18 agreed to start, and monitor, a process to move toward gender equality in climate change decision-making positions, and COP20:

> also known as the Lima work programme on gender, requested the secretariat to include in this report information regarding the implementation by the secretariat of decisions that include a gender approach, in keeping with applicable gender-related policies under the Convention.
>
> *(UNFCCC 2015:3)*

The Women and Gender Constituency (WGC), formed in 2009 and recognized as one of the nine official constituencies by the UNFCCC in 2011, works with the UNFCCC secretariat, national governments, NGOs, and other stakeholders to ensure that 'women's issues and gender justice' are addressed by the Convention (WGC 2015). However, the extent to which these initiatives and processes can achieve systemic change, bearing in mind the caveats concerning gender mainstreaming discussed in this chapter, is questionable.

This dominant masculinity in climate change decision-making in industry, business, and government, and indeed of privileging climate change as 'the' pre-eminent environmental problem of its time (see MacGregor 2014), could potentially be challenged by gender sensitive environmental lobbying, but in the UK (and many other places) the environmental movement is similarly characterized by cultures of masculinity.

## Cultures of masculinity in environmental non-governmental organizations

Generally, as Rakibe Kulcur's (2013) research nicely illustrates, mainstream ENGOs are not sympathetic to nuances of gender. In her interviews with key players in UK ENGOs, there is a clear, and sometimes apparently wilful, lack of understanding of the role gender plays in the construction, production, and resolution of environmental issues, as well as their impacts. The available, and stark, facts of the men and women who are employed, promoted, and appointed to senior positions in management and on the boards of ENGOs are augmented by revealing interviews in which (mostly male) senior decision makers argue that gender is not an issue for generic (primarily conservation oriented) ENGOs, but instead for women's, or perhaps development, organizations. Employment practices that resist flexible working and demand long and unsociable hours while offering only limited term contracts appear to be gendered, as they do not easily accommodate caring responsibilities, most commonly performed by women. Kulcur's women interviewees revealed how, for example,

> You don't really see many female managers at all. I've been quite alone in that regard . . . even when they are women, the culture itself felt very male . . . there is a way

of working that I have noticed in the environmental movement that is very male, is very macho.

*(quoted in Kulcur 2013:206)*

This respondent concludes that she has 'had so many sexist remarks' and that 'moving into the environmental sector turned me into a much stronger feminist than I think I was before' (Kulcur 2013:206–207). Those women who are promoted tend not to have children or caring responsibilities. One of Kulcur's male respondents suggested that the number of female managers who did not have children 'maybe . . . proves the point that the women who don't have children go higher up in the career ladder . . . whereas if you look at the men . . . well, two out of three have children' (213).

One of Kulcur's main conclusions is that ENGOs are failing to erode gendered working practices as they appear to mimic the masculinist institutional structures and concerns of those organizations from which they seek funding. At one point in her research Kulcur was asked by a male chief executive officer whether she has children, and when she affirmed that she did (she had one daughter at that point), his response was 'There you go, it is too late, you've ruined your career [laughs]' (216).

Years of representing WEN at government briefings and environmental gatherings have impressed on me just how masculinist the mainstream environmental organizations can be. At one meeting convened by the UK's DEFRA in the early 2000s, I recall the combative stance of the CEOs of two leading environmental organizations, dressed in sweaters and jeans, standing at the back of the room, conspicuously challenging civil servants at every opportunity. My neighbour at this event was a woman who had once led the Green Party. I was surprised to hear her admit to feeling intimidated by these alternative 'masters of the universe', such that she failed to add her voice to the debate. This is a good illustration of feminist theorist Iris Marion Young's argument that the dominant style of communication and discussion in Western society is one that values the 'assertive and confrontational', rather than the 'tentative, exploratory or conciliatory' (1997:64). This, she says, encourages those with a sense of entitlement, while effectively silencing the less privileged, including women, who 'often feel intimidated by the argument requirements'.

Where women are conspicuous, however, is in the marketing of environmental campaigns. Consider, for example, the People for the Ethical Treatment of Animals' (PETA) campaign to ban fur using the near naked bodies of young and slender women (for evidence, type 'PETA I'd rather go campaign' in Google images), or more recently, in the winter of 2013, the focus on one of the minority of women protestors against drilling for oil in the Arctic becoming the 'poster girl' of the 'Free the Arctic 30'. One Twitter response (Digital Spy) asked 'Anyone else tempted to join Greenpeace to meet hot girls like [the woman portrayed]?', which generated threads of sexual innuendo. However insulting these responses are, I think Greenpeace has to take a share of responsibility for using this young woman's photograph – vulnerable and behind bars – to the virtual exclusion of images from the rest of the Arctic 30. A review of the photographs and short autobiographical reasons for joining the campaign reveal eight of the thirty to be women, with a noticeably younger age average than the twenty-two men (*The Guardian* 2013). It could be argued that the image of the woman used represented the only British woman on board the Arctic Sunrise, although there were also five British men, who did not feature nearly so prominently.

Seager's (1993) groundbreaking research in the 1990s, in her book *Earth Follies*, revealed how few women had senior positions in US ENGOs. In 2014, environmental justice scholar Dorceta Taylor published a comprehensive report on the 'state of diversity' in US environmental organizations (including mainstream ENGOs, foundations and government agencies), in which she finds that although some gains have been made by white women, men are still much more likely than women to hold powerful positions.[5]

## The future of gender justice and climate justice

So how might the aims of the *Women's Manifesto on Climate Change* regarding action, information, and recognition be taken forward in such a masculinist world? Recalling Fraser's (2000) work on recognition, which places it alongside distribution within the context of justice, it can be seen that strategies to achieve more women in decision-making will not, in themselves, change the lack of attention to women's voices, although this is still a worthwhile aim. The environmental justice literature argues that those who have the least, in terms of resources and power, bear the brunt of environmental problems (see Di Chiro 2008; Walker 2013). Given that those who have the most to lose in a material sense from solving these problems have an interest in preserving the prevailing status quo, any situation in which decision-making is concentrated within an elite group is unlikely to alter this arrangement. Feminist standpoint theory may also be useful here because it argues that those who are most on the periphery of systems of power and privilege – those with epistemic privilege – can better see its faults (Harding 2003). They are therefore more reliable critics than powerful elites. The privileged among women who are admitted to positions of power in climate change policy- and decision-making are, on current evidence, the highly educated and credentialized, typically with no dependents to care for or with the wherewithal to buy high quality care services. They consequently lack this perspective of the outsider. Attending to numerical gender balance alone, therefore, is unlikely to significantly disrupt the system, which has created the conditions for anthropogenic climate change, in order to create the structural social change that is needed.

Paradoxically, evidence of truly engrained sexism and male entitlement, privilege and power provided, for example, by the 'Everyday Sexism' project in the UK (everydaysexism.com); by the repressive reaction toward women protesters in the Middle East (FIDH 2013); and by widespread international concern about male violence against women in India occasioned by the gang rape and murder of a young woman on a bus in Delhi in 2013 (BBC 2012), appears to have raised the profile of, and renewed commitment to, feminism by a new generation of women and some men, and some of this may be slowly encroaching on the environmental movement. For example, the 'Federation of Young Greens' in Europe produced a manifesto comprising five areas, albeit addressed separately: gender and LGBTQ+; migration and free movement; social Europe; democratic Europe; energy, climate change, and agriculture (FYEG 2013). FoE's 'Big Ideas Project', launched in 2014 to identify ten main themes critical to the next thirty-five years, identifies women's empowerment as key to achieving environmental sustainability as one of these ten 'big ideas' (FoE 2015).

Social media is also a platform for alternative grassroots environmental action; witness, for instance, the activity of Avaaz and 38 Degrees in recent climate protests. If these environmental and feminist organizations can speak to each other more directly, then the potential for gender sensitive climate decisions is likely to increase. There is, then, potential for the few women's environmental groups, and the *Women's Manifesto for Climate Change* to intervene to encourage this dialogue, although, to date, these groups have a low social media presence.

Research into how environmental decision-making and campaigning is gendered is currently scarce and has a low profile in the field of environmental politics and social movements. As a relatively low priority for research funding,[6] arguments have often relied on a small number of reports of practical projects and personal experiences, small scale ethnographic research and generalizations of varying reliability. A much higher consideration needs to be accorded to examining gender relations, which entails studies of men and masculinities as well as those of women and femininities. More attention also needs to be given to how gender norms, roles, and relations affect, structure, and result from environmental problems, including climate change. This work needs to articulate practice with research, and be grounded in a broad social justice context.

## Conclusion

In this chapter I have argued that women's role in climate change advocacy in the Global North is, in many ways, a reaction to the marginalization of women in environmental politics – both formal and informal. Using the development of the *Women's Manifesto of Climate Change* as a starting point to examine women's roles and achievements in climate change campaigning, I explored how gender is addressed in policy-making and how environmental campaigning generally is blind to gender concerns. Advocacy to raise gender as an issue in climate change, therefore, requires more than the insertion of gender into policy, or even, the insertion of more women into climate change policy-making. It requires challenges to the social structure in which institutions, from government and businesses to NGOs, deeply embed gender inequalities. Groups such as the WEN are those most marginalized in environmental campaigning and could, therefore, be said to hold 'epistemic privilege' in this arena. The recognition of women's concerns, reflected in the *Women's Manifesto of Climate Change*, can be scaled-up to illustrate the general lack of recognition of women's collective voices in campaigning. But recognition is usually claimed rather than given, and I suggest that some cause for hope in new movements for gender and climate justice emerging from unorthodox protests and campaigns, to which WEN has contributed.

## Notes

1  Every year in the UK the political parties' annual conferences are scheduled in the same order, with the minor parties earlier (e.g., Green Party, Liberal Democrats), followed by the Labour Party, and with the Conservative Party meeting closing the party conference season. This chronological order, Labour before Conservative, is used to discuss WEN's involvement in fringe events at both conferences.
2  For further details of the manifesto, see: www.wen.org.uk/climate-change/
3  Information retrieved from websites on 10th February 2016: www.gov.uk/government/organisations/ department-of-energy-climate-change; www.gov.uk/government/organisations/department-for-transport; www.gov.uk/government/organisations/department-for-environment-food-rural-affairs
   Numbers may have changed since the time of writing. In July 2016 Theresa May (the UK's second woman prime minister) disbanded the Department of Energy and Climate Change.
4  For example, in 2009, *The Lancet* and the Institute for Global Health Commission (University College London) argued that climate change was the biggest global health threat of the twenty-first century and called for a 'public health movement that frames the threat of climate change for humankind as a health issue' (2009:1696). See: www.ucl.ac.uk/global-health/project-pages/lancet1/ucl-lancet-climate-change. pdf. The EU holds that climate change and its impacts are 'the greatest environmental, social and economic threats our planet is facing', and that this 'is becoming a key international problem of the 21st century'. See: http://ec.europa.eu/research/environment/index_en.cfm?pg=climate
5  Taylor's (2014) report highlights the fact that the domination of US environmental organizations by white people is a much more striking problem than the imbalanced male-female ratio in leadership. She finds, for example, that 'despite the growth in the ethnic minority population in the US, the percentage of minorities on the boards or general staff of environmental organizations does not exceed 16% in the three types of institutions studied' (Taylor 2014:2). Her research revealed that while 76.9 per cent of the presidents and 71.3 per cent of the chairs of the boards of environmental conservation and preservation societies sampled were male, 88.7 per cent of leadership positions in the same organizations were held by people who are white (2014:49–50).
6  But see the EU's Horizon 2020 research programme, launched in 2013, which calls for greater gender balance among researchers and more consideration of gender issues in research.

# References

*BBC News* (2012) 'Delhi bus gang rape: Uproar in Indian parliament', BBC Online. Available at: www.bbc.co.uk/news/world-asia-india-20765869 (accessed 15 February 2016).

Bond, R. and Cleevely, E. (2010) 'National federation of women's institutes: Women organising for a healthy climate', in Dankleman, I. (ed) *Gender and Climate Change: An Introduction*. London: Earthscan, 244–246.

Buckingham, S. (2010) 'Call in the women', *Nature* 468: 502.

Buckingham, S. and Kulcur, R. (2017) 'Gender balancing climate change decision making in government departments and ENGOs in the UK: Implications for women and the workplace', in Griffin-Cohen, M. (ed) *Gender, Climate Change and Labour*. London: Routledge.

Buckingham, S., Reeves, D. and Batchelor, A. (2005) 'Wasting women: The environmental justice of including women in municipal waste management', *Local Environment* 10(4): 427–444.

Davies, M. (2011) *Women on Boards*. London: HM Government.

Di Chiro, G. (2008) 'Living environmentalisms: Coalition politics, social reproduction, and environmental justice', *Environmental Politics* 17(2): 276–298.

Ergas, C. and York, R. (2012) 'Women's status and carbon dioxide emissions: A quantitative cross-national analysis', *Social Science Research* 41: 965–976.

European Commission, *Gender Equality Documents*. Online. Available at: http://ec.europa.eu/justice/gender-equality/document/index_en.htm (accessed 10 February 2016).

*The Everyday Sexism Project*. Online. Available at: http://everydaysexism.com/.

Fédération internationale des ligues des droits de l'Homme, Nazra for Feminist Studies, New Women Foundation and the Uprising of Women in the Arab World (2013) *Egypt: Keeping Women Out; Sexual Violence Against Women in the Public Sphere*. Paris: FIDH.

Fraser, N. (2000) 'Rethinking recognition', *New Left Review* 3: 107–120.

Friends of the Earth (ed) (2015) *Why Women Will Save the Planet*. London: Zed Books.

*Friends of the Earth* (FoE) Online. Available at: www.foe.co.uk/what_we_do/about_us/big_ideas_change_the_world_40167.html (accessed 19 September 2014).

FYEG (2013) *Common Manifesto for the 2014 Elections to the European Parliament*. Online. Available at: www.fyeg.org/sites/fyeg.org/files/pdf/policy-papers/FYEGManifesto2013.pdf.

*GenderCC*. (2015) Online. Available at: http://gendercc.net/ (accessed 15 February 2016).

Goldenberg, S. (2014) 'Why are so many white men trying to save the planet without the rest of us?', *The Guardian*. Online. Available at: www.theguardian.com/commentisfree/2014/may/08/white-men-environmental-movement-leadership (accessed 17 August 2016).

Grubb, M. and Yamin, F. (2001) 'Climatic collapse at the Hague: What happened, why, and where do we go from here?', *International Affairs* 77(2): 261–276.

*The Guardian* (2013) Who are the Greenpeace Arctic 30?. Online. Available at: www.theguardian.com/environment/ng-interactive/2013/oct/14/greenpeace (accessed 17 September 2014).

Harding, S. (ed) (2003) *The Feminist Standpoint Theory Reader: Intellectual and Political Control*. London: Routledge.

Harris, P. and Lock, A. (2002) 'Sleaze or clear blue water? The evolution of corporate and pressure group representation at the major UK party conferences', *Journal of Public Affairs* 2(3): 136–151.

Kenrick, J. (2006a) 'Let's make it easier to turn consumers green', *The Independent, Climate Clinic*.

Kulcur, R. (2013) *Environmental Injustice? An Analysis of Gender in Environmental Non-Governmental Organizations in the United Kingdom and Turkey*. University PhD thesis, Brunel, London. Online. Available at: http://bura.brunel.ac.uk/handle/2438/7680 (accessed 28 November 2014).

Lancet and University College London Institute for Global Health Commission (2009) 'Managing the health effects of climate change', *The Lancet Volume* 373(9676): 1693–1733.

MacGregor, S. (2010) 'A stranger silence still: The need for feminist social research on climate change', *Sociological Review* 57(2): 124–140.

MacGregor, S. (2014) 'Only resist: Feminist ecological citizenship and the post-politics of climate change', *Hypatia* 29(3): 617–633.

McRobbie, A. (2009) *The Aftermath of Feminism: Gender, Culture and Social Change*. London: Sage Publications.

McSmith, A. (2000) 'French anger at 'macho' Prescott', *The Telegraph* 28th November. Online. Available at: www.telegraph.co.uk/news/uknews/1375979/French-anger-at-macho-Prescott.html (accessed 26 August 2016).

Magnusdottir, G. L. and Kronsell, A. (2014) 'The (in)visibility of gender in Scandinavian climate policy making', *International Feminist Journal of Politics* 17(2): 308–326.

Metcalf, K. et al. (2015) 'The power of grassroots action for women's empowerment and the environment', in Friends of the Earth (ed) *Why Women Will Save the Planet*. London: Zed Books, 194–203.

*The Nappy Alliance* (2007) Online. Available at: www.parliament.uk/documents/lords-committees/science-technology/st1nappyalliance.pdf (accessed 17 September 2014).

Nelson, J. (2012) 'Is dismissing the precautionary principle the manly thing to do? Gender and the economics of climate change', *Research Note #013*. Institute for New Economic Thinking. New York. Online. Available at: http://ineteconomics.org/sites/inet.civicactions.net/files/Note-13-Nelson.pdf (accessed 6 June 2014).

Röhr, U. (2009) 'A view from the side? Gendering the climate change negotiations', *Women Gender and Research* 3–4: 52–63.

Röhr, U. and Hemmati, M. (2008) 'A gender sensitive climate regime?', in Grovers, V. (ed) *Global Warming and Climate Change: Kyoto Ten Years and Still Counting*. Oxford: Science Publishers.

Röhr, U., Ssitzner, M., Stiefel, E. and v. Winterfeld, U. (2008) *Gender Justice as the Basis for Sustainable Climate Policies*. Bonn: German NGO Forum on Environment and Development/genanet.

Seager, J. (1993) *Earth Follies: Feminism, Politics and the Environment*. London: Earthscan.

Seager, J. (2009) 'Death by degrees: Taking a feminist hard look at the 2° climate policy', *Kvinder, Kin og Foraksning – Women Gender and Research* 3–4: 11–21.

Sutton, L. (2006a) 'Women on front-line in war against climate threat', *The Independent, Climate Clinic.*

Sutton, L. (2006b) 'Women on front-line in war against climate threat', *The Independent, Climate Clinic.*

Taylor, D. (2014) 'The state of diversity in environmental organizations: Mainstream NGOs, foundations, government agencies', *Green 2.0*. Online. Available at: http://orgs.law.harvard.edu/els/files/2014/02/FullReport_Green2.0_FINALReducedSize.pdf (accessed 3 April 2016).

UNFCCC (2012) 'Promoting gender balance and improving the participation of women in UNFCCC negotiations and in the representation of Parties in bodies established pursuant to the Convention or the Kyoto Protocol', *FCCC/CP/2012/8/Add.3.*

UNFCCC (2015) 'Report on Gender Composition', *FCCC CP/2015/6 page 3* http://unfccc.int/resource/docs/2015/cop21/eng/06.pdf (accessed 3 January 2017).

Walker, G. (2013) *Environmental Justice: Concepts, Evidence and Politics*. London: Routledge.

*Womens' and Gender Constituency* (WGC) (2015). Online. Available at: http://womengenderclimate.org/about-us/ (accessed 15 February 2016).

Women's Environmental Network (2010) *Gender and the Climate Change Agenda: The Impacts of Climate Change on Women and Public Policy*. London: Women's Environmental Network.

Women's Environmental Network (WEN) (No Date) *Why Women and Climate Change?* London: Women's Environmental Network Briefing.

Women's Environmental Network (WEN) and National Federation of Women's Institutes (NWFI) (2007) *Women's Manifesto on Climate Change*. London: WEN and NFWI. Online. Available at: www.wen.org.uk/your-wen/climate-change/ (accessed 9 July 2014).

Young, I. M. (1997) *Intersecting Voices: Dilemmas of Gender, Political Philosophy, and Policy*. Princeton, NJ: Princeton University Press.

# 27

# CHANGING THE CLIMATE OF PARTICIPATION

## The gender constituency in the global climate change regime

*Karen Morrow*

## Introduction

The adoption of the concept of sustainable development by the 1992 United Nations Conference on Environment and Development (UNCED) and the associated imperative to mainstream the 'bottom-up' civil society participation in international environmental law and policy that it entails (WCED 1987) was, in principle, little short of revolutionary in its potential to re-shape global governance (Morrow 2015). This approach was made manifest in Principle 10 of the Rio Declaration (UN 1992a) and (in ostensibly more practical terms) in the 'blueprint' for sustainable development in *Agenda 21* (UN 1992b). In practice, however, the impact of this advance was severely curtailed from the outset. There were a number of reasons for this curtailment, one of which was that state and institutional 'buy-in' to sustainable development, despite enjoying a high public profile, in fact operated in a rather shallow manner, largely 'siloing' the issue in the soft law outcomes of the conference and effectively side-lining it in respect of its hard law outcomes. This was very clear in the context of climate change, which at the first UNCED was identified not as a sustainability issue, to be subjected to the new governance approach, but rather as a technical matter suitable for a traditional top-down state-centric approach. Arguably the initial narrow statist and technocratic approach taken excluded the voices of important stakeholders from the debate shaping the emerging international law climate change regime, an issue that has been one of the less discussed factors impeding legal progress in this area (Morrow 2013). Nonetheless, even here participation did make an – arguably somewhat tokenistic – appearance in the regime's founding document, the Framework Convention on Climate Change (UNFCCC; UN 1992c), specifically in Art. 4.1.(i). This provision obliges parties to the convention to promote public awareness and to 'encourage the widest participation in this process including that of non-governmental organizations'.

The need for the UNFCCC regime (and not just its signatory states) to extend its reach beyond the traditional parameters of a top-down approach into more bottom-up forms of participation seems to have become evident quite early on. This is evidenced by the regime's institutions, notably its secretariat, reaching out to draw other actors into the regime and in particular a number of the major groups[1] that had been identified in *Agenda 21* specifically: environmental; business and industry; non-governmental organizations (NGOs); local government and municipal authorities; indigenous peoples; and research and independent organizations and trade unions. Women as a major group were notably absent from this initiative. While women are to some degree active within other major groups, they tend to be underrepresented within them in numerical terms, and it is only within a gender constituency context that they are consistently in a position to articulate women's perspectives as prime considerations. In any event, the identity of those groups chosen to participate in the UNFCCC processes underlines the domination of hard science and economics in this area of international governance at the expense of social factors. Furthermore, the absence of women from this privileged category of stakeholder groups speaks eloquently of the failure to actualize a systemic approach toward gender across the UN and of a longstanding failure of the UNFCCC process and its institutions to appreciate the significance of gender to its activities. This failure was particularly mystifying, as not only were women recognized as a key constituency in the sustainability sphere alongside other groups that were included by the climate change regime, but also in light of the UN's longstanding (though admittedly oftentimes problematic) institutional commitment to gender mainstreaming[2] (see, for example, Moser and Moser 2005).

Policy and law can and have played a key role in regard to fostering women's participation in global governance processes, through for example, raising awareness of existing rights and how to access them and providing further rights of access to both general and specific legal and policy information (Brody et al. 2008:17). Furthermore, as I explain in the discussion that follows, harnessing the potential for transplanting law and policy norms from other established areas in which they flourish can prompt an expansion of rights activism into new spheres.

The women's movement saw the need to engage with climate change issues from a gender perspective early on; though after an abortive attempt to set up a women's NGO forum at the first FCCC Conference of Parties (COP1, Berlin 1995; Wamukonya and Skutsch 2001), the issue languished for a number of years. The catalyst for re-visiting gender in the context of climate change came from the more general discussion of gender issues as part of the 2002 World Summit on Sustainable Development (WSSD) process. This heritage is clear in the subsequent goal of the women/gender grouping[3] in seeking formal constituency status which identified its agenda as being:

> to formalise the voice of the women's and gender civil society organisations present and regularly active in UNFCCC processes . . . [drawing] upon global commitments to gender equality and women's rights, especially as they relate to climate change, and toward the achievement of the Millennium Development Goals and related commitments.
> *(GenderCC 2011: Article 1)*

However, the UNFCCC secretariat only approved the women/gender grouping's application for provisional constituency status in 2009. COP16 (Cancun) in 2010 saw the provisional women/gender constituency advocating for a rights-based approach to participation (Agostino 2010). Full constituency status was finally granted to the women/gender constituency just prior to COP17 (Durban) in 2011, and at last gender began to emerge as a discernible and distinct institutional priority within the UNFCCC regime. This at long last allowed the women/gender group to have hard-won official observer status in the UNFCCC negotiations (Morrow 2013).

This chapter focusses on women's participation in the global climate change regime and seeks evidence of the use of feminist (specifically ecofeminist) epistemologies and transversal political strategies to accommodate difference while also forging a basis for coherent participation in global environmental governance. Women's interaction with the global law and policy community more generally has long been the subject of feminist scholarly scrutiny (see, for example, Charlesworth et al. 1991). This enquiry has expanded into the rapidly emerging field of global environmental governance (see, for example, Gupta 2006) and to the developing global climate change regime (Lambrou and Piana 2006).

## Making the case for women's/gender constituency status in the UNFCCC regime

Having delineated the timeline for full recognition of the women's/gender constituency in the UNFCCC process, I now briefly consider how the case was made for this development and the role of activist and theoretical ecofeminism and transversal politics (discussed later) in prompting and shaping women's practical engagement with the international polis in this area. Advocating women's participation in the climate change regime is predicated on the proposition that their involvement is necessary in order to effectively address the gender issues raised. There are a number of reasons for this, ranging from matters of principle to practical considerations and, in this section, I will consider some of the most significant of these reasons.

### *Why gender? Why women?*

It is now widely understood that women are both agents of and affected by environmental degradation that may and often does impact differentially on female and male actors in ways that are intimately shaped by gender considerations. One important manifestation of this knowledge has been the development of ecofeminism which can be viewed as a broad-based perspective that combines scholarship and activism founded on the 'recognition of a shared societal classification of women and the environment and the application of feminist scrutiny to the particularized impacts of environmental degradation on women' (Morrow 2013:377).

As its nomenclature suggests, ecofeminism is the progeny of both ecological/environmental and feminist thought (Rocheleau et al. 2006), but it also enjoys a degree of hybrid vigour and has not been limited in its development to synthesizing its conceptual inheritance, developing into a rich (if contentious) area of discourse in its own right. Of particular significance for my purposes here is ecofeminism's enthusiastic incorporation of theoretical elements alongside grassroots activism (see, for example, Shiva 1993:70). The ability to accommodate such apparently divergent approaches arguably makes ecofeminism fertile ground for the combination of macro and micro concerns that are required in order to address climate change. Significantly, dominant social ecofeminist approaches view relationships between women and the environment as socially rooted and enforced/reinforced by an intricately interlinked web of societal mechanisms (Sandilands 1999). This approach regards the sphere of the 'personal' as extending beyond the individual, into families, communities, host ecosystems, and ultimately the biosphere. This being the case, it also seeks to account for the complex interrelating influences in addition to gender that situate women as environmental actors – notably 'race' (embracing the concerns of people of colour and indigenous peoples), class, sexual orientation, age, disability, and the concerns of other species and non-human nature – through the concept of compound disadvantage. This approach strives to accommodate the diverse experiences and identities of women and to recognize that each situating component (individually and in combination) has the potential to interact with cross-cutting gender considerations in complex and often unpredictable ways.

In ecofeminist thought, sustainable decision-making processes must accommodate the complexities of gender (incorporating both female *and* male) perspectives alongside the concerns of nature. In so doing, difference is stressed (and must be accommodated), as is equality between participants. These initial foci remain foundational at all stages. In light of these commitments, securing women's participation as a matter of entitlement, rather than at the discretion of decision-makers in law and policy-making processes, is a central concern. At the same time, the concepts of personal agency and civil society activism that underpin bottom-up approaches to participation in international sustainability and environmental law and policy more generally intersect to a degree with the principles and priorities of ecofeminism. The latter, with its strong emphasis on both individual and collective participation, can be presented as promoting a specific conception of the broader feminist notion of engaged citizenship (Lister 2003). In this context, and being habituated to gender mainstreaming (discussed later) in other aspects of the UN system, women pressed for many years for inclusion in the climate change regime (discussed previously), ultimately pursing a well-developed participation agenda to their desired ends. Their tactics in seeking inclusion are honed by long experience of engagement in both the international and domestic arenas (Verchick 1996).

Such cohesion as there now is within ecofeminism, forging an actively transversal approach (discussed later) to accommodate multiple incarnations of difference rather than imposing a false homogeneity on women as a group, has been hard-won. At the same time, as seen with regard to progressing the role of the women/gender constituency in the UNFCCC, the strategies developed and the techniques employed in the development of ecofeminism are also proving apposite in the latter context.

## *Regime functionality*

The complexity and extent of the problems subsumed under the umbrella term 'climate change' is considerable in its own right and only compounded when inevitably enmeshed with a host of other major issues such as health, resource scarcity, food security, environmental disasters, conflict, and migration. The unprecedented scale and complexity of the issues involved means that effective engagement with climate change will require significantly more ambitious and creative endeavours than have been demonstrated thus far. At the very least, given the nature of the causes of climate change, an effectual regime to address it cannot meaningfully be confined to statecraft; the magnitude of the problems involved being such that individual behavioural change is also required in response to the altered social, economic, and environmental realities involved. We are all, to a greater or lesser extent, both agents of and potential victims of climate change – in effect we are all stakeholders in this global phenomenon.

The statist model invoked by the UNFCCC as initially envisaged exhibited an inbuilt institutional bias (Morrow 2013) that ignored or even effectively excluded many voices, notably those of women, from the law and policy debate. This was at best short-sighted, as women too are drivers of and contribute to the societal practices that generate climate change, making their engagement a necessary element to addressing it. Concomitantly, gendered societal roles and responsibilities ensure that women hold considerable, though often latent or under-exploited, capacity to offer practical insights into addressing many of the manifestations of climate change and are therefore potentially powerful agents in this regard. Thus women's participation in climate change governance is a matter of practical necessity as women need to be 'on board' with responses and have significant contributions to make to the climate change debate in general and on adaptation and mitigation in particular (Brody et al. 2008).

## A matter of principle

Even if practical considerations did not support the case for women's full involvement in the climate change debate, matters of principle make it a moral imperative. Climate change is already having, and will continue to have, a disproportionate impact on the most vulnerable in society despite them being least implicated in its causes. The entrenched societal gender inequalities referred to previously result in women being among those most disadvantaged by the impacts of climate change and least well placed socially, legally, and economically to respond to them (Parikh, n.d.; Brody et al. 2008). Compound disadvantage also operates to ensure that women are among the most deleteriously affected members of other disadvantaged groups in this regard, notably indigenous peoples and refugees (Brody et al. 2008). Even if this state of affairs did not make a rudimentary appeal to justice, the most recent incarnation of the UN's own long-standing institutional commitment (ECOSOC 1997) to address systemic gender inequality though gender mainstreaming would seem to require that such an obvious manifestation of it be addressed. Gender mainstreaming, the latest approach to addressing gender inequality embraced by the UN, may be defined as

> the process of assessing the implications for women and men of any planned action, including legislation, policies or programmes, in all areas and at all levels. It is a strategy for making women's as well as men's concerns and experiences an integral dimension of the design, implementation, monitoring and evaluation of policies and programmes in all political, economic and societal spheres so that women and men benefit equally and inequality is not perpetuated. The ultimate goal is to achieve gender equality.
>
> *(ECOSOC 1997)*

Gender mainstreaming sits well with core ecofeminist strategies for tackling the ills associated with patriarchal domination of women and the environment and in particular supports calls for women's participation in policy and decision-making processes. Mainstreaming notionally seeks to propagate internal organizational change and foster a more profound enculturation of gender at an institutional and societal level. This two-pronged approach is necessary because, for gender mainstreaming to succeed, both attitudes and practices need to change. One problem is that, ambitious as it is, gender mainstreaming is less radical than agenda-setting, involving the integration of gender considerations into existing policy areas, rather than requiring or constituting a full-scale re-orientation of policy agendas (Bhatta 2001; see also Arora-Jonsson in this handbook). Thus gender-mainstreaming is evolutionary, not revolutionary, in its approach; it ultimately seeks (albeit substantial) attitude change in existing institutional praxis and not its rout. As climate change policy was still very much mutable in the mid-1990s when the gender mainstreaming initiative emerged as a UN institutional priority, this arguably allowed it to slip through the net on mainstreaming. Had it been applied from the outset, it could have addressed what has become apparent as one of the major flaws of the climate change regime and avoided a situation where women became disadvantaged and effectively marginalized across its institutions and processes. Nonetheless, even where gender mainstreaming is pursued it does not represent a 'magic bullet'; for example, it does not, in and of itself, actually overcome the impacts of pre-existing power differentials – this is dependent on the commitment of policy and decision-makers (Benschop and Verloo 2006).

## A 'representative' role

In principle, 'women' ostensibly represent a cohesive group that may notionally be readily represented by inclusion of a gender constituency in institutional arrangements – at least in the rarefied world of the administration of civil society by international governmental organizations which tend, in a gross oversimplification that sacrifices accuracy to convenience, to treat gender as synonymous with 'women's' issues. Convenient as such an approach may be for institutions, it tends to gloss over the fact that gender considerations apply to both women and men, the enormous diversity among women, and the fact that forging a workable and 'representative' constituency (insofar as this can be claimed for an unelected body which time and space preclude discussing in detail here) that can legitimately claim to speak for women actually presents a hugely difficult task. Claims to play a (what is perhaps best termed) quasi-representative role in this context require broad participation by women globally in developing strategies and positions. However, ecofeminist approaches are well equipped to accommodate the considerable diversity that such participation brings to the fore and habitually employ a range of approaches, strategies, and methodologies to forge alliances that have been also used to good effect in the climate change context (Morrow 2013). These include focused campaigning; broader consensus-building activities; general network and specific coalition construction around discrete matters of shared concern; and developing and sharing skill sets. In each of these areas, new technologies have been harnessed to good effect to develop a more consistent global reach for these activities than has been attainable hitherto. Furthermore, and significantly given the more established position of other major groups in the climate change regime, these activities are not exclusively focused within the women's movement; they are also applied in reaching out to other civil society actors where experience of compound disadvantage creates shared and cross-cutting communities of interest.

While agenda setting may be the ultimate goal for the gender constituency, for a relatively disempowered group, it can be problematic, and more incremental approaches therefore tend to predominate. The following section considers the application of a number of ecofeminist-informed approaches that have served to aid in constructing the gender constituency in the global climate change regime.

## *Transversal politics and coalition-building*

For civil society, the task of coalition-building across administratively convenient constituencies that are in fact comprised of highly heterogeneous groups is a key challenge. Transversal politics, which eschews the ethnocentricity and exclusionary practices of assimilatory politics and the essentialism and reification of identity politics (Yuval-Davis 1999), are increasingly employed by feminists as a means of developing collective identity and action. At its most basic, transversal politics is based on standpoint epistemology; 'the encompassment of difference by equality'; and a clear differentiation between 'positioning, identity and values' (Yuval-Davis 1999:95). It can be defined as: 'an alternative political ethos characteristic of heterogeneous coalitions which prizes openness, dialogue and unity of purpose among diverse entities' (Murtagh 2008:22). Transversal politics appears to offer an excellent opportunity to build upon the recognition of intersectionality that is a key response to the ecofeminist conception of compound disadvantage, as it can, among other things, potentially capitalize on the politics of multiple overlapping identities, identifying important elements of commonality that can promote coalition building. In its recognition of the importance of lived experience, the contingent nature of knowledge and the need for debate and dialogue that results, and its conscious attempt to accommodate difference without resort to a smothering imposition of homogeneity, transversal politics sits particularly well with ecofeminist thought.

The story of the gender constituency's battle for recognition in the global climate change regime has involved practical manifestations of transversal politics in its invocation of active and engaged multiple citizenships that are also globally and transnationally located (Yuval-Davis 1997:5). This type of innovative approach offers an exciting means to progress beyond the deadlock that inevitably ensues from a need for total agreement in forging subject-specific alliances, requiring instead an openness to dialogue as a means to arriving at a common perspective. However, its very flexibility represents a serious challenge to more traditional and entrenched means of doing the business of politics that can, in domestic contexts at least, make transversal politics the subject of misunderstanding and even outright hostility (Murtagh 2008). That said, it is arguably more readily suited to the porous and fluid nature of modern international politics where there is perhaps more conceptual space for alternative modes of engagement, including those founded on feminist thought, particularly in light of the (albeit controversial; see Amoore and Langley 2004) growth of global civil society that has been one of the by-products of globalization and the dominance of neoliberal discourse (Marchand 2003).

The quest for official constituency status in the global climate change regime was mandated by the women's caucus at COP14 (Poznan 2008). In order to establish its credentials as representing the interests and expertise of women across the globe, one of the key strategies adopted was to forge a coalition. This coalition was headed by an umbrella organization called GenderCC – Women for Climate Justice. Originally founded at COP 9 (Milan 2003), GenderCC is a global network of women, gender activists, and experts on gender and climate justice issues representing all world regions. Given subsequent developments which have seen extraordinarily rapid advancement for the gender cause after years of glacial progress, the influence of GenderCC on rallying women to action and in relatively short order successfully pressing for institutional change has been little short of miraculous. It also speaks to the importance of providing a figurehead (in both organizational and symbolic terms) in solidifying the identity of what could otherwise be viewed as a somewhat amorphous group.

## Fostering participation and inclusiveness within the gender constituency

The promotion of inclusiveness through adopting open, participatory dialogue in its own affairs is a hallmark of ecofeminist methodology and one that has been very much present in the development of the gender constituency in the global climate change regime. In part, this is a matter of principle, following through the thinking on women's participation in global institutional processes to its logical conclusion by applying it internally. At the same time, fostering inclusion through participation is also a response to ecofeminism's activist roots, which emphasize the need to respect and incorporate women's lived experience in decision-making processes and outcomes. This is not to the exclusion of scientific or technical or scholarly concerns, but as an important source of relevant material in its own right, thus ensuring that conclusions arrived at are based on the most complete information possible.

An inclusive and participatory approach featured strongly in the gender constituency's activities in developing a strategic position from which to fight its corner in the quest for recognition in the global climate change regime. A key example of this approach in the process was the negotiation and agreement of a charter behind which women could rally. The draft Charter of the Women's and Gender Constituency (GenderCC 2011) was fashioned through an inclusive dialogue undertaken by a global coalition of women's groups comprised of Women in Europe for a Common Future (WECF); ENERGIA (International Network on Gender and Sustainable Energy); the Women's Environment and Development Organisation (WEDO); and GenderCC. The principles invoked in the charter, both in draft and as eventually adopted in augmented form after a lengthy consultative process (GenderCC 2016) strongly echo the core priorities of ecofeminism. They include democratic and participatory governance; respect for divergent positions; and wide and inclusive membership (in terms of age, region, and background; GenderCC 2016: Article 2) These principles are to be pursued through the cultivation of a 'flexible governance structure' (GenderCC 2016: Article 7), employing open, active, consensus-building communication strategies (GenderCC 2016: Article 8). The Charter's objectives likewise echo an ecofeminist agenda, by prioritizing making women's voices and experiences heard; feeding women's views into all aspects of ongoing climate change discourse; and promoting co-operation with other constituencies and caucuses in the search for constructive and mutually reinforcing alliances (GenderCC 2016: Article 3). In line with its own constituent practices, the constituency also specifically committed to a framework for the pursuit of a 'just and gender-responsive climate framework' (GenderCC 2016: Article 4). In its continuing endeavours interfacing with the climate change regime, the constituency promises a flexible, transparent, and accountable governance structure (GenderCC 2016: Article 6).

## Women's leadership and climate change

At the same time as women were pressing for participation rights in the global climate change regime, another important strand of gender activism was emerging. At COP 16 (Cancun) in 2010, through a NGO-sponsored capacity building and networking initiative, the then provisional women/gender constituency was also pressing for a leadership role for women in respect of climate justice (Jackson 2010). In particular, the Mary Robinson Foundation's Climate Justice Initiative (MRFCJI) sought to promote a more directional role for women in climate change in the run-up to COP16. The conception of leadership involved was a broad and purposive one and in order to promote a range of gender aspects the MRFCJI established an informal women's leadership network. This drew in diverse representatives from UN institutions, governments, civil society, and the philanthropic and private sectors. The approach that emerged from the MRFCJI process exhibits a number of features that display ecofeminist characteristics, in particular in advocating gender equality in UNFCCC sub-programmes, full participation for women in decision-making, collaborative sharing and extrapolation of good practice, and networking. Progress on developing women's leadership was augmented at COP16 itself by establishing a troika consisting of the three female ministers holding the relevant portfolios from the states hosting COP 15 (Copenhagen), 16, and 17 (Durban; Sebastian and Ceplis 2010), in order to play a more pronounced role in promoting the women's agenda in the COP17 process. This approach has subsequently been continued and expanded upon in the Troika+ initiative.[4]

In the wake of official confirmation of the status of the gender constituency at COP 17 (2011), there has of course been a degree of institutional change within the global climate change regime itself, but women continue to seek to lead and drive debate in the quest for further progress. For example, another important dimension of the ongoing work of the MRF-CJI is providing a research base that is informing the debate on 'gender balance' (of which more below) in the UNFCCC process. It subsequently published a report recommending that targets be set (no less than 40 per cent and no more than 60 per cent for either gender) for regime bodies and state delegations, and that sanctions be imposed for non-compliance with them (MRFCJI 2013).

In terms of developing women's leadership in the global climate change regime, the appointment of Mary Robinson herself as the UN special envoy for climate change is encouraging (UN News Centre 2014). Not only is her committed advocacy of an active role for women in this context secured as part of her indicated intention to continue working with her foundation in climate justice of value in its own right, but she is also a strong role model with a proven track record of leadership in human rights and environmental issues within the UN system.

## Changing the climate of participation?

There have been a number of encouraging developments with regard to gender within the UNFCCC regime in the wake of the granting of constituency status. Most significantly COP 18 (in Doha, 2012) led to the adoption of Decision 23/CP.18 on 'Promoting gender balance and improving the participation of women in UNFCCC negotiations and in the representation of Parties in bodies established pursuant to the Convention or the Kyoto Protocol' (UNFCCC 2012a). This formalized a new institutional commitment to address gender issues in the context of climate change and adopted 'gender balance' as a goal for the regime and has set in motion interesting developments, some of which are considered later in this chapter.

Additionally, COP 18 and COP 19 (Warsaw, 2013) both featured a specific 'Gender Day' as part of the official COP meeting. The presence of gender issues was not limited to a single tokenistic gesture: the former also featured the UNFCCC subsidiary body for implementation delivering a report on 'Gender and Climate Change' (UNFCCC 2013c). The latter included a workshop on gender balance in the UNFCCC (UNFCCC 2013b) and showcased grassroots good practice on addressing climate change across a range of 'lighthouse activities' (such as climate change resilient affordable housing; the one million women movement; and the Adaptation for Smallholder Agriculture Programme; Momentum for Change 2013).

The UNFCCC is also beginning to bring gender to the fore in respect of the climate change regime's substantive activities – for example, the Clean Development Mechanism (CDM; UNFCCC 2012b). Its approach here, however, appears to be somewhat anodyne and does not really convey a full understanding of the extent of what is required. For example, despite making references to gender mainstreaming, the document 'CDM and Women' seemingly views gender as something that can be successfully addressed as a mere 'add on' to an originally gender-blind regime. Long experience would suggest otherwise, and it is evident that much remains to be done to realize gender mainstreaming in the CDM.

Gender also came to the fore in the context of climate change in association with the 2012 United Nations Conference on Sustainable Development – Rio+20 – with the joint liaison group of the three secretariats of the treaties signed at Rio in 1992, producing a report on the importance of gender in implementing the long-term objectives of their respective regimes (CBD et al. 2012). The UNFCCC's contribution to this document indicated its understanding in principle of climate change as a gendered issue and the need to pursue gender mainstreaming and women's agency in addressing its impacts, particularly through the CDM. The coverage offered seemed to indicate a concrete attempt by the UNFCCC to bring itself more into line with the broader UN institutional approach to gender, as it had indicated in principle was its aim in Decision 23/CP.18 (UNFCCC 2012a). This trajectory was seemingly reinforced by the adoption at COP 20 of Decision 18/CP.20, referring to developments thus far and initiating the two-year Lima Work Programme on Gender (LWPG) under the UNFCCC (UNFCCC 2014), which promised a more thoroughgoing engagement with gender by the regime machinery than hitherto. However, while the regime may arguably be attempting to set its house in order in this regard, this does not guarantee that its signatory states will respond to the invitation to do so positively – or indeed at all. This would seem to be borne out by the Paris Agreement, the most significant outcome of COP 21 (in Paris, 2015) and the guiding document for future action on climate (UNFCCC 2015), which, if viewed as an acid test for the regime's engagement with gender, makes for discouraging reading. Despite significant discussion of gender (not least prompted by the gender constituency) in the run up to the COP, it receives a scant three mentions in the agreement: appearing once in the preamble, which refers to gender equality and empowerment of women; and twice in the substantive agreement in Articles 7 (adaptation) and 11 (capacity building), which hardly amounts to 'mainstreaming'. Nonetheless, these initiatives considered collectively at least indicate that gender is now enjoying some visibility in the global climate change regime – this in itself represents an improvement and indicates that the regime can no longer be described as entirely gender blind – which is a good, if inexcusably belated and as yet painfully slow, start.

## Conclusion: a Damascene conversion?

The granting of constituency status has certainly opened doors for women's fuller participation in the global climate change regime as this is the vehicle through which official observer participation is pursued. The UNFCCC has also committed in principle to encourage (but significantly not *to require*, which is beyond its power) 'balanced geographic and perspective representation' at workshops mandated by the COPs and the regime's subsidiary body, where much of the real business of the regime is done (UNFCCC undated). Much will of course depend on the response of signatory states as to whether such participation manifests as a matter of form or substance. Furthermore, merely allowing women access to the regime does not constitute meaningful participation; they must also be enabled to secure a proportionate influence on its development and operation. This depends in part on the regime's willingness to accommodate the necessary power shift that is involved, but it is also a more complex question as other structural and procedural factors will come into play. These include lack of resources to facilitate participation; lack of representation; lack of access to information; lack of technical capacity to engage with scientific materials; limited advocacy skills; and financial and procedural barriers. For women, the ability to pursue participation is further hindered by gendered social, economic, cultural, legal, and educational barriers (Brody et al. 2008).

At least gender is now finally, if not always prominently, present as a concern within the global climate change regime – a fact indicated by its presence on the main UNFCCC website, which recognizes that gender is a significant cross-cutting issue that is relevant across the range of its activities, noting the 'gender and . . . ' relationship in regard to adaptation, financial support, mitigation, and technology support. There is also a specific commitment to both institutional and human resource capacity-building support to foster 'gender balance' in all the aforementioned aspects of the climate change regime. The rationale for the UNFCCC's emerging, more gender-aware approach is multifaceted: the key element focuses of course on securing the effectiveness of convention regime initiatives in their own right but supporting strands include the following: not exacerbating other gender inequality/vulnerability issues; promoting solutions to other gender inequality/vulnerability issues; and supporting broader gender mainstreaming with respect to technology. Significantly, in terms of advancing convention initiatives, ensuring 'the equal participation of men and women in the decision-making and implementation phases of [convention regime] activities' are identified as significant (UNFCCC 2013d).

The emerging approach taken toward gender in the global climate change regime, while representing a considerable improvement on what has gone before, does however remain ambiguous at best. On the one hand the avoidance of the established terms 'gender mainstreaming' and 'gender equality' in favour of the rather vague (in the UNFCCC's usage, if not elsewhere – see, for example, MREJF 2013 – discussed previously) term 'gender balance' in a seemingly deliberate departure from the recognized lexicon, gives pause for thought and could, were one inclined to be uncharitable, indicate avoidance of key aspects of the established gender regime. It is also significant that, throughout its ongoing initiatives, the UNFCCC's tone and approach is necessarily but also determinedly hortatory rather than compulsory. This limits its influence and impact on signatory state behaviour, which ultimately directs the regime – as is amply demonstrated in the relative paucity of gender coverage in the Paris Agreement. On the other hand, in terms of gendering the internal machinery of the UNFCCC, more may potentially be achievable – though it is at the time of writing too early to fully evaluate the impact of the LWPG. Thus far it may be said that the approach adopted toward building and publicizing a database of women's representation in regime institutions and in signatory state delegations seems to offer a positive start in providing measureable, evidenced baseline for action (UNFCCC 2013a). However, it should be kept in mind that even ostensible organizational cooperation is no guarantee of concrete progress in addressing gender equality issues as the potential for constructive dialogue, let alone action, can be fatally compromised by wildly differing interpretations of key concepts once analysis passes beyond the superficial (Benschop and Verloo 2006). This is arguably the stage at which the UNFCCC's broader engagement with gender currently rests, not least as evident in the disappointing approach to gender evident in the Paris Agreement. Realizing effective participation requires a thoroughgoing change in organizational practices and while such may be emerging in supporting areas of the regime architecture, they are as yet scantly represented in the main arena. At a minimum, it is necessary that policies, procedures, and processes are put in place that are capable of addressing women's more general lack of power in respect of both policy and decision-making processes (Bhatta 2001). Failure to address adequately these structural problems acts not only to the detriment of women's exercise and enjoyment of hard-won participation rights, but arguably also goes to the viability of societal responses to the substantive issues themselves. Finally, while addressing gender issues is often characterized as the proverbial 'win-win' concept, it can be perceived as a threat to a multiplicity of entrenched institutional values and practices and as conflicting with established mainstream policy goals – and this would seem to be a real possibility in the context of the global climate change regime.

At the time of writing, it remains to be seen whether initiatives under the UNFCCC represent mere lip-service to tackling the manifest gender inequality issues in the global climate change regime (if so, they will deliver little); but if they represent the beginning of full gender mainstreaming, they are potentially revolutionary. COP21 suggests that while gender issues are now 'live' within the global climate change regime, they are yet to gain substantial traction in terms of its central legal sphere. What we seem to be seeing is the (long-delayed) start of a long process of gendering global climate change governance, and it is clear that further substantive progress will depend not only on the efforts of the secretariat but on the willingness of signatory states to demonstrate the necessary political will to drive the process forward – which is evidently even now by no means a given.

## Notes

1 The 'major groups' identified in *Agenda 21* are business and industry; children and youth; farmers; indigenous peoples; local authorities; science and technology; workers and trade unions; and NGOs and women.

2 Gender mainstreaming was first adopted in UN policy in the wake of the Fourth United Nations World Conference on Women in Beijing in 1995 under the Beijing Declaration and Platform for action (UN 1995).

3 While the major group in question is commonly referred to in the UN institutional context as 'women', internally the constituency adopts a more inclusive approach, preferring the term 'women and gender' in acknowledgement of the fact that the issues involved are not confined to 'women's' concerns.

4 This high-level leadership network now comprises more than fifty-five members and continues to be actively engaged in fostering gender balance and improved participation in the UNFCCC regime. For further information, see www.mrfcj.org/our-work/troika/ (accessed 18 April 2016).

# References

Agostino, A. (2010) *Statement to the High Level Segment of the COP 10 December 2010.* Online. Available at: https://unfccc.int/files/meetings/cop_16/statements/application/pdf/101210_cop16_hls_icae.pdf (accessed 4 August 2014).

Amoore, L. and Langley, P. (2004) 'Ambiguities of a global civil society', *Review of International Studies* 30: 89–110.

Benschop, Y. and Verloo, M. (2006) 'Sisyphus' sisters: Can gender mainstreaming escape the genderedness of organizations?', *Journal of Gender Studies* 15(1): 19–33.

Bhatta, G. (2001) 'Of geese and ganders: Mainstreaming gender in the context of sustainable human development', *Journal of Gender Studies* 10(1): 17–32.

Brody, A., Demetriades, J. and Esplen, E. (2008) *Gender and Climate Change: Mapping the Linkages.* Brighton: BRIDGE. Online. Available at: http://www.bridge.ids.ac.uk/reports/Climate_Change_DFID_draft.pdf (accessed 13 June 2014).

CBD, UNCCD, and UNFCCC (2012) *The Rio Conventions: Action on Gender.* Online. Available at: http://unfccc.int/resource/docs/publications/roi_20_gender_brochure.pdf (accessed 23 June 2014).

Charlesworth, H., Chinkin, C. and Wright, S. (1991) 'Feminist approaches to international law', *The American Journal of International Law* 85(4): 613–645.

ECOSOC (1997) *Res 1997/2 Agreed Conclusions on Gender Mainstreaming.* Online. Available at: www.un.org/womenwatch/osagi/pdf/ECOSOCAC1997.2.PDF (accessed 4 August 2014), p3.

GenderCC (2011): *Charter of the Women's and Gender Constituency Under the UNFCCC* (draft). Online. Available at: www.gendercc.net/fileadmin/inhalte/Dokumente/UNFCCC_conferences/Constituency/Women_Gender_Constituency_Charter_final.pdf (accessed 13 June 2014).

GenderCC (2016): *Charter of the Womens' and Gender Constituency.* Online. Available at: http://womengenderclimate.org/wp-content/uploads/2014/04/WGC_Charter_2016.pdf (accessed 18 April 2016).

Gupta, K. S. (2006) 'Gender and international environmental negotiations – How far and how much more?' *Papers on International Environmental Negotiation, Vol XV PON Harvard Law School.* Online. Available at: www.oas.org/dsd/Tool-kit/Documentos/ModuleV/Gupta%20Reading.pdf. (accessed 20 October 2014).

Jackson, S. (2010) 'Mary Robinson Foundation (Climate Justice)/Realizing Rights (The Ethical Globalization Initiative)', *Women's Leadership on Climate Justice: Planning for Cancun and Beyond,* 17/09/2010. Online. Available at:www.mrfcj.org/pdf/Meeting_Report_Womens_Leadership_on_Climate_Justice_17Sep2010.pdf (accessed 10 June 2014).

Lambrou, Y. and Piana, G. (2006) 'Gender: The missing component of the response to climate change', *Food and Agriculture Organization of the United Nations.* Online. Available at: www.eldis.org/vfile/upload/1/document/0708/DOC21057.pdf (accessed 20 October 2014).

Lister, R (2003) *Citizenship: A Feminist Perspective* (second edition). Washington Square, NY: New York University Press.

Marchand, M. M. (2003) 'Challenging globalization: Towards a feminist understanding of resistance', *Review of International Studies* 29: 145–160.

Mary Robinson Foundation – Climate Justice Initiative (2013) *The Full View: Advancing the Goal of Gender Balance in Multilateral and Intergovernmental Processes.* Online. Available at: www.mrfcj.org/pdf/2013–06–13-The-Full-View.pdf (accessed 7 August 2014).

Momentum for Change (2013) *Momentum for Change; Women for Results – Sponsored by the Rockefeller Foundation.* Online. Available at: http://unfccc.int/secretariat/momentum_for_change/items/7318.php (accessed 13 June 2014).

Morrow, K. (2013) 'Ecofeminism and the environment: International law and climate change', in Davies, M. and Munro, V. (eds) *The Ashgate Research Companion to Feminist Legal Theory*. Farnham: Ashgate, 377–394.

Morrow, K. (2015) 'Sustainability, environmental citizenship and the ongoing challenges of reshaping supranational environmental governance', in Grear, A. and Kotze, A. (eds) *Research Handbook on Human Rights and the Environment*. Cheltenham: Edward Elgar, 200–218.

Moser, C. and Moser, A. (2005) 'Gender mainstreaming since Beijing: A review of success and limitations in international institutions', in Porter, F. and Sweetman, C. (eds) *Mainstreaming Gender in Development: A Critical Review*. Oxford: Oxfam Focus on Gender, 11–23.

Murtagh, C. (2008) 'A transient transition: The cultural and institutional obstacles impeding the Northern Ireland women's coalition in its progression from informal to formal politics', *Irish Political Studies* 23(1): 21–40.

Parikh, J. (n.d.) 'Is climate change a gender issue?', *UNDP India* (Draft). Online. Available at: www.disasterwatch.net/climatechange/gndr_climt07.pdf (accessed 6 August 2014).

Rocheleau, D., Thomas-Slayter, B. and Wangari, E. (2006) 'Gender and the environment: A feminist political ecology perspective', in Haenn, N. and Wilk, R. (eds) *The Environment in Anthropology: A Reader in Ecology, Culture and Sustainable Living*. New York: New York University Press, 27–33.

Sandilands, C. (1999) *The Good-Natured Feminist: Ecofeminism and the Quest for Democracy*. Minneapolis: University of Minnesota Press.

Sebastian, J. and Ceplis, D. (CARES) (2010) *Perspective on Gender and Climate Change at Cancun*. Online. Available at: www.aic.ca/gender/pdf/Gender_and_Climate_Cancun.pdf (accessed 10 June 2014).

Shiva, V. (1993) 'The impoverishment of the environment: Women and children last', in Mies, M. and Shiva, V. (eds) *Ecofeminism*. London: Zed Books, 70–90.

UN (1992a) *Rio Declaration on Environment and Development*. Online. Available at: www.unep.org/Documents. Multilingual/Default.asp?documentid=78&articleid=1163 (accessed 10 June 2014).

UN (1992b) *Earth Summit: Agenda 21: The United Nations Programme of Action from Rio*. Online. Available at: www.un.org/esa/dsd/agenda21/res_agenda21_00.shtml (accessed 10 June 2014).

UN (1992c) *Framework Convention on Climate Change (FCCC)*. Online. Available at: http://unfccc.int/resource/docs/convkp/conveng.pdf (accessed 10 June 2014).

UN (1995) *Beijing Declaration and Platform for Action*. Online. Available at: www.un.org/womenwatch/daw/beijing/pdf/BDPfA%20E.pdf (accessed 10 June 2014).

UNFCCC (2012a) Decision 23/CP.18 on 'Promoting gender balance and improving the participation of women in UNFCCC negotiations and in the representation of Parties in bodies established pursuant to the Convention or the Kyoto Protocol', *FCCC/CP/2012/8/Add.3*. Online. Available at: http://unfccc.int/files/bodies/election_and_membership/application/pdf/cop18_gender_balance.pdf (accessed 7 August 2014).

UNFCCC (2012b) *CDM and Women*. Online. Available at: http://unfccc.int/resource/docs/publications/cdm_and_women.pdf (accessed 26 June 2014).

UNFCCC (2013a) *Report on Gender Composition UNFCCC/CP/2013/4*. Online. Available at: http://unfccc.int/resource/docs/2013/cop19/eng/04.pdf (accessed 7 August 2014).

UNFCCC (2013b) *Workshop on Gender, Climate Change and the UNFCCC Workshop on Gender, Climate Change and the UNFCCC*. Online. Available at: http://unfccc.int/files/adaptation/application/pdf/in_session_workshop_agenda_web.pdf (accessed 11 August 2013).

UNFCCC (2013c) *Subsidiary Body for Implementation 'Gender and Climate Change' FCCC/SBI/2013/L.16*. Online. Available at: http://unfccc.int/resource/docs/2013/sbi/eng/l16.pdf (accessed 7 August 2014).

UNFCCC (2013d) *Linking Gender and Climate Change*. Online. Available at: http://unfccc.int/gender_and_climate_change/items/7516.php (accessed 13 June 2014).

UNFCCC (2014) *Decision 18/CP.20 'Lima Work Programme on Gender*. Online. Available at: http://unfccc.int/resource/docs/2014/cop20/eng/10a03.pdf#page=35 (accessed 18 April 2016).

UNFCCC (2015) *The Paris Agreement*. Online. Available at: https://unfccc.int/resource/docs/2015/cop21/eng/l09.pdf (accessed 18 April 2016).

UNFCCC (n.d.) *Constituencies and observer participation at workshops*. Online. Available at: http://unfccc.int/files/parties_and_observers/ngo/application/pdf/20063103_constituencies_and_workshops.pdf (accessed 13 June 2014).

UN News Centre (2014) *Ban Appoints Former Irish President Mary Robinson as Special Envoy for Climate Change*. 14 July 2014. Online. Available at: www.un.org/apps/news/story.asp?NewsID=48265#.U99pTlJ0zMw. (accessed 4 August 2014).

Verchick, R. M. M. (1996) 'In a greener voice: Feminist theory and environmental justice', *Harvard Women's Law Journal* 19: 23–88.

Wamukonya, N. and Skutsch, M. (2001) *Is there a Gender Angle to the Climate Change Negotiations?* Online. Available at: www.unep.org/roa/amcen/Projects_Programme/climate_change/PreCop15/Proceedings/Gender-and-climate-change/IsthereaGenderAngletotheClimateChangeNegiotiations.pdf. (accessed 10 June 2014).

WCED (World Commission on Environment and Development) (1987) *Our Common Future* (the Brundtland Report). Oxford: Oxford University Press. Online. Available at: http://conspect.nl/pdf/Our_Common_Future-Brundtland_Report_1987.pdf. (accessed 4 August 2014).

Yuval-Davis, N. (1997) 'Women, citizenship and difference', *Feminist Review* 57(Autumn): 4–27.

Yuval-Davis, N. (1999) 'What is "transversal politics"?', *Soundings* 12(summer): 94–98.

# 28

# PLANNING FOR CLIMATE CHANGE

## REDD+SES as gender-responsive environmental action

*Marcela Tovar-Restrepo*

## Introduction

Over the past twenty years, a broad scientific consensus has emerged on the fact that climate change is one of the most urgent issues of our time, bringing environmental and socio-economic implications that threaten both industrialized and less industrialized world regions. A much smaller community of scholars and practitioners has documented the linkages between climate change and gender inequality, showing differentiated impacts on men and women because of the gender division of labour and differences in use, control, and ownership of assets and natural resources (Masika 2002; Dankelman 2010; Tovar-Restrepo 2010; Arora-Jonsson 2011). The central argument is that climate change exacerbates existing gender inequality and so strategies for addressing it must take into account not only gender but also other *intersecting* markers of power and identity such as income, ethnicity, race, religion, ability/disability, age, literacy, migratory status, and geographical location (Crenshaw 1989; Khosla and Masaud 2011; Bastia 2014). All of these factors lead to differences in exposure to risk and vulnerability in the face of climate changes. Climate change impacts disproportionately affect poor, rural and indigenous women in non-industrialized countries and yet they are less able to cope and recover than men (Enarson 2000; Dankelman 2009; WEDO-GGCA-IUCN-UNDP 2009). Thanks to the work of many women's advocacy organizations, some gender-sensitive policies have been included in multilateral climate change and environmental agreements such as the United Nations Framework Convention on Climate Change (UNFCCC) and Reducing Emissions from Deforestation and Forest Degradation (REDD+; see Box 28.1). However, even though there have been a few improvements in this regard, climate change planning continues to ignore debates on gender and fails to address differentiated vulnerability, impacts, and resilience conditions between men and women.

This chapter provides an overview of the connections between climate change and gender, using action research on REDD+ that was conducted in 2011 in Tanzania, Nepal, Ecuador, and Brazil to demonstrate the needs and benefits of mainstreaming gender, age, location, and ethnicity when trying to achieve more sustainable human settlements. This research project

---

## Box 28.1   What is REDD+?

REDD+ stands for: 'Reducing emissions from deforestation and forest degradation plus sustainable management of forests, conservation of forest carbon stocks and enhancement of forest carbon stocks'.

Degradation and deforestation of the world's tropical forests are cumulatively responsible for about 10 per cent of net global carbon emissions. Thus tackling the destruction of tropical forests is core to any concerted effort to combat climate change. REDD is a policy mechanism that is part of the UNFCCC negotiations. It intends to incentivize a break from historic trends of increasing deforestation rates and greenhouse gases emissions. It is a framework through which developing countries are rewarded financially for any emissions reductions achieved associated with a decrease in the conversion of forests to alternate land uses. Having identified current and/or projected rates of deforestation and forest degradation, a country taking remedial action to effectively reduce those rates will be financially rewarded relative to the extent of their achieved emissions reductions. In its infancy, REDD was first and foremost focused on reducing emissions from deforestation and forest degradation. However, in 2007 the Bali Action Plan, formulated at COP-13 to the UNFCCC, stated that a comprehensive approach to mitigating climate change should include '[p]olicy approaches and positive incentives on issues relating to reducing emissions from deforestation and forest degradation in developing countries; and the role of conservation, sustainable management of forests and enhancement of forest carbon stocks in developing countries'. A year later, this was further elaborated on as the role of conservation, sustainable management of forests and enhancement of forest carbon stocks was upgraded so as to receive the same emphasis as avoided emissions from deforestation and forest degradation. Finally, in 2010, at COP-16 as set out in the Cancun Agreements, REDD became REDD-plus (REDD+), to reflect the new components. REDD+ now includes:

1   Reducing emissions from deforestation;
2   Reducing emissions from forest degradation;
3   Conservation of forest carbon stocks;
4   Sustainable management of forests;
5   Enhancement of forest carbon stocks.

Within its remit, REDD+ has the potential to simultaneously contribute to climate change mitigation and poverty alleviation, while also conserving biodiversity and sustaining vital ecosystem services. This potential for multiple benefits raises the crucial question of to what extent the inclusion of development and conservation objectives may help or hinder the overall success of, and negotiations for, a future REDD+ framework (explicitly for climate change mitigation). Having said this, prospective co-benefits can easily transform into prospective co-detriments, making the earlier question arguably irrelevant. Aside from whether consideration of such factors will promote or hamper the success and negotiations of a REDD+ framework, they are unquestionably important for the creation of a sustainable and equitable REDD+ process.

*Source*: http://theredddesk.org/what-redd#toc-2

from which my data are taken was conducted by the Women's Environment and Development Organization (WEDO; see Box 28.2) in partnership with and the REDD+ Social and Environmental Standards Initiative (REDD+SES; see Box 28.3).[1] The purpose was to 'unpack and address the links between gender, safeguards, and standards in REDD+ [in order] to move beyond the conceptual level and generate suggestions for strengthening REDD+ from in-country research based on the lives of women and men in forest communities' (Owen in WEDO-REDD+SES 2013). Research findings presented here are primarily oriented to policy and planning and seek to contribute to the broader theoretical agenda within feminist research on climate change which, as MacGregor (2010) has pointed out, is urgently needed. Building on lessons learned from this research, I present guidelines that, from a feminist perspective, should be taken into account in climate change planning processes. I argue that actions taken to mitigate and/or adapt to climate change should be designed, implemented, and monitored from a gender perspective in order to achieve sustainable resource management, to improve livelihoods, and to promote gender equality. My argument resonates with the main conclusions and evidence presented by the research project.

---

### Box 28.2　The Women's Environment and Development Organization (WEDO)

The Women's Environment and Development Organization (WEDO) was established in 1990 by a US Congresswoman (Bella Abzug) and a US journalist (Mim Kelber). It is a global women's advocacy organization working to promote human rights, gender equality, and the integrity of the environment. Its mission is to ensure women's rights and economic and environmental justice and to advocate for the inclusion of sustainable development principles in national policies, programs, and practices.

WEDO's central purpose is to mobilize and empower women to participate in conferences, forums, and other policy-making processes, so that their voices are heard and their perspectives taken into account in traditionally male dominated policy areas such as the environment, development, or population. WEDO organizes women from all over the world to allow them to contribute to these decision-making processes, principally (but not exclusively) at the international level, such as at the UN. In November 1991, for example, WEDO organized the World Women's Congress for a Healthy Planet, which produced a strategy document which it presented to the UN Conference on the Environment and Development (UNCED). This subsequently became *Women's Action Agenda 21*, and was included in the UN's *Agenda 21* and the Rio Declaration of 1992.

WEDO's work includes running and participating in conferences; capacity building and training work; awareness-raising; and facilitating networks of relevant NGOs and other stakeholders. It works in partnerships with governments, civil society organizations including women's, human rights, environmental and development organizations, intergovernmental organizations, and other stakeholders. It also runs projects, currently under three broad themes of Women's Leadership, Sustainable Development, and Global Governance.

In 2006 WEDO won the Champion of the Earth award by the United Nations Environment Program for its work on sustainable development.

*Website*: http://www.wedo.org
(*Source*: Doyle et al. 2015)

---

**Box 28.3    REDD+ Social and Environmental Standards
Initiative (REDD+SES)**

The REDD+ Social and Environmental Standards initiative aims to build support for government-led REDD+ programs that make a significant contribution to human rights, poverty alleviation, and biodiversity conservation. Recognizing that REDD+ has the potential for serious risks to indigenous peoples, local communities, and women, along with the potential for social and environmental co-benefits, REDD+SES is a comprehensive framework of key issues to address the social and environmental performance of a REDD+ program. REDD+SES is intended for use by governments, NGOs, financing agencies, and other stakeholders to support the design and implementation of government-led REDD+ programs implemented at national or state/provincial/regional level and for all forms of fund-based or market-based financing. The standards provide guidance in designing REDD+ programs using a multi-stakeholder approach and also provide a mechanism for reporting on the social and environmental performance of REDD+ programs. REDD+SES consists of Principles, Criteria, and Indicators (PCI). While the Principles and Criteria are consistent across countries, the Indicators are adaptable at the country level. The process for using REDD+SES is informed by 'Guidelines for the use of REDD+SES at Country Level'. The Climate, Community, and Biodiversity Alliance (CCBA) and CARE International serve as the international secretariat of the REDD+SES initiative with technical support from the Proforest Initiative. Countries currently participating in the REDD+SES initiative include Brazil (State of Acre), Ecuador, Indonesia (Central Kalimantan), Nepal, and Tanzania since 2010, and Guatemala, Liberia, Mexico, Indonesia (East Kalimantan), Peru (Region of San Martin), and Brazil (State of Amazonas) since 2012. For more information, visit www.redd-standards.org.

*Source:* WEDO/REDD+SES 2013:16

---

The chapter is divided into three sections. In the next section, I present key concepts and linkages between gender and climate change, explaining how these links are relevant to adaptation and mitigation strategies such as REDD+. I then discuss the main research findings, highlighting issues to be taken into account when implementing a gender-responsive action plan. Finally, I suggest a set of guidelines for gender-responsive climate change policy and planning processes based on the research findings.

## Climate change and gender: key concepts and linkages

According to the Intergovernmental Panel on Climate Change (IPCC; 2007), climate change refers to a significant variability in weather patterns over an extended period of time, typically decades or longer. It is linked to carbon emissions commonly produced by human activities, such as clearing forests and burning fossil fuels. Climate change effects are principally higher temperatures in the climate system, including air and ocean temperatures, and an increase in the intensity and frequency of natural disasters, such as flooding or hurricanes that threaten rural and urban ecosystems. Total anthropogenic greenhouse gas emissions continued to increase from 1970 to 2010, with larger absolute decadal increases toward the end of this period, the highest in human history. Without additional efforts to combat climate change, emissions growth is expected to persist, resulting in temperature increases in 2100 from 3.7°C to 4.8°C compared to pre-industrial levels (IPCC 2014).

Climate change is often presented in scientific language as a problem affecting all humans, but social scientific research shows dramatic variation in its effects on different populations. Kaijser and Kronsell (2014) explain that a feminist intersectionality approach[2] is useful in showing how different individuals and groups relate differently to climate change, due to their situatedness in power structures based on context-specific and dynamic social categorizations. They write:

> The responsibility, vulnerability, and decision-making power of individuals and groups in relation to climate change can be attributed to social structures based on characteristics such as gender, socio-economic status, ethnicity, nationality, health, sexual orientation, age, and place. Moreover, the impacts of climate change, as well as strategies for mitigation and adaptation, may reinforce or challenge such structures and categorisations.
>
> *(Kaijser and Kronsell 2014:420)*

Most negative climate change impacts are faced by poor women and men living in rural and urban areas in low and middle-income countries who have the fewest resources. Extensive research has demonstrated how gender roles and identity constructions determine forms of vulnerability and inequality in climate change events. One observation is that because of social norms and expectations about what it is to be masculine, men are more likely to carry out activities that affect their health and safety, such as pursuing rescue actions or migrating to new and unknown environments. For example, in the case of Hurricane Mitch that hit Honduras in 1998, more men than women died while performing salvage activities (Buvinic et al. 1999). During cyclone floods in Bangladesh in 1991, female mortality was greater because cultural norms of femininity prevented women from having swimming skills (Baden et al. 1994).

Although men are also harmed by climate change in specific ways, it is arguably more important to focus on women because they are generally more vulnerable than men. They are more vulnerable because of their lower socio-economic status and unequal power positioning derived from patriarchal relations (Kabeer 2003). Vulnerable women are those with high exposure to external stresses and shocks, and with high sensitivity to change and low adaptive capacity to adjust in response to actual or expected changes due to their lack of secure access to the assets on which secure livelihoods are built. These tangible and intangible assets are defined as a stock of financial, human, natural, or social resources that can be acquired, developed, improved, and transferred across generations. Assets are linked to capabilities that women and men use to build livelihoods and strengthen their agency to reproduce, challenge, or change the rules that govern the control, use, and transformation of these assets and resources (Moser 2011; Moser and Stein 2011, 2014). More specifically, poor immigrant or ethnic minority women in low-income countries are more likely to be exposed to climate extremes having a great impact on their wealth and capital goods, health, access to technologies, education, services and information, and opportunities to generate productive assets. As community leaders, caregivers, and heads of households, women face an increase of under-paid and non-paid hours of care-work devoted to their domestic and community spheres resulting from the effects of climate change (Moser 2011; Tovar-Restrepo and Blomstrom 2013). Moreover, under conditions of increasing distress and anxiety, women have reported greater levels of depression, conflict, and sexual violence (Osei-Agyemang 2007).

Despite these negative impacts, women are more than simply 'vulnerable victims' of climate hazards. As a report by WEDO et al. (2009) has documented, women have different capacities and strategies to cope with short- and mid-term climate change crises. They play a crucial role in building more resilient settlements through natural resource management and political participation in climate change decision-making. For this reason, their participation is essential when designing and implementing climate change adaptation and mitigation plans in both rural and urban contexts.[3] Adaptation and mitigation are convergent strategies that should increase resilience and reduce emissions, while helping communities to adapt to and cope with immediate shocks – for example, projects that address conservation and sustainable livelihoods (Drexhage 2006). Adaptation and mitigation need to be framed by a complex understanding of resilience that moves beyond the mainstream meaning provided by the IPCC. The IPCC (2007) defines resilience as people's ability to absorb climate change impacts and disturbances, strengthening their capacity to adapt to stress and change through self-organization.

Resilience has been extensively discussed (Schoon 2005; Swanstrom 2008; Rao 2013), as it has become a commonly used concept in climate change planning. Different critiques have pointed out the scientific, technical, or physical character that has been given to this term, ignoring the social implications and power relations that are at stake when defining it (Satterthwaite et al. 2007; Fainstein 2010; Rodin 2014). They draw attention to the human dimensions of resilience-building initiatives and to how politics and power mediate the roles of actors involved in these processes, stressing the fact that resilience should transform unequal power relations and institutions (Pelling 2010; Bahadur and Tanner 2014). It is important to echo some of these reflections that highlight the political and social dimensions embedded in the idea of resilience, where contextual needs of different social groups must be taken into account (Satterthwaite 2013; Satterthwaite and Dodman 2013). These works urge practitioners to implement bottom-up initiatives that transform existing hierarchical dominant structures (Shaw 2012). Nevertheless, while these critiques reveal some needed improvements to qualify understandings of resilience, there is still an extended practice of ignoring the gender and intersectional perspectives in most definitions, analysis, and action plans that seek sustainable and resilient human settlements (see, for example, Davoudi 2012 or Wilkinson 2012). They obliterate the fact that unequal gender relations are the most pervasive and ubiquitous forms of inequality. This omission has also permeated adaptation and mitigation strategies that put emphasis on maintaining functioning systems by using top-down approaches that can reinforce gender gaps and women's vulnerability.

In this regard, it is crucial to address contributions from researchers working in women's advocacy organizations and gender and environment scholars that provide important insights into the resilience debate. These have shown how building resilience requires addressing access to, control of, ownership, and management of assets, and acknowledging gender equality and equity issues that are closely linked to forms of vulnerability and differentiated climate change impacts. In order to support this claim, the WEDO-REDD+ project took into account a set of principles when working on its climate change mitigation strategy, specifically in regard to deforestation and the lives of people in forest communities. The strategy states that in order to transform unequal power relations that are embedded in cultural norms, institutions, and behaviours, climate change policies, and actions should be:

> *Gender sensitive and gender responsive* – by considering socio-cultural norms and discriminations in order to acknowledge the different rights, roles, and responsibilities of women and men in a community, and the relationships between them. Gender sensitive policies, programs, administrative and financial activities, and organizational procedures will differentiate between the capacities, needs, and priorities of women and men; ensure that the views and ideas of both women and men are taken seriously; consider the implications of decisions on the situation of women relative to

men; and take actions to address inequalities or imbalance between women and men. These actions might include including planning, programming, and budgeting.

*Gender transformative* – by recognizing gender as a central dimension to achieve positive development outcomes; by transforming unequal gender relations, promoting shared power and control of resources; and guaranteeing gender-balanced participation in decision-making that supports women's empowerment.

The WEDO-REDD+ project sought to translate these principles into concrete actions during its fieldwork, projecting its outcomes into policy and climate change planning activities as described in the following section.

## REDD+SES as climate change planning in Brazil, Ecuador, Nepal, and Tanzania

The REDD+SES is an initiative designed in 2009 to respond to climate change by reducing carbon emissions and deforestation while contributing to human rights, poverty alleviation, and biodiversity conservation. It seeks to protect forests and extend climate change mitigation measures into areas of conservation, sustainable forest management, and enhancement of carbon stocks. Forests are crucial for mitigating climate change effects and providing food resources, energy, and water provisions especially for rural populations from non-industrialized countries. REDD+SES is a comprehensive framework of key issues, including principles, criteria, and indicators that are intended for use in addressing the social and environmental performance of its program implementation, recognizing the potential risks and benefits to different social groups such as indigenous peoples, local communities, and women. The standards provide guidance in designing REDD+ programs, using a multi-stakeholder approach that provides a mechanism for reporting on the social and environmental performance of REDD+ programs.[4]

In February 2012 the REDD+SES initiative began a comprehensive process of reviewing the principles, criteria, and indicators (the content) and the guidelines for using REDD+SES on a national level (the process). This led to a partnership between the REDD+SES secretariat and WEDO to undertake a year-long action research project in four countries using REDD+SES: Brazil (State of Acre), Ecuador, Nepal, and Tanzania. The partners identified research as a necessary tool for understanding context-specific issues in order to strengthen the REDD+ gender dimension, taking into account ethnicity and location as primary identity markers of inequality in these contexts. By linking capacity-building strategies to the research process, the project enhanced the skills of stakeholders to address gender considerations. A main outcome was a practical guide on how REDD+SES programs could effectively address gender equality and the advancement of women's rights. This tool consists of three easy and practical 'action checklists' to ensure that their strategies and programs address gender considerations. The target audience is policy makers, program officers, and practitioners – those who will be developing the REDD+ national strategy or program. However, the action checklists may be adapted for a number of different situations, processes, programs, or projects, particularly within the forest sector. This instrument can also be used for evaluation and monitoring of the incorporation of gender considerations throughout program development and implementation.

The project investigated the following five context-specific issues:

1    gender-differentiated relationships with forests, specifically, use and control of forest resources;
2    gender inequalities women face in issues related to forest conservation strategies;

3    challenges, best practices and opportunities identified in REDD+ pilot projects;
4    women's knowledge, capacities, and networks; and
5    risks and opportunities for women in REDD+.

These issues were investigated with a view to developing suggestions for addressing the gender dimension in each country's REDD+SES process.[5] Given the space limit, only the first four issues are discussed in this section of the chapter (the full report is available online; WEDO-REDD+ 2013).

## Methodology

Three types of qualitative research methods were used between March and July 2012. First, participatory workshops were held with policy makers and representatives from national and local women's organizations, including women from ethnic minorities. Second, site visits and stakeholder interviews were conducted in communities where forestry projects or pilot programs have been developed. The interviews served to document grassroots women's perspectives on gender-differentiated access and control of forest resources; identify traditional gender inequalities and discriminations; explore actions taken to address gender considerations; determine specific risks and opportunities for women in forest-related (or REDD+) projects; and list actions they would like to see in future projects. Third, interviews were held with key figures including government officials, major stakeholders, implementing partners, and donors to determine the extent to which the gender dimension has been incorporated into initiatives at the national and local levels.

## Research findings

What follows is a summary discussion of four of the five key issues that were investigated by the research project.

### Gender-differentiated relationships with forests: use and control of resources

Forest resources constitute crucial assets for women and men in the context of climate change events. As mentioned earlier, forests ensure food security and access to energy and water supply, and guarantee biological diversity. The research documented the gendered access to and use of forest resources, showing how women and men are forest managers and primary users of forest biodiversity. Their unique knowledge, experience, and leadership, both formal and informal, contribute to the sustainability of forest ecosystems, especially in the case of indigenous communities. As a result of cultural norms and social roles, women's lives and livelihoods can be highly dependent on and affected by the health of their local ecosystems (see Aguilar et al. 2011). Research findings show a gender-differentiated relationship to forests in the following ways:

- Women's and men's livelihood dependence on forests is different.
- Women and men obtain different products and receive different benefits from forests.
- Women and men have different knowledge, access to, and control over forests.
- Women and men contribute in different ways to forest conservation and management.

The results detailed in Table 28.1 show that women are important forest stakeholders who contribute to the success of forest-related initiatives with specific perspectives, knowledge, and

*Table 28.1* Gender-differentiated relationship with forests in the four project countries

|  | Brazil (Acre) | Ecuador | Nepal | Tanzania |
|---|---|---|---|---|
| **Gender-differentiated activities in forests** | *Women and men:* many activities are similar, but specific roles may differ (e.g., in Brazilian nut extraction, men collect nuts and women crack them) | *Women:* activities related to maintaining households<br><br>*Men:* labour-intensive activities and forest monitoring | *Women:* forest product collection for household needs<br><br>*Men:* logging, making decisions about forest activities, and technical work | *Women and men:* many activities are similar, with the following differences:<br><br>*Women:* collect water and wood for fuel<br><br>*Men:* collect wood for timber |
| **Gender-differentiated products obtained from forests** | *Women:* medicinal plants used for home births<br><br>*Men:* wood and game (from hunting) | *Women and men:* many products obtained are similar, with the following differences:<br><br>*Women:* seeds for handcrafts and non-forest timber products (NFTP)<br><br>*Men:* wood | *Women:* NFTP for household needs<br><br>*Men:* NFTP to sell, and game (from hunting) | *Women:* products for household use<br><br>*Men:* products to use in economic activities |
| **Gender-differentiated benefits (cash and non-cash) obtained from the forests** | *Women and men:* receive cash and non-cash benefits from product exchanges<br><br>*Men:* control the financial returns | *Women and men:* extract local products to sell<br><br>*Women:* obtain non-cash benefits to improve their families' livelihoods<br><br>*Men:* tend to sell products and control money | *Women and men:* products sold for cash differ<br><br>*Women:* responsible for agriculture and receive more benefits when water sources increase | *Women and men:* receive non cash benefits<br><br>*Women:* receive little money from selling products<br><br>*Men:* receive money from selling products |
| **Gender-differentiated impact of forest loss** | *Women and men:* impacts both, but it has a different impact depending on resource<br><br>*Women:* collect water; thus water loss affects them more | *Women and men:* effects include loss of resources (including NTFP), lack of work sources, loss of traditional medicine, and loss of family unity<br><br>*Women:* increase in household labour requirements, lack of food security, and longer distances to collect water | *Women:* domestic work becomes more time intensive, decrease in water resources, and reduced crop and other food production, including cattle<br><br>*Men:* time intensive collection of products, limits employment opportunities from forest, migration of | *Women:* walk longer distance to fetch water and firewood, and lose areas to collect fruits and vegetables<br><br>*Men:* no production of timber, firewood, honey, medicine, and log extraction, which decreases their income |

*Table 28.1* (Continued)

| | Brazil (Acre) | Ecuador | Nepal | Tanzania |
|---|---|---|---|---|
| | | *Men:* lack of animals for hunting, and migration | men in search of employment, and increased alcohol use/dependence due to stress from unemployment | |
| **Gender- differentiated effects of forest conservation** | *Women and men:* positive impact as it secures natural resource access, increases income, and improves quality of life | *Women and men:* can have a negative effect if it affects income *Women:* can have a negative effect on agricultural practices, food security, and family welfare | *Women and men:* increased food security *Women:* breaking traditional boundaries and personal development *Men:* increased income generation opportunities | N/A (not discussed) |

*Source*: Please see www.wedo.org/wp-content/uploads/leafbyleaf_booklet1_web.pdf

skills. Gender-blind initiatives that do not recognize this reality will continue to reinforce inequalities and will not achieve social, developmental, or environmental benefits, especially at the community level.

## Inequalities in women's access to and control over forest-related resources

The research found that women tend to lack or have less access to land and property ownership, tenure, and rights. They also are less likely to be recognized as forest stakeholders and land users and therefore lack full and effective participation, particularly in decision-making. There are gender inequalities in the distribution of benefits; women have less access to and/or control over benefits relative to men. Table 28.2 shows the results of a detailed analysis of the barriers women face in regards to access to and control over forest-related resources.

These results demonstrate the need for making the REDD+ process gender sensitive and targeting these gaps by, first, transforming gender stereotypes, especially as they pervade the forestry sector, and second, by empowering local women as decision makers and rights holders and contributing to the enhancement of local livelihoods. In addition, there is a need to build gender awareness among policy makers and program/project designers and practitioners.

## Forest management pilot projects: challenges, best practices, and opportunities

In Nepal and Tanzania it was possible to document challenges, opportunities, and best practices in forest management pilot projects that women's networks have pursued in relation to REDD+. In Nepal these networks have advocated for the inclusion of the gender dimension in both the REDD+ National Strategy and the REDD+SES country process. In the REDD+SES process

*Table 28.2* Women's access to and control over forest-related resources

| Issue: 'Do women have . . .?' | Brazil (Acre) | Ecuador | Nepal | Tanzania |
|---|---|---|---|---|
| **Access to forest resources** | YES: rely on it for survival | YES: to support their families and communities | YES: extract many resources | YES: collect many products |
| **Control over cash generated by activities in the forests** | NO: sales and financial management done by men | YES: as long as cash comes from sale of products or handcrafts<br><br>NO: (larger-scale) sales and financial management done by men<br><br>NO: in benefit-sharing schemes, such as PES, it has been documented that in both private and community modalities payments are made to men | NO: men tend to make decisions about cash | VARIES: based on location: in some villages women control cash from resources they sell; in others men control cash |
| **Opportunity to own land or forests** | YES: when sufficient financial resources | NO: because they do not receive inheritance according to traditional community governance systems; few exceptions | YES: can own private lands and Forest Act gives women user rights | NO: face many challenges to owning land |
| **Access to and control over tools and equipment** | YES: simple tools, but not specialized or mechanized equipment | NO: tools and equipment are used for men's work | YES: simple tools but not machines or vehicles | YES: can use all tools |
| **Access to and control over new technologies** | NO: have limited technology | NO: men have access to training and formal education; most men control internet and cell phones | YES: local technologies available for rural areas<br><br>NO: high tech instruments | YES: in urban areas but limited in rural areas<br><br>NO: they do not have control of phones |
| **Access to and control over credit** | NO: law that confers credit rights is recent and needs to be enforced | YES: through development banks<br><br>NO: complicated through traditional bank system | YES: can obtain credit without mortgage<br><br>NO: not involved in decision-making | YES: access to some loans<br><br>NO: limiting conditions imposed by income generating institutions |

Table 28.2 (Continued)

| Issue: 'Do women have . . .?' | Brazil (Acre) | Ecuador | Nepal | Tanzania |
|---|---|---|---|---|
| **Opportunity to participate in forest related activities** | *YES*: as part of community organizations<br><br>*NO*: many cannot go to the city for meetings regarding forest programs/ projects | *YES*: can be involved in some activities and serve on the boards, but their family support influences the degree greatly | *YES*: spend most of their time in the forest | *NO*: some activities are difficult for women, but it depends on the activities |
| **Request to participate in forest projects** | *YES*: to communal organizations | *YES*: involved, but usually when there are no monetary benefits | *YES*: but only sometimes, especially when there is no cash remuneration; women-led organizations are neglected | *YES*: some women are in the natural resource committee |
| **Opportunity and time to participate in forest projects** | *YES*: when projects are undertaken in the communities | *NO*: because of many daily chores, they cannot participate | *NO*: economic problems, lack education and skills, and there are social restrictions | *YES*: because they arrange time for it |

*Source:* Please see http://www.wedo.org/wp-content/uploads/leafbyleaf_booklet1_web.pdf

women were recognized as a separate stakeholder represented by the organization HIMAWANTI. Tanzania, on the other hand, had made advances in developing its National REDD+ Strategy and Action Plan by 2012. Table 28.3 is provided as an example of the findings regarding the pilot projects.

## Women's knowledge, capacities, and networks

As agents of change, women possess knowledge, capacities, and networks that are crucial in building resilience and mitigating climate change hazards. Results from workshops demonstrated that rural and indigenous women have traditional practices and knowledge that are directly relevant to sustainable natural resource management. These can be mobilized through:

- capacity building on climate change mitigation actions, especially REDD+SES;
- developing mitigation program components such as REDD+SES principles, criteria and indicators;
- recommendations to mainstream gender into adaptation and mitigation actions, including REDD+; and
- providing best practices and lessons learned that are scaled-up nationally and internationally.

Women in Nepal and Tanzania possessed important knowledge about forest resources, as well as forest management capacities. For example, Nepal's development of context and gender-specific

Table 28.3 REDD+ pilot projects in Nepal that have successfully addressed risks and maximized opportunities for women

| Name of the project | Objective | Location | Initial challenges | Good practices developed and implemented |
|---|---|---|---|---|
| Carbon Trust Fund Project | 1. Pilot payment for REDD+ through sustainable forest management | Gorkha, Chitwan, and Dolakha watershed areas included 105 groups within three watershed areas | • Women did not have sufficient knowledge about REDD+<br>• Carbon fund allotted 15 per cent fund to women, but provided a weak basis for claiming the funds. How and where women could invest was not specified. | • Interaction and workshop programs for the representatives of groups<br>• Women received credit, with minimal or no interest, for income-generating activities such as farming and tailoring; the credit was provided based on economic status of the recipient |
| Annapurna Conservation Area (ACAP), Buffer Zone, and Community Forest | 1. Eco-tourism development<br>2. Sustainable development<br>3. Increase participation in conservation and development | Ghandruk, Annapurna Conservation Area | • Initial participation of women was very low because men did not consider it important<br>• Men interfered in women's decision-making process; decisions made by women were rejected by men. Examples: Men decided placement of water tap from which women fetched water Women had to request permission to leave home to attend meetings Women were generally underestimated, and their leadership was not accepted by society | • Mothers' group was formed<br>• Opportunities opened for women in the community to attend meetings, listen, understand, and discuss relevant information<br>• Women started planning and implementing<br>• Gender-specific training and education<br>• Men were given a space for working in women-led programs and were invited to attend meetings and programs organized by women<br>• Daycare centre was established in 1992, which now has an endowment<br>• Noteworthy: ACAP received an international award, which helped men acknowledge the importance of women's contributions in conservation and development |
| Training of Teachers for Indigenous People | 1. Training of trainers (ToT), indigenous peoples, and ethnic groups on climate change and REDD+ | Bajakhet, Khasru, Lamjung | • Women, indigenous, ethnic, and pro-poor groups and Dalit had 15 per cent quota for participation. However, the information was kept secret by chair and secretary of the group. When confronted, they responded that women also belong to ethnic, indigerous, poor groups, and no distinctio.1 was necessary.<br>• Men always participated, even when mandatory participation of women was mentioned in a formal letter. | • During the ToT, facilitators explicitly called upon women to actively participate to balance the degree of participation between women and men and minimize the opportunity for men to dominate |

Source: Please see http://www.wedo.org/wp-content/uploads/leaflapf-booklet1.mah.pdf

contents relating to REDD+ is leading to gender-sensitive measures and paradigm shifts in the forest sector. In Tanzania the pilot projects initiated by various organizations and community networks[6] provided a unique opportunity to exchange ideas and experiences about context-specific knowledge and practices. In the cases of Ecuador and Brazil, local experts and professionals with research skills and knowledge about environmental legislation and gender were identified as potential contributors to successful climate change program implementation, including REDD+. It is in Acre, Brazil in particular where there has been important research on local forest conservation and payment for environmental services such as the work done by Grupo de Pesquisa e Extensão em Sistemas Agroflorestais do Acre (PESACRE) on land reform initiatives and models for forest conservation including women's and men's different perspectives and needs.

Women's and environmental networks are invaluable for socializing knowledge and capacities while promoting participation. The identified links between the networks in the four countries make up multi-stakeholder platforms and privileged entry points for climate change actions. Networks play an important role in bridging national and international decision-makers and environmental platforms, such as in the cases of Nepal and Ecuador where both professional and grassroots women's networks focus on sustainable natural resource management. In Nepal the networks HIMAWANTI and Women Leading for Change in Natural Resources (WLCN) worked with the Ministry of Environment. In the cases of Brazil and Tanzania, formal and informal networks were identified as potential platforms to build on their experience and expertise, as with Acre's indigenous women's network that focuses on protecting traditional knowledge and conservation practices, or Acre's research institute PESACRE that has worked with gender issues, land reform actions, and environmental restoration. In Tanzania, informal women's networks called Upatu, working as financial support systems within communities, were also acknowledged as potential tools to work on conservation and benefit-sharing as a REDD+ component.

## General outcomes and REDD+SES process

One of the patterns observed in the four countries was that despite many efforts, gender equality is not yet a reality, and there are significant differences between women and men in the full enjoyment of their rights. Women experience gender-based discrimination in decision-making processes, benefit distribution, access and control of cash and forest products, benefit sharing, land tenure, capacity building, and access to information. Forest resources are highly important in women's livelihoods because they provide food, energy sources, income generation, shelter, water provision, access to bio-diverse products, and traditional medicine resources. Inequitable access, control, or ownership of these assets make women more vulnerable to climate change hazards and decreases their adaptive capacity to adjust to abrupt changes such as droughts or flooding. Moreover, it has collective harmful effects by preventing the sustainable conservation of forests and therefore impeding efforts to reduce carbon emissions. In this regard, in order to achieve REDD+ objectives, project participants identified the following required actions:

- Informing women about their rights
- Respecting and complying with women's rights
- Determining barriers and inequalities that limit women's rights, access, and control
- Improving relations between women and men, especially in the forest sector
- Including women in decision-making structures
- Ensuring full and effective participation of women at every stage of REDD+ initiatives

A main insight about the process was that capturing the gender dimension in a REDD+ program is key to transforming gender relations in the forest sector by positively impacting gender equality. To effectively implement gender-sensitive policies it is crucial to engage in a comprehensive process that first identifies and strengthens in-country enabling conditions; then develops an overall strategic action plan to carry out a gender-responsive process of interpretation and implementation of the policies; and finally proposes a series of local efforts and projects to implement the strategic action plan. Moreover, the research described herein revealed that the development of a gender-sensitive REDD+ process requires a step-wise method that identifies the gender considerations and obtains baseline information, and then effectively incorporates them into the program or strategy design. The main steps include:

- Conduct an analysis of gender-differentiated use, access to, and control of forest resources, and of the gender inequities that are observed in many forest-related processes (e.g., participation, transparency, distribution of benefits).
- Carry out a gender-differentiated analysis of the potential positive and negative social impacts – that is, the risks and opportunities.
- Understand the current situation of the country with regard to policies (environmental, gender, sustainable development), climate change initiatives, forestry programs, and gender equality.
- Identify gender equality and women's rights issues that should be included in a REDD+ program, including a gap and opportunity analysis.
- Propose concrete suggestions to address gender equality and women's rights in the REDD+ program, particularly in the safeguards and standards.

## Conclusion

Women and men have context-specific roles as natural resource managers that contribute to climate change mitigation and adaption activities in their households, workplaces, communities, and countries. However, these tend to be overlooked by gender-blind policies and plans that can increase gender inequalities. Feminist environmental scholars have long recognized gender inequalities that cause millions of women around the world to live in societies that impose barriers to the full realization and enjoyment of their rights (cf. Agarwal 2016). If gender inequalities are not properly addressed at the beginning of and at every stage of climate change mitigation and adaptation actions and plans, then the success and sustainability of the initiative can be jeopardized. From an activist perspective, planners, policy makers, and practitioners should ensure that the entire design, implementation, and monitoring process of climate change initiatives are gender sensitive.

The case presented in this chapter is an exemplary mitigation initiative seeking to mainstream gender into climate change policy in order to achieve gender equality and resilient human settlements and communities. Important advances could be made in climate change mitigation if REDD+ program implementations introduce gender and intersectionality perspectives by taking into account men and women from different age and ethnic groups, with different living traditions and localities. This experience has proved once more that climate change actions must evaluate the country- and context-specific situations to determine which gender and other inequalities are most relevant to the process and which can be addressed (along with those which cannot). Particularly from a gender perspective, REDD+ safeguards and standards must rigorously identify, analyze, and pose solutions for empowering women and upholding international and national-level mandates for gender equality and human rights.

Empirical results from this project can be extrapolated to climate change planning that seeks to adapt and mitigate climate extremes by creating gender aware planning processes. Generating research projects, promoting community organization initiatives, and implementing bottom-up planning methodologies that take into account localized and situated knowledges of women and men, can improve results when preventing climate change. Taking into account perspectives and needs of diverse men and women in climate change mitigation processes is an important step toward improving resilience among communities.

A critical examination of the resilience concept suggests that in order effectively to combat climate change and to achieve real sustainable adaptability, there must be gender-sensitive and gender-transformative measures and principles integrated into policies, plans, and programs at the national level (such as Climate Change National Action Plans) or city level (Climate Change City Action Plans). Most commonly, these plans seek to reduce greenhouse gas emissions, generate renewable energy, improve energy efficiency, cut transportation and land-use related emissions, and reduce emissions from waste management. Gender awareness can be mainstreamed into all these planning sectors. It would ensure that women's knowledge, capacities, needs, and priorities are taken into account equally with men's. It also would guarantee that budget planning and decision-making processes respond to women's necessities and ensure gender-balanced participation. But most importantly, it would question unequal power relations based on gender roles, norms, and cultural practices that should lead to women's empowerment and full control of tangible and intangible assets. In the case of REDD+ these assets would also include key issues such as knowledge, networks, financial means, technology, information, and capacities to strengthen women's agency and autonomy.

## Notes

1 Andrea Quesada Aguilar was the lead author who conducted the research project on REDD+SES and its related report 'From research to action, leaf by leaf: getting gender right in REDD+SES' (WEDO-REDD+ 2013; WEDO 2012b). Eleanor Blomstrom (WEDO) and Raja Jarrah (CARE) were supporting authors of projects mapping gender-sensitive REDD+ strategies in Ghana, Cameroon, and Uganda (WEDO 2012a, 2012b, 2012c). The research and publication were made possible thanks to the generous contributions from the Norwegian Agency for Development Cooperation (Norad), the Ford Foundation and CARE. The Climate, Community and Biodiversity Alliance (CCBA), and CARE International serve as the international secretariat of the REDD+SES Initiative, and the partners are thankful for their support during the research. The research in Brazil was conducted in the State of Acre in collaboration with the IMC of the State Government of Acre. WEDO was supported by a local research associate, who is both coordinator of the Rede Acreana de Mulheres e Homens (RAMH) and State Coordinator for Validation and Monitoring of System of Incentives for Environmental Services (SISA), as well as representatives from CARE Brazil and the CARE HIMA pilot project in Tanzania, who supported field visits and workshops.
2 Kimberlé Crenshaw (1989) describes the intersections existing between different forms of identity and discriminatory practices. The feminist intersectionality approach analyzes issues of power and various identity markers, rejecting separate essentialist categories such as class, race, or ethnicity. It analyzes how different forms of discrimination intersect and aims to explain the particular experience of different groups of women on the basis of gender, income, religion, age, race, and class simultaneously (Yuval-Davis 2007; Bastia 2014).
3 Adaptation is defined as adjustments in ecological, social, or economic systems in response to actual or expected climatic stimuli and their effects or impacts. This term refers to changes in processes, practices, and structures to moderate potential damages or to benefit from opportunities associated with climate change. Mitigation refers to an anthropogenic intervention to reduce the sources or enhance the sinks of greenhouse gases.
4 See redd-standards.org.
5 In order to complement the entire research process and to improve recommendations, the following research questions were formulated: (a) What are the barriers to women's full and effective participation in REDD+ governance/decision-making, and how might these barriers be (or have they been) overcome? (b) What are the potential positive and negative social impacts of REDD+ on the interests and rights of women in the country? (c) How is gender being addressed in the REDD+ national process in particular

with respect to governance and social impacts? (d) How is gender being addressed in forest-related projects in the country, in particular with respect to governance and social impacts?

6 These groups include: MJUMITA, Tanzania Forest Conservation Groups (TFCG), Tanzania Traditional Energy Development and Environment Organization (TaTEDO), and Hifadhi ya Misitu ya Asili Piloting REDD in Zanzibar through Community Forest Management (CARE HIMA).

# References

Agarwal, B. (2016) *Gender Challenges*. Oxford: Oxford University Press.

Aguilar, L., Shaw, D. and Quesada-Aguilar, A. (2011) *Forests and Gender*. Gland: IUCN and New York: WEDO. Online. Available at: https://portals.iucn.org/library/efiles/documents/2011-070.pdf (accessed June 2014).

Arora-Jonsson, S. (2011) 'Virtue and vulnerability: Discourses on women, gender and climate change', *Global Environmental Change* 21(2): 744–751.

Baden, S., Green, C., Goetz, A. M. and Guhathakurta, M. (1994) *Background Report on Gender Issues in Bangladesh*. Bridge Report No. 26. Brighton: Institute for Development Studies, University of Sussex.

Bahadur, A. and Tanner, T. (2014) 'Transformational resilience thinking: Putting people, power and politics at the heart', *Environment and Urbanization* 26: 200–214.

Bastia, T. (2014) 'Intersectionality, migration and development', *Progress in Development Studies* 14(3): 237–248.

Buvinic, M., Vega, G., Bertrand, M., Urban, A.-M., Grynspan, R. and Truitt Nakata, G. (1999) *Hurricane Mitch: Women's Needs and Contributions*. Inter-American Bank Washington, DC. Online. Available at: http://publications.iadb.org/handle/11319/5215?locale-attribute=en (accessed July 2008).

Crenshaw, K. (1989) 'Demarginalizing the intersection of race and sex: A black feminist critique of anti-discrimination doctrine, feminist theory and antiracist politics', *University of Chicago Legal Forum*: 139–167.

Dankelman, I. (2009) 'Bearing the burden', *UN Chronicle* 46(3–4): 50–53.

Dankelman, I. (2010) 'Climate change, human security and gender', in Dankelman, I. (ed) *Gender and Climate Change: An Introduction*. London: Earthscan, 55–72.

Davoudi, S. (2012) 'Resilience: A bridging concept or a dead end?', *Planning Theory and Practice* 13(2): 300–308.

Doyle, T., McEachern, D. and MacGregor, S (2015) *Environment and Politics* (fourth edition). London: Routledge.

Drexhage, J. (2006) *Climate Change Situation Analysis*. Switzerland: IUCH-IISD.

Enarson, E. (2000) *Gender and Natural Disasters*, IPCRR Working Paper no 1, International Labour Organization (ILO), Geneva.

Fainstein, S. (2010) *The Just City*. Ithaca, NY: Cornell University Press.

Intergovernmental Panel on Climate Change (IPCC) (2007) *Fourth Assessment Report: Climate Change 2007*. Online. Available at: www.ipcc.ch/publications_and_data/publications_and_data_reports.shtml (accessed July 2014).

Intergovernmental Panel on Climate Change (IPCC) (2014) *Summary for Policymakers, In: Climate Change 2014, Mitigation of Climate Change. : Contribution of Working Group III to the Fifth Assessment Report of the Intergovernmental Panel on Climate Change*. Cambridge and New York, NY: Cambridge University. Online. Available at: http://report.mitigation2014.org/spm/ipcc_wg3_ar5_summary-for-policymakers_approved.pdf (accessed July 2014).

Kabeer, N. (2003) *Gender Mainstreaming in Poverty Eradication and the Millennium Development Goals: A Handbook for Policy-makers and Other Stakeholders*. Sussex: International Development Research Centre, Canadian International Development Agency.

Kaijser, A. and Kronsell, A. (2014) 'Climate change through the lens of intersectionality', *Environmental Politics* 23(3): 417–433.

Khosla, P. and Masaud, A. (2011) 'Cities, climate change and gender: a brief overview', in Dankelman, I. (ed) *Gender and Climate Change: An Introduction*. London: Earthscan, 78–97.

MacGregor, S. (2010) 'A stranger silence still: The need for feminist social research on climate change', *Sociological Review* 57(1): 124–140.

Masika, R. (2002) *Gender, Development and Climate Change*. Oxford: Oxfam.

Moser, C. (2011) 'A conceptual and operational framework for pro-poor asset adaptation to urban climate change', in Hoornweg, D. (ed) *Cities and Climate Change*. Washington, DC: World Bank, 225–255.

Moser, C. and Stein, A. (2011) 'Implementing urban participatory climate change adaptation appraisals: A methodological guideline', *Environment and Urbanization* 23(2): 463–485.

Moser, C. and Stein, A. (2014) 'Asset planning for climate change adaptation: Lessons from Cartagena, Colombia', *Environment and Urbanization* 23(2): 166–183.

Osei-Agyemang, M. (2007) 'Temperatures rising: Understanding the relationship between climate change, conflict and women', *Women and Environment* 74/75(Spring–Summer): 21–24.

Pelling, M. (2010) *Adaptation to Climate Change: From Resilience to Transformation.* London: Routledge.

Rao, P. (2013) 'Building climate resilience in coastal ecosystems in India: Cases and trends in adaptation practices', in Filho, W. Leal (ed) *Climate Change and Disaster Risk Management.* Heidelberg: Springer, 335–349.

Rodin, J. (2014) *The Resilience Dividend: Being Strong in a World Where Things Go Wrong.* New York: Public Affairs.

Satterthwaite, D. (2013) 'The political underpinnings of cities' accumulated resilience to climate change', *Environment and Urbanization* 25(2): 381–391.

Satterthwaite, D. and Dodman, D. (2013) 'Towards resilience and transformation for cities within a finite planet', *Environment and Urbanization* 25: 291–298.

Satterthwaite, D., Huq, S., Pelling, M., Reid, H. and Romero Lankao, P. (2007) 'Adapting to climate change in urban areas: The possibilities and constraints in low- and middle-income nations', *Human Settlements Discussion Paper Series.* London: Human Settlements Group and Climate Change Group, International Institute for Environment and Development.

Schoon, M. (2005) 'A short historical overview of the concepts of resilience, vulnerability and adaptation', Workshop in Political Theory and Policy Analysis, Working Paper W05–4, 29 January, Indiana University, Bloomington, IN.

Shaw, K. (2012) 'Reframing resilience: Challenges for planning theory and practice', *Planning Theory and Practice* 13(2): 308–312.

Swanstrom, T. (2008) *Regional Resilience: A Critical Examination of the Ecological Framework.* Berkeley: Institute of Urban and Regional Development.

Tovar-Restrepo, M. (2010) 'Gender, ethnicity and climate change in Colombia', in Dankelman, I. (ed) *Gender and Climate Change: An Introduction.* London: Earthscan, 145–152.

Tovar-Restrepo, M. and Blomstrom, E. (2013) 'Green economies, job opportunities and women', in Röhr, U. (ed) *Sustainable Economy and Green Growth.* Berlin: Genanet and The German Federal Ministry for Environment, Nature Conservation and Nuclear Energy, 48–50.

WEDO (2012a) *Gender and Cameroon's REDD+ Road Map.* New York: Women's Environment and Development Organization. Online. Available at: www.wedo.org/wp-content/uploads/cameroon_case_study.pdf (accessed 5 November 2014).

WEDO (2012b) *Gender and Uganda's REDD+ Road Map.* New York: Women's Environment and Development Organization. Online. Available at: www.wedo.org/wp-content/uploads/uganda_case_study.pdf (accessed 5 June 2014).

WEDO (2012c) *Mainstreaming Gender Considerations into REDD+ Processes in Ghana.* New York: Women's Environment and Development Organization. Online. Available at: www.wedo.org/wp-content/uploads/REDDghana_case_study-1.pdf (accessed 5 June 2014).

WEDO-GGCA-IUCN-UNDP (2009) *Training Manual on Gender and Climate Change.* Online. Available at: http://cmsdata.iucn.org/downloads/eng_version_web_final_1.pdf (accessed 5 November 2014).

WEDO-REDD+ (2013) *From Research to Action, Leaf by Leaf: Getting Gender Right in the REDD+ Social and Environmental Standards.* Online. Available at: www.wedo.org/library/wedo-launches-from-research-to-action-leaf-by-leaf-getting-gender-right-in-redd-ses (accessed 5 November 2014).

Wilkinson, C. (2012) 'Urban resilience: What does it mean in planning practice?', *Planning Theory and Practice* 13(2): 319–324.

Yuval-Davis, N. (2007) 'Intersectionality, citizenship and contemporary politics of belonging', *Critical Review of International Social and Political Philosophy* 10(3): 561–574.

# PART IV

# Futures

# 29

# PRAGMATIC UTOPIAS

## Intentional gender-democratic and sustainable communities

*Helen Jarvis*

## Introduction

While some aspects of social and economic life have changed significantly since the industrial revolution and through the post-industrial era, domestic living arrangements remain stubbornly rooted in traditional gender roles and a rigid model of separate family dwelling. Despite persuasive feminist critique and evidence of viable alternatives (notably the Israeli Kibbutz and the extended family compounds typical of many African and Central Asian countries), the pattern of dwelling and internal arrangement of domestic space in Western societies remains conservative and inward looking. In Britain, for example, apart from the humblest accommodation for the working classes (which often had shared cooking and washing facilities), the family has been housed in a self-contained dwelling with the interior divided into a number of strongly demarcated spaces, each classified according to gender-defined activities. The norm has been established as one of conservative emphasis on privacy (Lawrence 1982) and more recently a treadmill of investment in comfort, cleanliness, and convenience (Shove 2003).

The rigid separation of public and private spaces that provides exclusive facilities for small family units arguably presents a major obstacle to improving both the position of women and the quality of the environment (Chouinard 1989; Seyfang 2010). We find evidence of historically entrenched male bias in architecture and town planning in the segregated geography of residential location, as well as in housing design and domestic technology. In effect, women have been 'kept in their place' by the separate zoning of housing in dormitory suburbs, and residential blocks that are set apart from sites of employment and public life (Roberts 1991:153). The ghettoization of the domestic sphere has been reproduced not only by physical separation, but also by cultural norms of 'respectable femininity' that drive women to devote their working lives to intensive caring and mothering and to creating the impression of an ideal home. The mundane, typically unpaid, feminized activities of feeding, clothing, washing, sheltering, and caring for family and neighbours are rendered invisible and disregarded by the 'tyranny' of single family dwelling (Jarvis 2013).

In turn, social and material conditions that reproduce persistent patriarchal gender relations also coincide with negative consequences for the planet. Conventional housing corresponds with higher rates of carbon emissions and energy consumption than for any individual mode of transport or industrial sector (Buckingham 2004; Crabtree 2006). A heavy housing-related carbon footprint is attributed to the wasteful separation of privatized sites of consumption. Thus American sociologist Harvey Molotch (2003) observes that one solution to the problem of people buying excess 'stuff', and then facing the problem of how to reuse or recycle the stuff that is not needed, is to promote collective access and use of goods and services via *cooperative arrangements.*

To some extent, we are witnessing just such a cultural shift in a growing number of 'sharing' and 'solidarity' economies in the overdeveloped Global North. While in some high-profile spheres of consumption (e.g., ZipCars, Airbnb, etc.), mutual exchange and trust are replacing cash and 'ownership' as the new currency, many of these 'niche markets of green consumption' simply reproduce unsustainable, unjust consumption-led capitalism in novel ways (Seyfang 2010). A more radical solution, perhaps, would cultivate 'efficiencies of propinquity' through multiple households living more collectively in the manner of a traditional village or tribe (Jarvis 2011). In this context it is illuminating to examine historical and contemporary intentional community arrangements that replace separation (fixed gender roles, fixed spatial boundaries) with creative scope for ecologically sustainable and gender democratic societies to be realized.

Indeed, scholars from many disciplines, including gender studies, environmental studies, sociology, history, geography, architecture, and planning, have chosen to make intentional communities the focus of research and publication, both as a category and scale of purposeful social organizing and as a diverse continuum of experimentation. Varied motivations and the impulse to live communally are such that gender democracy is not always prioritized within the intentional community ethos. It is for this reason that in this chapter I offer critical reflection on the positive connotations of collaboration and purpose, including the question of whether intentional communities offer the potential for *some* or *all* residents to shape and influence domestic arrangements in socially progressive and sustainable ways. For example, efforts to challenge patriarchal norms can compete – rather than correspond – with parallel motivations and efforts to deliver an ecological, affordable, and community-based approach to future housing construction (Chatterton 2013; Pickerill 2015). I argue that it is important to recognize the quest for gender equality as being discrete from ecological sustainability, while also acknowledging that these intentions are not mutually exclusive. Moreover, while shared space and collective self-management can summon forth new forms of citizenship, everyday practices of home-making remain deeply implicated in relations of paid and unpaid work, and this has profound implications for dimensions of difference including gender, class, disability, and age.

## Building differently to live differently: a pragmatic utopia

Although we tend to think of particular moments and places as 'revolutionary' there has never been a time when non-conformists and dissenting groups have not sought to challenge or transform the status quo to some extent. Thus renewed interest in community ownership of housing, motivated in part by issues of affordability and supportive neighbourhoods for an ageing population, can claim earlier precedent in extensive critical writing on 'placeless sprawl'. In the 1960s Herbert Gans (1967) published a searing indictment of what he observed as racist, sexist, and homophobic intolerance in the pressure to conform in dormitory suburbs such as Levittown, in the United States, for example. In the absence of meaningful solidarity and association, non-traditional families including single parents and gay or lesbian couples, were excluded from locally constructed definitions of family (Gans 1967:415–416). In that decade, dissatisfaction with poor access to affordable housing among low-income families led to the adoption of Community

Land Trusts in the United States. Influenced by a mix of Native American ideas on stewardship of common land and the civil rights movement, these citizen-led non-profit organizations sought to collectively purchase and manage property on behalf of the local community. The sixties became widely known as the quintessential 'counter-cultural epoch' because it witnessed three distinct but interdependent strands of civil mobilization; an emerging ecofeminist movement; a transnational women's movement; and a peace movement characterized by high-profile direct action including the illegal occupation of military sites as communal peace camps (see the chapter by Thompson and MacGregor in this handbook).

Scholarship on utopianism probably represents the best known, if widely misunderstood story of ordinary people building differently in order to live differently. Yet it is misleading to interpret 'intentionality' in terms of a quest for 'utopia' as if it were a blue-print alternative or fixed goal. Utopia is a term first coined by Thomas More in the sixteenth century as a play on the two Greek words that supply the 'u' sound, eu (good) and ou (not). When taken together with topos (place) – the root of the second part of the word – utopia could be construed as a 'good place' or a 'somewhere that does not exist' (Gold 2008:69; Jarvis et al. 2009). This tendency to view any imagined alternative to mainstream society as a fantasy of 'no-place' is problematic for the politics of challenging patriarchy and materialism in alternative models of intentional community development. Consequently, there is a move within ecofeminist scholarship to reclaim a dynamic process from the static notion of utopia more frequently used as a pejorative term (of abuse, e.g., 'fantasy' or 'ego') of naïve idealism (Schehr 1997:30).

In 'Looking for the blue: the necessity of utopia', sociologist Ruth Levitas seeks to liberate the concept of utopia from a place and goal (of master planning), to replace it with a 'utopian method' of unsettling and challenging the dominant culture of the day (2007:289). She argues that we need to pay greater attention to the dynamic process of 'orientation' and 'yearning' and to reclaim this creative journey of experimentation from the static notion of utopia. This way she recognizes the process of utopian thinking as creative and transformational elements of social change – both prevalent and necessary. She reminds us that as a method of analysis, utopianism is about uncovering processes that are already entailed in experimentation: existential quests (i.e., 'looking for the blue') coexist with a narrower utopia in political discourse that she calls 'looking for the green'. By contrast, 'looking for the green' (a viable mode of living within ecological limits) requires a utopian approach that must be understood creatively 'as a method rather than a goal' (Levitas 2007:290). Burke (2004) similarly argues that in order for imagination to flow there has to be space for creativity and experimentation – hence we need to critically examine the gendered power relations that arise in the process of imagining, collaborating in, and realizing intentional communities, noting how this may variously liberate or exclude individual women and men from creative spaces and processes.

## Living together: defining intentional community

The umbrella term 'intentional community' (IC) is widely used to describe a variety of experiments in 'living together', as well as successive human struggles to pursue socio-spatial justice (Kanter 1976). Embedded within the intentional community tradition are expressions of resistance to dominant social norms and expectations of home, work, and family life: motivations for challenging the status quo can be progressive and creative rather than solely reacting in opposition to dominant norms (Sargisson 2000).

Feminist scholars have drawn attention to progressive experiments in urban design, including collective, ideological, and matriarchal communities from around the world, in an effort to theorize everyday social reproduction and space-time interdependence (Fromm 1991, 2000; Jarvis et al. 2009:144). This approach indicates that neighbour relations are more meaningful and mutually supportive when homes and communities are co-produced – 'self-made' rather than 'ready-made'. We also learn that collaborative housing offers practical as well as social support for the upheaval of life-course transitions such as separation or death of a partner or spouse, children leaving home, and all that is required in a practical sense to provide care for immediate family (Maxey 2004; Manzella 2010). This brings to mind the popular African proverb (used by Hillary Clinton as the title of a 1996 publication on social responsibility): 'it takes a village to raise a child'. The implied ethic of shared care envisions a more harmonious, creative, and just society in which children's, older people's, and women's needs, and the social reproduction of all peoples and natures, are valued as central motives for action (Jarvis 2005; Jarvis et al. 2009:133). These are the defining characteristics of gender democracy that are reported to attract women in particular to intentional community. However, while some expressions of mutual cooperation and sharing are growing in popularity, largely as a by-product of economic austerity and an ageing population, mainstream Western society appears unwilling to voluntarily share domestic space or household amenities 'except in extraordinary circumstances' (Hemmens et al. 1996:17).

Emphasis on 'intentionality' is rooted in collaborative housing and community, in opposition to top-down notions of 'master planning'. This is why intentional communities often pursue anti-establishment development approaches that challenge professional expertise, cultivating instead a do-it-yourself (DIY) culture of self-build and direct action. For example, in the autonomous community of Christiania, which has occupied a former military site in the Danish capital Copenhagen since 1971, residents flout not only urban policies but also traditional gender roles bound up in conventional expectations of who gets to build a house where and with what method and materials. From the outset, the unspoken rule of the 'Christiania way' was to renovate and adapt rather than to tear down existing buildings and to build with reclaimed materials at minimum cost (Jarvis 2013). This messy and protracted craft process of self-build suggests the liberation of housing construction from its conventional association with a male-dominated commercial industry, where 'the tools of the trade are linked to assumptions about strength and toughness, and knowledge of a particular language and code of behaviour' (Pringle and Winning 1998:221). The same would be true of other examples of housing restoration work, but here the skills are learned and traded through a 'barn-raising' collaborative ethos, against the grain of stereotyped definitions of women's and men's competencies (see also Pickerill and Maxey 2009).

At the same time, other intentional communities flourish as self-governing entities that were designed, but not built, by community members. The common thread to the IC definition, therefore, is collaboration to ensure that neither the individual nor the group is submerged by the other. This excludes hierarchical, military, totalitarian, or charismatic spiritual cults from this definition. As with the assumed simplicity of any umbrella term, the picture is complicated by many culturally specific ways that community groups and scholars qualify the nature of collective, communal, collaborative, or cooperative association. Emphasis on intentionality (shared purpose) differentiates 'communities which people consciously create for themselves [from] those which arise naturally through humans living or working in close proximity' (Metcalf 2004:8). Shared spaces for 'living together' are crucial to the IC definition because the potential to challenge conventional gender relations requires that community members are close enough that they can carry out a shared lifestyle, within a shared culture and with a common purpose.

Much in the way that environmentalism encompasses 'multiple shades of green, from light to dark' (O'Riordan 1981), degrees of sharing vary from the highest level of pooled income (such as the kibbutz or commune), to looser arrangements combining private and shared domestic resources (such as with cooperatives, ecovillages, and cohousing). Groups that embrace notions

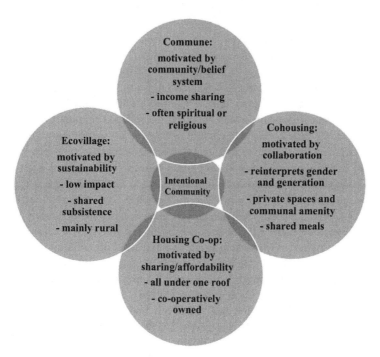

*Figure 29.1*   Four main 'types' of intentional community identified by primary collective motivation

of collective activity and shared physical space do not necessarily define themselves as an intentional community and the 'label' that is applied to any 'alternative' or 'counter-cultural' living arrangement is frequently contested. Consequently, the four main categories of IC identified in Figure 29.1 represent a simplified reality: by suggesting a primary motivation for each category, it is easier to differentiate between the largely collective economy of the commune and the pragmatic blend of shared facilities and separate living spaces found in cohousing. In practice, it can be impossible to identify one common vision: each IC is typically motivated by several intersecting intentions (such as social justice, gender democracy, low-impact living, self-reliance, sharing, self-growth, and aspects of spirituality rooted in an ethic of care). Nonetheless, it is constructive to emphasize a common vision or purpose because it distinguishes the IC concept from a widely used 'fuzzy' notion of community that 'can mean almost anything, or next to nothing' (Metcalf 2004:7). Accordingly, IC is not just about sharing money, land, housing or mutual care, but also about the reason for sharing: a vision and values that are negotiated and agreed in common by consensus.

## The ambivalent legacy of his-story

The early origins of communal settlement and mutual cooperation can be traced as far back as Plato's *Republic* in the fourth century BC and more reliably to the sixteenth century Anabaptist and Digger movements (Metcalf 1995; Coates 2007). Historical evidence helps to distinguish the quest for gender democracy as a persistent, yet frequently marginalized, impulse for alternative types of community-based housing. As already suggested, these can be understood variously as a reaction *against* hegemonic gender divisions and power relations as much as by a way of re-imagining and *creating* (as if from a blank page) a better future world. Inevitably these historical projects illustrate the way that patriarchy functions on multiple levels that cannot be reduced to an idealized 'blue-print' for gender democracy or equality.

Seventeenth century England was a deeply patriarchal society in which the father was the absolute leader of the family. Both the Leveller and Digger movements sought to reform hierarchical social relations with an agrarian lifestyle based on small self-reliant egalitarian rural colonies. The Levellers were a group of farmers led by the disciplined communist Gerrard Winstanley who was known as the True Leveller. They were among the first social democrats in English history. Significantly, this movement opened up modest opportunities for women to engage in direct action such as organizing demonstrations and mass petitions. Similarly, the Diggers were one of a number of nonconformist dissenting groups that emerged around this time (Beynon 2012).

Time and again, the stories of IC projects in the nineteenth and twentieth centuries illustrate the persistent disregard of women as active agents ('architects') in the process of imagining and realizing alternative models. In 1830, for instance, the French philosopher Charles Fourier railed against the isolated single-family dwelling as one of the greatest obstacles to improving the position of women. He published his proposals to eradicate poverty and support women's rights, most notably by challenging traditional marriage, affirming sexual difference, and advocating education and employment based on merit rather than sex. Indeed, he is credited with coining the feminist moniker. Yet there is little evidence of him engaging in any practical way (through consultation with women) in a 'female perspective'. While Fourier did not practice or set out to realize his own socialist utopia (beyond a refusal to marry), his ideas directly inspired the male founders of several ICs to engineer the socialization of domestic work. For example, the Brook Farm transcendentalist community founded by Unitarian minister George Ripley in the US state of Massachusetts in the 1840s sought to distribute work and leisure equally among men and women so as to liberate time for intellectual pursuits and create harmony and balance in community relations (Hayden 1978:275; Hayden 1976).

Similarly, Ebenezer Howard, the British architect of the Garden City movement, realized a vision of inclusive urban design that was directly inspired by socialist feminist ideals popularized in the late 1900s by the feminist author and social reformer Charlotte Perkins Gilman. Because of his male privilege and his architectural training, Howard was able to realize Gilman's ideas in his proposal for a 'cooperative quadrangle', which was intended to release women from isolated domestic drudgery. This saw garden apartments arranged around a collective kitchen, dining room, and open space. Several quadrangles were built between 1911 and 1930, designed specifically for single female professionals, although they never became standard provision in the garden cities (Hayden 1984:90). And Gilman's intervention remained unacknowledged in Howard's published work.

In historical terms, possibly the best known communal experiment was that of New Harmony, Indiana, in the nineteenth century. This represented the second attempt by the prominent Welsh social reformer Robert Owen to build a model town based on communitarian ideals. The first and more successful of his communities was the smaller mill-town of New Lanark founded in Scotland in 1816. Owen espoused a 'community of equality' and cited three 'monstrous evils' that combined to thwart 'mental independence': private property, religion, and conventional marriage. He described the kind of marriage he sought to promote as a 'natural marriage'. In practice, however, historical archives suggest that many women who had joined New Harmony 'in order to realize equality of the sexes' found that 'domestic chores became (their) exclusive and expected duty, despite equal education alongside men'. More significantly, in 'natural marriage' women served as 'community wives' to cook, sew, and clean for the entire village (Sutton 2004:42).

As Manzella (2010:35) observes, while the nineteenth century was an especially fertile time for experiments in communal living; the historical record reveals this largely through popular preoccupation with sensational forms of open marriage. Thus, the Oneida Community, located in the original homeland of the Oneida tribe, in the northeast United States, under the charismatic leadership of John Humphrey Noyes, is best known for experimenting with group or 'complex' marriage in which the community (and ultimately Noyes) supervised heterosexual relations that could involve any number of members (Schaefer and Zellner 2008:63). Romantic attachments were discouraged (in Biblical terms) as representing selfish orientations that failed to recognize the spirit of the Pentecost (Manzella 2010:34). In group marriage, sexual equality interpreted everyone as being married to everyone else.

Whereas preoccupation with 'group marriage' remains problematic to intentional communities research, communitarian experiments have arguably had a powerful and progressive impact in the loosening of traditional heterosexual and nuclear family ties, opening up spaces and expressions for challenging 'new normal' family forms. In this sense, Manzella notes that early intentional communities served an important function in reinterpreting and adapting family ties in (post-colonial) ways to variously suit 'frontier' and 'pioneer' conditions; thus Shakers defined family as single males and females living in separate quarters with a common sense of mission, while the Oneida Community defined family as plural marriage with shared children (2010:40). More generally, the lasting influence of North American intentional communities from the nineteenth century is the definition of family as an extended rather than nuclear concept and of community ties other than those of blood kin. This understanding paved the way for contemporary ICs to redefine 'family as community' to compensate for what has been lost (or never firmly established) in the nuclear family. In a pragmatic sense, modern communalism reconstitutes the traditional notion of the tribe or village in order to rescue the support functions (of inter-generational care and mutual reciprocity) of the extended family that have been inadequately replaced by commercial venues and services. This does not mean the nuclear family has disappeared from contemporary communities. Rather, it means that nuclear families may thrive within a larger non-kin family (Manzella 2010:41–42).

The Digger movement inspired the development of hundreds of communes on the West Coast of the United States in 1960s (Boal et al. 2012). This model is recognized as the inspiration behind 'back to the land' 'off grid' ecovillages that have proliferated in rural areas around the world, as is evident from the extensive reach of the Global Ecovillage Network, established in 1991. What characterized and distinguished IC formation in the 1970s was the simultaneous expression of disenchantment with mainstream material cultures and widespread international experimentation with novel forms of communal living witnessed in the United States, United Kingdom, Australia, and Northern Europe. For example, hundreds of self-organizing land-sharing communities were established in Australia at this time (Curry et al. 2001), with an estimated 251 concentrated in the 'rainbow' region of North East New South Wales alone (Irvine 2003). Indeed, the 1973 Aquarius Festival was explicitly modelled on the US Woodstock Music and Art Festival, and this alone attracted 5,000 students to an iconic community experience (Hannan 2002). Experimental developments of ecologically oriented community life and low cost housing coincided with a deep restructuring of the dairy industry and this made it possible for groups of young people with very limited assets to collectively purchase cheap farmland (Dunstan 1975). While the Leveller and Digger movements sought to challenge deeply held patriarchal legal and social structures, the harsh realities of farming on land that was illegally occupied, combined with daily struggles to resist violent eviction, typically reinforced traditional gender roles that defined farming skills in terms of physical strength. Rebecca Laughton (2008) makes a similar observation in the context of those ICs today that seek to live off the land. She notes that 'labour-intensive pre-modern' farming practices often reinforce traditional gender roles, especially where young children or babies are present and in communities where values of local food self-reliance coincide with humanistic cultures interpreted as mother-centred, such as those with extended breast-feeding (Laughton 2008:247).

## Cohousing as a 'new normal' non-sexist neighbourhood?

Collaborative housing (also called cohousing) is a type of intentional community made up of private homes with additional shared facilities in which residents actively participate in the design, planning and governance of the community as a whole. The contemporary cohousing concept is inspired by the Swedish 'kollectivhus' and a similar Danish 'living together apart' arrangement known as *bofællesskab* dating from the late 1960s (Vestbro 1992), but it captures the enduring ideals of a much longer communal imagination. Swedish cohousing in particular emerged from a concerted effort to bring about greater equality between men and women and to support dual earning and caring roles. Common meals and other services were designed to reduce the burden of housework and to make it possible to combine personal careers based on paid employment with family and community life. In the many places around the world where the cohousing concept has taken root, commitment to shared meals is widely held as the benchmark of gender-democratic shared housekeeping (Hayden 1980).

In the Swedish context, cohousing covers fully fledged collectives (which may be funded by the state but which are governed non-hierarchically by the collective) often built as high density blocks in urban areas with a wide range of shared amenities, or rural ecovillages with separate dwellings and shared food production, and collective 'cluster houses', which are designed to combine fully equipped private apartments (or town houses) with collective living space. Cohousing is intended to make it easier for neighbours to share activities such as eating together, childcare, and food production such as gardening; it is increasingly popular among older people and non-traditional families such as lone mothers (Horelli and Vepsä 1994).

Dick Urban Vestbro (1997) usefully differentiates between two periods of experimentation in collective housing in Sweden that reflect broader shifts in feminist thinking. The modernist collective housing unit or 'family hotel' dating from the 1930s through the 1960s featured a clear division of labour between occupants and employed staff (Caldenby and Walldén 1979). The middle-class tenants employed domestic staff to provide them with meals that were paid on the basis of a monthly subscription. While the radical modernists endorsed collective housing as a means to promote equality between men and women, Vestbro and Horelli (2013:323) argue that these 'hotels' were based not on cooperation, but on the social division of labour. They attracted criticism for this reason as a 'special solution for privileged people' and the Labour Party considered it impossible to provide subsidies to this model of collective housing (Vestbro 1992). After meal services were suspended in one family hotel, a group of women, called BIG, *Bo i Gemenskap* ('live in community'), rejected the idea of separating productive and reproductive work. They did not agree with the modernist view that housework should be minimized. Instead they argued that cooking and caring for children together with others is enjoyable, saves time, and should be regarded as a valuable contribution to society (Vestbro and Horelli 2013:325). In this 'self-work' arrangement residents organize in small teams to cook for the whole community. Residents agree to share defined common tasks such as cooking, cleaning, and administration by rotation irrespective of sex. This arrangement, which combines modestly apportioned private space with common facilities for shared daily use and non-hierarchical collective self-governance, became the most popular form of cohousing from the 1970s. Collaborative 'self-work' regimes resonate with feminist ideology of the 1960s, which emphasized the emancipatory power of solidarity in collective activity. Whether or not in practice, communal kitchens are emancipatory remains the subject of debate (Shroeder 2007).

The international phenomenon of cohousing can be identified by three waves of development: first, in northern European cities from the 1960s, with a view to improving the lives of working parents and their children through more efficient and egalitarian housekeeping; second, in the United States in 'cosmopolitan' metropolitan areas since the 1980s, with a view to recreating socially inclusive 'traditional' close-knit communities and building a sustainable alternative to 'place-less sprawl'; third, in Australia and South-East Asia in peri-urban to rural areas, engaging with the ecovillage ideals to combine cohousing with strong environmental conservation measures including aspects of self-sufficiency with respect to local food production and 'off-grid' renewable energy (Williams 2005). A good proportion of first and second wave cohousing groups are women-only; some are intended for older women (such as the aptly named Older Women's Cohousing group, OWCH, in London). Some are intended for mixed seniors (usually over age fifty), while the majority is intergenerational and mixed.

Cohousing in the United States can appear (both aesthetically and organizationally) to lack a radical vision. It is nevertheless highly influential both as the fastest growing form of intentional community and as a 'new normal' way of cultivating mutual support within and between households on a 'parochial scale of trust and knowing' (Lofland 1973). For example, in a study of the Elder Spirit Cohousing community in the United States, Anne Glass (2009) found that 80 per cent of senior residents turn to neighbours rather than to distant kin to facilitate local self-reliance. As another West Coast US IC resident observes, 'lots of people are drawn to cohousing because, at its best, it's supposed to be a beautiful blend of community and capitalism – it's not a commune' (Jarvis 2015:101). In this context it is important to stress the active participation and collaboration of residents in self-governance. This is necessary to clearly distinguish cohousing from commercial condominiums or gated communities that also have common spaces and shared facilities but which do not cultivate community-based micro-structures of social organizing that endow local meaning and shape to the way common spaces and facilities are used. Practical examples of social organizing around sharing that characterize cohousing (in the United States and elsewhere) include collective and reciprocal childcare, pooled ownership of transport and large domestic appliances, tools and machinery, and cultural expectations that everyday possessions such as books, toys, recipes, and DVDs are routinely circulated on loan. On-line calendars are typically used to coordinate and apportion common-use facilities such as guest rooms for which each household has access on a time-share basis. In this sense the infrastructure of daily life in cohousing include not only the mechanisms to challenge domestic activities, possessions or roles as 'his', 'hers', or 'exclusive' but also the circuits of learning and influence that can be progressive and transformative. As one West Coast US IC resident observes, for example,

> in cohousing I have a life situation and a set up that encourages me to have less stuff, to live in a small home, to share more, to live more simply . . . .you've got a common pool of knowledge about living simply.
>
> *(Jarvis 2011)*

This suggests that the cohousing model has the potential to transform mainstream dwelling, precisely because it modifies without abandoning familiar notions of privacy, property, community, and sharing.

## Our story: the enduring legacy of the women's peace movement

Striking parallels are revealed between the complex intersection of actors, intentions, and settings needed to cultivate 'efficiencies of propinquity' and similarly sustained participation in new social movements (Passy and Giugni 2000). Cynthia Hamilton describes the way that women's actions in the early 80s shifted the form and values of solidarity from

> walking into your local CND meeting (where) it's a very bureaucratic set-up, invariably run by blokes, to a completely different way of doing things. We never sat in rows. We introduced ourselves and tried to keep the groups fairly small. . . . .Everyone got a chance to express themselves and their feelings.
>
> *(Hamilton 1989:130)*

This emphasis on expressing feelings can be observed as a legacy of the 'tribal council circle', originally derived from indigenous cultures and widely adopted in the Quaker movement. The open forum of the tribal-council circle was adopted with particularly cathartic affect in the women's peace camps (Roseneil 1995). It is typical for women-only and mixed intergenerational groups to draw inspiration from the way women organized daily life in the enduring peace camps such as Greenham Common through 'highly productive intellectual openness' (Roseneil 1995:67). In a tribal council circle, a talking stick is passed around from member to member, allowing only the person holding the stick to speak. This enables all those present to be heard, especially those who would feel intimidated by adversarial debate. This is evident at Twin Oaks, which was founded in 1967 in rural central Virginia, with a mission 'to promote secular values of cooperation, sharing, nonviolence, equality and ecology' (Twin Oaks 2014). The Twin Oaks community is self-supporting economically, income-sharing and partly self-sufficient. Each member works forty-two hours a week in the community's business and domestic areas. Each member receives housing, food, health care, and personal spending money from the community.

Conscientious listening is central to the 'non-violent' open communication style adopted by Twin Oaks, and this combines with wider social learning. On the one hand gender democracy is manifest in terms of an absence of leadership, in a non-hierarchical gender division of labour and decision-making. On the other hand, in more subtle ways, egalitarian intentions are also instilled in a culture of non-violent community and a shared ethos that commits individual members to challenge and rewrite oppressive and sexist language and behaviour in mainstream society. In this way, 'calm' communication, nurturing, and compassionate language becomes the superior cultural capital intended to replace the taken for granted privilege and domination of loud, confident, aggressive, or intimidating voices (Flanigan 2011:xviii). In theory at least, meeting in the circle, where there is no up or down, beginning or end, a non-hierarchical culture is enshrined which promotes openness toward each other's concerns and emphasis on non-judgmental experimentation.

Similarly, it is important to acknowledge the influence of intersecting intentions that emphasize spiritual values because these typically provide further scope to disrupt dominant ethnocentric and androcentric assumptions. It can be argued that it is in the blurred relations between ecology and spirituality and between ecology and human sexuality that activists and scholars find the nuanced analysis of society and nature's interrelatedness needed to re-imagine a harmonious and sustainable future (Sbicca 2012). For example, the Brazilian shamanic IC of Terra Mirim rescues the ancient lineage of the Goddess Mother as an embodied practice of people living in harmony with each other and nature. Faith rests on a spiritual-natural affective 'encounter' rather than institutionalized religious practice. In this context, shared rituals and ceremonies play a fundamental role in the enactment of a feminized (rather than women-only) space: visitors and residents comment on the feminine culture and 'energy' that the shamans claim is rooted in 'nurture and abundance' and cultivated in relation to four food types: spiritual (contemplation), psychic (understanding), emotional (love), and physical (local seasonal food production and solidarity economies; Alba Maria 2014). Elsewhere there are also examples of women-only communities such as those founded in the 1970s to practice the politics of gay rights and women's liberation in a 'separate lesbian world'. The Pagoda Community in Florida, for instance, is one of about one hundred below-the-radar intentional women's communities in North America to practice a separate lesbian feminist 'utopia' on grounds of matriarchy (Unger 2010).

## Summary and concluding remarks: re-imagining gender democracy

Intentional communities are frequently viewed as 'laboratories for testing and demonstrating new ideologies and social structures' (Forster 1998:39). Yet, as I have shown in this chapter, there has generally been limited theorizing of the gender norms and relations constructed and reproduced in a group setting where order and action is shaped by shared arrangements for daily living. Research has drawn attention to resource sharing within virtual communities (such as freecycle; Nelson et al. 2007), for specific populations of students and young professionals (Heath and Kenyon 2001) and institutional or semi-institutional health care facilities (Parr 2000), but not situations of collaboration in building, funding and managing community-based housing (but see Vestbro and Horelli 2013 specifically on cohousing). Further research is needed to examine the extent to which regional cultures of patriarchy, individualism, and competitiveness are modified in a group setting by governance practices intended to replace 'macho' adversarial agenda-setting practices with creative and compassionate dialogue rooted in conscientious listening.

Home and community are major sites of consumption, waste, and inequality, and the contradictions and dilemmas of 'idealized' Western material cultures of home-making raise significant concerns for the promotion of 'green' homes. This chapter situates renewed interest in novel forms of collective and communal living, notably intentional communities, in a well-rehearsed critique of the 'arrested development' of mainstream, private single family dwelling. The umbrella term 'intentional community' was introduced in Figure 29.1 as encompassing four 'types' of shared space and collaboration (communes, cooperatives, cohousing, and ecovillages). This typology highlights an interdependent scale of dwelling that challenges sexist and materialistic living arrangements by attempting to combine and redistribute productive and reproductive work between households. While it is entirely possible to design village-like communities within cities, rarely do 'master-planned' 'urban village' developments take the 'soft infrastructures' of participatory governance into account. This is why it is instructive to explore the ambiguous intentions and multiple realities of gender equality and ecological sustainability in more communal settings. Notions of solidarity and autonomy help distinguish the vision of sharing and participation in cohousing from historical examples of totalitarian or ideologically exclusive communes.

Perhaps inevitably, evidence from the historical record and contemporary demonstration communities reveal a mixed picture. The social scale relations of sharing, collaboration, and consensus governance are complex, fragile, and difficult to 'engineer'. Notwithstanding the recurring motivation of distaste for misogyny and materialism and enduring efforts to subvert the conventional nuclear family and single family home, we find paradoxical evidence to suggest that 'back to the land' sustainability initiatives can serve to reinforce traditional gender roles because the environmental agenda overshadows issues of social justice. Similarly, emphasis on non-violent, consensus-based communication can reinforce gender separated rather than inclusive egalitarian

*Helen Jarvis*

group settings. The social and material networks that cultivate conviviality and sharing in a consensus community setting are not always benign or sufficient to combat persistent gender inequalities. Even when ideological commitments to gender equality are widespread in the intentional community group, gender divisions can be normalized and taken for granted by the way democratic social relations and cooperation are enacted. While sexist attitudes are outwardly challenged, gender imbalances are witnessed in the persistent undervaluation of the emotional labour most frequently constructed as 'women's work'.

Cohousing represents a pragmatic grassroots movement that has grown out of dissatisfaction with individual dwelling. While it accounts for a tiny fraction of new housing construction in the United Kingdom, the United States, and Australia, it is the subject of growing political attention and popular desire. While it may not prove to be the most 'radical' model of collective living over the long term, it represents a plausible shift toward fundamentally rethinking how and where people live, to promote sustainability and gender justice in the future. The energy efficiency arguments alone (e.g., fewer building materials, combined heat and power) are compelling; added to these are the need to address the social isolation and absence of reciprocal welfare characteristic of the rising number of smaller households, many with high support needs. The challenges facing groups wishing to establish alternative, gender democratic, sustainable cohousing, or more radical communal arrangements are nevertheless daunting, and the failure rate of ICs is high. In large part this is because, unlike mythical utopias, intentional communities are not island states. As one resident of an Australian rural IC observed, 'it's almost like you have to kind of keep shaking the other world off to come into this one – of negotiation, sharing and consensus' (Jarvis 2015:101). This scale of intentional community reflects regional cultural variation that function through multiple scales of history, patriarchy, and state welfare regulation. In short, while there are numerous practical examples of the way shared intentions, collective work, and participatory democracy foster non-exploitative mutual support, this is a fragile scale of welfare and self-reliance that is prone to depletion, especially when hollowed out by debt, ageing, disability, and a political economy that renders social reproduction work invisible by the privileged status assigned to wage employment.

# References

Alba Maria (2014) *Shaman Alba Maria on Shamanism*. Online. Available at: http://shamans-journey.blogspot.co.uk/2014/10/shaman-alba-maria-on-shamanism-science.html (accessed 12 August 2015).

Beynon, G. (2012) *Women and the English Civil War*. Online. Available at: www.internationalsocialist.org.uk/index.php/2012/06/women-and-the-english-civil-war/#sthash.c8TXoiwp.dpuf (accessed 12 August 2015).

Boal, I., Stone, J., Watts, M. and Winslow, C. (eds) (2012) *West of Eden: Communes and Utopia in Northern California*. Oakland, CA: PM Press.

Buckingham, S. (2004) 'Ecofeminism in the twenty first century', *The Geographical Journal* 170(2): 146–154.

Burke, G. (2004) 'Knowing place: The role of immersive pedagogy within the context of a community-based art and environment project', *Australian Art Education* 28(1–2): 6–21.

Caldenby, C. and Walldén, A. (1979) *Collective Housing Units: Soviet Union and Sweden Around 1930*. Stockholm: The Swedish Research Council T11: 197.

Chatterton, P. (2013) 'Towards an agenda for post-carbon cities: Lessons from Lilac, the UK's first ecological, affordable cohousing community', *International Journal of Urban and Regional Research*: 1654–1674, on-line first: doi:10.1111/1468–2427.12009.

Chouinard, V. (1989) 'Social reproduction and housing alternatives: Cooperative housing in postwar Canada', in Dear, M. and Wolch, J. (eds) *The Power of Geography: How Territory Shapes Social Life*. Sydney: Allen and Unwin, 222–237.

Coates, C. (2007) *Writing and Printing and Editing in Diggers and Dreamers*. London: Diggers and Dreamers.

Crabtree, L. (2006) 'Disintegrated houses: Exploring ecofeminist housing and urban design options', *Antipode* 38(4): 711–734.

Curry, G., Koczberski, G. and Selwood, J. (2001) 'Cashing in, cashing out: Rural change on the south coast of Western Australia', *Australian Geographer* 32: 109–124.

Dunstan, G. (1975) 'Nimbin: The vision and the reality', in Smith, M. and Crossley, D. (eds) *The Way Out: Radical Alternatives in Australia*. Melbourne: Lansdowne Press, 19–27.

Flanigan, J. (2011) 'Utopian gender: Counter discourses in a feminist community', *Dissertations Paper 459*. Online. Available at: http://scholarworks.umass.edu/open_access_dissertations/459 (accessed 12 August 2015).

Forster, P. M. (1998) 'Communities and academics: A developing dialogue', *Community, Work and Family* 1: 39–49.

Fromm, D. (1991) *Collaborative Communities: Cohousing, Central Living and Other New Forms of Housing With Shared Facilities*. New York: Van Nostrand Reinhold.

Fromm, D. (2000) 'American cohousing: The first five years', *Journal of Architectural and Planning Research* 17(2): 94–109.

Gans, H. (1967) *The Levittowners: Life and Politics in a New Suburban Community*. Harmondsworth: The Penguin Press.

Glass, A. (2009) 'Aging in a community of mutual support: The emergence of an elder intentional cohousing community in the United States', *Journal of Housing for the Elderly* 23(4): 283–303.

Gold, J. R. (2008) 'Modernity and utopia', in Hall, T., Hubbard, P. and Short, J. R. (eds) *The Sage Companion to the City*. London: Sage Publications, 67–87.

Hamilton, C. (1989) 'Women in politics: Methods of resistance and change', *Women's Studies International Forum* 12: 129–135.

Hannan, M. (2002) 'Music making in the village of Nimbin', *Transformations* 2. Online. Available at: www.cqu.edu.au/transformations (accessed 27 July 2011).

Hayden, D. (1976) *Seven American Utopias: The Architecture of Communitarian Socialism, 1790–1975*. Cambridge, MA: MIT Press.

Hayden, D. (1978) 'Two utopian feminists and their campaigns for kitchenless houses', *Signs* 4(2): 274–290.

Hayden, D. (1980) 'What would a non-sexist city be like? Speculations on housing, urban design, and human work', *Signs* 5(3): 170–187.

Hayden, D. (1984) *Redesigning the American Dream: The Future of Housing, Work and Family Life*. New York and London: W.W. Norton.

Heath, S. and Kenyon, L. (2001) 'Single young professionals and shared household living', *Journal of Youth Studies* 4(1): 83–100.

Hemmens, G. C., Hoch, C. J. and Carp, J. (eds) (1996) *Under One Roof: Issues and Innovations in Shared Housing*. New York: State University Press.

Horelli, L. and Vepsä, K. (1994) 'In search of supportive structures for everyday life', in Altman, I. and Churchman, A. (eds) *Women and the Environment: Human Behaviour and Environment* (Vol. 13). New York: Plenum, 201–226.

Irvine, G. (2003) 'Creating communities at the end of the rainbow', in Wilson, H. (ed) *Belonging in the Rainbow Region: Cultural Perspectives on the NSW North Coast*. Lismore, NSW: Southern Cross University, 1–5. Excerpt. Online. Available at: http://elementaleducation.com/wp-content/uploads/Community-LandHoldingOptions.pdf.

Jarvis, H. (2005) *Work/Life City Limits: Comparative Household Perspectives*. Basingstoke: Palgrave.

Jarvis, H. (2011) 'Saving space, sharing time: Integrated infrastructures of daily life in cohousing', *Environment and Planning A* 43: 560–577.

Jarvis, H. (2013) 'Against the "tyranny" of single-family dwelling: Insights from Christiania at 40', *Gender, Place & Culture* 20(8): 939–959.

Jarvis, H. (2015) 'Towards a deeper understanding of the social architecture of cohousing: Evidence from the UK, USA and Australia', *Urban Research and Practice* 8(1): 93–105.

Jarvis, H., Kantor, P. and Cloke, J. (2009) *Cities and Gender*. London: Routledge.

Kanter, R. M. (1976) 'Roots versus restlessness: Cooperative households, the city, and recurrent issues in American family life', *The Massachusetts Review* 17(2): 331–353.

Laughton, R. (2008) *Surviving and Thriving on the Land: How to Use Your Time and Energy to Run a Successful Smallholding*. Padstow: Green Books.

Lawrence, R. J. (1982) 'Domestic space and society: A cross-cultural study', *Comparative Studies in Society and History* 24(1): 104–130.

Levitas, R. (2007) 'Looking for the blue: The necessity of utopia', *Journal of Political Ideologies* 12: 289–306.

Lofland, L. (1973) *A World of Strangers*. Prospect Heights, IL: Waveland Press.

Manzella, J. C. (2010) *Common Purse, Uncommon Future: The Long, Strange Trip of Communes and Other Intentional Communities.* Santa Barbara, CA: Praeger.

Maxey, L. (2004) 'The participation of younger people within intentional communities: Evidence from two case studies', *Children's Geographies* 2(1): 29–48.

Metcalf, B. (1995) *From Utopian Dreaming to Communal Reality: Cooperative Lifestyles in Australia.* Sydney: University of New South Wales Press.

Metcalf, B. (2004) *The Findhorn Book of Community Living.* Findhorn: The Findhorn Press.

Molotch, H. (2003) *Where Stuff Comes From: How Toasters, Toilets, Cars, Computers and Many Other Things Come to Be as They Are.* London: Routledge.

Nelson, M. R., Rademacher, M. A. and Paek, H.-J. (2007) 'Downshifting consumer = upshifting citizen? An examination of the local freecycle community', *Annals of the American Academy of Political and Social Science* 611: 141–156.

O'Riordan, T. (1981) *Environmentalism.* London: Pinon Ltd.

Parr, H. (2000) 'Interpreting the "hidden social geographies" of mental health: Ethnographies of inclusion and exclusion in semi-institutional places', *Health & Place* 6(3): 225–237.

Passy, F. and Giugni, M. (2000) 'Life-spheres, networks and sustained participation in social movements: A phenomenological approach to political commitment', *Sociological Forum* 15: 117–144.

Pickerill, J. (2015) 'Bodies, building and bricks: Women architects and builders in eight eco-communities in Argentina, Britain, Spain, Thailand and USA', *Gender, Place & Culture* 22(7): 901–919.

Pickerill, J. and Maxey, L. (eds) (2009) *Low Impact Development: The Future in Our Hands.* Leeds: Creative Commons.

Pringle, R. and Winning, A. (1998) 'Building strategies: Equal opportunities in the construction industry', *Gender, Work and Organization* 5(4): 220–229.

Roberts, M. (1991) *Living in a Man-made World: Gender Assumptions in Modern Housing Design.* London: Routledge.

Roseneil, S. (1995) *Disarming Patriarchy: Feminism and Political Action at Greenham.* Buckingham: Open University Press.

Sargisson, L. (2000) *Utopian Bodies.* London: Routledge.

Sbicca, J. (2012) 'Eco-queer movement(s): Challenging heteronormative space through (re)imagining nature and food', *European Journal of Ecopsychology* 3: 33–52.

Schaefer, R. T. and Zellner, W. W. (2008) *Extraordinary Groups: An Examination of Unconventional Lifestyles 8th Edition.* New York: Wroth Publishers.

Schehr, R. C. (1997) *Dynamic Utopia: Establishing Intentional Communities as a New Social Movement.* Westport, CT: Bergin and Garvey.

Seyfang, G. (2010) 'Community action for sustainable housing: Building a low-carbon future', *Energy Policy* 38: 7624–7633.

Shove, E. (2003) *Comfort, Cleanliness and Convenience: The Social Organisation of Normality.* Oxford: Berg.

Shroeder, K. (2007) 'A feminist examination of community kitchens in Peru and Bolivia', *Gender, Place and Culture* 13(6): 663–668.

Sutton, R. P. (2004) *Communal Utopias and the American Experience: Secular Communities 1824–2000.* Santa Barbara: Greenwood Publishing.

*Twin Oaks* (2014) Online. Available at: www.twinoakscommunity.org/ (accessed 12 August 2015).

Unger, N. (2010) 'From jook joints to sisterspace: The role of nature in lesbian alternative environments in the United States', in Mortimer-Sandilands, C. and Erickson, B. (eds) *Queer Ecologies: Sex, Nature, Politics, Desire.* Bloomington, IN: Indiana University Press, 173–198.

Vestbro, D. U. (1992) 'From central kitchen to community cooperation: Development of collective housing in Sweden', *Open House International* 17(2): 30–38.

Vestbro, D. U. (1997) 'Collective housing in Scandinavia: How feminism revised a modernist experiment', *Journal of Architectural and Planning Research* 14(4): 329–342.

Vestbro, D. U. and Horelli, L. (2013) 'Design for gender equality: The history of co-housing ideas and realities', *Built Environment* 38(3): 315–335.

Williams, J. (2005) 'Designing neighbourhoods for social interaction: The case of cohousing', *Journal of Urban Design* 10(3): 195–227.

# 30

# FEMINIST FUTURES AND 'OTHER WORLDS'

## Ecologies of critical spatial practice

*Meike Schalk, Ulrika Gunnarsson-Östling, and Karin Bradley*

[W]e can choose to create new discourses and counter-technologies of economy and to construct strategic forms of interplace solidarity, bringing to the fore ways to make other worlds possible.

(Gibson-Graham 2008:623)

## Introduction

Scholars working in the field of gender and environment, including ecofeminists, feminist political ecologists, and new materialist feminists, share a criticism of human domination of the environment. From this common stance, they reject mainstream approaches to sustainable development as anthropocentric and androcentric.[1] Instead of technical measurements and 'green growth' scenarios within hegemonic systems, these scholars approach contemporary threats such as climate change, uneven social development, and environmental injustice by calling for radically new ethical frameworks to change existing structures that exploit nature, animals, and humans. As Sanati et al. argue, 'The crisis that is created as a result of unsustainable capitalist patriarchal growth and its technologies cannot be solved and compensated for by more of the same' (2011:90). A central feature of this call for change is an ethics that privileges emotions, relationships, and experiences over impartial and rational moral reasoning to determine what is demanded in the face of environmental challenges.

Feminist and environmentalist critiques have been strongly interrelated since the 1970s. In the fields of feminist architecture and urban studies, for example, scholars have developed criticisms of the urban 'manmade environment', encompassing, since the 1980s, the concept of *spatial justice*. This concept is based on the idea that the built environment should not exclude or discriminate. It also addresses the relationships between those who build and make decisions about built environments and those who dwell in them (Hayden 1980, 1981; Matrix 1984; Young 1991; Weisman 1992; Sandercock 1998). Today, parts of this body of feminist-environmental critique have become absorbed into mainstream spatial research and practice, where it is rarely given the credit it deserves. Arguably, there has also been a loss of radical desire to challenge existing structures. In response to these observations, we suggest that there is a need to rethink feminist environmental critique in the fields of planning, architecture, and futures studies. In a time largely devoid of utopian or radical approaches, there are good reasons to bring back the feminist agenda for altering practice and subjectivity (Braidotti 1994; Petrescu 2007) in order to address the environmental challenges facing contemporary societies.

In this chapter we explore practical and pedagogical approaches, tools, and methods for cultivating more socio-environmentally just relations that are inspired by feminist spatial critique. The practices we consider stem from the desire to counteract unsustainable and socially unjust structures and the need to organize society differently. Feminist spatial practices, in our understanding, work toward more socio-environmentally just relations by performing 'other worlds' (Petrescu 2007; Gibson-Graham 2008; Stengers 2008; Braidotti 2013). These practices happen both inside and outside the academy and involve the 'productive power of making' to bring new kinds of social and economic realities into existence (Gibson-Graham 2008:614). As a refusal to accept the neoliberal mantra that 'there is no alternative', they take on systemic and structural change through micropolitical and microsocial practices. We see these as radical and normative approaches toward change, happening in the here and now, and thus we refer to them also as *lived utopias*. Central to our exploration of these approaches are the examples of the former British feminist design cooperative Matrix (1980–1994), and the contemporary European network Eco Nomadic School (established in 2011), which share the objective of transforming the roles of producers of the built environment by shifting focal viewpoints and considering marginalized practices, demystifying dominant socio-economic relations as the norm, and actively building a 'personal practice' (Gibson-Graham 2008).

Working from our positions in the fields of urban planning, architecture, and futures studies, we discuss these practices in combination with key insights from ecofeminism, feminist political ecology, and feminist new materialism. We argue that feminist spatial practice envisions structural and systemic change through social, economic, and aesthetic alternatives on the micro level, and that they act as seeds of transformation. Feminist futures are therefore not restricted to women, but encompass alternative future forms of human and nonhuman relations that imply radical societal transformation of systems and structures that create and sustain gender hierarchy. We explore practice by asking: How are the ethical rationales understood, performed, and envisioned? What subjectivities do they entail? And what insights can we gain from them for future environmental practice, planning, and architecture?

The chapter has five sections. This introduction is followed by a (dis)positioning from the viewpoint of our different disciplinary fields in order to interpret feminist spatial practices. A third section maps out a theoretical framework of feminist spatial practice extending from the economic geographers J. K. Gibson-Graham's notions of 'diverse economies' and ethical practice through to techniques of 'ontological reframing, rereading for difference, and cultivating creativity' (2008:613).[2] Two practices and their approaches, ethos, and development of methods and tools are discussed, through the lens of Gibson-Graham's techniques, in the fourth section. Fifth and finally, there is a discussion of the tactics and strategies that are employed in the cases of feminist spatial practice followed by a debate on its capacity to engender change.

## (Dis)positions

Many critics see the environmental crisis as being connected to societal and political crises and, above all, to a crisis of meaning and relations. For example, Félix Guattari, in *The Three Ecologies* (1989), broadens the notion of ecology and speaks of environmental, social, and mental ecologies, taking ecology beyond mere environmental concerns to include social relations and human subjectivity. His critique resembles feminist critiques when he addresses the experiences and effects of the linear developmental model, notions of hierarchy, and competition as driving forces in the economy – in other words, the dominant notions of legitimate knowledge and power relations between genders and species (Haraway 1988, 2003; Harding 2008).

Futures studies often understands radical change in terms of technological development and behavioural change in the approach to sustainable development (Åkerman 2011; Höjer et al. 2011). While the intent is to invite a plurality of futures, social structures – such as gender, race and class hierarchies – are seldom explicitly analyzed (Gunnarsson-Östling 2011). Planning discourse on justice has intensified in the last decades (Harvey and Potter 2009; Campbell 2010; Fainstein 2010; Brenner et al. 2011), but planning practice is still criticized for its inability to plan for socio-environmental justice (Bullard 2000; Agyeman 2005; Bradley et al. 2008). Architectural practice has the ability to create and communicate 'other worlds' through images but often denies the political and ethical dimensions of design (Felton et al. 2012).

We claim that four decades of feminist critical analyses in these three fields have paved the way for a diversified planning and building discourse and have evoked changes in policy-making attitudes. We have seen changes in planning policies such as disabled access regulations, in documents on gender mainstreaming, in economic measurements such as gender budgeting, and in governmental shifts to involve citizens in participatory processes that shape environments. Despite these efforts, however, planning and building practice has hardly changed. Participation is rarely about sharing power with citizens, but rather about consultation and information (Lindholm et al. 2015). In the current economic climate, spatial injustice is increasing, as gentrification and segregation in most major cities demonstrate. On a political level, clearly, current policies may highlight 'green growth' and technical innovation, but they leave social innovation, alternative value-creating models, and sufficient consumption without the support they need (Mont et al. 2014; see also chapters by Mellor and Littig in this volume). The hard work of questioning mainstream sustainable development paths is often carried out by non-governmental organizations and in the micropolitical and microsocial practices of citizen initiatives. Linking discourse and practice requires other modes of practice to enter the conversation about desired futures.

Feminist spatial practice is inspired by the feminist architecture theorist Jane Rendell's (2006) concept of critical spatial practice, which includes everyday activities and creative practices that involve social critique, self-reflection, social change, and efforts to resist the dominant social order of global corporate capitalism. A professional critical and feminist spatial practice does not respond to set briefs and preformulated questions; it demands rethinking the terms of engagement and procedures and may reformulate issues and questions. It is a critical and projective practice. In the early 2000s, the terms *post-critical, post-theoretical,* and *projective* were alternately used to oppose an interpretation of criticality as a pessimistic prognosis of architecture practice from the outside, with a more optimistic outlook for the profession through an internal architecture discourse that was supposed to focus on the making of architecture (Somol and Whiting 2003). In contrast, we argue that a feminist spatial practice must always be both critical and projective.

## Diverse economies: a theoretical framework for feminist futures

We argue that a feminist spatial perspective is a productive way to rethink the dominant sustainable urban development path. So far, this path has not led to the necessary actions to address climate change, recurring financial crises, social and spatial injustice, and the overuse of natural resources (Swyngedouw 2011; Bradley and Hedrén 2014). Since the 1980s, however, a second wave of feminist critique of the *man*made built environment has seen urban planning as a patriarchal practice that excludes the experiences of women and diverse groups in the city (Hayden 1980, 1981; Matrix 1984; Weisman 1992; Eichler 1995; Sandercock 1998; Fenster 2002). Ecofeminism, with its theoretical analysis of the intertwined domination of nature and women, emerged as a movement in the 1980s. Feminist political ecology research, stressing the social construction of gender and nature relations, developed in the 1990s partly as a critique of some aspects of ecofeminism. It highlighted that environmental problems have particularly negative effects on women and other marginalized groups (Rocheleau et al. 1996). In the last decade, 'new' materialist feminist theorists have embraced posthumanist approaches and see opportunities for community building toward new/different social and institutional practices that can create more resilient futures (Gibson-Graham 2008; Stengers 2008; Braidotti 2013; Gibson-Graham et al. 2013; Petrescu 2013).

These critical strands have contributed in different ways with their analyses of environmental and labour patterns as gendered constructions. They have encouraged self-organization, activism, and resistance that have materialized in temporary and more permanent forms such as in women's peace camps, or in numerous feminist housing projects all over the world (see Jarvis in this volume). We see these activities as lived utopias, meaning lifeways in the here and now that practice alternative ways of living, producing, and consuming, that deviate from mainstream market economies. Feminist practices are reviewed here through Gibson-Graham's concept of 'diverse economies', an alternative approach to organizing life, which they set out in their 2008 essay (based on a lecture delivered at the Association of American Geographers meeting in 2006), 'Diverse Economies: Performative Practices for "Other Worlds"'. Gibson-Graham see structural and systemic change as a performative ontological project building upon and drawing from alternative practice and subjectivity. They speak of ontological reframing, rereading for difference, and cultivating creativity that emerges from an experimental, performative, and ethical orientation to the world.

It is worth discussing briefly Gibson-Graham's notion of diverse economies. It was developed in the late 1980s from feminist economic analysis that has demonstrated that nonmarket transactions and unpaid household work constitute 30 to 50 per cent of economic activity in both rich and poor countries (Ironmonger 1996). However, as radical economic geographers, they claim that 'marginal' economic practice and forms of enterprise are actually more prevalent and account for more hours worked and more value produced than the capitalist sector (see Figure 30.1). They criticize the mainstream focus of capitalist economics on the market – calling it a form of 'discursive violence' – and emphasize the importance of representing economy differently (Gibson-Graham 2008:615).

The diverse economies concept extends far beyond mainstream economic thinking with its narrow focus on exchange value, monetary activities, and traditional labour relations. It builds on the necessity to change perspective, or what they call *ontological reframing*. In their three-step program, ontological reframing is followed by re-reading for difference and cultivating creativity. They state that while we cannot ignore the power of past discourse and its materialization in durable technologies, infrastructures, and behaviour, we can actively work toward creating 'new discourses and counter-technologies of economy' (2008:623). In their reading of possibilities for systemic and structural change, Gibson-Graham have departed from a Marxist understanding and theorization of capitalist restructuring on macro levels, as they see here little scope of action for micromovements working for transformation. In response, they have asked how theory and epistemology could advance what they wanted *to do* in the world. Hence they have dropped their structuralist approach to social explanation and adopted an approach that theorizes the contingency of social outcomes, rather than the unfolding of structural logics. This gives them '(and

*Figure 30.1* The economy as an iceberg

*Source*: Image from J. K. Gibson-Graham, *Take Back the Economy* (2013:11), courtesy of Katherine Gibson

the world) more room to move' and to enlarge the space of the ethical and political (Laclau and Mouffe 1985; Gibson-Graham 2008:615).

Gibson-Graham see their own practice as researchers involved in participatory action research as a learning environment for the making of 'other worlds' collectively with other people. Part of this practice involves foregrounding the social and economic experiments that are happening worldwide and helping to proliferate them through research, by analyzing, highlighting, and conceptualizing economic relations outside of the capitalist mainstream. This is one way of foregrounding marginalized and hidden activities, in order to 'make them more real and more credible as objects of policy and activism' and thus open an imaginative space for alternatives (Gibson-Graham 2008:616). Here 'other worlds' can be performed (Butler 1993; Kosofsky-Sedgwick 2003; Law and Urry 2004). Gibson-Graham point to the performative effect of the familiar representations of capitalism dampening and discouraging noncapitalist initiatives. Without its systemic embodiment, however, capitalism's dominance became an open question rather than an initial assumption. Thus 'the diverse economies research program is a performative onto-logical project – part of bringing new economies into being – rather than a realist epistemological project of capturing and assessing existing objects' (Gibson-Graham 2008:616). In this way the strategy of making difference visible does not automatically create new paths forward, but it can generate new possibilities, different strategies, and alternatives to hegemonic experience that create conditions that enlarge the field of credible experiences, thus widening the possibilities for social experimentation (Santos 2006).

According to Gibson-Graham (2008), one of the prerequisites of change is the becoming of different subjects. Alternative discourse makes it possible to construct subjectivity and become aware of new opportunities for subject identification in a process independent of social structures and in a 'praxis of ethical learning' (Varela 1992). They state: 'The co-implicated processes of changing the world are what we identify as an ethical practice', and the three techniques of reframing, rereading for difference, and cultivating creativity enlarge the space of agency for all sorts of participants. All of them involve creativity in that they push us to make something new from what is at hand and from where we stand (Gibson-Graham 2008:618). 'Other worlds' are thus constituted not only on the macroscale of societal futures, policy, and planning, but also on the microscale of everyday practices, relations that may be transformed by practice in planning and architecture, and individuals and communities. This means everybody can be part of making change. It means not putting all our eggs in one basket and waiting for global agreements to solve the world's environmental problems. It means commencing change here and now.

## Two critical spatial practices: Matrix and the Eco Nomadic School

Narratives of feminist and/or radical alternative futures have emerged outside academia in art, architecture, and planning practice with a track record of criticism in the form of methods, activities, processes, and realized works (atelier d'architecture autogérée [aaa] 2007; Petrescu 2007; Schalk 2007, 2012; Trogal 2012). These are important, though undertheorized, cases. In Guattari's words, they are new social and aesthetic practices, and new practices of the self in relation to the other. They come into being through the articulation of an emerging subjectivity and environment while reinventing themselves and reappropriating 'universes of value' (Guattari 1989:45). To get social and political practice to work for humanity, Guattari suggests, it is essential to organize new micropolitical and microsocial practices, new solidarities, and a new gentleness.

In this section we look specifically at two feminist spatial practices, one historic and one contemporary, that experiment with, create, and live different socio-economic realities. They perform what we have called *lived utopias*. They are, first, the former feminist design cooperative Matrix (UK, 1980–1994), which aimed to transform power relations by inventing a new professional language, changing labour relations, and reproducing knowledge involving transversal pedagogies. Distributed across France, Romania, the UK, the Netherlands, and Germany, the pan-European Eco Nomadic School (ENS) network is our second example. Here we focus specifically on the workshop *Rural Women's Economies* (Höfen, Sulzbach, Southern Germany, October 2012). Through mutual learning and the teaching of ecocivic practices, ENS wants to reinforce democratic values by transferring local and gendered knowledge and skills to a highly diverse collection of participants in remote urban, suburban, and rural contexts. This practice approaches resilience by means of a critique that radically reconfigures social and economic relations and rethinks economies, producer-consumer relations, and the redistribution of power. We analyze the written and visual material from these two practices – manifestos, catalogues, websites, and other texts and films – in addition to gathering data through participation in a workshop with the Eco Nomadic School and an interview with Julia Dwyer, a former member of Matrix. Our aim is to analyze their perspectives and conditions of practice, to understand how their alternative futures are envisioned.

## *Matrix*

We realized we had to find ways of talking about the qualities of the space; how light or dark, soft or hard, high or wide the space should be. We needed to find a language accessible to everyone involved. We have continued thinking about this. It means starting from feelings about the spaces women know and their everyday experiences in them, and using that information to gradually build up a picture of the new space . . .

Because women do not have a long history of being builders or architects, every project is like pioneering. Most women . . . do not have mothers and grandmothers who have done it before, and prove they will be able to do it too. This question of confidence affects day-to-day work. . . . How do we establish standards of our own, ways that suit our skills and expectations?

*(Bradshaw 1984:94, 104)*

Matrix formed as a feminist design cooperative and was active during the 1980s and early 1990s in London. According to the former members, Julia Dwyer and Anne Thorne, 'twenty-five women collaborated over 14 years in a cooperatively-structured practice to explore the ways in which theory and practice of architecture could respond to affect social relations' (2007:41). Matrix was organized as a workers' cooperative with a nonhierarchical managerial structure, equal pay, and collaborative work. It was by no means an exceptional appearance in London at the time. Matrix was formed by and became integral to a broad network of various feminist and critical initiatives and professional groups: 'It was at the heart of a network of feminist architects, builders, and academics' (Dwyer and Thorne 2007:41; Dwyer 2012a).[3]

The intention was to work together as women, to develop a feminist approach to design through practical projects and theoretical analysis. Other aims were to communicate feminist design ideas widely; to look critically at the way the built environment affects women in society; to share skills and help develop an understanding of how women are 'placed' in a manmade environment; to use that knowledge to subvert it; and to start some ideas about how things could be different (Matrix 1984). Ultimately the question was how to involve women 'in making decisions about or in creating the environment' at all stages – recognizing needs, obtaining finances, organizing, designing, building, and using it – to create more connections between architects, builders, and users, recognizing these relationships also as class issues (Bradshaw 1984:89,102), and to challenge norms.

The problem, according to Matrix members, was that the built environment was predominantly modelled on the needs and experiences of one social group – men – yet was seen as neutral. For example, the transport system was designed for journeys to paid jobs but not for journeys with children and the handling of prams, the separation of home and workplace ignored the needs of women who stayed home, and there was a lack of suitable places to meet in the city, especially for immigrant women. This gendering of physical space disregarded the experience, needs, and desires of women and could not respond to a variety of lifestyles and cultures. The cause was the predominantly male decision-making power structure in the 1980s in the UK and elsewhere (see Figure 30.2).

Matrix members produced the book, *Making Space: Women and the Man Made Environment* (1984), an exhibition on housing design, *Home Truth*, and architectural designs. The cooperative worked in two main areas: design projects, such as health-care centres and spaces for women and children, and technical aid, which were publicly funded.[4] Technical aid resulted in a number of workshops and publications such as *A Job Designing Buildings* (1986) that addressed women considering a career in architecture. Matrix was interested in increasing the number of women

*Figure 30.2* Book cover of *Making Space* (1984)

*Source:* Photo by Meike Schalk

entering the building design profession. The objective was to advise women on how to take control of their own environment and work situation (Awan et al. 2009; Dwyer 2012b).

The Matrix design cooperative developed tools for participatory processes that involved users and builders in a different way. Architects had to train everyone who was part of the designing and building process – including the architects themselves, builders and clients – to better understand each other and the process. Matrix members adapted conventional architectural drawing and worked with large flexible models like dollhouses and interactive plans. These new devices helped avoid presenting 'fait accompli' solutions (Bradshaw 1984:96) and got everyone involved in understanding the tasks, enabling discussions, and making suggestions. In part, this education built up a form of transversal (or intersecting) knowledge by changing roles and letting people other than the architects do the drawings; in collaborative projects with builders (e.g., the Women's Building Co-op), architects could act as builders and builders and clients could act as architects.

As a 'design collective' rather than an 'architectural practice', Matrix valued nonarchitects as highly as architects. It was influenced by contemporary criticism of professionalism and architects' professional institutions by groups such as the New Architecture Movement (NAM). 'We have learned from working with women who have not been trained as architects. They have questioned conventional assumptions about design and have been excited by the possibility of creating buildings that suit their needs' (Dwyer and Thorne 2007:42).

A lack of transparency and communication was identified as the main obstacle to women's empowerment in architecture. 'Because architects' skills are less visible than builders', it is even more important that architects' skills should be demystified and made clear and accessible' (Bradshaw 1984:104). Therefore, finding pedagogies, tools, methods, and procedures that enhanced transparency, invited debate, and made collaboration possible in the designing and building process was a central concern. Matrix members argued that 'the ideology underlying how information is organized, whom you listen to, what questions you ask, which parts of the process could be open to group involvement – these are not generally discussed by architects or by those who employ them' (Bradshaw 1984:101). The manual, *Building for Childcare*, for example, advised clients and users what to have to mind in a designing and building process: how budgets should be calculated and timetables set up, how to allot time for consultation meetings and public discussion, and what specialists are involved in building. The manual advised users/clients to accompany the architects to meetings with the specialists on structure, services, and fire regulations to be able to participate in all decisions made at early stages. It also encouraged clients and users to prompt the architects to present their plans in legible ways that stimulated, rather than inhibited, discussion. Both communication with clients and users and with builders was in focus:

> Aware of the unequal class position of builders in the production of building, and of the mutual disrespect which sometimes resulted from this, the women builders argued that the building process should be far more collaborative and that methods should be adapted to make this possible, including addressing the language used by the professionally trained architects, which they suggested, distanced them from clients and builders.
>
> *(Dwyer and Thorne 2007:42)*

To improve the exchange between builders and architects and to find a framework for working together based on support and mutual trust, some Matrix members felt there was a need for double skills (consequently, Fran Bradshaw trained as a bricklayer). However, the hierarchies and professional roles, the decision-making patterns of builders, clients, and architects were experienced as difficult to change:

> Exploring ways of working together takes place within a divided and exploitative building industry. . . . The assumptions that go with conventional roles within the building industry are powerful. The definition of jobs, which skills are considered necessary in the creation of buildings and how they are relatively valued and paid for – these are all issues of importance.
>
> *(Bradshaw 1984:105)*

Matrix dissolved as a design cooperative in the beginning of the 1990s in large part due to the economic crisis and the disappearance of public commissions and technical aid funding, which was connected to the rise of neoliberal agenda in the UK under Margaret Thatcher at that time. A Matrix principle was to not take private commissions, and it became difficult for the cooperative to survive economically.[5] Looking back over the history of their cooperative, Matrix members have arrived at a number of critical insights into their demise. One view at Matrix was that ideology had been too overarching in terms of impact on the individuals involved; instead, projects should be driven by accepting all empirical components as important, with a subtext of anti-authoritarianism. Instead of an overall ideology, small patches of resistance would then be more useful, because one would not have to take care of *everything*. A further point of self-criticism concerned the lack of flexibility in the face of change. Julia Dwyer even wondered if cooperative structures were doomed to fail. Cooperation, she said, puts everyone in the same situation despite their varied lives, and co-ops had to adjust. 'But to become continually different, also in terms of architecture, means constant reflection and change' (2012b:n.p.).

Despite this self-criticism, we claim that Matrix developed a new form of ethical and aesthetic practice, tools, and artefacts that continue to inspire feminist architects, planners, and builders. Today, as in the 1980s, numerous critical participatory projects by feminist spatial practitioners are reemerging. These recall Matrix's work, and indeed they can learn from Matrix's creative practice as well as from their mistakes. The Matrix contribution is not only to a discourse on socio-environmentally just relations but also to an aesthetic discourse in architecture. Its construction of equal, nonhierarchical, and close relations between users, builders, designers, and the needs of clients and workers are understood in a much more comprehensive way than in a conventional planning and building process predominantly oriented toward the market. Thus the work of Matrix continues to provide the opportunity to rethink the entire building process along more just and sustainable lines, from a feminist perspective.

In Gibson-Graham's (2008) understanding, Matrix was performing 'other worlds'. Their feminist spatial practice generated new possibilities for social experimentation, different strategies for intervening in a streamlined planning and building processes with demands for recognizing difference, and most importantly, alternatives to hegemonic experience. The knowledge produced at Matrix has been handed on in the tradition of open universities through workshops, the publication of manuals and manifestos, and teaching. Manuals are sought to empower their users; they can teach theories and methods that enable others to pursue an alternative practice. Since then, more feminist initiatives have recognized the importance of developing pedagogies for critical practice and valuing the knowledge produced through redesigning one's own practice and by rethinking strategies, tools and methods, collaborations, working procedures, and economies.[6] The main outcome is another form of knowledge production created in common and communicated via the participants over time. We call Matrix's practice a lived utopia. Lived utopia is a double paradox that produces a productive tension between the assumed impossibility of fully realizing the utopia of a just practice within an unjust system and, simultaneously, the real possibility of making ethical choices by performing, inhabiting, and living 'other worlds' in the here and now. The awareness in combination with these acts has the power to bring about transformation.

## The Eco Nomadic School: Rural Women's Economies civic seminar, October 2012

Like the political-pedagogical agenda of Matrix, the Eco Nomadic School (ENS) performs 'other worlds' by addressing the issue of (re-)learning the alternative practice of everyday ecologies within the framework of nomadic classrooms and involving a highly diverse group of participants. Distributed across France, Romania, the Netherlands, the UK, and Germany, ENS is an initiative committed to creating 'environments for mutual learning and teaching ecocivic practices' (aaa 2009). The aim is to reinforce democratic values by (1) enabling the transfer of local and gendered knowledge and skills on issues of resilience in remote urban, suburban, and rural contexts, and (2) diffusing ecocivic knowledge, skills, and values on a European scale. The central mission is to connect an ecological ethos with the notion of citizenship.

The project is based on a partnership between a collection of organizations already active in the transmission of ecological skills and knowledge. These are atelier d'architecture autogérée (aaa) in France, a not-for-profit organization; the Agency research centre of the School of Architecture at the University of Sheffield; Myvillages, an artist collective; and the Community Foundation for Local Development/Fundatia Communitara de Dezvoltare Local (FCDL), a foundation in the town of Brezoi in Romania that furthers social and cultural regional sustainability. ENS has several locations: a metropolitan suburban city, Colombes, near Paris; a postindustrial urban area (also a Transition Town) called Todmorden in the UK; a suburban rural area of Franconia in southern Germany; and an isolated rural area, Brezoi, in Romania. Funding for the project came from the European Commission's Lifelong Learning Programme – Grundtvig, and from various local sources.[7]

In study trips, site visits, common participatory training workshops, civic seminars, and 'live projects',[8] the ENS teaches and learns ecological practices, such as reuse, recycling, urban agriculture, building ecologically, and alternative economies. The civic seminar, *Rural Women's Economies* (which took place in the villages of Höfen, Sulzbürg, Frensdorf and Birkach in October 2012), brought together the partners, interested participants, researchers, and practitioners, in the wider network of ENS, from Rotterdam, Berlin, Budapest, London, and Stockholm and local women's organizations from the Höfen and Sulzbürg area.[9] The program's structure allowed for engagement on different levels and in accordance with individual interests and knowledge; presentations and discussions took place in German, English, and French. The aim of the workshop was to examine gendered rural practices in different regions and to foreground the knowledge in sustainable practice as a point of departure for developing educational strategies and methods for future ecocivic practice.

The civic seminar addressed issues related to 'women's rural economies and production' from a *subsistence perspective* as a model that could become extended to urban contexts (Bennholdt-Thomsen and Mies 1999). Like Gibson-Graham's (2008) technique of ontological reframing, the subsistence perspective suggests a radical shift. Instead of extending from the urban middle-class perspective of the Global North as the norm, a subsistence perspective adopts a view 'from below', particularly rural women's perspectives in the Global South, enabling 'people to produce and reproduce their own life, to stand on their own feet and to speak in their own voice' (Bennholdt-Thomsen and Mies 1999:3). Carrying out and experiencing gendered rural everyday practice, such as the making of sauerkraut as a common act, served as a personal entry into a theoretical discussion that linked material, know–how, and perspectives, and opened speculation on future outlooks (see Figure 30.3). When discussing social practices in relation to social innovation or sustainable consumption and change, the sociologist Elizabeth Shove defines three elements of social practice: *material*, *competence*, and *meaning* (Shove et al. 2012). In relation to gendered rural practice, we argue for the elements *material*, *know-how*, and *standpoint*. Competence is more of a precondition, and standpoint or perspective (as defined by feminist theorists such as Haraway 1988; Bennholdt-Thomsen and Mies 1999; Harding 2004) enables us to demystify seemingly stable ideological constructions and deconstructs those structures, which otherwise appear static and overpowering.

The day, 'All About White Cabbage', took place in the communal kitchen of the Peasant Museum in Frensdorf. Groups and individual guests prepared several cabbage dishes together according to local recipes with ingredients they had brought 'from home', with herbs, vinegar, and side dishes. The purpose was an exchange of local knowledge on food preparation and conservation. Other activities offered varied from curated site visits to relevant institutions (such as the Peasant Museum in Frensdorf[10] and Haus der Bäuerin, a communal facility aimed to ease women's household chores and to provide social space for the village, in Birkach),[11] to exemplary self-initiated and self-organized activities (such as the market in Neumarkt, run by the local farmers' association), and to the village shop in Sulzbürg, a not-for-profit organization managed by a collective of local women. Another form of knowledge transfer was the curated and

*Figure 30.3* 'Rural Women's Economies' civic seminar, 2012

*Source*: Photo by Kathrin Böhm, myvillages

self-created group discussion. Presenting participants and contributors showed and told about the objects and food they brought.[12] The civic seminar ended with a joint collection of the issues and questions that had evolved for a concluding discussion, and an ENS meeting formulated future goals and projected common future activities.

The program of the civic seminar focused both on practice and skills, but also on necessary institutions and environments for learning and exchanging experience and knowledge. In the end, three conclusions were drawn. First, the ENS was discussed as a possible prototype for creating European networks and 'interplace solidarities' (as referred to in the epigraph by Gibson-Graham given previously) across urban and rural environments. For mutual learning and for creating change, common experience was recognized as important. Thus, the nomadic aspect of visiting each other was seen as useful for learning about the different traditions on site. Second, connecting social practice in a full cycle was crucial: growing vegetables, organizing vegetable gardens, harvesting and cooking together, organizing shops, markets and restaurants, and making the furniture for the gardens together. Farmers' markets and the women farmers' association were seen as especially important for the reproduction and exchange of knowledge and to keep existing practices alive. Third, women's producer roles in the countryside were deemed stronger than in the city, where consumption mattered more, and where useful skills had been lost. All the workshops were about practicing and teaching in order to keep skills, or relearning lost skills from each other. It was concluded that people could relearn in an urban context and thus get inspiration from rural women's economies.

The temporary activities of the ENS network present another form of lived utopia, distinct from Matrix the cooperative. While Matrix's work testifies to the need for constant struggle, ENS brings together various actors organized in different forms, for recurring civic seminars. Here, ENS performs 'other worlds' in form of rehearsals for learning and teaching about ecocivic practices as a precondition for change.

## Concluding discussion

Critical spatial practice assumes the explicit motivation of performing 'other worlds', a practice involving the demystification of dominance and the imagination of alternative futures (Gibson-Graham 2008). Its take on structural change is through micropolitical and microsocial practices, or lived utopias, in which there is agency even in 'molecular domains' (Guattari 1989; Gibson-Graham 2006; Petcou and Petrescu 2014) – including the development of activist practice and pedagogical models in the 'here and now'.

In this chapter we have discussed shifting values and norms, as exemplified by an ethical approach to feminist spatial practice and the critique of mainstream economics. We have presented two practices and how they related to, or possibly contributed to, more just socio-environmental relations. We have also inquired into the creation of new roles for professionals and co-producers, the redistribution of responsibilities, and the emergence of new subjectivities that we regard as feminist futures. The micropolitics of self-transformation are critical to greater social change and the macropolitical agenda. They involve developing receptivity to a politics of becoming, in which new forms of subjectivity may be cultivated (Connolly 2002).

Gibson-Graham's (2006, 2008) interest in building new worlds involves credible, diverse economies, and practices that already exist, in which interdependency between people and environment is ethically negotiated. These economies and practices can be recognized now and constructed in the future. Rather than deeming communal economic experiments unviable because they depend on grants, gifts, state subsidies, long staff hours, volunteer labour, unstable markets, and so on, Gibson-Graham study their strategies of survival and support their efforts to learn from experience. Highlighting these experimental efforts as credible possibilities helps them to find ways of changing what they wish to change.

In futures studies, one often thinks the other way around; futures are depicted and described for enabling change. As a research field, futures studies is characterized by a plurality of approaches, most using scenarios as a tool to explore the future. Scenarios can be predictions – criticized for colonization of the future since they make us prepare for probable developments – or explorations of possible and even preferable futures. The idea is then to depict alternative futures – not only the most possible ones. By imagining other futures, we facilitate discussion about the change we want here and now. Thus, instead of only critiquing current trends, we actually ought to describe how another society could be organized and thus open up for debates about important, but maybe overlooked, matters that can affect the future.

In addition, Gibson-Graham's (2008) technique of re-reading for difference has a number of effects. It produces a recognition of differences (as in the case of Matrix) and situated knowledges (as seen in the example of ENS). It opens the performance of dominance not only to research but also to practice, and thus it allows new participants to enter conversation about sustainable resource use, rights, and community development. Gibson-Graham point to the importance of shifting focal viewpoints and considering marginalized practices, demystifying dominant socio-economic relations as the norm and actively building a personal practice.

Can these micropolitical and microsocial practices engender change? Gibson-Graham believe they already do transform the world, not through a focus on large structural shifts in the first place, but through the performing of 'small patches of resistance' (Dwyer 2012b) and 'ecocivic knowledge' (ENS), or lived utopias. An understanding of the environment in which Matrix developed (and disappeared) shows that these practices do not emerge in a vacuum but in interdependency with other initiatives, networks, and institutions. To make possible more diversified landscapes of critical spatial practice in design, planning, and building, we need not only to transform our own practice but also to reclaim institutional programs for change.

## Notes

1 *Sustainable development*, as defined in the Brundtland Report (1987), focuses on humans as the beneficiaries of sustainable development. Though the Brundtland Report is often discussed as a radical document, its focus on humans contrasts with an ecofeminist understanding of interspecies justice (see Gaard in this handbook).

2 J. K. Gibson-Graham is the pen name of two feminist economic geographers, Julie Graham and Katherine Gibson, who wrote together for many years until Julie Graham's death in 2010. It is common to use plural nouns (etc.) when referring to them. Katherine Gibson still writes under this name.

3 Many members of Matrix had also been members of the New Architecture Movement (NAM) in the late 1970s, a mixed group of socialist architects. In 1978, around twenty women started the Feminist Design Collective, which split in 1980. Then Matrix was initiated (Bradshaw 1984). A number of other project-based groups of women architects, builders, and academics emerged at the same time, such as Lambeth Women's Workshop, the Women Builders Cooperative, and Women and Manual Trade. Membership in these initiatives often overlapped.

4 During the 1980s governmental funding was available for voluntary organizations that gave advice on design and related technical issues (the equivalent in the United States were the community design centres).

5 But there is no coherent idea within the group as to why Matrix in this form ended (Dwyer 2012b). Former members went their own way professionally: Anne Thorne Architects founded a women's practice with Fran Bradshaw as a partner in 1996, and in 1999 other former members of Matrix initiated Taking Place, a group with some Matrix ambitions in a less collectivist form.

6 Art criticism has recognized an 'educational turn' in the second half of the 1990s. Art, architecture, and curatorial projects have focused on pedagogical processes and programs and on alternative ways to exchange knowledge and research practice. In the centre is not an aesthetic object. Instead, the focus

is on the educational process and the use of discursive, pedagogical methods, and situations inside and outside of institutions.

7 The Eco Nomadic School (since 2011) derives from the previous cross-European research and action network Rhyzom – local cultural practices and trans-local disseminations.

8 Live projects are an educational initiative at the University of Sheffield's School of Architecture. Students work with and for organizations in real time with real budgets for an allotted period. See: www.liveprojects.org.

9 The Rural Women's Economies civic seminar was curated by artist Kathrin Böhm from Myvillages and organized together with the Peasant Museum Bamberger Land and rural feminist sociologist Heide Inhetveeten.

10 'To provide and to economize' was the topic of the guided tour through the Peasant Museum in Frensdorf; other guided tours included 'Change and Trade in a Migration Village', through Sulzbürg, and 'Talking Business' to the Village Shop in Sulzbürg and the farmers' market in Neumarkt.

11 'Houses of the female peasant' were part of a governmental programme to modernize and collectivize rural women's everyday chores. They appeared in the 1950s in southern Germany as communal meeting places in rural communities for food processing and storage, a bath house, a communal kitchen, a small abbatoir, and social facilities. Many of these are still active. The institution catered to women farmers, but it also kept them in the realm of the household and separated them from the agricultural work on the farm.

12 The Communal Village House in Höfen, organized by the Höfer women's group under the theme 'Women, Economy, and Money – Rural Women as Business Secretaries', is an example. Participants brought account books of household kitties (pots of money for collective use). Another group discussion, 'Sites of Production and Models of Trade in Rural Areas', took up previously presented case studies of the village shop, a cultural project, and the Odaia economy in Brezoi, and discussed their potential for local development in future scenarios (www.internationalvillageshop.net). The third session was 'All About Herbs'. Local knowledge about recipes for food, medicine, liquor, cosmetics, and treatment were tested and exchanged in a transnational comparison. The last session was 'Precautious and Sustainable Economies', with input from sociologist and activist Elisabeth Meyer-Renschhausen, one of the initiators of the urban gardening organization Allmende-kontor in Berlin (www.allmende-kontor.de).

# References

Agyeman, J. (2005) *Sustainable Communities and the Challenge of Environmental Justice*. New York: New York University Press.

Åkerman, J. (2011) *Transport Systems Meeting Long-Term Climate Targets: A Backcasting Approach*. Doctoral dissertation, Stockholm: KTH – Royal Institute of Technology, Sweden.

atelier d'architecture autogérée (aaa) and European Platform for Alternative Practice and Research on the City (PEPRAV) (2007) *Urban Act: A Handbook for Alternative Practices*. Online. Available at: www.urban-tactics.org/dissemination/urbanact-a-handbook-for-alternative-practice-aaa-peprav-2007/

atelier d'architecture autogérée (aaa) (2009) *Rhyzom*. Online. Available at: www.rhyzom.net/nomadicschool (accessed 28 February 2015).

Awan, N., Schneider, T. and Till, J. (2009) *Spatial Agency*. Online. Available at: www.spatialagency.net (accessed 26 January 2012).

Bennholdt-Thomsen, V. and Mies, M. (1999) *The Subsistence Perspective*. London: Zed Books.

Bradley, K., Gunnarsson-Östling, U. and Isaksson, K. (2008) 'Exploring environmental justice in Sweden: How to improve planning for environmental sustainability and social equity in an "eco-friendly" context', *Projections* 8: 68–81.

Bradley, K. and Hedrén, J. (eds) (2014) *Green Utopianism: Perspectives, Politics and Micro-Practices*. London: Routledge.

Bradshaw, F. (1984) 'Working with women', in Matrix (ed) *Making Space: Women and the Man-Made Environment*. London: Pluto Press, 89–105.

Braidotti, R. (1994) *Nomadic Subjects*. New York: Columbia University Press.

Braidotti, R. (2013) *The Posthuman*. Polity: Cambridge.

Brenner, N., Marcuse, P. and Mayer, M. (eds) (2011) *Cities for People, Not for Profit*. Abingdon: Routledge.

Bullard, R. D. (2000) *Dumping in Dixie: Race, Class and Environmental Quality*. Atlanta: Westview Press.

Butler, J. (1993) *Bodies That Matter*. Abingdon: Routledge.

Campbell, H. (2010) 'The idea of planning: Alive or dead? Who cares?', *Planning Theory & Practice* 11: 471–475.

Connolly, W. E. (2002) *Neuropolitics: Thinking, Culture, Speed*. Minneapolis: University of Minnesota Press.

Dwyer, J. (2012a) 'Inscription as a collective practice: Taking place and "the other side of waiting"', in Edquist, H. and Vuaghan, L. (eds) *The Design Collective: An Approach to Practice*. Newcastle: Cambridge Scholars Publishing, 35–53.

Dwyer, J. (2012b) *Interview with Julia Dwyer by Meike Schalk*.

Dwyer, J. and Thorne, A. (2007) 'Evaluating Matrix: notes from inside the collective', in Petrescu, D. (ed) *Altering Practices*. London: Routledge, 39–56.

Eichler, M. (ed) (1995) *Change of Plans: Towards a Non-sexist, Sustainable City*. Toronto: Garamond Press.

Fainstein, S. (2010) *The Just City*. Ithaca, NY: Cornell University Press.

Felton, E., Zelenko, O. and Vaughan, S. (eds) (2012) *Design and Ethics: Reflections on Practice*. Abingdon: Routledge.

Fenster, T. (2002) 'Planning as control: Cultural and gendered manipulation and misuse of knowledge', *Hagar – International Social Science Review* 3(1): 67–84.

Gibson-Graham, J. K. (2006) *A Postcapitalist Politics*. Minneapolis: University of Minnesota Press.

Gibson-Graham, J. K. (2008) 'Diverse economies: Performative practices for "other worlds"', *Progress in Human Geography* 32(5): 613–632.

Gibson-Graham, J. K., Cameron, J. and Healy, S. (2013) *Take Back the Economy*. Minneapolis: University of Minnesota Press.

Guattari, F. (1989) *The Three Ecologies*. London: Bloomsbury.

Gunnarsson-Östling, U. (2011) *Just Sustainable Futures: Gender and Environmental Justice Considerations in Planning*. Doctoral dissertation, KTH Royal Institute of Technology, Stockholm.

Haraway, D. (1988) 'Situated knowledges', *Feminist Studies* 14(3): 575–599.

Haraway, D. (2003) *The Companion Species Manifesto*. Chicago: Prickly Paradigm Press.

Harding, S. (2004) *The Feminist Standpoint Theory Reader*. New York: Routledge.

Harding, S. (2008) *Science From Below: Feminisms, Postcolonialities, and Modernities*. Durham: Duke University Press.

Harvey, D. and Potter, C. (2009) 'The right to the just city', in Marcuse, P., Connolly, J., Novy, J., Olivo, I., Potter, C. and Steil, J. (eds) *Searching for the Just City: Debates in Urban Theory and Practice (Questioning Cities)*. Abingdon: Routledge, 40–51.

Hayden, D. (1980) 'What would a non-sexist city be like?', *Signs* 5(3) Supplement. Women and the American City, 170–187.

Hayden, D. (1981) *The Grand Domestic Revolution*. Cambridge, MA: MIT Press.

Höjer, M., Gullberg, A. and Pettersson, R. (2011) 'Backcasting images of the future city: Time and space for sustainable development in Stockholm', *Technological Forecasting and Social Change* 78(5): 819–834.

Ironmonger, D. (1996) 'Counting outputs, capital inputs and caring labor: Estimating gross household product', *Feminist Economics* 2(3): 37–64.

Kosofsky-Sedgwick, E. (2003) *Touching Feeling: Affect, Pedagogy, Performativity*. Durham, NC: Duke University Press.

Law, J. and Urry, J. (2004) 'Enacting the social', *Economy and Society* 33(3): 390–410.

Lindholm, T., Oliveira e Costa, S. and Wiberg, S. (2015) *Medborgardialog – demokrati eller dekoration?* Stockholm: Arkus skrift nr. 72.

Matrix (1984) *Making Space: Women and the Man-Made Environment*. London: Pluto Press.

Mont, O., Heiskanen, E., Power, K. and Kuusi, H. (2014) 'Lessons from Nordic Council of Ministers study "Improving Nordic policymaking by dispelling myths on sustainable consumption"', *Nordic Working Papers*. Norden. Nordic Council of Ministers, Copenhagen. NA2013:915. Online. Available at: http://dx.doi.org/10.6027/NA2013–915.

Petcou, C. and Petrescu, D. (2014) 'R-URBAN: Strategies and tactics for participative utopias and resilient practices', in Bradley, K. and Hedrén, J. (eds) *Green Utopianism*. London: Routledge, 258–278.

Petrescu, D. (ed) (2007) *Altering Practices*. London: Routledge.

Petrescu, D. (2013) 'Gardeners of commons', in Rawes, P. (ed) *Relational Architectural Ecologies*. Abingdon: Routledge, 261–274.

Rendell, J. (2006) *Art and Architecture: A Place Between*. London: IB Tauris.

Rocheleau, D., Thomas-Slayter, B. and Wangari, E. (eds) (1996) *Feminist Political Ecology*. Abingdon: Routledge.

Sanati, F., Hatamian, H. N. and Tengku Mahadi, T. S. (2011) 'An analysis of the ecofeminist viewpoint on industrialization and environmental degradation in Starhawk's the fifth sacred thing', *Journal of Sustainable Development* 4(4): 86–90.

Sandercock, L. (1998) *Towards Cosmopolis: Planning for Multicultural Cities.* London: John Wiley.

Santos, B. d. S. (2006) *The Rise of the Global Left.* London: Zed Books.

Schalk, M. (2007) 'Urban curating : a critical practice towards greater "connectedness"', in Petrescu, D. (ed) *Altering Practices Feminist Politics and Poetics of Space.* London: Routledge, 153–166.

Schalk, M. (2012) 'Altering Berlin', *Nordic Journal of Architecture* 3(2): 58–66.

Shove, E., Pantzar, M. and Watson, M. (2012) *The Dynamics of Social Practice.* Thousand Oaks: Sage Publications.

Somol, R. and Whiting, S. (2003) 'Notes around the Doppler effect and other moods of modernism', *Perspecta* 33, Mining Autonomy, 72–77.

Stengers, I. (2008) 'Experimenting with refrains: Subjectivity and the challenge of escaping modern dualism', *Subjectivity* 22: 38–59.

Swyngedouw, E. (2011) 'Whose environment? The end of nature, climate change and the process of post-politicization', *Ambiente & Sociedade* 14(2): 69–87.

Trogal, K. (2012) *Caring for Space.* Doctoral dissertation, University of Sheffield, The School of Architecture.

Varela, F. (1992) *Ethical Know-how: Action, Wisdom, and Cognition.* Stanford: Stanford University Press.

Weisman, L. K. (1992) *Discrimination by Design.* Champaign: University of Illinois Press.

World Commission on Environment and Development (1987) *Our Common Future* ('Brundtland Report'). Oxford: Oxford University Press.

Young, I. M. (1991) *Justice and the Politics of Difference.* Princeton: University Press.

# 31

# ORCA INTIMACIES AND ENVIRONMENTAL SLOW DEATH

## Earthling ethics for a claustrophobic world

*Margret Grebowicz*

In December 2014, twenty-seven-year-old Yang Jinhai broke into a tiger pen in a zoo in Southern China in hopes that the tigers would eat him alive. The *Time* magazine headline read 'Depressed Man Tries to Feed Himself to Tigers, Rejected'. It echoed another recent failure to get eaten alive, namely that of anaconda snake scientist and activist Paul Rosolie, whose Discovery Channel special 'Eaten Alive' disappointed viewers who had tuned in to see just that. The *New York Post* announced, 'Viewers livid after Anaconda Man fails to get eaten alive' (Morabito 2014). Could part of the success of *Blackfish* (2013), the documentary film about Sea World whale trainer Dawn Brancheau, who was not just killed but also partly eaten by her beloved orca, Tilikum, be due to the public expectation finally being fulfilled? She was killed immediately following a 'Dine with Shamu' show. Though the cause of her death was drowning and blunt trauma to the head, several moments in the film imply that she was eaten, or something like it – 'he still has her' and 'his mouth had to be pried open'.

Contrast this fatality in an American theme park with ecofeminist philosopher Val Plumwood's crocodile attack, which nearly cost her her life on a solo canoeing outing in Australia's remote Kakadu National Park in 1985. Ten years after the attack, when she finally felt ready to write about it, in a piece called 'Being Prey' (1996), she revealed what the encounter with the saltwater crocodile had taught her: that humans are in fact not at the top of the food chain. We are apex predators only in Anthropocene conditions. In other words, it is only now that human activity impacts the planet in a historically unprecedented way that we can be considered at the top of the food chain rather than prey for bigger predators. The crocodile attack was a sort of return to nature for Plumwood, an encounter with a real apex predator; the biggest terrestrial predator on Earth, hypercarnivorous, opportunistic, fond of ambush, and with the strongest bite of any animal alive today. It was in many ways an expected move for an ecofeminist thinker: to knock humans down to size in the area where human exceptionalism has taken perhaps its most perverse form: the question of who eats whom.

But the *Blackfish* narrative dramatically departs from any kind of holistic naturalism. Since humans are not a natural part of any orca diet (no hominid is a natural part of any marine mammal diet), the event of Brancheau's death reeks of perversion of nature. While becoming crocodile prey reminded Plumwood in the most spectacular way that she is part of an ecosystem, repositioning her, however briefly, in her proper place vis-à-vis her attacker, Tilikum ate Brancheau precisely because he had been removed from his proper place. The human-made ecosystems in which he has lived his entire life, first Sealand and later Sea World, are part of the monstrosity that media theorists call the 'military entertainment complex' (cf. Lenoir 2000). The film is an argument for the personhood of orcas, but this personhood is demonstrated not by the usual means (signs of intellectual complexity, capacity for communication, elaborate social structures), but by Tilikum's aggression, presented as something like a revolutionary act of violence, anti-colonial, proletarian, or both.

This chapter considers these situations through the ethics found in Donna Haraway's (2007) work on companion species and contact zones, work that feminist theory has been slower to take up than her celebrated essay 'A Cyborg Manifesto' (1991; see chapters by Merrick and Sandilands in this handbook). Just as the cyborg work showed us that we humans were not not-machines, it is often assumed that the companion species work in *When Species Meet* (2007) shows that we are not not-animals. Indeed, Haraway's later work focuses on excavating the animality that has acted on us spectrally since Carolus Linnaeus both codified and denied it in the same gesture as he circumscribed that curious animal that knows itself to be 'man'. But *When Species Meet* also makes another important but overlooked contribution to theory. 'Companion species' is not a figure, but a relationship, something we do together rather than something we individually are. This shift to the relationship as the smallest unit of analysis is necessary because we are living in conditions of 'mutual use'. In a world in which using, killing, eating, objectifying, commodifying others, and being-commodity are no longer merely optional, a reality in which we can no longer be innocent, Haraway calls for attention to relations of use among species in conditions of 'permanent complexity' (2007:75). The central question of *When Species Meet* is 'how can responsibility be practiced among earthlings?', not among humans, subjects-of-a-life, or agents, but among *earthlings*, given the permanent material and moral complexity of their situation (77).

From the perspective of the relationship between gender and environment, earthlings, who are themselves not gendered, open an important area for feminist theory to explore further, namely how 'mutual use' might intervene in received political categories like gender and labour. If using each other is indeed permanent and irreducibly complex, what does this mean for future-oriented, liberation projects/movements like feminism, Marxism, and Marxist feminism, for instance? Given the focus of this handbook on the ecological feminist tradition of theorizing the gender-environment nexus, however, my aim in this chapter will be to work out what is happening on the 'environment' end of things. I focus on the permanence of environmental crisis, turning from the relatively intact, if contested, category 'nature' (in which Plumwood situated her crocodile attack and on which much ecofeminism continues to rely) to *interspecies contact* in conditions which Bill McKibben (2006) calls 'the end of nature'. McKibben's position, that a 'true' nature unimpacted by human activity no longer exists, is now at the heart of the notion of the Anthropocene. The question for environmental ethics is no longer *what does Haraway's work contribute to environmental ethics?* But rather, *how does the loss of nature shape relation itself, reimagining who counts as an agent, how agency manifests itself, and what constitutes a relationship?* Earthlings, in relations of mutual use and conditions of irreducible complexity and claustrophobia, are Haraway's attempt at an answer, and thus her contribution to not only what we call environmental ethics, but also to the reimagining of what counts as ethics and what makes an environment in the first place.

## Earthling ethics and Mars

It is important to note that unlike McKibben, Haraway herself is not committed to any claims about the end of nature, or to the memory of a pre-Anthropocene nature. Earthling ethics is an ethics 'after' nature for the simple reason that, for Haraway, there is no truth of the world prior to what contact between beings reveals. In contrast to feminist standpoint theory, especially philosopher Sandra Harding's (1993) notion of 'strong objectivity', knowledge comes about not as the result of a particular standpoint or even situatedness, from which some denotative truth about the world becomes knowable, however limitedly and contestably, by a partial, located knower. The only kind of truth-telling that interests Haraway in *When Species Meet* is not denotative at all. She focuses on the greeting:

> This sort of truth or honesty is not some trope-free, fantastic kind of natural authenticity that only animals can have while humans are defined by the happy fault of lying denotatively and knowing it. Rather, this truth telling is about co-constitutive naturecultural dancing, holding in esteem, and regard open to those who look back reciprocally.
>
> *(Haraway 2007:27)*

The purest form of interaction, the greeting is meta-interactive, announcing that interaction will take place, rules will be made, a relationship will be allowed to grow. Nothing denotative has taken place, but the parties to the greeting have announced to each other their desire to interact, and it is here, Haraway would say, that something like truth takes place, as actors and world come into being as the ongoing products of relationships. Response is ecological from day one, for all ethics is environmental, after the end of nature.

In his book *Molecular Red: Theory for the Anthropocene*, McKenzie Wark (2015) draws a direct (if dotted) line from Haraway to American science fiction writer Kim Stanley Robinson, whose *Mars trilogy* opens questions around what counts as nature, and what counts as anthropogenic change, among many other important environmental questions. Literary theorist Ursula K. Heise agrees with Wark that Mars stands for Earth in Robinson's books, as

> a world where, in keeping with McKibben's vision, there is no swath of 'nature' left that is not impacted by humans. . . . On both planets, humans henceforth live in terraformed or 'areoformed' environments they themselves have created, whether intentionally or unintentionally.
>
> *(Heise 2011:466–467)*

Wark connects Haraway and Robinson around the subject of their rejection of holistic or traditionally ecological ontologies of nature. He points out that Robinson resists the tendency

> to see nature as an *ecology*, as like a market, and markets as therefore also, by reverse substitution, 'natural'. The emphasis is rather on the instability of the relations of the new Martian species to each other and their world, 'all of them monsters together'. There may be patches of relative ecological stability, but they are local and temporary.
>
> *(Wark 2015:209)*

But I think this is a much stronger claim than Haraway is willing to make. She is silent about how nature works, committing neither to ecological stability nor to the instability of a place like Robinson's terraformed Mars. It is precisely because we can't say conclusively that the world is this way or that way that all we have is contact with others, 'rich and largely uncharted, material-semiotic, flesh-to-flesh, and face-to-face connection' (Haraway 2007:235). She calls this process of world-making 'autre-mondalisation', or other-worlding, but again, Haraway's otherworld is unmistakably this one. Returning to Robinson, there is a scene in *Red Mars* in which protagonist Frank Chalmers, having received his Mars assignment, leaves Washington, D.C., for some time alone in the Shenandoah Valley, a particularly scenic part of the Virginia wilderness:

> Then he parked in a scenic overlook and walked off into the forest, and sat down between the roots of a big tree. No one around, a warm fall night, the earth dark, and furry with trees. Cicadas cycling through their alien hum, crickets creaking their last mournful creaks, sensing the frost that would kill them. He felt so odd . . . could he really leave this world behind? Sitting there on the earth he had wished he could slide down a crack like a changeling and reemerge something else, something better, something mighty, noble, long-lived – something like a tree. But nothing happened, of course. He lay on the ground, cut off from it already. A Martian already.
>
> *(Robinson 1993:413–414)*

Haraway would argue that Chalmers missed the most important lesson of his outing. In running away from the encounter, he had missed the opportunity for a rich, uncanny, productive, unsettling meeting with this-other-world of earthlings.

## Consuming in captivity

Why 'other'? Because what the Anthropocene is for Haraway has something to do with conditions of what we might call generalized captivity. Australian philosopher Glenn Albrecht (2005) has invented a name for the sadness particular to the Anthropocene: 'solastalgia' is a form of pining for a lost environment, a version of homesickness that does not require actually leaving home, but is instead the experience of home as already gone. He writes that twenty-first century people are

> suffering symptoms eerily similar to those of indigenous populations that are forcibly removed from their traditional homelands. But nobody is being relocated; they haven't moved anywhere. It's just that the familiar markers of their area, the physical and sensory signals that define home, are vanishing.
>
> *(in Thompson 2007:n.p.)*

Until recently, the American wilderness provided a great escape from the affective afflictions of modernity, for both American and foreign tourists. As American nature writer Wallace Stegner famously wrote in defence of the Wilderness Act of 1964, which established the US Wilderness Preservation System, 'We simply need that wild country available to us, even if we never do more than drive to its edge and look in. For it can be a means of assuring ourselves of our sanity as creatures, a part of the geography of hope' (The Wilderness Society 1994:68). More recently, in an interview with film-maker Ken Burns, park ranger-turned-crime writer Nevada Barr states, 'I think we require national parks for our psychic stability and sanity. We need national parks because we psychologically need to have a place to go when we can't be "here" anymore' (Duncan 2009:196).

The Wilderness Act established wilderness domains as spaces 'where man himself is a visitor who does not remain', thus speaking directly to the anthrophobia at the heart of our desire to get away from it all. That the American wilderness had to be forcibly de-peopled in order to become the fantasy of an original 'world without us' is old news to anyone interested in First Nations/ indigenous history and the history of the American West more generally. Environmental historian William Cronon (1995) has criticized wilderness from precisely this perspective, as a form of something like false consciousness. We can live out our not-so-wild lives better just knowing that an alternative exists out there, beyond the threshold of the mundane home. In his influential essay, 'The Trouble with Wilderness', Cronon argues that experiencing ourselves ahistorically means evading responsibility:

> We inhabit civilization while holding some part of ourselves – what we imagine to be the most precious part – aloof from its entanglements. By imagining that our true home is in the wilderness, we forgive ourselves the homes we actually inhabit. In its flight from history, in its siren song of escape, in its reproduction of the dangerous dualism that sets human beings outside of nature – in all of these ways, wilderness poses a serious threat to responsible environmentalism at the end of the twentieth century.
>
> *(Cronon 1995:n.p.)*

Of course, the oceans were never human habitats, so oceanscapes answer our desires for wild spaces without people relatively unproblematically. Indeed, the take-home message of *Blackfish* is that wilderness is the answer. The film ends with precisely the siren song of escape, as black dorsal fins deftly cut the glimmering waters of the Pacific Northwest. The former Sea World trainers tear up at the sight of orcas swimming in pods in the wild, open waters, in sharp contrast to Sea World's despairing captives.

But while most terrestrial wilderness is de-historicized when we wilfully forget human habitation, ocean wilderness is de-historicized when we wilfully forget human impact. Stacy Alaimo writes that the disconnection between terrestrial humans and 'the vast liquid habitats that cover much of the planet' makes it easier to distance ourselves from what is in fact an enormous human presence inside oceans in the following forms, to name just a few:

> Climate change. Ocean acidification. Dead zones. Oil 'spills'. Industrial fishing, overfishing, trawling, long lines, shark finning. Bycatch, bykill. Ghost nets. Deep-sea mining. Habitat destruction. Dumping. Radioactive, plastic, and micro-plastic pollution. Ecosystem collapse. Extinction.
>
> *(Alaimo 2014:188,186)*

*National Geographic* reports that the oceans are a 'toxic sink', and because orcas are apex predators, they serve as a measure of ocean ecosystem health (Handwerk 2005). As pollutants bioaccumulate, the animals highest on the food chain are the most toxic. This makes for a whole new imaginary of multispecies captivity: we are captive to toxicity itself. In the BBC documentary 'Planet Earth, The Future', Roger Payne, President of The Ocean Alliance, describes the breast milk of women in populations that rely heavily on a marine mammal diet, like the Japanese and Inuit, who eat whale meat:

> So for example, any woman of childbearing age, if she's nursing her infant in that tenderest of all mammalian acts, what she is actually doing is dumping her lifetime's accumulation of pollutants into that infant. And if her milk was in containers other than her breasts, she would not be allowed to take it over state lines, it's that polluted. We can dodge that bullet by simply feeding formula to our children; not an option for a whale.
>
> *(BBC 2006)*

As these linkages show, and as Rachel Carson taught, toxicity is not unidirectional, and it doesn't stop at the environmental level. Its circulation between the social and the environmental, and between non-human and human animals creates what Lauren Berlant (2011) calls 'slow death' or a situation in which the very things one must do in order to have a life are the things which lessen quality of life. As marine mammals living in the wild are declared the most toxic animals on the planet, human milk banks compete with each other online, each claiming to have the purest breast milk for sale. The newest market for human milk is male high-endurance athletes, who drink it as an energy drink to increase 'performance'. But it turns out there are other bullets to dodge besides pollution: the risks of buying unregulated breast milk are the same as those of buying unregulated sex: HIV, syphilis, and hepatitis (Despain 2014). And there is something of what Berlant (2011) calls 'cruel optimism' about everything that is presented to first-worlders as an antidote to solastalgia. Buying more stuff makes first-worlders sadder, so they buy more stuff. Ultra-running to clear their heads and get away from it all destroys their joints and leaves a significant environmental footprint (e.g., there are over a thousand races worldwide, most in protected wilderness areas, which are thereby becoming polluted). And disturbingly, but perhaps not surprisingly, a budding sex industry is emerging around the breast milk black market – men visiting women to buy the milk straight from their breasts, including fetishists of that tenderest of all mammalian acts, which in this case is called 'adult nursing', are sometimes buying traditional sex also – and as this market grows, the people most likely to be on its most exploited end (for both breast milk and bought sex) are underprivileged women (Roberts 2014). If Nietzsche's dictum in *Twilight of the Idols*, 'that which does not kill us makes us stronger', was a sort of mantra for modernity, the present moment seems to announce something different. When life-building and the attrition of life become indistinguishable processes, that which does not kill us kills us.

According to Berlant, we are living in times in which crisis is no longer an event, but an environment. Unlike an event, which is 'calibrated according to its intensities and kinds of impact', an environment 'can absorb how time ordinarily passes, how forgettable most events are, and overall how people's ordinary perseverations fluctuate in patterns of undramatic attachment and identification' (Berlant 2011:100–101). This seems precisely to describe the way we experience environmental crisis, in which single catastrophes, which once signified much more powerfully in their own right, have been reduced to mere symptoms of more general and totalizing conditions like climate change and what conservationists call 'collapse'. Sustainability has become about optimistically sustaining something that is unliveable in the first place, and what today passes for 'wellness' answers to first world, late capitalist values: reproduction, optimized performance, consumerism, and upward mobility. Consider the viral Hyundai 'suicide' car ad, pulled from the Internet and YouTube in 2013 because it was deemed offensive (Woodard and Meyer 2013). The ad shows a middle-aged man trying to commit suicide in the garage of his very nice single-family home by inhaling his car's exhaust fumes. In the course of his attempt, he discovers that the new Hyundai is a zero-emissions vehicle. The text across the screen announces the good news: the fumes can't kill him! What is sustained by the zero-emissions green consumerism advertised here is not just the environment, but the man's low-grade despair, from which there is no exit. He opens the garage door and walks out dejectedly, his head hung low, returning to his suburban, single-family home, continuing to live his unremarkably normal and also unliveable life, because he must.

Indeed, Berlant argues that the attrition of life under late capitalism generates new forms of agency that no longer locate the subject in the drama of decision of the sort that suicide would have stood for in the old days. Lateral or interruptive agency temporarily interrupts the pressure of relentless life-building, offering 'small vacations from the will itself' (Berlant 2011:116). We kill time, spread out, by eating, smoking, sometimes by having sex, spacing out, watching cat videos, posting to Instagram, all disaffected ways of interrupting the self-as-project. But Berlant's model doesn't help us to understand that young Chinese man Yang Jinhai, who is now being treated for depression, as if his problem were the flat-affect emptiness associated with depression, not specifically the desire to be eaten alive by tigers (Liljas 2014). *As if the issue was not desire at all.* And yet, his disappointment at being rejected resembles that of a jilted lover. Clearly, there are agencies and desires at work here, not merely escapist fantasies. *Blackfish* underscores that Tilikum is 'the most successful sire in captivity', including the uncomfortable footage of his semen being manually 'harvested'. Between that and the controversy around Brancheau's long, golden pony-tail, which Sea World insisted was the reason the whale dragged her into the water, the whole thing starts to sound like a crime of passion. Quick semiotic slips between violence and eros, sex and eating, and desire and death keep the audience suspended in a state of horror, equal parts aversion and attraction. Tilly's murderous, perverted despair is our own. It is not Brancheau but Tilly who is presented as the new figure of consuming in captivity, trapped not only in his tank but in the socio-ecologically toxic environment we quickly come to recognize as the same one in which we are trapped.

Gregory Bateson (2000) might have attempted to think such events with the help of his concept of 'eco-mental system'. One of the original thinkers of the environment in terms of relation, Bateson locates mental health not in the subject, but in what he calls the unit of evolutionary survival – namely, organism plus environment. He calls this unity of organism and environment 'mind'. For Haraway, contact or response is the only way 'out', if you will, of ecosystems that Bateson describes as having been 'driven insane' (2000:491–492). She focuses on those sites where species meet in 'unnatural' conditions not of their own making: mostly the experimental laboratory and pet keeping, but also curiosities like National Geographic's Crittercam program, or perhaps Discovery Channel's anaconda program, Southern Chinese zoos, and Sea World Orlando. The focus here is precisely on asymmetrical, forced, awkward, often horrible conditions we have not chosen but in which we are in difficult proximity to other animals, in other words, relations of mutual use. While it is still true that hell is other people, it is perhaps less true that there is no exit. The exit is also other people, and the people are animals. One good example of this may be found in Ingrid Visser's orca research. She is a marine zoologist in New Zealand, founder of the Orca Research Trust, and the only scientist to swim alongside wild orcas while photographing them. But from Haraway's perspective, the most important part of Visser's work is not the science itself, but the invention of a new greeting: when they see her boat, some of the orcas Visser knows immediately swim up to it, and she sticks her face in the water and blows bubbles, to which the orcas respond by blowing bubbles back.[1] Unremarkable, were it not for the fact that orcas do not blow bubbles at each other in greeting.

## Conclusion: dense ontology

Some find Haraway's foregrounding of greetings with 'higher-order', charismatic animals like dogs, cats, and apes anthropomorphic and objectionable for various reasons. For example, cultural theorist Dominic Pettman (2011) offers the most robust critique of Haraway, one which takes the need for deep relation seriously but is simultaneously sceptical of proximity. He zeroes in on a logic of mutuality and 'full partnership' in Haraway that, he shows, misses out on the significance and pleasure of more oblique, abstract, minimal, and even unidirectional forms of relation with other kinds of animals, especially ones that are ocular but without 'face' in the traditional sense (Pettman 2011:88–90). Pettman is especially drawn to J. A. Baker's account of his love for per-egrine falcons in *The Peregrine*, a cooler and 'more sparse ontology' than the 'enmeshed, reaching, potentially claustrophobic mode of contact' he sees in what he playfully calls Haraway's 'lesbian bestiality' (Pettman 2011:96).

Indeed, one could read the orca bubble-blowing encounter as a great example of such mutuality, since the orcas are aping or mirroring (choose your metaphor) the human, and the bubble blowing smacks of a mouth-to-mouth resuscitation worthy of Haraway's 'warm drooling tongue-licks' (Pettman 2011:96), even if orca French kisses would be much saltier. But Haraway has already beaten us to the claustrophobia charge – it is precisely at the heart of her critique of our eco-mental illness. She does not prescribe proximity, but takes it for granted as our permanent condition. With no more 'outside' of nature to save us from ourselves, the Anthropocene *is* ontologically claustrophobic. The desire for ontological sparseness is a wilful forgetting of this, a dream of wide open spaces and of an ethics of relation that nonetheless surreptitiously counts on the big sky and the deep blue sea, and thus on an uncontaminated nature into which to escape, for its ontological support. But in the absence of such a wilderness, do our imaginaries of non-interference and cool distance not also require revising?

Furthermore, when Haraway (2007) emphasizes the mutual in relations of use, or 'co-' and the 'intra-' of meeting and greeting, her focus is not on the animals' response, but on the humans'. It is we, the species allegedly most capable of empathy, moral agency, reflection, and sociality, who have failed at response. Pettman might object that the bubble-blowing orca is simply telling the human what she wants to hear, already locked into a codependent, intelligible and clearly anthropocentric relationship in which domesticity kills desire and familiarity breeds contempt. But I think that this misses the point of Haraway's shift of emphasis. That the bubble-blowing orca happens to be aping the human is beside the point. The point is that for a split second neither the human nor the orca are aping themselves. Rather than being returned to their true natures when species meet, the parties to the encounter are denaturalized or queered by the meeting.

My favourite example of such a possibility is in Terry Bisson's (1993) short story 'Bears Discover Fire', which takes place in the present, nowhere special (semi-rural Kentucky), with characters who are nobodys (working class, white, mostly male, uninteresting). The setting is very close to the Shenandoah Valley in which 'nothing happened, of course', to Frank Chalmers, and indeed, nothing happens here, except that the news reports that the bears in the local forests are sitting around bonfires at dusk.

> 'They don't hibernate anymore', I said. 'They make a fire and keep it going all winter'.
> 'I declare', Mother said, 'What'll they think of next!'
>
> *(Bisson 1993:14)*

In the end, Mother uneventfully dies of old age, but right before she dies, she goes out to the forest to sit peacefully with the bears, where her cold body is found at dawn. That is literally the end of the story. Bisson manages to fully integrate daily life and a denaturalized nature in precisely the way Haraway likes, and the story is peppered with mundane, unsentimental earthling moments like 'I cut a little firewood and stacked it to one side, just to be neighborly' and 'I looked around the circle at the bears and wondered what *they* saw' (1993:7, 22). Of course, this is fictional, and we all know it to be impossible – humans are the only animals to use fire, all other animals fear it, and wild animals don't just suddenly act not in accordance with their nature. That is, until they do.

Relations of mutual use are inescapable and their complexity is permanent, but earthlings are not completely, exhaustively determined by this. The presence of others means that at any moment, at every moment, there exists the possibility of reconfiguring relation, the where, how, and who of it. Such creative reconfiguring becomes absolutely necessary when living together must take place in unliveable conditions.

## Note

1 'The Woman Who Swims with Killer Whales' Clip 3. Online. Available at: https://vimeo.com/39250296

## References

Alaimo, S. (2014) 'Oceanic origins, plastic activism, and new materialism at sea', in Iovino, S. and Opperman, S. (eds) *Material Ecocriticism*. Bloomington and Indianapolis: Indiana University Press, 186–203.

Albrecht, G. (2005) 'Solastalgia, a new concept in human health and identity', *Philosophy Activism Nature* 3: 41–44.

Bateson, G. (1972/2000) *Steps to an Ecology of Mind*. Chicago: University of Chicago Press.

Berlant, L. (2011) *Cruel Optimism*. Durham, NC: Duke University Press.

Bisson, T. (1993) *'Bears Discover Fire' and Other Stories*. New York: Orb.

Blackfish (2013) [film] Directed by Gabriela Cowperthwaite.

Cronon, W. (1995) *The Trouble With Wilderness*. Online. Available at: www.williamcronon.net/writing/Trouble_with_Wilderness_Main.html (accessed 5 June 2015).

Despain, D. (2014) *The Really Weird Trend of Breast Milk as Energy Beverage*. Online. Available at: www.outsideonline.com/1926846/really-weird-trend-breast-milk-energy-beverage (accessed 12 May 2015).

Duncan, D. (and Burns, K.) (2009) *The National Parks: America's Best Idea*. New York: Knopf Doubleday.

Handwerk, B. (2005) 'Killer Whales are most toxic arctic animals', *Study reports*. Online. Available at: http://news.nationalgeographic.com/news/2005/12/1213_051213_killer_whales.html (accessed 12 May 2015).

Haraway, D. J. (1991) 'A cyborg manifesto: Simians, cyborgs, and women', in Haraway, D. J. (ed) *Simians, Cyborgs and Women: The Reinvention of Nature*. New York: Routledge, 149–181.

Haraway, D. J. (2007) *When Species Meet*. Minneapolis: University of Minnesota Press.

Harding, S. (1993) 'Re-thinking standpoint epistemology: What is strong objectivity?', in Alcoff, L. and Potter, E. (eds) *Feminist Epistemologies*. New York and London: Routledge, 49–82.

Heise, U. K. (2011) 'Martian ecologies and the future of nature', *Twentieth-Century Literature* 57.3 and 57.4 (Fall/Winter): 466–467.

Lenoir, T. (2000) 'All but war is simulation: The military-entertainment complex', *Configurations* 8(3): 289–335.

Liljas, P. (2014) *Depressed Man Tries to Feed Himself to Tigers, Rejected*. Online. Available at: http://time.com/8192/depressed-man-tries-to-feed-himself-to-tigers-gets-rejected/ (accessed 2 January 2015).

McKibben, B. (1989, 2006) *The End of Nature*. New York: Random House.

Morabito, A. (2014) *Viewers Livid After Anaconda Man Fails to Get Eaten Alive*. Online. Available at: http://nypost.com/2014/12/08/anaconda-man-fails-to-get-eaten-alive-for-discovery-special/ (accessed 15 January 2015).

Pettman, D. (2011) *Human Error*. Minneapolis: University of Minnesota Press.

Planet Earth: The Future (2006) [TV series] Produced by BBC Natural History Unit.

Plumwood, V. (1996) 'Being prey', *Terra Nova* 1(3): 32–44.

Roberts, G. (2014) *Breastfeeding Prostitution Ring Raided in China, Where Men Pay to Suckle Young Mums*. Online. Available at: www.mirror.co.uk/news/weird-news/breastfeeding-prostitution-ring-raided-police-4897565 (accessed 12 May 2015).

Robinson, K. S. (1993) *Red Mars*. New York: Bantam Books.

Thompson, C. (2007) *Clive Thompson on How the Next Victim of Climate Change Will be Our Minds*. Online. Available at: www.wired.com/techbiz/people/magazine/16-01/st_thompson.

Wark, M. (2015) *Molecular Red: Theory for the Anthropocene*. New York, Verso.

*The Wilderness Act* (1964) Online. Available at: http://wilderness.nps.gov/document/wildernessAct.pdf (accessed 2 January 2015).

The Wilderness Society (1994) *The Wilderness Act Handbook*. Washington, DC: Wilderness Society.

The Woman Who Swims with Killer Whales [Clip 3] (2011) [documentary] Produced by Big Wave TV. Online. Available at: https://vimeo.com/39250296.

Woodard, C. and Meyer, F. (2013) *Hyundai Yanks Suicide Ad*. Online. Available at: www.usatoday.com/story/money/cars/2013/04/25/hyundai-suicide-ad-commercial/2113461/ (accessed 26 April 2013).

# 32

# THE END OF GENDER OR DEEP GREEN TRANSMISOGYNY?

*Laura Houlberg*

In May of 2013 the radical American environmental organization called Deep Green Resistance (DGR) released a YouTube video explaining their position as a radical feminist group whose definition of 'women' and 'men' include only people categorized as such at birth. In other words, they positioned themselves as a 'trans-exclusive' organization whose gender politics bar transgender people. Specifically, they bar transgender women from being recognized as 'women' or as an oppressed group under patriarchy. The moment was critical, not because DGR has a particularly large or influential hold on current dialogue around gender and environment, but instead because it marked one of the first public stances on gender and gender identity made by an openly identified 'feminist' environmental activist organization (The Letter Collective 2014). It was an infuriating moment for many observers, although not unexpected due to DGR's past actions and policies. However, as understanding of transgender people's lives, as well as knowledge and activism about the violence used to uphold the binary gender system, is quickly increasing in the United States (and some other countries), I want to draw attention to the views of Deep Green Resistance as a warning for how an environmentally concerned *politics of naturalness* can be complicit in oppression when applied in specific ways to gender. In this chapter, therefore, I tackle this moment, and its underpinning ideology, by contextualizing DGR's position in a way that (1) situates contemporary green conversations about gender within a larger history of American environmentalism, and (2) creates space for a more inclusive environmentalism of the future.

In her book, *The Ecological Other*, Sarah Jaquette Ray (2013) illuminates how modern environmental movements are capable of reinforcing social oppressions. She does this by focusing specifically on how mainstream environmentalist rhetoric excludes and even demonizes disabled people, indigenous people, and undocumented immigrants. Inspired by Ray, I am concerned with similar dynamics of power and the questions she asks in her book:

> in what ways does environmentalism – as a description of nature, as a social movement, and as a code of behavioral imperatives – play a role in the exploitation of land and bodies? Along what implicit lines do these environmental codes distinguish between good and bad bodies?
>
> *(Ray 2013:1–2)*

As I deconstruct DGR's quest to exclude transgender women from their movement, I argue that these efforts are not simply the results of second wave feminism's gender essentialist past, nor are they a move to correct or to cut ties with this history. Rather, these radical environmental politics align sinisterly with deeper, bloodier beginnings of the environmental movement in the United States – beginnings arguably grounded in ableism, racism, colonialism, and misogyny.

Queer, feminist, and environmental scholars from a range of disciplines have begun the necessary exploration of this history, realizing that the borderlands of their disciplines teem with strangeness and possibility. I argue in what follows that we have reached a pinnacle in our need to address the material effects of what a politics of 'natural' means for people, especially women, and especially queer and transgender (or trans, for short) women. While cisgender (a word describing those who are not transgender) queer women have successfully begun to create dialogue about un/naturalness and sexuality within the discipline of environmental studies, there has yet to emerge a strong presence of conversations centring trans people, specifically the perspectives of trans women. Greta Gaard's 'Moving Toward a Queer Ecofeminism' (1997); Annette and Noel Gough's 'Tales From Camp Wilde: Queer(y)ing Environmental Education Research' (2003); and Catriona Mortimer-Sandilands's 'Unnatural Passions? Notes Toward a Queer Ecology' (2005) have all begun the process of making connections between queerness and environment (see Butler and Seymour in this handbook). However, these works still revolve around cisgender subjects and cisgender queerness. It becomes apparent that there is a huge gap in who is writing and speaking about environmental issues and the role of nature in society, imagination, and identity, as it is difficult to locate major works about gender and environment written by trans authors. This is especially concerning when environmentally-minded groups like DGR throw attacks into the ether; where are the organizations and the literature to inform others, especially younger people beginning to understand their relationships to gender and environment, that visions of environmental justice like DGR's are anything but emancipatory? I want to expose the barriers that trans women face when entering these conversations so that the exclusionary framing in current environmental thought might one day be eradicated.

## In pursuit of a common language

The interdisciplinary nature of the fields of environmental studies and gender studies, while contributing to thorough and unique analyses, also means that many people may be entering this conversation from a background that may not include gender, trans, or queer theory. To help bridge this gap, and in the interests of developing a common language, I will begin by clarifying the vocabulary I use in this chapter.

Two of the most important words to define from the very beginning are 'cisgender' and 'transgender'. A trans person is someone whose gender differs from the one they were assigned at birth. The word 'trans' by itself was created to function as an umbrella term for all people who self-define their gender as anything different from their birth assignment. In the context of this chapter, when used by itself or in front of 'people', trans should be read as all-encompassing of non-cisgender identities. A 'cisgender' person, on the other hand, is someone who does not identify as having a gender different from the one they have been assigned. The word 'cis' was popularized in the 1990s by trans people who wanted an alternative way to refer to non-trans people, rather than using words like 'natural', 'biological', 'normal', 'genetic', or 'real'. According to Emi Koyama, '"cis" is real – even if carelessly articulated'; 'cis' is preferable to the aforementioned words because 'it treats "cis" and "trans" as linguistic equivalents', rather than treating one as more normal or natural or otherwise standard and the other abnormal, artificial, or exceptional (2013:n.p.).

'Transmisogyny' is perhaps best defined as the confluence of misogyny (the hatred of women) and transphobia, including 'negative attitudes, expressed through cultural hate, individual and state violence, and discrimination' that are specifically targeted toward trans women and trans feminine people (Kacere 2014:n.p.). Some ways in which this phenomenon manifests are described in Julia Serano's (2012) essay, 'Transmisogyny Primer'. She writes that 'the majority of violence committed against gender-variant individuals targets individuals on the trans female/feminine spectrum' (2012:n.p.). In the media, 'jokes and demeaning depictions of gender-variant people primarily focus on trans female/feminine spectrum people' and these individuals are also 'routinely sexualized' (Serano 2012). While transphobia is regarded as a generalized system of oppression affecting all trans people, transmisogyny is specific to the oppression that trans feminine people face.

## Who is Deep Green Resistance?

DGR describes itself as an organization of radical environmentalists dissatisfied with the ineffectiveness of mainstream environmentalism. Founded in 2011 in the United States by Derrick Jensen, Lierre Keith, and Aric McBay,[1] the organization now has active chapters in at least seven countries worldwide. It mobilizes around issues of global warming, rapid species extinction, and the over-consumption of fossil fuels, stating on its website – in a section titled 'Guiding Principles' – that 'the only honest solution is to stop industrial civilization from burning fossil fuels' and that 'this culture needs to be destroyed before it consumes all life on this planet' (DGR 2015a).

The goal of DGR, as elaborated on their website, is to 'deprive the rich of their ability to steal from the poor and the powerful of their ability to destroy the planet' (a permutation of an ecologically minded Robin Hood). While they admit that this is 'a vast undertaking', members believe that the collapse of industrial civilization is possible. DGR's plan involves a complex network of belowground and aboveground organizing that is committed to 'fighting back' against exploitation and injustice in every facet of civilization, not only issues of direct ecological significance. At first glance they at least appear to be operating under noble motives. Some of their stated principles are that DGR 'works to end abuse at the personal, organizational, and cultural levels', attempts to 'eradicate domination and subordination' from their personal interactions, and seeks 'to promote solidarity between oppressed peoples' (DGR 2015b).

Despite DGR's claim that they work to promote solidarity, since 2012 the group has generated a great deal of controversy in radical environmentalist circles. Surprisingly, this controversy is not over the fact that the organization sees 'civilization as the institution that is destroying life on Earth' (DGR 2015a) and in response has created a strategy for catalyzing the collapse of global civilization through what they call Decisive Ecological Warfare. It is also not due to their militant underground resistance network that plans to engage in direct action against banks, coal-fired power plants, and other exploitative institutions (DGR 2015c). The reason why the organization recently has been banned from numerous conferences, speaking events, and radical websites has to do with their policy on gender, specifically their refusal to recognize the legitimacy of the genders of trans people.

DGR aligns their organization with radical feminism, though a more accurate description would be trans-exclusive radical feminism, a branch of second wave feminist thought (championed by writers such as Janice Raymond, Sheila Jeffreys, and the late Mary Daly), which actively rejects the idea that trans women are women, and instead, accuses them of fetishization, deceit, and most extremely, rape.[2] Since 2012, numerous accounts of DGR's discrimination against trans people, specifically trans women, have been made public through personal blogs, as well as articles on radical news sites, by trans and cis people from within, and outside of, the organization.

Some of this discrimination has been enacted through the deliberate use of the wrong pronouns for trans women, denying trans women access to women's spaces and gender appropriate housing at DGR's conferences, delegitimizing and erasing trans women's oppression through their trans-exclusive radical feminist analysis, and spreading false information about the tenets of trans-inclusive feminism through their materials and lectures (GenderTrender 2013).

DGR's anti-trans policies and actions are rooted in the organization's trans-exclusive radical feminism, as well as their particular flavor of radical environmentalism; transmisogyny is built into DGR's structure and values. In the forty-minute video on DGR's YouTube channel, Rachel Ivy, a young, white, liberal arts graduate, presents DGR's official policy on gender in slideshow form. Ivy begins the presentation by clarifying that she is 'not presenting this topic for debate, not in the slightest . . . this represents DGR's policy' (The End of Gender 2013). From the very beginning, DGR emphasizes that they do not allow for productive conversations around gender. Furthermore, Ivy describes their trans-exclusive policy as 'the core of DGR'. 'This is the reason why I joined DGR', she states, '[and] this is the reason why the women I look up to are in DGR, and if it changed, we would all leave' (The End of Gender 2013). Since DGR is one of the only radical environmentalist organizations that also outspokenly identifies with feminist politics, it has attracted many feminists who are both aware, and unaware, of the transmisogyny underlying the organization's principles. However, many women have left the organization for precisely the same reason Ivy is defending (The End of Gender 2013).

## Deep Green transmisogyny

Why is DGR so invested in gender? How does this focus on gender relate back to DGR's political vision? The answer is in the organization's assertion that 'gender is unnatural', an idea they justify by construing gender as solely a cultural artifact, a symptom of civilization that must be dismantled in order to overthrow society (The End of Gender 2013). Useful here is Serano's idea of gender artifactualism, 'the tendency to conceptualize and depict gender as being primarily or entirely a cultural artifact' (2013:117). It is by portraying gender as merely an oppressive cultural artifact that DGR's investment in gender aligns with their political ideas that position the 'natural' as morally superior and the 'artifactual' as inferior, even harmful.

While some radical feminists, cis lesbians, and ecofeminists have been accused of gender essentialism (the idea that there are innate, essential differences between men and women, usually defined, in regards to women, as a 'female essence' that binds all women together), Serano posits that what is often being used in these analyses is gender artifactualism. Social constructionism falls somewhere in the middle of essentialism and artifactualism, and is the belief that

> gender does not arise in a direct and unadulterated manner from biology, but rather is shaped to some extent by culture – by socialization, gender norms, and the gender-related ideology, language, and labels that constrain and influence our understanding of the matter.
>
> *(Serano 2013:117–118)*

While essentialism is the belief that all aspects of gender are inherent, and artifactualism is the belief that gender is entirely constructed, social constructionism acknowledges that gender is an infinitely complicated mixture of biology and culture. Serano herself identifies as a social constructionist, and she points out that many feminists who think they are using a social constructionist framework are actually using gender artifactualism. When this happens, any acknowledgement of the role, or possible role, of biology in creating and understanding gender, queerness, femininity, and transness is accused of being biological determinism, the idea that biology dictates or determines a fixed outcome.

Since women, genderqueers, and trans people have had their identities, behaviours, and bodies pathologized by scientific and medical institutions for centuries, some feel this definition of an entirely artifactual gender can be liberating. If there is no scientific or medical basis for difference, then difference can become obsolete, and with it, the ability to build hierarchies upon those differences. However, what gender artifactualism actually does is destroy 'any possibility that there might be non-social or intrinsic factors that influence or predispose one to cross-gender identification' (Serano 2013:119), meaning that the logic of gender artifactualists like DGR goes, according to Serano, like this: '1) Gender is a cultural artifact; 2) Transsexuals mistake gender to be something real (rather than recognizing it as artificial); 3) Therefore, transsexuals reify the gender system' (121). DGR's trans-exclusive radical feminism is not gender essentialist, because they actively reject the idea of an innate gender. They instead see gender as a classification that would disappear without the enforcement of a sex caste system (The End of Gender 2013). So if gender is a cultural artifact and has no meaning outside of the caste system, then an organization whose primary priority is to end civilization would, of course, reject gender in and of itself. For DGR, gender is unnatural, so true ecological justice must reject gender, to call for the 'end of gender'.

In *The Ecological Other*, Ray describes the pervasive and enduring doctrine of American environmentalism as this: 'The crisis of nature is a crisis of the body, and recovering our connection to nature requires not only getting out of it, but disciplining the body away from its reliance on technology and the "crutches" of society' (2013:32). My argument is that DGR uses gender artifactualism to erase the subjectivity of trans people, and by defining femininity as artificial and inherently subordinate, specifically targets trans women. Trans women, in DGR's analysis, are depicted as reliant on the 'crutches' of gender and femininity, and therefore as a symptom of a society that must be overthrown. This analysis is based in DGR's investment in naturalness, as a part of its radical environmentalist ethic. This conceptual framework creates 'green transmisogyny' – transmisogyny rooted in insecurities of naturalness and its relation to environmental futures. However, as we can learn from disability and trans scholars, the 'unmediated contact between man [*sic*] and nature' is impossible, as theorists of both fields 'contend every body's encounter with the physical world is always mediated' (Ray 2013:40). In other words, the 'naturalness' that DGR chases is a distant mirage, though their insistence on its existence follows a long history of using the socially constructed idea of naturalness to oppress others. The relation between its trans-exclusive radical feminism and its radical environmentalism is not serendipitous, but constitutively constructed.

## More white than green

DGR's definition of gender and gender politics relies on the white supremacist, colonialist project of the gender binary. As a result, they leave out alternative ways of experiencing and understanding gender from their utopian imagining. There are many cultures who have (and have had) more than two genders, and did not base their society along a rigid, binarist gender hierarchy, but these ways of knowing gender are left out of DGR's analysis.

Among indigenous Native American societies, there are many examples of non-binary gender systems. For example, pre-colonial Navajo societies recognized four genders: men, women, masculine female-assigned people, and feminine male-assigned people (Nanda 1999). In Mohave society, a young male-assigned person may decide to become an alpha, and partake in a ceremony to change their gender, adopt a traditionally feminine name, and wear feminine clothing. They are then lauded as exceptional healers among their communities. With the emergence of the term 'Two-Spirit' in the 1990s – a specific Native American identity that takes into account their intersecting oppressions along the lines of race, colonialism, queerness, sexuality, and transness – there has been growing recognition of the non-binary systems of gender that indigenous people had in place before colonialism (Nanda 1999:13). DGR's stance that transfeminine people are somehow an affront, or a threat, to cis women, and that they uphold patriarchy, demonstrates an ignorance of non-colonialist gender systems, demonizes those that they claim to be in solidarity with, and forwards a specifically white and patriarchal agenda.

This is certainly not the first time that environmentalism and the construction of the 'natural' have contributed to the eradication of indigenous peoples and their cultures. Colonialism has been very much an environmental movement, in the way that it has sought to dominate across environments. Environmentalism in the United States became a social movement alongside the construction of 'wilderness', with the decision by President Roosevelt to construct national parks such as Yellowstone in the late nineteenth century. The violent displacement of Native American people from these areas in order to preserve empty land for white tourists and visitors is just one example of how early environmentalism and colonialism colluded against Native Americans, though the history of environmentalism in the United States since then is fraught with even more examples.

In her essay, 'Colonialism, Two-Spirit Identity, and the Logics of White Supremacy', Phoenix Singer shows how white supremacy seeks not only to colonize indigenous people through attacks on their bodies, but also attempts to colonize their minds. 'To fully destroy resistance', she writes, is not achievable through only attacks on the physical bodies of the oppressed; 'one must also dominate the mind and the spirit' (Singer [n.d.]:5). Singer refers to the boarding schools that young Native American children were sent to, where Christianity and patriarchy forcibly replaced historical indigenous cultures, as an example of the colonialism of the mind. I argue that DGR continues this colonial process by denying indigenous non-binary gender identities, and imposing their own binarist analysis that seeks to eradicate gender itself, albeit by unclear means. Like some white environmentalists in the United States before them, DGR centres whiteness and the colonial project of gender, regardless of their claims of building solidarity with indigenous peoples.

## Disentangling the knot

It is important to understand that DGR's framework for understanding gender falls apart easily under the slightest pressure. There are four main flaws in DGR's definition of gender that make their trans-exclusivity illogical. The first is that their definition of gender mistakenly conflates gender identity, gender role, and gender expression. The second is that they define femininity as 'ritualized displays of submission to males', thus naturalizing masculinity by portraying femininity as constructed and inherently subordinate (The End of Gender 2013). The third flaw is that DGR makes no distinction between difference and hierarchy, and asserts that difference itself creates hierarchy. Finally, the DGR framework portrays the genders of trans people as voluntary and politically motivated. In this section, I deconstruct each of these claims to illuminate the contradictory nature of their arguments.

In the YouTube video I mentioned earlier, Ivy explains DGR's definition of gender as 'a hierarchical system which maintains the subordination of females as a class to males as a class through force'. Additionally, they argue that 'gender is not natural or voluntary, since no person is naturally subordinate to another'. The solution she proposes for redressing this oppressive gender system? 'Overthrow male power and thus the entire gender system', asserts Ivy, reading the statement for DGR (The End of Gender 2013).

In addition to seeing gender as a class system, DGR's notion of gender is a conflation of gender identity, gender expression, and gender role. Arguably like all feminists, DGR members question assigned gender roles, and for good reason. Feminism is founded on the rejection of compulsory roles assigned by gender, and the devaluation of typically feminine tasks or roles.[3] However, gender identity is simply the gender with which someone identifies, and is not inherently linked to gender role (Serano 2009:23–26). DGR compounds the conflation of gender role and identity by adding gender expression. But while gender identity, expression, and role are often connected in many cultures, they can also be discrete aspects of a person's experience of gender, and are capable of operating independently of each other. For example, the gender roles and expressions available for European women have changed drastically since the late nineteenth century Victorian era, but mainstream conceptions of gender are still based around the identities of 'men' and 'women' (Gender Spectrum 2015).

DGR argues that gender identity and gender expression are loci of hierarchical power dynamics, but take the argument so far as to define femininity itself as 'ritualized displays of submission to males' (The End of Gender 2013). While it is true that women are often defined as deviations from, or in opposition to, men (though not as equals), DGR's definition of femininity reinforces, rather than challenges, the positioning of women and femininity as having lesser value. However, we should challenge this idea that femininity is defined by its submission. Plenty of powerful women have embodied both feminine gender expressions and strength. Singer Beyoncé Knowles, politicians such as Hillary Clinton and Marina Silva, theorist bell hooks, media writer Janet Mock, and comedian Margaret Cho, are just a few examples of women who embody femininity, but also occupy leadership positions in male-dominated spaces. DGR also fails to acknowledge the femininity of queer women, like Margaret Cho, whose femininity is not preened for a male gaze and therefore cannot be understood as simply a 'display of submission to males'. What DGR does by equating femininity, women, and submission is strip women of agency. Arguing that femininity is inherently less valuable or natural than masculinity reinforces patriarchal notions of masculinity's innate superiority and naturalness.

In a patriarchal society such as the United States, gender identity, expression, and the roles of men and women are not simply different; women and femininity are marked as lesser, while masculinity and men are rewarded with social privileges, thus creating a hierarchy. However, DGR does not make a distinction between difference and hierarchy, as they believe difference itself is what creates the hierarchy. 'Without gender there cannot be oppression', states Ivy in the video, ignoring the ways in which people of the same gender have, and do, oppress each other through white supremacy, classism, ableism, fat phobia, heterosexism, and more. This leads to another point regarding DGR's position on gender: DGR does not acknowledge in their gender analysis that the gender binary has been a colonialist project. The definition of gender that DGR both employs and critiques is a definition that has been created through the violence of white people inflicted onto indigenous and colonized people. To not acknowledge the wealth of meaning and identities that 'gender' has been tied to in cultures around the globe is to again centre whiteness, which also happens to be a historically important investment of American environmentalism (Ray 2013).

Using the concept of naturalness to reinforce masculinity is not a new rhetorical move – in fact, environmentalism has been doing so since its inception. At the emergence of American environmentalism in the 1890s, notions of 'nature' and 'wilderness' were shaped against a backdrop of a feminizing city. As immigrants moved into US cities, the urban landscape became a source of insecurity for white, straight men with class privilege. Led by wealthy, white men in positions of power, and fueled by anxiety over the 'closing of the frontier', new swaths of 'untouched' land became the landscapes for purifying American masculinity. Nature turned into a place of escape (if it could be afforded), and bodily fitness (in terms of ability, whiteness, and masculinity) became a sign of connection to the wilderness. Similar to the views of DGR today, the bodies who could thrive in nature were the ones who *deserved* to inhabit it.

The last major flaw in DGR's reasoning around gender is their claim that trans people's genders are deliberate political statements. In the DGR video, Ivy refers to trans people as 'gender outlaws' (The End of Gender 2013), referencing the title of trans activist Kate Bornstein's (1994) groundbreaking memoir. But while Bornstein was attempting to describe what it feels like to have an identity outside the mainstream conception of gender, Ivy interprets 'gender outlaws' to mean that all trans people's genders are simply political choices, or a way to 'escape' or be an 'outlaw' to gender (Bornstein 1994). 'When I was a liberal this was really attractive', Ivy says, 'because it left it all up to me. If I wanted to escape gender, I could do it' (The End of Gender 2013). This claim does not stand up to empirical reality. There are many trans people who come to an understanding about their gender long before being exposed to trans, queer, or feminist theory, and many trans people will never be exposed to those discourses (TransWhat? [n.d.]). To say that gender identity is absolutely not linked to biological predispositions, as DGR argues, discounts the deep, inexplicable feelings that many trans people have about gender, often early in life as children (Serano 2009, 2013). Not only does Ivy misinterpret the reason why trans people transition by seeing it as an intentionally political act, but she completely misses the mark with the idea that somehow trans people want to escape or are capable of escaping gender at all (The End of Gender 2013).

Trans people are faced with gender roles, norms, identities, and gendered assumptions constantly in their daily lives, and are forced to think about it much more often than cisgender people just in order to live comfortably and to survive. Trans people are often not allowed to express their gender in the way they would like because they receive inordinate amounts of pressure to present themselves in a way that is masculine or feminine enough to avoid discrimination and violence or to gain access to medical care. This attempt to self-present in a way that will minimize the threat of being mis-gendered or attacked is often misinterpreted as trans people 'dressing as, or appearing as, the traditional gender stereotype' and then distorted by cissexists to mean that trans people misunderstand gender to be a sort of costume (The End of Gender 2013). In reality, there are butch trans women, femme trans men, and non-gender-binary people of all types of expressions, and all of these gender expressions are legitimate. However, when not presenting traditional expressions of their genders, cissexists often use this non-conformity as evidence that trans people's genders are inauthentic. This presumption of inauthenticity can often lead to violence as those seeking to uphold the gender binary quell the threat that transness poses. Trans people live genuine genders in a world that constantly delegitimizes them. Contrary to DGR's claims that identifying as trans advertises an 'escape' from gender, transness opens both the possibility of violence at the hands of people wishing to uphold a rigid gender binary, as well as begins to describe a multitude of ways to have relationships to gender outside of a gender binary. Neither of these openings describes an escape from thinking about or interacting with gender or a gendered society (Serano 2013).

Since DGR assumes that trans people's genders are entirely political positions, Ivy makes false connections between ineffective, individual-based environmentalist strategies, such as those championed by companies who launch green-washed campaigns as a way to attract consumers, and trans people's gender identities. 'Dressing as or presenting as the traditional gender stereotype of the opposite sex is no more effective than living in a hut in the woods somewhere' and expecting civilization to end, says Ivy. 'It doesn't make any political difference on its own', she continues (The End of Gender 2013). Living in a hut in the woods to protest civilization is an entirely political act, and she is right that it does not do much, if anything, on its own. Trans people's genders, though, are not solely voluntary political choices – they are deeply felt identities – and the mere existence of trans people across cultures, regions, and histories is proof that the definition of gender that Ivy uses, as well as the notion of gender essentialism, is inaccurate. Trans people are not all political, are not all feminists, and are not all post-modern queer or gender theorists. Ivy's assertion that trans people think they destroy or escape the gender system simply by living their authentic selves discounts the wealth of different experiences that trans people have.

Julia Serano, the transgender American writer, activist, and biologist, addresses this type of claim directly and beautifully in her book *Excluded* (2013). She writes, 'The assumption that we can subvert or overthrow the gender system by simply engaging in certain gendered or sexual behaviors (but not others) seems pretty silly' (2013:137). She notes that while gender non-conforming people have existed in various ways throughout history, 'our mere presence has never once simply made sexism vanish into thin air'. She continues, 'I would have to be pretty full of myself to believe that I could undo the gender system simply by behaving in one way or another' (137). Rather, Serano argues, sexism and cissexism occur because of double standards that exist in our society, or 'when we assume that some people are less valid or natural than others because of their sex, gender, or sexuality' (137). Serano's argument calls for a change in the way people perceive each other's identities and expressions, not the erasure of identity and expression.

## Toward green transdisciplinarity

I am interested in how we who explore the connections between environment and gender can create dialogues and theories that eradicate green transmisogyny. For inspiration, I suggest looking toward the actions of organizations that have stated their disagreement with DGR's policies regarding gender, as well as the work of trans people within environmentalism. Additionally, the future depends on the engagement of younger people (the next generation of social change agents) who are just beginning to explore their own relationships to their environments and gender identity; they deserve inclusive communities and movements, and the tools with which to imagine better futures.

Since DGR's official presentation of their trans-exclusive policy, it has been heartening to see other radical environmental organizations speak out against their analysis and actions. For example, Earth First! Newswire, self-described as 'Media from the Frontlines of Ecological Resistance', is an important informational hub for people organizing around environmental issues. In 2013 they released a statement online confirming that they would 'no longer print or in any way promote DGR material' on their website or in their printed journal (Earth First! 2013). 'While we don't need to agree with an individual or organization to find their words or actions relevant for discussion', they explained, 'we will not continue to include those whose core expression of values continues to promote exclusion and oppression' (Earth First! 2013). They proceeded to summarize their concerns with DGR's analysis following similar arguments as mine, and also to call attention to the positive material impacts that trans people have made in environmental movements. 'Trans people are people', they write, 'people who have worked on the [Earth First!] Journal collective and stood on the front lines of the ecological resistance' (Earth First! 2013).

Another moment of resistance to DGR's position was the defection of DGR's Portland, Oregon, chapter in 2013. After an argument, and brief physical contact, occurred between members of DGR and a handful of trans and queer activists at the 2013 Law and Disorder conference (held in Portland), leaders of the Portland chapter published an open letter of resignation from DGR on Earth First's website. In the letter, they wrote that they 'have become dismayed with Derrick Jensen and Lierre Keith's insistence on exaggerating and manipulating the facts about what occurred at the Law and Disorder conference in order to gain public sympathy and to aggressively push their trans-phobic agenda' (Resistance Portland 2013). Among these exaggerations and manipulations, they cited DGR's intentional mis-gendering of the trans activists as an attempt to 'spin the event as an act of male violence against women' (Resistance Portland 2013). They closed their letter with invitations to those who would also like to leave DGR, and introduced their newly independent organization's new name, Resistance Portland. Their urging of others to follow their renewed focus on 'those who are killing the planet' rather than attacking trans people with ideology, 'and to build uncompromising organizations in the face of oppression and civilization with us', appears indicative of a positive new wave of environmental organizing (Resistance Portland 2013). One that can include a robust analysis of gender that protects and values trans people of all cultures in environmental organizing.

To be clear, this work is already happening in other environmental organizations around the United States. For example, the Trans and/or Women's Action Camp (TWAC) is an 'action camp for folks who identify as female, transgender, transsexual, gender queer and gender variant' where information about recent environmental organizing, as well as strategies for direct action, can be shared, without involving cisgender men (TWAC About [n.d.]). The camp is one week long, held in rural areas across the United States (including in Oregon, California, and Florida), and culminates in an act of direct resistance, usually in solidarity with other groups from the area. TWAC states on their website that 'women and trans folks have always been powerhouses of political action' and the camp provides an accountable, safer, space to gather, heal, and plan together (TWAC About: no date).

Ariel Howland, a self-identified radical transgender and genderqueer woman, has written about her personal experience as a regular attendee of the camp. Reflecting positively, she has noted that over her five years of attending the camp, 'while TWAC as a whole makes some mistakes they are putting a lot of effort into including transgender folks including trans women' (Howland 2014:1). Among these efforts, she notes pronoun check-ins,[4] workshops that specifically address transmisogyny, and an overall sense of eagerness among cis campers to learn more about issues that affect trans communities. Coupled with the impressive amount of fundraising that TWAC does to ensure that all interested people can attend, TWAC appears to be a much more inclusive and motivating setting than DGR's retreats, which have also been criticized for not making enough space for disagreement or discussion among members. Overall, TWAC creates an exciting new space for cis and trans people to come together to do important, directly effective work around environmental issues.

## New tools

The canon of gender and environment literature could do with a similar renovation. As young people begin to understand their identities and relationships to their environments, they need to have works to turn to for guidance in the canon of environmental studies. In this section, I describe some key works by trans writers that I believe contribute valuable perspectives to discussions of gender and environment, and draw compelling blueprints for the future.

One example of canonical trans studies literature that should also be understood as environmental literature is Susan Stryker's (1994) 'My Words to Victor Frankenstein Above the Village of Chamounix: Performing Transgender Rage'. This groundbreaking essay became the first article by an openly transgender author to be published in a peer-reviewed academic journal. In the essay, Stryker likens herself to 'the monster'. She writes, 'I am too often perceived as less than fully human due to the means of my embodiment' (1994:238). As the 'monster', she positions herself in opposition to, and critical of, 'naturalness', arguing that 'the Nature you bedevil me with is a lie' (240). She emphasizes her experience as a transsexual woman, rather than a transgender or trans woman, to call attention to the role medical intervention played in shaping her identity. Stryker argues that the motivations of the doctors who created sex reassignment or sex affirmation techniques are rooted in the 'pursuit of immortality through the perfection of the body', similar to the impulse of Mary Shelley's Dr. Frankenstein (242). The motivations for developing these techniques are 'aligned with a deeply conservative attempt to stabilize gendered identity in service of the naturalized heterosexual order'. In this way, Stryker argues that sex affirmation surgeries are corrective, developed to 'contain and colonize the radical threat posed by a particular transgender strategy of resistance to the coerciveness of gender' (244).

Stryker argues that while these procedures and techniques are intended to 'generate naturalness' (1994:242), they actually place the subject 'in an unassimilable, antagonistic, queer relationship to a Nature in which it must nevertheless exist' (243). While throughout the essay she takes on the subject position of 'the monster', or the unnatural creature, Stryker argues that all people (trans or not) are subject to a 'gendering process that sustains the illusion of naturalness' (243–250). The assumed 'naturalness' of pairing certain genders with certain bodies deserves interrogation. From the lack of, or mis-, representation of non-binary genders in popular culture and media, to the siege of violence against trans women, the gender binary is more than inconvenient, it inflicts violence on those it does not describe (Mogul et al. 2011). 'Nature', Stryker writes, 'exerts such hegemonic oppression' (1994:250).

The essay 'Love Your Monsters' by French post-environmental theorist Bruno Latour (2011) uses the story of Frankenstein to get across a similar message about the illusion of naturalness. Post-environmentalism calls for us to adopt a 'compositionist' approach, 'one that sees the process of human development as neither liberation from Nature nor as a fall from it, but rather as a process of becoming ever-more attached to, and intimate with, a panoply of nonhuman natures' (Latour 2011:n.p.). Some of the intimacy that Latour is referring to is apparent within his comparison of French and American national parks. In France, these parks are seen as rural ecosystems, whereas in the United States there is more intervention, 'at always greater levels of detail, with ever more subtle care – to keep them 'natural enough' for Nature-intoxicated tourists to remain happy' (2011:n.p.). The intervention required to maintain the illusion of naturalness is precisely the situation that Stryker is writing about. In order to preserve 'naturalness', greater levels of intervention are required, soon blurring the lines of what is natural and what is not. The logic itself is circular. What is unnatural? Why do we go through great lengths to protect Nature when it resists this control?

Both Latour and Stryker, located in post-environmentalism and trans studies respectively, are concerned with questions of naturalness, and how the things we deem 'natural' are more often than not culturally or socially constructed. In both essays, Frankenstein's monster is not a character from a horror film. To Latour, our creations deserve love and care, the same affection we would show our own children. Stryker reminds us of the Latin root of the word 'monster', *monstrum*, which means 'divine portent', itself formed on the root of the verb *monere*, 'to warn'. Throughout history, Styker writes, monsters served a role similar to angels, messengers sent to say, 'Pay attention: something of profound importance is happening' (1994:240). Between these two essays alone, a wealth of possibility exists for conversations between ecological and queer and trans scholars.

Eva Hayward is another good example of someone whose scholarship productively illuminates issues of gender, corporeality, and nature. A student of Donna Haraway, her interdisciplinary work in art, marine ecology, and queer studies gives her a unique perspective on inter-species relationships. Her essay 'Lessons from a Starfish' (2008) is a beautiful account of her relationship with the song 'The Cripple and the Starfish' by Antony and the Johnsons. The essay suggests her corporeality as a trans woman as being similar to that of a starfish, who can grow back limbs from its own flesh. Rather than describing herself in the way that Susan Stryker articulates – as a 'monster', or as 'othered' from Nature – Hayward suggests a link to non-human animals whose bodies also undergo an experience of separation, change, and rejuvenation. Neither of these descriptions is more right than the other, but they offer interesting ways to interpret all people's relationships between their bodies and non-human bodies.

Additionally, Eli Clare (1999), a genderqueer trans man, writes in his memoir *Exile and Pride* about his experience as a rural queer, balancing issues of gender, sexuality, ecological destruction, small town politics, and the urban emphasis of both queer and environmental activism. Of course, while Clare is not a trans woman, his work illuminates important connections between environmental studies and gender studies that could be elaborated by people of many genders. My hope is that future environmentalist and post-environmentalist movements understand the unnaturalness that has categorized queer people and issues as inherently flawed, and therefore dedicate time and energy toward incorporating these frameworks, problems, and goals into the study of environment.

## Conclusion

When envisioning the future, I am brought back to Sarah Jaquette Ray's description of environmentalism as 'a form of social control' (2013:16). She writes that 'by othering groups perceived as threats', environmentalism is able to 'draw on and perpetuate ideas of nature that reinforce racial and social hierarchies' (16). As I have argued in this chapter, even radical groups that use the rhetoric of social justice can perpetuate these hostile and violent ideologies, and in fact can develop their own types of 'green' oppression. Green transmisogyny is not new, in fact it has been a thick rope binding together much of environmentalism, even some facets that theorize about gender and environment with a self-described feminist lens.

The work of trans scholars and activists should, and will, guide toward cohesive and groundbreaking terrain en route to creating more just visions of gender and of environment. Rather than envisioning an 'end of gender' by unknown means, as DGR calls for, I see a more promising vision forming in communities like Trans and/or Women's Action Camp (TWAC), where marginalized voices are brought to the centre in coalition with one another. To follow Stryker's advice, what is needed is examining the 'seams and sutures' in ourselves, to understand the powers at play that create the mediating boundaries between us and our environments and identities, and to confront the 'discourses of fear and policies of social control that continue to influence environmentalism today' (1994:16). Only when we intentionally and devotedly break down our own constructions can we build a new future for all.

## Notes

1 Jensen is an American author, self-described 'indigenist', and critic of mainstream environmentalism (see www.derrickjensen.org). Keith is a trans-exclusive radical feminist, environmentalist and food activist (see www.lierrekeith.com). McBay is the primary contributor to Deep Green Resistance's strategy for collapsing civilization, but left the organization in early 2012 (see www.aricmcbay.org).
2 Janice Raymond is well-known for her 1994 book *The Transsexual Empire*, in which she includes her now famous line, 'All transsexuals rape women's bodies by reducing the real female form to an artifact, appropriating this body for themselves' (1994:104). Inspired in part by Raymond's work, Sheila Jeffreys wrote further about trans women in her essay 'Transgender Activism: A Lesbian Feminist Perspective', claiming that trans women construct a 'conservative fantasy of what women should be. They are inverting an essence of womanhood which is deeply insulting and restrictive' (Jeffreys 1997). Mary Daly, who was Janice Raymond's dissertation advisor, claimed that while 'surgeons and hormone therapists of the transsexual kingdom . . . can be said to produce feminine persons . . . they cannot produce women'

(Daly 1978). Together, perhaps along with Germaine Greer, they are three of the most frequently quoted trans-exclusive radical feminists.

3 This is not to say that feminine roles are bad or oppressive in themselves. Some women find joy in motherhood or caregiving. Others have no interest in politics. Others enjoy sewing and other stereotypically female activities. Problems arise, however, when these roles are devalued, cast as being less important than traditionally masculine roles, and when people are forced into performing these roles because of their gender.

4 It has become common in some communities and organizations for meetings to start with a pronoun check-in, where participants introduce themselves with their name and the pronouns by which they wish to be addressed, such as 'My name in Joan and my pronouns are "she" and "her"' or 'I'm Freddie and my pronouns are "zie" and "hir"'.

# References

Bornstein, K. (1994) *Gender Outlaw: On Men, Women, and the Rest of Us.* New York: Routledge.

Clare, E. (1999) *Exile and Pride.* Cambridge: South End Press.

Daly, M. (1978) *Gyn/ecology: The Metaethics of Radical Feminism.* Boston: Beacon Press.

Deep Green Resistance (2015a) *Why Deep Green Resistance?* Online. Available at: http://deepgreenresistance.org/en/who-we-are/about-deep-green-resistance (accessed 6 September 2015).

Deep Green Resistance (2015b) *Guiding Principles of Deep Green Resistance.* Online. Available at: http://deepgreenresistance.org/en/who-we-are/guiding-principles-of-deep-green-resistance (accessed 6 September 2015).

Deep Green Resistance (2015c) *Decisive Ecological Warfare.* Online. Available at: http://deepgreenresistance.org/en/deep-green-resistance-strategy/decisive-ecological-warfare (accessed 6 September 2015).

Earth First! Newswire (2013) *Deep Green Transphobia.* Online. Available at: http://earthfirstjournal.org/newswire/2013/05/15/deep-green-transphobia (accessed 1 February 2016).

The End of Gender: Revolution, Not Reform (2013) *Video, Deep Green Resistance.* Online. Available at: www.youtube.com/watch?v=Ot8cBm0YmXo (accessed 7 September 2015).

Gaard, G. (1997) 'Toward a queer ecofeminism', *Hypatia* 12: 114–137.

GenderTrender (2013) *Trans vs. Feminism.* Online. Available at: http://gendertrender.wordpress.com/2013/05/16/trans-vs-feminism-video-footage-of-queertrans-activists-at-the-law-and-disorder-conference-following-last-weekends-portland-attack (accessed 6 September 2015).

Gough, N. and Gough, A. (2003) 'Tales from Camp Wilde: Queer(y)ing environmental education research', *Canadian Journal of Environmental Education* 8: 4–66.

Hayward, E. (2008) 'More lessons from a starfish: Prefixial flesh and transspeciated selves', *Women's Studies Quarterly* 36(3 and 4): 64–85.

Howland, A. (2014) *Trans and Women's Action Camp Reportback: A Transgender Perspective.* Online. Available at: http://twac.files.wordpress.com/2014/08/twac-reportback-by-ariel-howland.pdf (accessed 1 February 2016).

Jeffreys, S. (1997) 'Transgender activism: A lesbian feminist perspective', *Journal of Lesbian Studies* 1: 55–74.

Kacere, L. (2014) *Transmisogyny: What It Is and What We Can Do About It.* Online. Available at: http://everydayfeminism.com/2014/01/transmisogyny/ (accessed 7 September 2015).

Koyama, E. (2013) *'Cis' Is Real – Even If It Is Carelessly Articulated.* Online. Available at: http://eminism.org/blog/entry/399 (accessed 4 September 2015).

Latour, B. (2011) 'Love your monsters', in Shellenberger, M. and Nordhaus, T. (eds) *Love Your Monsters: Postenvironmentalism and the Anthropocene.* The Breakthrough Institute. Online. Available at: http://thebreakthrough.org/index.php/journal/past-issues/issue-2/love-your-monsters (accessed 8 September 2015).

The Letter Collective (2014) *A Toxic Culture of Violence and Shame: How DGR's Denial of Transphobia Exposes Worse Tendencies.* Online. Available at: http://earthfirstjournal.org/newswire/2014/02/23/a-toxic-culture-of-violence-and-shame-how-dgrs-denial-of-transphobia-exposes-worse-tendencies/ (accessed 4 September 2015).

Mogul, J. L., Ritchie, A. J. and Withlock, K. (2011) *Queer (In)justice: The Criminalization of LGBT People in the United States.* Boston: Beacon Press.

Mortimer-Sandilands, C. (2005) 'Unnatural passions? Notes toward a queer ecology', *Invisible Culture: An Electronic Journal for Visual Studies*, 9. Visual & Cultural Studies Program, University of Rochester.

Nanda, S. (1999) *Gender Diversity: Crosscultural Variations.* Long Grove, IL: Waveland Press.

Ray, S. J. (2013) *The Ecological Other.* Tucson: University of Arizona Press.

Raymond, J. (1994) *The Transsexual Empire: The Making of the She-Male.* Boston: Beacon Press.

Resistance Portland (2013) *Deep Green Resignation and Reclamation.* Online. Available at: http://earthfirst-journal.org/newswire/2013/05/16/deep-green-reclamation/ (accessed 1 February 2016).

Serano, J. (2009) *Whipping Girl.* Berkeley: Seal Press.

Serano, J. (2012) *Transmisogyny Primer.* Online. Available at: www.juliaserano.com/av/TransmisogynyPrimer-Serano.pdf (accessed 4 September 2015).

Serano, J. (2013) *Excluded.* Berkeley: Seal Press.

Singer, P. (n.d.) *Colonialism, Two-Spirit Identity, and the Logics of White Supremacy.* Online. Available at: www.academia.edu/2259929/Colonialism_Two-Spirit_Identity_and_the_Logics_of_White_Supremacy (accessed 7 September 2015).

Stryker, S. (1994) 'My words to Victor Frankenstein', *GLQ: A Journal of Lesbian and Gay Studies* 1(3): 237–254.

TransWhat? (n.d.) *Misconceptions Debunked.* Online. Available at: http://transwhat.org/debunked (accessed 7 September 2015).

TWAC (n.d.) *About.* Online. Available at: https://twac.wordpress.com/about/ (accessed September 2015).

# 33

# WELCOME TO THE WHITE (M)ANTHROPOCENE?

## A feminist-environmentalist critique

*Giovanna Di Chiro*

### Introduction: vulnerability and resilience in the human age

'Women carry the weight of a falling sky', writes Barbara Kingsolver in *Ms.* magazine, referring to the heavy burden that falls unequally on women's shoulders to respond to the life-threatening risks associated with escalating climate change (2015:43). 'From the Andes to the South Asian tropics to the African Plains', she continues, women from impoverished and vulnerable communities in the Global South rise up to deal with the problems of ever-increasing floods, droughts, food and fuel shortages, and higher rates of infectious diseases and other health crises brought about by warming temperatures and increasingly unpredictable weather (45). Not only are women the first responders, Kingsolver contends, but they are often the first to adapt to climate change 'bringing outsized energy' and creative solutions to mitigate its effects and to build 'resilience' (47).

Researchers focusing on gender, environment, and climate change have long documented the disproportionate 'vulnerability' to environmental disasters that women from around the world face, and how their voices are rarely heard by decision-makers when drafting climate policy or by planners when weighing sustainable development options (Seager and Hartmann 2005; Cuomo 2011; Pelter and Capraro 2015; Arora-Jonsson in this handbook). This feminist-environmentalist critique has influenced international debates on environment and development (e.g., the women in/and development [WID, WAD] and gender and developments [GAD] debates of the 1990s) and has been 'mainstreamed' in the rhetoric of many international institutions, notably in UN conventions and policy statements (Razavi and Miller 1995; Morrow, this volume). At the start of the Beijing+20 meetings in March 2015 in New York City, three internationally known feminist leaders[1] argued that when addressing the world's growing rates of poverty, mitigating the worsening impacts of climate change, and designing and financing effective paths to sustainable development, it is imperative to prioritize human rights and, in particular, women's and gender equality. In planning for the historic COP21 held in December 2015 in Paris, they argued for the importance of listening to and learning from those women who are most directly and negatively impacted by climate change:

> In many homes around the world, women are at the heart of the household's nexus of water, food, and energy – and thus often know firsthand about the challenges and potential solutions in these areas. In our conversations with women around the world,

we hear about their struggles, but also their ideas, many of which, if applied, could facilitate change. Women are the most convincing advocates for the solutions that they need, so they should be at the forefront of decision-making on sustainable development and climate-change mitigation.

*(Robinson et al. 2015)*

While feminist-environmentalists have challenged the 'women as victims' trope in disaster management theory and policy, and rightly point to the importance of 'listening to women's voices' and learning from women's ingenuity and resourcefulness (as in the previous quote), some worry that the other side of the 'victim' stereotype – women as climate 'heroes' – emerges in the recent fixation on climate 'adaptation' and 'resilience' and the championing of the 'green economy' through local eco-entrepreneurialism (Cote and Nightingale 2012; MacGregor 2014; Di Chiro 2015; Harcourt and Nelson 2015). While the 195 parties to the Paris Agreement have promised to address climate mitigation to keep global warming 'to well below 2 degrees Celsius' and, through the Green Climate Fund, to provide what many consider a paltry $100 billion a year in aid to developing countries to implement emissions reduction technologies and to minimize climate change impacts, neither of these promises is legally binding. Eschewing the dream of protecting *Our Common Future* (WCED 1987) through sound international climate policy and well-financed sustainable development, a global, eco-neoliberal agenda has dominated international discussions on climate policy. The responsibility for climate adaptation has devolved to the individual, and the romanticization of 'climate resilience' in the face of disturbance and disruption, especially undertaken by those most vulnerable, including women from the Global South, are the key talking points of the day (Di Chiro 2003; Ribot 2013; Anguelovski et al. 2014). Individual responsibility for climate adaptation is located either at the scale of the individual nation state (determining its own Intended Nationally Determined Contributions [INDCs][2]), the local community (drafting its own 'climate compact' and non-profits creating a 'shadow state' to provide social services), or the individual consumer (eating local, buying green; Gilmore 2009; Klein 2014a; Nightingale 2015).

The recent calls for resilience emanating from the international climate science and policy establishment are embedded in the gendered and racialized power dynamics of global political and economic systems. While women of colour and their children are the primary victims of climate change (and those expected to adapt to its worst impacts), it is (predominantly) white, upper class men who are the primary spokespersons, decision makers, and pontificators in all spheres of climate science, economics, and politics (Hemmati and Röhr 2009; MacGregor 2010; Dankelman 2012; Buckingham, this volume).[3] Despite the mainstreaming of WID, WAD, and GAD in UN contexts, the historic, two-week climate meeting held in Paris offered only one 'high level' plenary panel to commemorate 'Gender Day' (December 8, 2015). Moreover, to the dismay of Ireland's Mary Robinson, one of the keynote speakers on the Gender Day panel, '[the UNFCCC conference] is a very male world. When it is a male world, you have male priorities' (quoted in Harvey 2015). If women from around the world bear 'the weight of a falling sky' and have been active leaders in climate justice movements calling for action on mitigation and adaptation policies, as Mary Robinson laments, then their contributions are largely drowned out by the torrent of 'mansplaining' (Solnit 2012) that dominates mainstream climate science and climate politics.[4]

In recent years, mansplaining has risen to even greater heights with the proposal by an international panel of climate scientists to christen the earth's current geological epoch after *Man* himself, and to rename the present time the *Anthropocene* (the 'Age of Man'). After extensive scientific assessments, the Anthropocene Working Group (82 per cent of whom are men, and the majority from Global North countries)[5] concluded that *Man*kind has become such a dominant force of nature, so drastically depleting and altering earth's systems through *his* high levels of anthropogenic emissions, extractions, and exterminations, that *he* has punted the planet out of the 10,000 years of relative climate stability recently enjoyed in the *Holocene* into a new eponymous epoch. Following in the tracks of the masculinist and colonialist naming practices of Western religion, science, and politics (think Adam, Columbus, and Linneaus), Anthropocene is unsurprisingly self-referential. Taking its place as the latest hegemonic frame reiterating 'genesis, and its endless repetitions' (Haraway 1997:60), the Anthropocene retells the masculinist origin/self-birthing story that inevitably culminates in *Man* as the master creation, the Master of the Universe, and now its destroyer and, possibly, its saviour. Mirroring the race, gender, and class composition of other climate and environmental research and policy arenas, the Anthropocene might more appropriately be coined the *Man*thropocene (Raworth 2014).[6]

## Anthropocene as the new normal: 'Man and Nature' redux

In this chapter, I examine what I consider to be the boundedness and limitations of Anthropocene discourse as a political ecological strategy for the twenty-first century. I argue that the pan-humanism of the concept of Anthropocene reflects and shores up neoliberal, individualist, entrepreneurial forms of 'resilience', which trade on the notion that if 'we' (humans) are *all* to blame for the climate crisis, then *no one* is to blame and, therefore, *no one* is responsible, so we're all left to our own devices to become more resilient. The story of Anthropocene conceals the gendered, racialized, and exploitative global capitalist system that is driving ecological and climatological destruction and destabilizing the relative predictability of the planet's Holocene epoch. Moreover, the preoccupation with Anthropocene as the new human-nature construct reinforces individualistic approaches to environmental and climate responsiveness, which stereotypically casts women in the roles of either vulnerable climate victims or hardy climate heroes. But, as I will argue, the Anthropocene's revival of liberal humanism is not the only contemporary political narrative addressing human responsibility and agency (or lack of it) in the face of climate catastrophe. Refocusing the lenses of accountability for the current climate crisis and how to adapt to it, and engaging very different concepts of 'resilience' and 'common futures', environmental justice and feminist scholars and activists are creating innovative research and action collaborations that are envisioning a more robust perspective of the 'collective we' and putting forward new policies and practices for just, sustainable, and genuinely resilient communities.

## *The hospitality of the Anthropocene: a mixed reception*

As if to invite the UN's 'family of nations' to a gala celebration, the opening event of the 2012 Rio+20 United Nations Conference on Sustainable Development featured the screening of a video entitled: 'Welcome to the Anthropocene'.[7] The three-minute, fast-paced video consists of a screen-size image of the globe superimposed with an uninterrupted succession of the hockey stick-shaped graphs illustrating the 'great acceleration' of human activities in the past 250 years including steadily rising $CO_2$ emissions, tropical forest loss, and population growth. In the soothing tones of a gracious hostess, the British-accented female voiceover in the video invites the audience to reflect on the 'relentless pressure' humanity has inflicted on the planet now that 'we have entered the Anthropocene', yet we can have confidence that 'our creativity, energy, and industry offer hope' to shape our future.[8]

The Rio+20 'welcome to the party' video is upbeat and even celebratory about the human zeal, ingenuity, and progress symbolized by the Anthropocene. The story told in this UN video climaxes with the eco-modernist 'green economy' policy framework promoting both market-based approaches to climate mitigation (e.g., the Clean Development Mechanism), and the advancement of new 'geoengineering' technologies (e.g., carbon dioxide removal or solar radiation management).[9] To date, there are still no binding emissions reductions policies, adaptation strategies, or action plans agreed upon by all UN member states. And, as many have observed, the only step required of parties to the 2015 UNFCCC convention in Paris were the self-determined climate action plans (INDCs) that many critics believe represent the forsaking of a commitment to 'our common future' and a retreat to national sovereignty. According to some environmental analysts, the UN's Anthropocene 'party' has been a big flop (Conca and Dabelko 2014; Jamieson 2014).

Within the academic field of environmental studies, the 'Welcome to the Anthropocene' meme has been deployed, on the one hand, to garner critical academic and political analysis on humanity's role in anthropogenic climate change and, on the other, to mobilize technological optimism about humanity's capacity to fix it. For example, to promote a 'can-do' attitude among academics attending the 2014 annual conference of the Association for Environmental Science and Studies (AESS), in his keynote talk titled 'Paths to a "Good" Anthropocene', science writer Andrew Revkin put a positive spin on the idea of 'The Great Acceleration' of the advance of human civilization, by describing the familiar scientific graphs depicting exponentially rising human population, resource use, and waste as the 'the astonishing pulse of *us!*'[10] Emphasizing the sunny side of the Anthropocene, Revkin's optimism suggests that humans need a strong dose of motivational 'anthropophilia' to get through these tough times. He muses: 'We have to accept ourselves, flaws and all, in order to move beyond what has been something of an *unconscious, species-scale pubescent growth spurt, enabled by fossil fuels in place of testosterone*' (emphasis added; 2011:n.p.).

Revkin's buoyant enthusiasm expresses a kind of (m)Anthropocenic euphoria likening modernity to a hormone-like, carbon dioxide-induced, Big Bang eruption of 'masculinist self-birthing' (Haraway 1992:331).[11] The unconscious sexism in equating the naturalness of human and masculine exceptionalism in the repeated telling of the Story of Man is nothing new, and demonstrates Revkin's obliviousness or unwillingness to engage with decades of feminist-environmentalist and ecofeminist analyses on the topic of the rise of Western modernity and its social and ecological consequences (Merchant 1992/2005; Mies and Shiva 1993/2014; Plumwood 1994). As one of the most recent framings of Universal Man, the construction of the neologism Anthropocene assumes that the Anthropos at the root of the term has no sex, gender, class, or race. Yet in Revkin's talk, the examples of people possessing what he calls the 'human traits' of innovation, resourcefulness, and enthusiasm – those who are developing cutting-edge environmental sustainability projects – are, almost exclusively, white, male, academic, and Euro-American.[12] This plenary lecture at the largest professional association of environmental studies scholars in the United States did not even gesture to the fact that women from around the world disproportionately bear the 'weight of a falling sky', nor that women activists, scientists, and community researchers are diligently innovating and implementing solutions to environmental problems large and small (Harcourt and Escobar 2005; Shiva 2005/2015). Moreover, as ethicist Clive Hamilton (2013) has argued, technological optimists like Revkin de-escalate political urgency to fight climate change by championing individualistic, personal lifestyle, and techno-utopian consumer-based solutions, rather than calling for collective action to challenge the unsustainability of global capitalism. The universal 'we' and 'us' embodied in the species idiom of Anthropocene obscure the extensive scholarship on diverse human histories and resurgent 'naturecultures' (Haraway 1992) that are imagining and producing effective approaches to climate mitigation, adaptation, and sustainability.

A more critical treatment of the 'Welcome to the Anthropocene' motif in the environmental studies context in the United States was exemplified in a 2014 talk by philosopher Ned Hettinger titled 'Age of Man Environmentalism and Respect for an Independent Nature'.[13] In this talk, Hettinger argued that the discourse of the Anthropocene, together with its unapologetic anthropocentrism, 'manifests a culpable failure to appreciate the profound role non-human nature continues to play on Earth and an arrogant overvaluation of human's role and authority'. Worse, it has 'helped spawn "Age of Man Environmentalism" (AME)' by 'downplaying the importance of nature preservation, restoration, and re-wilding and it will have us simply become managers of the earth we have created, promoting ecosystem invention and geo-engineering' (Hettinger 2014:4). As a member of a large group of scholars, writers, and activists concerned about human hegemony and the relentless 'domestication of wild nature' (e.g., Wuerthner et al. 2014), Hettinger criticizes academics and conservationists who have been seduced by the Anthropocene concept, yet in his critique he reproduces the gendered framing of Man and Nature in his nostalgia for a particularly North American variety of environmentalism that *used* to value preservation and the conservation of *real* wilderness and real nature. His Age of 'Man Environmentalism' well describes the gendered, racialized, and dichotomous constructions of nature and society intrinsic to many Western philosophical standpoints, and as ecofeminists, environmental justice scholars, and other critics have shown, such binary thinking lies at the root of the exploitative and unsustainable economies that have brought us to the edge of climate catastrophe in the first place (Merchant 1992/2005; Mies and Shiva 1993/2014; Seager 1993).

Other critics of the ascendance of Anthropocene as the new framing of the relationship of Man and Nature argue that it is the *wrong* word because it doesn't require humans to take responsibility for our reign of terror on the earth. For example, humanities scholar Kathleen Dean Moore writes:

> We are bringing the Holocene Epoch to a dismal end, and we need to face the full horror of what we are doing. We are recklessly destroying the ecological and geophysical conditions under which our lives and the lives of countless other creatures evolved, making us all suddenly maladapted. Even as we doom ourselves, we destroy the prospects of other beings.
>
> *(K. Moore 2013:n.p.)*

More apt descriptions of human impact, Moore continues, might be 'Unforgiveable Crimescene' or the 'Obscene Epoch' to foreground the 'horror of what we are doing'. Keeping with the theme of humanity as villain, referring to the 'poverty of our nomenclature', Eileen Crist argues that the story of the Anthropocene would only be told from the point of view of the victors, not those whom it has killed and displaced, and so the choice of the term makes sense; it secures the silencing of nonhuman others and is the perfect representation of the 'human superiority complex' (2013:133). Anthropocene boosters, Crist writes, use the neutral language of 'change' and not more appropriate words such as 'extirpation' or 'ecocide':

> The vocabulary that we are 'changing the world' – so matter-of-factly portraying itself as impartial and thereby erasing its own normative tracks even as it speaks – secures its ontological ground by silencing the displaced, killed, and enslaved whose homelands have been assimilated and whose lives have, indeed, been changed forever; erased, even.
>
> *(Crist 2013:133)*

While this strong criticism of the takeover, assimilation, and killing of non-human nature by self-aggrandizing and rapacious humans might just as well be describing the history of colonialism and the impoverishment of both humans and nature that unfolded in its aftermath, Crist's rejection of Anthropocene as the 'wrong word' rarely goes there. Crist uses the term 'poverty' in her article as a metaphor to signify the flaws of Anthropocene as a discourse (not about the conditions of hunger and destitution produced by unjust and ecocidal economic policies), and only once refers to the Anthropocene's 'human enterprise' as aggrandizing 'most especially its privileged subgroups' and not all of its members (2013:143). For Crist, Hettinger, and other scholars critical of the human hubris of the Anthropocene, the overly 'humanitarian' fixation on social justice embraced by environmental and climate justice movements becomes untenable.

Crist and her co-editors of the volume *Keeping the Wild* (Wuerthner et al. 2014) dedicated their book to Michael Soulé, one of founders of the field of conservation biology who has long criticized the 'social siege' of nature by the postmodern humanities and social sciences who have apparently conspired together for many years to take over environmental studies (Soulé and Press 1998). Wary of the anthropocentrism embedded in the 'humanitarianism' that has been invading environmental studies programs and nature conservation organizations, in his chapter for Crist's edited volume, Soulé writes:

> How people define 'saving life', 'caring for life', or 'saving the world' is all over the map. In 1989 I discovered, to my dismay, that 95 per cent of my students in the Environmental Studies department at the University of California-Santa Cruz interpreted 'saving the world' to mean kindness directed at under-privileged sections of humanity, whereas I meant saving all of nature with the emphasis on wild creatures. I was depressed for a week.
>
> *(Soulé 2014:69)*

Soulé's 'depression' speaks volumes about the question of *whose* lives are deemed worthy of mattering in charting the Anthropocene's deadly impacts and in recognizing the historical accountabilities and social responsibilities for addressing these problems.

The question of 'whose lives matter' in environmental science and studies arguments that take for granted the universal humanism in the Anthropocene story can be seen clearly in a popular science context: the Pulitzer Prize-winning book *The Sixth Extinction: An Unnatural History* by science and environmental writer Elizabeth Kolbert (2014). Echoing the slogan used in the UN's Rio+20 video discussed previously, Kolbert titled one of her book's chapters 'Welcome to the Anthropocene' (2014:92). Kolbert's riveting investigation chronicles the extensive scientific research documenting the Anthropocene's destructive impacts on the earth's diverse ecosystems, and explains how scientists have drawn the conclusion that humanity is ushering in the 'sixth great extinction' in the planet's history. Kolbert travels the globe touring scientists' research sites to witness the physical imprint of human activities that have brought about mass extinctions of non-human plant and animal species including extinctions that occurred in the distant past – the marine Graptolites in Scotland, the Mastodon in France, and the Great Auk in Iceland – and evidence of species declines in more recent times, such as the die-offs of reef-building corals in Australia's Great Barrier Reef caused by ocean acidification, and the disappearance of golden frogs due to the introduction of invasive species in the rainforests of Panama.

Kolbert's choice of particular human protagonists in her story, once again, epitomizes the demographics of the (m)Anthropocene: the vast majority of scientific experts she visits and writes about on her fact-finding journey are Northern white men. In admiration of the dedication of these scientific researchers, Kolbert describes how their recordings of the Anthropocene's destructive path has often meant working in isolation for years on end, sometimes focusing on the life history of just one particular species living on a remote reef, island, or cave. While the stories of her scientist-protagonists are told in decidedly heroic terms, Kolbert brands the human species as a whole in largely pejorative ones: 'man the killer' (2014:230), 'a weedy species' (266), and humans as genetically hard-wired for serial killing and self-destructiveness. Such murderous tendencies, Kolbert concludes, belies the convenient myth that 'man once lived or ever would live in harmony with nature' (235).

In the final pages of her book, Kolbert laments that humanity's responsibility for having caused the sixth great extinction of life forms on earth 'will, unfortunately, be our most enduring legacy' (269). Her take-home message, or call to action, is that we should be so alarmed by the evidence of human recklessness, that we should wake up and reject anthropocentrism and be more concerned about the survival of the millions of non-human species whose demise 'we' are ensuring. Kolbert ends with the following reflection on the main lesson that should be gleaned from the information brought to light in her book:

> Obviously, the fate of our own species concerns us disproportionately. But at the risk of sounding *anti-human* – some of my best friends are humans! – *I will say, that it is not, in the end, what's most worth attending to.* Right now, in the amazing moment that to *us* counts as the present, *we* are deciding . . . which evolutionary pathways will remain open and which will forever be closed.
>
> *(Kolbert 2014:268–269, emphasis added)*

While it is clear that Kolbert's research on the impacts of the Anthropocene presents a sobering account of the severity of the current environmental crisis, it is important to observe how her use of species discourse functions to foreground the deaths of millions of plants and animals as 'worthy' of our attention (and rightly so), but does so at the expense of seeing the connections between the injustices of such appalling non-human species extinctions and the injustices of the *disproportionate* mortality rates and killings of *particular* groups of human beings. Environmental justice and climate justice scholars have for many years expounded on this connection between the exploitation of non-human nature and the disproportionate impact of environmental depredation on poor communities and communities of colour around the world; that is, the fate of only particular members of our own species appears to 'concern us disproportionately'.

The previous proponents *and* critics of the neologism Anthropocene deploy the species-totalizing discourse of Universal Man. The uncritical use of the universal 'we', as adopted in the 'Welcome to the Anthropocene' meme, ignores the particular human histories that are largely responsible for the ecological and climatological disasters the earth is facing, and it overlooks the vastly unequal social, economic, and environmental conditions in which millions of people presently live. With its vacillation between dire warnings of the human-caused catastrophe on the one hand, or its buoyant excitement about the planet-wide powers and breathtaking gifts the human species possesses enabling it to rise to meet this new challenge on the other, the (m)Anthropocene does not account for the diversity of human presence on earth. Anthropocene ecopolitics, often mired in defeatism and denial, engenders an apocalyptic, '*post*-political condition', where democratic debate, public policy-making, and collective action is replaced by technocratic administration or individual lifestyle change (MacGregor 2014:618). The urgency to curtail the 'destructiveness of the human species' can lead to a resurgence of *anti*-humanism, which surfaces in renowned ecologist E.O. Wilson's book *Half Earth* (2016), where he proposes that the world's leaders must set aside half the planet for conservation and wilderness reserves and forcibly relocate the majority of the (impoverished) human population into managed and controlled urban spaces (for a review, see Fletcher and Büscher 2016). The Anthropocene seamlessly morphs into the *Mis*Anthropocene (Patel 2013).[14]

But, for whom is the new Anthropocene narrative (and its Mis-anthropocenic tendencies) politically mobilizing? Residents of environmental justice communities from around the world, predominantly low-income people of colour in the industrialized Global North and impoverished communities from Global South nations, are deeply concerned about unequal exposure to polluted air and water, resource and species destruction, rising sea levels, and unpredictable and extreme weather brought about by climate change. Yet, members of these populations, who face the severest impacts of climate change (and who Wilson would herd into urban centres), would be disinclined to become politically energized either by Wilson's *Half Earth* proposal, by Soulé's anti-humanism, or by Kolbert's suggestion that addressing the survival of human beings is not the issue most 'worthy' of our attention in this moment of ecological apocalypse. For many US environmental justice activists, many of whom are women leaders in the Black Lives Matter movement fighting against the disproportionate 'herding' and incarceration rates and premature deaths from unequal toxic exposures faced by Black communities (discussed further later on), the Anthropocene looks and sounds like a familiar story: a resurgence of environmental racism and eco-colonialism by another name. Welcome to the *WhiteMan*thropocene?

## Minding the social and environmental justice gap

Environmental justice (EJ) research has well documented that it is poor communities and communities of colour around the world who have borne the brunt of modernity's 'Great Acceleration' while reaping few of the rewards (Faber 2008; Steady 2009; Taylor 2014). Telling the story of environmental decline and catastrophe very differently, EJ (and, more recently, climate justice) scholars and activists foreground the deep history of environmental racism when analyzing the *disproportionate* impact of the history of fossil-fuel driven, modern industrial development (Martinez-Alier 2004; Carmin and Agyeman 2011; Di Chiro 2013; Schlosberg and Collins 2014). The critiques of the human hubris and anthropocentrism embedded in Anthropocene discourse point to the imperative to recognize the anthropogenic devastation wrought on the non-human world, but by not recognizing the deeper history of colonialism, often fail to address the persistent dehumanization, racism, sexism, homo/transphobia, eugenics, and other social injustices experienced by human groups who are still not 'welcomed' as fully human (Escobar 1994/2011; Ray 2013). Recognizing these shortcomings of Anthropocene and its limited capacity to generate the collective 'we' necessary to mobilize the political force to address anthropogenic climate change, some authors choose either not to use the term or to make it do different kinds of ideological and political work (Gibson-Graham 2011; Malm and Hornborg 2014; Haraway 2015).

Drawing on feminist political ecology and feminist science studies, Donna Haraway maintains that the Anthropocene story, which favours either 'game over' climate politics or 'geoengineers to the rescue' plot lines, leads not to better stories imagining 'more livable presents and more livable futures', but often instead to despair and denial (2014:n.p.). Arguing in support of a 'regenerative', joyful, and clear-eyed eco-politics, Haraway states: 'We need stories that are non-despairing, non-cynical, non-defeatist, and not in denial about the possibilities of flourishing on a damaged planet' (2014:n.p.). If we need a 'big story' to demarcate the earth's current predicament, Haraway considers the more historically accurate 'Capitalocene' or the related 'Plantationocene'[15] – the era in which an assemblage of political, cultural, economic, scientific, and technological apparatuses fuelled by fossil energy and hetero-patriarchal colonialist ambitions becomes consumed with 'making more fossils as fast as possible'.[16] For Haraway, however, the Anthropos-centrism in the stories of Anthropocene and Capitalocene makes both insufficient, too readily lending themselves to 'cynicism, defeatism, and self-certain and self-fulfilling predictions, like "game over, too late" discourse'. She supports instead the crafting of a new name: *Chthulucene* ('after the diverse earth-wide tentacular powers and forces'; the intercultural, genderqueer, human-nonhuman entities with names such as Naga, Gaia, Terra, Spider Woman, Pachamama, and many others) for our current time (Haraway 2015, 2016). Rather than re-centering 'Man' in earth's story ('humans have never acted alone'), Haraway calls instead for the flourishing of collaborative, intra-active stories of *sympoiesis* (together-making) peopled by diverse human and non-human players cultivating anti-genocidal multispecies assemblages taking responsibility for 'ongoingness' on a damaged planet.

### Flourishing communities matter: rethinking resilience, leaping forward (not bouncing back)

The 'politics of naming' in the current era of climate crisis grapples with the questions of who 'we' are at this moment in earth's and human's history and who 'we' want to be as 'we' imagine possible futures. As I have argued previously, the trending Anthropocene concept burst onto the scene as one of the most visible naming projects in the early twenty-first century. While most debates about the term tend to take at face value the scientific claims of the advent of the Anthropocene and accept the universal humanism embedded in the mainstream analyses of anthropogenic climate change, some scholars and environmental analysts have challenged its pan-species assumption and have pointed out that not all humans are equally responsible for climate change nor do all suffer the consequences equally. Moreover, the Anthropocene Working Group's proposal to rename the earth's current geological epoch after *ourselves* largely remains an academic exercise in Euro-Australo-North American climate conversations and has not gained traction in the world of environmental justice and climate justice politics. This would seem a problem, since EJ communities are the most directly harmed by the severe disturbances of climate change, and women are those at the frontlines of disaster response. As Barbara Kingsolver contends, 'The developed world could learn from the resilience of women', as well as from the 'ready sacrifices they make for the health of their land and a more secure future' (2015:47). With current debates about climate policy mired in the white (m)Anthropocene, environmental and climate justice leaders (the majority of whom are women of colour) are building innovative and proactive discourses that go by the names of 'just resilience', 'just sustainability', and 'just transition', highlighting the voices and experiences of those communities around the world who know what it means to engage in 'ongoingness'. In the remaining sections of this chapter I examine examples, largely from US-based contexts, of resurgent eco-politics that are integrating, not dichotomizing, humans and their environments in this moment of ecological deterioration and climate instability.

### Environmental human rights

Using an intersectional environmental approach to creating climate solutions, members of environmental justice and climate justice communities 'affirm the sacredness of Mother Earth, ecological unity, and interdependence of all species' (Principles of Environmental Justice 1991), while at the same time advocate for an *environmental human rights* perspective as the most effective responses to a damaged planet and runaway climate change. This multidimensional approach to theorizing and organizing for environmental and climate justice resonates with and grows out of women of colour and post-colonial feminist analyses of 'intersectionality': the critical focus on how structures and relationships of power are organized through the interlocking institutional, cultural, and ideological systems of gender, race, class, sexuality, ability, age, among other categories of difference (e.g., Cho et al. 2013; Kaijser and Kronsell 2014). Insisting on seeing the connections between environmental integrity *and* human well-being and the dignity of marginalized populations, EJ activists and scholars generate a potent intersectional analysis that is rare in the dominant climate science and policy framework. For members of these communities, many facing the ongoing brutality of racism, colonialism, and environmental injustices, and whose claims to full humanity and human rights are still not guaranteed, the pan-humanism or anti-humanism of the Anthropocene's narrative of the universal 'we' just doesn't make historical or political sense (Di Chiro 2008).

For example, in Harlem, New York, the well-established EJ organization West Harlem Environmental Action (WEACT) strongly criticizes the paradigm of domination and environmental injustice underlying the US history of progress and manifest destiny, which has left a legacy of toxic environments and poor health in communities of colour and low-income communities and has contributed to the current global warming crisis. A leader in the climate justice movement in the US, WEACT sees the connections between its EJ work in New York City and the activist histories of abolitionism, anti-colonial struggle, civil rights activism, and the founding of the Black Lives Matter movement as a 'new civil rights movement' in 2012 (Tillet 2015). Grounded in the eco-politics of intersectional environmentalism, WEACT aims to build solidarity and diverse collaborations enabling ongoingness, resiliency, and sustainable futures for African American communities and for all marginalized communities who have been disproportionately affected by and excluded from decision-making on environmental and climate policies in the United States and around the globe (Shepard and Corbin-Mark 2009).

Criticizing the normalized demographics of scientists, academics, and government agencies focusing on climate issues, WEACT's climate justice policy analyst Jalonne White-Newsome argues, 'when you're in a room with environmentalists or the Environmental Protection Agency (EPA) talking about climate or energy policy and you don't see any faces of colour, then you should know that that conversation is incomplete'.[17] To address the cumulative effects of living in a polluted environment now made worse by climate change, White-Newsome and WEACT simultaneously develop strategies for climate mitigation, adaptation, and community resilience. This includes designing proactive climate policies with diverse community organizations and local and national governments to support locally generated, renewable energy initiatives and to enhance civic engagement for the meaningful participation of EJ communities to shape strategies for climate mitigation and adaptation.

Quite the opposite of the anti-humanist slant of the Anthropocene story, White-Newsome's EJ perspective maintains that 'working together to achieve climate justice for *those most marginalized will provide climate benefits for all*'.[18] Responses to climate chaos must 'mind the EJ gap' as she puts it, and in collaboration with EJ communities most directly harmed, must develop participatory and scientifically sound solutions to sustainability.

## *People-powered living economies*

Refusing the apocalyptic and misanthropic rhetoric inclined toward cynicism and angst, climate justice advocates like White-Newsome are taking action to push for policies to reduce the fossil fuel–based pollution that both creates global warming and endangers human health. At the same time, they are building partnerships for 'integral development'[19] (collective human rights to livelihood integrated with the rights of Mother Earth) to create a 'just transition' toward climate-friendly economies and thriving, resilient communities around the world. Representing new idioms of *possibilism*, these proactive solutions originate from those communities least responsible and most directly impacted by climate change. For example, the New York City

Environmental Justice Alliance (NYC-EJA), a network of city-based EJ organizations, and United Puerto Ricans' Organization of Sunset Park (UPROSE), a multi-racial, intergenerational EJ organization in Brooklyn, are leading the community-based 'mitigation, adaptation, and resilience' efforts in this mega-city. Eddie Bautista, NYC-EJA's executive director, argues, however, that the conventional understanding of the concept of resilience as the ability to 'bounce back' after a disturbance must be reframed to take into account the history of environmental injustices. This commonly understood definition of resilience, he argues, 'presupposes that the status quo is the preferred state of being'. But, he continues, 'we don't want to bounce back to an inequitable system that's choking us. Poverty is resilient. We don't want to bounce back. We want to leap forward'.[20]

In the aftermath of the flooding of New York City's lower boroughs in 2012 from Super Storm Sandy, in the spirit of 'leaping forward', NYC-EJA and UPROSE established the Climate Justice Community Resiliency Center, the city's first community-led planning project dedicated to 'just adaptation' and community resiliency, and they organize an annual Youth Climate Justice conference teaching young people how to take action on climate change.[21] Comparable with the demographic profile of populations who are endangered by climate-fuelled crises like Super Storm Sandy, residents in this global city who are most at risk are low-income women of colour, children, and the elderly. The youth leaders of NYC-EJA and UPROSE who are on the frontlines of the climate resiliency initiative argue that the rising climate justice movement will not be '*pale, male, and stale*' (Adler 2014). These environmental/climate justice initiatives illustrate the spirit of 'enlightened anthropocentrism' (Chakrabarty 2013): regenerative people power, not human hubris.

Also focusing on regenerative eco-politics, and grounding their climate activism in the 'collective continuance' of their communities and the 'systems of responsibilities' they assume as members of diverse indigenous (First Nations and Native American) groups, many indigenous women activists see themselves as 'enablers of adaptation and mitigation efforts' (Powys-Whyte 2014:600). In contrast to the Anthropocene's labelling humans as the controllers and tormentors of non-human nature, indigenous theories of the interdependence of humans and the environment produce structures of organization integrating 'political, societal, cultural, religious, and familial institutions that tie together humans and multiple living, non-living, and spiritual beings, and natural interdependent collectives, including forested areas, species habitats, and water cycles' (Powys-Whyte 2014:601).

Diverse coalitions of indigenous activists directly challenge the 'false solutions to destroy the Earth's balance, assassinate the seasons, unleash severe weather havoc, privatize life and threaten the very survival of humanity' (Kari-Oca Declaration 2012)[22] and engage in ecologically sustainable practices of 'embodied resilience' (Lewallen 2014). For example, regenerative political alliances among young EJ activists and indigenous communities across the Americas have emerged to fight the extraction of shale gas and oil on indigenous lands and to demand that institutions of higher education divest their financial endowments from fossil fuel stocks and re-invest in a renewable economy (Grady-Benson and Sarathy 2015).[23]

A new generation of young women indigenous leaders catalyzed the Idle No More movement in late 2012 to contest the Canadian government's passing of legislation that would further undercut indigenous land and water rights, weakening their access to traditional livelihoods and their rights to self-determination. Idle No More activists including Crystal Lameman (Beaver Lake Cree), Leanne Betasamosake Simpson (Mississauga Nishnaabeg), and Eriel Tchekwie Deranger (Athabasca Chipewyan) forcefully critique the climate-destroying, exploitative, and extractivist mind-set of modern, industrial society, yet they do not explain this as a problem of humans vs. nature. Resisting the hetero-patriarchal, genocidal, and ecocidal industrial worldview that lies at the heart of settler colonialism, and that has largely created the climate crisis, Lameman's, Simpson's, and Deranger's activism expresses the interconnectedness of naturecultures and conceptualizes an eco-politics grounded in multi-species relationality, what some have referred to as cosmo-vision (LaDuke 1999; Walsh 2011). In her book *Dancing on Our Turtle's Backs* (2011), Simpson tells stories of resistance, flourishing, and resurgence in the face of the ongoing havoc of settler colonialism visited upon First Nations and indigenous communities by the Canadian and US governments and corporations in the current era of social, ecological, and climatological chaos. She relates Nishnaabeg stories told to her by her grandmother and other elders about life and responsibility to all earth's creatures and about the value of reciprocity among all 'relations' who participate in the community. Fighting against tar sands development in First Nations' territories in Canada, Deranger argues that

> Colonization came with the imposition of patriarchy. The real power of our communities came from our women as we were matriarchal societies. Our women today are reclaiming our roles as leaders of our community, as part of this resurgence of our people, not just in the climate movement but in all of the different movements to reclaim our health, sacred lands, and indigeneity.
>
> *(quoted in Chitnis 2016:n.p.)*

The '*inhuman humanism*' (Luciano 2015) of the Anthropocene (or, more aptly, the *WhiteManthro*pocene) control narrative cannot account for these human stories of relationality, responsibility, and collective continuance (Simpson 2011).

'Organizing for resilience' in frontline communities, the Climate Justice Alliance (CJA) and the Movement Generation (MG) Justice and Ecology Project, leaders of a wide network of environmental and climate justice organizations headquartered in the United States, created the 'Our Power' campaign in 2013 to forge a 'just transition away from unsustainable energy toward more resilient, equitable and living economies to address the root causes of climate change'.[24] Launching the 'Summer of Our Power' in 2015 'in recognition of our interrelated, interdependent, and complementary relationship with Mother Earth', the CJA and MG aimed to build the local capacity of environmental and climate justice groups to mobilize globally 'on the road to Paris' and beyond. The alliance organizes conferences and workshops focused on developing equitable and sustainable approaches to regional food systems, public transportation, community-generated renewable energy, zero waste, affordable and durable housing, cultural revival, and ecosystem restoration and stewardship. Imagining the possibility of 'building the bigger *we*' by creating multi-racial, multi-class, and transnational coalitions for climate justice and respect for the rights of Mother Earth/ Pachamama, the Our Power movement[25] responds to the present and future realities of global climate change not with cynicism or the arrogance of the Earthmasters (Hamilton 2013), but with active hopefulness for a just transition toward living economies for all.[26]

## Conclusion: sustainability for all

As I discussed previously, the 'pale, male, and stale' attributes of mainstream environmental and climate organizations have been challenged for decades by a host of environmental justice advocates, ecofeminists, and Global South scholars and activists. Yet, just at the moment when activists and researchers from environmental justice and feminist movements have raised public awareness around the world that it is poor and marginalized women who 'carry the weight of the falling sky', the proponents of the climate consensus have come up with the Anthropocene: we're *all* to blame and we *all* must mend our ways and become resilient. Feminists of all races, genders, sexualities, and ethnicities recognize this familiar manoeuvre of those in power to profess 'collectivity' as a tactic to deflect historical accountability and 'differentiated' responsibilities, in this case, for climate change. As many Global South critics have argued, not all passengers inhabiting 'Spaceship Earth' enjoy equal conditions for eking out a life (de Araujo Castro 1998). In the United States, the painful reality of *unequal* opportunities for life, liberty, and the pursuit of happiness, and the *disparate* risks of death experienced by African Americans has come to the fore with the rise of the Black Lives Matter (BLM) movement. First organized in 2012 as a social media hashtag (#BlackLivesMatter) by a group of young, queer, Black women in response to the acquittal of the killer of unarmed seventeen-year-old boy Trayvon Martin, the movement has grown rapidly to become one of the most important forces organizing against police violence and *differential* extermination of people of colour in the country. One of the organizers, Alicia Garza, explains the political inspiration behind her co-founding the movement:

> Black Lives Matter is an ideological and political intervention in a world where Black lives are systematically and intentionally targeted for demise. It is an affirmation of Black folks' contributions to this society, *our humanity, and our resilience in the face of deadly oppression.*
> *(Garza 2014:n.p.)*[27]

The central purpose of the #BLM social media action was to compel the public to focus for at least a moment on the specificities of anti-Black racism in the United States and its legacy of killing Black bodies in astonishingly high rates, but it was not long until the hashtag stirred up opposition (Taylor 2016). Refusing to accept the #BLM's highlighting the precariousness of Black life, a segment of the twittersphere and a handful of public officials countered with the rebuttal '*all lives matter*'. The neutral, universal humanism of 'all lives matter' refuses to see that not all lives are understood to be *worthy of mattering*, 'which is precisely why it is most important to name the lives that have not mattered, and are struggling to matter in the way they deserve' (Butler and Yancy 2015). In fact, many activists in the BLM movement have powerfully deployed the environmentalists' language of extinction, and argue that they consider themselves to be *endangered species*. The versions of universal humanism embedded in the white (m)Anthropocene meme and the 'all lives matter' retort to the BLM movement deflect attention (and responsibility) from the root causes of social and environmental injustices and from the recognition of their differential impacts.

Together with more than fifty organizations representing thousands of Black people, in 2016 members of the BLM drafted a policy platform supporting the broader Movement for Black Lives (M4BL), addressing issues concerning the lives of Black people in North America and globally. While not explicitly emphasizing 'environmental' or 'climate' issues as elements contributing to the targeted demise of Black lives, the BLM and the M4BL policy platform focus on investment in education, health, and safety of Black lives, including investing in renewable energy, and divestment from exploitative forces such as prisons, police violence, and fossil fuels.[28] The BLM and the newly formed M4BL have significantly influenced the emergence of a stronger intersectional analysis on climate justice in the United States and is expanding internationally (cf., Klein 2014c; Mock 2014; Smith 2014). Well known for her critiques of the 'shock doctrine' underlying global capitalism, Naomi Klein (who acknowledges that she came late to the climate conversation) recently published a book, *This Changes Everything: Capitalism vs. the Climate* (2014b), and a documentary film based on the book, that incisively analyzes the connections between the human rights objectives of both the BLM and climate justice movements. She writes:

> Thinly veiled notions of racial superiority have informed every aspect of the non-response to climate change so far. Racism is what has made it possible to systematically

look away from the climate threat for more than two decades. It is also what has allowed the worst health impacts of digging up, processing and burning fossil fuels – from cancer clusters to asthma – to be systematically dumped on indigenous communities and on the neighborhoods where people of colour live, work and play. The South Bronx, to cite just one example, has notoriously high asthma rates – and according to one study, a staggering 21.8 per cent of children living in New York City public housing have asthma, three times higher than the rate for private housing. The choking of those children is not as immediately lethal as the kind of choking that stole Eric Garner's life, but it is very real nonetheless.

*(Klein 2014c:n.p.)*

As discussed previously, African American communities in the United States are more likely to exist in regions that have been and will continue to be most negatively impacted by climate change, and Black women, men, and youth have been on the frontlines of the environmental and climate justice movements (Taylor 2014). A commitment to climate policies and international climate mobilization on the basis that Black lives matter would demand hopeful and effective technological and economic innovations and investments in the most 'vulnerable' parts of the world (from Nairobi, to Ferguson, to Port-au-Prince), and as WEACT's Jalonne White-Newsome argued previously, it would provide climate benefits for *all*, including all human, non-human, biotic, and abiotic components of our earth.

As leaders of the intersectional Our Power climate justice movement proclaim, their communities' lives *matter*. Furthermore, they are working to achieve climate justice by focusing attention on those lives that have not been deemed worthy of mattering and are building movements for climate resilience and a just transition to sustainable societies with the goal of creating 'sustainability for *all*'. Not a retreat to the façade of Anthropocenic universalism, to the individualism of green consumerism, or to the techno-fixes of the green economy, this concept of 'green for all' aims to tell a story and develop practices of *collective* continuance (Powys-Whyte 2014) in support of just and flourishing communities. The generativity of the strategies to reduce emissions and build community-based just sustainability initiatives proposed by many women activists, EJ organizers, and indigenous leaders from around the world, including

- innovations in small-scale agriculture and agro-forestry;
- decentralized, community-controlled renewable energy;
- anti-gentrification urban greening initiatives;
- community-based flood management and water catchment systems;
- free public transportation and health care; and
- indigenous land rights and cultural heritage contesting fossil fuel extraction and promoting living economies;

cannot be embodied in the gendered, racialized, and ethnocentric environmental politics of the Anthropocene.

## Notes

1 These three women are Mary Robinson, UN Secretary General Special Envoy on Climate Change; Christiana Figueres, then Executive Secretary of UN Framework Convention on Climate Change (UNFCCC); and Amina Mohammed, UN Secretary General Special Advisor on Post-2015 Development Planning).

2 Intended Nationally Determined Contributions (INDCs) are post-2020 carbon-mitigation and adaptation action plans that parties to the convention of the UNFCCC were required to submit in advance of the Paris meetings in December 2015.

3 Sexism and the impunity of male dominance in the international climate establishment was made manifest in February 2015 when Rajendra Pachauri, the longtime chair of the Intergovernmental Panel on Climate Change (IPCC), resigned from his position after a sexual harassment suit was filed against him by a female employee working at his research institute, The Energy and Resources Institute, in Delhi. See http://grist.org/news/ipcc-chief-pachauri-resigns-over-sexual-harassment-charges/.

4 The already minimal statements on gender equality that had appeared in earlier UNFCCC outcome documents and that had been bracketed or all but removed in the outcome document at COP-20 in Lima, would remain in brackets in the final text of the Paris Agreement. The concern for gender equality in supporting climate responsive policies for mitigation and adaptation also remains vague and non-committal: under the agreement, industrialized, Annex I countries are not held liable for global warming and will not pay any loss and damage compensation to those who are the victims of climate change, a disallowance that the Women and Gender Constituency (WGC) of the UNFCCC argues will drive greater numbers of people living in countries most vulnerable to climate change, particularly women, into poverty (WGC 2015; Paul 2016).

5 According to the Subcommission on Quaternary Stratigraphy, http://quaternary.stratigraphy.org/workinggroups/anthropocene/ (accessed 4 February 16).

6 On 29 August 2016, the Anthropocene Working Group announced that the thirty-five-member panel had unanimously agreed that the Anthropocene – the new geological epoch dominated by the human species – was determined to have begun in 1950. See 'The Anthropocene is here: scientists', 29 August 2016, http://phys.org/news/2016–08-anthropocene-scientists.html (accessed 3 September 2016).

7 The video was produced by the International Geosphere-Biosphere Programme (IGBP). Available at: www.anthropocene.info/en/home.

8 'Welcome to the Anthropocene' (www.anthropocene.info/en/home).

9 The 'eco-modernist' approach to climate change is well represented by Ted Nordhaus and Richard Shellenberger (2015) and the organization they founded called the Breakthrough Institute, http://thebreakthrough.org/.

10 Available at www.youtube.com/watch?v=VOtj3mskx5k.

11 Revkin is not alone in using bio-chemical metaphors to discuss climate change and to posit hormonal and essentialist explanations for human male delusions of grandeur. References to the 'climate on steroids' (Sierra Club, Environmental Defense Fund) and media headlines like 'Juiced by Climate Change: Extreme Weather On Steroids' (Climate Progress) and 'Carbon Doping: Hurricane Sandy is Climate on Steroids' (Friends of the Earth) are used liberally by mainstream environmental organizations.

12 Similar upbeat enthusiasm about the human awesomeness and imagination that can be redirected to address climate change that also seems to be the exclusive domain of the white males of the species can be found in Diane Ackerman's book, *The Human Age: The World Shaped by Us* (2014). Ackerman is likewise beguiled by naming the current age the Anthropocene after 'us' because 'it highlights the enormity of our impact on the world. We are dreamsmiths and wonder-workers. What a marvel we've become, a species with planetwide powers and breathtaking gifts. That's a feat to recognize and celebrate. It should fill us with pride and astonishment' (308).

13 Keynote lecture delivered by Ned Hettinger at the annual conference of the International Society of Environmental Ethics (ISEE). Highlands Retreat Center, Allenspark, Colorado, June 9–12, 2014.

14 Due to limitations of space and the focus of my analysis, I do not take up the field of feminist 'critical posthumanism' in this article. The critiques of the Anthropocene levied by scholars such as Alaimo (2010), Braidotti (2013), and Åsberg (2014) raise important analyses about the problems with liberal humanism and concentrate on the anthropocentrism in the Anthropocene's reassertion of the human-nonhuman boundary.

15 In a commentary published in *Environmental Humanities*, Haraway credits Jason Moore (2013) as having first coined the term Capitalocene, and Scott Gilbert as proposing the Plantationocene (Haraway 2015). Anna Tsing's *The Mushroom at the End of the World* (2015) also builds on an analysis of Anthropocene as being driven by the history of the political economy of the plantation system.

16 Also pointing to the culture of capitalism as the root of the problem, Jussi Parikka titles his book '*The Anthrobscene*' to 'index the profound wastefulness of contemporary capitalism' (Parikka 2015:6).

17 'Climate Justice and Environmental Justice: Honoring the Past, Looking Toward the Future', Washington, D.C., 26 February 2014. www.epa.gov/environmentaljustice/events/20th-anniversary.html.

18  'Climate Justice and Environmental Justice: Honoring the Past, Looking Toward the Future'.
19  In Bolivia and Ecuador 'integral development' is embodied in the concept '*buen vivir*' ('living well' or 'collective well-being'). See Gudynas (2011).
20  Interview with Eddie Bautista, *City Atlas New York*, http://newyork.thecityatlas.org/people/eddie-bautista/.
21  Climate Justice Community Resiliency Center, http://uprose.org/?page_id=1547.
22  'Kari-Oca 2 Declaration'. Indigenous Environmental Network, 21 June 2012. www.ienearth.org/kari-oca-2-declaration.
23  Fossil Fuel Divestment Student Network, http://studentsdivest.org/.
24  Climate Justice Alliance, www.ourpowercampaign.org/cja/.
25  Our Power Convening, 6–9 August 2014, https://storify.com/OurPower/richmond2014.
26  Examples of dynamic, climate justice political assemblages include: Movement Generation Justice and Ecology Project (http://movementgeneration.org/), *buen vivir* (Gudynas 2011), living economies/community economies (J. K. Gibson-Graham et al. 2013; Shiva 2005/2015), 'green for all' (www.greenforall.org/), 'Earthseed and the Black Permaculture Network (http://earthseedconsulting.com/).
27  Despite the 'herstory' of the #BLM movement, many Black women activists have pointed out that the media attention has often focused on Black men as the targets and victims of extrajudicial violence and killing (Winfrey Harris 2015). Using the taglines, #SayHerName and 'Black Women's Lives Matter' too, activists and scholars have demanded greater visibility of women's experiences and awareness of their contributions to this 'new civil rights movement' (Tillet 2015).
28  The Movement for Black Lives Platform, https://policy.m4bl.org/invest-divest/ (accessed 3 September 2016).

# References

Ackerman, D. (2014) *The Human Age: The World Shaped by Us.* New York: W. W. Norton.
Adler, B. (2014) 'At this year's big climate rally, most of the people won't be pale, male, and stale', *Grist*. Online. Available at: http://grist.org/climate-energy/at-this-years-big-climate-rally-most-of-the-people-wont-be-pale-and-male-and-stale/ (accessed 15 May 2016).
Alaimo, S. (2010) *Bodily Natures: Science, Environment, and the Material Self.* Bloomington, IN: Indiana University Press.
Anguelovski, I., Chu, E. and Carmin, J. (2014) 'Variations in approaches to urban climate adaptation: Experiences and experimentation from the global South', *Global Environmental Change* 27: 156–167.
Araujo Castro, de J. A. (1998) 'Environment and development: The case of developing countries', in Conca, K. and Dabelko, G. D. (eds) *Green Planet Blues: Environmental Politics From Stockholm to Rio* (second edition). Boulder, CO: Westview Press, 30–38.
Åsberg, C. (2014) 'Resilience is cyborg: Feminist clues to the post disciplinary environmental humanities of critique and creativity', *Resilience: Journal of Environmental Humanities* 1: 5–7.
Braidotti, R. (2013) *The Posthuman.* Cambridge, UK: Polity.
Butler, J. and Yancy, G. (2015) 'What's wrong with "all lives matter?"', *New York Times*. Online. Available at: http://opinionator.blogs.nytimes.com/2015/01/12/whats-wrong-with-all-lives-matter/?_r=0 (accessed 15 May 2016).
Carmin, J. and Agyeman, J. (eds) (2011) *Environmental Inequalities Beyond Borders: Local Perspectives and Global Injustices.* Cambridge, MA: MIT Press.
Chakrabarty, D. (2013) 'History on an expanded canvas: The Anthropocene's invitation', *Keynote Address*. Online. Available at: www.youtube.com/watch?v=svgqLPFpaOg or www.hkw.de/en/programm/projekte/2014/anthropozaen/anthropozaen_2013_2014.php (accessed 15 May 2016).
Chitnis, R. (2016) 'How women-led movements are redefining power, from California to Nepal', *Yes! Magazine*. Online. Available at: www.yesmagazine.org/people-power/how-women-led-movements-are-redefining-power-from-california-to-nepal-20160308 (accessed 15 May 2016).
Cho, S., Crenshaw, K. W. and McCall, L. (2013) 'Toward a field of intersectionality studies: Theory, applications, and praxis', *Signs* 38(4): 785–810.
Conca, K. and Dabelko, G. (2014) *Green Planet Blues: Critical Perspectives on Global Environmental Politics.* Boulder, CO: Westview Press.
Cote, M. and Nightingale, A. (2012) 'Resilience thinking meets social theory: Situating change in socio-ecological systems research', *Progress in Human Geography* 36(4): 475–489.

Crist, E. (2013) 'On the poverty of our nomenclature', *Environmental Humanities* 3: 129–147.

Cuomo, C. (2011) 'Climate change, vulnerability, and responsibility', *Hypatia* 26(4): 690–714.

Dankelman, I. (ed) (2012) *Gender and Climate Change: An Introduction.* New York: Routledge.

Di Chiro, G. (2003) 'Beyond ecoliberal "common futures": Toxic touring, environmental justice, and a transcommunal politics of place', in Moore, D., Kosek, J. and Pandian, A. (eds) *Race, Nature, and the Politics of Difference.* Chapel Hill: Duke University Press, 204–232.

Di Chiro, G. (2008) 'Living environmentalisms: Coalition politics, social reproduction, and environmental justice', *Environmental Politics* 17(1): 276–298.

Di Chiro, G. (2013) 'Climate justice now! Imagining grassroots ecocosmopolitanism', in Adamson, J. and Ruffin, K. (eds) *American Studies, Ecocriticism, and Citizenship.* New York: Routledge, 204–219.

Di Chiro, G. (2015) 'Environmental justice and the Anthropocene meme', in Gabrielson, T., Hall, C., Meyer, J. M. and Schlosberg, D. (eds) *Oxford Handbook on Environmental Political Theory.* New York: Oxford University Press, 362–381.

Escobar, A. (1994/2011) *Encountering Development: The Making and Unmaking of the Third World.* Princeton: Princeton University Press.

Faber, D. (2008) *Capitalizing on Environmental Injustice: The Polluter-Industrial Complex in the Age of Globalization.* Lanham, MD: Rowman and Littlefield Publishers.

Fletcher, R. and Büscher, B. (2016) 'Why E. O. Wilson is wrong about how to save the Earth', *Aeon.* Online. Available at: https://aeon.co/opinions/why-e-o-wilson-is-wrong-about-how-to-save-the-earth (accessed 15 May 2016).

Garza, A. (2014) 'A Herstory of the #BlackLivesMatter Movement', *Feminist Wire*, October 7. Online. Available at: www.thefeministwire.com/2014/10/blacklivesmatter-2/ (accessed 15 May 2015).

Gibson-Graham, J. K. (2011) 'A feminist project of belonging for the Anthropocene', *Gender, Place and Culture* 18(1): 1–21.

Gibson-Graham, J. K., Cameron, J. and Healy, S. (2013) *Take Back the Economy.* Minneapolis: University of Minnesota Press.

Gilmore, R. W. (2009) 'In the shadow of the shadow state', in Incite: Women of Colour Against Violence (ed) *The Revolution Will Not Be Funded: Beyond the Non-Profit Industrial Complex.* Cambridge, MA: South End Press, 41–52.

Grady-Benson, J. and Sarathy, B. (2015) 'Fossil fuel divestment in US higher education: Student-led organizing for climate justice', *Local Environment* 21(6): 661–668. http://dx.doi.org/10.1080/13549839.2015.1009825.

Gudynas, E. (2011) 'Buen vivir: Today's tomorrow', *Development* 54(4): 441–447.

Hamilton, C. (2013) *Earthmasters: The Dawn of the Age of Climate Engineering.* New Haven: Yale University Press.

Haraway, D. (1992) 'The promises of monsters: A regenerative politics for inappropriate/d others', in Grossberg, L., Nelson, C. and Treichler, P. (eds) *Cultural Studies.* New York: Routledge, 295–337.

Haraway, D. (1997) *Modest_Witness@Second_Millennium.FemaleMan©_ Meets_OncoMouse™: Feminism and Technoscience.* New York: Routledge.

Haraway, D. (2014) 'Anthropocene, Capitalocene, Chthulucene: Staying with the trouble', Anthropocene: Arts of Living on a Damaged Planet Conference, UC Santa Cruz. Online. Available at: http://vimeo.com/97663518 (accessed 15 May 2016).

Haraway, D. (2015) 'Anthropocene, Capitalocene, Plantationocene, Chthulucene: Making kin', *Environmental Humanities* 6: 159–165. Online. Available at: http://environmentalhumanities.org/arch/vol6/6.7.pdf (accessed 15 May 2016).

Haraway, D. (2016) *Staying With the Trouble: Making Kin in the Chthulucene.* Durham, NC: Duke University Press.

Harcourt, W. and Escobar, A. (eds) (2005) *Women and the Politics of Place.* West Hartford, CT: Kumarian Press.

Harcourt, W. and Nelson, I. (eds) (2015) *Practising Feminist Political Ecologies: Moving Beyond the 'Green Economy'.* London: Zed Books.

Harvey, F. (2015) 'COP21 is too male dominated and has male priorities, says UN special envoy', *The Guardian.* Online. Available at: www.theguardian.com/environment/2015/dec/08/cop21-is-too-male-dominated-and-has-male-priorities-says-un-special-envoy (accessed 15 May 2016).

Hemmati, M. and Röhr, U. (2009) 'Engendering the climate-change negotiations: Experiences, challenges, and steps forward', *Gender and Development* 17(1): 19–32.

Hettinger, N. (2014) 'Valuing naturalness in the "Anthropocene": Now more than ever', in Wuerthner, G., Crist, E. and Butler, T. (eds) *Keeping the Wild: Against the Domestication of Earth.* Washington, DC: Island Press, 174–179.

Jamieson, D. (2014) *Reason in a Dark Time.* Oxford: Oxford University Press.

Kaijser, A. and Kronsell, A. (2014) 'Climate change through the lens of intersectionality', *Environmental Politics* 23(3): 417–433.

Kingsolver, B. (2015) 'The weight of a falling sky', *Ms. Magazine* 25(1): 43–47.

Klein, N. (2014a) 'The change within: The obstacles we face are not just external', *The Nation.* Online. Available at: www.thenation.com/article/179460/change-within-obstacles-we-face-are-not-just-external?page=0,1 (accessed 15 May 2016).

Klein, N. (2014b) *This Changes Everything: Capitalism vs. The Climate.* New York: Simon and Schuster.

Klein, N. (2014c) 'Why #BlackLivesMatter should transform the climate debate', *The Nation.* Online. Available at: www.thenation.com/article/what-does-blacklivesmatter-have-do-climate-change/ (accessed 15 May 2016).

Kolbert, E. (2014) *The Sixth Extinction: An Unnatural History.* New York: Henry Holt and Company.

LaDuke, W. (1999) *All Our Relations: Native Struggles for Land and Life.* Cambridge, MA: South End Press.

Lewallen, A. (2014) 'Resilience embodied', *Resilience: A Journal of the Environmental Humanities* 1(1).

Luciano, D. (2015) 'The inhuman Anthropocene', *LA Review of Books.* Online. Available at: http://avidly.lareviewofbooks.org/2015/03/22/the-inhuman-anthropocene/ (accessed 15 May 2016).

MacGregor, S. (2010) 'Gender and climate change: From impacts to discourses', *Journal of Indian Ocean Region* 6(2): 223–238.

MacGregor, S. (2014) 'Only resist: Feminist ecological citizenship and post-politics of climate change', *Hypatia* 29(3): 617–633.

Malm, A. and Hornborg, A. (2014) 'The geology of mankind? A critique of the Anthropocene narrative', *The Anthropocene Review* 1(1): 1–8.

Martinez-Alier, J. (2004) *The Environmentalism of the Poor.* London: Edward Elgar.

Merchant, C. (1992/2005) *Radical Ecology: The Search for a Livable World.* New York: Routledge.

Mies, M. and Shiva, V. (1993/2014) *Ecofeminism.* Halifax, NS: Fernwood Publications.

Mock, B. (2014) 'Why environmentalists should support the Black Lives Matter protests', *Grist.* Online. Available at: http://grist.org/living/why-environmentalists-should-support-the-black-lives-matter-protests/ (accessed 15 May 2016).

Moore, J. (2013) 'Anthropocene or Capitalocene?', Jason W. Moore. Online. Available at: https://jasonwmoore.wordpress.com/2013/05/13/anthropocene-or-capitalocene/ (accessed 15 May 2016).

Moore, K. D. (2013) 'Anthropocene is the wrong word', *Earth Island Journal.* Online. Available at: www.earthisland.org/journal/index.php/eij/article/anthropocene_is_the_wrong_word/ (accessed 15 May 2016).

Nightingale, A. (2015) 'Challenging the romance with resilience: Communities, scale and climate change', in Harcourt, W. and Nelson, I. (eds) *Practising Feminist Political Ecologies: Moving Beyond the 'Green Economy'.* London: Zed Books, 182–208.

Nordhaus, T. and Shellenberger, M. (2015) 'An ecomodernist manifesto', *Manifesto.* Online. Available at: www.ecomodernism.org/manifesto/ (accessed 15 May 2016).

Parikka, J. (2015) *The Anthrobscene.* Minneapolis: University of Minnesota Press.

Patel, R. (2013) 'Misanthropocene?', *Earth Island Journal.* Online. Available at: www.earthisland.org/journal/index.php/eij/article/misanthropocene/ (accessed 15 May 2016).

Paul, S. (2016) 'Paris delivers historic climate treaty, but leaves gender untouched', *Inter Press Service.* Online. Available at: www.ipsnews.net/2015/12/paris-delivers-historic-climate-treaty-but-leaves-gender-untouched/ (accessed 15 May 2016).

Pelter, Z. and Capraro, C. (2015) 'Climate justice for all: Putting gender justice at the heart of the Paris Climate Change Agreement', *ACT Alliance.* Online. Available at: www.christianaid.org.uk/Images/Climate-justice-for-all-May-2015.pdf (accessed 15 May 2016).

Plumwood, V. (1994) *Feminism and Mastery of Nature.* New York: Routledge.

Powys-Whyte, K. (2014) 'Indigenous women, climate change impacts, and collective action', *Hypatia* 29(3): 599–616.

Principles of Environmental Justice (1991) The First National People of Colour Environmental Leadership Summit, 24–27 October 1991, Washington, DC.

Raworth, K. (2014) 'Must the Anthropocene be a Manthropocene?', *The Guardian.* Online. Available at: www.theguardian.com/commentisfree/2014/oct/20/anthropocene-working-group-science-gender-bias (accessed 15 May 2016).

Ray, S. J. (2013) *The Ecological Other: Exclusion in American Culture.* Tucson, AZ: University of Arizona Press.

Razavi, S. and Miller, C. (1995) 'From WID to GAD: Conceptual shifts in the Women and Development discourse', *United Nations Research Institute Occasional Paper series* (United Nations Research Institute for Social Development) 1:2. Online. Available at: www.unrisd.org/80256B3C005BCCF9/%28httpPub-lications%29/D9C3FCA78D3DB32E80256B67005B6AB5?OpenDocument (accessed 15 May 2016).

Revkin, A. (2011) 'Embracing the anthropocene', *DOT Earth*, May 20. Online. Available at: http://dotearth. blogs.nytimes.com/2011/05/20/embracing-the-anthropocene/?_php=trueand_type=blogsand_r=0 (accessed 15 May 2016).

Revkin, A. (2014) 'Paths to a 'Good' anthropocene', Association for Environmental Science and Studies Conference, Keynote Address, 11–14 June 2014, PACE University, New York.

Ribot, J. (2013) 'Risk and blame in the Anthropocene: Multi-scale climate change analysis', Conference Paper #7, Conference on Food Sovereignty: A Critical Dialogue, 14–15 September 2013, Yale University.

Robinson, M., Mohammed, A. and Figueres, C. (2015) 'Gender equality and earth's future', *Global Gender and Climate Alliance*. Online. Available at: www.project-syndicate.org/commentary/gender-equali-ty-sustainable-development-by-mary-robinson-et-al-2015–03 (accessed 15 May 2016).

Schlosberg, D. and Collins, L. (2014) 'From environmental to climate justice: Climate change and the dis-course of environmental justice', *WIREs Clim Change*. doi:1002/wcc.275.

Seager, J. (1993) *Earth Follies: Coming to Feminist Terms With the Global Environmental Crisis*. New York: Routledge.

Seager, J. and Hartmann, B. (2005) *Mainstreaming Gender in Environmental Assessment and Early Warning*. Nairobi: UNEP.

Shepard, P. and Corbin-Mark, C. (2009) 'Climate justice', *Environmental Justice* 2(4): 163–166.

Shiva, V. (2005/2015) *Earth Democracy*. Cambridge, MA: South End Press.

Simpson, L. B. (2011) *Dancing on Our Turtle's Back: Stories of Nishnaabeg Re-Creation, Resurgence, and a New Emergence*. New York: Arbeiter Ring Publishing.

Smith, D. (2014) 'Why the climate movement must stand with Ferguson', *CommonDreams*. Online. Avail-able at: www.commondreams.org/views/2014/08/21/why-climate-movement-must-stand-ferguson (accessed 15 May 2016).

Solnit, R. (2012) 'Men explain things to me', *Guernica*. Online. Available at: www.guernicamag.com/daily/rebecca-solnit-men-explain-things-to-me/ (accessed 15 May 2016).

Soulé, M. (2014) 'The "new" conservation', in Wuerthner, G., Crist, E. and Butler, T. (eds) *Keeping the Wild: Against the Domestication of Earth*. Washington DC: Island Press, 66–80.

Soulé, M. and Press, D. (1998) 'What is Environmental studies?', *BioScience* 48(5): 397–405.

Steady, P. C. (2009) *Environmental Justice in the New Millennium: Global Perspectives on Race, Ethnicity, and Human Rights*. New York: Palgrave MacMillan.

Taylor, D. (2014) *Toxic Communities*. New York: New York University Press.

Taylor, K. Y. (2016) *From #BlackLivesMatter to Black Liberation*. Chicago: Haymarket Books.

Tillet, S. (2015) 'Female visibility matters', *New York Times Magazine*. Online. Available at: www.nytimes. com/2015/08/07/magazine/female-visibility-matters.html?_r=0 (accessed 15 May 2016).

Tsing, A. L. (2015) *The Mushroom at the End of the World: On the Possibility of Life in Capitalist Ruins*. Prince-ton: Princeton University Press.

Walsh, C. (2011) 'Afro and indigenous life: Visions in/and politics: (De)colonial perspectives in Bolivia and Ecuador', *Bolivian Studies Journal* 18: 47–67.

Wilson, E. O. (2016) 'Half earth', *Aeon*. Online. Available at: https://aeon.co/essays/half-of-the-earth-must-be-preserved-for-nature-conservation (accessed 15 May 2016).

Winfrey Harris, T. (2015) 'Making black women's lives matter', *Fusion*. Online. Available at: http://fusion. net/story/132822/making-black-womens-lives-matter/ (accessed 15 May 2016).

Women and Gender Constituency (WGC) (2015) 'A reality check on the Paris Agreement: Women demand climate justice', *Women and Gender Constituency*. Online. Available at: http://womengenderclimate.org/a-reality-check-on-the-paris-agreement-women-demand-climate-justice/ (accessed 15 May 2016).

World Commission on Environment and Development (WCED) (1987) *Our Common Future: The Brundt-land Report*. Oxford: Oxford University Press.

Wuerthner, G., Grist, E. and Butler, T. (eds) (2014) *Keeping the Wild: Against the Domestication of Earth*. Washington, DC: Island Press.

# INDEX

Printed in the United States
by Baker & Taylor Publisher Services